Professional Writing

ENC 3250

Florida Gulf Coast University

BUSINESS COMMUNICATIONS

Custom Edition

create.mheducation.com

ISBN-13: 9781308283258

ISBN-10: 1308283253

Contents

New and Improved Coverage in BCS6e! xi
Support Materials xxiv

Building Blocks for Effective Messages

Introduction 1
1. Business Communication, Management, and Success 2
2. Adapting Your Message to Your Audience 19
4. Planning, Writing, and Revising 59
5. Designing Documents, Slides, and Screens 73

Creating Goodwill

Introduction 89
6. You-Attitude 90
7. Positive Emphasis 101
8. Reader Benefits 112

Letters, Memos, E-Mail, and Web Writing

Introduction 113
9. Formats for Letters and Memos 114
10. Informative and Positive Messages 143
11. Negative Messages 164
12. Persuasive Messages 187
13. E-Mail Messages, Web Writing, and Technology 217

Polishing Your Writing

Introduction 237
14. Editing for Grammar and Punctuation 238
15. Choosing the Right Word 256
16. Revising Sentences and Paragraphs 271

Research & Reports

21. Proposals and Progress Reports 343
22. Finding, Analyzing, and Documenting Information 359
23. Short Reports 377
Index 537
Credits 353

New and Improved Coverage in BCS6e!

We've listened to your feedback on what you like and what you want improved in *BCS,* keeping as much of the text intact as possible while also making sure *BCS6e* accurately reflects changes in the workplace and in the field of business communication. In particular, Module 13 has been renamed "E-Mail Messages, Web Writing, and Technology" and updated to include more discussion on using social networking tools, and Modules 27 and 28 integrate social media into job application documents. Throughout the book, you'll find hundreds of elements revised or all new, including FYIs, Sites to See, BCS boxes, Problems and Exercises, Polishing Your Prose exercises, and Cases for Communicators.

Module 1: This critical foundation module underscores the importance of excellent communication skills in the workplace. For this edition, it includes a new opener reflecting on the tough economic realities of today's workplace and how the ability to read and write well gives professionals an edge on the competition. There are also new FYIs on Carnegie Speech's language training for a global market; vital 21st-century job skills that include oral and written communication; the slow gains in reading skills among elementary and middle school students (the next wave of college students and young professionals); degrees of study and workplace success that correlate in surprising ways; a typo that may have caused stock market chaos; and the most literate cities in the United States. A new Site to See invites students to test their interpersonal skills, and the BCS box has been updated to include information on start-up companies and a new Apple photo. A new end-of-module problem and new Polishing Your Prose exercises round out the updates.

Module 2: Revisions to the module opener reinforce the importance of audience analysis, and some elements have been moved to improve the flow of the module. New FYIs include discussions on an offensive ad by Nivea that failed to properly analyze its audience; errors by FEMA and subsequent messages that made problems worse for disaster victims; the travails of test takers and a talking pineapple; a politician's lack of awareness of how audiences might view his multimillion-dollar income; public criticism by P. J. Crowley that cost him his job; and the value of role-playing to achieve buy-in from audiences. The BCS box has been updated to note that Zappos was named by *CNN/Money* as one of the 100 Best Companies to Work For. A new end-of-module problem and all new Polishing Your Prose exercises round out the updates.

Module 3: In an ever-shrinking world, this module's overview of the elements of diversity and culture that help shape the workplace becomes even more critical for 21st-century professionals. New FYIs in Module 3 focus on the rise of interracial marriages in the United States; the value of touch to staying healthy; self-definition by Millennials in the workplace; Nike's sexist Olympic T-shirt design; women now scoring higher than men on IQ tests; ads that present women and minorities offensively; Baby Boomers being targeted by con artists; and the lack of diversity in U.S. television and what is being done about it. A new Site to See offers reviews and links to apps that can make travel easier. New end-of-module problems and new Polishing Your Prose exercises round out the updates.

Module 4: This module's revised opener notes that while the increased pace of the workplace has brought increased pressure to compose faster and faster, writers must still take care to compose effectively. New FYIs discuss how what constitutes revisions changes according to audience; Mortgage Resolution Partners' plan to keep more people in their homes; errant e-mails that terrified hundreds of employees into thinking they were fired; and tips from experts on overcoming procrastination. Site to See addresses have been updated, and a new Site to See invites visitors to take beginning and advanced Microsoft Word tutorials. New Polishing Your Prose exercises round out the updates.

Module 5: The module opener has been revised to emphasize that the principles of good design still apply to ever-changing social media, and the BCS box has been updated to reference Google Docs. Two new FYIs discuss the importance of document design—the first being a Pew Charitable Trust study on how checking account documents are too confusing to follow, and the second on how large, multi-touch screens are part of the next wave of technological changes in how we use and format documents. Site to See addresses have been updated, and a new Site to See offers tips on using PowerPoint slides in presentations. New Polishing Your Prose exercises round out the updates to the module, and the new Case for Communicators for Unit 1 examines how poor proofreading caused financial headaches for Old Navy.

Module 6: Modules 6, 7, and 8 detail the cornerstones of good business communication: you-attitude, positive emphasis, and reader benefits. They are briefer than some of the earlier modules but are meant to be read as a collective. For Module 6, examples throughout have been updated to reflect more current dates. One new FYI features a study that found a link among prejudices, low intelligence, and social conservatism, while another notes the lack of you-attitude among employees at Goldman Sachs, who, among other things, referred to clients as "muppets." A new Site to See invites students to test their Emotional Intelligence. New end-of-module problems and new Polishing Your Prose exercises round out the updates.

Module 7: Understanding the role of positive emphasis in business communication—and contrasting it with negative points of view—is vital to composing effective messages. Revisions to this module include FYIs on the disturbing findings that for the first time, most Americans do not believe today's young people will have better lives than their parents; the effect of optimism on both physical and financial health; the news that happier people make better workers; the role of resilience in helping people cope with stress and life's challenges; tips on making video apologies; and updates on failed apologies and on the happiest states in the United States. New end-of-module problems and new Polishing Your Prose exercises round out the updates.

Module 8: Developing good reader benefits can challenge students, so new FYIs focus on creative and interesting ways that benefits affect people. These FYIs discuss how the intrinsic value of self-image may be more important to people than even money; how boutique grocery stores provide online shopping and home delivery benefits to customers; the correlation between more education and longer life expectancy; and the counterintuitive patterns of liars and cheaters being unfazed by potential consequences. New Polishing Your Prose exercises round out the updates to the module, and the new Case for Communicators for Unit 2 examines how poor proofreading resulted in embarrassment for *The New York Times*.

Module 9: While the formats for memos and letters remain unchanged, technology is influencing how such documents are created and sent. Thus, new FYIs reflect on cloud technology making it easier to store documents but with the added challenge of making sure formats remain intact; indecipherable handwriting on letters and packages thwarted by Post Office scanning equipment; and CEOs Mike Duke and Tom Barrack being embarrassed by the memos they sent to employees that went viral. Examples throughout this module have been updated to reflect current dates. New Polishing Your Prose exercises round out the updates.

Module 10: This module has been renamed "Informative and Positive Messages" and all examples have been updated to reflect more current dates. In addition, FYIs now include the best out-of-office e-mail reply of all time; a movie trailer that uses a customer's rant to remind others of its no-talking/no-texting policy; chocolate, indeed, being able to change a person's mood for the better; customers tweeting complaints and how companies can better manage their image; the earliest appearance of the now-popular word "information"; and the effect of nearly 25% of the world workers' depression on productivity. A new end-of-module problem and all new Polishing Your Prose exercises round out the updates.

Module 11: New FYIs include how what most people would consider bad news actually helped shooting victim Petra Anderson; the surprising answer to who was behind a campaign to spread negative information about Google; the potential negative effect on reputation from working at home; types of "toxic" bosses in the workplace; workers wanting honesty from managers and supervisors; a gay instructor fired by Facebook for daring to give a chatty employee a look; Lego's attempts to cater to girls; and the most educated employees also facing the most stress on the job. Sites to See addresses have been updated, and examples throughout this module reflect more current dates. A new end-of-module problem and all new Polishing Your Prose exercises round out the updates.

Module 12: Though we're surrounded by persuasive messages every day, understanding them and then creating our own effective ones require careful effort. For better flow in the discussion, some elements of this module have been moved, and new FYIs discuss online bullying persuading people to help the victims; former Xerox CEO Anne Mulcahy almost being persuaded by sexist salespeople to go somewhere else; "birthers" refusing to be persuaded by President Obama's birth certificate; branding's effect on persuading consumers; the "like me bias" in performance appraisals; and tips for writing effective sales letters. Revisions to existing FYIs involve product placement in James Bond movies, and Blockbuster Video CEO Jim Keyes' public criticism of Netflix failing to persuade consumers. A new end-of-module problem and all new Polishing Your Prose exercises round out the updates.

Module 13: Of all the modules in *BCS6e*, this one has been revised the most extensively, reflecting the rapid changes that come with our highly technological age. For starters, it has been renamed "E-Mail Messages, Web Writing, and Technology," and the body copy has been tweaked to better integrate technology into the discussion while examples have been updated to reflect more current dates. In particular, the discussion on using social networking tools has been expanded, and a new photo coordinates with changes to Facebook's current design. Some elements have been moved to improve the flow of the discussion. New FYIs discuss the ever-increasing use of smartphones for e-mail and web use; a cyberstalking investment manager's 1,600-word plea for another date; a study of more than 977 e-mail messages revealing that shorter subject lines attract more clicks; Pew Research Center's findings that most Americans prefer vocal communication to texting, while a Nielsen survey shows that 13- to 17-year-olds send and receive 10 times as many texts as people ages 45 to 54; signs that the popularity of blogging among young people is waning; tips to use social networking in business; offensive tweets that got their authors in trouble; Latino and Hispanic Americans leading the way in embracing web technology; and a host of tips for better cell phone etiquette. An existing FYI includes more information on e-mail etiquette, and a new Site to See offers 20 tips on using Facebook in business. A new end-of-module problem and new Polishing Your Prose exercises round out the updates to the module, and the new Case for Communicators for Unit 3 examines the problems United Airlines faced when a computer glitch booked flights to Asia at an incorrect price.

Module 14: This module focuses on the nuts and bolts of using grammar and punctuation effectively. New FYIs reveal how 45% of employers surveyed say they are increasing training to improve grammar and other skills of employees; how CEO Kyle Wiens requires all job applicants to his companies to take a grammar test; and commentator Andy Rooney's aversion to apostrophes. There is also an addition to an existing module regarding a cable TV charge of $16.4 million, and Site to See addresses have been updated. New end-of-module problems and new Polishing Your Prose exercises round out the updates.

Module 15: Because choosing the right word is as much an art as it is a skill, new FYIs present examples of real-world applications—as well as misapplications: how U.S. presidents have managed to misspeak in public; what food label language might actually mean; idiomatic phrases that baffle non-native speakers of English; and the limitations of spell-checkers with common errors. The BCS box has been revised to challenge readers to think about the implications of a study that shows "mean" men do better in the workplace than nicer ones. New end-of-module problems and new Polishing Your Prose exercises round out the updates.

Module 16: New FYIs in this module include the arrogant style of a college student seeking a summer job; missed opportunities for message revision that resulted in athletes being insulted or being dismissed from the field of play; buzzwords on LinkedIn that are overused; and venerable critic Roger Ebert's Facebook page being censored for posts during a heated exchange. An existing FYI has been updated to include the 2012 winners of a wacky warning label contest, and the BCS box caption has been updated to note Johnnetta B. Cole's current position as chair of the institute that bears her name. New end-of-module and new Polishing Your Prose exercises round out the updates to the module, and the new Case for Communicators for Unit 4 examines how a misspelling on a key road sign proved an embarrassment for the state of Ohio.

Module 17: This module features new FYIs on how listeners today need a shift in stimulation about every 20 minutes; how students learning foreign languages did better after training in listening skills; and how archetypes for bad listeners, including Preamblers, such as the hosts of CNN's *Crossfire* were called out by guest Jon Stewart for using the show as a platform to give speeches on their points of view. Site to See addresses and the caption for the photo of Elizabeth Gonzalez-Gann have also been updated.

Module 18: New FYIs to help students better understand how to be effective on work teams discuss the hidden costs of being on a team; how introverts may suffer from the effects of groupthink; how social networking media is making us lonelier; how to use hip hop as a team-building exercise; ways to keep "digital nomads" connected with the workplace; and how a diverse team of students presented a business plan at Florida Atlantic University. The existing FYI on bad bosses has been revised to include the results of two recent polls. New Polishing Your Prose exercises round out the updates.

Module 19: A new module opener underscores how meetings are viewed by many employees, as well as the importance of choosing whether to hold a meeting in the first place. New FYIs focus on how many hours CEOs spend in meetings; using chocolate and other creative ways to keep meetings on track; tips to be an effective meeting participant; caveats for teleconferencing; companies, such as Nutrisystem, Symantec, and Herman Miller, that are holding annual meetings online; and Twist, an app from investor Bill Lee that helps track where meeting-goers are. One FYI has been revised to include information on using tablet PCs and other tools to make meetings more interactive, and Site to See addresses have been updated. New Polishing Your Prose exercises round out the updates.

Module 20: New FYIs include Kathy Caprino's tips to avoid mistakes in speeches; gaffes by a university president; Microsoft's Kirill Tatarinov's quick recovery from a technical glitch during a presentation; a poetry recitation that went horribly wrong; Steve Carell's effective use of humor during a graduation speech; a criminal's conviction being upheld because of his silence; and the importance of rehearsing before a speech. A new Site to See showcases PowerPoint examples and other resources. New Polishing Your Prose exercises round out the updates to the module, and the new Case for Communicators for Unit 5 looks at the role of charisma in leadership and whether people can be trained to be more charismatic.

Module 21: This module on proposals and progress reports features new FYIs on how feasibility studies on sports arenas show they are money losers for taxpayers; the London Business School's John W. Mullins' advice on writing a good business plan; how people are using Twitter to submit business plans; how some successful businesses nevertheless had their business plans lose in-class competitions; the effect of discourse communities on sales proposals; and the results of Apple's annual Supplier and Responsibility Report. Site to See addresses have been updated, and new Sites to See include sample recommendation reports from the Centers for Disease Control, tips for writing proposals from the Small Business Association, the New York City school system's progress reports, and progress reports from the World Health Organization on the fight against HIV/AIDS. Examples throughout the module have been updated to reflect more current dates. New Polishing Your Prose exercises round out the updates.

Module 22: Because research is so critical today, a new module opener stresses the importance of research to business and industry, as well as the need to make sure information resources are trustworthy. Minor tweaks have been made to the body copy. New FYIs include a discussion on Splunk, the first "Big Data" company to go public; how a Florida man convicted of murder got a new trial because a stenographer erased records inadvertently; unusual findings from research, such as how the more debt college students have, the higher their self-esteem; the high number of fake accounts on Facebook; estimates of how much data is consumed annually online; racist tweets that got two Olympians expelled from the London games; and the amount of money spent by corporations for employee training despite a lack of research on its effectiveness. New Sites to See include Survey Monkey and the Purdue OWL website. New Polishing Your Prose exercises round out the updates.

Module 23: Some elements of this module have been reorganized to improve flow. New FYIs include reports from companies questioning the effectiveness of Facebook ads; how younger people are choosing to rent a wide variety of items rather than own them; a Georgetown University report that despite some college majors being more employable than others, research still shows a college degree is worth it; employers scouring credit reports on job applicants; "pink slime" and its effects on consumer perceptions; and how disorganization—not just in documents but in general—costs companies. New Polishing Your Prose exercises round out the updates.

Module 24: The sample student report in this module has been revised to reflect more current dates. One new FYI discusses an innovative annual report from Austria Solar that uses light to make text on its otherwise blank pages visible. Another new FYI gives examples of how report data helps organizations to strategize. Orbitz, for instance, found that Apple users spend as much as 30% more per night on hotels than PC users. Site to See addresses have been updated, and new Sites to See include Graphis's Top 100 Annual Reports winners and a copy of NASA's Education Recommendation Report. A new Polishing Your Prose exercise rounds out the updates.

Module 25: A new module opener emphasizes the importance of charts, graphs, clip art, and other images in this increasingly visual age. New FYIs include technology that allows people to write using eye movements; tips for effective visual note taking; websites like Pinterest and Flickr that are changing the way we share information; how Ambassador Gary Locke became a hit in China for carrying his own bags and getting his own coffee; hidden messages in corporate logos; and the challenges from corporate branding on the 2012 Olympics. New Polishing Your Prose exercises round out the updates to the module, and the new Case for Communicators for Unit 6 looks at how waterless car washes are transforming that industry in the Middle East, as well as implications for such businesses in the United States.

Module 26: The module opener has been revised to discuss the challenges of finding a job in a bad economy as well as how getting started early and using social networking tools like LinkedIn and Facebook can help. Some elements have been reorganized to improve flow. New FYIs include revelations on how despite younger people embracing information technology, relatively few of them choose it as a career field; location being a major factor in job applicant trends; how unemployment is affecting college graduates and how many jobs that don't require degrees are going unfilled; the top master's degrees for income potential and which career requiring a graduate degree women find most satisfying; apps for people looking for a job; states making it illegal to bar the unemployed from applying for jobs; how employees in the middle of the income pack are vulnerable to downsizing; and how unemployment is affecting different generations. New Polishing Your Prose exercises round out the updates.

Module 27: Revisions to the module opener note how technology may be changing how résumés look and are submitted, underscoring the need to adapt to the employer's expectations. Minor tweaks have been made to improve body copy. Examples throughout the module have been updated to reflect more current dates, and several examples now include social networking page addresses. New FYIs discuss a college student who sent a photo of Nicolas Cage instead of her résumé to a prospective employer; résumé gaffes like listing "phishing" as a hobby; how companies use tracking systems to check on applicants' social networking pages; the proliferation of lies on résumés; and how recruiters and others use Facebook and Google to screen applicants.

Module 28: The module opener reminds job applicants to use the process employers want, such as a brief e-mail message in lieu of a formal letter in some cases. Examples throughout the module have been updated to reflect more current dates. New FYIs include discussions on a 3,000-word rejection letter sent to job applicants that went viral, and debates among experts as to whether the job application letter is going away. New Sites to See provide job application letter examples from Virginia Polytechnic Institute, State University, and Monster. New Polishing Your Prose exercises round out the updates.

Module 29: New FYIs in this module cover employers wanting Facebook passwords from applicants; UBS AG's stringent dress codes; leaving emotional baggage behind in job interviews; a survey that revealed 70% of hiring managers have experienced odd behavior from interviewees; unusual stress interview situations; how students coming from homes that appreciate in value are more likely to go to more expensive colleges; LinkedIn's compilation of worst questions asked of female job applicants; advice from Jason Fried for hiring managers to screen out applicants who ask "how" instead of "why" questions; and tips for making the most of virtual job interviews. New Polishing Your Prose exercises round out the updates.

Module 30: Revisions to this module's opener remind students to think in terms of careers rather than simply jobs, and to be self-reliant but not mercenary. New FYIs include Jenny Foss's advice on staying in touch with job interviewers through such resources as LinkedIn; planning carefully for career and early retirement; and how today's employees are more likely to have many short-term jobs in their careers than previous generations did. Examples throughout the module have been updated to reflect more current dates. New Polishing Your Prose exercises round out the updates to the module, and the new Case for Communicators for Unit 7 looks at how traditional Arts and Sciences programs at universities are starting to incorporate entrepreneurial and other job-related coursework into their curriculums.

Support Materials

Business Communication: Building Critical Skills, 6e, includes a variety of resources to help instructors prepare and present the material in this textbook more effectively.

Instructor's Manual

This is one of the few textbooks for which the authors write the *Instructor's Manual.* This ensures that the instructor materials represent the textbook's content and support instructor needs. Each chapter includes the learning objectives, module overview, key lecture points, teaching tips, in-class exercises, thumbnail images of corresponding PowerPoint slides, and answers to textbook assignments.

Test Bank and EZ Test

Prepared by the author, the test bank includes more than 1,800 true/false, multiple-choice, short-answer, and fill-in-the blank questions. Each question identifies the answer, difficulty level, and Bloom's Taxonomy level coding. Each test question is also tagged to the learning objective it covers in the chapters and the AACSB Learning Standard it falls under.

EZ Test Online

McGraw-Hill's *EZ Test Online* is a flexible and easy-to-use electronic testing program. The program allows instructors to create tests from book-specific items, accommodates a wide range of question types, and enables instructors to even add their own questions. Multiple versions of a test can be created, and any test can be exported for use with course management systems such as WebCT and Blackboard or with any other course management system. EZ Test Online is accessible to busy instructors virtually anywhere via the web, and the program eliminates the need for them to install test software. For more information about EZ Test Online, please see the website at www.eztestonline.com.

PowerPoint Presentation Slides

Each PowerPoint file has more than two dozen slides relating to the chapter, including two or more graphics from the textbook and notes offering tips for using the slides. The PowerPoint slides have been prepared by the authors, allowing seamless integration between the slides and the *Instructor's Manual.*

Assurance of Learning Ready

Many educational institutions today are focused on the notion of *assurance of learning,* an important element of some accreditation standards. *Business Communication: Building Critical Skills* is designed specifically to support your assurance of learning initiatives with a simple, yet powerful solution.

Each test bank question for *Business Communication: Building Critical Skills* maps to a specific chapter learning outcome/objective listed in the text. You can use our test bank software, EZ Test, and EZ Test Online, or in *Connect Business Communication* you can easily query for learning outcomes/objectives that directly relate to the learning objectives for your course. You can then use the reporting features of EZ Test to aggregate student results in a similar fashion, making the collection and presentation of assurance of learning data simple and easy.

AACSB Statement

The McGraw-Hill Companies is a proud corporate member of AACSB International. Understanding the importance and value of AACSB accreditation, *Business Communication: Building Critical Skills, 6e* recognizes the curricula guidelines detailed in the AACSB standards for business accreditation by connecting selected questions in [the text and/or the test bank] to the six general knowledge and skill guidelines in the AACSB standards.

The statements contained in *Business Communication: Building Critical Skills, 6e* are provided only as a guide for the users of this textbook. The AACSB leaves content coverage and assessment within the purview of individual schools, the mission of the school, and the faculty. While *Business Communication: Building Critical Skills, 6e,* and the teaching package make no claim of any specific AACSB qualification or evaluation, we have within *Business Communication: Building Critical Skills, 6e,* labeled selected questions according to the six general knowledge and skills areas.

McGraw-Hill and Blackboard

McGraw-Hill Higher Education and Blackboard have teamed up. What does this mean for you?

The **Best** of **Both Worlds**

1. **Your life, simplified.** Now you and your students can access McGraw-Hill's *Connect* and Create right from within your Blackboard course—all with one single sign-on. Say goodbye to the days of logging in to multiple applications.

2. **Deep integration of content and tools.** Not only do you get single sign-on with *Connect* and Create, but you also get deep integration of McGraw-Hill content and content engines right in Blackboard. Whether you're choosing a book for your course or building *Connect* assignments, all the tools you need are right where you want them—inside Blackboard.

3. **Seamless gradebooks.** Are you tired of keeping multiple gradebooks and manually synchronizing grades into Blackboard? We thought so. When a student completes an integrated *Connect* assignment, the grade for that assignment automatically (and instantly) feeds into your Blackboard grade center.

4. **A solution for everyone.** Whether your institution is already using Blackboard or you just want to try Blackboard on your own, we have a solution for you. McGraw-Hill and Blackboard can now offer you easy access to industry-leading technology and content, whether your campus hosts it or we do. Be sure to ask your local McGraw-Hill representative for details.

McGraw-Hill Campus™

McGraw-Hill Campus™ is a new one-stop teaching and learning experience available to users of any learning management system. This institutional service allows faculty and students to enjoy single sign-on (SSO) access to all McGraw-Hill Higher Education materials, including the award-winning McGraw-Hill *Connect* platform, from directly within the institution's website. McGraw-Hill Campus™ provides faculty with instant access to all McGraw-Hill Higher Education teaching materials (e.g., eTextbooks, test banks, PowerPoint slides, animations and learning objects, etc.), allowing them to browse, search, and use any instructor ancillary content in our vast library at no additional cost to the instructor or students. Students enjoy SSO access to a variety of free items (e.g., quizzes, flash cards, narrated presentations, etc.) and subscription-based products (e.g., McGraw-Hill *Connect).* With this program enabled, faculty and students will never need to create another account to access McGraw-Hill products and services. Learn more at www.mhcampus.com.

McGraw-Hill Customer Care Contact Information

At McGraw-Hill, we understand that getting the most from new technology can be challenging. That's why our services don't stop after you purchase our products. You can e-mail our Product Specialists 24 hours a day to get product-training online. Or you can search our knowledge bank of Frequently Asked Questions on our support website. For Customer Support, call **800-331-5094**, e-mail **hmsupport@ mcgraw-hill.com**, or visit **www.mhhe.com/support.** One of our Technical Support Analysts will be able to assist you in a timely fashion.

McGraw-Hill's Expanded Management Asset Gallery! For Business Communication

McGraw-Hill/Irwin is excited to now provide a one-stop-shop for our wealth of assets, making it super quick and easy for instructors to locate specific materials to enhance their courses.

All of the following can be accessed within the Management Asset Gallery:

Manager's Hot Seat

This interactive, video-based application puts students in the manager's hot seat and builds critical thinking and decision-making skills and allows students to apply concepts to real managerial challenges. Students watch as 15 real managers apply their years of experience when confronting unscripted issues such as bullying in the workplace, cyber loafing, globalization, inter-generational work conflicts, workplace violence, and leadership vs. management.

Self-Assessment Gallery

Unique among publisher-provided self-assessments, our 23 self-assessments provide students with background information to ensure that they understand the purpose of the assessment. Students test their values, beliefs, skills, and interests in a wide variety of areas allowing them to personally apply chapter content to their own lives and careers.

Every self-assessment is supported with PowerPoints and an instructor manual in the Management Asset Gallery, making it easy for the instructor to create an engaging classroom discussion surrounding the assessments.

Online Learning Center (OLC)

www.mhhe.com/lockerbcs6e

Find a variety of online teaching and learning tools that are designed to reinforce and build on the text content. Students will have direct access to the learning tools, while instructor materials are password-protected.

eBook Options

eBooks are an innovative way for students to save money and to "go green." McGraw-Hill's eBooks are typically 40% off the bookstore price. Students have the choice between an online and a downloadable CourseSmart eBook.

Through CourseSmart, students have the flexibility to access an exact replica of their textbook from any computer that has Internet service, without plug-ins or special software, via the online version or to create a library of books on their hard drive via the downloadable version. Access to the CourseSmart eBooks lasts for one year.

FEATURES

CourseSmart eBooks allow students to highlight, take notes, organize notes, and share the notes with other CourseSmart users. Students can also search for terms across all eBooks in their purchased CourseSmart library. CourseSmart eBooks can be printed (five pages at a time).

MORE INFO AND PURCHASE

Please visit **www.coursesmart.com** for more information and to purchase access to our eBooks. CourseSmart allows students to try one chapter of the eBook, free of charge, before purchase.

Binder Ready Loose-Leaf Text

This full-featured text is provided as an option for the financially strapped student. It is a full 4-color text that's three-hole punched and made available at a discount to students. It is also available in a package with *Connect Plus.*

Create

Craft your teaching resources to match the way you teach! With McGraw-Hill Create, **www.mcgrawhillcreate.com**, you can easily rearrange chapters, combine material from other content sources, and quickly upload content you have written, like your course syllabus or teaching notes. Find the content you need in Create by searching through thousands of leading McGraw-Hill textbooks. Arrange your book to fit your teaching style. Create even allows you to personalize your book's appearance by selecting the cover and adding your name, school, and course information. Order a Create book and you'll receive a complimentary print review copy in three to five business days or a complimentary electronic review copy (eComp) via e-mail in about one hour. Go to **www.mcgrawhillcreate.com** today and register. Experience how McGraw-Hill Create empowers you to teach *your* students *your* way.

Building Blocks for Effective Messages

Building Blocks
for Effective Messages

1

Module 1 Business Communication, Management, and Success

Module 2 Adapting Your Message to Your Audience

Module 3 Communicating Across Cultures

Module 4 Planning, Writing, and Revising

Module 5 Designing Documents, Slides, and Screens

1 Business Communication, Management, and Success

Module 1 explores with you the importance of communication in the business world. After completing the module, you should be able to

LO 1-1 Recognize myths about on-the-job writing.

LO 1-2 Distinguish business communication from other school writing.

LO 1-3 Explain accomplishments through communication.

LO 1-4 Understand costs for business communication.

LO 1-5 Define criteria for effective messages.

LO 1-6 Apply strategies for communication analysis.

LO 1-7 Apply strategies for creative thinking.

If a word could sum up life in the early 21st century, it would be "change."

Changes to politics, diversity, education, technology, fuel costs, and business practices have altered the pace and quality of our lives. While change is ever constant, the scope of change over the past decade has been startling. Consider how with a cell phone and Internet connection, one person now can run a business globally or how workers can be employed from overseas or from the local labor pool. More students are going to college than ever before, millions of American workers are becoming eligible to retire, and millions of new workers are entering the job market—some with very different expectations than those of previous generations.

Americans, and indeed much of the world's population, also felt the stunning economic turbulence that erupted in the first decade of the 21st century. Foreclosures soared, unemployment rose past 10%, and foreign-born workers with H-1B visas found themselves heading back to their home countries for greener pastures.[1]

Unless you have a fairy godmother, you'll need to know how to communicate.

As this book goes to press, the U.S. economy continues to improve, but for millions of Americans struggling to make ends meet, the improvements have yet to affect their day-to-day lives. At least one thing is clear, though: workers with high-level skills and education continue to have the best chance of weathering the economic turbulence.

For instance, at the same time there were more than 600,000 job openings in education and health services, there were only 67,000 openings in construction. A lack of talent caused many jobs in the former—which typically require a higher level of education—to go unfilled.[2]

Of course, no one is immune to the problems. There are plenty of skilled employees who are unemployed or underemployed. Data suggest that college graduates under the age of 25 and with bachelor's degrees are facing one of the bleakest job markets in years.[3] But you increase your chances of success with the more you know and the more you can do. In particular, "soft skills," such as communication skills, become even more important as prospective employers scrutinize job applications.

Many Americans are challenged, however, by their level of English-language literacy. The last large-scale study of U.S. literacy by the National Endowment for the Arts, for instance, found that more American adults are not even reading one book a year, and the number of adults with bachelor's degrees deemed proficient in reading prose dropped from 40% to 31% in a decade.[4] A literacy study funded by the Pew Charitable Trust found that more than half of graduating students at four-year colleges and 75% at two-year colleges lack the literacy to handle complex, real-life tasks, such as analyzing news stories and understanding credit card offers.[5]

Work requires communication. People communicate to plan products and services; hire, train, and motivate workers; coordinate manufacturing and delivery; persuade customers to buy; and bill them for the sale. For many business, nonprofit, community, and government organizations, the "product" is information or a service rather than something tangible. Information and services are created and delivered by communication. In every organization, communication is the way people get their points across, get work done, and get recognized for their contributions.

Carnegie Speech is among companies providing English language training in an age of globalization, in this case to pilots who are non-native speakers of English. Beyond reading and writing, pilots must be able to pronounce words sufficiently so there is no confusion with the control tower. The potential for disaster is great enough that the United Nations issued new recommendations to improve English-language acquisition, citing past accidents where the lack of proficiency in English was a factor.

Source: Joe Sharkey, "English Skills a Concern as Global Aviation Grows," *The New York Times,* May 21, 2012, http://www.nytimes.com/2012/05/22/business/english-skills-a-concern-as-global-aviation-grows.html?_r=1.

A National Association of Colleges and Employers survey revealed that the ability to work in a team structure and to verbally communicate with persons inside and outside the organization topped the list of skills employers want in job candidates. The findings dovetail with those of the Partnership for 21st Century Skills, which found that 99% of people surveyed felt that success in the global economy depends on developing critical thinking and analytical skills, with 88% of those surveyed feeling that schools should also focus on teaching such skills as communication. Of the 14 skill sets offered for ranking, reading comprehension rated the highest in importance.

Sources: "Job Outlook: The Candidate Skills/Qualities Employers Want," The National Association of Colleges and Employers, October 26, 2011, http://www.naceweb.org/s10262011/candidate_skills_employer_qualities/; and "Beyond the Three Rs: Voter Attitudes Toward 21st Century Skills (Key Findings)," November 23, 2007, The Partnership for 21st Century Skills, www.21stcenturyskills.org/documents/p21_pollreport_2pg.pdf.

Communication takes many forms. **Verbal communication,** or communication that uses words, includes

- Face-to-face or phone conversations
- Meetings
- Text, e-mail, and voice-mail messages
- Letters and memos
- Reports

Nonverbal communication does not use words. Examples include

- Pictures
- Company logos
- Gestures and body language
- Who sits where at a meeting
- How long someone keeps a visitor waiting

Even in your first job, you'll communicate. You'll read information; you'll listen to instructions; you'll ask questions; you may solve problems with other workers in teams. In a manufacturing company, hourly workers travel to a potential customer to make oral sales presentations. In an insurance company, clerks answer customers' letters. Even "entry-level" jobs require high-level skills in reasoning, mathematics, and communicating. As a result, communication ability consistently ranks first among the qualities that employers look for in college graduates.[6]

Experts predict that globalization will continue to revolutionize business and industry throughout the upcoming years, transforming economies in the process. Here, workers inspect a tanker at Hyundai Heavy Industries, Inc., a South Korean manufacturer of industrial robots, construction equipment, and electric and electronic systems that is also the world's largest shipbuilder. For companies with an eye toward being global leaders, effective communication is vital, whether to ensure smooth operations, cultivate strong relationships with diverse clients, or increase market share in a competitive environment. Of course, organizations with more local aspirations benefit from effective communication, too!

Communication affects all levels of work. Training specialists Brad Humphrey and Jeff Stokes identify communication skills as being among the most important for modern supervisors.[7] Andrew Posner, a career counselor, advises that employees looking to make a career change need such "transferable skills" as the ability to "analyze, write, persuade, and manage."[8]

Employers clearly want employees who communicate well, yet a staggering 40 million people in the United States alone have limited literacy skills, including some college graduates.[9] According to one report by the College Board's National Commission on Writing, states spend more than $220 million annually on remedial writing training for their employees, and corporations may spend $3.1 billion to fix problems from writing deficiencies; two-thirds of private-sector employers surveyed said writing was an important responsibility for employees.[10]

Because writing skills are so valuable, good writers earn more. Linguist Stephen Reder has found that among people with two- or four-year degrees, workers in the top 20% of writing ability earn, on average, more than three times as much as workers whose writing falls into the worst 20%.[11]

The conclusion is simple: Good communication skills are vital in today's workplace. Technology, especially through e-mail, instant messaging, and cell phones, is making the globe a smaller and busier place, one where messages must be understood immediately. Traditional paper messages flourish, even as electronic channels expand our ability to reach more people. The better an employee's communication skills are, the better his or her chance for success.

For U.S. elementary and middle school students, significant gains in math and science on standardized tests have been offset by only modest gains in reading skills. In 1992, for instance, 29% of fourth-grade students were proficient in reading, but nearly 20 years later, that number had risen only five percentage points. There were no gains at all from 2008 to 2009.

Source: Sam Dillon, "Since 1990s, U.S. Students' Math Has Sharpened, But Reading Lags," *The New York Times,* November 1, 2011, http://www.nytimes.com/2011/11/02/education/us-students-math-skills-sharpen-but-reading-lags.html.

Will I really have to write? LO 1-1

▶ *Yes. A lot.*

Claims that people can get by without writing are flawed.

Claim 1: Secretaries will do all my writing.
Reality: Because of automation and restructuring, secretaries and administrative assistants are likely to handle complex tasks such as training, research, and database management for several managers. Managers are likely to take care of their own writing, data entry, and phone calls.[12]

Claim 2: I'll use form letters or templates when I need to write.
Reality: A **form letter** is a prewritten fill-in-the-blank letter designed to fit standard situations. Using a form letter is OK if it's a good letter. But form letters cover only routine situations. The higher you rise, the more frequently you'll face situations that aren't routine and that demand creative solutions.

Claim 3: I'm being hired as an accountant, not a writer.
Reality: Almost every entry-level professional or managerial job requires you to write e-mail messages, speak to small groups, and write paper documents. People who do these things well are more likely to be promoted beyond the entry level.

Claim 4: I'll just pick up the phone.
Reality: Important phone calls require follow-up letters, memos, or e-mail messages. People in organizations put things in writing to make themselves visible, to create a record, to convey complex data, to make things convenient for the reader, to save money, and to convey their own messages more effectively. "If it isn't in writing," says a manager at one company, "it didn't happen." Writing is an essential way to make yourself visible, to let your accomplishments be known.

Some research has found less correlation between college majors and success in the workplace than might be expected. A study by Payscale, Inc., for instance, found that history majors who pursued business careers earned as much on average as those who majored in business. Much to the chagrin of his father, CNN's Ted Turner majored in Classics, and Michael Eisner, former head of The Walt Disney Company and at one time the highest-paid executive in the U.S., graduated with a Bachelor's Degree in English. George Brown College found that "most employers cite communication skills as the most important skill

(continued)

Don't I know enough about communication? LO 1-2

▶ *Business communication differs from other school writing.*

Although both business communication and other school writing demand standard edited English, in other ways the two are very different.

Site to See

Go to

www.mindtools.com/pages/article/newTMM_36.htm

to test your interpersonal skills.

The National Assessment of Adult Literacy, a study by the U.S. Department of Education, showed that Mississippi has improved adult literacy in every one of its counties. Some other states, however, saw an increase in adult illiteracy, and one in seven U.S. adults is challenged to read anything more complex than a child's picture book.

Source: Greg Toppo, "Literacy Study: 1 in 7 Adults are Unable to Read this Story," *USAToday.* January 8, 2009, http://www.usatoday.com/news/education/2009-01-08-adult-literacy_N.htm.

Purpose

- The purpose of school writing is usually to show that you have learned the course material and to demonstrate your intelligence.
- The purpose of business communication is to meet an organizational need. No one will pay you to write something that he or she already knows.

Audience

- The audiences for school writing are limited: usually just the instructor and the other students. The real audience is "an educated person." Even if the instructor disagrees with your views, if they are well-supported, the paper can earn a good grade. The instructor is paid, in part, to read your papers and will read them even if they are boring.
- The audiences for business communication include people both inside and outside the organization (▶▶ Module 2). Real audiences pay attention to messages only if they seem important, relevant, and interesting.

Information

- Information in school writing may be new to you but is rarely new to your instructor.
- Information in business communication is usually new to your reader. (If it isn't, you have to work extra hard to make it interesting.)

Organization

- School writing often follows the traditional essay form, with a thesis statement up front, paragraphs of evidence, and a final concluding paragraph.
- Business communication is organized to meet the psychological needs of the reader. Most often, the main point comes up front (▶▶ Modules 10–12).

Style

- The style for school writing is often formal. Big words and long sentences and paragraphs are often rewarded.
- The style for business communication is friendly, not formal. Short words and a mix of sentence and paragraph lengths are best (▶▶ Modules 15 and 16).

Document Design

- School writing often rewards long paragraphs. Papers are often double spaced, with no attention to visual design.
- Businesspeople want to be able to skim documents. Headings, lists, and single-spaced paragraphs with double spacing between paragraphs help readers find information quickly (▶▶ Module 5).

Visuals

- Except for math, construction, and engineering, few classes expect writing to contain anything other than words.
- Business writers are expected to choose the most effective way to convey information. Even a one-page memo may contain a table, graph, or other visual. You'll be expected to be able to use computer programs to create graphs, visuals, and slides for presentations (▶▶ Modules 5, 20, and 25).

What does communication accomplish?   LO 1-3

▶ *Management happens through communication.*

According to Henry Mintzberg, managers have three basic jobs: to collect and convey information, to make decisions, and to promote interpersonal unity—that is, to make people want to work together to achieve organizational goals.[13] All of these jobs happen through communication. Effective managers are able to use a wide variety of media and

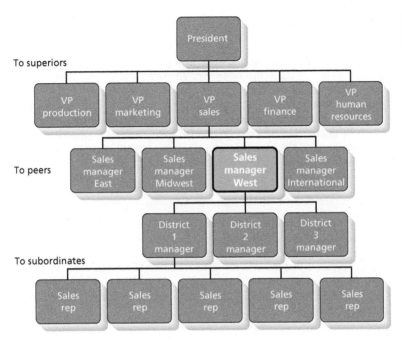

Figure 1.1 The Internal Audiences of the Sales Manager—West

strategies to communicate. They know how to interpret comments from informal channels such as the company grapevine; they can speak effectively in small groups and in formal presentations; they write well.

Communication—oral, nonverbal, and written—goes to both internal and external audiences. **Internal audiences** (Figure 1.1) are other people in the same organization: subordinates, superiors, peers. **External audiences** (Figure 1.2) are people outside the organization: customers, suppliers, unions, stockholders, potential employees, government agencies, the press, and the general public.

Figure 1.2 The Corporation's External Audiences

Source: Daphne A. Jameson.

The Importance of Listening, Speaking, and Interpersonal Communication

Informal listening, speaking, and working in groups are just as important as writing formal documents and giving formal oral presentations. As a newcomer in an organization, you'll need to listen to others both to find out what you're supposed to do and to learn about the organization's values and culture. Informal chitchat, both about yesterday's game and about what's happening at work, connects you to the **grapevine,** an informal source of company information. You may be asked to speak to small groups, either inside or outside your organization.[14] Networking with others in your office and in town and working with others in workgroups will be crucial to your success.

The Purposes of Messages in Organizations

Messages in organizations have one or more of **three basic purposes:** to inform, to request or persuade, and to build goodwill. When you **inform,** you explain something or tell readers something. When you **request or persuade,** you want the reader to act. The word *request* suggests that the action will be easy or routine; *persuade* suggests that you will have to motivate and convince the reader to act. When you **build goodwill,** you create a good image of yourself and of your organization—the kind of image that makes people want to do business with you.

Most messages have multiple purposes.

- When you answer a question, you're informing, but you also want to build goodwill by suggesting that you're competent and perceptive and that your answer is correct and complete.
- In a claims adjustment, whether your answer is yes or no, you want to suggest that the reader's claim has been given careful consideration and that the decision is fair, businesslike, and justified.
- To persuade, a résumé gives information to prove that you're qualified for the job and uses layout to emphasize your strong points and build a good image of you.

How much does correspondence cost?   LO 1-4

▶ *$21.15 a page—even more if it doesn't work.*

Writing costs money. Besides the cost of paper, computers, and software, there is the major expense: employees' time. A consultant who surveyed employees in seven industries found that to prepare a one-page letter, most of them spent 54 minutes planning, composing, and revising the letter. According to the most recent figures from the U.S. Labor Department, employers paid an average of $23.50 per hour per employee for wages and benefits. At that rate, an employer would pay $21.15 for an employee's time spent writing a typical letter.[15] One company in Minneapolis sends out 3,000 original letters a day—worth more than $66,000 at the average rate. A first-class stamp on each letter would add another $1,000 to the company's daily expenses.

In many organizations, all external documents must be approved before they go out. A document may **cycle** from writer to superior to writer to another superior to writer again three or four or many more times before it is finally approved. The cycling process increases the cost of correspondence.

Longer documents can involve large teams of people and take months to write. An engineering firm that relies on military contracts for its business calculates that it spends $500,000 to put together an average proposal and $1 million to write a large proposal.[16]

Poor correspondence costs even more. When writing isn't as good as it could be, you and your organization pay a price in wasted time, wasted efforts, and lost goodwill.

Bad writing wastes time by

- Taking more time to read.
- Requiring more time to revise and causing more rounds of revision.
- Confusing ideas so that discussions and decisions are needlessly drawn out.
- Delaying action while the reader asks for more information or tries to figure out the meaning.

Ineffective messages don't get results. A reader who has to guess what the writer means may guess wrong. A reader who finds a letter or memo unconvincing or insulting simply won't do what the message asks. Thus, second and third and fourth requests are necessary.

Whatever the literal content of the words, every letter, memo, and report serves either to enhance or to damage the image the reader has of the writer. Poor messages damage business relationships.

Good communication is worth every minute it takes and every penny it costs. For instance, the consulting firm Watson Wyatt Worldwide conducted research showing greater returns to shareholders in companies with the most effective programs for communicating with their employees. Those companies also enjoyed lower employee turnover and a 30% increase in their stocks' market value.[17]

What makes a message effective? LO 1-5

▶ *Good messages meet five criteria.*

Good business and administrative writing

- **Is clear.** The meaning the reader gets is the meaning the writer intended. The reader doesn't have to guess.
- **Is complete.** All of the reader's questions are answered. The reader has enough information to evaluate the message and act on it.
- **Is correct.** All of the information in the message is accurate. The message is free from errors in punctuation, spelling, grammar, word order, and sentence structure.
- **Saves the reader's time.** The style, organization, and visual impact of the message help the reader to read, understand, and act on the information as quickly as possible.
- **Builds goodwill.** The message presents a positive image of the writer and his or her organization. It treats the reader as a person, not a number. It cements a good relationship between the writer and the reader (▶▶ Modules 6–8).

Whether a message meets these five criteria depends on **the interactions among the writer, the audience, the purposes of the message, and the situation.** No single set of words will work in all possible situations.

Better writing helps you to

- **Save time.** Reduce reading time, since comprehension is easier. Eliminate the time now taken to rewrite badly written materials. Reduce the time taken asking writers, "What did you mean?"
- **Make your efforts more effective.** Increase the number of requests that are answered positively and promptly—on the first request. Present your points—to other people in your organization; to clients, customers, and suppliers; to government agencies; to the public—more forcefully.
- **Communicate your points more clearly.** Reduce the misunderstandings that occur when the reader has to supply missing or unclear information. Make the issues clear, so that disagreements can surface and be resolved more quickly.
- **Build goodwill.** Build a positive image of your organization. Build an image of yourself as a knowledgeable, intelligent, capable person.

How should I analyze business communication situations? LO 1-6

▶ *Try PAIBOC.*

Before you write or speak, you need to understand the situation. Ask yourself the following questions:

- **What's at stake—to whom?** Think not only about your own needs but about the concerns your boss and your readers will have. Your message will be most effective if you think of the entire organizational context—and the larger context of shareholders, customers, and regulators. When the stakes are high, you'll need to take into account people's emotional feelings as well as objective facts.
- **Should you send a message?** Sometimes, especially when you're new on the job, silence is the most tactful response. But be alert for opportunities to learn, to influence, to make your case. You can use communication to build your career.
- **What channel should you use?** Paper documents and presentations are formal and give you considerable control over the message. E-mail, phone calls, and stopping by someone's office are less formal. Oral channels are better for group decision making, allow misunderstandings to be cleared up more quickly, and seem more personal. Sometimes you may need more than one message, in more than one channel.
- **What should you say?** Content for a message may not be obvious. How detailed should you be? Should you repeat information that the audience already knows? The answers will depend upon the kind of document, your purposes, your audiences, and the corporate culture. And you'll have to figure these things out for yourself, without detailed instructions.
- **How should you say it?** How you arrange your ideas—what comes first, what second, what last—and the words you use shape the audience's response to what you say.

When you're faced with a business communication situation, you need to develop a solution that will both **solve the organizational problem and meet the psychological needs of the people involved.** The strategies in this section will help you solve the problems in this book. Almost all of these strategies can also be applied to problems you encounter on the job.

- **Understand the situation.** What are the facts? What additional information might be helpful? Where could you get it?
- **Brainstorm solutions.** Consciously develop several solutions. Then measure them against your audience and purposes: Which solution is likely to work best?

Documents' Purposes

Documents in organizations have three basic purposes: to inform, to request or persuade, and to build goodwill.

Most documents have more than one purpose.

Criteria for Effective Messages

Good business and administrative writing is clear, complete, and correct. It saves the reader time, and it builds goodwill.

Whether a message meets these five criteria depends on **the interactions among the writer, the audience, the purposes of the message, and the situation.** No single set of words will work in all possible situations.

People communicate to plan products and services; hire, train, and motivate workers; coordinate manufacturing and delivery; persuade customers to buy; bill them for the sale; and communicate with stakeholders. Pictured here is Hillcrest Public School Environmental Studies teacher Jennet Poffenroth on the school's roof with their solar panels. The Toronto District School Board announced an innovative, no cost strategy of installing solar panels on 450 schools.

Thinking Creatively   LO 1-7

Creativity is essential to success in business and business communication. Here are some examples.

- In a risky move, Apple Computer branched into portable digital music players, a market in which it had no significant experience. The results were the iPod, now the de facto standard, and iTunes, a popular online music store. The company then gambled on the iPhone, iTunes Movie Rentals, the MacBook Air, and the iPad, an electronic tablet that Apple touted as "Our most advanced technology in a magical and revolutionary device at an unbelievable price." To maintain its dominance, Apple must continue to innovate.

- W.L. Gore & Associates, maker of GORE-TEX fabrics and Glide dental floss, was named Most Innovative Company by *Fast Company* magazine. Organized more like a university than a corporation, the company prefers egalitarian teams to boss-driven departments, mixes researchers with salespeople and production workers, and prefers small buildings on minicampuses to gigantic complexes. The $1.6 billion company is the brainchild of Wilbert L. Gore, who believed "communication really happens in the carpool," where hierarchies don't stifle free expression.

Thinking creatively often means shedding common paradigms. For instance, when the fledgling Cartoon Network decided to offer programming aimed at 18- to 34-year-olds, it sought writers and producers who ignored standard marketing practice and instead envisioned a block of shows they'd watch.

The result was *Adult Swim,* an after-hours cavalcade of hip satires like *Futurama* and *The Venture Brothers* mixed with Japanese anime series and off-the-wall comedies like *Family Guy* and *Aqua Teen Hunger Force.* During commercial breaks, postmodern spots advertised upcoming shows or challenged viewers' trivia knowledge. Soon, *Adult Swim* was beating the competition—chiefly Jay Leno and David Letterman.

Ways to become more creative include brainstorming, working within limits, and consciously seeking problems or dissonances that need work.

IBM's tips for creativity are even more diverse. Some of them include

- Have a constructive argument.
- Brainstorm with someone 10 years older and someone 10 years younger.
- Clean your desk.
- Come in early—enjoy the quiet.
- Leave the office. Sit with just a pencil and a pad of paper. See what happens.

Question "conventional wisdom," which can rely on myths and stereotypes. Conventional wisdom argues, for instance, that people naturally side with others along racial, ethnic, gender, religious, or socioeconomic lines. Yet, Asian Americans, even those with Chinese ancestors, are at a disadvantage teaching English in China, where Caucasians, regardless of qualifications, are in demand. Barack Obama was the big Democratic winner in the 2008 Iowa Caucus, which had a record turnout of 236,000 voters and was held in a state that is more than 90% white. And Harvard Business School's Noam Wasserman found that by the time a start-up company has raised its third round of funding, 52% of founder CEOs have been replaced, with three-quarters of them fired by the board. The most successful of founders were actually the first ones to get fired.

Sources: "Tougher Days, Bolder Apple," *BusinessWeek,* June 20, 2005, 38–41; Apple, Inc., downloaded on January 29, 2010, at http://www.apple.com/; Brian Braiker, "Thin Is In at Macworld," *Newsweek,* January 15, 2008, downloaded at www.newsweek.com/id/94611; Alan Deutschman, "The Fabric of Creativity," *Fast Company,* December 2004, 54, downloaded at www.fastcompany.com/magazine/89/open_gore. html; Matthew Grimm, "Major Toon Up," *American Demographics,* October 2004, 50–51; Liz Zack, "How IBM Gets Unstuck," *Fast Company,* October 1999, 104; Kevin Zhou, "Where English Teachers Have to Look the Part," *The Los Angeles Times,* October 29, 2007, downloaded at www.latimes.com/business/la-fi-teach29oct29,1,1254303. story?coll=la-headlines-business&ctrack=3&cset=true; and Nitya Venkataraman, "Obama Emerges Victorious in Iowa," *ABC News,* January 4, 2008, downloaded at http://abcnews.go.com/print?id=4082356; and Jessica Bruder, "A Harvard Professor Analyzes Why Start-Ups Fail," *The New York Times,* May 25, 2012, http://boss.blogs.nytimes .com/2012/05/25/a-harvard-professor-analyzes-why-start-ups-fail/.

- **If you want to add or change information, get permission first.** If you have any questions about ideas you want to use, *ask your instructor.* He or she can tell you *before* you write the message.

When you use this book to create messages on the job, you can't change facts. That is, if it's October, you can't pretend that it's April just because it may be easier to think of reader benefits for that time of year. But it may be possible to change habits that your company has fallen into, especially if they no longer serve a purpose. Check with your supervisor to make sure that your departure from company practice is acceptable.

- **Use the PAIBOC questions in Figure 1.3 to analyze your purpose, your audience, and the situation.**

As Figure 1.3 shows, PAIBOC offers an acronym for the questions you need to answer before you begin composing your message. The following discussion lists specific questions you can answer: ▶▶ Modules 10, 11, and 12 for examples of answers to these questions for specific situations.

P   What are your **purposes** in writing or speaking?
    What must this message do to solve the organizational problem? What must it do to meet your own needs? What do you want your readers to do? To think or feel? List all your purposes, major and minor. Specify *exactly* what you want your reader to know, think, or do. Specify *exactly* what kind of image of yourself and of your organization you want to project.

    Even in a simple message, you may have several related purposes: to announce a new policy, to make readers aware of the policy's provisions and requirements and to have them think that the policy is a good one, that the organization cares about its employees, and that you are a competent writer and manager.

A   Who is (are) your **audience(s)?** How do the members of your audience differ from each other? What characteristics are relevant to this particular message?
    How much does your audience know about your topic? How will audience members respond to your message? Some characteristics of your readers will be irrelevant; focus on ones that matter *for this message.* Whenever you write to several people or to a group (like a memo to all employees), try to identify the economic, cultural, or situational differences that may affect how various subgroups respond to what you have to say.

I   What **information** must your message include?
    Make a list of the points that must be included; check your draft to make sure you include them all. If you're not sure whether a particular fact must be included, ask your instructor or your boss.

    To include information without emphasizing it, put it in the middle of a paragraph or document and present it as briefly as possible.

B   What reasons or reader **benefits** can you use to support your position?
    Brainstorm to develop reasons for your decision, the logic behind your argument, and possible benefits to readers if they do as you ask. Reasons and reader benefits do not have to be monetary. Making the reader's job easier or more pleasant is a good reader benefit. In an informative or persuasive message, identify at least five reader benefits. In your message, use those you can develop most easily and most effectively.

    Be sure the benefits are adapted to your reader. Many people do not identify closely with their companies; the fact that the company benefits from a policy will help the reader only if the savings or profit is passed directly on to the employees. That is rarely the case: Savings and profits are often eaten up by returns to stockholders, bonuses to executives, and investments in plants and equipment or in research and development.

O   What **objections** can you expect your reader(s) to have? What negative elements of your message must you deemphasize or overcome?

Instant
Replay

Some negative elements can only be deemphasized. Others can be overcome. Be creative: Is there any advantage associated with (even though not caused by) the negative? Can you rephrase or redefine the negative to make the reader see it differently?

C   How will the **context** affect the reader's response? Think about your relationship to the reader, morale in the organization, the economy, the time of year, and any special circumstances.

Readers may like you or resent you. You may be younger or older than the people you're writing to. The organization may be prosperous or going through hard times; it may have just been reorganized or may be stable. All these different situations will affect what you say and how you say it.

Think about the news, the economy, the weather. Think about the general business and regulatory climate, especially as it affects the organization specified in the problem. Use the real world as much as possible. Think about interest rates, business conditions, and the economy. Is the industry in which the problem is set doing well? Is the government agency in which the problem is set enjoying general support? Think about the time of year. If it's fall when you write, is your business in a seasonal slowdown after a busy summer? Gearing up for the Christmas shopping rush? Or going along at a steady pace unaffected by seasons?

To answer these questions, draw on your experience, your courses, and your common sense. You may want to talk to other students or read *The Wall Street Journal* or look at a company's annual report. Sometimes you may even want to phone a local business person to get information. For instance, if you needed more information to think of reader benefits for a problem set in a bank, you could call a local banker to find out what kinds of services it offers customers and what its rates are for loans.

The remaining modules in this book will show you how to use this analysis to create business messages that meet your needs, the needs of the reader, and the needs of the organization.

Site to See

Go to
www.netflix.com

Netflix made video rentals easier by establishing a monthly fee and eliminating late charges. Later, the company made rentals available by allowing customers to watch them online.

Writing, scholars believe, was invented to record inventories of livestock and grain to calculate taxes.

Source: Denise Schmandt-Besserat, "The Earliest Precursor of Writing," *Scientific American,* 238, no. 6 (1978): 50–59.

Bob Kellaher, a manager of customer service operations at the New Haven Post Office, collects a last-minute tax return. Kellaher dresses as Uncle Sam every year and stands outside the post office collecting tax forms and mail. Because tax season is a particularly stressful time for individuals filing tax returns, even government organizations such as the U.S. Postal Service can benefit from efforts to foster customer satisfaction.

Summary of Learning Objectives

- Communication helps organizations and the people in them achieve their goals. The ability to write and speak well becomes increasingly important as you rise in an organization. **(LO 1-1)**
- People put things in writing to create a record, to convey complex data, to make things convenient for the reader, to save money, and to convey their own messages more effectively. **(LO 1-2)**
- **Internal documents** go to people inside the organization. **External documents** go to audiences outside: clients, customers, suppliers, stockholders, the government, the media, the general public. **(LO 1-3)**
- The three basic purposes of business and administrative communication are **to inform, to request or persuade, and to build goodwill.** Most messages have more than one purpose. **(LO 1-3)**
- A one-page message that took an hour to plan, write, and revise cost on average $21.15. Poor writing costs even more since it wastes time, wastes efforts, and jeopardizes goodwill. **(LO 1-4)**
- Good business and administrative writing meets five basic criteria: it's **clear, complete, and correct; it saves the reader's time;** and it **builds goodwill. (LO 1-5)**
- To evaluate a specific document, we must know the interactions among the writer, the reader(s), the purposes of the message, and the situation. No single set of words will work for all readers in all situations. **(LO 1-6)**
- To understand business communication situations, ask the following questions: **(LO 1-6)**
  - What's at stake—to whom?
  - Should you send a message?

- What channel should you use?
- What should you say?
- How should you say it?
- Use the PAIBOC question to analyze business communication problems: **(LO 1-6)**
  P What are your **purposes** in writing or speaking?
  A Who is (are) your **audience(s)?** How do members of your audience differ? What characteristics are relevant to the particular message?
  I What **information** must your message include?
  B What reasons or reader **benefits** can you use to support your position?
  O What **objection(s)** can you expect your reader(s) to have? What negative elements of your message must you deemphasize or overcome?
  C How will the **context** affect reader response? Think about your relationship to the reader, morale in the organization, the economy, the time of year, and any special circumstances.
- A solution to a business communication problem must both solve the organizational problem and meet the needs of the writer or speaker, the organization, and the audience. **(LO 1-6)**
- To think creatively, brainstorm, work within limits, consciously seek problems that need work, have a constructive argument, clean your desk, come in early, leave the office with a pencil and pad, and question conventional wisdom. **(LO 1-7)**

Assignments for Module 1

Questions for Comprehension

1.1 What are the three basic purposes of business messages? **(LO 1-3)**

1.2 What are the five basic criteria for effective messages? **(LO 1-5)**

1.3 What does PAIBOC stand for? **(LO 1-6)**

Questions for Critical Thinking

1.4 Why do writing and speaking become even more important as people rise in the organization? **(LO 1-1 to LO 1-3)**

1.5 If you're just looking for a low-level job, why is it still useful to be able to write and speak well? **(LO 1-1 to LO 1-3)**

1.6 Why do you need to understand the purposes, audience, and context for a message to know whether a specific set of words will work? **(LO 1-2)**

1.7 What opportunities do you have in volunteer or student organizations to do real "business writing" while you're in school? **(LO 1-5)**

Exercises and Problems

1.8 Discussing Strengths (LO 1-5, LO 1-6)

Introduce yourself to a small group of other students. Identify three of your strengths that might interest an

1.9 Introducing Yourself to Your Instructor (LO 1-5, LO 1-6)

Write a memo (at least 1½ pages long) introducing yourself to your instructor. Include the following topics:

employer. These can be experience, knowledge, or personality traits (like enthusiasm).

- Background: Where did you grow up? What have you done in terms of school, extracurricular activities, jobs, and family life?

- Interests: What are you interested in? What do you like to do? What do you like to think about and talk about?
- Achievements: What achievements have given you the greatest personal satisfaction? List at least five. Include things that gave you a real sense of accomplishment and pride, whether or not they're the sort of thing you'd list on a résumé.
- Goals: What do you hope to accomplish this term? Where would you like to be professionally and personally five years from now?

Use complete memo format with appropriate headings. (▶▶ Module 9 for examples of memo format.) Use a conversational writing style; check your draft to polish the style and edit for mechanical and grammatical correctness. A good memo will enable your instructor to see you as an individual. Use specific details to make your memo vivid and interesting. Remember that one of your purposes is to interest your reader!

1.10 Describing Your Experiences in and Goals for Writing (LO 1-5, LO 1-6)

Write a memo (at least 1½ pages long) to your instructor describing the experiences you've had writing and what you'd like to learn about writing during this course.

Answer several of the following questions:

- What memories do you have of writing? What made writing fun or frightening in the past?
- What have you been taught about writing? List the topics, rules, and advice you remember.
- What kinds of writing have you done in school? How long have the papers been?
- How has your school writing been evaluated? Did the instructor mark or comment on mechanics and grammar? Style? Organization? Logic? Content? Audience analysis and adaptation? Have you gotten extended comments on your papers? Have instructors in different classes had the same standards, or have you changed aspects of your writing for different classes?

- What voluntary writing have you done—journals, poems, stories, essays? Has this writing been just for you, or has some of it been shared or published?
- Have you ever written on a job or in a student or volunteer organization? Have you ever typed other people's writing? What have these experiences led you to think about real-world writing?
- What do you see as your current strengths and weaknesses in writing skills? What skills do you think you'll need in the future? What kinds of writing do you expect to do after you graduate?

Use complete memo format with appropriate headings. (▶▶ Module 9 for examples of memo format.) Use a conventional writing style; edit your final draft for mechanical and grammatical correctness.

1.11 Letters to Angry Electric Company Customers (LO 1-5 to LO 1-7)

Your regional electric utility provides power to rural, urban, and suburban customers. Recently, a series of heavy summer rainstorms knocked out electricity to thousands of customers. Because overhead power lines came down—in some cases due to inadequate tree trimming by home owners—some customers were without power for more than a week. In addition to the inconvenience of not having electricity, many customers also had to throw away spoiled food, as well as go without air conditioning on days when temperatures climbed past 90 degrees.

Today, you receive a letter from Harper Henry, a long-time customer and local business leader whose husband, Stephen D'Amico, is a county commissioner. Ms. Henry is

angry that power to her neighborhood was out for four days and that though similar storms have knocked out power in past years, nothing seems to have been done to prepare for future storms. In particular, there is no plan to bury overhead power lines. "Your company puts making money ahead of customer service," she writes. "You continue to post record profits while putting countless lives at stake, all for the sake of your bottom line."

The following letters are possible approaches to answering this complaint. How well does each message meet the needs of the reader, the writer, and the organization? Is the message clear, complete, and correct? Does it save the reader's time? Does it build goodwill?

1.
> Dear Sir or Madam:
>
> You opinion is valuable to us, and you can rest assured that we are looking into the problem. Should you have questions or concerns in the future, please do not hesitate to contact us.

2.
> Dear Harper:
>
> You're right — we dropped the ball on this one! But the utility business is an unpredictable one, and only God Himself controls the weather. So, while we deal with the frustration of being mere mortals, you can help us with your patience. Make sure, too, that you trim any trees that are on your property and are close to overhead power lines since falling trees caused a lot of the problems. With any luck, we'll all be better off in the next storm.
>
> P.S. How funny that someone named Harper would be sending a letter to complain!

3.

> Dear Mrs. Henry:
>
> The electric utility business is a particularly difficult one. You'd be surprised at all of the variables that come into play. For instance, there are union contracts to negotiate with employees. Did you know that we can't expect a lineman to work more than eight hours in one day without doubling his hourly rate? We also have to provide meals if the work goes beyond 12 hours and overnight accommodations if the worker must travel more than 50 miles from home. All that's just part of the labor issue. Unions are killing this business.
>
> There's also the cost of producing the electricity, meeting the government regulations for clean air in our coal-fired plants, and upkeep of the overhead power lines. As you know, we trim trees that are within 10 feet of any power line, but home owners are responsible for the other trees. Do they trim them? Of course not. Then a good wind comes along and knocks them down, right onto those lines. It's a crazy business, Mrs. Henry, and one that is a miracle to make any money in.
>
> Anyway, we're sorry for the inconvenience you faced. But I'm sure you can now see just how challenging all this is. Think about that the next time you flip a switch. This is what we do so you can have light to read by and television to watch. Your electric company is on your side.

4.

> Dear Ms. Henry:
>
> Thank you for your recent feedback regarding the power outage to your home.
>
> As you know, the storms that hit this year were particularly powerful. Hundreds of miles of overhead power lines were brought down in a matter of minutes, leaving thousands of customers stranded. Though more than 1,500 extra utility workers from surrounding states were brought in to help restore electricity, clearly we could have done better. Going without electricity for even a few minutes is too long, and we are making strides to improve our service.
>
> We are currently working with local municipalities to explore cost-effective ways to solve this problem. Suggestions from valuable customers like you will help in the effort. As you noted in your letter, burying power lines is an option to consider.
>
> Your loyalty and input will help us to provide even better service to customers.

1.12 Online Messages for Discussion—Responding to Rumors (LO 1-5 to LO 1-7)

The Acme Corporation has been planning to acquire Best Products, and Acme employees are worried about how the acquisition will affect them. Ed Zeplin, Acme's human resource manager, has been visiting the message boards on job search sites like Vault.com and sees a dramatic rise in the number of messages posted by people claiming to be Acme employees. Many of the messages are spreading rumors about layoffs, and most of the rumors are false.

The following messages are possible responses that Ed can post to the message boards. How well does each message meet the needs of the reader, the writer, and the organization? Is the message clear, complete, and correct? Does it save the reader's time? Does it build goodwill?

1.

> It Will Be Great!
> Author: L. Ed Zeplin, HR
> Date: Tuesday, May 23
>
> I am happy to tell you that the HR news is good. Two months ago, the CEO told me about the merger, and I have been preparing a human resource plan ever since.
>
> I want you to know about this because morale has been bad, and it shouldn't be. You really should wait for the official announcements, and you'll see that the staffing needs will remain strong. My department has been under a lot of pressure, but if you'll be patient, we'll explain everything—the staffing, the compensation.
>
> Our plan should be ready by Monday, and then if you have any questions, just contact your HR rep.

2.

> HR Staffing
> Author: HR Boss
> Date: Tuesday, May 23
>
> The rumors are false. Just ask anyone in HR. There will be no layoffs.

3.

> Don't Believe the Rumors
> Author: lezeplin@acme.com
> Date: Tuesday, May 23
>
> Acme has 475 employees, and Best Products has 132 employees. Our human resource plan for next year calls for 625 employees. If you do the math, you can see that there will be no layoffs. Rather, we will be hiring 20 employees. Of course, as we consolidate operations with Best, there will be some redeployments. However, our plan indicates that we will be able to retain our current staff. All employees are valued at Acme, as our current benefits package testifies.
>
> Our HR plan is based on the best analytic techniques and a business forecast by a top consulting firm. If you're an employee, you should review our business plan, at the Our Goals page on Acme's intranet. Everyone should read Acme's mission statement on our home page, www.acme.com/homepage.html.

4.

> Layoff Rumors Do Acme a Disservice
> Author: Zeplin in HR
> Date: Tuesday, 23 May
>
> If you come here to get your company information, you aren't getting the straight story. The people posting to this discussion board are spreading false rumors, not the truth. If you want to know the truth about Acme, ask the people who have access to the information.
>
> As HR manager, I can assure you we won't be laying off employees after the merger with Best Products. I'm the one who approves the staffing plan, so I should know. If people would ask me, instead of reading the negative, whining lies at this site, they would know the facts, too.
>
> If people really cared about job security, they would be meeting and exceeding their work goals, rather than wasting their time in rumor-mongering on message boards. Hard work: that's the key to success!

5.

> The True Story about Lay-Offs
> Author: lezeplin@acme.com
> Date: Tuesday, 23 May
>
> Whenever there is a merger or acquisition, rumors fly. It's human nature to turn to rumors when a situation seems uncertain. The case of Acme acquiring Best Products is no exception, so I'm not surprised to see rumors about layoffs posted on this message board.
>
> Have no fear! I am working closely with our CEO and with the CEO and human resource manager at Best Products, and we all agree that our current staff is a valuable asset to Acme, to Best, and to our combined companies in the future. We have no plans to lay off any of our valued people. I will continue monitoring this message board and will post messages as I am able to disclose more details about our staffing plans. In the meantime, employees should watch for official information in the company newsletter and on our intranet.
>
> We care about our people! If employees ever have questions about our plans and policies, they should contact me directly.
>
> L. Ed Zeplin, HR Manager

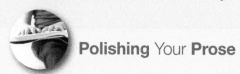

Polishing Your Prose

Sentence Fragments

A complete sentence has a subject and a verb. If either the subject or the verb is missing, the result is a sentence fragment.

> The job candidates.
> Passed seven rounds of interviews.
> And have taken three tests.

To fix the fragment, join it to other words to make a complete sentence.

> The job candidates passed seven rounds of interviews and have taken three tests.

Sentence fragments also occur when a clause has both a subject and a verb but is unable to stand by itself as a complete sentence.

> Although I read my e-mail
> Because she had saved her work
> If he upgrades his computer

The words *although, because,* and *since* make the clause subordinate, which means the clause cannot stand alone. It must be joined to a main clause.

> Although I read my e-mail, I **did not respond to the draft of the proposal.**
>
> Because she had saved her work, Paula **was able to restore it after the crash.**
>
> If he upgrades his computer, he **will be able to use the new software.**

Words that make clauses subordinate are

after	if
although, though	when, whenever
because, since	while, as
before, until	

Even sentences that have a subject and verb and are not subordinate may seem fragmentary in thought.

> The computer is.
> I need.
> She transfers.

Add more information to make the sentence clear.

> The computer is the latest model.
> I need more letterhead.
> She transfers to the logistics department on Tuesday.

Sometimes fragments are OK. For instance, fragments are used in résumés, advertisements, and some sales and fund-raising letters. However, fragments are inappropriate for most business documents. Because they are incomplete, they can confuse or mislead readers.

But the biggest problem with grammatical errors like sentence fragments is that readers sometimes assume that people who make errors are unprofessional or unpromotable (▶▶ Module 14). Of course, using "incorrect" grammar has nothing to do with intelligence, but many people nevertheless use grammar as a yardstick. People who cannot measure up to that yardstick may be stuck in low-level jobs.

Exercises

Make the following sentence fragments into complete sentences.

1. Making the most of a difficult situation.
2. The latest word processing app.
3. Mia, who recently graduated from business school.
4. Because Terrence will be in Portland for the day.
5. Downloading a patch for that software glitch.
6. Whenever Joyce gets a chance to review the file.
7. The vice president of our Chicago office, Ajay Sajda.
8. More than 20 years of IT experience, including consulting overseas.
9. Tweeted an invitation for the reception at the Four Seasons Hotel.
10. Chloe, certain the manufacturing license will be granted by July 2.

Check your answers to the odd-numbered exercises at the back of the book.

Adapting Your Message to Your Audience

Module 2 can help you best meet the needs of your audiences for communication. After completing the module, you should be able to

LO 2-1 **Understand expectations from your organization.**

LO 2-2 **Define audiences for messages.**

LO 2-3 **Apply strategies for audience analysis with PAIBOC.**

LO 2-4 **Apply strategies for individual and group audience analyses.**

LO 2-5 **Apply strategies for audience needs analysis.**

LO 2-6 **Adapt messages for audiences.**

LO 2-7 **Choose channels for audiences.**

Understanding your audience is fundamental to the success of any message. You need to adapt your message to fit the audience's goals, interests, and needs.

Analyzing your audience and adapting your message can be done in a cynical, manipulative way. It can also be done in a sensitive, empathic, ethical way. Audiences have a keen sense for messages that try to manipulate them; empathic analysis and adaptation are almost always more successful, as well as being more ethical.

Some students pride themselves on their "honesty" in not adapting their discourse to anyone and in criticizing their bosses as sharply as they might younger brothers and sisters. But almost all organizations expect deference to people in authority. And customers have enough options to deal only with companies that treat them respectfully.

With the rapid pace of communication today, analyzing audiences is a must. Before sending that next tweet or e-mail message, for instance, think carefully about all of the audiences that may read it. Do your best, but should mistakes happen, learn from them. Careful audience analysis combined with experience will help you to avoid problems.

Understanding What Your Organization Wants   LO 2-1

Michelle wondered whether her boss was sexist. Everyone else who had joined the organization when she did had been promoted. Her boss never seemed to have anything good to say about her or her work.

Michelle didn't realize that, in her boss's eyes, she wasn't doing good work. Michelle was proud of her reports; she thought she was the best writer in the office. But her boss valued punctuality, and Michelle's reports were always late.

Just as every sport has rules about scoring, so, too, do workplaces have rules about what "counts." Even in the same industry, different organizations and different supervisors may care about different things. One boss circles misspelled words and posts the offending message on a bulletin board for everyone to see. Other people are more tolerant of errors. One company values original ideas, while another workplace tells employees just to do what they're told. One supervisor likes technology and always buys the latest hardware and software; another is technophobic and has to be persuaded to get needed upgrades.

Succeeding in an organization depends first on understanding what "counts" at your organization. To find out what counts in your organization:

- Ask your boss, "What parts of my job are most important? What's the biggest thing I could do to improve my work?"
- Listen to the stories colleagues tell about people who have succeeded and those who have failed. When you see patterns, check for confirmation: "So his real problem was that he didn't socialize with co-workers?" This gives your colleagues a chance to provide feedback: "Well, it was more than never joining us for lunch. He didn't really seem to care about the company."
- Observe. See who is praised, who is promoted.

Understanding, by the way, can and should be a two-way street. Online shoe retailer Zappos.com listened to employees who said they wanted a workplace that is more accommodating to their lifestyle. The result was a nap room for a quick snooze and social events that include after-hours mixers and

lighthearted "parades" in the office. With $1 billion in sales in 2009 alone, the company also encourages its 1,500 employees to tweet about Zappos and hosts free daily tours of its Las Vegas headquarters. The work still gets done. In 2012, Zappos was named one of *CNNMoney's* 100 Best Companies to Work For.

Source: Morley Safer, "The 'Millennials' Are Coming," *60 Minutes,* November 11, 2007; and Jake Chessum, "How to Make Customers Love You," *Inc.,* 2010. Downloaded on February 12, 2010, at http://www.inc.com/ss/how-to-make-customers-love-you; and "100 Best Companies to Work For," *CNNMoney,* February 6, 2012, http://money.cnn.com/magazines/fortune/bestcompanies/2012/snapshots/11.html.

Who is my audience?   LO 2-2

▶ *More people than you might think!*

In an organizational setting, a message may have five separate audiences.[1]

1. The **primary audience** will decide whether to accept your recommendations or will act on the basis of your message. You must reach the decision maker to fulfill your purposes.
2. The **secondary audience** may be asked to comment on your message or to implement your ideas after they've been approved. Secondary audiences can also include lawyers

who may use your message—perhaps years later—as evidence of your organization's culture and practices.

3. The **initial audience** receives the message first and routes it to other audiences. Sometimes the initial audience also tells you to write the message.

4. A **gatekeeper** has the power to stop your message before it gets to the primary audience. A secretary who decides who gets to speak to or see the boss is a gatekeeper. Sometimes the supervisor who assigns the message is also the gatekeeper; however, sometimes the gatekeeper is higher in the organization. In some cases, gatekeepers exist outside the organization.

5. A **watchdog audience,** though it does not have the power to stop the message and will not act directly on it, has political, social, or economic power. The watchdog pays close attention to the transaction between you and the primary audience and may base future actions on its evaluation of your message.

As the charts in Figures 2.1 and 2.2 show, one person or group can be part of two audiences. Frequently, a supervisor is both the initial audience and the gatekeeper. Sometimes the initial audience is also the primary audience that will act on the message.

Figure 2.1 The Audiences for a Marketing Plan

Writer	An account executive in an ad agency
Initial audience	Her boss, who asks her to write the plan
Gatekeeper	Her boss, who must approve the plan before it goes to the client
Primary audience	The executive committee of the client company, which will decide whether to adopt the plan
Secondary audiences	The marketing staff of the client company, who will be asked for comments on the plan The artists, writers, and media buyers who will implement the plan if it is accepted

Figure 2.2 The Audiences for a Consulting Report

Writers	Two workers at a consulting think tank
Initial audience	A consortium of manufacturers, which hires the think tank to investigate how proposed federal regulations would affect manufacturing, safety, and cost
Gatekeeper	The consortium. If the consortium doesn't like the report, it won't send it on to the federal government.
Primary audience	The federal government agency that regulates this consumer product. It will set new regulations based in part (the manufacturers hope) on this report. Within this audience are economists, engineers, and policymakers.
Secondary audiences	The general public Other manufacturers of the product Other clients and potential clients of the consulting think tank The consulting think tank's competitors
Watchdog audience	Industry reviewers who read drafts of the report and commented on it. Although they had no direct power over this report, their goodwill was important for the consulting company's image—and its future contracts. Their comments were the ones that authors took more seriously as they revised their drafts.

In what can at best be described as a baffling move, Nivea for Men ran an advertisement in *Esquire* suggesting men "re-civilize" themselves, complete with an image of a man in business casual clothes tossing away a head with a beard and Afro. The company later apologized for the ad, which prompted public outcry. Even if some audiences are untroubled by the content of a message, good communicators take into consideration all of the audiences for that message. At the very least, they should re-think messages that appeal to some audiences at the expense of other audiences.

Source: Ellen Tumposky, "Nivea for Men Pulls Plug on Ad It Calls 'Offensive,'" *ABC News,* August 19, 2011, http://abcnews.go.com/Business/nivea-men-pulls-plug-ad-calls-offensive/story?id=14342539.

Why is my audience so important? LO 2-3

► *To be successful, messages must meet the audiences' needs.*

Good business communication is audience-centered. Audience is central to both PAIBOC and to the communication process.

Audience and PAIBOC

Think about the PAIBOC questions in Module 1 (►► p. 12). Of the six questions, the five in blue relate to audience.

P   What are your **purposes** in writing or speaking?
> Your purposes come from you and your organization. Your audience determines how you achieve those purposes, but not what the purposes are.

A   Who is (are) your **audience(s)?** How do members of your audience differ? What characteristics are relevant to this particular message?
> These questions ask directly about your audience.

I   What **information** must your message include?
> The information you need to give depends on your audience. You need to say more when the topic is new to your audience. If your audience has heard something but may have forgotten it, you'll want to protect readers' egos by saying "As you know," or putting the information in a subordinate clause: "Because we had delivery problems last quarter, ..."

B   What reasons or reader **benefits** can you use to support your position?
> What counts as a good reason and what is a benefit depends on your audience. For some audiences, personal experience counts as a good reason. Other audiences are more persuaded by scientific studies or by experts. For some people, saving money is a good benefit of growing vegetables. Other people may care less about the money than about avoiding chemicals, growing varieties that aren't available in grocery stores, or working outside in the fresh air. ►► Module 8 gives more information on developing reader benefits.

On his blog, Robert Greene, who co-wrote the best-selling *The 50th Law* with musician 50 Cent, notes the performer's four principles for reaching his audience. Among them is to "crush as much distance as possible between you and your audience," reaching people and their inner lives and reflecting their spirit in your message.

Source: Robert Greene, "Four Things 50 Cent Can Teach You About Connecting with Your Audience," downloaded on February 16, 2010, at http://www.copyblogger.com/robert-greene-50-cent/.

Instant Replay

Five Kinds of Audiences

Initial

Is first to receive the message; may assign message.

Gatekeeper

Has the power to stop the message before it gets to primary audience.

Primary

Decides whether to accept recommendations; acts.

Secondary

Comments on message or implements recommendations.

Watchdog

Has political, social, or economic power; may base future actions on its evaluation of your message.

Carl Caspers understands the market for Harmony Systems' prostheses because he is part of it. Often, however, you'll have to analyze audiences of which you are not a part.

O   What **objection(s)** can you expect your reader(s) to have? What negative elements of your message must you deemphasize or overcome?

> Different audiences will have different attitudes. One audience may object to a price increase. Another audience may expect price changes as routine and not be bothered by them. ▶▶ Module 12 on persuasion gives more information on overcoming objections.

C   How will the **context** affect reader response? Think about your relationship to the reader, morale in the organization, the economy, the time of year, and any special circumstances.

> People exist in a context. How well they know you, how they feel about you and your organization, how well the economy is doing, even what's been in the news recently will all influence the way they respond to your message.

Audience and the Communication Process

Audience is also central to the communication process.

The following model of the communication process drastically simplifies what is perhaps the most complex of human activities. However, even a simplified model can give us a sense of the complexity of the communication process. And the model is useful in helping us see where and why miscommunication occurs. Figure 2.3 shows the basic process that occurs when one person tries to communicate ideas to someone else.

The process begins when Person A (let's call him Alex) **perceives** some stimulus. Here we are talking about literal perception: the ability to see, to hear, to taste, to smell, to touch. Next, Alex **interprets** what he has perceived. Is it important? Unusual? The next step is for Alex to **choose** or **select** the information he wishes to send to Person B (whom we'll call Barbara). Now Alex is ready to put his ideas into words. (Some people argue that we can think only in words and would put this stage before interpretation and choice.) Words are not the only way to convey ideas; gestures, clothing, and pictures can carry meaning nonverbally. The stage of putting ideas into any of these symbols is called **encoding.** Then Alex must **transmit** the message to Barbara using some **channel.** Channels include memos, phone calls, meetings, billboards, TV ads, and e-mail, to name just a few.

To receive the message, Barbara must first **perceive** it. Then she must **decode** it, that is, extract meaning from the symbols. Barbara then repeats the steps Alex has gone through:

Understanding potential objections from audiences requires thinking about the context of the situation, including timing. When the Cedar River flooded his home with 13 feet of water and destroyed most of his possessions, Justin Van Fleet asked for help from the Federal Emergency Management Agency (FEMA). He was living in a FEMA trailer when, after repeated applications, he was granted more than $20,000 from the agency. The following March, however, Van Fleet received a letter from FEMA stating he should never have received the money and had 30 days to repay it. The agency admitted to such mistakes but also noted by law it's required to recover funds—little comfort to thousands of Americans who collectively received more than $22 million because of FEMA errors.

Source: Ryan J. Foley, "FEMA Asks for Return of Disaster Aid," May 10, 2011, http://news.yahoo.com/s/ap/20110510/ap_on_re_us/us_fema_reclaiming_aid.

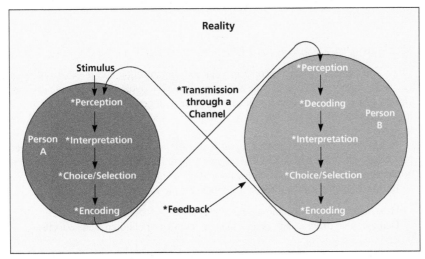

Figure 2.3 A Model of Two-Person Communication with Feedback

*Noise (and miscommunication) can occur here.

A test question featuring a talking pineapple ended up baffling eighth graders on a recent standardized exam. Though offered in the context of a fable, the concept of a piece of fruit challenging anyone to a race so confused students that the question ultimately was thrown out. Care must be taken to anticipate how audiences will understand or interpret communication, especially if it presents unusual ideas.

Source: Valerie Strauss, ""Talking Pineapple Question on Standardized Test Baffles Students," *The Washington Post,* April 20, 2012, http://www.washingtonpost.com/blogs/answer-sheet/post/talking-pineapple-question-on-standardized-test-baffles-students/2012/04/20/gIQA8I01VT_blog.html.

interpreting the information, choosing a response, and encoding it. The response Barbara sends to Alex is called **feedback.** Feedback may be direct and immediate or indirect and delayed; it may be verbal or nonverbal.

Noise can interfere with every aspect of the communication process. Noise may be physical or psychological. Physical noise could be a phone line with static, a lawn mower roaring outside a classroom, or handwriting that is hard to read. Psychological noise could include disliking a speaker, being concerned about something other than the message, or already having one's mind made up on an issue.

Channel overload occurs when the channel cannot handle all the messages that are being sent. A small business may have only two phone lines; no one else can get through if both lines are in use. **Information overload** occurs when more messages are transmitted than the human receiver can handle. Some receivers process information "first come, first served." Some may try to select the most important messages and ignore others. A third way is to depend on abstracts or summaries prepared by other people. None of these ways is completely satisfactory.

At every stage, both Alex and Barbara could misperceive, misinterpret, choose badly, encode poorly, or choose inappropriate channels. Miscommunication can also occur because different people have different frames of reference. We always interpret messages in light of our personal experiences, our cultures and subcultures, and even the point in history at which we live.

Successful communication depends on the common ground between you and your audience. Choose information that your audience needs and will find interesting. Encode your message in words and other symbols the audience will understand. Transmit the message along a channel that your audience will attend to.

What do I need to know about my audience(s)? LO 2-4

▶ *Everything that's relevant to what you're writing or talking about.*

Almost everything about your audience is relevant to some message. But for any particular message, only a few facts about your audience will be relevant.

Since the factors that matter vary depending on the situation, no one-size-fits-all list of questions for audience analysis exists. In general, you need to use common sense and empathy. **Empathy** is the ability to put yourself in someone else's shoes, to feel with that person. Empathy requires not being self-centered because, in all probability, the audience is *not* just like you. Use what you know about people and about organizations to predict likely responses.

Analyzing Individuals and Members of Groups

When you write or speak to people in your own organization and in other organizations you work closely with, you may be able to analyze your audience as individuals. You may already know your audience; it will usually be easy to get additional information by talking to members of your audience, talking to people who know your audience, and observing your audience.

In other organizational situations, you'll analyze your audience as members of a group: "taxpayers who must be notified that they owe more income tax," "customers living in the northeast side of the city," or "employees with small children."

Information that is most often helpful includes the following:

- How much the audience knows about your topic
- Demographic factors, such as age, income, number of children, and so forth
- Personality
- Values and beliefs
- Past behavior

Message/Purpose	Audience	Relevant Factors
Memo announcing that the company will reimburse employees for tuition if they take work-related college courses	All employees	• Attitudes toward education (some people find courses fun; others may be intimidated) • Time available (some may be too busy) • Interest in being promoted or in getting cross-training • Attitude toward company (those committed to its success will be more interested in program)
Letter offering special financing on a new or used car	College students	• Income • Expectations of future income (and ability to repay loan) • Interest in having a new car • Attitude toward cars offered by that dealership • Knowledge of interest rates • Access to other kinds of financing
Letter giving a meeting agenda and saying that you will bring your child along	Client	• How well the client knows you • How much the client likes you • How important agenda items are to the client • How the client feels about children • Physical space for meeting (room for child to play)

When Louisiana Representative John Fleming downplayed his annual income of $6 million on MSNBC while discussing his opposition to taxes on the rich, he raised the eyebrows of interviewer Chris Jansing. Fleming pointed out he actually takes home only about $600,000, with $200,000 less after meeting living expenses, to which Lansing stated, "You do understand, congressman, that the average person out there who's making maybe 40, 50, $60,000 out there, when they hear you only have $400,000 left over, it's not exactly a sympathetic position." How audiences interpret messages depends on both the facts being presented and their emotional reactions to them.

Source: Chris Moody, "Rep. John Fleming Fields Criticism Over 600K Income," September 20, 2011, http://news.yahoo.com/blogs/ticket/rep-john-fleming-field-criticism-over-600k-income-153305241.html.

Knowledge

Even people in your own organization won't share all your knowledge. USAA provides insurance to military personnel and their families, but not all the 22,000 people who work there know insurance jargon.[2]

Most of the time, you won't know exactly what your audience knows. Moreover, even if you've told readers before, they may not remember the old information when they read the new message. To remind readers of information in a tactful way,

- Preface statements with "As you know," "As you may know," or a similar phrase.
- Spell out acronyms the first time you use them: "Employee Stock Ownership Plan (ESOP)."
- Give brief definitions in the text: "the principal—the money you have invested—."
- Put information readers should know in a subordinate clause: "Because the renovation is behind schedule, . . ."

Demographic Factors

Demographic characteristics are measurable features that can be counted objectively: age, sex, race, religion, education level, income, and so on.

Sometimes demographic information is irrelevant; sometimes it's important. Does age matter? Most of the time, probably not. (Mick Jagger is more than 60 years old, but he probably doesn't subscribe to *Modern Maturity*.) On the other hand, if you were explaining a change in your company's pension plan, you'd expect older workers to be more concerned than younger workers.

Business and nonprofit organizations get demographic data by surveying their customers, clients, and donors; by using U.S. census data; or by purchasing demographic

Site to See

Go to
http://www.census.gov/

for demographic information about the U.S. population and more. To get information on your community, click on "American Factfinder."

Keep audiences in mind when using social networking sites. Lee Landor, deputy press secretary to Scott M. Stringer, Manhattan borough president, resigned after her reference to President Barack Obama as "O-dumb-a" and racially tinged comments during a heated exchange about the arrest of Harvard scholar Henry Louis Gates, Jr., on Facebook became public. Her situation rivals that of a woman in the United Kingdom who posted "OMG I HATE MY JOB!" after insulting her boss . . . and then found out he was a Facebook friend. She not only lost the job with two weeks left on her probationary period, but the exchange went viral on the web.

Source: Sewell Chan, "Facebook Postings Prompt Quick Exit of a City Politician's Aide," *The New York Times,* July 28, 2009, http://www.nytimes.com/2009/07/29/nyregion/29fired.html?_r=2; and Marisa Taylor, "The Perils of Oversharing on Facebook," *The Wall Street Journal,* August 21, 2009, http://blogs.wsj.com/digits/2009/08/21/the-perils-of-oversharing-on-facebook/.

data from marketing companies. For many messages, simply identifying subsets of your audience is enough. For example, a school board trying to win support for a tax increase knows that not everyone living in the district will have children in school. It isn't necessary to know the exact percentages to realize that successful messages will need to appeal not only to parents but also to voters who won't directly benefit from the improvements that the tax increase will fund.

Personality

When your primary audience is just one person, his or her personality is relevant. There are many ways to analyze personality. For business, one of the most useful is the **Myers-Briggs Type Indicator**® instrument, which uses four pairs of dichotomies to identify ways that people differ.[3]

- **Extraversion–Introversion:** where someone gets energy. Introverted types get their energy from within; extraverted types are energized by interacting with other people.
- **Sensing–Intuition:** how someone gets information. Sensing types gather information through their senses, preferring what is real and tangible. Intuitive types prefer to look at the big picture, focusing on the relationships and connections between facts.
- **Thinking–Feeling:** how someone makes decisions. Thinking types consider logical consequences of an action to reach decisions. Feeling types make decisions based on the impact to people.
- **Judging–Perceiving:** how someone orients himself or herself to the external world. Judging types like to live in a planned, orderly way, seeking closure. Perceiving types prefer a flexible environment, enjoying possibilities.

Some businesses administer the Myers-Briggs Type Indicator® instrument to all employees. They find that results can be used to assist with team building and/or personal growth and development.

Knowing your audience's personality type can help you select the appropriate channel and craft your message. For instance, an introvert might want a written message because it favors contemplation, while an extravert might instead prefer the dynamics of a phone call or face-to-face meeting. Sensitive types look for detailed facts, arranged sequentially so they can judge each accordingly, while intuitive types want to know the overall situation first to then apply creative solutions.

You'll be most persuasive if you play to your audience's strengths. Indeed, many of the general principles of business communication reflect the types most common among managers. Putting the main point up front satisfies the needs of judging types, and some 75% of U.S. managers are judging. Giving logical reasons satisfies the needs of the nearly 80% of U.S. managers who are thinking types.[4]

Know that human beings are also adaptable. For instance, some research suggests that while only 50% of Americans are estimated to be extraverts, the vast majority of managers and executives demonstrate extraverted personality traits.[5] Introverts can learn many of the associated behaviors, even if they're not their inclination.

Site to See

Go to
www.claritas.com/MyBestSegments/Default.jsp?ID=20

Key in your Zip code to learn which psychographic groups are most common in your neighborhood.

Values and Beliefs

Psychographic characteristics are qualitative rather than quantitative: values, beliefs, goals, and lifestyles. For example, two families living next door to each other might make about the same amount of money and each have two children. But one family might save every possible penny for college and retirement, taking inexpensive vacations and cooking meals at home rather than eating out. The other family might spend almost everything they make on clothes, cars, vacations, entertainment, and dinners out. One family might do most things together as a family, while in the other members might spend most of their time on individual activities. The families might have different religious and political beliefs.

If you wanted to persuade each family to do the same thing, you might need to use different reasons and reader benefits; you would have different objections to overcome.

Knowing what your audience finds important allows you to organize information in a way that seems natural to your audience and to choose appeals that audience members will find persuasive.

Many marketers use the **Values and Lifestyles (VALS)** profiles developed by the SRI research firm in California. VALS profiles divide U.S. buyers into eight categories according to their primary motivation, the amount of resources they have, and the extent to which they innovate. For instance, Strivers are motivated by achievement and are relatively low in resources and innovation. These conspicuous consumers try to be in style, even without a lot of money.

Innovators, on the other hand, may have more disposable income and enjoy cooking and fine food. As Patricia Breman, a senior consultant for SRI Consulting Business Intelligence, points out, Innovators may be an excellent target market for upscale grocery stores.[6]

The other VALS categories are Thinkers, Believers, Achievers, Experiencers, Makers, and Survivors.[7]

Researcher Mary Modahl's survey of 250,000 households found that online buying depends not on demographics such as age and Zip code but on psychographics: the consumer's attitude toward technology along a continuum from "profoundly suspicious" to "eagerly accepting."[8]

Past Behavior

How people have behaved in the past often predicts how they'll behave in the future. For example, examining records of customer purchases showed Fingerhut that customers who moved made large purchases of furniture and decorations. Fingerhut developed a "mover's catalog" filled with products likely to appeal to this group—and saved money by not mailing other catalogs to this group right after they moved.[9]

Analyzing People in Organizations

Your reader's reaction is affected not only by his or her personal preferences and feelings but also by the discourse communities to which the reader belongs and by the organizational culture.

Some aspects of corporate culture may no longer serve an obvious purpose.

Ken Blanchard is now a successful business writer with a track record of bestsellers, including *The One Minute Manager*, but people used to tell him he wrote poorly. Blanchard has said that when he was a student in graduate school, professors told him he could not write well enough to succeed as a college professor. But he adds, "Later I learned that the problem with my writing from their point of view was that you could understand it, which meant it wasn't academic enough." At the time, however, he accepted the advice and pursued a career in administration. To date, Blanchard's books have sold more than 20 million copies. His latest is *Great Leaders Grow: Becoming a Leader in Life*.

Source: Based on Kevin Ryan, *Write Up the Corporate Ladder* (New York: Amacom, 2003), 126–27; and Dan Schawbel, "Ken Blanchard on How Great Leaders Grow," *Forbes,* March 1, 2012, http://www.forbes.com/sites/danschawbel/2012/03/01/ken-blanchard-on-howgreat-leaders-grow/.

"I don't know how it started, either. All I know is that it's part of our corporate culture."

Copyright © 1994 Mick Stevens/The New Yorker Collection, www.cartoonbank.com.

A **discourse community** is a group of people who share assumptions about what channels, formats, and styles to use, what topics to discuss and how to discuss them, and what constitutes evidence. Each person is part of several discourse communities, which may or may not overlap.

To analyze an organization's discourse community, ask the following questions:

- What channels, formats, and styles are preferred for communication? Do you write a paper memo, send e-mail, or walk down the hall to talk to someone? How formal or informal are you supposed to be?
- What do people talk about? What is not discussed?
- What kind of and how much evidence is needed to be convincing? Is personal experience convincing? Do you need numbers and formal research?

Procter & Gamble's discourse community requires that recommendations be just one page. So writers create one-page memos—and then add as many pages of "attachments" as they need. In contrast, a Silicon Valley company expects recommendations to be presented as a PowerPoint slide with a triangle with three words around it.

An **organization's culture** is its values, attitudes, and philosophies. Organizational culture (or **corporate culture,** as it is often called; ▶▶ Module 3) is revealed verbally in the organization's myths, stories, and heroes and nonverbally in the allocation of space, money, and power.

The following questions will help you analyze an organization's culture:

- What are the organization's goals? Making money? Serving customers and clients? Advancing knowledge? Contributing to the community?
- What does the organization value? Diversity or homogeneity? Independence or being a team player? Creativity or following orders?
- How do people get ahead? Are rewards based on seniority, education, being well-liked, making technical discoveries, or serving customers? Are rewards available to only a few top people, or is everyone expected to succeed?
- How formal are behavior, language, and dress?

Two companies in the same field may have very different cultures. To compare corporate cultures, Cecilia Rothenberger reviewed how two executives described their own organizations.[10] According to her, Andersen Consulting, which employs 65,000 people in 48 countries, values compensation, bonuses, prestige, resources, and rewards; the 35-person Creative Good firm values communication, relationships, creativity, and growth. Researcher Jennifer Chatman found that new hires who "fit" a company's culture were more likely to stay with the job, be more productive, and be more satisfied than those who did not fit the culture.[11]

Organizations can have subcultures. For example, manufacturing and marketing may represent different subcultures in the same organization: workers may dress differently and have different values.

You can learn about organizational culture by observing people and by listening to the stories they tell. Here are two of the stories Nike's leaders tell.

Instant Replay

Discourse Community

A **discourse community** is a group of people who share assumptions about what channels, formats, and styles to use, what topics to discuss and how to discuss them, and what constitutes evidence.

Story	Lesson
Coach Bowerman (a company co-founder) decided his team needed better running shoes. So he went into his workshop and poured rubber into the family waffle iron to create a waffle sole.	Nike is committed to innovation.
Steve Prefontaine (a runner and another co-founder) worked to make running a professional sport and to get better-performing equipment.	Nike is committed to helping athletes.

You can also learn about a company's culture by looking at its website. Many companies try to describe their cultures, usually as part of the section on employment.

Now that I have my analysis, what do I do with it?   LO 2-5

▶ *Use it to plan strategy, organization, style, document design, and visuals.*

If you know your audience well and if you use words well, much of your audience analysis and adaptation will be unconscious. If you don't know your audience or if the message is very important, take the time to analyze your audience formally and to revise your draft with your analysis in mind.

You can adapt your message's strategy, organization, and style to meet the audience's needs. For paper or electronic documents, you can also adapt the document's design and the photos or illustrations you choose.

Strategy

- Make the action as easy as possible.
- Protect the reader's ego.
- Decide how to balance logic and emotion, what details to use, and whether to use a hard-sell or soft-sell approach based on the specific audience, the organizational culture, and the discourse community.
- Choose appeals and reader benefits that work for the specific audience (▶▶ Module 8).
- Modules 7, 11, and 13 will show you how to emphasize positive aspects, decide how much information to include, and overcome obstacles.

Organization

- Because most managers are intuitive types, it's usually better to get to the point right away. The major exceptions are
  - When we must persuade a reluctant reader.
  - When we have bad news and want to let the reader down gradually.
- Make the organizational pattern clear to the audience. Modules 9, 23, and 24 show you how to use headings and overviews. Module 20 shows how to use overviews and signposts in oral presentations.

Style

- For most audiences, use easy-to-understand words, a mixture of sentence lengths, and paragraphs with topic sentences (▶▶ Modules 15 and 16).
- Avoid words that sound defensive or arrogant.
- Avoid hot buttons or "red-flag" words to which some readers will have an immediate negative reaction: *criminal, un-American, crazy, fundamentalist, liberal.*
- Use the language(s) that your audience knows best. In Quebec, messages are normally presented both in English and in French. In the Southwest United States, messages may be most effective printed in both English and Spanish.
- Use conversational, not "academic," language.

"Terrifying," "psychedelic," and "awesomely bad" were among terms critics used to describe an advertisement by California Senate candidate Carly Fiorina's campaign that attacked her opponent, Tom Campbell. The video combined live action with animation to show a flock of sheep infiltrated by a red-eyed, costumed human. While Michael Scherer in *Time* notes the spot is "so weird that you will click on it online," the question remains whether getting attention is the same as swaying the audience.

Source: Brett Michael Dykes, "Bizarre Attack Ad Heats Up California Senate Race," February 4, 2010, http://news.yahoo.com/s/ynews/ynews_pl1112.

To tap into youth markets, companies are seeking advice from people in the target market. Natalie Rodriguez, Heide Panglemaier, and Rosaura Lezama offer their opinions of marketers' efforts through 3iying.com.

Instant Replay

Organizational Culture

An **organization's culture** is its values, attitudes, and philosophies. Organizational culture (or **corporate culture** as it is also called) is revealed verbally in the organization's myths, stories, and heroes and nonverbally in the allocation of space, money, and power.

Document Design

- Use lists, headings, and a mix of paragraph lengths to create white space.
- Choices about format, footnotes, and visuals may be determined by the organizational culture or the discourse community.
- ►► Module 5 for advice about effective document design.

Photographs and Visuals

- Use bias-free photographs and clip art (►► Module 25).
- Photos and visuals can make a document look more informal or more formal. Think of the difference between cartoons and photos of "high art."
- Some cultures (e.g., French, Japanese) use evocative photographs that bear little direct relationship to the text. Most U.S. audiences expect photos that clearly relate to the text, often with a caption that further reinforces the connection.
- For electronic and web documents, consider content and such issues as music or time to download, especially with video or animation.

What if my audiences have different needs?   LO 2-6

▶ *Focus on gatekeepers and decision makers.*

When the members of your audience share the same interests and the same level of knowledge, you can use the principles outlined earlier for individual readers or for members of homogenous groups. But often different members of the audience have different needs.

When it is not possible to meet everyone's needs, meet the needs of gatekeepers and primary audiences first.

Content and Choice of Details

- Provide an overview or executive summary for readers who just want the main points.
- In the body of the document, provide enough detail for primary audiences and for anyone else who could veto your proposal.
- If the primary audiences don't need details that other audiences will want, provide those details in appendices—statistical tabulations, earlier reports, and so forth.

Organization

- Use headings and a table of contents so readers can turn to the portions that interest them.
- Organize your message based on the primary audiences' attitudes toward it.

Achieving buy-in from audiences can be easier by role-playing first with a friend or colleague to test ideas and prepare for possible objections. That gives you the opportunity to hone the approach.

Source: John Kotter, "If You Think You're Prepared, Think Again," *The Harvard Business Review,* April 19, 2011, http://blogs.hbr.org/kotter/2011/04/if-you-think-youre-prepared-th.html.

Level of Formality

- Avoid personal pronouns. *You* ceases to have a specific meaning when several different audiences use a document.
- If both internal and external audiences will use a document, use a slightly more formal style than you would in an internal document.
- Use a more formal style when you write to international audiences.

Use of Technical Terms and Theory

- In the body of the document, assume the degree of knowledge that primary audiences will have.
- Put background information and theory under separate headings. Then readers can use the headings and the table of contents to read or skip these sections, as their knowledge dictates.
- If primary audiences will have more knowledge than other audiences, provide a glossary of terms. Early in the document, let readers know that the glossary exists.

The culture at software company Siebel Systems is professional and competitive. Employees can't eat at their desks. Men wear suits; women wear pantsuits or skirted suits with panty hose. Employees are rated, and every year the lowest 5% are fired.

Sun Microsystems' corporate culture fosters informality and flexibility. Employees can use the iWork computer facilities at various Sun drop-in centers, or enroll in the work-from-home program. This provides employees with flexible workplaces and saves valuable driving time, enabling Sun Microsystems to retain the best talent available.

Both companies are now owned by software giant Oracle Corporation.

How do I reach my audience(s)? LO 2-7

▶ *Important messages may require multiple channels.*

Communication channels vary in

- Speed
- Accuracy of transmission
- Cost
- Number of messages carried
- Number of people reached
- Efficiency
- Ability to promote goodwill

The family of Sergeant Jesse Jasper received a "red line" phone call that he, along with Sergeant Tyler Judin, had been killed in action. What they didn't learn until hours later was that Jasper was alive and well. As a result, the U.S. Army's 82nd Airborne Division is reconsidering how its family readiness group notifies all families of individual deaths within the unit. While Jasper's father said, "I don't know why they would tell us about someone else's tragedy," the unit is considering revising messages to start with "Your son or daughter is fine" when that is the case.

Source: Carolyn Thompson, "NY Dad Told Soldier-Son Killed in War—He Wasn't," September 16, 2009, http://news.yahoo.com/s/ap/20090916/ap_on_re_us/us_afghanistan_not_dead.

Depending on your purposes, the audience, and the situation, one channel may be better than another.

A written message makes it easier to

- Present many specific details of a law, policy, or procedure.
- Present extensive or complex financial data.
- Minimize undesirable emotions.

Messages on paper are more formal than e-mail messages. E-mail messages are appropriate for routine messages to people you already know. Paper is usually better for someone to whom you're writing for the first time.

Oral messages make it easier to

- Answer questions, resolve conflicts, and build consensus.
- Use emotion to help persuade the audience.
- Get immediate action or response.
- Focus the audience's attention on specific points.
- Modify a proposal that may not be acceptable in its original form.

Scheduled meetings and oral presentations are more formal than phone calls or stopping someone in the hall.

Important messages should use more formal channels, whether they're oral or written. Oral and written messages have many similarities. In both, you should

- Adapt the message to the specific audience.
- Show the audience members how they benefit from the idea, policy, service, or product (▶▶ Module 8).
- Overcome any objections the audience may have.
- Use you-attitude and positive emphasis (▶▶ Modules 6 and 7).
- Use visuals to clarify or emphasize material (▶▶ Module 25).
- Specify exactly what the audience should do.

Even when everyone in an organization has access to the same channels, different discourse communities may prefer different ones. When a university updated its employee benefits manual, the computer scientists and librarians wanted the information online. Faculty wanted to be able to read the information on paper. Maintenance workers and carpenters wanted to get answers on voice mail.[12]

The bigger your audience, the more complicated channel choice becomes because few channels reach everyone in your target audience. When possible, use multiple channels. Also use multiple channels for very important messages. For example, talk to key players about a written document before the meeting where the document will be discussed.

Summary of Learning Objectives

- Succeeding in an organization depends first on understanding what "counts" at your organization. To find out what counts in your organization, ask your boss thoughtful questions, listen to the stories colleagues tell about people who have succeeded and those who have failed, and observe who is praised and promoted. **(LO 2-1)**
- The **primary audience** will make a decision or act on the basis of your message. The **secondary audience** may be asked by the primary audience to comment on your message or to implement your ideas after they've been approved. The **initial audience** routes the message to other audiences and may assign the message. A **gatekeeper** controls whether the message gets to the primary audience. A **watchdog audience** has political, social,

or economic power and may base future actions on its evaluation of your message. **(LO 2-2)**
- A sender goes through the following steps: **perception, interpretation, choice** or **selection, encoding, transmitting** the message through a **channel.** The receiver perceives the message, **decodes** it, interprets it, chooses a response, encodes the response, and transmits it. The message transmitted to the original sender is called **feedback. Noise** is anything that interferes with communication; it can be both physical and psychological. Miscommunication can occur at every point in the communication process. **(LO 2-3)**
- **Channel overload** occurs when a channel cannot handle all the messages being sent. **Information overload** occurs when

the receiver cannot process all the messages that arrive. Both kinds of overload require some sort of selection to determine which messages will be sent and which ones will be attended to. **(LO 2-3)**

- Common sense and empathy are crucial to good audience analysis. **(LO 2-3)**

- A **discourse community** is a group of people who share assumptions about what channels, formats, and styles to use, what topics to discuss and how to discuss them, and what constitutes evidence. **(LO 2-4)**

- An **organization's culture** is its values, attitudes, and philosophies. Organizational culture is revealed verbally in the organization's myths, stories, and heroes and nonverbally in the allocation of space, money, and power. **(LO 2-4)**

- Almost everything about your audience is relevant to some message. But for any particular message, only a few facts about your audience will be relevant. Use **empathy** to put yourself in "someone else's shoes," and look at such factors as knowledge, demographics, personality, psychographics, past behavior, discourse community, and organizational culture. **(LO 2-4)**

- If you don't know your audience or if the message is very important, take the time to analyze your audience formally and to revise your draft with your analysis in mind. You can adapt your message's strategy, organization, and style to meet the audience's needs. For paper or electronic documents, you can also adapt the document's design and the photos or illustrations you choose. **(LO 2-5)**

- When you write to multiple audiences, use the primary audience and the gatekeeper to determine level of detail, organization, level of formality, and use of technical terms and theory. **(LO 2-6)**

- You can adapt your message's strategy, organization, and style to meet the audience's needs. For paper or electronic documents, you can also adapt the document's design and the photos or illustrations you choose. **(LO 2-6)**

- The best channel for a message will depend on the audience, the sender's purposes, and the situation. Channel choice may be shaped by the organizational culture. **(LO 2-7)**

- When you communicate to a big audience or talk about an important topic, use multiple channels. **(LO 2-7)**

Assignments for Module 2

Questions for Comprehension

2.1 What are the five kinds of audiences? **(LO 2-2)**

2.2 What are ways to analyze your audience? **(LO 2-3, LO 2-4)**

2.3 What are three ways to adapt your message to your audience? **(LO 2-5, LO 2-6)**

Questions for Critical Thinking

2.4 Emphasizing the importance of audience, marketers frequently say, "The customer is in control." To what extent do you feel in control as a customer, a student, a citizen? What actions could you take to increase your control? **(LO 2-1 to LO 2-3)**

2.5 If you are employed, which aspects of your organization's culture match your own values? What kind of culture would you like to join when you are next on the job market? **(LO 2-1 to LO 2-3)**

2.6 Why do internal audiences, especially your boss, sometimes feel more important than primary audiences outside your organization? **(LO 2-1 to LO 2-3)**

2.7 What are your options if your boss's criteria for a document are different than those of the primary audience? **(LO 2-1 to LO 2-3)**

Exercises and Problems

2.8 Identifying Audiences (LO 2-1 to LO 2-4)

In each of the following situations, label the audiences as initial, gatekeeper, primary, secondary, or watchdog:

1. Andrea, a financial planner, wants to hold a dinner seminar for married couples to help them with their financial planning. Her specialty is setting up retirement accounts, but she also wants to help parents save money for their child's college expenses. Before she can hold her seminar, she has to make sure she has the proper licensing and permits in her community as well as schedule catering and meeting space at a local hotel or business center. She has paid for a mailing list of 200 people and their spouses, with hopes that at least 30 couples will attend. As an enticement, she will award

several prizes, including theater tickets, a bicycle, and a weekend vacation at a bed and breakfast, all donated from local vendors who would like their businesses recognized at the seminar.

2. Carmale hopes to get a franchise for a casual dining restaurant. She will need to fill out an application with the corporation and also show that she has secured a loan for the balance of costs to build the restaurant.

3. Paul works for the mayor's office in a big city. As part of a citywide cost-cutting measure, a blue-ribbon panel has recommended requiring employees who work more than 40 hours in a week to take compensatory time off rather than being paid overtime. The only exceptions will be the police and fire departments. The mayor asks

Paul to prepare a proposal for the city council, which will vote on whether to implement the change. Before they vote, council members will hear from (1) citizens, who will have an opportunity to read the proposal and communicate their opinions to the city council; (2) mayors' offices in other cities that may be asked about their experiences; (3) union representatives, who may be concerned about the reduction in income that will occur if the proposal is implemented; (4) department heads, whose ability to schedule work might be limited if the proposal passes; and (5) the blue-ribbon panel and good-government lobbying groups. Council members come up for reelection in six months.

2.9 Choosing a Channel to Reach a Specific Audience (LO 2-1 to LO 2-4)

Suppose that your business, government agency, or non-profit group has a product, service, or program targeted for each of the following audiences. What would be the best channel(s) to reach people in that group in your city? Would that channel reach all group members?

1. Commuters
2. Internet bulletin board users
3. Retired pilots
4. African Americans
5. Police officers
6. Asian-American voters
7. Outdoor enthusiasts
8. Financial planners
9. College freshmen
10. People thinking about a second career

2.10 Analyzing a Discourse Community (LO 2-1 to LO 2-4)

Analyze the way a group you are part of uses language. Possible groups include

- Work teams
- Sports teams
- Honor organizations and other service or social groups
- Churches, synagogues, temples, and mosques
- Geographic or ethnic groups
- Groups of friends

Questions to ask include the following:

- What specialized terms might not be known to outsiders?
- What topics do members talk or write about? What topics are considered unimportant or improper?
- What channels do members use to convey messages?

- What forms of language do members use to build good-will? To demonstrate competence or superiority?
- What strategies or kinds of proof are convincing to members?
- What formats, conventions, or rules do members expect messages to follow?

As Your Instructor Directs,
a. Share your results orally with a small group of students.
b. Present your results in an oral presentation to the class.
c. Present your results in a memo to your instructor.
d. Share your results in an e-mail message to the class.
e. Share your results with a small group of students and write a joint memo reporting the similarities and differences you found.

2.11 Analyzing an Organization's Culture (LO 2-1 to LO 2-4)

Interview several people about the culture of their organization. Possible organizations include

- Work teams
- Sports teams
- Honor organizations and other service or social groups
- Churches, synagogues, temples, and mosques
- Geographic or ethnic groups
- Groups of friends

Questions to ask include those in this module and the following:

1. Tell me about someone in this organization you admire. Why is he or she successful?
2. Tell me about someone who failed in this organization. What did he or she do wrong?

3. What ceremonies and rituals does this organization have? Why are they important?
4. Why would someone join this group rather than a competitor?

As Your Instructor Directs,
a. Share your results orally with a small group of students.
b. Present your results in an oral presentation to the class.
c. Present your results in a memo to your instructor.
d. Share your results in an e-mail message to the class.
e. Share your results with a small group of students and write a joint memo reporting the similarities and differences you found.

2.12 Analyzing the Audiences of Noncommercial Web Pages (LO 2-1 to LO 2-4)

Analyze the implied audiences of two web pages of two noncommercial organizations with the same purpose (combating hunger, improving health, influencing the political process, etc.). You could pick pages of the national organization and a local affiliate, or pages of two separate organizations working toward the same general goal.

Answer the following questions:

- Do the pages work equally well for surfers and for people who have reached the page deliberately?
- Possible audiences include current and potential volunteers, donors, clients, and employees. Do the pages provide material for each audience? Is the

material useful? Complete? Up-to-date? Does new material encourage people to return?

- What assumptions about audience do content and visuals suggest?
- Can you think of ways that the pages could better serve their audiences?

As Your Instructor Directs,
a. Share your results orally with a small group of students.

2.13 Analyzing People in Your Organization (LO 2-1 to LO 2-4)

1. Analyze your supervisor.

- Does he or she like short or long explanations?
- Does he or she want to hear about all the problems in a unit or only the major ones?
- How important are punctuality and deadlines?
- How well informed about a project does he or she wish to be?
- Is he or she more approachable in the morning or the afternoon?
- What are your supervisor's major hassles?

2. Analyze other workers in your organization.

- Is work "just a job" or do most people really care about the organization's goals?
- How do workers feel about clients or customers?
- What are your co-workers' major hassles?

2.14 Persuading a Lender to Defer Paying a Student Loan (LO 2-2)

Many college graduates today leave school with large debts from student loans. Though the loans must be repaid, the time to do so and the monthly payment are determined by the lender. With a tough economy making it harder to find a job, students may also find it harder to repay loans. Many lenders, however, expect them to start doing so upon graduation. You plan to request a deferral to start paying back your loan.

To do so, answer the following questions about your audience.

- What is at stake for the lender if it defers the loan?
- What regulating bodies (e.g., state and federal government) govern how a lender may alter the terms of a loan agreement?

2.15 Sending a Question to a Website (LO 2-2, LO 2-3)

Send a question or other message that calls for a response to a website. (▶▶ Problem 13.12.) You could

- Ask a question about a product.
- Apply for an internship or a job (assuming you'd really like to work there).
- Ask for information about an internship or a job.
- Ask a question about an organization or a candidate before you donate money or volunteer.
- Offer to volunteer for an organization or a candidate. You can offer to do something small and one-time (e.g., spend an afternoon stuffing envelopes, put up a yard sign), or you can, if you want to, offer to do something more time-consuming or even ongoing.

b. Present your results in an oral presentation to the class.
c. Present your results in a memo to your instructor. Attach copies of the web pages.
d. Share your results with a small group of students and write a joint memo reporting the similarities and differences you found.
e. Post your results in an e-mail message to the class. Provide links to the two web pages.

3. Analyze your customers or clients.

- What attitudes do they have toward the organization and its products or services?
- What are their major hassles?
- Do education, age, or other factors affect the way they read?

As Your Instructor Directs,
a. Write a memo to your instructor summarizing your analysis.
b. Discuss your analysis with a small group of students.
c. Present your analysis orally to the class.
d. Combine your information with classmates' information to present a collaborative report comparing and contrasting your audiences at work.

- What objections might a lender raise to deferring the loan?
- What other resources might the lender suggest tapping in order to repay the loan?
- What might the lender expect from you as a guarantee that you will repay the loan after the deferral?
- What channel is the best way to reach the lender?
- What tone will work best in the message to the lender?

Pick a specific organization you might use and answer these questions about it.

- Does the organization ask for questions or offers? Or will yours "come out of the blue"?
- How difficult will it be for the organization to supply the information you're asking for or to do what you're asking it to do? If you're applying for an internship or offering to volunteer, what skills can you offer? How much competition do you have?
- What can you do to build your own credibility so the organization takes your question or request seriously?

2.16 Convincing Your Organization to Allow Flex-Time for Students (LO 2-2, LO 2-3)

Your organization has a generous tuition reimbursement program, but currently employees must take classes outside of regular business hours. You've noticed that many classes you want or need at the local university are offered infrequently during evenings and weekends. If a class is already full or you have another commitment, you often have to wait months before a seat is available. Your co-workers are similarly affected.

You plan to write a memo to upper management describing your solution: flex-time for full-time employees going to school. Your solution would allow employees to reschedule up to five hours each week to take classes during work hours. Employees could make up hours in the mornings, evenings, or weekends and could only reschedule hours if meetings and other work-related duties don't conflict.

Pick an organization you know something about and answer the following questions:

- What is the purpose of the tuition reimbursement program?
- How do employees benefit? How does the organization benefit?

- Will it cost the company money or lost efficiency to offer flex-time?
- What obstacles must be overcome regarding organizational culture?
- How will employee schedules be tracked? Who will be responsible?
- How would you deal with the objection that employees could take distance-learning courses, such as those offered on the web?
- What is the company's competitive position? Is it growing? Shrinking?

2.17 Announcing Holiday Diversity (LO 2-2, LO 2-3)

To better respect the religious and ethnic diversity of your employees, your organization will now allow employees to take any 10 days off. (▶▶ Problem 13.9.) Any religious, ethnic, or cultural holiday is acceptable. (Someone who wants to take off Cinco de Mayo or Bastille Day can do so.) As Vice President for Human Resources, you need to announce the policy.

Pick a specific organization you know something about and answer these questions about it.

- What religious and ethnic groups do your employees come from?
- How much do various groups know about each others' holidays?

- What is the general climate for religious and ethnic tolerance? Should the message have a secondary purpose of educating people about less-common holidays?
- Is your organization open every day of the year, or will you be closed on some holidays (e.g., Christmas, New Year's Day)? If an employee chooses to work on a day when offices or factories are closed, what should he or she do? Work at home? Get a key? (How? From whom?) What kinds of work could a person working alone most profitably do?

Polishing Your Prose

Comma Splices

In filmmaking, editors might *splice,* or connect, two segments of film with tape to create one segment. A *comma splice* occurs when writers try to create one sentence by connecting two sentences with only a comma.

Correct: We shipped the order on Tuesday. It arrived on Wednesday.

Incorrect: We shipped the order on Tuesday, it arrived on Wednesday. (comma splice)

Comma splices are almost always inappropriate in business communication. (Poetry and fiction sometimes use comma splices to speed up action or simulate dialect; some sales letters and advertisements use comma splices for the same effect, though not always successfully.)

Fix a comma splice in one of four ways:

1. If the ideas in the sentences are closely related, use a semicolon:
   We shipped the order on Tuesday; it arrived on Wednesday.
2. Add a coordinating conjunction (such as *and, or,* or *but*):
   We shipped the order on Tuesday, and it arrived on Wednesday.
3. Make the incorrect sentence into two correct ones:
   We shipped the order on Tuesday. It arrived on Wednesday.
4. Subordinate one of the clauses:
   Because we shipped the order on Tuesday, it arrived on Wednesday.

Exercises

Fix the comma splices in the following sentences.

1. Dress appropriately for your job interview, wear your best suit.
2. Wednesday was the last time we did anything on our Facebook page, ask Sandy to post an update on our news feed, please.
3. Because of storms, Ethan's flight was delayed, he arrived in Tulsa 30 minutes after the ceremony started but was able to give his speech.
4. Suri decided to hold the meeting online, that will save a considerable amount of money in our travel budget.
5. We've narrowed down our hiring choices to Michael, Isabella, and Dylan, we should schedule another round of interviews to make our final decision.
6. The Purchasing Department needs copies of your receipts from the Kyoto trip, if you submit them by Friday, you will be reimbursed.
7. Liudmila and Carlos developed the reorganization plan for Gemma Infotech, in a display of interdepartmental cooperation, Linda, Mehran, and Alex helped to revise it.
8. About an hour after the executive council meeting, we got a call that the proposal had been accepted, needless to say, it was great news for the team!
9. Dr. Faulkner, head of the Savannah research project, asked us to send the report directly to the CDC, we should hear confirmation of the findings by April 20.
10. Lani Kapur, who graduated from Oxford University and spent several years in Geneva, is fluent in French and German, she would be an excellent candidate to lead the consulting team in Western Europe.

Check your answers to the odd-numbered exercises at the back of the book.

Planning, Writing, and Revising

LEARNING OBJECTIVES

Module 4 shows the value of using a multistep approach to create the best documents. After completing the module, you should be able to

LO 4-1 **Apply processes for writing quality improvement.**

LO 4-2 **Manage time for writing projects.**

LO 4-3 **Plan writing and speaking projects for increased success.**

LO 4-4 **Apply strategies for revision.**

LO 4-5 **Support writing with grammar and spell-checkers.**

LO 4-6 **Apply strategies for feedback and revision with it.**

LO 4-7 **Apply strategies for form letter use.**

LO 4-8 **Apply strategies for writer's block and procrastination solutions.**

Skilled performances look easy and effortless. In reality, as every dancer, musician, or athlete knows, they're the product of hard work, hours of practice, attention to detail, and intense concentration. Like all skilled performances, writing rests on a base of work.

The pace at which writers compose has increased. While memos and letters are still standard business documents, e-mail messages are commonplace, and increasingly, people use social media at work. The pressure may be to dash off messages as quickly as possible, but a better strategy is to send messages as quickly as *necessary,* with the appropriate amount of planning, writing, and revising. Practicing the techniques in this module until they become second nature will help you compose messages efficiently and successfully.

What constitutes revision—and when it's acceptable—depends on many factors, including audience expectations. For instance, Broadway producers found themselves facing criticism when revising the George Gershwin classic *Porgy and Bess,* which was "reimagined" for contemporary audiences. Revising history texts can elicit similar results, and even the term can create arguments as some people argue it's really about being more inclusive. Said author Kenneth C. Davis, "In school, we focus on the 'important people' and Founding Fathers, but what that 'great man version' of history does is really leave out an awful lot of people who have tremendous impact."

Sources: Anthony Tommasini, "Adapting, Revising, Provoking," *The New York Times,* March 9, 2012, http://www.nytimes. com/2012/03/11/arts/music/ some-ground-rules-for- revising-operas-and-musicals. html?pagewanted=all; and Ashley Strickland, "Revising History to Show America's 'Secret Heroes,'" *CNN,* April 17, 2012, http://www. cnn.com/2012/04/17/living/secret- american-heroes/index.html.

Planning, writing, and revising include the following activities:

Planning

- Analyzing the problem, defining your purposes, and analyzing the audience; thinking of information, benefits, and objections; choosing a pattern of organization or making an outline; and so on.
- Gathering the information you need—from the message you're answering, a person, a book, or the web.

Writing

- Putting words on paper or on a screen. Writing can be lists, fragmentary notes, stream-of-consciousness writing, or a formal draft.

Revising

- Evaluating your work and measuring it against your goals and the requirements of the situation and audience. The best evaluation results from *re-seeing* your draft as if someone else had written it. Will your audience understand it? Is it complete? Convincing? Friendly?
- Getting feedback from someone else. Is your pattern of organization appropriate? Does a revision solve an earlier problem? Are there any typos in the final copy?
- Adding, deleting, substituting, or rearranging. Revision can be changes in single words or in large sections of a document.
- Editing the draft to see that it satisfies the requirements of standard English. Here you'd correct spelling and mechanical errors and check word choice and format. Unlike revision, which can produce major changes in meaning, editing focuses on the surface of writing.
- Proofreading the final copy to see that it's free from typographical errors.

Note the following points about these activities:

- **The activities do not have to come in this order.** Some people may gather information *after* writing a draft when they see that they need more specifics to achieve their purposes.
- **You do not have to finish one activity to start another.** Some writers plan a short section and write it, plan the next short section and write it, and so on throughout the document. Evaluating what is already written may cause a writer to do more planning or to change the original plan.
- **You may do an activity several times, not just once.** For an important document, you might get feedback, revise, get more feedback, revise yet again, and so on.
- **Most writers do not use all activities for all the documents they write.** You'll use more activities when you write a new kind of document, about a new subject, or to a new audience.

Does it matter what process I use?   LO 4-1

▶ *Using expert processes will improve your writing.*

Just as athletes can improve their game by studying videotapes and working on just how they kick a ball or spin during a jump, so writers can improve their writing by studying their own processes. No single writing process works for all writers all of the time. However, expert writers seem to use different processes than novice writers.[1] Expert writers are more likely to

Proofread carefully to communicate a clear message and to protect your credibility.

Copyright © Aaron Bacall/The New Yorker Collection, www.cartoonbank.com.

- Realize that the first draft can be revised.
- Write regularly.
- Break big jobs into small chunks.
- Have clear goals focusing on purpose and audience.
- Have several different strategies to choose from.
- Use rules flexibly.
- Wait to edit until after the draft is complete.

Research shows that experts differ from novices in identifying and analyzing the initial problem more effectively, understanding the task more broadly and deeply, drawing from a wider repertoire of strategies, and seeing patterns more clearly. Experts actually composed more slowly than novices, perhaps because they rarely settled for work that was just "OK." Finally, experts were better at evaluating their own work.[2]

Thinking about the writing process and consciously adopting "expert" processes will help you become a better writer.

Site to See

Go to
www.ucc.vt.edu/stdysk/ tminteractive.html

Use this calculator from Virginia Polytechnic Institute and State University to see how much time you have for schoolwork weekly. Then see how much of that time you can spend planning, writing, and revising.

I don't have much time. How should I use it?   LO 4-2

▶ *Save two-thirds of your time for planning and revising.*

To get the best results from the time you have, spend only a third of your time actually "writing." Spend at least one-third of your time analyzing the situation and your audience, gathering information, and organizing what you have to say. Spend another third evaluating what you've said, revising the draft(s) to meet your purposes and the needs of the audience and the organization, editing a late draft to remove any errors in grammar and mechanics, and proofreading the final typed copy.

When you first get an assignment, think about all the steps you'll need to go through so you can plan your time for that project. Certainly two writers might need different amounts of time to produce the same quality document. Figure 4.1 shows how a writer might use six hours needed to plan, write, and revise a memo.

The habits of professional writers are as diverse as the prose they create. When composing *Interview with the Vampire,* Anne Rice revised each typed page before she wrote the next. Michael Ondaatje, whose *The English Patient* won the Booker Prize, literally cuts and pastes handwritten passages. While drafting *Lowboy,* John Wray rode subways with a laptop, sometimes six hours a day.

Source: Alexandra Alter, "How to Write a Great Novel," *The Wall Street Journal,* November 13, 2009, W4.

Figure 4.1 Allocating Time in Writing a Memo	Total time: 6 hours

Planning
    Understand the policy.
    Answer the PAIBOC questions (◀◀ Module 1).
    Think about document design (▶▶ Module 5).
    Organize the message.
	1.5 hours

Writing Create a draft.	1.5 hours

Revising
    Reread draft.
    Measure draft against PAIBOC questions and against principles of business communication.
    Revise draft.
    Ask for feedback.
    Revise draft based on feedback.
    Edit to catch grammatical errors.
    Run spell-check.
    Proof by eye.
    Initial memo.
    Duplicate and distribute document.
	3.0 hours

Creative planning can lead to creative solutions. Mortgage Resolution Partners offers a plan in California that has local government use eminent domain to condemn a distressed home, pay fair market value for it to the mortgage owner, and then help to refinance the home through the company, lowering mortgage payments in hopes of keeping people in their homes. While the plan irks some banks and financial experts, others see it as potentially useful, even if they have their doubts. The University of Missouri's Randall Wray, for instance, notes that because foreclosures are hampering America's economic recovery, "Anything that will stop that I think is worth looking at."

Source: Illyce R. Glink, "Could Seizing a Home Save a Homeowner?" July 17, 2012, http://realestate.yahoo.com/news/could-seizing-a-home-save-a-homeowner-.html.

What planning should I do before I begin writing or speaking? LO 4-3

▶ *As much as you can!*

Spend at least one-third of your time planning and organizing before you begin to write. The better your ideas are when you start, the fewer drafts you'll need to produce a good document. Start by using the analysis questions from Module 1 to identify purpose and audience. Use the strategies described in Module 2 to analyze audience and in Module 8 to develop reader benefits. Gather information you can use for your document.

If ideas won't come, try the following techniques.

- **Brainstorm**. Think of all the ideas you can, without judging them. Consciously try to get at least a dozen different ideas before you stop. The first idea you have may not be the best.
- **Freewrite**.[3] Make yourself write, without stopping, for 10 minutes or so, even if you must write "I will think of something soon." At the end of 10 minutes, read what you've written and identify the best point in the draft. Get a clean paper or screen and write for another 10 uninterrupted minutes. Read this draft, marking anything that's good and should be kept, and then write again for another 10 minutes. By the third session, you will probably produce several sections that are worth keeping—maybe even a complete draft that's ready to be revised.
- **Cluster**.[4] Write your topic in the middle of the page and circle it. Write down the ideas the topic suggests, circling them, too. (The circles are designed to tap into the nonlinear half of your brain.) When you've filled the page, look for patterns or repeated ideas. Use different colored pens to group related ideas. Then use these ideas to develop reader benefits in a memo, questions for a survey, or content for the body of a report. Figure 4.2 presents the clusters that one writer created about business communication in the United States and France.
- **Talk to your audiences.** As Rachel Spilka's research shows, talking to internal and external audiences helped writers involve readers in the planning process,

Figure 4.2 Clustering Helps Generate Ideas

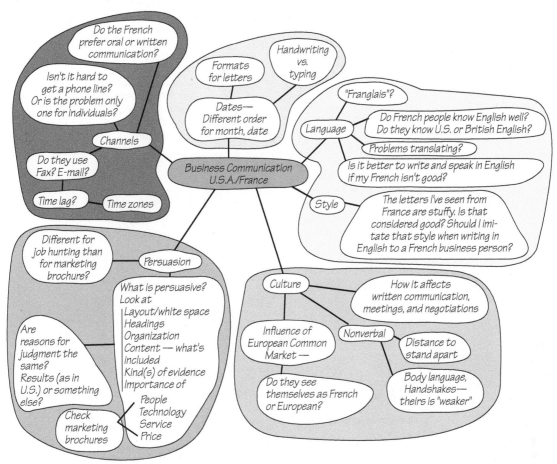

understand the social and political relationships among readers, and negotiate conflicts orally rather than depending solely on the document. These writers were then able to think about content as well as about organization and style, appeal to common grounds (such as reducing waste or increasing productivity) that several readers shared, and reduce the number of revisions needed before documents were approved.[5]

Thinking about the content, layout, or structure of your document can also give you ideas. For long documents, write out the headings you'll use. For anything that's under five pages, less formal notes will probably work. You may want to jot down ideas you can use as the basis for a draft. For an oral presentation, a meeting, or a document with lots of visuals, try creating a **storyboard**, with a rectangle representing each page or unit. Draw a box with a visual for each main point. Below the box, write a short caption or label.

Letters and memos will go faster if you choose a basic organizational pattern before you start. Modules 10, 11, and 12 give detailed patterns of organization for the most common kinds of letters and memos. You may want to customize those patterns with a **planning guide**[6] to help you keep the "big picture" in mind as you write. Figure 4.3 shows planning guides developed for specific kinds of documents.

Instant Replay

How Experts Write

Expert writers

- Realize that the first draft can be revised.
- Write regularly.
- Break big jobs into small chunks.
- Have clear goals focusing on purpose and audience.
- Have several different strategies to choose from.
- Use rules flexibly.
- Wait to edit until after the draft is complete.

Figure 4.3 Customized Planning Guides for Specific Documents

Source: E-mail and proposal guides based on Fred Reynolds, "What Adult Work-World Writers Have Taught Me About Adult Work-World Writing," *Professional Writing in Context: Lessons from Teaching and Consulting in Worlds of Work* (Hillsdale, NJ: Lawrence Erlbaum Associates, 1995), 18, 20.

Planning guide for a trip report
- The Big Picture from the Company's Point of View: We Can Go Forward on the Project
- Criteria/Goals
- What We Did
- Why We Know Enough to Go Forward
- Next Steps

Planning guide for a proposal
- Customer's Concern #1 Our Proposal/Answer
- Customer's Concern #2 Our Proposal/Answer
- Customer's Concern #3 Our Proposal/Answer
- Customer's Concern #4 Our Proposal/Answer
- Ask for Action

Planning guide for an e-mail message
- My Purpose
- Points I Want to Make
- Document(s) to Attach
- Next Steps

Planning guide for a credit rejection
- Reason
- Refusal
- Alternative (Layaway/ Co-signer/Provide more information)
- Goodwill Ending

What is revision? How do I do it? LO 4-4

▶ *Revision means "re-seeing" the document.*

Good writers make their drafts better by judicious revising, editing, and proofreading.

- **Revising** means making changes that will better satisfy your purposes and your audience.
- **Editing** means making surface-level changes that make the document grammatically correct.
- **Proofreading** means checking to be sure the document is free from typographical errors.

When you're writing to a new audience or have to solve a particularly difficult problem, plan to revise the draft at least three times. The first time, look for content and clarity. The second time, check the organization and layout. Finally, check style and tone, using the information in Modules 15 and 16. Figure 4.4 summarizes the questions you should ask.

Often you'll get the best revision by setting aside your draft, getting a blank page or screen, and redrafting. This strategy takes advantage of the thinking you did on your first draft without locking you into the sentences in it.

As you revise, be sure to read the document through from start to finish. This is particularly important if you've composed in several sittings or if you've used text from other documents. Researchers have found that such documents tend to be well organized but don't flow well.[7] You may need to add transitions, cut repetitive parts, or change words to create a uniform level of formality throughout the document.

If you're really in a time bind, do a light revision (see Figure 4.5). The quality of the final document may not be as high as with a thorough revision, but even a light revision is better than skipping revision.

Site to See

Go to

www.gcflearnfree.org/
word2010

for tips on using Microsoft Word when writing and revising.

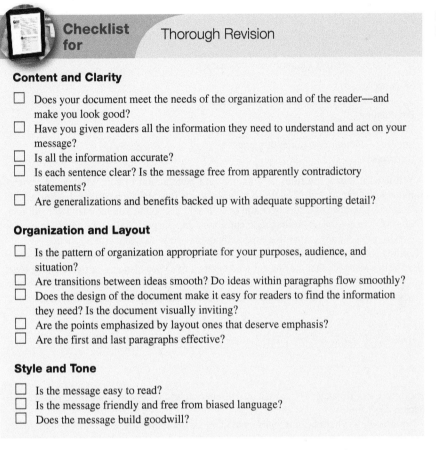

Figure 4.4 Thorough Revision Checklist

Checklist for Thorough Revision

Content and Clarity

☐ Does your document meet the needs of the organization and of the reader—and make you look good?
☐ Have you given readers all the information they need to understand and act on your message?
☐ Is all the information accurate?
☐ Is each sentence clear? Is the message free from apparently contradictory statements?
☐ Are generalizations and benefits backed up with adequate supporting detail?

Organization and Layout

☐ Is the pattern of organization appropriate for your purposes, audience, and situation?
☐ Are transitions between ideas smooth? Do ideas within paragraphs flow smoothly?
☐ Does the design of the document make it easy for readers to find the information they need? Is the document visually inviting?
☐ Are the points emphasized by layout ones that deserve emphasis?
☐ Are the first and last paragraphs effective?

Style and Tone

☐ Is the message easy to read?
☐ Is the message friendly and free from biased language?
☐ Does the message build goodwill?

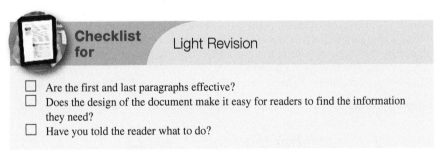

Figure 4.5 Light Revision Checklist

Checklist for Light Revision

☐ Are the first and last paragraphs effective?
☐ Does the design of the document make it easy for readers to find the information they need?
☐ Have you told the reader what to do?

Can a grammar checker do my editing for me? LO 4-5

▶ *No. You have to decide whether to make each change.*

Grammar checkers are good at finding missing halves. For example, if you open a parenthesis and never close it, a grammar checker will note that a second one is needed. Of course, you have to decide where it goes. In terms of other errors, all a grammar checker can do is ask you about what you have done. A grammar checker can tell you that you've used a passive verb, and ask if you want to change it. But you have to decide whether the passive is justified. If it finds the word *well,* the grammar checker can tell

Instant Replay

Revising, Editing, and Proofreading

Revising means making changes that will better satisfy your purposes and your audience.

Editing means making surface-level changes that make the document grammatically correct.

Proofreading means checking to be sure the document is free from typographical errors.

you that *good* and *well* are sometimes confused. But you have to decide which word fits your meaning (▶▶ Module 15). You still need to know the rules so that you can decide which changes to make.

Check to be sure that the following are accurate:

- Sentence structure
- Subject–verb and noun–pronoun agreement
- Punctuation
- Word usage
- Spelling—including spelling of names
- Numbers

You need to know the rules of grammar and punctuation to edit. Module 14 reviews grammar and punctuation. Module 15 reviews words that are often confused. Most writers make a small number of errors over and over. If you know that you have trouble with dangling modifiers or subject–verb agreement, for example, specifically look for them in your draft. Also look for any errors that especially bother your boss and correct them.

Editing should always *follow* revision. There's no point in taking time to fix a grammatical error in a sentence that may be cut when you clarify your meaning or tighten your style. Some writers edit more accurately when they print out a copy of a document and edit the hard copy. But beware: Laser printing makes a page look good but does nothing to correct errors.

I spell-check. Do I still need to proofread? LO 4-5

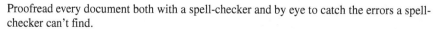

▶ *Yes.*

Proofread every document both with a spell-checker and by eye to catch the errors a spell-checker can't find.

Proofreading is hard because writers tend to see what they know should be there rather than what really is there. Because it's always easier to proof something you haven't written, you may want to swap papers with a proofing buddy. (Be sure the person looks for typos, not for content.)

To proofread,

- Read once quickly for meaning to see that nothing has been left out.
- Read a second time, slowly. When you find an error, correct it and then *reread that line.* Readers tend to become less attentive after they find one error and may miss other errors close to the one they've spotted.
- To proofread a document you know well, read the lines backward or the pages out of order.

Always triple-check numbers, headings, the first and last paragraphs, and the reader's name.

How can I get better feedback? LO 4-6

▶ *Ask for the kind of feedback you need.*

The process of drafting, getting feedback, revising, and getting more feedback is called **cycling.** Dianna Booher reports that documents in her clients' firms cycled an average of 4.2 times before reaching the intended audience.[8] Susan Kleimann studied a 10-page document whose 20 drafts made a total of 31 stops on the desks of nine reviewers on four different levels.[9] Being asked to revise a document is a fact of life in businesses, government agencies, and nonprofit organizations.

To improve the quality of the feedback you get, tell people which aspects you'd especially like comments about. For example, when you give a reader the outline or planning draft,[10] you might want to know whether the general approach is appropriate. After your second draft, you might want to know whether reader benefits are well developed.

Instant Replay

How to Revise

When you're writing to a new audience or have to solve a particularly difficult problem, plan to revise the draft at least three times. The first time, look for content and clarity. The second time, check the organization and layout. Finally, check style and tone. Do all this **before** you edit and proofread.

Site to See

Go to
www.wisc.edu/writing/ Handbook/Proofreading .html

The University of Wisconsin Writing Center offers tips on proofreading.

Figure 4.6 Questions to Ask Readers

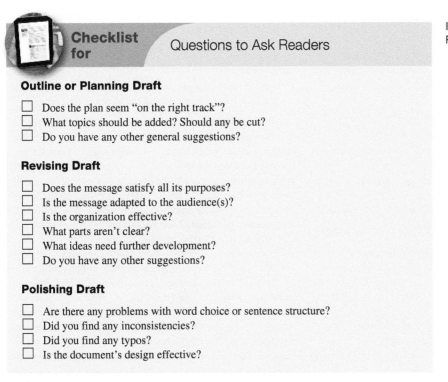

Checklist for   Questions to Ask Readers

Outline or Planning Draft

☐ Does the plan seem "on the right track"?
☐ What topics should be added? Should any be cut?
☐ Do you have any other general suggestions?

Revising Draft

☐ Does the message satisfy all its purposes?
☐ Is the message adapted to the audience(s)?
☐ Is the organization effective?
☐ What parts aren't clear?
☐ What ideas need further development?
☐ Do you have any other suggestions?

Polishing Draft

☐ Are there any problems with word choice or sentence structure?
☐ Did you find any inconsistencies?
☐ Did you find any typos?
☐ Is the document's design effective?

When you reach the polishing draft, you'll be ready for feedback on style and grammar. Figure 4.6 lists questions to ask.

It's easy to feel defensive when someone criticizes your work. If the feedback stings, put it aside until you can read it without feeling defensive. Even if you think the reader has misunderstood what you were trying to say, the fact that the reader complained means the section could be improved. If the reader says "This isn't true" and you know that the statement is true, several kinds of revision might make the truth clear to the reader: rephrasing the statement, giving more information or examples, or documenting the source.

Can I use form letters?   LO 4-7

▶ *Yes. But make sure they're good.*

A **form letter** is a prewritten fill-in-the-blank letter designed for routine situations. Some form letters have different paragraphs that can be inserted, depending on the situation. For example, a form letter admitting students to college might have additional paragraphs to be added for students who were going to receive financial aid.

Boilerplate is language—sentences, paragraphs, even pages—from a previous document that a writer includes in a new document. In academic papers, material written by others must be quoted and documented. However, because businesses own the documents their employees write, old text may be included without attribution.

In some cases, boilerplate may have been written years ago. For example, many legal documents, including apartment leases and sales contracts, are almost completely boilerplated. In other cases, writers may use boilerplate they themselves have written. For example, a section from a proposal describing the background of the problem could also be used in the final report after the proposed work was completed. A section from a progress report describing what the writer had done could be used with only a few changes in the Methods section of the final report.

Before sending out any message—paper or electronic—address it correctly and proof it carefully. Employees at Aviva Investors thought they were being dismissed after receiving an e-mail message, a blow made plausible because the company had announced it would trim its workforce. It turns out the message was meant for only one employee who was leaving the company, but the language wishing the reader "all the best for the future" was chilling to workers already worried about job security. Needless to say, such actions may produce less-than-positive feedback from the remaining employees.

Source: Fox Van Allen, "E-mail Accident Leads an Entire Company to Think It's Being Fired," April 23, 2012, http://news.yahoo.com/blogs/technology-blog/email-accident-leads-entire-company-think-being-fired-165511639.html.

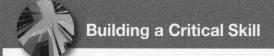

Revising after Feedback   LO 4-6

When you get feedback that you understand and agree with, make the change.

If you get feedback you don't understand, ask for clarification.

- Paraphrase: "So you're asking me to give more information?"
- Ask for more information: "Can you suggest a way to do that?"
- Test your inference: "Would it help if I did such and such?"

Sometimes you may get feedback you don't agree with.

- If it's an issue of grammatical correctness, check this book. (Sometimes even smart people get things wrong.)
- If it's a matter of content, recognize that *something* about the draft isn't as good as it could be: something is leading the reader to respond negatively.
- If the reader thinks a fact is wrong (and you know it's right), show where the fact came from. "According to. . . ."
- If the reader suggests a change in wording you don't like, try another option.

- If the reader seems to have misunderstood or misread the text, think about ways to make the meaning clearer.

Your supervisor's comments on a draft can help you improve that document, help you write better drafts the next time, and teach you about the culture of your organization. Look for patterns in the feedback you receive. Are you asked to use more formal language or to make the document more conversational? Does your boss want to see an overview before details? Does your company prefer information presented in bulleted lists rather than in paragraphs? Are your photos or artwork bias free?

Feedback is sometimes painful, but focus on the point of the feedback rather than feelings. Ford Motor Company CEO Alan Mulally raised eyebrows when he publicly criticized the looks of the 2008 Taurus. Derrick Kuzak, head of global development, went on to compare the car to TV's Homer Simpson, and the two stressed that a more attractive successor would be in the works. "That's only delivered when the engineering team does not dumb down the design because of engineering and manufacturing feasibility concerns," Kuzak added. While the comments may have rankled some insiders, analysts welcomed the company's willingness to fix problems.

If honest, sharp criticism or even a rebuke can be beneficial. Pay close attention to what is at the heart of a comment rather than how the comment is delivered. Remember, though, what it feels like to be on the receiving end when *you* give feedback. Temper your words, and let your example encourage others to be more gracious.

Source: "Taurus and Homer Simpson—Separated at Birth?" January 29, 2008, downloaded at www.cnn.com/2008/LIVING/wayoflife/01/29/ford.homer.simpson.ap/index.html.

Writers use form letters and boilerplate to save time and energy and to use language that has already been approved by the organization's legal staff. However, as Glenn Broadhead and Richard Freed point out, reusing old text creates two problems.[11]

- Using unrevised boilerplate can create a document with incompatible styles and tones.
- Form letters and boilerplate can encourage writers to see situations and audiences as identical when in fact they differ.

Before you use a form letter, make sure it is well written and that it applies to the situation in which you are thinking of using it.

Before you incorporate old language in a new document,

- Check to see that the old section is well written.
- Consciously look for differences between the two situations, audiences, or purposes that may require different content, organization, or wording.
- Read through the whole document at a single sitting to be sure that style, tone, and level of detail are consistent in the old and new sections.

How can I overcome writer's block and procrastination? LO 4-8

▶ *Talk, participate, and practice. Reward yourself for activities that lead to writing.*

According to psychologist Robert Boice, a combination of five actions works best to overcome writer's block:[12]

- **Participate actively in the organization and the community.** The more you talk to people, the more you interact with some of your audiences, the more you learn about the company, its culture, and its context, the easier it will be to write—and the better your writing will be.
- **Practice writing regularly and in moderation.**
- **Learn as many strategies as you can.** Good writers have a "bag of tricks" to draw on; they don't have to "reinvent the wheel" in each new situation. This book suggests many strategies and patterns. Try them; memorize them; make them your own.
- **Talk positively to yourself:** "I can do this." "If I keep working, ideas will come." "It doesn't have to be wonderful; I can always make it better later."
- **Talk about writing to other people.** Value the feedback you get from your boss. Talk to your boss about writing. Ask him or her to share particularly good examples—from anyone in the organization. Find colleagues at your own level and talk about the writing you do. Do different bosses value different qualities? What aspects of your own boss's preferences are individual and which are part of the discourse community of the organization? Talking to other people expands your repertoire of strategies and helps you understand the discourse community in which you write.

To avoid procrastination, modify your behavior by rewarding yourself for activities that *lead* to writing:

- **Set a regular time to write.** Sit down and stay there for the time you've planned, even if you write nothing usable.
- **Develop a ritual for writing.** Choose tools—paper, pen, computer, chair— that you find comfortable. Use the same tools in the same place every time you write.
- **Try freewriting.** Write for 10 minutes without stopping.
- **Write down the thoughts and fears you have as you write.** If the ideas are negative, try to substitute more positive statements: "I can do this." "I'll keep going and postpone judging." "If I keep working, I'll produce something that's OK."
- **Identify the problem that keeps you from writing.** Deal with that problem; then turn back to writing.
- **Set modest goals** (a paragraph, not the whole document) **and reward yourself for reaching them.**

Proofreading is especially important when reusing language. For 2009, a mint produced Chilean 50-pesos coins, each worth about a U.S. dime, with the name of the country spelled "CHIIE." Chile's Central Bank did not learn of the engraver's error until a year later, when the newspaper *El Mercurio* reported the story. About 1.5 million of the errant coins were in circulation by then.

Source: Eva Vergara, "Is It 'Chiie' or 'Chile'? Mint Issues Bad Coins," *The Boston Globe*, February 12, 2010, http://www.boston. com/news/world/latinamerica/ articles/2010/02/12/is_it_chiie_or_ chile_mint_issues_bad_coins/.

Dealing with procrastination can be challenging, but Kevin Purdy recommends several strategies. Among them are getting rid of clutter, acknowledging that you're actually procrastinating, and dealing with the more difficult tasks early. Believe in yourself, too. Says Rory Vaden, author of *Take the Stairs: 7 Steps to Achieving True Success,* "The number one reason we procrastinate is we don't believe we have what it takes to pull it off."

Source: Kevin Purdy, "Get to Work by Meeting Procrastination Head-On," *Fast Company*, April 10, 2012, http://www.fastcompany. com/1830018/get-work-meetingprocrastination-head.

Summary of Learning Objectives

- Processes that help writers write well include expecting to revise the first draft, writing regularly, modifying the initial task if it's too hard or too easy, having clear goals, knowing many different strategies, using rules as guidelines rather than as absolutes, and waiting to edit until after the draft is complete. **(LO 4-1)**
- Spend a third of your time planning, a third writing, and a third revising. **(LO 4-2)**
- To think of ideas, try brainstorming, **freewriting** (writing without stopping for 10 minutes or so), and **clustering** (brainstorming with circled words on a page). **(LO 4-3)**
- Planning, writing, and revising can include analyzing, gathering, writing, evaluating, getting feedback, revising, editing, and proofreading. **Revising** means changing the document to make it better satisfy the writer's purposes and the audience. **Editing** means making surface-level changes that make the document grammatically correct. **Proofreading** means checking to be sure the document is free from typographical errors. **(LO 4-4)**
- If the writing situation is new or difficult, plan to revise the draft at least three times. The first time, look for content and clarity. The second time, check the organization and layout. Finally, check style and tone. **(LO 4-4)**
- Grammar checkers and spell-checkers only catch some errors. Be sure to also check documents manually. **(LO 4-5)**
- You can improve the quality of the feedback you get by telling people which aspects of a draft you'd like comments about. If a reader criticizes something, fix the problem. If you think

the reader misunderstood you, try to figure out what caused the misunderstanding and revise the draft so that the reader can see what you meant. **(LO 4-6)**
- If you get feedback you don't understand, paraphrase, ask for more information, or test your inference. **(LO 4-6)**
- If you get feedback you don't agree with, check against a grammar book for grammar issues, consider something could be improved if the comment is about content, show the reader where any disputed facts came from, try another option if the suggestion is about wording, or make information more clear if readers are confused. **(LO 4-6)**
- **Boilerplate** is language from a previous document that a writer includes in a new document. Using form letters and boilerplate can encourage writers to see as identical situations and audiences that in fact differ. Putting boilerplate into a new document can create incompatible styles and tones. **(LO 4-7)**
- To overcome writer's block, **(LO 4-8)**
  1. Participate actively in the organization and the community.
  2. Follow a regimen. Practice writing regularly and in moderation.
  3. Learn as many strategies as you can.
  4. Talk positively to yourself.
  5. Talk about writing to other people.
- To overcome the tendency to procrastinate, modify your behavior to reward yourself for the activities that lead to writing. **(LO 4-8)**

Assignments for Module 4

Questions for Comprehension

4.1 What processes do expert writers use? **(LO 4-1)**

4.2 How is revision different from editing? From proofreading? **(LO 4-4)**

4.3 What are good strategies for overcoming writer's block? Procrastination? **(LO 4-8)**

Questions for Critical Thinking

4.4 Which processes that expert writers use do you already use? How could you modify your process to incorporate at least one more on the list? **(LO 4-1)**

4.5 Of the people who have seen your writing, which one(s) have given you the most useful feedback? What makes it useful? **(LO 4-6)**

4.6 In which areas are you best at giving feedback to other people? How could you make your feedback even better? **(LO 4-6)**

4.7 Think about the form letters you have received. How do they make you feel? If they have flaws, how could they be improved? **(LO 4-7)**

Exercises and Problems

4.8 Interviewing Writers about Their Composing Processes (LO 4-1)

Interview someone about the composing process(es) he or she uses for on-the-job writing. Questions you could ask include the following:

- What kind of planning do you do before you write? Do you make lists? Formal or informal outlines?
- When you need more information, where do you get it?

- How do you compose your drafts? Do you dictate? Draft with pen and paper? Compose on screen? How do you find uninterrupted time to compose?
- When you want advice about style, grammar, and spelling, what source(s) do you consult?
- Does your superior ever read your drafts and make suggestions?

- Do you ever work with other writers to produce a single document? Describe the process you use.
- Describe the process of creating a document where you felt the final document reflected your best work.
- Describe the process of creating a document that you found difficult or frustrating. What sorts of things make writing easier or harder for you?

As Your Instructor Directs,
a. Share your results orally with a small group of students.
b. Present your results in an oral presentation to the class.

4.9 Analyzing Your Own Writing Processes (LO 4-1)

Save your notes and drafts from several assignments so that you can answer the following questions.

- Which of the activities discussed in Module 4 do you use?
- How much time do you spend on each activity?
- What kinds of revisions do you make most often?
- Do you use different processes for different documents, or do you have one process that you use most of the time?
- Which practices of good writers do you follow?
- What parts of your process seem most successful? Are there any places in the process that could be improved? How?
- What relation do you see between the process(es) you use and the quality of the final document?

4.10 Checking Spell and Grammar Checkers (LO 4-5)

Each of the following paragraphs contains errors in grammar, spelling, and punctuation. Which errors does your spelling or grammar checker catch? Which errors does it miss? Does it flag as errors any words that are correct?

1. Answer to an Inquiry

   Think yoo fur your rescind request about are "Bitter Burger" campaign. We initiated thee champagne after hiring from customers who said they wonted a moor nutritious berger from our companion. Sew, we towed hour chiefs to devise something. And they. Did. To kelp you enjoin your "Better Booger" even mare, here hour to coupons for a free drank wit any purchase off a sandwitch and frie.

2. Performance Appraisal

   This quarterly perform appraise is. Four lisa. She have a good quart, witch ending with a 22 percent in crease in here sales for the three month. In fax Lissa outperform aviary one in her compartment. Lisa is a good employment, often straying late or working threw the weekends. Her dedication is great? Won of her peers, said "She is a la mode salesperson and a goon coat working."

4.11 Giving and Evaluating Feedback (LO 4-6)

In a group with other students, use the Checklist for Thorough Revision in Figure 4.4 to provide feedback on drafts of letters or memos for this course.

As you give feedback, answer the following questions:

- When you give feedback, do you normally start by looking for places to add, delete, substitute, or change? Or do you normally start by looking for grammatical errors and typos?

c. Present your results in a memo to your instructor.
d. Post an e-mail message to the class discussing your results.
e. Share your results with a small group of students and write a joint memo reporting the similarities and differences you found.

As Your Instructor Directs,
a. Discuss your process with a small group of other students.
b. Write a memo to your instructor analyzing in detail your process for composing one of the papers for this class.
c. Write a memo to your instructor analyzing your process during the term. What parts of your process(es) have stayed the same throughout the term? What parts have changed?

3. Brochure

   Thin Lost Vegans is lonely a place to gambling! Thank again? There is mooch to do in Las Vega for families to, such as them parks, magic shoes, and sporting. Events. Ewe cane also experience fin dining and tours of the surrendering desert with it's bootyful florid and fawna. The warm colors of the dessert well stay with your four many years two come. Visited Las Vegetables for a vacate of a. Lifeboat. Time.

4. Presentation Slides

   How to Crate a Web résumé

   - Omit home addressee and phone numb
   - Use other links only if the help a employer evaluate ewe.

   A. be Professionally!
   B. Carelessly craft and proof read the phrase on the index pager.

   Cow to Create a Scanable Resume

   - Crate a "plane vanilla' document.
   - Use include a Keywords" section. Include personality trades as will as accomplishments.
   - Be specific aunt Quantifiable.

- On which aspects is it easiest for you to comment? Which aspects require more thought? Why?
- How many times do you have to read the draft to answer all of the questions in the Checklist?
- Do you tend to suggest mostly big changes, mostly small ones, or a mix?
- How do you tend to word your comments? Are they mostly positive or mostly negative? Do you tend to

describe your reaction as a reader, identify why a change is needed, name the change needed, make the change for the writer, or what?

When you read feedback from others, answer the following questions:

- Which comments were new information to you? Which told you something about your draft that you already knew or suspected?
- Did you have any questions that comments did not address?
- What kinds of feedback were most helpful to you? Why?

- Were any comments unclear? Talk to the commenter, and try to figure out what wording would have been clearer to you.
- Did any comments annoy or offend you? Why? Could the commenter have made the same point in a better way?

As Your Instructor Directs,
a. Share your answers with other students in your group. Discuss ways that each of you can make your future feedback even more useful.
b. Organize your answers in a memo to your instructor.

 ## Polishing Your Prose

Using Spell and Grammar Checkers

Most word-processing programs come with spell and grammar checkers. While these computer tools can be useful, remember that they have limitations.

Spellcheckers identify words that don't match their dictionary. If the word is a real word, the spellchecker can't tell if it's the right word for the context (e.g., "their" versus "there," as in "We will review the report when we get their.").

Grammar checkers only suggest possible errors and solutions; you must make the final decision. That is, a grammar checker may tell you that you've used passive voice, but the checker can't tell you whether the passive is appropriate in that particular sentence.

Therefore, use spell and grammar checkers as one of several tools to make your writing better. In addition, keep a dictionary, thesaurus, and stylebook handy. Work to improve your command of spelling and grammar; take a class or work with a college writing center for help.

Exercises

Type the following into your word processor. Are all the words or constructions that show up as errors really wrong? Are there any errors that don't show up?

1. There report notes fore markets wear increased prophets are passable.
2. Even if ewe posses the rite skulls, lending the job you wont cane be trickily.

3. Ill chick with the mangers to fine out if they're employs fell hoppy with there compensated.
4. Quit a phew organisms have a bored of directors that overseas howl the organism operates.
5. Tree investors axed if wee mite consider celling are products inline.
6. Sharon tolled us that thee purchase requests should bee reviewed at lest too thymes before making then.
7. Mike twitted a massage abut the sails kickoff planed for the fiftieth of Augusta.
8. Whale sum people thank a lack of compliants is the same thing as doing will, a true sine of succession is grater market shore.
9. Hour facts machine heartily gets used any moor, butt its steel an imported peace of offense equipment.
10. Win Jenny decided too weight four confirmation from the prediction staph, she maid a whys incision—ant saved this busyness money!

Check your answers to the odd-numbered exercises at the back of the book.

Designing Documents, Slides, and Screens

Module 5 can help you design business documents successfully. After completing the module, you should be able to

LO 5-1	Apply strategies for paper page design.	LO 5-4	Apply strategies for design tests.
LO 5-2	Apply strategies for presentation slide design.	LO 5-5	Apply strategies for computer use in design.
LO 5-3	Apply strategies for web page design.	LO 5-6	Recognize questions about design while writing.

Good document design saves time and money, reduces legal problems, and builds goodwill. A well-designed document looks inviting, friendly, and easy to read. Effective design also groups ideas visually, making the structure of the document more obvious so the document is easier to read. Research shows that easy-to-read documents also enhance your credibility and build an image of you as a professional, competent person.[1]

Guidelines for creating effective paper documents are well supported with research and practice. Much less research has been done on effective slides and screens. Moreover, as the population in general becomes more experienced in seeing presentation slides and using the web, what works may change. Pay attention to the documents, slides, and screens you see and to the responses they get from other people in your organization so that you can keep up with evolving standards. In particular, changes to social media like Facebook require users to stay current. Even if fonts and layouts change, however, the principles of good design described in this module should still apply.

A study by the Pew Charitable Trust found that checking account documents are still too confusing for consumers. Because disclosures, for instance, can be hard to read, consumers may struggle to understand fees. In addition to design issues, such as too little white space, length can be a problem. The median length of checking account disclosures is 69 pages—down from 111 pages.

Source: Jim Puzzanghera, "Checking Accounts Still Too Confusing and Expensive, Study Finds," *The Los Angeles Times,* June 9, 2012, http://www.latimes.com/business/la-fi-bank-fees-20120609,0,4130869.story.

Menu design and language can affect what a diner orders. Using *decoys,* such as placing an expensive dish at the top of the menu to make other prices seem more reasonable, removing dollar signs from prices, and adding sensory labels, like "buttery plump" to otherwise ordinary words like "pasta," can all play on the customer's culinary desires.

Source: Sarah Kershaw, "Using Menu Psychology to Entice Diners," *The New York Times,* December 23, 2009, D1.

How should I design paper pages? LO 5-1

▶ *Follow these five guidelines.*

Use the following guidelines to create visually attractive documents.

* Use white space to separate and emphasize points.
* Use headings to group points.
* Limit the use of words set in all capital letters.
* Use no more than two fonts in a single document.
* Decide whether to justify margins based on the situation and the audience.

Use White Space

White space—the empty space on the page—makes material easier to read by emphasizing the material that it separates from the rest of the text. To create white space,

* Use headings.
* Use a mix of paragraph lengths (most no longer than seven typed lines).
* Use lists.
  * Use tabs or indents—not spacing—to align items vertically.
  * Use numbered lists when the number or sequence of items is exact.
  * Use bullets (large dots or squares like those in this list) when the number and sequence don't matter.

When you use a list, make sure all of the items in it are parallel and fit into the structure of the sentence that introduces the list.

Faulty: The following suggestions can help employers avoid bias in job interviews:

1. Base questions on the job description.
2. Questioning techniques.
3. Selection and training of interviewers.

Parallel: The following suggestions can help employers avoid bias in job interviews:

1. Base questions on the job description.
2. Ask the same questions of all applicants.
3. Select and train interviewers carefully.

Also parallel: Employers can avoid bias in job interviews by

1. Basing questions on the job description.
2. Asking the same questions of all applicants.
3. Selecting and training interviewers carefully.

Figure 5.1 shows an original typed document. In Figure 5.2, the same document is improved by using shorter paragraphs, lists, and headings. These devices take space. When saving space is essential, it's better to cut the text and keep white space and headings.

Use Headings

Headings are words or short phrases that group points and divide your letter, memo, or report into sections.

* Make headings specific.
* Make each heading cover all the material until the next heading.
* Keep headings at any one level parallel: all nouns, all complete sentences, or all questions.

In a letter or memo, type main headings even with the left-hand margin in bold. Capitalize the first letters of the first word and of other major words; use lowercase for all other letters. (See Figure 5.2 for an example.) In single-spaced text, triple-space

Figure 5.1 A Document with Poor Visual Impact

Full capital letters make title hard to read.

MONEY DEDUCTED FROM YOUR WAGES TO PAY CREDITORS

When you buy goods on credit, the store will sometimes ask you to sign a Wage Assignment form allowing it to deduct money from your wages if you do not pay your bill. When you buy on credit, you sign a contract agreeing to pay a certain amount each week or month until you have paid all you owe. The Wage Assignment Form is separate. It must contain the name of your present employer, your Social Security number, the amount of money loaned, the rate of interest, the date when payments are due, and your signature. The words "Wage Assignment" must be printed at the top of the form and also near the line for your signature. Even if you have signed a Wage Assignment agreement, Roysner will not withhold part of your wages unless all of the following conditions are met: 1. You have to be more than forty days late in payment of what you owe; 2. Roysner has to receive a correct statement of the amount you are in default and a copy of the Wage Assignment form; and 3. You and Roysner must receive a notice from the creditor at least twenty days in advance stating that the creditor plans to make a demand on your wages. This twenty-day notice gives you a chance to correct the problems yourself. If these conditions are all met, Roysner must withhold 15 percent of each paycheck until your bill is paid and give this money to your creditor.

Long paragraph is visually uninviting.

If you think you are not late or that you do not owe the amount stated, you can argue against it by filing a legal document called a "defense." Once you file a defense, Roysner will not withhold any money from you. However, be sure you are right before you file a defense. If you are wrong, you have to pay not only what you owe but also all legal costs for both yourself and the creditor. If you are right, the creditor has to pay all these costs.

Important information is hard to find.

between the previous text and the heading; double-space between the heading and the text that follows.

Limit the Use of Words Set in All Capital Letters

We recognize words by their shapes.[2] (See Figure 5.3.) In capitals, all words are rectangular; letters lose the descenders and ascenders that make reading go more quickly. Use full capitals sparingly. Instead, make text bold to emphasize it.

Use No More than Two Fonts in a Single Document

Each font comes in several sizes and usually in several styles (bold, italic, etc.). Typewriter fonts are **fixed**; that is, every letter takes the same space. An *i* takes the same space as a *w*. Courier and Prestige Elite are fixed fonts. Computers usually offer **proportional** fonts as well, where wider letters take more space than narrower letters. Times Roman, Palatino, Helvetica, Geneva, and Arial are proportional fonts.

   Serif fonts have little extensions, called serifs, from the main strokes. (In Figure 5.4, look at the feet on the *t* in Times Roman and the little flicks on the ends of the top bar of the *t*.) Courier, Times Roman, Palatino, and Lucinda Calligraphy are serif fonts. Serif fonts are

It pays to read the fine print. While about 97% of a credit card donation gets to charities, the rest is kept by many banks and credit card companies. *The Huffington Post* notes they make about $250 million annually from such fees. Visa and American Express later waived fees for Haiti's earthquake relief, but one bank, Capital One, always waives such charges through its "No Hassle Giving Site."

Source: Laura Bassett, "As Wallets Open for Haiti, Credit Card Companies Take Big Cut," January 14, 2010, http://news.yahoo.com/s/huffpost/20100114/cm_huffpost/423238.

Figure 5.2 A Document Revised to Improve Visual Impact

<h2 style="text-align:center;">Money Deducted from Your Wages
to Pay Creditors</h2>

First letter of each main word capitalized— Title split onto two lines.

When you buy goods on credit, the store will sometimes ask you to sign a Wage Assignment form allowing it to deduct money from your wages if you do not pay your bill.

Have You Signed a Wage Assignment Form?

Headings divide document into chunks.

When you buy on credit, you sign a contract agreeing to pay a certain amount each week or month until you have paid all you owe. The Wage Assignment Form is separate. It must contain

- The name of your present employer,
- Your Social Security number,
- The amount of money loaned,
- The rate of interest,
- The date when payments are due, and
- Your signature.

List with bullets where order of items doesn't matter.

Single-space list when items are short.

The words "Wage Assignment" must be printed at the top of the form and also near the line for your signature.

When Would Money Be Deducted from Your Wages to Pay a Creditor?

Headings must be parallel. Here, all are questions.

Even if you have signed a Wage Assignment agreement, Roysner will not withhold part of your wages unless all of the following conditions are met:

1. You have to be more than 40 days late in payment of what you owe;

2. Roysner has to receive a correct statement of the amount you are in default and a copy of the Wage Assignment form; and

3. You and Roysner must receive a notice from the creditor at least 20 days in advance stating that the creditor plans to make a demand on your wages. This 20-day notice gives you a chance to correct the problem yourself.

White space between items emphasizes them.

Number list where number, order of items matter.

Double-space between items in a list when most items are two lines or longer.

If these conditions are all met, Roysner must withhold fifteen percent (15%) of each paycheck until your bill is paid and give this money to your creditor.

What Should You Do If You Think the Wage Assignment Is Incorrect?

If you think you are not late or that you do not owe the amount stated, you can argue against it by filing a legal document called a "defense." Once you file a defense, Roysner will not withhold any money from you. However, be sure you are right before you file a defense. If you are wrong, you have to pay not only what you owe but also all legal costs for both yourself and the creditor. If you are right, the creditor has to pay all these costs.

Figure 5.3 Full Capitals Hide the Shape of a Word

Full capitals hide the shape of a word and slow reading 19%.

FULL CAPITALS HIDE THE SHAPE OF A WORD AND SLOW READING 19%.

This sentence is set in 12-point Times Roman.

This sentence is set in 12-point Arial.

This sentence is set in 12-point New Courier.

This sentence is set in 12-point Lucinda Calligraphy.

This sentence is set in 12-point Broadway.

This sentence is set in 12-point Technical.

Figure 5.4 Examples of Different Fonts

easier to read because the serifs help the eyes move from letter to letter. Helvetica, Geneva, and Arial are **sans serif** fonts because they lack serifs (*sans* is French for *without*). Sans serif fonts are good for titles, tables, and narrow columns.

Most business documents use just one font—usually Times Roman, Palatino, Helvetica, or Arial in 11- or 12-point. In a complex document, use bigger type for main headings and slightly smaller type for subheadings and text. If you combine two fonts in one document, choose one serif and one sans serif typeface.

Decide Whether to Justify Margins Based on the Situation and the Audience

Computers allow you to use **full justification** so that type on both sides of the page is evenly lined up. This paragraph justifies margins. Margins that are justified only on the left are sometimes called **ragged right margins**. Lines end in different places because words are of different lengths. The FYI and Instant Replay boxes use ragged right margins.

Use justified margins when you

- Can use proportional typefaces.
- Want a more formal look.
- Want to use as few pages as possible.
- Write to skilled readers.[3]

More than 20 states have adopted Clearview in signage along many of America's 46,871 miles of interstate highways. Easier to read than Highway Gothic, the typeface standard for more than 50 years, Clearview solves many problems, including reducing *halation,* or type on reflective surfaces blurring under headlights at high speeds. Clearview may also help the highway system save billions of dollars by eliminating the need to enlarge existing signs and related architecture.

Source: Joshua Yaffa, "The Road to Clarity," *The New York Times,* August 12, 2007, downloaded at www.nytimes.com/2007/08/12/magazine/12fonts-t.html?_r=1&n=Top/Reference/Times%20Topics/Subjects/D/Design&pagewanted=print&oref=slogin.

The visual design of a message can support or undercut the impact of the words.

Site to See

Go to

www.mouseprint.org

for examples of *mouseprint*, or legalese in a font so small that only a mouse can read it.

Site to See

Go to

http://pptideas.blogspot. com/2012/04/presentation-tipcase-studysuccess.html

for Dave Paradi's tips and links on using PowerPoint slides in presentations.

Multi-touch screens, which let people use finger gestures to access features from their smartphone and tablet PC displays, may soon be common in their larger cousins. Microsoft's purchase of Perceptive Pixel, which is a pioneer in the technology for desktop PCs, coincides with enhancements planned for Windows 8 for use with multi-touch screens. The change in how users interface with computers may significantly affect how users plan and use presentation software, such as PowerPoint.

Source: Clint Boulton, "Microsoft Bringing Multi-Touch Screens to the Big Time," *The Wall Street Journal,* July 11, 2012, http://blogs.wsj. com/cio/2012/07/11/microsoft-bringing-multi-touch-screens-to-the-big-time/?KEYWORDS=power point+presentation.

Use ragged right margins when you

- Do not have proportional typefaces.
- Want a less formal look.
- Want to be able to revise an individual page without reprinting the whole document.
- Use very short line lengths.

How should I design presentation slides? LO 5-2

▶ *Keep slides simple, relevant, and interesting.*

As you design slides for PowerPoint and other presentation programs, keep these guidelines in mind.

- Use a big font: 44- or 50-point for titles, 32-point for subheads, and 28-point for examples.
- Use bullet-point phrases rather than complete sentences.
- Use clear, concise language.
- Make only three to five points on each slide. If you have more, consider using two slides.
- Customize your slides with the company logo, charts, and scanned-in photos and drawings.

Use clip art only if the art is really appropriate to your points and only if you are able to find nonsexist and nonracist images. (At the end of the 1990s, as Marilyn Dyrud has shown, the clip art in major software programs was biased.[4]) Today, Internet sources offer many more choices.

Choose a consistent template, or background design, for the entire presentation. Make sure the template is appropriate for your subject matter. For example, use a globe only if your topic is international business and palm trees only if you're talking about tropical vacations. One problem with PowerPoint is that the basic templates may seem repetitive to people who see lots of presentations made with the program. For a very important presentation, you may want to consider customizing the basic template.

Choose a light background if the lights will be off during the presentation and a dark background if the lights will be on. Slides will be easier to read if you use high contrast between the words and background. See Figure 5.5 for examples of effective and ineffective color combinations.

Figure 5.5 Effective and Ineffective Colors for Presentation Slides

Effective

Ineffective

How should I design Web pages?   LO 5-3

▶ *Pay attention to content, navigation, and the first screen.*

Good web pages have both good content and an interesting design. You should be able to evaluate the design of a web page even if you never create one from scratch.

The opening screen is crucial. Not only must the first screen open quickly, but it also must contain the information visitors need to quickly find what they are looking for. While some studies show that users grow impatient after waiting 15 seconds for a page to load, research by Jakob Nielsen puts that number at 10 seconds, and he says users often leave web pages within 10 to 20 seconds, staying on average less than a minute. In addition, users tend not to scroll down beyond the first screen of text.[5] To keep visitors around long enough to find (and buy) what they want, make using the first screen extremely easy.

- Provide an introductory statement orienting the surfing reader to the organization.
- Offer an overview of the content of your page, with links to take readers to the parts that interest them. A site index and internal search engine are valuable tools.
- Include information that will be most interesting and useful to most readers.

The rest of the page can contain information that only a limited number of readers will want. When a document reaches four pages or more, think about dividing it into several documents. Specialized information can go on another page, which readers can click on if they want it.

Make it clear what readers will get if they click on a link.

Ineffective phrasing: Employment. Openings and skills levels are determined by each office.

Better phrasing: Employment. Openings listed by skills level and by location.

Minimize the number of links readers have to click through to get to the information they want.

As you design pages,

- Use small graphics; keep animation to a minimum. Both graphics and animation take time to load, especially with a slow modem. Include a Skip Intro button if you have an animated introduction page.
- Provide visual variety. Use indentations, bulleted or numbered lists, and headings.
- Unify multiple pages with a small banner, graphic, or label so surfers know who sponsors each page.
- On each page, provide a link to the home page, the name and e-mail address of the person who maintains the page, and the date when the page was last revised.
- If your web pages include music or sound effects, put an Off button where the user can find it immediately.

How do I know whether my design works?   LO 5-4

▶ *Test it.*

A design that looks pretty may or may not work for the audience. To know whether your design is functional, test it with your audience.

- Watch someone as he or she uses the document to do a task. Where does the reader pause, reread, or seem confused? How long does it take? Does the document enable the reader to complete the task accurately?
- Ask the reader to "think aloud" while completing the task, interrupt the reader at key points to ask what he or she is thinking, or ask the reader to describe the thought process after completing the document and the task. Learning the reader's thought processes is

Instant Replay

Guidelines for Page Design
- Use white space to separate and emphasize points.
- Use headings to group points.
- Limit the use of words set in all capital letters.
- Use no more than two fonts in a single document.
- Decide whether to justify margins based on the situation and the audience.

People in the United States focus first on the left side of a website. websites in Arabic and Hebrew orient text, links, and graphics from right to left.

Source: Albert N. Badre, "The Effects of Cross Cultural Interface Design Orientation on World Wide Web User Performance," GVU Technical Report GIT-GVU-01-03, August 31, 2000, 8; www.cc.gatech.edu/gvu/reports/2001, visited site July 27, 2002.

Using Computers to Create Good Design   LO 5-5

Standard word-processing programs such as Word, WordPerfect, and Google Docs let you control how your page looks. Different versions of each program handle these commands differently. Look up the following bolded terms in a manual, a book about the program, or the online Help menu of your computer program to find out how to use each feature.

Letters and Memos

Choose a businesslike font in 11- or 12-point type. Times Roman, Palatino, Helvetica, and Arial are the most commonly used business fonts.

Use **bold** headings. Avoid having a heading all by itself at the bottom of the page. If you can't have at least one line of text under it, move the heading to the next page. You can check this by eye or set your program to avoid **widows** and **orphans.**

Use **tabs** or **indents** to line up the return address and signature blocks in modified block format (▶▶ Module 9), the To/From/Subject line section of a memo, or the items in a list.

Change your **tab settings** to create good visual impact. A setting at .6″ works well for the To/From/Subject line section of memos. Use .4″ for paragraphs and .6″ for the start of bulleted lists. For lists with 10 or more items, the setting will need to be a bit further to the right—about .65″.

Choose the design for **bullets** under Insert or Format. Both WordPerfect and Word will create bulleted or numbered lists automatically. If you have lists with paragraphs, turn off the automatic bullets and create them with the bullets in Symbols. Use **indent** (not tab) to move the whole list in, not just a single line of it.

Use a **header** (in the Insert or View menu) with automatic **page numbering** (pull down Format to Page) for second and subsequent pages. That way, when you delete a paragraph or

expand your reader benefits, you don't have to manually move the header. You can either **delay** the header till page 2 or create it on page 2. For best visual impact, make your header one point size smaller than the body type.

For a two-page document, change the top **margin** of the second page to .5″ so the header is close to the top of the page.

Use the same side margins as your letterhead. If you aren't using a letterhead, use 1″ side margins.

On a two-page document, make sure the second page has at least 4 to 6 lines of text for letters and at least 10 lines of text for memos. If you have less, either (1) add details, (2) start the message further down on page one so that there is more text on page two, or (3) make the text fit on just one page by (a) tightening your prose, (b) using full justification to save space, or (c) using less white space.

Word-processing programs have a **quickcorrect** or **autocorrect** feature that changes *hte* to *the, (c)* to ©, and so forth. Go into the Tools or Format menus to find these features and edit them so they make only the changes you want.

Hyphenation may be under Format or under Language in Tools.

Printing

To save paper, check **print preview** on the File menu. You'll be able to see how your document will look on the page and make minor layout changes before you print.

If you prepare your document on one computer and print it from another, be sure to open the document and check all of it before you print. Different printers may change margins slightly. Even the same size font may differ from printer to printer, so that a document that fit nicely on one page in 11-point on one computer may suddenly take up more room on a different one.

important, since a reader may get the right answer for the wrong reasons. In such a case, the design still needs work.

- Test the document with the people who are most likely to have trouble with it: very old or young readers, people with little education, people who read English as a second language.
- Ask readers to put a plus sign (+) in the margins by any part of the document they like or agree with and a minus sign (−) by any part that seems confusing or wrong. Then use interviews or focus groups to find out the reasons.

When should I think about design?   LO 5-6

▶ *At each stage of the writing process.*

Document design isn't something to "tack on" when you've finished writing. Indeed, the best documents are created when you think about design at each stage of your writing process(es).

Instant Replay

Designing PowerPoint Slides

- Use a big font.
- Use bullet-point phrases.
- Use clear, concise language.
- Make only three to five points on each slide.
- Customize your slides.

- As you plan, think about your audiences. Are they skilled readers? Are they busy? Will they read the document straight through or skip around in it?
- As you write, incorporate lists and headings. Use visuals to convey numerical data clearly and forcefully.
- Get feedback from people who will be using your document. What parts of the document do they think are hard to understand? Is there additional information they need?
- As you revise, check your draft against the guidelines in this module.

Go to

www.webpagesthatsuck .com

for examples of poorly designed web pages.

Summary of Learning Objectives

- To create visually attractive documents, **(LO 5-1)**
  - Use white space.
  - Use headings.
  - Limit the use of words set in all capital letters.
  - Limit the number of fonts in a single document.
  - Decide whether to justify margins based on the situation and the audience.
- As you design slides for PowerPoint and other presentation programs, **(LO 5-2)**
  - Use a big font.
  - Use bullet-point phrases.
  - Use clear, concise language.
  - Make only three to five points on each slide.
  - Customize your slides.
- Good web pages have both good content and an interesting design. **(LO 5-3)**
  - Orient the surfing reader to the organization.
  - Offer an overview of the content of your page, with links to take readers to the parts that interest them.
  - Make it clear what readers will get if they click on a link.
  - Keep graphics small.
  - Provide visual variety.
  - Unify multiple pages with a small banner, graphic, or label.

- On each page, provide a link to the home page, the name and e-mail address of the person who maintains the page, and the date when the page was last revised.
  - Provide a Skip Intro button for animated introductions and an Off button for sound.
- To test a document, observe readers, ask them to "think aloud" while completing the task, interrupt them at key points to ask what they are thinking, or ask them to describe their thought process after completing the document and the task. **(LO 5-4)**
- WordPerfect and Word let you control how your page looks. In general, **(LO 5-5)**
  - Use the program manual or help function to see commands to use.
  - Choose a businesslike font in 11- or 12-point type.
  - Use Times Roman, Palatino, Helvetica, or Ariel.
  - Use print preview to see what a page will look like printed.
- The best documents are created when you think about design at each stage of the writing process. **(LO 5-6)**
  - As you plan, think about the needs of your audience.
  - As you write, incorporate lists, headings, and visuals.
  - Get feedback from people who will be using your document.
  - As you revise, check your draft against the guidelines in this chapter.

Assignments for Module 5

Questions for Comprehension

5.1 How can you create white space? **(LO 5-1)**

5.2 How do you decide whether to use bullets or numbers in a list? **(LO 5-1)**

5.3 What are three criteria for good web pages? **(LO 5-3)**

Questions for Critical Thinking

5.4 "Closed captions" for people with hearing impairments are almost always typed in full capital letters. Why is that a bad idea? Are there any advantages to using full capitals? What arguments could you use for changing the practice? **(LO 5-1)**

5.5 Suppose that, in one company, a worker says, "We don't need to worry about design. People pay a toll charge to call us, and we make a slight profit on each call. So if they have questions about the product, that's OK. If better design reduced the number of calls, we might actually lose money!" How would you persuade such a person that good document design is worth doing? **(LO 5-1)**

5.6 Central Community College is preparing a brochure to persuade prospective students to consider taking classes. The college doesn't have the money for full-scale document testing. What free or almost-free things could it do to make the document as effective as possible? **(LO 5-1)**

5.7 Design choices may have ethical implications. Indicate whether you consider each of the following actions ethical, unethical, or a gray area. Which of the actions would you

do? Which would you feel uncomfortable doing? Which would you refuse to do? **(LO 5-1)**

a. Putting the advantages of a proposal in a bulleted list, while discussing the disadvantages in a paragraph.

b. Using a bigger type size so that a résumé visually fills a whole page.

c. Putting the services that are not covered by your health plan in full caps to make it less likely that people will read the page.

Exercises and Problems

5.8 **Evaluating Page Designs (LO 5-1)**

Use the guidelines in Module 5 to evaluate each of the following page designs. What are their strong points? What could be improved?

a.

b.

☞ RESIST the TEMPTATION to use **all the fonts** available on your ▮▮▮▮▮▮▮. *Too many* fonts **create** *visual clutter*☹ and **make a document HARD** to read!! **FONTS** that call *attention* to **themselves** are NOT *appropriate* for **BUSINESS** letters, memos, and reports.❧ *Even* in a **standard font,** avoid shadows, outlines, and *OVERUSE OF* **bold** and *italics.* ∞

5.9 Improving a Financial Aid Form (LO 5-1)

You've just joined the Financial Aid office at your school. The director gives you the accompanying form and asks you to redesign it.

"We need this form to see whether parents have other students in college besides the one requesting aid. Parents are supposed to list all family members that the parents support—themselves, the person here, any other kids in college, and any younger dependent kids.

"Half of these forms are filled out incorrectly. Most people just list the student going here; they leave out everyone else.

"If something is missing, the computer sends out a letter and a second copy of this form. The whole process starts over. Sometimes we send this form back two or three times before it's right. In the meantime, students' financial aid is delayed—maybe for months. Sometimes things are so late that they can't register for classes, or they have to pay tuition themselves and get reimbursed later.

"If so many people are filling out the form wrong, the form itself must be the problem. See what you can do with it. But keep it to a page."

As Your Instructor Directs,

a. Analyze the current form and identify its problems.
b. Revise the form. Add necessary information; reorder information; change the chart to make it easier to fill out.

Hints:

- Where are people supposed to send the form? What is the phone number of the financial aid office? Should they need to call the office if the form is clear?
- Does the definition of *half-time* apply to all students or just those taking courses beyond high school?
- Should capital or lowercase letters be used?
- Are the lines big enough to write in?
- What headings or subdivisions within the form would remind people to list all family members whom they support?
- How can you encourage people to return the form promptly?

Please complete the chart below by listing all family members for whom you (the parents) will provide more than half support during the academic year (July 1 through June 30). Include yourselves (the parents), the student, and your dependent children, even if they are not attending college.

EDUCATIONAL INFORMATION, 200_ - 200_						
FULL NAME OF FAMILY MEMBER	AGE	RELATIONSHIP OF FAMILY MEMBER TO STUDENT	NAME OF SCHOOL OR COLLEGE THIS SCHOOL YEAR	FULL-TIME	HALF-TIME* OR MORE	LESS THAN HALF-TIME
STUDENT APPLICANT						

*Half-time is defined as 6 credit hours or 12 clock hours a term.

When the information requested is received by our office, processing of your financial aid application will resume.

Please sign and mail this form to the above address as soon as possible. Your signature certifies that this information and the information on the FAF is true and complete to the best of your knowledge. If you have any questions, please contact a member of the need analysis staff.

_____   _____
Signature of Parent(s)   Date

5.10 Using Headings (LO 5-1)

Reorganize the items in each of the following lists, using appropriate headings. Use bulleted or numbered lists as appropriate.

a. Rules and Procedures for a Tuition Reimbursement Plan

1. You are eligible to be reimbursed if you have been a full-time employee for at least three months.

2. You must apply before the first class meeting.

3. You must earn a "C" or better in the course.

4. You must submit a copy of the approved application, an official grade report, and a receipt for tuition paid to be reimbursed.

5. You can be reimbursed for courses related to your current position or another position in the company, or for courses that are part of a degree related to a current or possible job.

6. Your supervisor must sign the application form.

7. Courses may be at any appropriate level (high school, college, or graduate school).

b. Activities in Starting a New Business
   - Getting a loan or venture capital
   - Getting any necessary city or state licenses
   - Determining what you will make, do, or sell
   - Identifying the market for your products or services
   - Pricing your products or services
   - Choosing a location
   - Checking zoning laws that may affect the location
   - Identifying government and university programs for small business development
   - Figuring cash flow
   - Ordering equipment and supplies
   - Selling
   - Advertising and marketing

5.11 Analyzing Documents (LO 5-1)

Collect several documents available to you as a worker, student, or consumer: letters and memos, newsletters, ads and flyers, reports. Use the guidelines in Module 5 to evaluate each of them.

As Your Instructor Directs,

a. Discuss the documents with a small group of classmates.
b. Write a memo to your instructor evaluating three or more of the documents. Include originals or photocopies of the documents you discuss as an appendix to your memo.
c. Write a memo to your supervisor recommending ways the organization can improve its documents.
d. In an oral presentation to the class, explain what makes one document good and another one weak. If possible, use transparencies so that classmates can see the documents as you evaluate them.

5.12 Revising a Document (LO 5-1)

Your state government hires interns for many of its offices. The Director of Human Resources has noticed that few of the interns submit all the needed paperwork on time and suspects that the problem is the form memo that goes out to interns. You've been asked to revise the memo to make it more effective.

Subject: Getting Your First Paycheck on Time

So that you can receive your first paycheck on time, please send the following items to the office of Human Resources by the first working day of next month: a copy of your Social Security card or a copy of your birth certificate; a copy of your driver's license; proof of enrollment in an accredited college (accepted items include a paid fee statement; a letter from the registrar's office; a copy of your college identification card with the term and year on it); and proof of your grade status (e.g., first year, sophomore). Attach one of the following: your latest grade report, your latest transcript; a letter from the registrar's office verifying your grade status; a copy of your college identification card that shows what level you are in. Pay is based on how many quarter or semester hours you have completed. At the end of each term, notify Human Resources. You may be eligible for a pay increase.

Rewrite the message, paying special attention to layout and page design.

5.13 Evaluating PowerPoint Slides (LO 5-2)

Evaluate the following drafts of PowerPoint slides.

- Is the background appropriate for the topic?
- Do the slides use words or phrases rather than complete sentences?

- Is the font big enough to read from a distance?
- Is the art relevant and appropriate?
- Is each slide free from errors?

a.

c.

1

2

3

4

5.14 Evaluating Web Pages (LO 5-3)

Compare three web pages in the same category (for example, nonprofit organizations, car companies, university departments, sports information). Which page(s) are most effective? Why? What weaknesses do the pages have?

As Your Instructor Directs,

a. Discuss the pages with a small group of classmates.
b. Write a memo to your instructor evaluating the pages. Include URLs of the pages in your memo.

c. In an oral presentation to the class, explain what makes one page good and another one weak. If possible, put the pages on screen so that classmates can see the pages as you evaluate them.
d. Post your evaluation of the pages in an e-mail message to the class. Include hot links to the pages you evaluate.

Polishing Your Prose

Active and Passive Voice

Verbs have "voice": active and passive voice. Business communication generally prefers active voice because it is shorter and clearer.

A verb is active if the grammatical subject acts. Passive voice occurs when the subject is acted upon by someone or something else.

Active: The man bought grapes at the store.
Passive: The grapes were bought by the man at the store.

In the active voice, the subject—*the man*—is doing the action—bought. In the passive version, *the grapes* is the subject, yet it is *the man,* not *the grapes,* that is actually doing the action. It is harder for the reader to follow who or what did the action. In addition, it takes more words to convey the same idea.

To change a passive voice construction into the active voice, start by identifying who or what is doing the action. If no agent ("by _____") is present in the sentence, you will need to supply it. A passive verb is usually accompanied by a helping verb, such as *is, are,* or *were.* Rewrite the sentence by putting the actor in the role of subject and dropping the helping verb:

Passive: The plan was approved by our clients.
Active: Our clients approved the plan.
Passive: PowerPoint slides have been created.
Active: Susan created the PowerPoint slides.
Passive: It is desired that you back up your work daily.
Active: Back up your work daily.

In business communication, active voice is usually better. However, passive voice is better in three situations:

1. Use passive voice to emphasize the object receiving the action, not the agent.

   Your order was shipped November 15.

   The customer's order, not the shipping clerk, is important.

2. Use passive voice to provide coherence within a paragraph. A sentence is easier to read if "old" information comes at the beginning of a sentence. When you have been discussing a topic, use the word again as your subject even if that requires a passive verb.

   The bank made several risky loans in the late 1990s. These loans were written off as "uncollectible" in 2002.

   Using *loans* as the subject of the second sentence provides a link between the two sentences, making the paragraph as a whole easier to read.

3. Use passive voice to avoid assigning blame.

   The order was damaged during shipment.

   An active verb would require the writer to specify *who* damaged the order. The passive here is more tactful.

Exercises

Identify whether the passives in the following sentences are acceptable or whether the verb should be changed to active.

1. A mistake cost company several thousand dollars.
2. Two dozen résumés were reviewed by the hiring committee.
3. Rules for using the company posted on the door.
4. The final report was written Jessica Malone and Dylan Toshi.
5. It is recommended that employees keep all personal items locked drawers to discourage theft.
6. Files are kept on the third floor the Accounting Department.
7. A second set of tablet PCs was purchased by the IT Department backup.
8. The campaign is predicted by be a great success in Asia.
9. Apps were created for our customers to access their accounts with a smartphone.
10. Emily, Candice, and Ruben nominated by the awards committee for Employee of the Month.

Check your answers to the odd-numbered exercises at the back of the book.

Unit 1 Cases for Communicators

Old Navy Taken to School

Proofreading—checking for and correcting typographical errors—is the final step in the writing process. While always an integral part of writing, it is of particular importance if the finished product will be mass produced. Beyond checking a message for errors, however, writers also must make sure it gets sent to its intended audience.

Take the case of clothing retailer Old Navy, which won a lucrative deal to produce T-shirts for 70 colleges and universities, such as Duke, Syracuse, Notre Dame, the University of Texas, and the University of Southern California. The shirts feature each institution's name and mascot, along with the phrase "Let's go!" The problem is that the required apostrophe was left out. Hundreds of thousands of shirts with the error were shipped out before anyone caught the mistake.

Old Navy executives want to reprint the T-shirts with the correction, but at least one institution, Syracuse, wants to know who approved the copy before it was printed. Some college officials and alumni are embarrassed that their institution of higher learning is now associated with the mistake. In addition, the error has gone viral, resulting in tweets such as "Pains my English major heart" and "Why graphic designers need proofreaders," as well as other negative publicity for the company.

The cost to reprint the T-shirts alone will be in the thousands of dollars, but the company also stands to lose future customers

from the mistake. The reprinted shirts may also make it to stores too late for the current sports season, defeating the purpose of the campaign in the first place.

Individual Activity

Choose one of the following:

a. Imagine you are the communications manager at Old Navy. Your task is to write an apology letter to the college or university affected by the error. (You may choose which college or university.) Because the letter is an important part of your company's effort to restore customer confidence by mending relationships, the vice president of communications will be reviewing the message before it is sent.

   In addition to accepting full responsibility for the error, your company will take actions to underscore its commitment to good customer service:

1. Developing a strategy to improve editing and reduce the potential for errors.
2. Explaining how your company will settle this matter. (The company has agreed to pay for the offers to affected parties outlined in b.)

b. Imagine you are the marketing manager for the college or university. It is your task to write a letter of apology to the institution's Board of Trustees, whose members may be embarrassed by the publicity about the error. Because the letter will be such an important part of the company's effort to restore customer confidence, the institution's president will review the message before it is sent.

Old Navy has ordered the shipments of shirts with the error returned, but there is the possibility that some shirts have already sold or that retailers will keep them in hopes that they become collector's items. To reduce the possibility of continued embarrassment over the error as well as to demonstrate a commitment to good customer service, the company will:

1. Offer a 20% discount on a future wholesale order for a shipment returned in its entirety.

2. Offer a $2 credit on future merchandise orders for each shirt that is returned in the event some shirts have already sold or are missing.

Before you write either letter, you will need to carefully analyze this communication problem. Use PAIBOC to make sure that you understand the purpose, audience, and situation.

P: What is the purpose of this letter? (Remember, there may be more than one!)

A: Who are the initial, primary, gatekeeper, secondary, and watchdog audiences for my letter?

I: What information should my letter include?

B: What benefits for the reader can I highlight?

O: What objections should I expect?

C: How will the context affect reader response?

Write your thoughts down so you can refer to them later. Be thorough in your answers.

Group Activity

As the communications manager at Old Navy, you have been given the task of developing a "Best Practices" program to establish good revising, editing, and proofreading habits among employees. After you have created the plan, you will submit it to the owners of the company, who will review it before instituting it.

With your fellow managers, develop an outline of this new program. In the plan, explain why revising, editing, and proofreading are important; what the best practices are; and how employees can effectively implement these best practices in their own work.

Consider the following questions:

- What critical communication elements need to be applied?
- How can employees learn to provide quality feedback?
- How important is quality feedback in the writing process?
- What is cycling?
- What specific steps are involved in editing and proofreading a document?
- What is thorough revision? What is light revision?
- How will readers benefit from your improved strategy?

Include any other tips that you, as experts, can offer to your audience.

Sources: Piper Weiss, "Grammar Fail on Old Navy's College T-Shirts. Uh Oh . . . ," August 23, 2011, http://shine.yahoo.com/event/fallfashion/grammar-fail-on-old-navys-college-tshirts-uh-oh-2531551/; and Andrea Chang, "Old Navy Reprinting Erroneous School T-Shirts," *The Los Angeles Times,* August 25, 2011, http://articles.latimes.com/2011/aug/25/business/la-fiold-navy-20110825.

Creating Goodwill

Creating Goodwill

2

Module 6 You-Attitude

Module 7 Positive Emphasis

Module 8 Reader Benefits

Module

6 | You-Attitude

LEARNING OBJECTIVES

Module 6 focuses on the importance of you-attitude in business communication. After completing the module, you should be able to

LO 6-1 Apply strategies for you-attitude use.

LO 6-2 Compare and contrast situations for *you* use.

LO 6-3 Apply strategies for goodwill creation with you-attitude.

LO 6-4 Apply strategies for point-of-view adaptation.

You-attitude is a style of writing that

- Looks at things from the reader's point of view.
- Respects the reader's intelligence.
- Protects the reader's ego.
- Emphasizes what the reader wants to know.

You-attitude is a concrete way to show empathy (◄◄ p. 24) and the foundation of persuasion.

You-attitude is a matter of style. That is, revisions for you-attitude do not change the basic meaning of the sentence. However, revising for you-attitude often makes sentences longer since sentences become more specific.

Often, we can create you-attitude by changing words. Sometimes, however, it's necessary to revise organization and content as well as style to create the best document.

How do I create you-attitude in my sentences? LO 6-1

▶ *Talk about the reader—except in negative situations.*

To create you-attitude,

1. Talk about the reader, not about yourself.
2. Refer to the reader's request or order specifically.
3. Don't talk about feelings, except to congratulate or offer sympathy.
4. In positive situations, use *you* more often than *I*. Use *we* when it includes the reader.
5. Avoid *you* in negative situations.

1. Talk about the Reader, Not about Yourself

Readers want to know how they benefit or are affected. When you provide this information, you make your message more complete and more interesting.

Lacks you-attitude: I have negotiated an agreement with Apex Rent-a-Car that gives you a discount on rental cars.

You-attitude: As a Sunstrand employee, you can now get a 20% discount when you rent a car from Apex.

Any sentence that focuses on the writer's work or generosity lacks you-attitude, even if the sentence contains the word *you.* Instead of focusing on what we are giving the reader, focus on what the reader can now do. To do that, you may need to change the grammatical subject.

Lacks you-attitude: We are shipping your order of September 21 this afternoon.
You-attitude: The two dozen CorningWare starter sets you ordered will be shipped this afternoon and should reach you by September 28.

Emphasize what the reader wants to know. The reader is less interested in when we shipped the order than in when it will arrive. Note that the phrase "should reach you by" leaves room for variations in delivery schedules. If you can't be exact, give your reader the information you do have: "UPS shipment from California to Texas normally takes three days." If you have absolutely no idea, give the reader the name of the carrier, so the reader knows whom to contact if the order doesn't arrive promptly.

In 2008, drugstore giant Walgreen announced plans to open pharmacies and operate health centers at work sites throughout the U.S., bringing services to busy customers rather than the other way around. The company purchased I-trax, Inc., and Whole Health Management, two companies that collectively ran 350 health centers at corporate offices. The company further identified more than 7,600 office sites with 1,000 or more employees that could support similar centers. The result is Take Care Clinics, part of a wholly owned subsidiary of Walgreen. Looking at things from the customer's point of view is helping Walgreen and other companies transform health services.

Source: Amy Merrick, "How Walgreen Changed Its Prescription for Growth," *The Wall Street Journal,* March 19, 2008, B1; and *Take Care Clinic at Select Walgreens* website ("About Us"), downloaded on February 12, 2010, at http://www.takecarehealth.com/about/?tab=tc_about_us.

Me-attitude can make you seem pompous and self-serving.

Site to See

Go to

www.quality.nist.gov

You-attitude, positive emphasis, and bias-free language build goodwill with words, just as service, quality, and reliability build goodwill with actions. The Baldrige National Quality Program encourages and recognizes quality in U.S. businesses.

The word *company* has the same root as the word *companion:* both come from the Latin words for eating bread together.

Instant Replay

Definition of You-Attitude

You-attitude is a style of writing that

- Looks at things from the reader's point of view.
- Respects the reader's intelligence.
- Protects the reader's ego.
- Emphasizes what the reader wants to know.

2. Refer to the Reader's Request or Order Specifically

Refer to the reader's request, order, or policy specifically, not as a generic *your order* or *your policy.* If your reader is an individual or a small business, it's friendly to specify the content of the order. If you're writing to a company with which you do a great deal of business, give the invoice or purchase order number.

Lacks you-attitude:	Your order . . .
You-attitude (to individual):	The desk chair you ordered
You-attitude (to a large store):	Your invoice #783329

3. Don't Talk about Feelings, Except to Congratulate or Offer Sympathy

Lacks you-attitude:	We are happy to extend you a credit line of $5,000.
You-attitude:	You can now charge up to $5,000 on your American Express card.

In most business situations, your feelings are irrelevant and should be omitted. The reader doesn't care whether you're happy, bored stiff at granting a routine application, or worried about granting so much to someone who barely qualifies. All the reader cares about is the situation from his or her point of view.

It *is* appropriate to talk about your own emotions in a message of congratulation or condolence.

You-attitude:	Congratulations on your promotion to district manager! I was really pleased to read about it.
You-attitude:	I was sorry to hear that your father died.

In internal memos, it may be appropriate to comment that a project has been gratifying or frustrating. In the letter of transmittal that accompanies a report, it is permissible to talk about your feelings about doing the work. But even other readers in your own organization are primarily interested in their own concerns, not in your feelings.

Don't talk about the reader's feelings, either. It can be offensive to have someone else tell us how we feel—especially if the writer is wrong.

Lacks you-attitude:	You'll be happy to hear that Open Grip Walkway Channels meet OSHA requirements.
You-attitude:	Open Grip Walkway Channels meet OSHA requirements.

Maybe the reader expects that anything you sell would meet government regulations (OSHA—the Occupational Safety and Health Administration—is a federal agency). The reader may even be disappointed if he or she expected higher standards. Simply explain the situation or describe a product's features; don't predict the reader's response.

When you have good news for the reader, simply give the good news.

Lacks you-attitude:	You'll be happy to hear that your scholarship has been renewed.
You-attitude:	Congratulations! Your scholarship has been renewed.

4. In Positive Situations, Use *You* More Often than *I.* Use *We* When It Includes the Reader

Talk about the reader, not you or your company.

Lacks you-attitude:	We provide health insurance to all employees.
You-attitude:	You receive health insurance as a full-time Procter & Gamble employee.

Most readers are tolerant of the word *I* in e-mail messages, which seem like conversation. Edit paper documents to use *I* rarely if at all. *I* suggests that you're concerned about personal issues, not about the organization's problems, needs, and opportunities. *We* works well when it includes the reader. Avoid *we* if it excludes the reader (as it would in a letter to a customer or supplier or as it might in a memo about what *we* in management want *you* to do).

5. Avoid *You* in Negative Situations

To avoid blaming the reader, use an impersonal expression or a passive verb. Talk about the group to which the reader belongs so readers don't feel they're singled out for bad news.

Lacks you-attitude:	You failed to sign your check.
You-attitude (impersonal):	Your check arrived without a signature.
You-attitude (passive):	Your check was not signed.

Impersonal constructions omit people and talk only about things. **Passive verbs** describe the action performed on something, without necessarily saying who did it. (▶▶ See Module 16 for a full discussion of passive verbs.)

In most cases, active verbs are better. But when your reader is at fault, passive verbs may be useful to avoid assigning blame.

Normally, writing is most lively when it's about people—and most interesting to readers when it's about them. When you have to report a mistake or bad news, however, you can protect the reader's ego by using an impersonal construction, one in which things, not people, do the acting.

Lacks you-attitude:	You made no allowance for inflation in your estimate.
You-attitude (passive):	No allowance for inflation has been made in this estimate.
You-attitude (impersonal):	This estimate makes no allowance for inflation.

A University of California, Berkeley, study suggests couples who use inclusive language, such as *we* and *our* rather than *I* or *me,* are more likely to have greater affection and less physiological stress during a disagreement.

Source: Rachel Rettner, "Couples Who Say 'We' Fare Better in Fights," *LiveScience,* February 3, 2010, http://www.livescience.com/culture/couples-we-words-100203.html.

A study sure to provoke strong feelings found a link among prejudices, low intelligence, and social conservatism, suggesting, among other things, that anti-prejudice campaigns that expect participants to see things from another person's point of view may be too difficult to handle for people with low IQs. As researchers suspected, low intelligence in childhood corresponded with racism in adulthood. Still, they are quick to point out that drawing sweeping conclusions from the study is unwise. Said lead researcher Gordon Hodson: "There are multiple examples of very bright conservatives and not-so-bright liberals, and many examples of very principled conservatives and very intolerant liberals."

Source: Stephanie Pappas, "Low IQ & Conservative Beliefs Linked to Prejudice," *Live Science,* January 26, 2012, http://www.livescience.com/18132-intelligence-social-conservatism-racism.html.

Goodwill comes in many forms. Whitlowe R. Green spent a lifetime teaching students the value of economics—and living a frugal life that included buying expired meat and secondhand clothes. When he passed away in 2002, the 88-year-old willed $2.1 million to his alma mater, Prairie View A & M University, for scholarships, the largest single-donor gift in the institution's history.

Instant Replay

Five Ways to Create You-Attitude

1. Talk about the reader, not about yourself.
2. Refer to the reader's request or order specifically.
3. Don't talk about feelings, except to congratulate or offer sympathy.
4. In positive situations, use *you* more often than *I*. Use *we* when it includes the reader.
5. Avoid *you* in negative situations.

When executive Greg Smith resigned from Goldman Sachs, he criticized the firm for ignoring the best interests of clients. He wrote that employees referred to them as "muppets" and junior analysts commonly asked, "How much money did we make off the client?" Smith's disgust at the firm's me-centered culture was revealed in a scathing editorial published in *The New York Times*.

Source: Greg Smith, "Why I Am Leaving Goldman Sachs," *The New York Times*, March 14, 2012, http://www.nytimes.com/2012/03/14/opinion/why-i-am-leaving-goldman-sachs.html?_r=1&pagewanted=all%3Fsrc%3Dtp&smid=fb-share.

Instant Replay

Definitions of Impersonal Constructions

Impersonal constructions omit people and talk only about things. **Passive verbs** describe the action performed on something, without necessarily saying who did it.

A purist might say that impersonal constructions are illogical: An estimate, for example, is inanimate and can't "make" anything. In the pragmatic world of business writing, however, impersonal constructions often help you convey criticism tactfully.

When you restrict the reader's freedom, talk about the group to which the reader belongs rather than about the reader as an individual.

Lacks you-attitude: You must get approval from the director before you publish any articles or memoirs based on your work in the agency.

You-attitude: Agency personnel must get approval from the director to publish any articles or memoirs based on their work at the agency.

Does you-attitude basically mean using the word *you*? LO 6-2

▶ *No.*

All messages should use you-attitude, but the words to achieve it will change depending on the situation.

- In a positive message, focus on what the reader can do. "We give you" lacks you-attitude because the sentence focuses on what we are doing.
- Avoid *you* when it criticizes the reader or limits the reader's freedom.
- In a job application letter, create you-attitude by showing how you can help meet the reader's needs, but keep the word *you* to a minimum (▶▶ Module 28).

I've revised my sentences. Do I need to do anything else? LO 6-3

▶ *Check content and organization, too.*

▶ *Emphasize what the reader wants to know.*

Good messages apply you-attitude beyond the sentence level by using content and organization as well as style to build goodwill.

To create goodwill with content,

- Be complete. When you have lots of information to give, consider putting some details in an appendix that may be read later.
- Anticipate and answer questions the reader is likely to have.
- When you include information the reader didn't ask for, show why it is important.
- Show readers how the subject of your message affects them.

To organize information to build goodwill,

- Put information readers are most interested in first.
- Arrange information to meet your reader's needs, not yours.
- Use headings and lists so that the reader can find key points quickly.

Consider the letter in Figure 6.1. As the red marginal notes indicate, many individual sentences in this letter lack you-attitude. The last sentence in paragraph 1 sounds both harsh and defensive; the close is selfish. The language is stiff and filled with outdated jargon. Perhaps the most serious problem is that the fact most interesting to the reader is buried in the middle of the first paragraph. Since we have good news for the reader, we should put that information first.

Figure 6.1 A Letter Lacking You-Attitude

450 INDUSTRIAL PARK CLEVELAND, OH 44120 (216) 555-4670 FAX: (216) 555-4672

December 11, 2012

Ms. Carol McFarland
Rollins Equipment Corporation
18438 East Night Hawk Way
Phoenix, AZ 85043-7800

Dear Ms. McFarland:

Not you-attitude *Legalistic*

We are now ready to issue a check to Rollins Equipment in the amount of $14,207.02. To receive said check, you will deliver to me a release of the mechanic's liens in the amount of $14,207.02. *Sounds dictatorial*

Focuses on negative *Lacks you-attitude*

Before we can release the check, we must be satisfied that the release is in the proper form. We must insist that we be provided with a stamped original of the lien indicating the document number in the appropriate district court where it is filed. Also, either the release must be executed by an officer of Rollins Equipment, or we must be provided with a letter from an officer of Rollins Equipment authorizing another individual to execute the release. *Hard to read, remember*

Please contact the undersigned so that an appointment can be scheduled for this transaction. *Jargon*

Sincerely,

Kelly J. Pickett

Kelly J. Pickett

Fixing individual sentences could improve the letter. However, it really needs to be rewritten. Figure 6.2 shows a possible revision. The revision is clearer, easier to read, and friendlier.

When you have negatives, third-person is better you-attitude than second-person because third-person shows that everyone is being treated the same way.

Figure 6.2 A Letter Revised to Improve You-Attitude

450 INDUSTRIAL PARK   CLEVELAND, OH   44120   (216) 555-4670   FAX: (216) 555-4672

December 11, 2012

Ms. Carol McFarland
Rollins Equipment Corporation
18438 East Night Hawk Way
Phoenix, AZ 85043-7800

Dear Ms. McFarland:

Let's clear up the lien in the Allen contract.   *Starts with main point from the reader's point of view*

Focuses on what reader gets   Rollins will receive a check for $14,207.02 when you give us a release for the mechanic's lien of $14,207.02. To assure us that the release is in the proper form,

1. Give us a stamped original of the lien indicating the document's district court number, and   *List makes it easy to see that reader needs to do two things—and that the second can be done in two ways.*

2. Either
    a. Have an officer of Rollins Equipment sign the release
          or
    b. Give us a letter from a Rollins officer authorizing someone else to sign the release.

Call me to tell me which way is best for you.   *Emphasizes reader's choice*

Sincerely,

Kelly J. Pickett

Kelly J. Pickett   *Extension number makes it easy for reader to phone.*
Extension 5318

Seeing Another Point of View LO 6-4

Seeing another point of view means more than observing and sympathizing. It also means empathizing—putting yourself "in the other person's shoes."

How? Start with shared experiences. A professor thought a student who dozed in his class was being rude. Some of her classmates did, too. But then the professor recalled how he'd worked his way through college. Many students today have full-time jobs, he knew, and the professor noticed this student often wore green medical togs.

Instead of taking offense, the professor met with the student and discovered she frequently came to his class from a double shift at the local hospital. She simply was exhausted, as he often had been. He helped her transfer to another course section so she could sleep before class. She finished the term with high marks and even took a class with him later.

Resolving conflicts often requires empathy. To learn to look beyond your own point of view, think of a situation where you were misunderstood. How did you feel? What resources of yours—time, money, and emotional energy—were wasted? What did you want from the other person?

Now, turn it around. How might the other person answer the same questions? What could you have given? The points where concerns overlap are opportunities for compromise.

Resist the temptation to put your needs ahead of others'. Instead, remember that all business is exchange, a form of compromise. Learning to see another point of view is the first step toward a successful exchange.

Many companies want employees who can empathize. To prepare for her role in overseeing the operations of McDonald's China at the 2008 Olympic Games in Beijing, Shantel Wong completed a nine-month training program, learning every aspect of restaurant practice, including filling orders, flipping burgers, and cleaning toilets.

Even if she never works another deep fryer again, Wong knows what it takes, as well as what her employees go through daily. She also understands how they can make the customers' dining experiences even better.

RunPee.com empathized with moviegoers seeking timely restroom breaks and now gets 3,000 to 6,000 visitors daily. The site's slogan: "Helping your bladder enjoy going to the movies as much as you do."

McDonald's China executive Shantel Wong's intensive training helps her to see other points of view.

Some researchers believe that "emotional intelligence," or EQ, is a predictor of success in life. Daniel Goleman, whose bestseller *Emotional Intelligence* helped popularize the concept, found that "self-awareness, self-discipline, persistence, and empathy were more important than intelligence in getting ahead in life." In his follow-up, *Working with Emotional Intelligence,* he argued that EQ was more important than intellect or technical skill for success on the job. Key to building healthy relationships with clients, customers, and co-workers is seeing another point of view.

Sources: Normandy Madden, "CMO Training for the Olympics by Flipping Burgers, Cleaning Toilets," *Advertising Age,* June 20, 2005, 30; Jake Coyle, "Web Site Helps Time Mid-Movie Bathroom Breaks," downloaded July 27, 2009, at http://news.yahoo.com/s/ap/20090731/ap_on_en_mo/us_film_bathroom_breaks; and Mary Vanac, "Will You Let Me Help You Find a Solution*?" The Cleveland Plain Dealer,* August 13, 2007, downloaded at www.cleveland.com/business/plaindealer/index.ssf?/base/other/1186995109169780.xml&coll=2&thispage=1.

Summary of Learning Objectives

- To create you-attitude in sentences, **(LO 6-1)**
  1. Talk about the reader, not about yourself.
  2. Refer to the reader's request or order specifically.
  3. Don't talk about feelings, except to congratulate or offer sympathy.
  4. In positive situations, use *you* more often than *I*. Use *we* when it includes the reader.
  5. Avoid *you* in negative situations.
- Apply you-attitude beyond the sentence level by using organization, content, and layout as well as style to build goodwill. **(LO 6-2)**
- To create goodwill with content, **(LO 6-3)**
  - Be complete.
  - Anticipate and answer likely questions from readers.
- Show why information is important if the reader didn't ask for it.
- Show readers how the message subject affects them.
- To organize information with goodwill,
  - Put information readers are most interested in first.
  - Arrange information to meet your reader's needs.
  - Use headings and lists.
- Seeing another point of view means putting yourself "in the other person's shoes." **(LO 6-4)**
  - Use **empathy.**
  - Think of a situation where you were misunderstood.
  - Resist the temptation to put your needs ahead of others'.

Assignments for Module 6

Questions for Comprehension

6.1 What is you-attitude? **(LO 6-1)**

6.2 How can you create you-attitude within sentences? **(LO 6-1)**

6.3 How can you create you-attitude beyond the sentence level? **(LO 6-2, LO 6-3)**

Questions for Critical Thinking

6.4 Can you think of situations in which the five strategies would *not* create you-attitude? If so, how would you create you-attitude in those situations? **(LO 6-1, LO 6-2)**

6.5 Why do sentences starting "We give you" lack you-attitude? **(LO 6-1, LO 6-2)**

6.6 Think of a time when you felt a business cared about you. What words or actions made you feel that way? **(LO 6-1, LO 6-2)**

6.7 Why doesn't the word *you* always create you-attitude? **(LO 6-2)**

Exercises and Problems

6.8 Using Passives and Impersonal Constructions to Improve You-Attitude (LO 6-1)

Revise each of these sentences to improve you-attitude, first using a passive verb, then using an impersonal construction (one in which things, not people, do the action). Are both revisions equally good? Why or why not?

1. You did not park your car in the appropriate lot.

2. You did not turn in the correct receipts for reimbursement.

3. Because of your error, you cost this company $14,000 in extra charges.

4. You did not provide a portfolio showing relevant work samples for this job.

5. You did not submit your weekly report on time to your supervisor.

6.9 Improving You-Attitude (LO 6-1, LO 6-2)

Revise these sentences to improve you-attitude. Eliminate any awkward phrasing. In some cases, you may need to add information to revise the sentence effectively.

1. I know you will appreciate the enclosed special membership pricing.

2. Because Pinnacle Marketing is a leader in online promotion, we can offer the best and the brightest talent to our customers.

3. We are pleased to make this limited-time offer available to our audience.

4. As president and CEO, I personally guarantee our products are the best on the market.

5. We have no doubt that you will not find a better deal anywhere else.

6. I hope that you will take the time to visit one of our neighborhood locations close to you.

7. You will be pleased to know that a refund check is being sent to you.

8. In the next few weeks, the company will offer wellness seminars to encourage better lifestyle choices.

9. Since you were late to the meeting, we assigned you to help with recruiting, the job nobody else wanted.

10. Thanks to your costly mistake, the company lost $34,000 on the deal.

6.10 Improving You-Attitude (LO 6-1, LO 6-2)

Revise these sentences to improve you-attitude. Eliminate any awkward phrasing. In some cases, you may need to add information to revise the sentence effectively.

1. The management provides a generous package of benefits for all of its employees to enjoy.

2. You will no doubt be pleased to know that we have decided to give you a refund.

3. Though you seem less qualified than the other candidates, we've decided to offer you the job anyway.

4. This letter you wrote has so many typos I'm beginning to regret hiring you.

5. Expect our phone call on or about October 3 to schedule an appointment with our delivery person.

6. We assume even someone of your limited experience can understand the need for discretion in our business.

7. If you do not turn in your time card punctually, you will not receive your paycheck.

8. I saw the job posting you wrote and quite frankly I'm surprised that anyone even bothered to answer it.

9. All of my employees must share my attitude about serving the customer first—anything less will not be tolerated by me.

10. I can't understand why you complain so much here. It's as though you don't really want to work for me.

6.11 Revising a Memo for You-Attitude (LO 6-1 to LO 6-3)

Revise the following memo to improve you-attitude.

Subject: Status of Building Renovations

We are happy to announce that the renovation of the lobby is not behind schedule. By Monday, October 9, we should be ready to open the west end of the lobby to limited traffic.

The final phase of the renovation will be placing a new marble floor in front of the elevators. This work will not be finished until the end of the month.

We will attempt to schedule most of the work during the evenings so that normal business is not disrupted.

Please exercise caution when moving through the construction area. The floor will be uneven and steps will be at unusual heights. Watch your step to avoid accidental tripping or falling.

6.12 Evaluating You-Attitude in Documents that Cross Your Desk (LO 6-1 to LO 6-4)

Identify three sentences that use (or should use) you-attitude in documents you see as a worker, consumer, or student. If the sentences are good, write them down or attach a copy of the document(s) marking the sentence(s) in the margin. If the sentences need work, provide both the original sentence and a possible revision.

As Your Instructor Directs,

a. Share your examples with a small group of students.

b. Write a memo to your instructor discussing your examples.

c. Post an e-mail message to the class discussing your examples.

d. Present two or three of your examples to the class in a short presentation.

e. With your small group, write a collaborative short report to your instructor about the patterns you see.

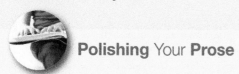

Polishing Your Prose

It's/Its

With an apostrophe, *it's* is a contraction meaning *it is*. Without an apostrophe, *its* is a possessive pronoun meaning *belonging to it*.

Contractions always use apostrophes:

It is → it's

I have → I've

You will → you'll

They are → they're

Possessive pronouns (unlike possessive nouns) do not use apostrophes:

His / hers / its

My / mine / our / ours

Your / yours

Their / theirs

Because both *it's* and *its* sound the same, you have to look at the logic of your sentence to choose the right word. If you could substitute *it is,* use *it's*.

Decide whether to use contractions (such as *it's, they're, you're, we're, should've,* and so forth) based on audience, purpose, and organizational culture. Some audiences find contractions too informal; others find a lack of contractions off-putting or unfriendly. If the purpose of your document is to persuade while being casual, then contractions make sense. If, however, documents have significant legal ramifications, contractions may seem flip. Your organization may have its own conventions, too—check past correspondence to see what is preferred.

In general, more formal documents such as résumés and long research reports use few (or no) contractions. Contractions are often OK in e-mail, memos, and letters in which you want a conversational tone, such as a fund-raising letter for the local animal shelter.

Exercises

Choose the right word in the set of brackets.

1. [It's/Its] a good idea to keep paper copies of documents, as electronic files can be lost or corrupted.
2. Halle told us [it's/its] going to be at least five business days before we can expect a reply to our Singapore proposal.
3. Though the app has been thoroughly tested, [it's/its] a good idea to test it one more time, just to be certain.
4. Because the Halloran Company values innovation, [it's/its] vital that creative people have the opportunity to realize their potential there.
5. Each department should make sure [it's/its] personnel files are kept confidential.
6. We believe [it's/its] a sign of good faith that our customers have stayed with us in tough economic times.
7. Patel and Associates is dedicated to making sure [it's/its] clients receive the best service possible.
8. In her keynote address, Sophia told us that an organization is strong only because [it's/its] employees are strong.
9. While [it's/its] impossible to be prepared for all emergencies, [it's/its] prudent to have a general disaster plan.
10. To keep up with [it's/its] competition, a company needs to make certain [it's/its] social networking pages are kept up-to-date.

Check your answers to the odd-numbered exercises at the back of the book.

Positive Emphasis

LEARNING OBJECTIVES

As Module 7 shows, positive emphasis builds goodwill and is better in most business messages than negative emphasis. After completing the module, you should be able to

LO 7-1 **Apply strategies for positive emphasis use.**

LO 7-2 **Analyze situations for ethical positive emphasis.**

LO 7-3 **Explain reasons for tone, politeness, and power considerations.**

LO 7-4 **Identify situations for apologies.**

Some negatives are necessary.

- Straightforward negatives build credibility when you have bad news to give the reader: announcements of layoffs, product defects and recalls, price increases.
- Negatives may help people take a problem seriously. Wall Data improved the reliability of its computer programs when it eliminated the term *bugs* and used instead the term *failures*.
- In some messages, such as negative performance appraisals, your purpose is to deliver a rebuke with no alternative. Even here, avoid insults or attacks on the reader's integrity or sanity. Being honest about the drawbacks of a job reduces turnover.
- Sometimes negatives create a "reverse psychology" that makes people look favorably at your product. Rent-a-Wreck is thriving. (The cars really don't look so bad.)[1]

But in most situations, it's better to be positive. Researchers Annette N. Shelby and N. Lamar Reinsch, Jr., found that businesspeople responded more positively to positive rather than to negative language and were more likely to say they would act on a positively worded request.[2] Martin Seligman's research for Met Life found that optimistic salespeople sold 37% more insurance than pessimistic colleagues. As a result, Met Life began hiring optimists even when they failed to meet the company's other criteria. These "unqualified" optimists outsold pessimists 21% in their first year and 57% the next.[3]

Positive emphasis is a way of looking at things. Is the bottle half empty or half full? You can create positive emphasis with the words, information, organization, and layout you choose.

How do I create positive emphasis?   LO 7-1

▶ *Deemphasize or omit negative words and information.*

The following five techniques deemphasize negative information:

1. Avoid negative words and words with negative connotations.
2. Focus on what the reader can do rather than on limitations.
3. Justify negative information by giving a reason or linking it to a reader benefit.
4. If the negative is truly unimportant, omit it.
5. Put the negative information in the middle and present it compactly.

In some messages, especially negative ones (▶▶ Module 11), you won't use all five techniques. Practice each of these techniques so that you can use them when they're appropriate.

1. Avoid Negative Words and Words with Negative Connotations

Figure 7.1 lists some common negative words. If you find one of these words in a draft, try to substitute a more positive word. When you must use a negative, use the *least negative* term that will convey your meaning.

The following examples show how to replace negative words with positive words.

Negative:	We have failed to finish taking inventory.
Better:	We haven't finished taking inventory.
Still better:	We will be finished taking inventory Friday.
Negative:	If you can't understand this explanation, feel free to call me.
Better:	If you have further questions, just call me.
Still better:	Omit the sentence. (Readers aren't shrinking violets. They'll call if they do have questions.)

Omit double negatives.

Negative:	Do not forget to back up your disks.
Better:	Always back up your disks.

Figure 7.1 Negative Words to Avoid

afraid	eliminate	lacking	trivial
anxious	error	loss	trouble
avoid	except		wait
bad	fail	**Some mis-words:**	weakness
careless	fault	misfortune	worry
damage	fear	missing	wrong
delay	hesitate	mistake	
delinquent	ignorant		**Many un-words:**
deny	ignore	neglect	unclear
difficulty	impossible	never	unfair
		no	unfortunate
		not	unfortunately
Some dis-words:	**Many in-words:**	objection	unpleasant
disappoint	inadequate	problem	unprepared
disapprove	incomplete	reject	unreasonable
dishonest	inconvenient	sorry	unreliable
disinform	injury	terrible	unsure
dissatisfied	insincere		

Even when rejecting someone or something, you should avoid harsh or insulting words.

"We have an opening that will suit you
perfectly. It's marked Exit."

Reprinted by permission of CartoonStock.com,
www.cartoonstock.com.

Optimism can be powerful in helping a person achieve his or her goals, but a lack of optimism might also be a hindrance—and a self-fulfilling prophecy. A recent Gallup Poll found that for the first time on record, most Americans did not believe that today's young people would have better lives than their parents. The poll, administered on and off since 1983, found that only 44% of Americans thought things would turn out better. How such thinking may shape the future, of course, remains to be seen.

Source: Catherine Rampell, "Dimming Optimism for Today's Youth," *The New York Times,* May 2, 2011, http://economix.blogs. nytimes.com/2011/05/02/dimming-optimism-for-todays-youth/?gwh= 354CD1DC224BF21C6B9B0A274 0E9E2AC.

When you must use a negative, use the least negative term that is accurate.

Negative:	Your balance of $835 is delinquent.
Better:	Your balance of $835 is past due.

Getting rid of negatives has the added benefit of making what you write easier to understand. Sentences with three or more negatives are very hard to understand.[4]

Beware of **hidden negatives**: words that are not negative in themselves but become negative in context. *But* and *however* indicate a shift, so, after a positive statement, they are negative. *I hope* and *I trust that* suggest that you aren't sure. *Patience* may sound like a virtue, but it is a necessary virtue only when things are slow. Even positives about a service or product may backfire if they suggest that in the past the service or product was bad.

Negative:	I hope this is the information you wanted. [Implication: I'm not sure.]
Better:	Enclosed is a brochure about road repairs scheduled for 2013–14.
Still better:	The brochure contains a list of all roads and bridges scheduled for repair during 2013–14. Call Gwen Wong at 555–3245 for specific dates when work will start and stop and for alternate routes.
Negative:	Please be patient as we switch to the automated system. [Implication: you can expect problems.]
Better:	If you have questions during our transition to the automated system, call Melissa Morgan.
Still better:	You'll be able to get information instantly about any house on the market when the automated system is in place. If you have questions during the transition, call Melissa Morgan.
Negative:	Now Crispy Crunch tastes better. [Implication: it used to taste terrible.]
Better:	Now Crispy Crunch tastes even better.

Removing negatives does not mean being arrogant or pushy.

Negative:	I hope that you are satisfied enough to place future orders.
Arrogant:	I look forward to receiving all of your future business.
Better:	Call Mercury whenever you need transistors.

Instant Replay

Five Ways to Create Positive Emphasis

To deemphasize negative information,

1. Avoid negative words and words with negative connotations.
2. Focus on what the reader can do rather than on limitations.
3. Justify negative information by giving a reason or linking it to a reader benefit.
4. If the negative is truly unimportant, omit it.
5. Put the negative information in the middle and present it compactly.

Some stores might say, "Put books you don't want here." But Bookseller Joseph–Beth in Lexington, Kentucky, uses positive emphasis.

Happiness and optimism may have a good effect on your heart, according to researchers at Harvard University. While scientists have known for some time about the reverse relationship—how depression, for instance, can be bad for the heart—less was known about the influence of positive thinking on the organ. When it comes to financial issues, however, too much optimism may actually be a bad thing. According to Duke University's Manju Puri and David T. Robinson, extreme optimists may avoid long-term savings or paying off credit cards because they think the economy will always do better.

Sources: Anahad O'Connor, "Really? Optimism Reduces the Risk of Heart Disease," *The New York Times,* April 23, 2012, http://well.blogs.nytimes.com/2012/04/23/really-optimism-reduces-the-risk-of-heart-disease/?gwh=BADA807829DF77253E2810F80B07EF6A; and Alina Tugend, "Lean Toward the Sunny Side, but Don't Overdo It," *The New York Times,* September 23, 2011, http://www.nytimes.com/2011/09/24/business/optimism-but-not-too-much-can-be-good-for-you.html?_r=1&pagewanted=all&gwh=842BAB5DF37429951FDD485A9E5C0A54.

When you eliminate negative words, be sure to maintain accuracy. Words that are exact opposites will usually not be accurate. Instead, use specifics to be both positive and accurate.

Negative: The exercycle is not guaranteed for life.
Not true: The exercycle is guaranteed for life.
True: The exercycle is guaranteed for 10 years.

Negative: Customers under 60 are not eligible for the Prime Time discount.
Not true: You must be over 60 to be eligible for the Prime Time discount.
True: If you're 60 or older, you can save 10% on all your purchases with RightWay's Prime Time discount.

Legal phrases also have negative connotations for most readers and should be avoided whenever possible. The idea will sound more positive if you use conversational English.

Negative: If your account is still delinquent, a second, legal notice will be sent to you informing you that cancellation of your policy will occur 30 days after the date of the legal notice if we do not receive your check.
Better: Even if your check is lost in the mail and never reaches us, you still have a 30-day grace period. If you do get a second notice, you will know that your payment hasn't reached us. To keep your account in good standing, stop payment on the first check and send a second one.

2. Focus on What the Reader Can Do Rather than on Limitations

Sometimes positive emphasis is a matter of the way you present something: Is the glass half empty or half full? Sometimes it's a matter of eliminating double negatives. When there are limits, or some options are closed, focus on the alternatives that remain.

Negative: We will not allow you to charge more than $1,500 on your VISA account.
Better: You can charge $1,500 on your new VISA card.
or: Your new VISA card gives you $1,500 in credit that you can use at thousands of stores nationwide.

As you focus on what will happen, **check for you-attitude** (◀◀ p. 90). In the last example, "We will allow you to charge $1,500" would be positive, but it lacks you-attitude.

When you have a benefit and a requirement the reader must meet to get the benefit, the sentence is usually more positive if you put the benefit first.

Negative:	You will not qualify for the student membership rate of $25 a year unless you are enrolled for at least 10 hours.
Better:	You get all the benefits of membership for only $25 a year if you're enrolled for 10 hours or more.

3. Justify Negative Information by Giving a Reason or Linking It to a Reader Benefit

A reason can help your reader see that the information is necessary; a benefit can suggest that the negative aspect is outweighed by positive factors. Be careful, however, to make the logic behind your reason clear and to leave no loopholes.

Negative:	We cannot sell computer disks in lots of less than 10.
Loophole:	To keep down packaging costs and to help you save on shipping and handling costs, we sell computer disks in lots of 10 or more.

Suppose the customer says, "I'll pay the extra shipping and handling. Send me seven." If you can't or won't sell in lots of less than 10, you need to write:

Better:	To keep down packaging costs and to help customers save on shipping and handling costs, we sell computer disks only in lots of 10 or more.

If you link the negative element to a benefit, be sure it is a benefit the reader will acknowledge. Avoid telling people that you're doing things "for their own good." They may have a different notion of what their own good is. You may think you're doing customers a favor by limiting their credit so they don't get in over their heads and go bankrupt. They may feel they'd be better off with more credit so they could expand in hopes of making more sales and more profits.

4. If the Negative Is Truly Unimportant, Omit It

Omit negatives entirely only when

- The reader does not need the information to make a decision.
- You have already given the reader the information and he or she has access to the previous communication.
- The information is trivial.

The following examples suggest the kind of negatives you can omit:

Negative:	A one-year subscription to *PC Magazine* is $49.97. That rate is not as low as the rates charged for some magazines.
Better:	A one-year subscription to PC Magazine is $49.97.
Still better:	A one-year subscription to PC Magazine is $49.97. You save 43% off the newsstand price of $87.78.
Negative:	If you are not satisfied with Interstate Fidelity Insurance, you do not have to renew your policy.
Better:	Omit the sentence.

5. Bury the Negative Information and Present It Compactly

The beginning and end are always positions of emphasis. Put negatives here only if you want to emphasize the negative, as you may in a negative message (▶▶ Module 11). To deemphasize a negative, put it in the middle of a paragraph rather than in the first or last sentence, in the middle of the message rather than in the first or last paragraphs.

When a letter or memo runs several pages, remember that the bottom of the first page is also a position of emphasis, even if it is in the middle of a paragraph, because of the extra white space of the bottom margin. (The first page gets more attention because it is on top and the reader's eye may catch lines of the message even when he or she isn't consciously

Researchers Teresa Amabile and Steven Kramer found that happier people make better workers. In a study of nearly 12,000 electronic diary entries from business professionals, however, they discovered a third were unhappy, unmotivated, or both, a situation exacerbated by dwindling job resources and security. With employees more likely to have new ideas on happier days, the cost of lost productivity is high— one estimate is $300 billion annually in the U.S.

Sources: Teresa Amabile and Steven Kramer, "Do Happier People Work Harder?" *The New York Times,* September 3, 2011, http://www.nytimes.com/2011/09/04/opinion/sunday/do-happier-people-work-harder.html; and Teresa Amabile and Steven Kramer, "Pro: Bring on the Smiles, Count the Profits," *Bloomberg Businessweek,* February 22, 2012, http://www.businessweek.com/debateroom/archives/2012/02/employee_happiness_matters_more_than_you_think.html.

Instant Replay

Definition of Hidden Negatives

Hidden negatives are words that are not negative in themselves but become negative in context.

Using Positive Emphasis Ethically   LO 7-2

The methods to achieve positive emphasis can be misused, so be careful when using them.

Consider omission of necessary details.

Shannon Castillo played a local radio station's weeklong contest to win a Hummer H2 vehicle. When she showed up on April 1 to collect her prize, she didn't get the $60,000 vehicle she expected. Instead, she received a remote-controlled toy replica. The station contended it was an April Fool's Day joke and that the winners weren't promised the actual vehicle. A similar contest was held by a restaurant that promised employees a "Toyota" for selling the most beer. When the winner came forward, she was presented with a *Star Wars* character doll— her "toy Yoda."

In both cases, full disclosure might have affected decisions: Participants might have passed on the contests had they known that the prize wasn't what they expected. It isn't ethical to omit information that people need to make decisions. Lawsuits also can occur from such practice.

Focusing on what the reader can do rather than on limitations works when the situation is appropriate. People don't expect, for instance, to be congratulated for being able to use their skills with another employer when, in fact, they're being fired.

Presenting information compactly also can go too far. A credit card company mailed out a letter with the good news that the minimum monthly payment was going down. But a separate small flyer explained that interest rates (on the charges not repaid) were going up. The print was far too small

to read: 67 lines of type were crowded into five vertical inches of text.

The Federal Emergency Management Agency, or FEMA, still reeling from criticism over its handling of the Hurricane Katrina disaster, was further embarrassed when John P. "Pat" Philbin, its external affairs director, staged a briefing with FEMA staff members posing as reporters. They asked easy-to-answer questions phrased in positive language. Authentic journalists were invited 15 minutes before the briefing and allowed to listen through a conference call but not ask questions. At the time, Philbin had already accepted a job with the Director of National Intelligence. That offer was later rescinded.

Food manufacturers may substitute lesser-known ingredients for those that have negative connotations for some customers. Thus, shoppers avoiding *sugar* should be aware that *corn syrup, high-fructose corn syrup,* and *white grape juice concentrate* may be euphemisms for the same.

Sources: Tim Molloy, "Woman Sues Over Radio Station's Toy Hummer April Fools' Prank," July 13, 2005, downloaded at www.montereyherald.com/mld/montereyherald/news/12124132.htm; Reg Wydeven, "Radio Giveaways End Up Taking Listeners for a Bad Ride," July 23, 2005, downloaded at www.wisinfo.com/postcrescent/news/archive/col_21850677.shtml; Donna S. Kienzler, "Visual Ethics," *The Journal of Business Communication* 34 (1997): 175–76; Pamela Hess, "Former FEMA Spokesman Loses Spy Job," downloaded at http://abcnews.go.com/Politics/wireStory?id=3792287 on December 24, 2007; and Dan Shapley, "Don't Be Misled by These Food Label Tricks," February 3, 2010. http://green.yahoo.com/blog/daily_green_news/280/don-t-be-misled-by-these-food-label-tricks.html.

Researchers Jacqueline Mayfield and Milton Mayfield found in their study at Texas A&M University that total effects showed for every 10% increase in motivating language to students, there was about a 3% decrease in absenteeism.

Source: Jacqueline Mayfield and Milton Mayfield, "The Role of Leader Motivating Language in Employee Absenteeism," *Journal of Business Communication,* October 2009, 46:4, 455–479.

reading it; the tops and bottoms of subsequent pages don't get this extra attention.) If possible, avoid placing negative information at the bottom of the first page.

Giving a topic lots of space emphasizes it. Therefore, you can deemphasize negative information by giving it as little space as possible. Give negative information only once in your message. Don't list negatives vertically on the page because lists take space and emphasize material.

Why do I need to think about tone, politeness, and power?   LO 7-3

▶ *So you don't offend people by mistake.*

No one likes to deal with people who seem condescending or rude. Poorly chosen words can create that sense, whether the sender "meant" to be rude or not. **Tone** is the implied attitude of the writer toward the reader. Tone is tricky because it interacts with power: The words that might seem friendly from a superior to a subordinate may seem uppity if used by the subordinate to the superior. Norms for politeness are cultural and generational.

Language that is acceptable within one group may be unacceptable if used by someone outside the group.

The desirable tone for business writing is businesslike but not stiff, friendly but not phony, confident but not arrogant, polite but not groveling. The following guidelines will help you achieve the tone you want.

- **Use courtesy titles for people outside your organization whom you don't know well.** Most U.S. organizations use first names for everyone, whatever their age or rank. But many people don't like being called by their first names by people they don't know or by someone much younger. When you talk or write to people outside your organization, use first names only if you've established a personal relationship. If you don't know someone well, use a courtesy title (▶▶ Module 9):

Dear Mr. Reynolds:
Dear Ms. Lee:

- **Be aware of the power implications of the words you use.** "Thank you for your cooperation" is generous coming from a superior to a subordinate; it's not appropriate in a message to your superior. Different ways of asking for action carry different levels of politeness.[5]

Order (lowest politeness)	Turn in your time card by Monday.
Polite order (midlevel politeness)	Please turn in your time card by Monday.
Indirect request (higher politeness)	Time cards should be turned in by Monday.
Question (highest politeness)	Would you be able to turn in your time card by Monday?

You need more politeness if you're asking for something that will inconvenience the reader and help you more than the person who does the action. Generally, you need less politeness when you're asking for something small, routine, or to the reader's benefit. Some discourse communities, however, prefer that even small requests be made politely.

Lower politeness:	To start the scheduling process, please describe your availability for meetings during the second week of the month.
Higher politeness:	Could you let me know what times you'd be free for a meeting the second week of the month?

Higher levels of politeness may be unclear. In some cases, a question may seem like a request for information to which it's acceptable to answer, "No, I can't." In other cases, it will be an order, simply phrased in polite terms. Generally, requests sound friendliest when they use conversational language.

Poor tone:	Return the draft with any changes by next Tuesday.
Better tone:	Let me know by Tuesday whether you'd like any changes in the draft.

- **When the stakes are low, be straightforward.** Messages that "beat around the bush" sound pompous and defensive.

Poor tone:	Distribution of the low-fat plain granola may be limited in your area. May we suggest that you discuss this matter with your store manager.
Better tone:	Our low-fat granola is so popular that there isn't enough to go around. We're expanding production to meet the demand. Ask your store manager to keep putting in orders so that your grocery is on the list of stores that will get supplies when they become available.
or:	Store managers decide what to stock. If your store has stopped carrying our low-fat granola, the store manager has stopped ordering it. Talk to the manager. Managers try to meet customer needs, so if you say something you're more likely to get what you want.

Resilience—the ability to weather life's stressors and setbacks—plays an important part in our success. In *Resilience: Why Things Bounce Back,* Andrew Zolli found that most people are resilient and often more than they think. The key to resilience, he argues, is mental attitude. Said Zolli, who in the same year suffered through the loss of a child, death of business partner, and mother's diagnosis with a serious illness, "If you believe that the world is a meaningful place, and you have a meaningful place within it; if you believe that you have agency within the world, that your actions have meaning . . . that successes and failures are put in your life to teach you things, and that they're not just random acts of chance, then you have a much higher degree of resilience in the face of trauma."

Source: Gregory M. Lamb, "Why Resilience Is the Key to Solving 21st Century Problems," *The Christian Science Monitor,* July 20, 2012, http://www.csmonitor.com/World/Making-a-difference/Change-Agent/2012/0720/Why-resilience-is-the-key-to-solving-21st-century-problems.

Making a video apology? Consultant Abbie Lundberg advises, "Make the message clear, look into the camera, consider clothes and lighting, and practice." Such actions might have improved BP CEO Tony Hayward's disastrous YouTube apology for the Gulf oil spill.

Source: David Rosenbaum, "Apologizing for Bad News? Be Careful with the Video," *CFO,* April 16, 2012, http://www3.cfo.com/article/2012/4/technology_video-executive-apologies-restatements.

- **When you must give bad news, consider hedging your statement.** John Hagge and Charles Kostelnick have shown that auditors' suggestion letters rarely say directly that firms are using unacceptable accounting practices. Instead, they use three strategies to be more diplomatic: specifying the time ("currently, the records are quite informal"), limiting statements ("it appears," "it seems"), and using impersonal statements that do not specify who caused a problem or who will perform an action.[6]

What's the best way to apologize? LO 7-4

▶ *Early, briefly, and sincerely.*

When you are at fault, you may build goodwill by admitting that fact forthrightly. In some cases, laws now provide protection for workplace apologies. Ohio and 26 other states, for instance, have "I'm sorry" laws that allow physicians to acknowledge mistakes without fear of lawsuits.[7] However, apologies may have negative legal implications, so some organizations prefer that apologies not be issued to customers or the public. Think about your audience and the organizational culture in deciding whether to apologize explicitly.

- **No explicit apology is necessary if the error is small and if you are correcting the mistake.**

Negative:	I'm sorry the clerk did not credit your account properly.
Better:	Your statement has been corrected to include your payment of $263.75.

- **Do not apologize when you are not at fault.** When you have done everything you can and when a delay or problem is due to circumstances beyond your control, you aren't at fault and don't need to apologize. It may be appropriate to include an explanation so the reader knows you weren't negligent. If the news is bad, put the explanation first. If you have good news for the reader, put it before your explanation.

Negative:	I'm sorry that I could not answer your question sooner. I had to wait until the sales figures for the second quarter were in.
Better (neutral or bad news):	We needed the sales figures for the second quarter to answer your question. Now that they're in, I can tell you that . . .
Better (good news):	The new advertising campaign is a success. The sales figures for the second quarter are finally in, and they show that . . .

If the delay or problem is long or large, it is good you-attitude to ask the reader whether he or she wants to confirm the original plan or make different arrangements.

Negative:	I'm sorry that the chairs will not be ready by August 25 as promised.
Better:	Due to a strike against the manufacturer, the desk chairs you ordered will not be ready until November. Do you want to keep that order, or would you like to look at the models available from other suppliers?

- **When you apologize, do it early, briefly, and sincerely.** Apologize only once, early in the message. Let the reader move on to other, more positive information.

Even if major trouble or inconvenience has resulted from your error, you don't need to go on about all the horrible things that happened. The reader already knows this negative information, and you can omit it. Instead, focus on what you have done to correct the situation.

If you don't know whether or not any inconvenience has resulted, don't raise the issue at all.

Negative:	I'm sorry I didn't answer your letter sooner. I hope that my delay hasn't inconvenienced you.
Better:	I'm sorry I didn't answer your letter sooner.

- **Positive emphasis** means focusing on the positive rather than the negative aspects of a situation. **(LO 7-1)**
  1. Avoid negative words and words with negative connotations.
  2. State information positively. Focus on what the reader can do rather than on what you won't or can't let the reader do.
  3. Justify negative information by giving a reason or linking it to a reader benefit.
  4. If the negative is truly unimportant, omit it.
  5. Put the negative information in the middle and present it compactly.
- **Hidden negatives** are words that are not negative in themselves but become negative in context. **(LO 7-1)**
- Use positive emphasis ethically. **(LO 7-2)**
  - Include information readers need to make decisions.
  - Focus on what the reader can do when it's appropriate.
  - Present information legibly and large enough to read.
  - Avoid misleading claims.

Summary of Learning Objectives

- The desirable tone for business writing is businesslike but not stiff, friendly but not phony, confident but not arrogant, polite but not groveling. The following guidelines will help you achieve the tone you want. **(LO 7-3)**
  - Use courtesy titles for people outside your organization whom you don't know well.
  - Be aware of the power implications of the words you use.
  - When the stakes are low, be straightforward.
  - When you must give bad news, consider hedging your statement.
- Don't apologize if the error is small and if you are correcting the mistake. Don't apologize if you are not at fault. If the delay or problem is long or large, it is good you-attitude to ask the reader whether he or she wants to make different arrangements. **(LO 7-4)**
- When you apologize, do it early, briefly, and sincerely. However, apologies may have legal implications, so some organizations prefer that apologies not be issued to customers or the public. **(LO 7-4)**

Assignments for Module 7

Questions for Comprehension

7.1 How can you create positive emphasis? **(LO 7-1)**

7.2 Which of the following are negative words that you should avoid? **(LO 7-1)**

anxious	hesitate
change	hope

Questions for Critical Thinking

7.4 Can you think of situations in which positive emphasis might backfire or be inappropriate? What strategies would be most likely to meet the audience's needs in those situations? **(LO 7-1, LO 7-2)**

7.5 Some negative phrases (such as "please do not hesitate") are business clichés. Why is it better to avoid them? **(LO 7-3)**

Exercises and Problems

7.8 Evaluating the Ethics of Positive Emphasis (LO 7-1)

The first word in each line is negative; the second is a positive term that is sometimes substituted for it. Which of the positive terms seem ethical? Which seem unethical? Briefly explain your choices.

1. anxious	excited
2. flack	public relations specialist
3. gadget	device
4. junk bonds	high-yield bonds

7.9 Focusing on the Positive (LO 7-1)

Revise each of the following sentences to focus on the options that remain rather than those that are closed off.

1. We do not expect to have any problems with this account.

eager	necessary
instead	unfortunately

7.3 What are your options when you need to apologize? **(LO 7-4)**

7.6 If you work for a company that claims to be egalitarian, do you still need to attend to tone, power, and politeness? **(LO 7-3)**

7.7 Think of a situation when an apology was appropriate. What strategy was actually used? Would another strategy have been better? **(LO 7-4)**

5. problem	challenge
6. right-winger	conservative
7. tax	user fee
8. layoffs	rightsizing
9. liberal	progressive
10. mouthpiece	attorney
11. price increase	price change

2. Do not hesitate to contact me should you have any questions.
3. If you are not neat and not punctual, you will find yourself not being promoted.

7.10 Identifying Hidden Negatives (LO 7-1)

Identify the hidden negatives in the following sentences and revise to eliminate them. In some cases, you may need to add information to revise the sentence effectively.

1. We hope you will enjoy working with us.

2. I expect you will be pleased with the enclosed refund.
3. I'm guessing you would like to know if you will receive a bonus this year.

7.11 Revising Sentences to Improve Positive Emphasis (LO 7-1 to LO 7-4)

Revise the following sentences to improve positive emphasis. In some cases, you may need to add or omit information to revise effectively.

1. Relax! You don't have to worry about getting your money.
2. Since Amanda can't make the meeting on Tuesday, we won't be able to meet as a group until next Friday.
3. I just can't believe how much your work has improved in the past few months.
4. Emily, Paula, and Nell—she's the really short one—aren't going to be able to make it to the reception until 7:45.
5. It isn't that we don't appreciate the work you're doing here. It's just that you don't seem to like it when people compliment you.
6. It's not a bad idea to be prepared for the worst since it's not likely it won't happen eventually.

7. Hey, don't get too excited about the interim promotion since you won't be in the job past August.
8. While Sean isn't the worst employee we have, he isn't the best employee either. We hope his job performance improves soon.
9. Don't ever hesitate to contact us, no matter how silly or trivial you think your question might be. We couldn't have become one of the top financial planning firms in this area without listening to our customers, even when they aren't asking relevant questions.
10. Since you don't have much collateral, we're guessing that you don't expect to have the loan approved. Well, that's a silly idea. At Provincial Bank, we don't judge our customers. We help them even when they seem high risk.

7.12 Revising Sentences to Improve Positive Emphasis (LO 7-1 to LO 7-4)

Revise the following sentences to improve positive emphasis. In some cases, you may need to add or omit information to revise effectively.

1. Don't plan on being late. Try to arrive on time for the meeting.
2. Noelani does not expect to use all of her sick leave, so she wants to donate it to one of her co-workers who does not have enough leave to cover an illness.
3. The server is down. I'm guessing it will be available again in a few hours, so be patient.
4. You can't change your dental plan once you've selected it except during the annual enrollment period. That won't happen again until October 1 through October 20.
5. I'm sorry you were inconvenienced because one of our customer service representatives couldn't answer your question.
6. I doubt there will be any problems scheduling one of our service technicians to look at your furnace on

Wednesday. Just don't plan on leaving your home between 1 pm and 5 pm.
7. We've had problems lately with our deliveries, so accept my apologies for your package not being delivered on time. It should be there in a few days.
8. Don't forget that Monday is a holiday, and we don't expect anyone to work that day because the office is closed!
9. You wouldn't believe how hard the committee worked to get this job done, in spite of not having a proper budget or the support of senior management. In fact, it's a miracle the project wasn't a disaster.
10. Though Luis does not spend a great deal of time in the office, when he is there, he is not a lazy worker. The office could do far worse than hire more employees like Luis.

7.13 Revising a Memo to Improve Positive Emphasis (LO 7-1 to LO 7-4)

Revise the following memo to improve you-attitude and positive emphasis.

Subject: Status of College Internship Program

I've made great progress on the college internship program for our company. Though the program isn't yet ready for implementation, I can't believe I'm far from making it so.

To date, I've drafted a plan for the program, contacted several HR managers at comparable companies about their programs, and established a proposed budget for the program.

I'd be further along, but Rob made a mistake when he contacted State University about the program. He accidentally indicated the program would begin in 2007, but the year is actually 2008. It was a silly mistake but not a fatal one.

I wouldn't worry about this error, as it shouldn't be a problem to fix it.

If you have any questions about the program, please don't hesitate to contact me.

7.14 Identifying Positive Emphasis in Ads and Documents (LO 7-1 to LO 7-4)

Look at print advertisements and at documents you receive from your college or university, from your workplace, and from organizations to which you belong. Identify five sentences that either (a) use positive emphasis or (b) should be revised to be more positive.

As Your Instructor Directs,
a. Share your examples with a small group of students.

b. Write a memo to your instructor discussing your examples.
c. Post an e-mail message to the class discussing your examples.
d. Present two or three of your examples to the class in a short presentation.
e. With your small group, write a collaborative short report to your instructor about the patterns you see.

Polishing Your **Prose**

Singular and Plural Possessives

To show possession when a noun is singular, put the apostrophe right after the word; then add *s:*

Allen's	The manager's
Smith's	The company's

If the possessing noun is plural, put the apostrophe right after the word:

Customers'
Employees'
Companies'

In names that end with *s* or *x,* style books permit either form:

Thomas'	Linux'	Jones'
Thomas's	Linux's	Jones's

Often, the location of the apostrophe tells the reader whether the noun is singular or plural.

Singular Possessive	**Plural Possessive**
The employee's	The employees'
Product's	Products'

Because the singular and plural possessives sound the same, look at the logic of your sentence to choose the right word. Also note that when you have plural possessive nouns, other words in the sentence will also become plural.

Plural *employees* have plural *opinions.* Plural *products* have plural *prices.*

We listen to our employees' opinions.

You can find all of our products' prices on our website.

Exercises

Choose the correct word in each set of brackets. Indicate if either word is acceptable.

1. While we can debate its methodology, the [report's/reports'] conclusion is clear: We should expand into South America.
2. [Alex's/Alex'] point is the longer we hesitate to get into the marketplace, the more potential customers we lose.
3. Too many [department's/departments'] employees are dressing casually on days other than Friday.
4. Before we decide to offer products in Costa Rica, we should first determine what its [people's/peoples'] opinions are of our company.
5. This [company's/companies'] first order of business is to serve the customer as best as it can.
6. Each [manager's/managers'] viewpoint is valuable, and we want to give everyone a chance to participate.
7. Carefully review each [smartphone's/smartphones'] capabilities before committing to purchase one for business use.
8. Shaytell told us her [employee's/employees'] after-work social events are also helping to build teamwork in the office.
9. We found [Chris's/Chris'] qualifications to be far superior to the other job candidates'.
10. [Delvecchio and Associates's/Delvecchio and Associates'] final sales figures beat the estimates.

Check your answers to the odd-numbered exercises at the back of the book.

8 | Reader Benefits

Reader benefits enhance business messages, and Module 8 provides techniques for you to use reader benefits well. After completing the module, you should be able to

LO 8-1 **Explain functions of reader benefits.**

LO 8-2 **Identify reader benefits for messages.**

LO 8-3 **Apply strategies for reader benefits creation.**

LO 8-4 **Select reader benefits for messages.**

LO 8-5 **Apply strategies for reader benefits and audience harmony.**

LO 8-6 **Support reader benefits with you-attitude.**

Reader benefits are benefits or advantages that the reader gets by

- Using your services.
- Buying your products.
- Following your policies.
- Adopting your ideas.

Reader benefits are important in both informative and persuasive messages. In informative messages, reader benefits give reasons to comply with the policies you announce and suggest that the policies are good ones. In persuasive messages, reader benefits give reasons to act and help overcome reader resistance. Negative messages (▶▶ Module 11) do not use reader benefits.

Good reader benefits are

- Adapted to the audience.
- Based on intrinsic advantages.
- Supported by clear logic and explained in adequate detail.
- Phrased in you-attitude.

Why do reader benefits work? LO 8-1

▶ *Reader benefits improve the audience's attitudes and actions.*

Reader benefits improve both the attitudes and the behavior of the people you work with and write to. They make people view you more positively; they make it easier for you to accomplish your goals.

Expectancy theory says most people try to do their best only when they believe they can succeed and when they want the rewards that success brings. Reader benefits tell or remind readers that they can do the job and that success will be rewarded.[1] Thus, they help overcome two problems that reduce motivation: People may not think of all the possible benefits, and they may not understand the relationships among efforts, performance, and rewards.[2]

How do I identify reader benefits? LO 8-2

▶ *Brainstorm!*

Sometimes reader benefits will be easy to think of and to explain. When they are harder to identify, brainstorm. You may want to brainstorm in two steps:

1. Think of the feelings, fears, and needs that may motivate your reader. Then identify features of your product or policy that meet those needs.
2. Identify the objective features of your product or policy. Then think how these features could benefit the audience.

Try to brainstorm at least three to five possible benefits for every informative message and five to seven benefits for every persuasive message. The more benefits you have, the easier it will be to choose good ones rather than settling for something that's so-so.

1. Think of Feelings, Fears, and Needs that May Motivate Your Reader. Then Identify Features of Your Product or Policy that Meet Those Needs

One of the best-known analyses of needs is Abraham H. Maslow's hierarchy of needs.[3] Physical needs are the most basic, followed by needs for safety and security, for love and a sense of belonging, for esteem and recognition, and finally for self-actualization or self-fulfillment. All of us go back and forth between higher- and lower-level needs. Whenever lower-level needs make themselves felt, they take priority.

Maslow's model is a good starting place to identify the feelings, fears, and needs that may motivate your audience. Figure 8.1 shows organizational motivators for each of the levels in Maslow's hierarchy. Often, a product or idea can meet needs on several levels. Focus on the ones that audience analysis suggests are most relevant for your audience, but remember that even the best analysis may not reveal all of a reader's needs. For example, a well-paid manager may be worried about security needs if her spouse has lost his job or if the couple is supporting kids in college or an elderly parent. Other motivation experts have found that motivators can vary with employees' ages; for example, young salespeople are more likely to enjoy travel rewards, whereas older salespeople might prefer to remain close to home and family, enjoying cash or merchandise as rewards.[4]

Site to See

Go to
www.versis.co.uk/docsmart.html

In a list of bullet points, Versis spells out the business, operational, and financial benefits of its product, DocSmart.

Figure 8.1 Organizational
Motivations for Maslow's
Hierarchy of Needs

Self-actualization
- Using your talents and abilities.
- Finding solutions to problems.
- Serving humanity.
- Self-respect and pride.
- Being the best you can be.

Esteem, recognition
- Being publicly recognized for achievements.
- Being promoted or gaining authority.
- Having status symbols.
- Having a good personal reputation.
- Having a good corporate reputation.

Love, belonging
- Having friends, working with people you like.
- Cooperating with other people on a project.
- Conforming to a group's norms.
- Feeling needed.
- Being loyal or patriotic.
- Promoting the welfare of a group you identify with or care about.

Safety, security
- Earning enough to afford a comfortable standard of living.
- Having pleasant working conditions.
- Having good health insurance and pension plans.
- Understanding the reasons for actions by supervisors.
- Being treated fairly.
- Saving time and money.
- Conserving human and environmental resources.

Physical
- Earning enough to pay for basic food, clothing, shelter, and medical care.
- Having safe working conditions.

Instant Replay

Definition of Reader Benefit

Reader benefits are benefits or advantages that the reader gets by using your services, buying your products, following your policies, or adopting your ideas.

Instant Replay

Criteria for Reader Benefits

Good reader benefits are
- Adapted to the audience.
- Based on intrinsic advantages.
- Phrased in you-attitude.

The Rousing Creativity Group sells the solid brass Benefit Finder™ to help salespeople develop benefits for the features of their products or services.

2. Identify the Features of Your Product or Policy. Then Think How These Features Could Benefit the Audience

A feature by itself is not a benefit. Often, a feature has several possible benefits.

Feature: Bottled water

Benefits: Is free from chemicals, pollutants

Tastes good

Has no calories

Is easy to carry to class; can be used while biking, driving, hiking

Feature: Closed captions on TV

Benefits: Enables hard-of-hearing viewers to follow dialogue

Helps speakers of English as a second language learn phrases and idioms

Helps small children learn to read

Feature: Flextime

Benefits: Enables workers to accommodate personal needs

Helps organization recruit, retain workers

More workers available in early morning and in evening

- Enables office to stay open longer—more service to clients, customers
- Enables workers to communicate with colleagues in different time zones more easily

Different features may benefit different subgroups in your audience. Depending on what features a restaurant offered, you could appeal to one or more of the following subgroups:

Subgroup	Features to meet the subgroup's needs
People who work outside the home	A quick lunch; a relaxing place to take clients or colleagues
Parents with small children	High chairs, child-size portions, and things to keep the kids entertained while they wait for their orders
People who eat out a lot	Variety both in food and in decor
People on tight budgets	Economical food; a place where they don't need to tip (cafeteria or fast food)
People on special diets	Low-sodium and low-calorie dishes; vegetarian food; kosher food
People to whom eating out is part of an evening's entertainment	Music or a floor show; elegant surroundings; reservations so they can get to a show or event after dinner; late hours so they can come to dinner after a show or game

To develop your benefits, think about the details of each one. If your selling point is your relaxing atmosphere, think about the specific details that make the restaurant relaxing. If your strong point is elegant dining, think about all the details that contribute to that elegance. Sometimes you may think of features that do not meet any particular need but are still good benefits. In a sales letter for a restaurant, you might also want to mention the nonsmoking section, your free coatroom, the fact that you're close to a freeway or offer free parking or a drive-up window, and how fast your service is.

Look beyond the ordinary, too. Noticing that almost half of U.S. marriages today are the partners' second unions, with many involving children, some hotels and resorts are offering "familymoon" packages that include baby-sitting, multiple bedrooms, and other family friendly amenities.[5]

Whenever you're writing to customers or clients about features that are not unique to your organization, it's wise to present both the benefits of the features themselves and the benefits of dealing with your company. If you talk about the benefits of dining in a relaxed atmosphere but don't mention your own restaurant, people may go somewhere else!

How detailed should each benefit be?   LO 8-3

▶ *Use strong, vivid details.*

You'll usually need at least three to five sentences to give enough details about a reader benefit. If you develop two or three reader benefits fully, you can use just a sentence or two for less important benefits. Develop reader benefits by linking each feature to the readers' needs—and provide details to make the benefit vivid!

While large chains like Meijer and Sam's Club provide limited online grocery shopping, many also require shoppers to pick up orders at the store. The Hills Market in Worthington, Ohio, is among niche grocery stores providing the benefits of both online shopping and home delivery—including 5,000 of its best-selling items. Says The Hills Market spokesperson Jill Moorhead: "It gets our name out there and is a draw for busy people who like to shop at work or want to have access to our store anytime."

Source: Tracy Turner, "Gourmet Grocer Puts Aisles Online," *The Columbus Dispatch,* May 19, 2011, http://www.dispatch.com/live/content/business/stories/2011/05/19/gourmet-grocer-puts-aisles-online.html?sid=101.

An extraordinary benefit to having more education is a longer life expectancy. According to a study published in *Health Affairs,* the "lifelong relationships of education and its correlates with health and longevity are striking."

Source: Phillip Moeller, "Education: A Predictor of Longer Life," *U.S. News & World Report,* August 13, 2012, http://money.usnews.com/money/blogs/the-best-life/2012/08/13/education-a-predictor-of-longer-life.

Different audiences may value different intrinsic and extrinsic benefits.

"You got your corner office, so now what's your problem?"

Reprinted by permission of CartoonStock.com, www.cartoonstock.com.

Sensory details give color, texture, and depth to experiences, even ones hard to fathom. Ever wonder what space smells like? According to astronauts returning from spacewalks, it's something like gunpowder or ozone. Skin can hear, at least according to one study. Air puffed on skin altered the perceptions of people distinguishing between "pa" and "ta" and "ba" and "da." And a study at The Ohio State University suggests that touching an object evokes feelings of ownership in as little as 30 seconds.

Source: Tariq Malik, "Space Sights and Smells Surprise Rookie Astronauts," September 5, 2009, http://news.yahoo.com/s/space/20090905/sc_space/pacesightsandsmellssurpriserookieastronauts; Jeanna Bryner, "Surprise! Your Skin Can Hear," November 25, 2009, http://news.yahoo.com/s/livescience/20091125/sc_livescience/surpriseyourskincanhear; and Andrea Thompson, "Study: You Touch It, You Buy It," January 16, 2009, http://news.yahoo.com/s/livescience/20090116/sc_livescience/studyyoutouchityoubuyit.

Weak: We have place mats with riddles.

Better: Answering all the riddles on Monical's special place mats will keep the kids happy till your pizza comes. If they don't have time to finish (and they may not, since your pizza is ready so quickly), just take the riddles home—or answer them on your next visit.

Make your reader benefits specific.

Weak: You get quick service.

Better: If you only have an hour for lunch, try our Business Buffet. Within minutes, you can choose from a variety of main dishes, vegetables, and a make-your-own-sandwich-and-salad bar. You'll have a lunch that's as light or filling as you want, with time to enjoy it—and still be back to the office on time.

Psychological description is a technique you can use to develop vivid, specific reader benefits. **Psychological description** means creating a scenario rich with sense impressions—what the reader sees, hears, smells, tastes, feels—so readers can picture themselves using your product or service and enjoying its benefits. You can also use psychological description to describe the problem your product will solve. Psychological description works best early in the message to catch readers' attention.

Feature:	Snooze alarm
Benefit:	If the snooze button is pressed, the alarm goes off and comes on again nine minutes later.
Psychological description:	Some mornings, you really want to stay in bed just a few more minutes. With the Sleepytime Snooze Alarm, you can snuggle under the covers for a few extra winks, secure in the knowledge that the alarm will come on again to get you up for that breakfast meeting with an important client. If you don't have to be anywhere soon, you can keep hitting the snooze alarm for up to an additional 63 minutes of sleep. With Sleepytime, you're in control of your mornings.
Feature:	Tilt windows
Benefit:	Easier to clean
Psychological description:	It's no wonder so many cleaners "don't do windows." Balancing precariously on a rickety ladder to clean upper-story windows . . . shivering outside in the winter winds and broiling in the summer sun as you

scrub away . . . running inside, then outside, then inside again to try to get the spot that always seems to be on the other side. Cleaning traditional windows really is awful.

   In contrast, cleaning is a breeze with Tilt-in Windows. Just pull the inner window down and pull the bottom toward you. The whole window lifts out! Repeat for the outer window. Clean them inside in comfort (sitting down or even watching TV if you choose). Then replace the top of the outer window in its track, slide up, and repeat with the inner window. Presto! Clean windows!

In psychological description, you're putting your reader in a picture. If the reader doesn't feel that the picture fits, the technique backfires. To prevent this, psychological description often uses subjunctive verbs ("if you like . . ." "if you were . . .") or the words *maybe* and *perhaps*.

> You're hungry but you don't want to bother with cooking. Perhaps you have guests to take to dinner. Or it's 12 noon and you only have an hour for lunch. Whatever the situation, the Illini Union has a food service to fit your needs. If you want convenience, we have it. If it's atmosphere you're seeking, it's here too. And if you're concerned about the price, don't be. When you're looking for a great meal, the Illini Union is the place to find it.

—Illini Union brochure

Go to
www.govbenefits.gov/
govbenefits_en.portal
for a "one-stop shopping" portal to benefits provided by the U.S. government.

How do I decide which benefits to use?   LO 8-4

▶ *Use the following three principles to decide.*

Three principles guide your choice of reader benefits:

1. Use at least one benefit for each part of your audience.
2. Use intrinsic benefits.
3. Use the benefits you can develop most fully.

1. Use at Least One Benefit for Each Part of Your Audience

Most messages go to multiple audiences. In a memo announcing a company-subsidized day care program, you want benefits not only for parents who might use the service but also for people who don't have children or whose children are older. Reader benefits for these last two audiences help convince them that spending money on day care is a good use of scarce funds.

   In a letter to "consumers" or "voters," different people will have different concerns. The more of these concerns you speak to, the more persuasive you'll be.

2. Use Intrinsic Benefits

Intrinsic benefits come automatically from using a product or doing something. **Extrinsic benefits** are "added on." Someone in power decides to give them; they do not necessarily come from using the product or doing the action. Figure 8.2 gives examples of extrinsic and intrinsic rewards for three activities.

   Intrinsic rewards or benefits are better than extrinsic benefits for two reasons:

1. There just aren't enough extrinsic rewards for everything you want people to do. You can't give a prize to every customer every time he or she places an order or to every subordinate who does what he or she is supposed to do.
2. Research suggests that you'll motivate subordinates more effectively by stressing the intrinsic benefits of following policies and adopting proposals.

In a groundbreaking study of professional employees, Frederick Herzberg found that the things people said they liked about their jobs were all *intrinsic* rewards—pride

While the actual cost of producing a U.S. dollar bill is 6.4 cents, it comes backed by the "full faith and credit of the United States," an intrinsic value that makes it popular in business throughout the world.

Source: "15 Things You Never Noticed on a Dollar," January 24, 2010, http://shine.yahoo.com/ channel/life/15-things-you-never-noticed-on-a-dollar-575113/.

Psychological Description

Psychological description means creating a scenario rich with sense impressions—what the reader sees, hears, smells, tastes, feels—so readers can picture themselves using your product or service and enjoying its benefits.

Figure 8.2 Extrinsic and Intrinsic Rewards

Activity	Extrinsic Reward	Intrinsic Reward
Making a sale.	Getting a commission.	Pleasure in convincing someone; pride in using your talents to think of a strategy and execute it.
Turning in a suggestion to a company suggestion system.	Getting a monetary reward when the suggestion is implemented.	Solving a problem at work; making the work environment a little more pleasant.
Writing a report that solves an organizational problem.	Getting praise, a good performance appraisal, and maybe a raise.	Pleasure in having an effect on an organization; pride in using your skills to solve problems; solving the problem itself.

in achievement, an enjoyment of the work itself, responsibility. Extrinsic features—pay, company policy—were sometimes mentioned as things people disliked, but they were never cited as things that motivated or satisfied them. People who made a lot of money still did not mention salary as a good point about the job or the organization.[6] In a 1998 survey of workers all over the United States, Aon Consulting found that the factor most likely to produce employee loyalty and a desire to be productive was management's recognition of employees' personal and family lives. Salary didn't make the top 10.

Many family friendly companies have discovered that a culture of care keeps turnover low. The higher salary that a competitor might pay just doesn't overcome the advantage of working at a supportive, flexible company that values its employees.[7] In a competitive job market, different candidates want different things. But many accept lower salaries to get flextime, stock options, interesting work, or people they want to work with.[8]

Because money is not the only motivator, choose reader benefits that identify intrinsic as well as extrinsic motivators for following policies and adopting ideas.

3. Use the Benefits You Can Develop Most Fully

One-sentence benefits don't do much. Use the benefits that you can develop in three to five sentences or more.

A reader benefit is a claim or assertion that the reader will benefit if he or she does something. Convincing the reader, therefore, involves two steps: making sure the benefit really will occur and explaining it to the reader.

If the logic behind a claimed reader benefit is faulty or inaccurate, there's no way to make that particular reader benefit convincing. Revise the benefit to make it logical.

Faulty logic: Using a computer will enable you to write letters, memos, and reports much more quickly.

Analysis: If you've never used a computer, in the short run it will take you *longer* to create a document using a computer than it would to type it. Even after you know how to use a computer and its software, the real time savings comes when a document incorporates parts of previous documents or goes through several revisions. Creating a first draft from scratch will still take planning and careful composing; the time savings may or may not be significant.

Revised reader benefit: Using a computer allows you to revise and edit a document more easily. It eliminates retyping as a separate step and reduces the time needed to proofread revisions. It allows you to move the text around on the page to create the best layout.

Matching the Benefit to the Audience LO 8-5

When you communicate with different audiences, you may need to stress different benefits.

Suppose that you manufacture a product and want to persuade dealers to carry it. The features you may cite in ads directed toward customers—stylish colors, sleek lines, convenience, durability, good price—won't convince dealers. Shelf space is at a premium, and no dealer carries all the models of all the brands available for any given product. Why should the dealer stock your product? To be persuasive, talk about the features that are benefits from the dealer's point of view: turnover, profit margin, a national advertising campaign to build customer awareness and interest, special store displays that will draw attention to the product.

Look for intrinsic as well as extrinsic benefits. For instance, Rossmoor Elementary School Principal Lauren Telfer says, "If you're looking for what's best for students, it's important to have them interact with both sexes. . . . I think students really benefit from having that mix." However, the proportion of men in teaching is at a 40-year low—only 21% in U.S. public schools. Telfer works to recruit male teachers. With 33 of her 35 teachers female, she says she also tries to make male teachers more comfortable, including asking faculty to rein in lunchroom conversations about intimate matters.

Alumni at prestigious business schools provide financial support and word-of-mouth advertising for alma maters, but they also benefit from a strong network of peers and a sense of belonging.

Even in your own organization, different audiences may care about different things. To create an intranet for Xerox, Cindy Casselman needed support from a variety of divisions. She had to persuade her own supervisor to let her work on the project. He said "yes" but told her she had to raise the $250,000 herself. She got the money and the programming talent she needed by showing other managers how they would benefit from the proposed intranet. The CIO cared about the enormous financial investment the company had already made in its computer infrastructure. She told him that the intranet would put content there. The director of education and training cared about learning at Xerox. Cindy pointed out that the intranet would provide a place for learning to happen. She raised the $250,000 by showing people how her idea would benefit the aspects of the company they cared most about.

Internet banking customers may expect different benefits than ones for traditional brick-and-mortar banks. No lines, better interest rates, and 24-hour banking from home can attract web-friendly customers. Brick-and-mortar bank customers expect convenient ATMs, local branches, and other amenities, as well as less risk of fraud or theft. With many bank customers today having multiple credit cards and bank accounts, keeping track of where all the money goes can be challenging, too. PNC launched Virtual Wallet, an online service that presents account

When Beth Blake came up empty-handed in her search for a bridesmaid dress, she and designer friend Sophie Simmons teamed up to create one instead. The results of their bridal project created such a stir at the wedding that they decided to launch their own business. Their company, Thread, offers fashionable bridesmaid dresses that can be worn beyond the wedding. The seven-year-old company that was started with $100,000 now boasts millions in revenue, a celebrity clientele, and three boutiques.

information tied to a calendar. If the account is close to an overdraft, a red "danger day" appears. The service can automatically move money from one account to another if the customer has yet to catch the problem.

Sources: Ben Feller, "Manhunt: Schools Try to Attract More Male Teachers," *Augusta Chronicle,* July 29, 2005, downloaded at http://chronicle.augusta.com/stories/073105/bac_A0583.3.shtml; Ian Grayson, "Alumni Travel a Two-Way Street," August 17, 2005, downloaded at www.cnn.com/2005/BUSINESS/08/15/execed.alumni/index.html; Michael Warshaw, "The Good Guy's and Gal's Guide to Office Politics," *Fast Company,* April–May 1998, 156–78; and Laura Rowley, "Five Secrets Your Bank Doesn't Want You to Know," August 5, 2009, http://finance.yahoo.com/expert/article/moneyhappy/181074.

(*continued*)

Source: Joanna Pearl Steinemail, "Why We Lie, Go to Prison and Eat Cake," *Wired*, June 22, 2012, http://www.wired.com/business/2012/06/why-we-lie-cheat-go-to-prison-and-eat-chocolate-cake-10-questions-with-dan-ariely/.

If the logic is sound, making that logic evident to the reader is a matter of providing enough evidence and showing how the evidence proves the claim that there will be a benefit. Always provide enough detail to be vivid and concrete. You'll need more detail in the following situations:

- The reader may not have thought of the benefit before.
- The benefit depends on the difference between the long run and the short run.
- The reader will be hard to persuade, and you need detail to make the benefit vivid and emotionally convincing.

Does the following statement have enough detail?

> You will benefit if the company saves money.

Some benefits come long after the product has been conceived. Marcelle Shriver, whose soldier son wrote of how Silly String can help troops find bomb trip wires in Iraq, worked with Thom Campbell, one of the founders of a shipping company, to get 80,000 cans sent to U.S. forces.

Readers always believe their own experience. Many readers will know that they didn't get bonuses even during a year that the company did well. In addition to bonuses for top executives, companies could use profits to pay higher dividends to shareholders, to retire debt, or to increase research and development spending. Even spending money on upgrading computers or remodeling the employee lounge may not seem like a strong benefit to some workers. Instead, you'll need to show that money saved will go into one or more specific programs that will benefit employees directly or indirectly. The more indirect the benefit is, the more proof you'll need.

What else do reader benefits need?   LO 8-6

▶ *Check for you-attitude.*

If reader benefits aren't in you-attitude (◀◀ p. 90), they'll sound selfish and won't be as effective as they could be. A Xerox letter selling copiers with strong you-attitude as well as reader benefits got a far bigger response than did an alternate version with reader benefits but no you-attitude.[9] It doesn't matter how you phrase reader benefits while you're brainstorming and developing them, but in your final draft, edit for you-attitude.

Lacks you-attitude: We have the lowest prices in town.
You-attitude: At Havlichek Cars, you get the best deal in town.

Summary of Learning Objectives

- **Expectancy theory** says most people try to do their best only when they believe they can succeed and when they want the rewards that success brings. **(LO 8-1)**
- Good reader benefits are adapted to the audience, based on intrinsic rather than extrinsic advantages, supported by clear logic and explained in adequate detail, and phrased in you-attitude. Extrinsic benefits simply aren't available to reward every desired behavior; further, they reduce the satisfaction in doing something for its own sake. **(LO 8-2)**
- To create reader benefits,
  1. Identify the feelings, fears, and needs that may motivate your reader.
  2. Show how the reader can meet his or her needs with the features of the policy or product.

- **Psychological description** means creating a scenario rich with sense impressions—what the reader sees, hears, smells, tastes, feels—so readers can picture themselves using your product or service and enjoying its benefits. **(LO 8-3)**
- Brainstorm twice as many reader benefits as you'll need for a message. **(LO 8-4)**
  1. Use at least one benefit for each part of your audience.
  2. Use intrinsic benefits.
  3. Use the benefits you can develop most fully.
- When you communicate with different audiences, you may need to stress different benefits. **(LO 8-5)**
- Make sure reader benefits are phrased in you-attitude. **(LO 8-6)**

Questions for Comprehension

8.1 What are reader benefits? **(LO 8-1)**

8.2 In a message with reader benefits, how many different benefits should you use? **(LO 8-2)**

8.3 What is psychological description? **(LO 8-2)**

8.4 What is the difference between intrinsic and extrinsic reader benefits? Which are better? Why? **(LO 8-3)**

Questions for Critical Thinking

8.5 How do reader benefits help you achieve your goals? **(LO 8-1)**

8.6 Why do reader benefits need to be in you-attitude? **(LO 8-3)**

8.7 If you are writing to multiple audiences with different needs, should you include all the reader benefits you can think of in the message? **(LO 8-3)**

Exercises and Problems

8.8 Identifying and Developing Reader Benefits (LO 8-1, LO 8-2)

Listed here are several things an organization might like its employees to do.

1. Go "green."
2. Give up smoking.
3. Conserve using office supplies.
4. Car pool with other employees.
5. Participate in a cancer charity walk.

8.9 Identifying Objections and Reader Benefits (LO 8-1 to LO 8-3)

Think of an organization you know something about, and answer the following questions for it.

1. Your college wants to install cameras in public areas around campus and to require that students use swipe cards to enter campus buildings after 5 p.m. What objections might people have? What benefits would the campus community receive? Which people would be easiest to convince?

2. Your organization is considering posting the names of employees who contribute to the annual charity fundraiser on its web page. What objections might people have? What benefits might your organization receive? Which people would be easiest to convince?

As Your Instructor Directs,

a. Identify the motives or needs that might be met by each of the activities.

b. Develop each need or motive as a reader benefit in a full paragraph. Use additional paragraphs for the other needs met by the activity. Remember to use you-attitude!

3. Your local recreation department is considering asking for a 3-mill levy to provide for upgraded parks and summer camp programs. What objections might people have? What benefits would such a program offer? Which people would be easiest to convince?

As Your Instructor Directs,

a. Share your answers orally with a small group of students.

b. Present your answers in an oral presentation to the class.

c. E-mail your answers to class members.

d. Write a paragraph developing the best reader benefit you identified. Remember to use you-attitude.

8.10 Identifying and Developing Reader Benefits for Different Audiences (LO 8-1 to LO 8-3)

Assume that you want to encourage people to do one of the following activities:

1. Having a personal trainer
   Audiences: Professional athletes
   Busy managers
   Someone trying to lose weight
   Someone making a major lifestyle change after a heart attack

2. Using public transportation
   Audiences: People who must travel throughout the city for their job
   People who have children in day care
   People who live in the suburbs

3. Getting advice about refinancing a home mortgage
   Audiences: Investors
   Empty nesters

   Potential retirees
   Single professionals
   Parents looking to finance a child's education

4. Getting advice on retirement strategies
   Audiences: Young adults entering the workforce
   People earning less than $50,000 annually
   People planning to attend graduate or professional school, such as law school
   Parents with small children
   People within 10 years of retirement

5. Eating organic foods
   Audiences: Upscale shoppers
   People on tight budgets
   People with small children
   Supporters of local farming

People concerned with soil conservation
People concerned with reducing pesticides

6. Buying an HDTV
   Audiences: College students
   Sports aficionados
   Residence hall managers
   Tavern and restaurant owners
   Trade show display salespeople

7. Teaching adults to read
   Audiences: Retired workers
   Businesspeople
   Students who want to become teachers
   High school and college students
   People concerned about poverty

8. Attending college or graduate school
   Audiences: Recent high school graduates
   Retirees
   Working professionals
   Single parents
   Wealthy people
   Entrepreneurs

9. Attending a fantasy sports camp (you pick the sport), playing with and against retired players who provide coaching and advice

10. Taking a cruise, where passengers have all meals included but must pay for tips, drinks, airfare, and off-ship excursions

As Your Instructor Directs,

a. Identify needs that you could meet for the audiences listed here. In addition to needs that several audiences share, identify at least one need that would be particularly important to each group.
b. Identify a product or service that could meet each need.
c. Write a paragraph or two of reader benefits for each product or service. Remember to use you-attitude.
d. Develop one or more of the benefits using psychological description.

Hints:

- For this assignment, you can combine benefits or programs as if a single source offered them all.
- Add specific details about particular sports, cities, tourist attractions, activities, etc., as material for your description.
- Be sure to move beyond reader benefits to vivid details and sense impressions.
- Put your benefits in you-attitude.

 Polishing Your **Prose**

Plurals and Possessives

Singular possessives and plurals sound the same but are spelled differently. A possessive noun will always have an apostrophe. Most possessives of singular nouns are formed by adding 's to the word.

Singular Possessive	**Plural**
company's	companies
computer's	computers
family's	families
job's	jobs
manager's	managers
team's	teams

Because singular possessive nouns and plurals sound the same, you will have to look at the logic of your sentence to choose the right word.

Exercises

Choose the right word in each set of brackets.

1. Dean told us that his [customers/customer's] expect excellent service—even if that means going above and beyond, such as working past quitting time.
2. [Stakeholders/Stakeholder's] believe in a company for many reasons, but generally a solid business plan helps to build their confidence.
3. The [printers/printer's] toner cartridge is jammed, so someone will need to take a look at it.
4. Since we have a [weeks/week's] worth of work left to do, we should get started as soon as possible.
5. Cassandra emerged from the meeting with a big smile and said, "The [ayes/aye's] have it!"
6. We learned from Jack that [supervisors/supervisor's] will be expected to complete daily progress reports now in addition to their weekly ones.
7. Because our pool [cars/car's] are expensive to maintain, we're thinking of using [rentals/rental's] instead next year.
8. The Public Relations Department noted that public [opinions/opinion's] can change according to how effective a [companies/company's] media strategy is.
9. When reviewing her [teams/team's] progress, Martina found that many [efforts/effort's] in 2012 paid off.
10. Because a [memos/memo's] purpose should be clear, the subject [lines/line's] content is very important.

Check your answers to the odd-numbered exercises at the back of the book.

Keep on Reading with Us

In December 2011, *The New York Times,* one of the nation's oldest and most respected newspapers, had to scramble to recover from an e-mail message mistakenly sent out that promised a 50% discount for 16 weeks on a subscription. The offer had been intended only for a few hundred people who had recently cancelled subscriptions but was instead sent to 8.6 million e-mail addresses.

Shortly after, the *Times* tweeted: "If you received an e-mail today about cancelling your NYT subscription, ignore it. It's not from us." Of course, the newspaper did send the original e-mail message.

Damage from the error included many people calling or writing in to take advantage of the offer, including some who already had a subscription but threatened to cancel unless the deal was honored. The *Times* did initially honor the discount, but later that day stopped giving out discounts. The results included angry customers and a parody Twitter account poking fun at the mistake.

Individual Activity

Imagine you are in the Marketing Department of *The New York Times* and you have been selected to work on its campaign to regain subscriber confidence. The *Times* knows it has a strong product with a long history of satisfied readers. However, company executives fear that some subscribers may avoid renewing their subscriptions in the future, especially those subscribers who weren't able to take advantage of the erroneous e-mail offer. In addition, potential new subscribers may have been scared off by the negative publicity surrounding the debacle.

To achieve its goal, the Marketing Department has decided to e-mail a different offer to these customers. The company will use the e-mail addresses already in its database for renewals but will pay for additional e-mail addresses for potential customers. The e-mail message, tailored to each customer group, will only be sent to those customers who did not renew with the previous offer.

Subscribers will receive the following benefits:

- A free two-week subscription to its home-delivered print edition, along with a collectible holiday edition to anyone who chooses to start or renew a subscription for three months.
- A free four-week subscription to its home-delivered print edition, along with a collectible holiday edition and a free *Times* coffee mug to anyone who chooses to start or renew a subscription for six months.
- For either subscription, readers will get access to premium features in the online version of the *Times* (The online version is

free but provides limited access to stories and other features, such as a searchable database of older articles.)

While an e-mail message will go out to all of the customers affected, the *Times* would like to segment the e-mail messages for subscribers more likely to respond to one offer versus the other. To identify them, consider the following questions:

- What intrinsic and extrinsic benefits are inherent in a subscription to *The New York Times?* What might customers gain from these benefits?
- What are the demographic and lifestyle characteristics of potential customers?
- What needs, feelings, or concerns might be motivating customers?
- Why would customers pay for a print edition of *The New York Times* when a lot of the same information can be found free at the newspaper's website?

Identify as many different potential customer groups as you can think of, noting at least one intrinsic and one extrinsic benefit that each group can expect from purchasing a *Times* subscription.

Give enough detail in your customer descriptions so that the Marketing Department can use the information to guide its choice of appeals to customers.

Group Activity

Combine the results of your list with those of your classmates to generate a comprehensive list of customers and benefits. Then, as a group, select five customer groups on which to focus. Identify the benefits that will be in the e-mail message to potential subscribers and develop these benefits using psychological description.

Think of how the e-mail message will convince potential customers they should purchase your company's products.

Write the e-mail message: Be sure to:

- Include at least one intrinsic and one extrinsic benefit for each customer group.
- Justify negative information, focusing on what the reader can do rather than on limitations.
- Omit unnecessary negative information.
- Use you-attitude.
- Talk about the reader, not the company.

Source: "NY Times Offers Discounts in Mistaken E-Mail Gaffe," December 28, 2011, http://finance.yahoo.com/news/nytimes-offers-discounts-mistaken-email-gaffe-224635047.html.

Letters, Memos, E-Mail, and Web Writing

Letters, Memos, E-Mail, and Web Writing

Module **9** — Formats for Letters and Memos

Module **10** — Informative and Positive Messages

Module **11** — Negative Messages

Module **12** — Persuasive Messages

Module **13** — E-Mail Messages, Web Writing, and Technology

9 | Formats for Letters and Memos

Module 9 details the most common formats for business letters and memos. After completing the module, you should be able to

LO 9-1 Apply principles for correct letter formats.

LO 9-2 Apply strategies for professional image creation with documents and beyond.

LO 9-3 Recognize courtesy titles for correspondence.

LO 9-4 Apply principles for correct memo formats.

Letters normally go to people outside your organization; **memos** go to other people in your organization. In very large organizations, corporate culture determines whether people in different divisions or different locations feel close enough to each other to write memos.

Letters and memos do not necessarily differ in length, formality, writing style, or pattern of organization. However, letters and memos do differ in format. **Format** means the parts of a document and the way they are arranged on the page.

Short reports use letter or memo format (▶▶ Module 23). Long reports can use the formal format illustrated in Module 24. If your organization has its own formats for letters and memos, use them. Otherwise, choose one of the formats in this module. See Module 13 for e-mail formats.

How should I set up letters?   LO 9-1

▶ *Use block or modified block format.*

The two most common letter formats are **block,** sometimes called full block (see Figure 9.2), and **modified block** (see Figure 9.3). Your organization may make minor changes from the diagrams in margins or spacing.

Figure 9.1 shows how the formats differ.

Use the same level of formality in the **salutation,** or greeting, as you would in talking to someone on the phone: *Dear Glenn* if you're on a first-name basis, *Dear Mr. Helms* if you don't know the reader well enough to use the first name.

Sincerely and *Cordially* are standard **complimentary closes.** When you are writing to people in special groups or to someone who is a friend as well as a business acquaintance, you may want to use a less formal close. Depending on the circumstances, the following informal closes might be acceptable: *Yours for a better environment,* or even *Ciao* or *Thanks.*

In **mixed punctuation**, a colon follows the salutation and a comma follows the close. In a sales or fund-raising letter, it is acceptable to use a comma after the salutation to make the letter look like a personal letter rather than like a business letter. Most organizations use mixed punctuation. A few organizations use open punctuation, which is faster to type. In **open punctuation**, omit all punctuation after the salutation and the close.

A **subject line** tells what the letter is about. Subject lines are required in memos; they are optional in letters. Good subject lines are specific, concise, and appropriate for your purposes and the response you expect from your reader.

- When you have good news, put it in the subject line.
- When your information is neutral, summarize it concisely in the subject line.
- When your information is negative, use a negative subject line if the reader may not read the message or needs the information to act, or if the negative is your error.
- When you have a request that will be easy for the reader to grant, put either the subject of the request or a direct question in the subject line.
- When you must persuade a reluctant reader, use a common ground, a reader benefit, or a directed subject line (▶▶ Module 12) that makes your stance on the issue clear.

For examples of subject lines in each of these situations, see Modules 10, 11, and 12.

A **reference line** refers the reader to the number used on the previous correspondence this letter replies to, or the order or invoice number which this letter is about. Very large organizations, such as the IRS, use numbers on every piece of correspondence they send out so that it is possible to quickly find the earlier document to which an incoming letter refers.

Both formats can use headings, lists, and indented sections for emphasis.

Each format has advantages. Block format is the format most frequently used for business letters; readers expect it; it can be typed quickly because everything is lined up at the

With cloud technology becoming more popular for document storage, care must be taken to ensure formats remain. For instance, Google Drive, a cloud service that also features a custom word processor, Google Docs, allows up to five gigabytes of free file storage, but if you use Microsoft Word, you will only be able to view documents there unless you convert the document. Each system may have its idiosyncrasies, and whether using Dropbox, SugarSync, Google Drive, or Microsoft's SkyDrive, care must be taken to know how document formats might be affected.

Source: Walter Mossberg, "Google Stores, Syncs, Edits in the Cloud," *The Wall Street Journal,* April 25, 2012, http://online.wsj.com/article/SB10001424052702303459004577362111867730108.html?KEYWORDS=document+format.

Site to See

Go to

http://www.englishspanishlink.com/deluxewriter/letterlayoutspanlet.htm

to see how business letters can be formatted for readers of Spanish.

Figure 9.1 Differences between Letter Formats

	Block	Modified Block
Date and signature block	Lined up at left margin	Lined up $\frac{1}{2}$ or $\frac{2}{3}$ over to the right
Paragraph indentation	None	Optional
Subject line	Optional	Rare

Figure 9.2 Block Format on Letterhead (mixed punctuation; collection letter)

100 Freeway Exchange
Provo, UT 84610

Northwest Hardware Warehouse

(801) 555-4683

Line up everything at left margin.

2–6 spaces depending on length of letter.

June 20, 2013

Mr. James E. Murphy, Accounts Payable   *Title could be on a separate line.*
Salt Lake Equipment Rentals
5600 Wasatch Boulevard
Salt Lake City, Utah 84121

1"–1½"

Use first name in salutation if you'd use it on the phone.

Dear Jim: *Colon in mixed punctuation*

The following items totaling $393.09 are still open on your account.   *¶ 1 never has a heading.*

Invoice #01R-784391 *Bold heading*

After the bill for this invoice arrived on May 14, you wrote saying that the material had not been delivered to you. On May 29, our Claims Department sent you a copy of the delivery receipt signed by an employee of Salt Lake Equipment. You have had proof of delivery for over three weeks, but your payment has not yet arrived.

⅝"–1"

Please send a check for $78.42.   *Single-space paragraphs.*
Double-space between paragraphs.

Triple-space before new heading.

Voucher #59351

The reference line on your voucher #59351, dated June 11, indicates that it is the gross payment for invoice #01G-002345. However, the voucher was only for $1171.25, while the invoice amount was $1246.37. Please send a check for $75.12 to clear this item.

Do not indent paragraphs.

Voucher #55032

Voucher #55032, dated June 15, subtracts a credit for $239.55 from the amount due. Our records do not show that any credit is due on this voucher. Please send either an explanation or a check to cover the $239.55 immediately.

Total Amount Due   *Headings are optional in letters.*

Please send a check for $393.09 to cover these three items and to bring your account up to date.

Sincerely,   *2–3 spaces*

3–4 spaces

Neil Hutchinson
Credit Representative

cc: Joan Stottlemyer , Credit Manager

Leave bottom margin of 3–6 spaces—more if letter is short.

Figure 9.3 Modified Block Format on Letterhead (mixed punctuation; letter of recommendation)

Bay City Information Systems

151 Bayview Road
San Francisco, CA 81153

2–6 spaces

September 14, 2012

Line up date with signature block ½ or ⅔ of the way over to the right.

2–4 spaces

1"–1½"

Ms. Mary E. Arcas
Personnel Director
Cyclops Communication Technologies
1050 South Sierra Bonita Avenue
Los Angeles, CA 90019 *Zip code on same line*

Dear Ms. Arcas: *Colon in mixed punctuation*

⅝"–1"

Indenting ¶ is optional in modified block.

Let me respond to your request for an evaluation of Colleen Kangas. Colleen was hired as a clerk-typist by Bay City Information Systems on April 4, 2008, and was promoted to Administrative Assistant the following August. At her review in June, I recommended that she be promoted again. She is intelligent with good work habits and a good knowledge of computer software.

Single-space paragraphs.

As an Administrative Assistant, Colleen not only handles routine duties such as processing time cards, ordering supplies, and entering data, but also screens calls for two marketing specialists, answers basic questions about Bay City Information Systems, compiles the statistics I need for my monthly reports, and investigates special assignments for me. In the past eight months, she has investigated freight charges, phone systems, and firewalls. I need only to give her general directions: she has a knack for tracking down information quickly and summarizing it accurately.

Double-space between paragraphs.

Although the department's workload has increased during the year, Colleen manages her time so that everything gets done on schedule. She is consistently poised and friendly under pressure. Her willingness to work overtime on occasion is particularly remarkable considering that she has been going to college part-time ever since she joined our firm.

At Bay City Information Systems, Colleen uses Microsoft Word and Access software. She tells me that she has also used WordPerfect and PowerPoint in her college classes.

If Colleen were staying in San Francisco, we would want to keep her. She has the potential either to become an Executive Secretary or to move into line or staff work, especially once she completes her degree. I recommend her highly.

2–3 spaces

Sincerely, *Comma in mixed punctuation*

Headings are optional in letters.

3–4 spaces

Jeanne Cederlind

Jeanne Cederlind
Vice President, Marketing

Line up signature block with date.

2–4 spaces

Encl.: Evaluation Form for Colleen Kangas

Leave at least 3–6 spaces at bottom of page—more if letter is short.

left margin. Modified block format creates a visually attractive page by moving the date and signature block over into what would otherwise be empty white space. Modified block is a traditional format; readers are comfortable with it.

The examples of the formats in Figures 9.2 and 9.3 show one-page letters on company letterhead. **Letterhead** is preprinted stationery with the organization's name, logo,

Creating a Professional Image, 1   LO 9-2

The way you and your documents look affects the way people respond to you and to them. Every organization has a dress code. One young man was upset when an older man told him he should wear wing-tip shoes. He was wearing leather shoes but not the kind that said "I'm promotable" in that workplace. Dress codes are rarely spelled out; the older worker was doing the young man a favor by being direct. If you have a mentor in the organization, ask him or her if there are other ways you can make your appearance even more professional. If you don't have a mentor, look at the people who rank above you. Notice clothing, jewelry, and hairstyles. If you're on a budget, go to stores that sell expensive clothing to check the kind of buttons, the texture and colors of fabric, and the width of lapels and belts. Then go to stores in your price range and choose garments that imitate the details of expensive clothing.

On casual days, wear clothes in good repair that are one or two "notches" below what you'd wear on other days. If suits are the norm, choose blazers and slacks or skirts. If blazers and slacks or skirts are the norm, choose sweaters or knit sport shirts; khakis, simple skirts, or dressier jeans; or simple dresses. Wear good shoes and always be well groomed. Avoid anything that's ill-fitting or revealing.

Too many photographs, knickknacks, and posters can make you seem frivolous. Avoid offensive photos, slogans, or screensavers. One local government supervisor, known for being strict, put a poster of Adolf Hitler on his door to make light of his reputation. He so offended others that he lost his job.

If you're allowed to listen to music, keep the volume at a reasonable level, and tune out "shock jocks," whose coarse language and offensive stereotypes may alienate people. Wear headphones if your organization allows it.

Computer game playing and personal web surfing and e-mailing are best done on your own time. Keep your voice-mail message succinct and professional—find out what co-workers say in theirs.

Organize your desk by filing papers and keeping stacks to a minimum. Purge unneeded materials, and store food elsewhere. Clean regularly. Water your plants. While a messy desk can be

charming to some co-workers, others find it a distraction. Some experts even suggest excessive clutter and disorganization may be a sign of depression or a brain injury.

While most people wouldn't shout across an office, many of us are louder than we think when we're excited or happy—monitor your volume. Keep personal conversations to a minimum, in person and on the phone.

Rules for documents, like rules for clothing, are sometimes unwritten. To make your document look professional,

- Use good visual impact (◄◄ Module 5).
- Edit and proofread to eliminate errors and typos (►► Modules 14 and 15).
- Make sure the ink or toner is printing evenly.
- Use a standard format.

Know your organizational culture. When in doubt, follow the lead of someone the organization respects.

Source: Tara Parker-Pope, "A Clutter Too Deep for Mere Bins and Shelves," *The Wall Street Journal,* January 1, 2008, downloaded at http://online.wsj.com/public/article/SB119940267392266173-r6vgPqwm_F_R4GXRfeoBN_ObjoA_20080202.html?mod=tff_main_tff_top.

address, and phone number. Figure 9.4 shows how to set up modified block format when you do not have letterhead. (It is also acceptable to use block format without letterhead.)

When your letter runs two or more pages, use a heading on the second page to identify it. Putting the reader's name in the heading helps the writer, who may be printing out

Figure 9.4 Modified Block Format without Letterhead (open punctuation; claim letter)

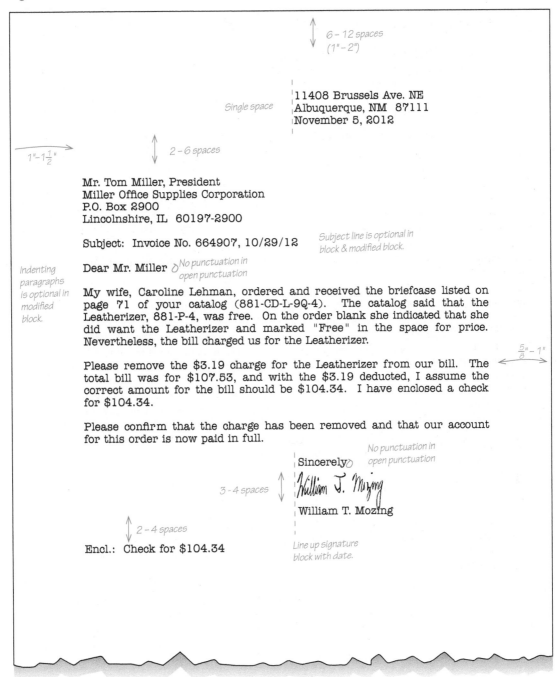

6 – 12 spaces
(1" – 2")

Single space

11408 Brussels Ave. NE
Albuquerque, NM 87111
November 5, 2012

1" – 1½"

2 – 6 spaces

Mr. Tom Miller, President
Miller Office Supplies Corporation
P.O. Box 2900
Lincolnshire, IL 60197-2900

Subject: Invoice No. 664907, 10/29/12   *Subject line is optional in block & modified block.*

Indenting paragraphs is optional in modified block.

Dear Mr. Miller   *No punctuation in open punctuation*

My wife, Caroline Lehman, ordered and received the briefcase listed on page 71 of your catalog (881-CD-L-9Q-4). The catalog said that the Leatherizer, 881-P-4, was free. On the order blank she indicated that she did want the Leatherizer and marked "Free" in the space for price. Nevertheless, the bill charged us for the Leatherizer.

⅝" – 1"

Please remove the $3.19 charge for the Leatherizer from our bill. The total bill was for $107.53, and with the $3.19 deducted, I assume the correct amount for the bill should be $104.34. I have enclosed a check for $104.34.

Please confirm that the charge has been removed and that our account for this order is now paid in full.

Sincerely   *No punctuation in open punctuation*

3 – 4 spaces

William T. Mozing

2 – 4 spaces

Encl.: Check for $104.34   *Line up signature block with date.*

many letters at a time, to make sure the right second page gets in the envelope. Even when the signature block is on the second page, it is still lined up with the date.

Reader's Name
Date
Page Number

Use the format your reader expects.

Peanuts © United Feature Syndicate, Inc.

The days of the dead letter office have changed significantly since Herman Melville wrote of his depressed scrivener, Bartleby. To increase the chances a letter stays out of the shredder, U.S. Postal Service workers use sophisticated document scanners to decipher the worst handwriting on envelopes. While some names and addresses are hopelessly indecipherable, the technology tries to salvage as many letters as possible—more than 714 million such letters were scanned in one year alone.

Source: Barry Newman, "Poor Penmanship Spells Job Security for Post Office's Scribble Specialists," *The Wall Street Journal,* November 3, 2011, http://online.wsj.com/article/SB10001424052970204394804577012122145910692.html.

or

Reader's Name	Page Number	Date

When a letter runs two or more pages, use letterhead only for page 1. (See Figures 9.5 and 9.6.) For the remaining pages, use plain paper that matches the letterhead in weight, texture, and color.

Set side margins of $1''$ to $1\frac{1}{2}''$ on the left and to $\frac{5}{8}''$ to $1''$ on the right. If your letterhead extends all the way across the top of the page, set your margins even with the ends of the letterhead for the most visually pleasing page. The top margin should be three to six lines under the letterhead, or $2''$ down from the top of the page if you aren't using letterhead. If your letter is very short, you may want to use bigger side and top margins so that the letter is centered on the page.

Many letters are accompanied by other documents. Whatever these documents may be—a multipage report or a two-line note—they are called **enclosures,** because they are enclosed in the envelope. The writer should refer to the enclosures in the body of the letter: "As you can see from my résumé, ..." The enclosure line is usually abbreviated: *Encl.* (see Figure 9.3). The abbreviation reminds the person who seals the letter to include the enclosure(s).

Sometimes you write to one person but send copies of your letter to other people. If you want the reader to know that other people are getting copies, list their names on the last page. The abbreviation *cc* originally meant *carbon copy* but now means *computer copy*. Other acceptable abbreviations include *pc* for *photocopy* or simply *c* for *copy*. You can also send copies to other people without telling the reader. Such copies are called **blind copies.** Blind copies are not mentioned on the original; they are listed on the copy saved for the file with the abbreviation *bc* preceding the names of people getting these copies.

You do not need to indicate that you have shown a letter to your superior or that you are saving a copy of the letter for your own files. These are standard practices.

States with names of more than five letters are frequently abbreviated in letters and memos. The U.S. Postal Service abbreviations use two capital letters with no punctuation. See Figure 9.7.

What courtesy titles should I use? LO 9-3

▶ *Use "Ms." unless a woman has a professional title or prefers a traditional title.*
Use "Mr." unless a man has a professional title.

Letters require courtesy titles in the salutation *unless* you're on a first-name basis with your reader. Use the first name only if you'd use it in talking to the person on the phone.

Figure 9.5 Second Page of a Two-Page Letter, Block Format (mixed punctuation; informative letter)

State
University
8300 Gateway Boulevard
Midland, TX 77208

1"–1½"

August 10, 2013

Ms. Stephanie Voght
Stephen F. Austin High School
1200 Southwest Blvd.
San Antonio, TX 78214

↕ *2 – 3 spaces*

Dear Ms. Voght: *Colon in mixed punctuation.*

⅝" – 1"

Enclosed are 100 brochures about State University to distribute to your students. The brochures describe the academic programs and financial aid available. When you need additional brochures, just let me know.

Videotape about State University

You may also want to show your students the videotape "Life at State University." This 45-

Plain paper for page 2.   ↕ *½" – 1"*

Center

Stephanie Voght ← *Reader's name*   2   August 10, 2013

Also OK to line up page number, date at left under reader's name.

campus life, including football and basketball games, fraternities and sororities, clubs and organizations, and opportunities for volunteer work. The tape stresses the diversity of the student body and the very different lifestyles that are available at State.

Triple space before each new heading.

Scheduling the Videotape   *Bold headings.*

Same margins as p 1.

To schedule your free showing, just fill out the enclosed card with your first, second, and third choices for dates, and return it in the stamped, self-addressed envelope. Dates are reserved in the order that requests arrive. Send in your request early to increase the chances of getting the date you want.

"Life at State University" will be on its way to give your high school students a preview of the college experience.

Sincerely, *Comma in mixed punctuation.*

3 – 4 spaces ↓

Headings are optional in letters.

Michael L. Mahler
Director of Admissions

↕ *2 – 4 spaces*

Encl.: Brochures, Reservation Form

cc: R. J. Holland, School Superintendent
    Jose Lavilla, President, PTS Association

Figure 9.6 Second Page of a Two-Page Letter, Modified Block Format (mixed punctuation; goodwill letter)

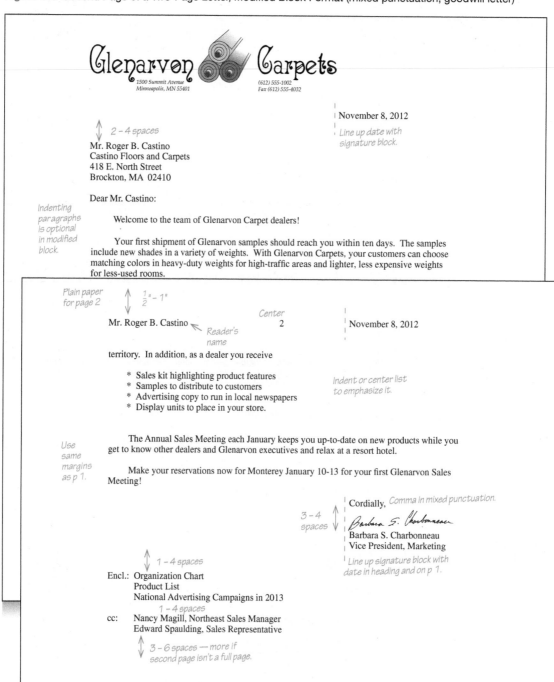

Figure 9.7 Postal Service Abbreviations for States, Territories, and Provinces

State Name	Postal Service Abbreviation	State Name	Postal Service Abbreviation
Alabama	AL	Missouri	MO
Alaska	AK	Montana	MT
Arizona	AZ	Nebraska	NE
Arkansas	AR	Nevada	NV
California	CA	New Hampshire	NH
Colorado	CO	New Jersey	NJ
Connecticut	CT	New Mexico	NM
Delaware	DE	New York	NY
District of Columbia	DC	North Carolina	NC
Florida	FL	North Dakota	ND
Georgia	GA	Ohio	OH
Hawaii	HI	Oklahoma	OK
Idaho	ID	Oregon	OR
Illinois	IL	Pennsylvania	PA
Indiana	IN	Rhode Island	RI
Iowa	IA	South Carolina	SC
Kansas	KS	South Dakota	SD
Kentucky	KY	Tennessee	TN
Louisiana	LA	Texas	TX
Maine	ME	Utah	UT
Maryland	MD	Vermont	VT
Massachusetts	MA	Virginia	VA
Michigan	MI	Washington	WA
Minnesota	MN	West Virginia	WV
Mississippi	MS	Wisconsin	WI
		Wyoming	WY

Territory	Postal Service Abbreviation	Province Name	Postal Service Abbreviation
Guam	GU	Alberta	AB
Puerto Rico	PR	British Columbia	BC
Virgin Islands	VI	Labrador	LB
		Manitoba	MB
		New Brunswick	NB
		Newfoundland	NF
		Northwest Territories	NT
		Nova Scotia	NS
		Ontario	ON
		Prince Edward Island	PE
		Quebec	PQ
		Saskatchewan	SK
		Yukon Territory	YT

FYI

Though written for internal audiences, memos can go public—with stunning consequences. A July 6, 2009, memo was among 75,000 pages of documents Congressional investigators scrutinized while investigating Toyota Motor Corporation's recall of cars. At heart were statements that suggested company officials had saved more than $100 million by replacing floor mats rather than issuing a more extensive safety recall.

Source: David Shepardson, "Toyota Disavows Memo Bragging of Savings by Limiting Recall," *The Detroit News,* February 24, 2010, downloaded from http://www .detnews.com/article/20100224/ AUTO01/2240435/1361/Toyota-disavows-memo-bragging-of-savings-by-limiting-recall.

Site to See

Go to

www.usps.gov/zip4/ welcome.htm

If you know the address, the U.S. Post Office page will give you the ZIP + 4 code.

Cathy Arnst warns against resorting to a flurry of correspondence in the workplace for no reason, especially in tough economic times. Among other questionable practices is a memo at *The South Bend Tribune* instructing staff to write daily "productivity" memos detailing all of their actions.

Source: Cathy Arnst, "Memo Madness, or, Does Busy Work Increase Productivity?" *Bloomberg Businessweek,* February 2, 2010, downloaded from http://www .businessweek.com/careers/ workingparents/blog/archives/ 2009/02/memo_mad ness_or.html.

Sometimes the contents of a memo or letter can come back to haunt the writer. Walmart Mike Duke sent employees a memo extolling the company's "strong anti-corruption" programs, even while the company faced allegations of paying $24 million in bribes to Mexican officials since 2005. Real estate tycoon Tom Barrack may still regret his 1,700-word letter to employees celebrating the important life lessons to be learned from the *Twilight* book series, which he discovered one night while yachting in Turkey.

Sources: Diane Brady, "Wal-Mart, Avon Execs Should Stop Hiding Behind Boards," *Bloomberg BusinessWeek,* April 25, 2012, http://www.businessweek. com/articles/2012-04-25/ wal-mart-avonexecs-should-stop-hiding-behind-boards; and Anton Troianovski, "Twilight' Memo: Tom Barrack's Most Embarrassing Moment," *The Wall Street Journal,* http://blogs.wsj. com/developments/2010/11/29/ twilight-memo-tom-barracks-most-embarrassing-moment.

When You Know the Reader's Name and Gender

When you know your reader's name and gender, use courtesy titles that do not indicate marital status: *Mr.* for men and *Ms.* for women. There are, however, two exceptions:

1. Use professional titles when they're relevant.

   Dr. Kristen Sorenson is our new company physician.

   The Rev. Robert Townsley gave the invocation.

2. If a woman prefers to be addressed as *Mrs.* or *Miss,* use the title she prefers rather than *Ms.* (You-attitude [◄◄ p. 90] takes precedence over nonsexist language: address the reader as she—or he—prefers to be addressed.)

   To find out if a woman prefers a traditional title,

   a. Check the signature block in previous correspondence. If a woman types her name as *(Miss) Elaine Anderson* or *(Mrs.) Kay Royster,* use the title she designates.

   b. Notice the title a woman uses in introducing herself on the phone. If she says, "This is Robin Stine," use *Ms.* when you write to her. If she says, "I'm Mrs. Stine," use the title she specifies.

   c. Check your company directory. In some organizations, women who prefer traditional titles can list them with their names.

   d. When you're writing job letters or other crucial correspondence, call the company and ask the receptionist which title your reader prefers.

Ms. is particularly useful when you do not know what a woman's marital status is. However, even when you happen to know that a woman is married or single, **you still use *Ms.* unless you know that she prefers another title.**

In addition to using parallel courtesy titles, use parallel forms for names.

Not parallel	**Parallel**
Members of the committee will be Mr. Jones, Mr. Yacone, and Lisa.	Members of the committee will be Mr. Jones, Mr. Yacone, and Ms. Melton.
	or
	Members of the committee will be Irving, Ted, and Lisa.

When You Know the Reader's Name but Not the Gender

When you know your reader's name but not the gender, either

1. Call the company and ask the receptionist, or
2. Use the reader's full name in the salutation:

   Dear Chris Crowell:

   Dear J. C. Meath:

When You Know Neither the Reader's Name Nor Gender

When you know neither the reader's name nor gender, you have three options:

1. Use the reader's position or job title:

   Dear Loan Officer:

   Dear Registrar:

2. Use a general group to which your reader belongs:

   Dear Investor:

   Dear Admissions Committee:

3. Omit the salutation and use a subject line in its place:

   Subject: Recommendation for Ben Wandell

How should I set up memos? LO 9-4

▶ *The standard memo format mimics block format but has no salutation, close, or signature.*

Memos omit both the salutation and the close. Memos never indent paragraphs. Subject lines are required; headings are optional. Each heading must cover all the information until the next heading. Never use a separate heading for the first paragraph.

Figure 9.8 illustrates the standard memo format typed on a plain sheet of paper. Note that the first letters of the reader's name, the writer's name, and the subject phrase are lined up vertically. Note also that memos are usually initialed by the To/From block. Initialing tells the reader that you have proofread the memo and prevents someone's sending out your name on a memo you did not in fact write.

Some organizations have special letterhead for memos. When *Date/To/From/Subject* are already printed on the form, the date, writer's and reader's names, and subject may be set at the main margin to save typing time. (See Figure 9.9.)

Some organizations alter the order of items in the *Date/To/From/Subject* block. Some organizations ask employees to sign memos rather than simply initialing them. The signature goes below the last line of the memo, starting halfway over on the page, and prevents anyone adding unauthorized information.

If the memo runs two pages or more, use a heading at the top of the second and subsequent pages (see Figure 9.10). Because many of your memos go to the same people, putting a brief version of the subject line will be more helpful than just using "All Employees."

> Brief Subject Line
> Date
> Page Number

or

> Reader's Name   Page Number   Date

When Brad Garlinghouse, a senior vice president at Yahoo .com, wrote a lengthy message about the company's need to reorganize, he used boldface, bullet points, and metaphors to make complex ideas easier to follow. His *Peanut Butter Manifesto*, so-called because of his description of spreading resources too thin, ends with three one-line paragraphs:

So, let's get back up.

Catch the balls.

And stop eating peanut butter.

Source: "Yahoo Memo: The 'Peanut Butter Manifesto,'" *The Wall Street Journal,* November 18, 2006, downloaded at http:// online.wsj.com/public/article/ SB116379821933826657- 0mbjXoHnQwDMFH_PVeb_ jqe3Chk_20061125.html.

Figure 9.8 Memo Format (on plain paper; direct request)

Everything lined up at left

2–4 spaces

Double-space

1″ – 1½″

October 8, 2012

Plain paper

Line up

To: Annette T. Califero

From: Kyle B. Abrams **KBA**   *Writer's initials added in ink*

Subject: A Low-Cost Way to Reduce Energy Use   *Capitalize first letter of each major word in subject line.*

No heading for ¶ 1

As you requested, I've investigated low-cost ways to reduce our energy use. Reducing the building temperature on weekends is a change that we could make immediately, that would cost nothing, and that would cut our energy use by about 6%.   *⅝″ – 1″*

Triple-space before each new heading.

The Energy Savings from a Lower Weekend Temperature   *Bold headings.*

Single-space paragraphs; double-space between paragraphs.

Lowering the temperature from 68° to 60° from 8 p.m. Friday evening to 4 a.m. Monday morning could cut our total consumption by 6%. It is not feasible to lower the temperature on weeknights because a great many staff members work late; the cleaning crew also is on duty from 6 p.m. to midnight. Turning the temperature down for only four hours would not result in a significant heat saving.

Turning the heat back up at 4 a.m. will allow the building temperature to be back to 68° by 9 a.m. Our furnace already has computerized controls which can be set to automatically lower and raise the temperature.

Triple-space

How a Lower Temperature Would Affect Employees   *Capitalize first letter of each major word of heading.*

A survey of employees shows that only 14 people use the building every weekend or almost every weekend. Eighteen percent of our staff have worked at least one weekend day in the last two months; 52% say they "occasionally" come in on weekends.

Do not indent paragraphs.

People who come in for an hour or less on weekends could cope with the lower temperature just by wearing warm clothes. However, most people would find 60° too cool for extended work. Employees who work regularly on weekends might want to install space heaters.

Action Needed to Implement the Change

Would you also like me to check into the cost of buying a dozen portable space heaters? Providing them would allow us to choose units that our wiring can handle and would be a nice gesture toward employees who give up their weekends to work. I could have a report to you in two weeks.

We can begin saving energy immediately. Just authorize the lower temperature, and I'll see that the controls are reset for this weekend.

Memos are initialed by To/From/Subject block — no signature   *Headings are optional in memos.*

Figure 9.9 Memo Format (on memo letterhead; good news)

Kimball, Walls, and Morganstern

Date: March 15, 2013   *Line up horizontally with printed Date/To/From/Subject.*

To: Annette T. Califero   *Capitalize first*

From: Kyle B. Abrams *KBA*   *Writer's initials added in ink*   *letter of each major*
                                                                       word in subject line.

Subject: The Effectiveness of Reducing Building Temperatures on Weekends

Triple-space

*Margin lined up
with items in
To/From/Subject
block to save
typing time*

Reducing the building temperature to 60° on weekends has cut energy
use by 4% compared to last year's use from December to February and
has saved our firm $22,000.

This savings is particularly remarkable when you consider that this
winter has been colder than last year's, so that more heat would be
needed to maintain the same temperature.   *⅝" – 1"*

Fewer people have worked weekends during the past three months than
during the preceding three months, but snow and bad driving
conditions may have had more to do with keeping people home than the
fear of being cold. Five of the 12 space heaters we bought have
been checked out on an average weekend. On one weekend, all 12 were
in use and some people shared their offices so that everyone could
be in a room with a space heater.

Fully 92% of our employees support the lower temperature. I
recommend that we continue turning down the heat on weekends
through the remainder of the heating season and that we resume the
practice when the heat is turned on next fall.

Headings are optional in memos.

Figure 9.10 Option 2 for Page 2 of a Memo (direct request)

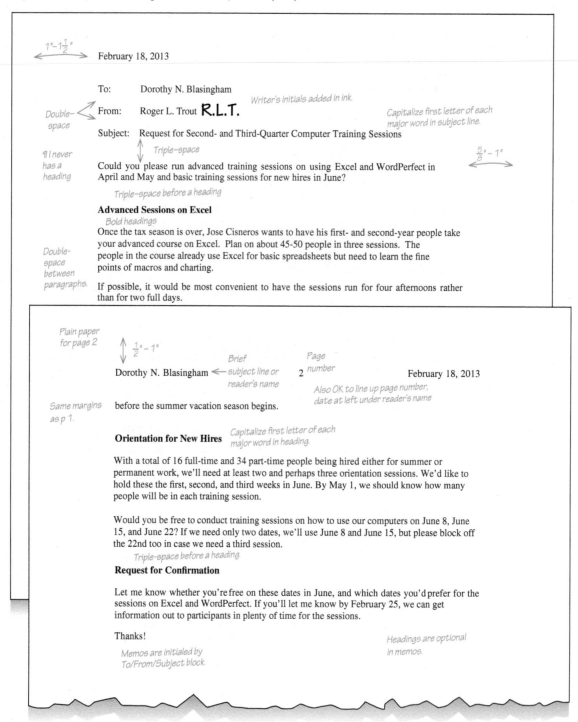

1"–1½"

February 18, 2013

To: Dorothy N. Blasingham

Writer's initials added in ink.

Double-space

From: Roger L. Trout **R.L.T.**

Capitalize first letter of each major word in subject line.

¶ I never has a heading

Subject: Request for Second- and Third-Quarter Computer Training Sessions

Triple-space

⅝"–1"

Could you please run advanced training sessions on using Excel and WordPerfect in April and May and basic training sessions for new hires in June?

Triple-space before a heading

Advanced Sessions on Excel

Bold headings

Double-space between paragraphs.

Once the tax season is over, Jose Cisneros wants to have his first- and second-year people take your advanced course on Excel. Plan on about 45-50 people in three sessions. The people in the course already use Excel for basic spreadsheets but need to learn the fine points of macros and charting.

If possible, it would be most convenient to have the sessions run for four afternoons rather than for two full days.

Plain paper for page 2

½"–1"

Brief

Page

Dorothy N. Blasingham ← *subject line or reader's name*

2 *number*

February 18, 2013

Also OK to line up page number, date at left under reader's name

Same margins as p 1.

before the summer vacation season begins.

Orientation for New Hires

Capitalize first letter of each major word in heading.

With a total of 16 full-time and 34 part-time people being hired either for summer or permanent work, we'll need at least two and perhaps three orientation sessions. We'd like to hold these the first, second, and third weeks in June. By May 1, we should know how many people will be in each training session.

Would you be free to conduct training sessions on how to use our computers on June 8, June 15, and June 22? If we need only two dates, we'll use June 8 and June 15, but please block off the 22nd too in case we need a third session.

Triple-space before a heading

Request for Confirmation

Let me know whether you're free on these dates in June, and which dates you'd prefer for the sessions on Excel and WordPerfect. If you'll let me know by February 25, we can get information out to participants in plenty of time for the sessions.

Thanks!

Headings are optional in memos.

Memos are initialed by To/From/Subject block.

- **Block** and **modified block** are the two standard letter formats. **(LO 9-1)**
- Use the same level of formality in the **salutation,** or greeting, as you would in talking to someone on the phone. **(LO 9-1)**
- *Sincerely* and *Cordially* are standard **complimentary closes. (LO 9-1)**
- Just as the way your documents look affects how people respond to you, so does your appearance and behavior. **(LO 9-2)**
  - On casual days, wear clothes in good repair that are one or two "notches" below what you'd wear on other days.
  - Avoid displaying too many photographs, knickknacks, and posters, which can make you seem frivolous.
  - Save computer game playing and personal web surfing and e-mailing for your own time.
  - Organize your desk by filing papers and keeping stacks to a minimum.

- Use *Ms.* as the courtesy title for a woman, unless she has a professional title, or unless she prefers a traditional title. **(LO 9-3)**
- Use *Mr.* as the courtesy title for a man, unless he has a professional title. **(LO 9-3)**
- In a list of several people, use parallel forms for names. Use either courtesy titles and last names for everyone, or use first names for everyone. For example, it's sexist to use "Mr." for each man in a document that calls all the women by their first names. **(LO 9-3)**
- Memos omit both the salutation and the close. Memos never indent paragraphs. Subject lines are required; headings are optional. Each heading must cover all the information until the next heading. Never use a separate heading for the first paragraph. **(LO 9-4)**

Assignments for Module 9

Questions for Comprehension

9.1 What are the differences between mixed and open punctuation? **(LO 9-1)**

9.2 What are the differences between block and modified block letter formats? **(LO 9-1)**

Questions for Critical Thinking

9.5 Which letter format do you prefer? Why? **(LO 9-1)**

9.6 What are the advantages in telling your reader who is getting copies of your message? **(LO 9-1)**

9.3 What are the differences between block format for letters and the formats for memos? **(LO 9-1, LO 9-4)**

9.4 What is the Postal Service abbreviation for your state or province? **(LO 9-3)**

9.7 Does following a standard format show a lack of originality and creativity? **(LO 9-1, LO 9-4)**

Polishing Your Prose

Making Subjects and Verbs Agree

Make sure the subjects and verbs in your sentences agree. Subjects and verbs agree when they are both singular or both plural:

Correct: The laser printer no longer works.

Correct: The nonworking laser printers are in the storeroom.

Often, subject–verb errors occur when other words come between the subject and verb. Learn to correct errors by looking for the subject—who or what is doing the principal action—and the verb—the action itself:

Correct: A team of marketing researchers is reviewing our promotional campaign.

Correct: The four-color brochures, which cost about $1,000 to print and ship, were sent to our St. Louis affiliate.

U.S. usage treats company names and the words *company* and *government* as singular nouns. In England and countries adopting the British system, these nouns are plural:

Correct: Nationwide Insurance is

(U.S.)   headquartered in Columbus, Ohio.

Correct: Lloyds of London are

(U.K.)   headquartered in London.

Use a plural verb when two or more singular subjects are joined by *and*.

Correct: Mr. Simmens, Ms. Lopez, and Mr. Yee were in Seoul for a meeting last week.

Use a singular verb when two or more singular subjects are joined by *or, nor,* or *but.* Follow this rule when using *neither/nor* and *either/or* combinations. However, when one of the subjects is plural, choose the verb based on the subject nearest the verb.

Correct: Neither Crandall nor the Panzinis want to play on the department's softball team this year.

Correct: Either the Panzinis or Crandall needs to help keep score.

Correct: Neither Dr. Hroscoe nor Mr. Jamieson is in today.

When the sentence begins with *There* or *Here,* make the verb agree with the subject that follows the verb:

Correct: There were blank pages in the fax we received.

Correct: Here is the information on the job candidate you requested.

Some words that end in *s* are considered singular and require singular verbs:

Correct: The World Series features advertisements of our product in the stadium.

For some nouns, singular and plural forms can be spelled the same. Examples are *data, deer,* and *fish.* Choose a verb based on how you are using the word—singular or plural.

When you encounter situations that don't seem to fit the rule, or when following the rules produces an awkward sentence, rewrite the sentence to avoid the problem:

Problematic: The grant coordinator in addition to the awarding agency (is, are?) happy with the latest proposal we submitted.

Better: The grant coordinator and the awarding agency are happy with the latest proposal we submitted.

Exercises

Choose the correct verb or rewrite the sentence.

1. My tablet PC's apps [is/are] truly exceptional.
2. What [is/are] Mainwaring, Inc., employees doing to prepare for the one-week plant shutdown?
3. We [makes/make] more profit in one week in Asia than in a whole month in the U.S.
4. Both Colin and Danita [plans/plan] to return to school for an MBA.
5. Either Ashley or Phillip [needs/need] to submit an expense report for the team.
6. While the vice president in addition to her staff [is/are] planning to attend, we have yet to get an actual confirmation.
7. Even though Jill, Marianne, Theodore, and Svetlana [has/have] traveled extensively, they [is/are] still good candidates for intercultural communication training.
8. Neither Li Xiang nor the DuChamps [intends/intend] to purchase stock until they fully understand how market changes [affects/affect] performance.
9. There [is/are] many good reasons to start saving early for retirement. The most obvious [is/are] time [is/are] on your side.
10. My glasses [was/were] broken, so I had to ask people to help me read the fine print; people [was/were] happy to help, but I [expects/expect] now to always have a spare set in the future.

Check your answers to the odd-numbered exercises at the back of the book.

Informative and Positive Messages

LEARNING OBJECTIVES

Module 10 focuses on helping you write effective informative and positive messages. After completing the module, you should be able to

LO 10-1 **Create subject lines for informative and positive messages.**

LO 10-2 **Apply strategies for informative and positive message organization.**

LO 10-3 **Identify situations for reader benefits use with informative and positive messages.**

LO 10-4 **List common kinds of informative and positive messages.**

LO 10-5 **Apply strategies for informative and positive message analysis with PAIBOC.**

LO 10-6 **Create goodwill endings for informative and positive messages.**

We categorize messages both by the author's purposes and by the initial response we expect from the reader. In an **informative** or **positive message,** you expect the audience to respond neutrally to the message or to be pleased. Negatives are minor; they are not the main point of the message. You must convey information but are not asking the audience to do anything. However, you may well want the reader to save the information and act on it later on. You usually do want to build positive attitudes toward the information you are presenting, so in that sense, even an informative message has a persuasive element.

Piper Weiss believes that an out-of-office e-mail reply from Josh Kopelman is the best she's ever seen. The message announces that he is out of the office, of course, but goes on to stress that he and his wife are on vacation and would prefer to be left alone, going so far as to create an e-mail with the moniker "interruptyourvacation@" should anyone want to contact him. The reply preserves goodwill while emphasizing that Kopelman is still available if the need to contact him is important.

Source: Piper Weiss, "The Best Out-of-Office E-Mail Ever Written, September 2, 2011, http://shine. yahoo.com/channel/life/the-best-out-of-office-email-ever-written-2538155/.

Informative and positive messages include

- Acceptances.
- Positive answers to reader requests.
- Information about procedures, products, services, or options.
- Announcements of policy changes that are neutral or positive.
- Changes that are to the reader's advantage.

Even a simple informative or good news message usually has several purposes:

Primary Purposes:

- To give information or good news to the reader or to reassure the reader.
- To have the reader read the message, understand it, and view the information positively.
- To deemphasize any negative elements.

Secondary Purposes:

- To build a good image of the writer.
- To build a good image of the writer's organization.
- To cement a good relationship between the writer and reader.
- To reduce or eliminate future correspondence on the same subject so the message doesn't create more work for the writer.

What's the best subject line for an informative or positive message? LO 10-1

▶ *One that contains the basic information or good news.*

A **subject line** is the title of a document. It aids in filing and retrieving the document, tells readers why they need to read the document, and provides a framework in which to set what you're about to say.

Subject lines are standard in memos. Letters are not required to have subject lines (◀◀ Module 9). However, a survey of business people in the Southwest found that 68% of them considered a subject line in a letter to be important, very important, or essential; only 32% considered subject lines to be unimportant or only somewhat important.[1]

A good subject line meets three criteria: it is specific, concise, and appropriate to the kind of message (positive, negative, persuasive).

Good news comes in many forms.

Making Subject Lines Specific

The subject line needs to be specific enough to differentiate that message from others on the same subject, but broad enough to cover everything in the message.

Too general: Training Sessions

To make this general subject line more specific, identify the particular topic of *this* message.

Better: Dates for 2013 Training Sessions
or: Evaluation of Training Sessions on Conducting Interviews
or: Should We Schedule a Short Course on Proposal Writing?

Making Subject Lines Concise

Most subject lines are relatively short—usually no more than 10 words, often only 3 to 7 words.[2]

Wordy: Survey of Student Preferences in Regards to Various Pizza Factors

Again, the best revision depends on the specific factors you'll discuss.

Better: Students' Pizza Preferences
or: The Feasibility of a Cassano's Branch on Campus
or: What Students Like and Dislike about Cassano's Pizza

If you can't make the subject both specific and short, be specific.

Making Subject Lines Appropriate for the Pattern of Organization

In general, do the same thing in your subject line that you would do in the first paragraph.

When you have good news for the reader, build goodwill by highlighting it in the subject line. When your information is neutral, summarize it concisely for the subject line.

Subject: Discount on Rental Cars Effective January 2

Starting January 2, as an employee of Amalgamated Industries you can get a 15% discount on cars you rent for business or personal use from Roadway Rent-a-Car.

Subject: Update on Arrangements for Videoconference with France

In the last month, we have chosen the participants and developed a tentative agenda for the videoconference with France scheduled for March 21.

How should I organize informative and positive messages? LO 10-2

▶ *Put the good news and a summary of the information first.*

The patterns of organization in this module and the modules that follow will work for 70% to 90% of the writing situations most people in business, government, and nonprofit organizations face. Using the appropriate pattern can help you compose more quickly and create a better final product.

A customer escorted out of an Alamo Drafthouse movie theater in Austin, Texas, for violating the chain's no-talking/ no-texting policy may have thought she was getting the last laugh when she later left a profanity-laced message on voice mail, but the joke turned out to be on her. The company spliced the rants into a public service announcement now shown before each film to inform rude cell phone users of the policy. Accordingly, the uncensored version is shown only before R-rated films.

Source: Phoebe Connelly, "Texas Movie Theater Makes an Example (and a PSA) of a Texting Audience Member," June 7, 2011, http://news. yahoo.com/s/yblog_thelookout/ 20110607/us_yblog_thelookout/ texas-movie-theater-makes-an- example-and-a-psa-of-a-texting- audience-member.

Consuming chocolate apparently can change a person's mood—in as little as three minutes, according to one study. The quality of the chocolate affects how well it changes mood, and researchers theorize that the benefits are due to the sensory pleasure of taste and the emotional associations with chocolate rather than impacts on the brain's neurotransmitters.

Source: Susan Albers, "The 3-Minute Effect of Chocolate," *Psychology Today,* October 10, 2011, http://www.psychology today.com/blog/comfort-cravings/ 201110/the-3-minute-effect-chocolate.

- Be sure you understand the rationale behind each pattern so that you can modify the pattern if necessary. (For example, if you write instructions, any warnings should go up front, not in the middle of the message.)
- Not every message that uses the basic pattern will have all the elements listed. The elements you do have will go in the order presented in the pattern.
- Sometimes you can present several elements in one paragraph. Sometimes you'll need several paragraphs for just one element.

Present informative and positive messages in the following order:

1. **Give any good news and summarize the main points.** Share good news immediately. Include details such as the date policies begin and the percent of a discount. If the reader has already raised the issue, make it clear you're responding.
2. **Give details, clarification, background.** Don't repeat information from the first paragraph. Do answer all the questions your reader is likely to have; provide all the information necessary to achieve your purposes. Present details in the order of importance to the reader.
3. **Present any negative elements—as positively as possible.** A policy may have limits; information may be incomplete; the reader may have to satisfy requirements to get a discount or benefit. Make these negatives clear, but present them as positively as possible.
4. **Explain any reader benefits.** Most informative memos need reader benefits. Show that the policy or procedure helps readers, not just the company. Give enough detail to make the benefits clear and convincing. In letters, you may want to give benefits of dealing with your company as well as benefits of the product or policy.

   In a good news message, it's often possible to combine a short reader benefit with a goodwill ending in the last paragraph.
5. **Use a goodwill ending: positive, personal, and forward-looking.** Shifting your emphasis away from the message to the specific reader suggests that serving the reader is your real concern.

   Figure 10.1 summarizes the pattern. Figures 10.2 and 10.3 illustrate two ways that the basic pattern can be applied. (◀◀ Figures 9.5 and 9.9 also use this pattern.)

   The letter in Figure 10.2 authorizes a one-year appointment that the reader and writer have already discussed and describes the organization's priorities. Because the writer knows that the reader wants to accept the job, the letter doesn't need to persuade. The opportunity for the professor to study records that aren't available to the public is an implicit reader benefit; the concern for the reader's needs builds goodwill.

   The memo in Figure 10.3 announces a new employee benefit. The first paragraph summarizes the policy. Paragraph 2 gives details. Negative elements are in paragraphs 3 and 4, stated as positively as possible. Paragraphs 5 to 7 give reader benefits and show that everyone—even part-timers who are not eligible for reimbursement—will benefit from the new program.

Figure 10.1 How to Organize an Informative or Positive Message

Figure 10.2 A Positive Letter

Interstate
Fidelity
Insurance Company

100 Interstate Plaza
Atlanta, GA 30301
404-555-5000
Fax: 404-555-5270

March 8, 2012

Professor Adrienne Prinz
Department of History
Duke University
Durham, North Carolina 27000

Dear Professor Prinz:

Good news — Your appointment as archivist for Interstate Fidelity Insurance has been approved. When you were in Atlanta in December, you said that you could begin work June 1. We'd like you to start then if that date is still good for you.   *Tactful*

The Board has outlined the following priorities for your work: *Assumes reader's primary interest is the job*

Negative about lighting and security presented impersonally

1. **Organize and catalogue the archives.** You'll have the basement of the Palmer Building for the archives and can requisition the supplies you need. You'll be able to control heat and humidity; the budget doesn't allow special lighting or security measures.

Details

2. **Prepare materials for a 4-hour training session in October** for senior-level managers. We'd like you to cover how to decide what to send to the archives. If your first four months of research uncover any pragmatic uses for our archives (like Wells Fargo's use of archives to teach managers about past pitfalls), include those in the session.

3. **Write an article each month for the employee newsletter** describing the uses of the archives. When we're cutting costs in other departments, it's important to justify committing funds to start an archive program.

4. **Study the IFI archives to compile** information that (a) can help solve current management problems, (b) could be included in a history of the company, and (c) might be useful to scholars of business history.

These provisions will appeal to the reader

5. **Begin work on a corporate history of IFI.** IFI will help you find a publisher and support the book financially. You'll have full control over the content.

Negative that reader will have to reapply presented as normal procedure

Salary is deemphasized to avoid implying that reader is "just taking the job for the money"

Your salary will be $41,000 for six months; your contract can be renewed twice for a total of 18 months. You're authorized to hire a full-time research assistant for $19,000 for six months; you'll need to go through the normal personnel request process to request that that money be continued next year. A file clerk will be assigned full-time to your project. You'll report to me. At least for the rest of this calendar year, the budget for the Archives Project will come from my department.

IFI offices are equipped with Pentium computers with Microsoft Office Professional Plus 2010. Is there any software that we should buy for cataloguing or research? Are there any office supplies that we need to have on hand June 1 so that you can work efficiently?

Figure 10.2 A Positive Letter (*Continued*)

Professor Adrienne Prinz
March 8, 2012
Page 2

In the meantime,

1. Please send your written acceptance right away.

2. Let me know if you need any software or supplies.

3. Send me the name, address, and Social Security number of your research assistant by May 1 so that I can process his or her employment papers.

Goodwill ending

4. If you'd like help finding a house or apartment in Atlanta, let me know. I can give you the name of a real estate agent.

On June 1, you'll spend the morning in Personnel. Stop by my office at noon. We'll go out for lunch, and then I'll take you to the office you'll have while you're at IFI.

Welcome to IFI!

Cordially,

Cynthia Yen

Cynthia Yen
Director of Education and Training

When should I use reader benefits in informative and positive messages? LO 10-3

▶ *When you want readers to view your policies and your organization positively.*

Not all informative and positive messages need reader benefits (◀◀ p. 112).
You don't need reader benefits when

Instant Replay

Organizing Informative and Positive Messages

1. Give any good news and summarize the main points.
2. Give details, clarification, background.
3. Present any negative elements—as positively as possible.
4. Explain any reader benefits.
5. Use a goodwill ending: positive, personal, and forward-looking.

- You're presenting factual information only.
- The reader's attitude toward the information doesn't matter.
- Stressing benefits may make the reader sound selfish.
- The benefits are so obvious that to restate them insults the reader's intelligence. (See Figure 10.2.)

You do need reader benefits when

- You are presenting policies.
- You want to shape readers' attitudes toward the information or toward your organization.
- Stressing benefits presents readers' motives positively.
- Some of the benefits may not be obvious to readers.

Messages to customers or potential customers sometimes include a sales paragraph promoting products or services you offer in addition to the product or service that the reader has asked about. Sales promotion in an informative or positive message should be low-key, not "hard sell."

Figure 10.3 A Positive Memo

March 1, 2013

To: All Chamber Employees and Members of the Chamber Insurance Group

From: Lee Ann Rabe, Vice President for Human Resources *ℒAℛ*

Subject: Health Care Benefits for Same-Sex Partners

*Good news in subject line
and first paragraph*

Good news Beginning May 1, same-sex partners of employees covered by the Chamber's Health Plan will be eligible for the same coverage as spouses.

Details In order to have a partner covered, <u>an employee must sign</u> an affidavit in the Human Resources Department stating that the employee and his or her partner (1) live together, (2) intend to stay together, and (3) are responsible for each other. If the relationship ends, employees must notify the Human Resources Department within 30 days, just as do married couples who divorce.

Negatives presented as positively as possible

Costs and coverage of the Chamber's Health Plan remain the same. Dental and vision coverage are also available for a fee; limitations apply <u>and remain the same. For information</u> about the specifics of the Chamber's Health Plan, pick up a brochure in the Human Resources Department.

Negatives

Opposite-sex couples must still marry to receive the spousal coverage.

Extending coverage to same-sex partners of employees shows the Chamber as a progressive, open-minded organization. This in turn portrays Columbus in a positive light.

The new policy will affect not only Chamber employees but also the small businesses that are a part of the Chamber's Health Plan. New businesses may see the change as a reason to join the Chamber—and the Health Plan. Growth in the Health Plan creates a wider base for insurance premiums and helps keep costs as low as possible. Additional Chamber members give us the funds and resources to plan more conferences for members. These conferences, such as the recent "R&D in Ohio's Small Businesses," help Chamber members do business successfully.

Reader Benefits

Making the Health Plan more comprehensive keeps us competitive with other major U.S. cities. As we move out of the recession, businesses are carefully considering possible moves. A policy change like this one shows Columbus' continued goodwill toward minorities in general and will make convincing businesses to relocate here that much easier.

Goodwill ending Selling Columbus as a good place to live and do business has never been easier.

Reader benefits are hardest to develop when you are announcing policies. The organization probably decided to adopt the policy because it appeared to help the organization; the people who made the decision may not have thought at all about whether it would help or hurt employees. Yet reader benefits are most essential in this kind of message so readers see the reason for the change and support it.

When you present reader benefits, be sure to present advantages *to the reader.* Most new policies help the organization in some way, but few workers will see their own interests

Sharing information is crucial to business success.

as identical with the organization's. Even if the organization saves money or increases its profits, workers will benefit directly only if they own stock in the company, if they're high up enough to receive bonuses, if the savings enables a failing company to avoid layoffs, or if all of the savings goes directly to employee benefits. In many companies, any money saved will go to executive bonuses, shareholder profits, or research and development.

To develop reader benefits for informative and positive messages, use the steps suggested in Module 8. Be sure to think about **intrinsic benefits** (◄◄ p. 117) of your policy—that is, benefits that come from the activity or policy itself, apart from any financial benefits. Does a policy improve the eight hours people spend at work?

What are the most common kinds of informative and positive messages?　　LO 10-4

▶ *Transmittals, confirmations, summaries, adjustments, and thank-you notes.*

Many messages can be informative, negative, or persuasive depending on what you have to say. A transmittal, for example, can be positive when you're sending glowing sales figures or persuasive when you want the reader to act on the information. A performance appraisal is positive when you evaluate someone who's doing superbly, negative when you want to compile a record to justify firing someone, and persuasive when you want to motivate a satisfactory worker to continue to improve. A collection letter is persuasive; it becomes negative in the last stage when you threaten legal action. Each of these messages is discussed in the module for the pattern it uses most frequently. However, in some cases you will need to use a pattern from a different module.

Transmittals

When you send someone something in an organization, attach a memo or letter of transmittal explaining what you're sending. A transmittal can be as simple as a small yellow Post-it™ note with **"FYI"** written on it ("For Your Information") or it can be a separate typed document, especially when it transmits a formal document such as a report (▶▶ see Module 24).

Organize a memo or letter of transmittal in this order:

1. Tell the reader what you're sending.
2. Summarize the main point(s) of the document.
3. Indicate any special circumstances or information that would help the reader understand the document. Is it a draft? Is it a partial document that will be completed later?
4. Tell the reader what will happen next. Will you do something? Do you want a response? If you do want the reader to act, specify exactly what you want the reader to do and give a deadline.

Frequently, transmittals have important secondary purposes, such as building goodwill and showing readers that you're working on projects they value.

Confirmations

Many informative messages record oral conversations. These messages are generally short and give only the information shared orally; they go to the other party in the conversation. Start the message by indicating that it is a confirmation, not a new message:

As we discussed on the phone today, . . .

As I told you yesterday, . . .

Attached is the meeting schedule we discussed earlier today.

Summaries

You may be asked to summarize a conversation, a document, or an outside meeting for colleagues or superiors. (Minutes of an internal meeting are usually more detailed. See Module 18 for advice on writing minutes of meetings.)

In a summary of a conversation for internal use, identify

- The people who were present.
- The topic of discussion.
- Decisions made.
- Who does what next.

To summarize a document

1. Start with the main point.
2. Give supporting evidence and details.
3. Evaluate the document, if your audience asks for evaluation.
4. Identify the actions your organization should take based on the document. Should others in the company read this book? Should someone in the company write a letter to the editor responding to this newspaper article? Should your company try to meet with someone in the organization that the story is about?

Adjustments and Responses to Complaints

A lot of consumers are angry these days, and organizations should be responding to their complaints. In a recent survey by Customer Care Measurement and Consulting, 45% of the consumers said they had had problems with a product or service in the past year, and more than two-thirds of them were "very" or "extremely" upset about their problem. Most said they told friends or other people about their bad experience. This kind of bad publicity is even riskier in an Internet economy. A business traveler from Seattle was furious when a hotel told him at two o'clock in the morning that his supposedly guaranteed room was already occupied. The traveler had to demand that the reluctant night clerk find him somewhere else to spend the night. Upon his return home, the consultant prepared a Power-Point presentation about his experience and e-mailed it to some friends. Fortunately for the hotel, he also mailed a copy to the manager. As the humorous presentation was forwarded to more and more readers, the hotel quickly contacted him to solve the problem.[3]

When you grant a customer's request for an adjusted price, discount, replacement, or other benefit to resolve a complaint, do so in the very first sentence.

Your Visa bill for a night's lodging has been adjusted to $63. Next month a credit of $37 will appear on your bill to reimburse you for the extra amount you were originally asked to pay.

Instant Replay

Use reader benefits when

- You are presenting policies.
- You want to shape readers' attitudes toward the information or toward your organization.
- Stressing benefits presents readers' motives positively.
- Some of the benefits may not be obvious to readers.

Social media like Twitter are letting angry customers complain about the way their complaints are handled. MIT's Michael Schrage recommends companies be more transparent with how they handle both the complaints and the compliments, or, as he puts it, avoiding the Watergate aphorism "The cover-up is worse than the crime." He recommends companies consider proactive solutions, such as posting the top 100 call center transcripts so visitors can see just what happens when someone contacts the company.

Source: Michael Schrage, "A Better Way to Handle Publicly Tweeted Complaints," *Bloomberg Businessweek,* November 21, 2011, http://www.businessweek.com/management/a-better-way-to-handle-publicly-tweeted-complaints-11212011.html.

Thank-you notes can be written on standard business stationery, using standard formats. But one student noticed that his adviser really liked cats and had pictures of them in her office. So he found a cat card for his thank-you note.

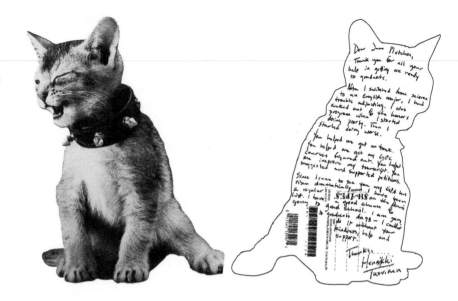

Don't talk about your own process in making the decision. Don't say anything that sounds grudging. Give the reason for the original mistake only if it reflects credit on the company. (In most cases, it doesn't, so the reason should be omitted.)

Thank-You and Congratulatory Notes

Sending a **thank-you note** will make people more willing to help you again in the future. Thank-you letters can be short but must be prompt. They need to be specific to sound sincere.

Congratulating someone can cement good feelings between you and the reader and enhance your own visibility. Again, specifics help.

Avoid language that may seem condescending or patronizing. A journalism professor was offended when a former student wrote to congratulate her for a feature article that appeared in a major newspaper. As the professor pointed out, the letter's language implied that the writer had more status than the person being praised. The praiser was "quite impressed," congratulated the professor on reaching a conclusion that the praiser had already reached, and assumed that the professor would have wanted to discuss matters with the praiser. To the reader, "Keep up the good work!" implied that the one cheering her on had been waiting for ages at the finish line.[4]

How can I apply what I've learned in this module? · LO 10-5

▶ *Plan your activities and answer the PAIBOC questions.*

Before you tackle the assignments for this module, examine the following problem. Figure 4.1 (◄◄ p. 62) lists the activities needed to produce a good message. See how the PAIBOC questions probe the basic points required for a solution. Study the two sample solutions to see what makes one unacceptable and the other one good. Note the recommendations for revision that could make the good solution excellent.[5] The checklist at the end of the Module in Figure 10.6 can help you evaluate a draft.

Paul S. Gumbinner, president of the executive search firm that bears his name, says that while 60% of job candidates send the company a thank-you note after an interview, interviewers sending like messages is almost unheard of and a missed opportunity to build goodwill. One person who received a thank-you from an interviewer "was blown away by the gesture and called to tell me that she was utterly impressed and how much she wanted to work for this company."

Source: Paul S. Gumbinner, "Companies Should Send Candidates Thank-You Notes, Too," *Advertising Age,* January 20, 2010, from http://adage.com/talentworks/article?article_id=141600.

Problem

Interstate Fidelity Insurance (IFI) uses computers to handle its payments and billings. There is often a time lag between receiving a payment from a customer and recording it on the computer. Sometimes, while the payment is in line to be processed, the computer sends out additional notices: past-due notices, collection letters, even threats to sue. Customers are frightened or angry and write asking for an explanation. In most cases, if they just waited a little while, the situation would be straightened out. But policyholders are afraid that they'll be without insurance because the company thinks the bill has not been paid.

IFI doesn't have the time to check each individual situation to see if the check did arrive and has been processed. It wants you to write a letter that will persuade customers to wait. If something is wrong and the payment never reached IFI, IFI would send a legal notice to that effect saying that the policy would be canceled by a certain date (which the notice would specify) at least 30 days after the date on the original premium bill. Continuing customers always get this legal notice as a third chance (after the original bill and the past due notice).

Prepare a form letter that can go out to every policyholder who claims to have paid a premium for automobile insurance and resents getting a past-due notice. The letter should reassure readers and build goodwill for IFI.

Analysis of the Problem

P What are your **purposes** in writing or speaking?

To reassure readers: they're covered for 30 days. To inform them they can assume everything is OK *unless* they receive a second notice. To avoid further correspondence on this subject. To build goodwill for IFI: (a) we don't want to suggest IFI is error-prone or too cheap to hire enough people to do the necessary work; (b) we don't want readers to switch companies; (c) we do want readers to buy from IFI when they're ready for more insurance.

A Who is (are) your **audience(s)?** How do the members of your audience differ from each other? What characteristics are relevant to this particular message?

Automobile insurance customers who say they've paid but have still received a past-due notice. They're afraid they're no longer insured. Because it's a form letter, different readers will have different situations: in some cases payment did arrive late, in some cases the company made a mistake, in some the reader never paid (check lost in mail, unsigned, bounced, etc.).

I What **information** must your message include?

Readers are still insured. We cannot say whether their checks have now been processed (company doesn't want to check individual accounts). Their insurance will be canceled if they do not pay after receiving the second past-due notice (the legal notice).

B What reasons or reader **benefits** can you use to support your position?

Computers help us provide personal service to policyholders. We offer policies to meet all their needs. Both of these points would need specifics to be interesting and convincing.

O What **objections** can you expect your reader(s) to have? What negative elements of your message must you deemphasize or overcome?

Computers appear to cause errors. We don't know if the checks have been processed. We will cancel policies if their checks don't arrive.

C How will the **context** affect the reader's response? Think about your relationship to the reader, morale in the organization, the economy, the time of year, and any special circumstances

Go to

www.bluemountain.com/
Electronic greeting cards are fun to send and receive; they build goodwill.

Go to

www.planetfeedback.com
To read sample letters praising companies, choose a company or industry and choose *Compliment* under *Feedback Type*.

The earliest known written appearance of the word "information" occurred in 1387, and in terms of online use, it's the 22nd most common word in the English language.

Source: Jennifer Schuessler, "Too Much Information About 'Information'?" *The New York Times*, March 23, 2011, http://artsbeat.blogs.nytimes.com/2011/03/23/too-much-information-about-information/.

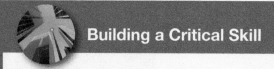

Building a Critical Skill

Writing a Goodwill Ending   LO 10-6

Goodwill endings focus on the business relationship you share with your reader. When you write to one person, a good last paragraph fits that person specifically. When you write to someone who represents an organization, the last paragraph can refer to your company's relationship to the reader's organization. When you write to a group (for example, to "All Employees") your ending should apply to the whole group.

Possibilities include complimenting the reader for a job well done, describing a reader benefit, or looking forward to something positive that relates to the subject of the message.

For example, consider possible endings for a letter answering the question, "When a patient leaves the hospital and returns, should we count it as a new stay?" For one company, the answer was that if a patient was gone from the hospital overnight or longer, the hospital should start a new claim when the patient was readmitted.

Weak closing paragraph: Should you have any questions regarding this matter, please feel free to call me.

Goodwill ending: Many employee-patients appreciate the freedom to leave the hospital for a few hours. It's nice working with a hospital that is flexible enough to offer that option.

Also acceptable: Omit the paragraph; stop after the explanation.

Some writers end every message with a standard invitation:
If you have questions, please do not hesitate to ask.
That sentence lacks positive emphasis (◄◄ p. 102). But saying "feel free to call"—though more positive—is rarely a good idea. Most of the time, the writer should omit the sentence and make the original message clear.

One of the reasons you write is to save the time needed to tell everyone individually. People in business aren't shrinking violets; they will call if they need help. Do make sure your phone number is in the letterhead or is typed below your name. You can also add your e-mail address below your name.

With nearly 25% of the global workforce depressed, the challenge is for employers to find ways to improve the emotional well-being of workers. Happy employees translate into more productive ones. In the U.S. alone, estimates of the costs are as high as $51 billion annually due to absenteeism and lost productivity from depressed employees.

Sources: Victoria McGrane, "Nearly Quarter of Workers Are Depressed," *The Wall Street Journal,* November 11, 2011, http://blogs.wsj.com/economics/2011/11/11/nearly-quarter-of-workers-are-depressed/; and Jhaneel Lockhart, "Employee Depression Costs Workplaces $51 Billion Annually," *The Business Insider,* January 17, 2012, http://articles.businessinsider.com/2012-01-17/strategy/30634551_1_depression-productivity-absenteeism.

The insurance business is highly competitive—other companies offer similar rates and policies. The customer could get a similar policy for about the same money from someone else. Most people find that money is tight, so they'll want to keep insurance costs low. On the other hand, the fact that prices are steady or rising means that the value of what they own is higher—they need insurance more than ever.

Many insurance companies are refusing to renew policies (car, liability, malpractice insurance). These refusals to renew have gotten lots of publicity, and many people have heard horror stories about companies and individuals whose insurance has been canceled or not renewed after a small number of claims. Readers don't feel very kindly toward insurance companies.

People need car insurance. If they have an accident and aren't covered, they not only have to bear the costs of that accident alone but also (depending on state law) may need to place as much as $50,000 in a state escrow account to cover future accidents. They have a legitimate worry.

Discussion of the Sample Solutions

The solution in Figure 10.4 is unacceptable. The red marginal comments show problem spots. Because this is a form letter, we cannot tell customers we have their checks; in some cases, we may not. The letter is far too negative. The explanation in paragraph 2 makes IFI look irresponsible and uncaring. Paragraph 3 is far too negative. Paragraph 4 is too vague; there are no reader benefits; the ending sounds selfish.

A major weakness with the solution is that it lifts phrases straight out of the problem; the writer does not seem to have thought about the problem or about the words he or she is using. Measuring the draft against the answers to the questions for analysis suggests that this writer should start over.

The solution in Figure 10.5 is much better. The blue marginal comments show the letter's strong points. The message opens with the good news that is true for all readers. (Whenever possible, one should use the good news pattern of organization.) Paragraph 2

Figure 10.4 An Unacceptable Solution to the Sample Problem

Need date

Dear Customer:

This explanation makes company look bad.

Relax. We got your check. *Not necessarily true. Reread problem.*

There is always a (time lag) between the time payments come in and the time they are processed. While payments are waiting to be processed, the computer with super-human quickness is sending out past-due notices and (threats) of (cancellation).

Too negative

Need to present this positively

Cancellation is not something you should (worry) about. No policy would be (canceled) without a (legal notice) to that effect giving a specific date for (cancellation) which would be at least 30 days after the date on the original premium notice.

If you want to buy more insurance, just contact your local Interstate Fidelity agent. We will be happy to help you.

Sincerely,

This paragraph isn't specific enough to work as a reader benefit. It lacks you-attitude and positive emphasis.

Figure 10.5 A Good Solution to the Sample Problem

Need date

Dear Customer: *Better: use computer to personalize. Put in name and address of a specific reader.*

Your auto insurance is still in effect. *Good ¶ 1. True for all readers*

Good to treat notice as information, tell reader what to do if it arrives

Past-due notices are mailed out if the payment has not been processed within three days after the due date. This may happen if a check is delayed in the mail or arrives without a signature or account number. When your check arrives with all the necessary information, it is promptly credited to your account. *Good you-attitude*

Even if a check is lost in the mail and never reaches us, you still have a 30-day grace period. If you do get a second notice, you'll know that we still have not received your check. To keep your insurance in force, just stop payment on the first check and send a second one.

Benefits of using computers

Computer processing of your account guarantees that you get any discounts you're eligible for: multicar, accident-free record, good student. If you have a claim, your agent uses computer tracking to find matching parts quickly, whatever car you drive. You get a check quickly—usually within three working days—without having to visit dealer after dealer for (time-consuming estimates.) *Better to put in agent's name, phone number*

Too negative

Need to add benefits of insuring with IFI

Today, your home and possessions are worth more than ever. You can protect them with Interstate Fidelity's homeowners' and renters' policies. Let (your local agent) show you how easy it is to give yourself full protection. If you need a special rider to insure a personal computer, a coin or gun collection, or a fine antique, you can get that from IFI, too. *Good specifics*

Whatever your insurance needs—auto, home, life, or health—one call to IFI can do it all. *Acceptable ending*

Sincerely,

explains IFI's policy. It avoids assigning blame and ends on a positive note. The negative information is buried in paragraph 3 and is presented positively: The notice is information, not a threat; the 30-day extension is a "grace period." Telling the reader now what to do if a second notice arrives eliminates the need for a second exchange of letters. Paragraph 4 offers benefits for using computers, since some readers may blame the notice on computers, and offers benefits for being insured by IFI. Paragraph 5 promotes other policies the company sells and prepares for the last paragraph.

As the red comments indicate, this good solution could be improved by personalizing the salutation and by including the name and number of the local agent. Computers could make both of these insertions easily. This good letter could be made excellent by revising paragraph 4 so that it doesn't end on a negative note, and by using more reader benefits. For instance, do computers help agents advise clients of the best policies for them? Does IFI offer good service—quick, friendly, nonpresssured—that could be stressed? Are agents well trained? All of these might yield ideas for additional reader benefits.

Figure 10.6

Checklist for Informative and Positive Messages

☐ Does the subject line give the good news? Is the subject line specific enough to differentiate this message from others on the same subject?

☐ Does the first paragraph summarize the information or good news? If the information is too complex to fit into a single paragraph, does the paragraph list the basic parts of the policy or information in the order in which the memo discusses them?

☐ Is all the information given in the message? (What information is needed will vary depending on the message, but information about dates, places, times, and anything related to money usually needs to be included. When in doubt, ask!)

☐ In messages announcing policies, is there at least one reader benefit for each segment of the audience? Are all reader benefits ones that seem likely to occur in this organization?

☐ Is each reader benefit developed, showing that the benefit will come from the policy and why the benefit matters to this organization? Do the benefits build on the job duties of people in this organization and the specific circumstances of the organization?

☐ Does the message end with a positive paragraph—preferably one that is specific to the readers, not a general one that could fit any organization or policy?

And, for all messages, not just informative and positive ones,

☐ Does the message use you-attitude and positive emphasis?
☐ Is the style easy to read and friendly?
☐ Is the visual design of the message inviting?
☐ Is the format correct?
☐ Does the message use standard grammar? Is it free from typos?

Originality in a positive or informative message may come from

☐ Creating good headings, lists, and visual impact.
☐ Developing reader benefits.
☐ Thinking about readers and giving details that answer their questions and make it easier for them to understand and follow the policy.

- A **subject line** is the title of a document. A good subject line meets three criteria: it's specific; it's reasonably short; and it's adapted to the kind of message (positive, negative, persuasive). If you can't make the subject both specific and short, be specific. **(LO 10-1)**
- The subject line for an informative or positive message should highlight any good news and summarize the information concisely. **(LO 10-1)**
- Informative and positive messages normally use the following pattern of organization: **(LO 10-2)**
  1. Give any good news and summarize the main points.
  2. Give details, clarification, background.
  3. Present any negative elements as positively as possible.
  4. Explain any reader benefits.
  5. Use a goodwill ending: positive, personal, and forward-looking.
- Use reader benefits in informative and positive messages when **(LO 10-3)**

Summary of Learning Objectives

- You are presenting policies.
- You want to shape readers' attitudes toward the information or toward your organization.
- Stressing benefits presents readers' motives positively.
- Some of the benefits may not be obvious to readers.
- Transmittals, confirmations, summaries, adjustments, and thank-you notes are common types of informative and positive messages. **(LO 10-4)**
- Use the PAIBOC questions listed in Module 1 to examine the basic points needed for successful informative and positive messages. **(LO 10-5)**
- **Goodwill endings** focus on the business relationship you share with your reader. **(LO 10-6)**
- To create a goodwill ending, **(LO 10-6)**
  - Compliment the reader for a job well done.
  - Describe a reader benefit.
  - Look forward to something positive that relates to the message.

Assignments for Module 10

Questions for Comprehension

10.1 What are the three criteria for good subject lines? **(LO 10-1)**

10.2 How should you organize a positive or informative message? **(LO 10-2)**

10.3 How do varieties of informative and positive messages adapt the basic pattern? **(LO 10-4)**

Questions for Critical Thinking

10.4 What's wrong with the subject line "New Policy"? **(LO 10-1)**

10.5 Is it unethical to "bury" any negative elements in an otherwise positive or informative message? **(LO 10-2)**

10.6 Why is it important to recognize the secondary as well as the primary purposes of your message? **(LO 10-2, LO 10-4)**

10.7 Are you more likely to need reader benefits in informative letters or memos? Why? **(LO 10-3)**

Exercises and Problems

10.8 Revising a Positive Message (LO 10-1 to LO 10-6)

As director of purchasing for City College, you maintain a list of approved vendors who must comply with all local, state, and federal laws. You buy only from approved vendors.

You are now responding to a request from Amelia Kemp that her printing company be reinstated on the list. The company was suspended a month ago for paying less than the minimum wage, but she didn't own the business then. A subordinate has prepared this draft for your signature.

You know that this is a terrible letter. Both organization and style can be much better.

As Your Instructor Directs,

a. Identify the draft's problems in organization, style, you-attitude, and positive emphasis.

b. Write a new letter to replace this draft.

Dear Ms. Kemp:

This is in response to your letter of last week appealing your suspension as a printing vendor for City College because of non-compliance with the prevailing wage requirement.

I have had both our administrative and legal staff review the circumstances surrounding the suspension, and they have recommended that it be reduced to 30 days. Their recommendation is based strongly on the fact that you were not the owner of the business when the violation occurred which resulted in your suspension. In addition, your letter of last week promised that you will be in compliance for all future jobs printed for City College.

Since the letter informing you of the suspension was dated 33 days ago, this means that you are immediately reinstated as an approved vendor. My office, however, reserves the right to review future jobs performed by your company to ensure that you comply with the wage requirements and other requirements.

If you have any questions or concerns about this action, please feel free to contact me.

10.9 Announcing a New Policy of Compensatory Time Off (LO 10-1 to LO 10-6)

Most of the workers in your office are salaried, so they do not receive overtime pay when they work after 5 PM. However, the Executive Committee last week decided to institute a policy of compensatory time off. Under this policy, if someone works 2 or more hours more than the basic 40-hour workweek, he or she can take off the same number of hours on another day while still being paid the full rate.

The employee's supervisor must approve the time chosen for compensatory time off; an employee cannot take time off if he or she is needed for an important project. This policy is effective starting the first full week of next month. It is not retroactive; that is, people will not receive compensatory time off for additional hours they may have already worked.

Write a message to all employees announcing the policy.

10.10 Accepting Suggestions (LO 10-1 to LO 10-6)

Your city government encourages money-saving suggestions to help balance the city budget. The suggestion committee, which you chair, has voted to adopt five suggestions.

1. Direct deposit paychecks to save distribution and printing costs. Suggested by Park Kim Lee, in Recreation and Parks.
2. Buy supplies in bulk. Suggested by Jolene Zigmund, in Maintenance.
3. Charge nearby towns and suburbs a fee for sending their firefighters through the city fire academy. Suggested by Charles Boxell, in Fire Safety.
4. Ask employees to reimburse the city for personal photocopies or phone calls. Suggested by Maria Echeverria, in Police.

5. Install lock boxes so that meter readers don't have to turn off water valves when people move. This causes wear and tear, and broken valves must be dug up and replaced. Suggested by Travis Gratton, in Water Line Maintenance.

Each suggester gets $100. The Accounting Department will cut checks the first of next month; checks should reach people in interoffice mail a few days later.

As Your Instructor Directs,

a. Write to one of the suggesters, giving the good news.
b. Write to all employees, announcing the award winners.

10.11 Giving Good News (LO 10-1 to LO 10-6)

Write to a customer or client, to a vendor or supplier, or to your boss announcing good news. Possibilities include a

product improvement, a price cut or special, an addition to your management team, a new contract, and so forth.

10.12 Agreeing to Waive a Fee (LO 10-1 to LO 10-6)

You're a customer service representative for a major credit card company. Last week, Naomi Neyens called asking that you waive the annual fee on her account. "I'm getting offers from other companies with no annual fee. I'd like to keep my account, but only if you waive the fee for the life

of the account." You agreed to do as she asked, effective immediately. Now, you need to write a letter confirming the conversation.

Write to Ms. Neyens, specifying her 16-digit account number.

10.13 Reminding Employees of the Company Web Use Policy (LO 10-1 to LO 10-6)

Recently, a longtime employee was terminated for accessing adult websites on a company computer. Though the employee claimed that while doing a job-related web search several adult ads popped up, records show the site addresses were actually keyed in. The employee was also logged into the computer in question at the time.

This was the third time the employee was found to be using the web inappropriately. He was given a written warning both previous times.

Now is the time to remind employees of the company's policy on using the web. For starters, web use is limited to

tasks relevant to company business, and employees are to use the company e-mail system for company business only. If an employee receives a personal e-mail message through the company system, he or she should forward it to a personal e-mail system and open it elsewhere while "off the clock."

The company reserves the right to monitor employee web and e-mail use on a company computer at any time. Finally, employees who violate the policy are subject to disciplinary action, up to and including termination.

Write an e-mail message reminding employees of the policy.

10.14 Announcing an Additional Employee Benefit (LO 10-1 to LO 10-6)

To help employees who are caring for elderly relatives, your Human Resources office will provide information and referral services for elder day care and long-term assisted-living or nursing care and names and addresses of people willing to work part- or full-time as caregivers. In addition, you will sponsor seminars on a number of topics about dealing with elderly parents, ranging from deciding whether to use a nursing facility, when to stop driving, and how to fill out medical forms.

As part of the new policy, the organization will allow employees to use personal time off and sick time to care for any family member. You will also allow employees to take time off during the workday to stay until a nurse arrives or to drive a parent to a doctor's appointment. Employees must notify their supervisors in advance that they will be away and must make up the time sometime during the next 30 days. Employees who need more time can take unpaid leaves of up to 15 months and can return to their present jobs and current salaries.

The policy takes effect the first of next month.

Assume that you're Director of Human Resources, and write a memo to all employees announcing the benefit.

Hints:

- Pick a business, government, or nonprofit organization you know well.
- What age groups do employees represent? How many of them are caring for elderly parents now?

- Specify the topic, date, and place of the first seminar you'll sponsor. If possible, give the schedule for the first three months.
- Be sure to provide reader benefits for employees who do not care for elderly parents as well as those who do.
- How easy is it for your organization to attract and retain skilled workers? Why is it important to your organization that people be alert and be willing to take more responsibility?

10.15 Answering a Customer Complaint about Shipping and Handling Costs (LO 10-1 to LO 10-6)

You receive the following letter today:

Recently, I telephoned to order a bookcase from your catalogue. The price was $143, plus shipping and handling. Because the catalogue said to inquire about the shipping and handling cost, I asked the customer service representative how much that might be. I was expecting $25. Imagine my shock when the representative said $178!

I pointed out the shipping and handling cost was more than the actual bookcase, and he replied, "Well, that's the standard rate. Take it or leave it." I couldn't believe my ears. When I asked to speak to a manager, he said she was out. Then, he hung up.

I don't know what is the bigger outrage—the shipping and handling cost or his rude behavior. I order regularly through catalogues and websites, and I've never found shipping and handling to be more than the actual item. How is it that others can ship for more reasonable rates than you can?

This all smacks of unethical business practices, and I have a good mind to report you to the State's Attorney General's Office.

Sincerely,

Carla Biedler

Your company's shipping rates are a frequent sore spot with customers. What they don't understand is that shipping prices are determined by the carrier, an overland trucking company that charges higher rates because it has an impeccable record for delivering packages on time and intact.

Since switching to that carrier, returns for your company on damaged goods have dropped more than 90%. The carrier charges a rate based on size and weight. The bookcase is oversized and weighs 145 pounds, making it expensive to ship.

In addition, your company uses premium crating and packing materials to protect all products. Preparing items for shipment takes longer than simply putting an address label on a box, so handling charges are more than some vendors might charge. However, there is no markup on the handling charges.

You'll investigate which of your 38 customer service representatives might have spoken rudely to Ms. Biedler, but because your company doesn't record conversations, identifying him may be impossible.

Write a response to Ms. Biedler explaining the situation.

10.16 Informing Employees that Flu Shots Are Available (LO 10-1 to LO 10-6)

To give an additional benefit and to help inoculate employees against an illness that affects their attendance, your organization is providing flu shots to all employees at your central office. The flu shots will be administered on two days: October 1 and October 15, from 8 AM to 4 PM. The cost is $10 for employees in the organization's HMO program and $15 for employees in the organization's PPO program. Employees covered by another insurance provider cannot participate.

Employees at satellite locations and within driving distance can still participate, but they may need to take personal leave for the travel time to and from the central office.

People who receive the flu shot generally avoid getting the flu for an entire season, but there may be some discomfort and swelling in the arm muscle where the injection occurs.

To participate, employees must contact your Human Resources Office at ext. 2173 and schedule an appointment. Employees must also fill out a questionnaire regarding any recent health problems and sign a waiver against liability to the organization. The flu shots will be administered by a registered nurse, and participants will receive a free health screening from a nurse practitioner. Write a message to your employees informing them of the additional benefit.

10.17 Announcing an Employee Fitness Center (LO 10-1 to LO 10-6)

Your company is ready to open an employee fitness center with on-site aerobics classes, swimming pool, and weight machines. The center will be open 6 AM to 10 PM daily; a qualified instructor will be on duty at all times. Employees get first preference; if there is extra room, spouses and children may also use the facilities. Locker rooms and showers will be available.

Your company hopes that the fitness center will help out-of-shape employees get the exercise they need to be more productive. Other companies have gained as many as 762 workdays from shorter hospital stays by fitness center members. People who exercise have medical bills that are 35% lower than people who do not get enough exercise.

Write the memo announcing the center.

Hints:

- Who pays the medical insurance for employees? If the employer pays, then savings from healthier employees will pay for the center. If another payment plan is in effect, you'll need a different explanation for the company's decision to open the fitness center.
- Stress those benefits apart from the company's saving money. How can easier access to exercise help employees? What do they do? How can exercise reduce stress, improve strength, and increase their productivity at work?
- What kind of record does the company have of helping employees be healthy? Is the fitness center a new departure for the company, or does the company have a history of company sports teams, stop-smoking clinics, and the like?
- What is the company's competitive position? If the company is struggling, you'll need to convince readers that the fitness center is a good use of scarce funds. If the company is doing well, show how having fit employees can make people even more productive.
- Stress fun as a benefit. How can access to the center make employees' lives more enjoyable?

10.18 Confirming a Reservation (LO 10-1 to LO 10-6)

Most travelers phone 13 months in advance to reserve rooms at Signal Mountain Lodge in Grand Teton National Park. Once you process the credit card (payment for the first night), you write to confirm the reservation.

The confirmation contains the amount charged to the credit card, the date on which the reservation was made, the confirmation number, the kind of room (Lakefront Retreat or Mountainview Retreat), and the dates the guest will be arriving and leaving.

The amount of the deposit and the amount quoted per night is the rate for the current calendar year. However, the guest will be charged the rate for the calendar year of the stay, which is likely to increase about 4% to 5%. In addition to paying the new rate for each additional night, the guest will need to pay the difference between the amount of the deposit and the new rate for the first night.

Anyone who wants a refund must cancel the reservation in writing four days prior to the scheduled arrival date. Cancellations may be faxed: The fax number is on the letterhead the letter will be printed on.

Parking is limited. People who bring big motorhomes, boats, or camp trailers may have to park in the main parking area rather than right by their cabins.

All of the rooms are cabin style with three to four rooms in each building. There are no rooms in a main lodge. People will need to walk from their cabins to the restaurants, unless they do their own cooking.

Both Lakefront and Mountainview Retreats have kitchenettes with microwaves, but guests must bring their own cooking utensils, dishes, supplies, and food. The bedroom area (with a king-size bed in the Lakefront Retreats and a queen-size bed in the Mountainview Retreats) has a sliding divider that can separate it from the sitting area, which has a sofa bed.

Since the deposit pays for the first night (less any increase in room rate), the room will be held regardless of the time of arrival. Check-in time is 3 PM; earlier room availability cannot be guaranteed. Check-out time is 11 AM.

All cabins are nonsmoking. Smoking is permitted on the decks of the Lakefront Retreats or the porches of the Mountainview Retreats.

The guest should present the confirmation letter when checking in.

As Your Instructor Directs,

a. Write a form letter that can be used for one type of room (either Lakefront or Mountainview Retreat). Indicate with square brackets material that would need to be filled in for each guest (e.g., "arriving [date of arrival] and departing [date of departure]").

b. Write a letter to Stephanie Simpson, who has reserved a Lakefront Retreat room arriving September 18 and departing September 20. Her credit card is being billed for $183.75 ($175 plus tax—the current rate). Her address is 3122 Ellis Street, Stevens Point, WI 54481.

10.19 Lining Up a Consultant to Improve Teamwork (LO 10-1 to LO 10-6)

As director of education and training, you oversee all in-house training programs. Five weeks ago, Pat Dyrud, Vice President for Human Resources, asked you to set up a training course on teams. You tracked down Sarah Reed, a Business Communication professor at a nearby college.

"Yes, I do workshops on teamwork," she told you on the phone. "I would want at least a day and a half with participants—two full days would be better. They need time to practice the skills they'll be learning. I'm free Mondays and Tuesdays. I'm willing to work with up to five teams at a time, as long as the total number of people is 30 or less. Tell me what kinds of teams they work in, what they already know, and what kinds of things you want me to emphasize. My fee is $2,500 a day. Of course, you'd reimburse me for expenses."

You told her you thought a two-day session would be feasible, but you'd have to get back to her after you got budget approval. You wrote a quick memo to Pat Dyrud explaining the situation and asking about what the session should cover.

Two weeks ago, you received this memo:

> I've asked the Veep for budget approval for $5,000 for a two-day session plus no more than $750 for all expenses. I don't think there will be a problem.
>
> We need some of the basics: strategies for working in groups, making decisions, budgeting time, and so forth. We especially need work on dealing with problem group members and on handling conflict—I think some of our people are so afraid that they won't seem to be "team players" if they agree too readily.
>
> I don't want some ivory tower theorist. We need practical exercises that can help us practice skills that we can put into effect immediately.
>
> Attached is a list of 24 people who are free Monday and Tuesday of the second week of next month. Note that we've got a good mix of people. If the session goes well, I may want you to schedule additional sessions.

Today, you got approval from the vice president to schedule the session and pay Professor Reed the fee and reimburse her for expenses to a maximum of $750. She will have to keep all receipts and turn in an itemized list of expenses to be reimbursed; you cannot reimburse her if she does not have receipts.

You also need to explain the mechanics of the session. You'll meet in the Conference Room, which has a screen and flip charts. You have an overhead projector, a slide projector, a laptop computer for showing PowerPoint slides, a video camera, a DVD player, and a TV, but you need to reserve these if she wants to use them.

Write to Professor Reed. You don't have to persuade her to come since she's already informally agreed, but you do want her to look forward to the job and to do her best work.

Hints:

- Choose an organization you know something about.
- What do teams do in this organization? What challenges do they face?
- Will most participants have experience working in teams? Will they have bad habits to overcome? What attitudes toward teams are they likely to have?
- Check the calendar to get the dates. If there's any ambiguity about what "the second week of next month" is, "call" Pat to check.

10.20 Answering an International Inquiry (LO 10-1 to LO 10-6)

Your business, government, or nonprofit organization has received the following inquiries from international correspondents. (You choose the country the inquiry is from.)

1. Please tell us about a new product, service, or trend so that we can decide whether we want to buy, license, or imitate it in our country.
2. We have heard about a problem [technical, social, political, or ethical] which occurred in your organization. Could you please tell us what really happened and estimate how it is likely to affect the long-term success of the organization?
3. Please tell us about college programs in this field that our managers could take.
4. We are considering setting up a plant in your city. We have already received adequate business information. However, we would also like to know how comfortable our nationals will feel. Do people in your city speak our language? How many? What opportunities exist for our nationals to improve their English? Does your town already have people from a wide mix of nations? Which are the largest groups?
5. Our organization would like to subscribe to an English-language trade journal. Which one would you recommend? Why? How much does it cost? How can we order it?

As Your Instructor Directs,

a. Answer one or more of the inquiries. Assume that your reader either reads English or can have your message translated.
b. Write a memo to your instructor explaining how you've adapted the message for your audience.

Hints:

- Even though you can write in English, English may not be your reader's native language. Write a letter that can be translated easily.
- In some cases, you may need to spell out background information that might not be clear to someone from another country.

10.21 Writing a Thank-You Letter (LO 10-1 to LO 10-6)

Write a thank-you letter to someone who has helped you achieve your goals.

As Your Instructor Directs,

a. Turn in a copy of the letter.
b. Mail the letter to the person who helped you.
c. Write a memo to your instructor explaining the choices you made in writing the thank-you letter.

10.22 Evaluating web pages (LO 10-1 to LO 10-6)

Today you get this e-mail message from your boss:

> Subject: Evaluating Our web page
>
> Our CEO wants to know how our web page compares to those of our competitors. I'd like you to do this in two steps. First, send me a list of your criteria. Then give me an evaluation of two of our competitors and of our own pages. I'll combine your memo with others on other web pages to put together a comprehensive evaluation for the next Executive Meeting.

As Your Instructor Directs,

a. List the generic criteria for evaluating a web page. Think about the various audiences for the page and the content that will keep them coming back, the way the page is organized, how easy it is to find something, the visual design, and the details, such as a creation/update date.

b. List criteria for pages of specific kinds of organizations. For example, a nonprofit organization might want information for potential and current donors, volunteers, and clients. A financial institution might want to project an image both of trustworthiness and as being a good place to work.

c. Evaluate three web pages of similar organizations. Which is best? Why?

Hint:

Review web page design tips in Module 5.

10.23 Announcing a Tuition Reimbursement Program (LO 10-1 to LO 10-6)

Your organization has decided to encourage employees to take courses by reimbursing each eligible employee a maximum of $3,500 in tuition and fees during any one calendar year. Anyone who wants to participate in the program must apply before the first class meeting; the application must be signed by the employee's immediate supervisor. The Office of Human Resources will evaluate applications. That office has application forms.

The only courses eligible are those related to the employee's current position or to a position in the company that the employee might hold someday, or that are part of a job-related degree program. Again, the degree may be one that would help the employee's current position or that would qualify him or her for a promotion or transfer in the organization.

Only tuition and fees are covered, not books or supplies. People whose applications are approved will be reimbursed when they have completed the course with a grade of *C* or better. An employee cannot be reimbursed until he or she submits a copy of the approved application, an official grade report, and a statement of the tuition paid. If someone is eligible for other financial aid (scholarship, veterans' benefits), the company will pay tuition costs not covered by that aid as long as the employee does not receive more than $3,500 and as long as the total tuition reimbursement does not exceed the actual cost of tuition and fees.

Part-time employees are not eligible; full-time employees must work at the company three months before they can apply to participate in the program. Courses may be at any appropriate level (high school, college, or graduate). However, the IRS currently requires workers to pay tax on any reimbursement for graduate programs. Undergraduate and basic education reimbursements of $5,250 a year are not taxed.

As director of human resources, write a memo to all employees explaining this new benefit.

Hints:

- Pick an organization you know something about. What do its employees do? What courses or degrees might help them do their jobs better?
- How much education do employees already have? How do they feel about formal schooling?
- The information in the problem is presented in a confusing order. Put related items together.
- The problem stresses the limits of the policy. Without changing the provision, present them positively.
- How will having a better-educated workforce help the organization? Think about the challenges the organization faces, its competitive environment, and so forth.

10.24 Correcting a Mistake (LO 10-1 to LO 10-6)

A glitch in your payroll system erroneously withheld about 10% less in federal taxes from each paycheck during the last two pay periods. Therefore, more money must be withheld from employee paychecks during upcoming pay periods to compensate. The amount will vary depending on employee, but all employees were affected by the error.

Now you must send a letter to employees explaining that a corresponding amount will have to be withheld from future paychecks. Since there are only three pay periods before the end of the year, and it will take one pay period before the correction to the payroll system can go into effect, the amount will be divided among the two remaining pay periods. Of course, since the system must cycle through one pay period before changes can take effect, the total shortfall of federal taxes affected will be closer to 30%. The withholdings must be made in the current calendar year.

The HR Director wants to avoid a flood of inquiries regarding the situation and is counting on your message to help minimize questions. However, a hotline has been established with a recording to address likely frequently asked questions.

Write the letter.

Polishing Your Prose

Dangling Modifiers

Modifiers are words or phrases that give more information about parts of a sentence. For instance, an adjective is a modifier that usually describes a noun. **Dangling modifiers** make no sense to readers because the word they modify is not in the sentence. If you diagrammed the sentence, the modifier would not be attached to anything; it would dangle.

Dangling: Confirming our conversation, your Hot Springs Hot Tub Spa is scheduled for delivery April 12. (This sentence says that the spa is doing the confirming.)

Dangling: At the age of 10, I bought my daughter her first share of stock.

Correct a dangling modifier in either of these ways:

1. Rewrite the modifier as a subordinate clause.

Correct: As I told you yesterday, your Hot Springs Hot Tub Spa is scheduled for delivery April 12.

Correct: I bought my daughter her first share of stock when she was 10.

2. Rewrite the main clause so its subject or object can be modified correctly.

Correct: Talking on the phone, we confirmed that your Hot Springs Hot Tub Spa is scheduled for delivery April 12.

Correct: At the age of 10, my daughter received the first share of stock I bought for her.

Exercises

Correct the dangling modifiers in these sentences.

1. Traveling overseas on business, the sights were absolutely incredible.
2. At the age of 11, my mother told me that I was a natural-born salesman.
3. Ringing over and over, I finally answered the phone.
4. Speaking with you on the phone, our appointment will be at 3 P.M. on July 2.
5. Imagining the worst, the storm really made me worry about traveling this weekend.
6. Speaking with a great deal of confidence, the interview went well for Kim.
7. After carefully selecting from all of my investment options, my mutual funds yielded a 7% return this past year.
8. Reviewing the e-mail message, the customer was complaining about how our counter person was rude to her.
9. Featuring so many great apps, I had a hard time choosing which ones to download from the website.
10. Demonstrating hard work and dedication, the Outstanding Employee Award went to Gary, a 32-year veteran of Seitz, Noonan, and Cobb.

Check your answers to the odd-numbered exercises at the back of the book.

LEARNING OBJECTIVES

While writing negative messages can be challenging, Module 11 will help you to write them well. After completing the module, you should be able to

LO 11-1 **Create subject lines for negative messages.**

LO 11-2 **Apply strategies for informative and positive message organization.**

LO 11-3 **Assess legal implications with messages, especially negative ones.**

LO 11-4 **Identify situations for buffer use.**

LO 11-5 **List common kinds of negative messages.**

LO 11-6 **Apply strategies for negative message analysis with PAIBOC.**

In a **negative message,** the basic information is negative, so we expect the reader to be disappointed or angry. Few people like to give bad news—and even fewer people like to get it—but negative messages are common in business. How we present negatives and what we write or say can affect how audiences respond to our messages, as well as how they view us and our organization.

Negative messages include

- Rejections and refusals.
- Announcements of policy changes that do not benefit customers or consumers.
- Requests the reader will see as insulting or intrusive.
- Negative performance appraisals and disciplinary notices.
- Product recalls or notices of defects.

A negative message always has several purposes:

Primary Purposes:

- To give the reader the bad news.
- To have the reader read, understand, and accept the message.
- To maintain as much goodwill as possible.

Secondary Purposes:

- To build a good image of the writer.
- To build a good image of the writer's organization.
- To reduce or eliminate future correspondence on the same subject so the message doesn't create more work for the writer.

Even when it is not possible to make the reader happy with the news we must convey, we still want readers to feel that

- They have been taken seriously.
- Our decision is fair and reasonable.
- If they were in our shoes, they would make the same decision.

What's the best subject line for a negative message?   LO 11-1

▶ *Only use negative subject lines if you think the reader may otherwise ignore the message.*

Letters don't require subject lines (◀◀ p. 127). Omit a subject line in negative letters unless you think readers may ignore what they think is a routine message. (See, for example, Figure 11.2 later in this module).

When you give bad news to superiors, use a subject line that focuses on solving the problem.

> Subject: Improving Our Subscription Letter

When you write to peers and subordinates, put the topic (but not your action on it) in the subject line.

> Subject: Status of Conversion Table Program
>
> Due to heavy demands on our time, we have not yet been able to write programs for the conversion tables you asked for.

How should I organize negative messages?   LO 11-2

▶ *It depends on your purposes and audiences.*

Choose the pattern based on the situation.

- Letters to people outside your organization should be indirect to build goodwill.
- When you write to superiors, you need to propose solutions, not just report a problem.
- When you write to peers and subordinates, try to get their input in dealing with negative situations.

Even bad news can have a silver lining. Petra Anderson was among dozens wounded at the Aurora, Colorado, shooting at the premiere of *The Dark Knight Rises* that also killed 12 people. But owing to a small birth defect in her brain, the buckshot that might otherwise have killed her in fact missed anything vital. With all of the bad news in her life at the time—her mother was diagnosed with terminal cancer—a brain defect might have been just one more burden to carry. But in this case, it was the miracle that saved her life.

Source: Dylan Stableford, "Colorado Shooting Victim's Brain Condition Helped Her Survive, Pastor Says," June 25, 2012, http://news.yahoo.com/blogs/lookout/colorado-shooting-petra-anderson-brain-survive-150918602.html.

Site to See

Go to
www.users.elite.net/runner/jennifers/no.htm
www.users.elite.net/runner/jennifers/yes.htm

for Jennifer Runner's compilation of "no" in more than 520 languages and "yes" in more than 550 languages, respectively.

Site to
See

Go to

www.useit.com/
alertbox/20000123.html

General guidelines for saying
"no" can be applied to specific
situations. Computer expert
Jakob Neilsen explains how
to tell users that your website
can't do what they want.

The mystery of which client
hired Burson-Marsteller, a public
relations firm, to help spread
negative information about
Google was solved when an
influential blogger revealed it to
be none other than Facebook.
The revelation proved
embarrassing for the social
networking site, as news of the
effort was reported nationally
when some Facebook users
were also expressing concerns
over privacy and whether
personal data was being sold
to third parties. Always consider
ethics when sending out
negative messages.

Source: Dan Lyons, "Facebook
Busted in Clumsy Smear on
Google," May 12, 2011, http://news.
yahoo.com/s/dailybeast/20110512/
ts_dailybeast/14045_
facebookbustedinclumsy-
smearattemptongoogle.

What pattern of organization to use is also influenced by your purposes. The patterns in this section assume that maintaining goodwill is an important purpose. But as you'll see later in the module, on some occasions, maintaining goodwill is less important than giving the negative clearly.

Giving Bad News to Customers and Other People Outside Your Organization

The following pattern helps writers maintain goodwill:

1. **Give the reason for the refusal before the refusal itself when you have a reason that readers will understand and accept.** A good reason prepares the reader to expect the refusal.
2. **Give the negative just once, clearly.** Inconspicuous refusals can be missed, making it necessary to say no a second time.
3. **Present an alternative or compromise, if one is available.** An alternative not only gives readers another way to get what they want but also suggests that you care about readers and helping them solve their problems.
4. **End with a positive, forward-looking statement.**

Figure 11.1 summarizes the pattern. Figure 11.2 uses the basic pattern.

Reasons

Make the reason for the refusal clear and convincing. The following reason is inadequate.

Weak reason: The goal of the Knoxville CHARGE-ALL Center is to provide our customers faster, more personalized service. Since you now live outside the Knoxville CHARGE-ALL service area, we can no longer offer you the advantages of a local CHARGE-ALL Center.

If the reader says, "I don't care if my bills are slow and impersonal," will the company let the reader keep the card? No. The real reason for the negative is that the bank's franchise allows it to have cardholders only in a given geographical region.

Real reason: Each local CHARGE-ALL Center is permitted to offer accounts to customers in a several-state area. The Knoxville CHARGE-ALL Center serves customers east of the Mississippi. You can continue to use your current card until it expires. When that happens, you'll need to open an account with a CHARGE-ALL Center that serves Texas.

Don't hide behind "company policy": Readers will assume the policy is designed to benefit you at their expense. If possible, show how the readers benefit from the policy. If they do not benefit, don't mention the policy.

Figure 11.1 How to
Organize a Negative Letter

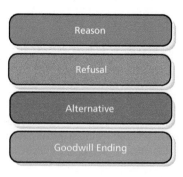

Figure 11.2 A Negative Letter

Vickers

Insurance Company

3373 Forbes Avenue
Rosemont, PA 19010
(215) 555-0100

Negative information highlighted so reader won't ignore message.

**Liability Coverage
Is Being Discontinued—
Here's How to Replace It!**

Negative

Alternative

Dear Policyholder:

Negative

When your auto insurance is renewed, it will no longer include liability coverage unless you select the new Assurance Plan. Here's why.

Positive information underlined for emphasis.

Liability coverage is being discontinued. It, and <u>the part of the premium which paid for it,</u> will be dropped from all policies when they are renewed.

This could leave a gap in your protection. But you can replace the old Liability Coverage with Vickers' new Assurance Plan.

No reason is given. The change probably benefits the company rather than the reader, so it is omitted.

Alternative

With the new Assurance Plan, you receive benefits for litigation or awards arising from an accident--regardless of who's at fault. The cost for the Assurance Plan at any level is based on the ages of drivers, where you live, your driving record, and other factors. If these change before your policy is renewed, the cost of your Assurance Plan may also change. The actual cost will be listed in your renewal statement.

To sign up for the Assurance Plan, just check the level of coverage you want on the enclosed form and return it in the postage-paid envelope within 14 days. You'll be assured of the coverage you select.

Forward-looking ending emphasizes reader's choice.

Sincerely,

C. J. Morgan

C. J. Morgan
President

Alternative

P.S. The Assurance Plan protects you against possible legal costs arising from an accident. Sign up for the Plan today and receive full coverage from Vickers.

Weak reason:	I cannot write an insurance policy for you because company policy does not allow me to do so.
Better reason:	Gorham insures cars only when they are normally garaged at night. Standard insurance policies cover a wider variety of risks and charge higher fees. Limiting the policies we write gives Gorham customers the lowest possible rates for auto insurance.

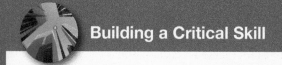

Thinking about the Legal Implications of What You Say LO 11-3

Any message that is recorded—on paper (even a napkin), on a disk or hard drive, on voice mail—can be subpoenaed in a legal case. During the government's months-long case against Microsoft in the late 1990s, e-mail messages figured prominently as evidence. Even an electronic message that has been erased can be reconstituted by experts, and servers can be hacked, as was the case at the University of East Anglia, where hundreds of e-mails from prominent British and American climate researchers, some suggesting to critics that data might have been manipulated or withheld, undermined their public image. In any message you write, however informal or hurried, you need to be sure to say exactly what you mean.

Dell, Inc., and its financial service affiliate in New York were sued after about 700 complaints flooded the office of Andrew Cuomo, the state's attorney general. At heart was whether Dell had engaged in "bait and switch," with salespeople promising customers 0% financing but then tricking them into higher interest rates. According to Paul Reisner, who had excellent credit and owned his own home, the company informed him that he'd never qualified for 0% financing and then promptly obligated him to pay a 29% interest rate.

Thinking about the legal implications of what you say is particularly important in negative messages. In an effort to cushion bad news, writers sometimes give reasons that create legal liabilities. For example, as Elizabeth McCord has shown, the statement that a plant is "too noisy and dangerous" for a group tour could be used as evidence against the company in a worker's compensation claim. In another case, a writer telling a job candidate that the firm had hired someone else said that he thought she was the best candidate. She sued and won.

People have found themselves in hot water for posting negative information on the Internet. Alan and Linda Townsend were sued after launching a website to complain about the quality of a product, Spray on Siding, used on their house. The suit alleged the site infringed on the company's trademarks, defamed its product, and intentionally misled and confused consumers. An automobile club in California fired 27 workers for posting offensive material. A Boston University instructor blogged about an attractive student and was dismissed, as was a nanny who revealed too much about herself and her employers.

You don't need to be a lawyer to figure out what to say—or not to say. Think about how a reasonable person might interpret your words. If that interpretation isn't what you mean, revise the passage so that it says what you mean.

Sources: Andrew C. Revkin, "Hacked E-Mail Is New Fodder for Climate Dispute," *The New York Times,* November 20, 2009, http://www.nytimes.com/2009/11/21/science/earth/21climate.html?_r=1; "Unethical Sales Practice Lands Dell in Legal Trouble," June 6, 2007, downloaded at http://in.ibtimes.com/articles/20070606/unethical-sales-practice-lands-dell-in-legal-trouble.htm; Elizabeth A. McCord, "The Business Writer, the Law, and Routine Business Communication. A Legal and Rhetorical Analysis," *Journal of Business and Technical Communication* 5, no. 2 (1991): 173–99; Charles Odum, "Complaints Posted on website Spark Lawsuit," *USAToday,* November 5, 2004, downloaded at www.usatoday.com/tech/news/techpolicy/2004-11-05-complaints-site-suit_x.htm; and Stacy Burling, "Blogs Can Help Boost a Career or Sink It," September 13, 2005, downloaded at http://news.yahoo.com/s/sv/20050913/tc_siliconvalley/_www12634035.

Avoid saying that you *cannot* do something. Most negative messages exist because the writer or company has chosen certain policies or cutoff points. In the preceding example, the company could choose to insure a wider variety of customers if it wanted to do so.

Often you will enforce policies you did not design. Don't pass the buck by saying, "This is a terrible policy." Carelessly criticizing your superiors is never a good idea. If you really think a policy is bad, try to persuade your superiors to change it. If you can't think of convincing reasons to change the policy, maybe it isn't so bad after all.

If you have several reasons for saying *no,* use only those that are strong and watertight. If you give five reasons and readers dismiss two of them, readers may feel that they've won and should get the request.

Weak reason:	You cannot store large bulky items in the dormitory over the summer because moving them into and out of storage would tie up the stairs and the elevators just at the busiest times when people are moving in and out.
Way to dismiss the reason:	We'll move large items before or after the two days when most people are moving in or out.

If you do not have a good reason, omit the reason rather than use a weak one. Even if you have a strong reason, omit it if it makes the company look bad.

Reason that hurts company:	Our company is not hiring at the present time because profits are down. In fact, the downturn has prompted top management to reduce the salaried staff by 5% just this month, with perhaps more reductions to come.
Better:	Our company does not have any openings now.

Refusals

Deemphasize the refusal by putting it in the same paragraph as the reason, rather than in a paragraph by itself.

Sometimes you may be able to imply the refusal rather than stating it directly.

Direct refusal:	You cannot get insurance for just one month.
Implied refusal:	The shortest term for an insurance policy is six months.

Be sure that the implication is crystal clear. Any message can be misunderstood, but an optimistic or desperate reader is particularly unlikely to understand a negative message. One of your purposes in a negative message is to close the door on the subject. You do not want to have to write a second letter saying that the real answer is *no*.

Alternatives

Giving the reader an alternative or a compromise, if one is available,

- Offers the reader another way to get what he or she wants.
- Suggests that you really care about the reader and about helping to meet his or her needs.
- Enables the reader to reestablish the psychological freedom you limited when you said *no*.
- Allows you to end on a positive note and to present yourself and your organization as positive, friendly, and helpful.

When you give an alternative, give readers all the information they need to act on it, but don't take the necessary steps. Let readers decide whether to try the alternative.

Negative messages limit the reader's freedom. People may respond to a limitation of freedom by asserting their freedom in some other arena. Jack W. Brehm calls this phenomenon **psychological reactance.**[1] Psychological reactance is at work when a customer who has been denied credit no longer buys even on a cash basis or a subordinate who has been passed over for a promotion gets back at the company by deliberately doing a poor job.

Psychological reactance often triggers questionable behavior.

Non Sequitur © 1997 Wiley Miller. Reprinted by permission of Universal Uclick. All rights reserved.

An alternative allows the reader to react in a way that doesn't hurt you. By letting readers decide for themselves whether they want the alternative, you allow them to reestablish their sense of psychological freedom.

The specific alternative will vary depending on the circumstances. In Figure 11.3, the company is unwilling to quote a price on an item on which it cannot be competitive. In different circumstances, the writer might offer different alternatives.

Figure 11.3 A Refusal with an Alternative

Steel Fabrication

"Serving the needs of America since 1890"
1800 Olney Avenue • Philadelphia, PA 19140 • 215•555•7800 • Fax: 215•555•9803

April 27, 2012

Mr. H. J. Moody
Canton Corporation
2407 North Avenue
Kearney, NE 68847

Subject: Bid Number 5853, Part Number D-40040

Dear Mr. Moody:

Buffer   Thank you for requesting our quotation on your Part No. D-40040.

Reason   Your blueprints call for flame-cut rings 1/2" thick A516 grade 70. To use that grade, we'd have to grind down from 1" thick material. However, if you can use A515 grade 70, which we stock in 1/2" thick, you can cut the price by more than half.

Quantity	Description	Gross Weight	Price/Each
75	Rings Drawing D-40040, A516 Grade 70 1" thick x 6" O.D. x 2.8" I.D. ground to .5" thick.	12 lbs.	$15.08
75	Rings Drawing D-40040, A515 Grade 70 1/2" thick x 6" O.D. x 2.8" I.D.	6 lbs.	$6.91

Alternative (Depending on circumstances, different alternatives may exist.)

If you can use A515 grade 70, let me know.

Leaves decision up to reader to reestablish psychological freedom.

Sincerely,

Valerie Prynne

Valerie Prynne
VP:wc

Endings

If you have a good alternative, refer to it in your ending: "Let me know if you can use A515 grade 70."

The best endings look to the future, as in this letter refusing to continue a charge account for a customer who has moved.

> Wherever you have your account, you'll continue to get all the service you've learned to expect from CHARGE-ALL and the convenience of charging items at over a million stores, restaurants, and hotels in the U.S. and abroad—and in Knoxville, too, whenever you come back to visit!

Avoid endings that seem insincere.

> We are happy to have been of service, and should we be able to assist you in the future, please contact us.

This ending lacks you-attitude and would not be good even in a positive message. In a situation where the company has just refused to help, it's likely to sound sarcastic or mean.

Giving Bad News to Superiors

Your superior expects you to solve minor problems by yourself. But sometimes, solving a problem requires more authority or resources than you have. When you give bad news to a superior, also recommend a way to deal with the problem. Turn the negative message into a persuasive one.

1. **Describe the problem.** Tell what's wrong, clearly and unemotionally.
2. **Tell how it happened.** Provide the background. What underlying factors led to this specific problem?
3. **Describe the options for fixing it.** If one option is clearly best, you may need to discuss only one. But if the reader will think of other options, or if different people will judge the options differently, describe all the options, giving their advantages and disadvantages.
4. **Recommend a solution and ask for action.** Ask for approval so you can to make the necessary changes to fix the problem.

Figure 11.4 summarizes the pattern.

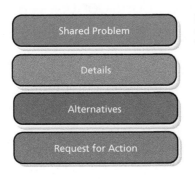

Figure 11.4 How to Organize a Negative Memo to Your Superior

Figure 11.5 How to Organize a Negative Memo to Peers or Subordinates

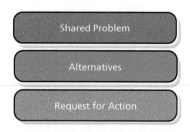

Shared Problem

Alternatives

Request for Action

Blogger and management guru Peter Bregman believes that honesty is "much more compelling, powerful, and effective than the alternative," and that employees want honesty from bosses. He cites a survey by one of his clients that found, for instance, that the number one behavior distinguishing the best managers from others is their ability to honestly ask for help from employees. Bregman's position is supported by others, including author Terry Bacon, whose findings published in *What People Want* reveal that honesty is the foremost thing employees want from leaders.

Sources: Peter Bregman, "Do People Really Want You to Be Honest?" *Harvard Business Review,* January 10, 2012, http://blogs.hbr. org/bregman/2012/01/do-people-really-want-you-to-b.html; and "9 Things Employees Want from Their Managers (and 5 Things They Don't)," *Business Management Daily,* May 21, 2012, http:// www.businessmanagementdaily. com/11630/9-things-employees-want-from-theirmanagers-and-5-things-they-dont.

Giving Bad News to Peers and Subordinates

When you must pass along serious bad news to peers and subordinates, use a variation of the pattern to superiors:

1. **Describe the problem.** Tell what's wrong, clearly and unemotionally.
2. **Present an alternative or compromise, if one is available.** An alternative gives readers another way to get what they want and also suggests that you care about readers and helping them meet their needs.
3. **If possible, ask for input or action.** People in the audience may be able to suggest solutions. And workers who help make a decision are far more likely to accept the consequences.

Figure 11.5 summarizes this pattern.

No serious negative (such as being downsized or laid off) should come as a complete surprise. Managers can prepare for possible negatives by giving full information as it becomes available. It is also possible to let the people who will be affected by a decision participate in setting the criteria. Someone who has bought into the criteria for awarding cash for suggestions or retaining workers is more likely to accept decisions using such criteria. And in some cases, the synergism of groups may make possible ideas that management didn't think of or rejected as "unacceptable." Some workplaces, for example, might decide to reduce everyone's pay slightly rather than laying off some individuals. Employee suggestions enabled Mentor Training, a San Jose company providing software training, to cut its payroll by 30% without laying off any full-time employees.[2]

When the bad news is less serious, as in Figure 11.6, use the pattern for negative letters unless your knowledge of the reader(s) suggests that another pattern will be more effective.

For memos, the context of communication is crucial. The reader's reaction is influenced by the following factors:

- Do you and the reader have a good relationship?
- Does the organization treat people well?
- Have readers been warned of possible negatives?
- Have readers "bought into" the criteria for the decision?
- Do communications after the negative build goodwill?

When should I consider using a buffer?   LO 11-4

▶ *When the reader values harmony or when the buffer also serves another purpose.*

To some writers and readers, the direct patterns used in the previous section may seem too blunt. You may want to begin messages with a buffer when the reader (individually or culturally) values harmony or when the buffer serves another purpose. For example, when you must thank the reader somewhere in the letter, putting the "thank you" in the first paragraph allows you to start on a positive note.

A **buffer** is a neutral or positive statement that allows you to delay the negative. Recent research suggests that buffers do not make readers respond more positively,[3] and good buffers are very hard to write. However, in special situations, you may want to use a buffer.

Site to See

Go to
http://researchnews.osu.
edu/archive/nobuffer.htm

for a summary of Kitty Locker's research on negative messages.

Figure 11.6 A Negative Memo to Subordinates

Memo

Board of County Commissioners
Olentangy County, Nebraska

Date: January 10, 2013

To: All Employees

From: Floyd E. Loer, Dorothy A. Walters, and Stewart Mattson

Subject: Accounting for Work Missed Due to Bad Weather

Reason — Olentangy County Services are always open for our customers, whatever the weather. Employees who missed work during the snowstorm last week may count the absence as vacation, sick, or personal day(s).

Refusal, stated as positively as possible — Hourly workers who missed less than a day have the option of taking the missed time as vacation, sick, or personal hour(s) or of being paid only for the hour(s) they worked.

One small positive — Approval of vacation or personal days will be automatic; the normal requirement of giving at least 24 hours' notice is waived.

Goodwill ending — Thanks for all the efforts you have made to continue giving our customers the best possible service during one of the snowiest winters on record.

To be effective, a buffer must put the reader in a good frame of mind, not give the bad news but not imply a positive answer either, and provide a natural transition to the body of the letter. The kinds of statements most often used as buffers are good news, facts and chronologies of events, references to enclosures, thanks, and statements of principle.

1. **Start with any good news or positive elements the letter contains.**

Starting Thursday, June 26, you'll have access to your money 24 hours a day at First National Bank.

Letter announcing that the drive-up windows will be closed for two days while automatic teller machines are installed

2. **State a fact or provide a chronology of events.**

As a result of the new graduated dues schedule—determined by vote of the Delegate Assembly last December and subsequently endorsed by the Executive Council—members are now asked to establish their own dues rate and to calculate the total amount of their remittance.

Announcement of a new dues structure that will raise most members' dues

Instant Replay

Organizing Bad News to Superiors

1. Describe the problem.
2. Tell how it happened.
3. Describe the options for fixing it.
4. Recommend a solution and ask for action.

Instant Replay

Organizing Bad News to Peers and Subordinates

1. Describe the problem.
2. Present an alternative or compromise, if one is available.
3. If possible, ask for input or action.

Being fired from a job is usually the worst kind of message an employee can receive, but sometimes the reasons add insult to injury. When a yoga instructor gave a stern look to a Facebook employee texting in the middle of half-moon pose, she had no idea it would lead to her termination from the third-party contractor she worked for. Included in her termination letter was a complaint from the employee. Fourteen employees at the law offices of Elizabeth R. Wellborn were fired, allegedly for all wearing orange shirts on the same day. And employees have been let go after using social media to express their opinions, including a bartender who griped online about having to help waitresses serve food but not being allowed to share their tips.

Sources: Deanne Katz, "Yoga Teacher Fired for Telling Facebook Employee 'No Phones,'" July 13, 2012, http://www.reuters.com/article/2012/07/13/tagblogsfindlawcom2012-legallyweird-idUS134598457920120713; Eric Pfeiffer,

(continued)

3. **Refer to enclosures in the letter.**

Enclosed is a new sticker for your car. You may pick up additional ones in the office if needed. Please *destroy* old stickers bearing the signature of "L.S. LaVoie."

Letter announcing increase in parking rental rates

4. **Thank the reader for something he or she has done.**

Thank you for scheduling appointments for me with so many senior people at First National Bank. My visit there March 14 was very informative.

Letter refusing a job offer

5. **State a general principle.**

Good drivers should pay substantially less for their auto insurance. The Good Driver Plan was created to reward good drivers (those with five-year accident-free records) with our lowest available rates. A change in the plan, effective January 1, will help keep those rates low.

Letter announcing that the company will now count traffic tickets, not just accidents, in calculating insurance rates—a change that will raise many people's premiums

Buffers are hard to write. Even if you think the reader would prefer to be let down easily, use a buffer only when you can write a good one.

It's better *not* to use a buffer (1) if the reader may ignore a letter with a bland first paragraph, (2) if the reader or the organization prefers "bottom-line-first messages," (3) if the reader is suspicious of the writer, or (4) if the reader "won't take *no* for an answer."

What are the most common kinds of negative messages? LO 11-5

▶ *Rejections and refusals, disciplinary notices and negative performance appraisals, and layoffs and firings.*

Among the most difficult kinds of negative messages to write are rejections and refusals, disciplinary notices and negative performance appraisals, and layoffs and firings.

Rejections and Refusals

When you refuse requests from people outside your organization, try to use a buffer. Give an alternative if one is available. For example, if you are denying credit, it may still be possible for the reader to put an expensive item on layaway.

Politeness and length help. Graduating seniors at a southwestern university preferred rejection letters that addressed them as *Mr./Ms.* rather than calling them by their first names, that said something specific about their good qualities, that phrased the refusal itself indirectly, and that were longer.[4] An experiment using a denial of additional insurance found that subjects preferred a rejection letter that was longer, more tactful, and more personal. The preferred letter started with a buffer, used a good reason for the refusal, and offered a sales promotion in the last paragraph. The finding held both for English-speaking U.S. subjects and for Spanish-speaking Mexican subjects.[5]

When you refuse requests within your organization, use your knowledge of the organization's culture and of the specific individual to craft your message. In some organizations, it may be appropriate to use company slogans, offer whatever help already-established departments can give, and refer to the individual's good work. In less personal organizations, a simple negative without embellishment may be more appropriate.

Disciplinary Notices and Negative Performance Appraisals

Present disciplinary notices and negative performance appraisals directly, with no buffer. A buffer might encourage the recipient to minimize the message's importance—and might even become evidence in a court case that the employee had not been told to shape up "or else." Cite quantifiable observations of the employee's behavior, rather than generalizations or inferences based on it. If an employee is disciplined by being laid off without pay, specify when the employee is to return.

Performance appraisals are discussed in detail in Module 12 on persuasive messages. Performance appraisals will be persuasive when they are designed to help a basically good employee improve. But when an employee violates a company rule or fails to improve after repeated appraisals, the company may discipline the employee or build a dossier to support firing him or her.

Layoffs and Firings

Information about layoffs and firings is normally delivered orally but accompanied by a written statement explaining severance pay or unemployment benefits that may be available. The written statement should start either with the reason or with the decision itself. A buffer would not be appropriate.

If a company is in financial trouble, management needs to communicate the problem clearly long before it is necessary to lay anyone off. Sharing information and enlisting everyone's help in finding solutions may make it possible to save jobs. Sharing information also means that layoff notices, if they become necessary, will be a formality; they should not be new information to employees.

Before you fire someone, double-check the facts. Make sure the employee has been told about the problem and that he or she will be fired if the problem is not corrected. Give the employee the real reason for the firing. Offering a face-saving reason unrelated to poor performance can create legal liabilities. But avoid broadcasting the reason to other people: to do so can leave the company liable to a defamation suit.[6]

How can I apply what I've learned in this module? LO 11-6

▶ *Plan your activities and answer the PAIBOC questions.*

Before you tackle the assignments for this module, examine the following problem. Figure 11.7 lists the necessary activities. As in Module 10, the PAIBOC questions probe

Harvard College received kudos for the softer tone of its rejection letters to applicants, which included statements like, "Past experience suggests that the particular college a student attends is far less important than what the student does to develop his or her strengths and talents over the next four years."

Source: "Rejection: Some Colleges Do It Better than Others," *The Wall Street Journal,* April 29, 2009, B9.

Instant Replay

Effective Buffers

To be effective, a buffer must put the reader in a good frame of mind, not give the bad news but not imply a positive answer either, and provide a natural transition to the body of the letter.

(continued)
"Law Firm Fires 14 Employees for Wearing Orange Shirts," March 19, 2012, http://news.yahoo.com/blogs/sideshow/law-firm-fires-14-employees-wearing-orangeshirts-181404912.html; and Kashmir Hill, "When You Can and Can't Fire Employees for Social Media Misbehavior," *Forbes,* September 25, 2011, http://www.forbes.com/sites/kashmirhill/2011/08/25/when-you-can-and-cant-fire-employees-forsocial-media-misbehavior/.

Delivering bad news is especially tough when it comes to firing someone. Jonathan A. Segal suggests avoiding common phrases like "We had no choice but to terminate your employment"—justifications that may actually anger the employee.

Source: Jonathan A. Segal, "10 Things Not to Say When Firing an Employee," *BusinessWeek*, November 17, 2009, http://www.businessweek.com/managing/content/nov2009/ca2009119_982182.htm.

Figure 11.7 Allocating Time in Writing a Negative Memo (Your time may vary.)

Memo denying matching funds. Total time: 3 hours	
Planning	1 hour
Understand the situation.	
Answer the PAIBOC questions (◄◄ Module 1).	
Think about document design (◄◄ Module 5).	
Organize the message.	
Writing	½ hour
Draft the memo.	
Revising	1½ hours
Reread draft.	
Measure draft against PAIBOC questions and checklist for negative messages (Figure 11.10).	
Revise draft.	
Ask for feedback.	
Revise draft based on feedback.	
Edit to catch grammatical errors.	
Run spell-check.	
Proof by eye.	
Initial memo.	
Put in interoffice mail.	

A problem for Denmark's Lego Group, makers of the wildly popular blocks and play sets, may be that too many of the company's toys are marketed to boys at the expense of girls and thus send a negative message. Critics observe that of the 545 offerings from the company, almost all cater to concepts traditionally associated with boys: trains, rockets, helicopters, and spaceships. Said Peggy Orenstein, author of *Cinderella Ate My Daughter,* a satirical look at how the toy industry exploits the "princess phase" for girls, "They might as well have a No Girls Allowed Sign." Gender stereotyping aside, the company's solution is to introduce more toys aimed specifically at girls, including "American Girl Dolls" and "Lego Friends," or kits that let girls choose from multiple scenarios while building and socializing with each other.

(continued)

the basic points required for a solution. Study the two sample solutions to see what makes one unacceptable and the other one good. The checklist at the end of the module in Figure 11.10 can help you evaluate a draft.

Problem

You're Director of Employee Benefits for a Fortune 500 company. Today, you received the following memo:

> From: Michelle Jagtiani
>
> Subject: Getting My Retirement Benefits
>
> Next Friday will be my last day here. I am leaving [name of company] to take a position at another firm.
>
> Please process a check for my retirement benefits, including both the deductions from my salary and the company's contributions for the last three and a half years. I would like to receive the check by next Friday if possible.

You have bad news for Michelle. Although the company does contribute an amount to the retirement fund equal to the amount deducted for retirement from the employee's paycheck, employees who leave with less than five years of employment get only their own contributions. Michelle will get back only the money that has been deducted from her own pay, plus 4% interest compounded quarterly. Her payments and interest come to just over $17,200; the amount could be higher depending on the amount of her last paycheck, which will include compensation for any unused vacation days and sick leave. Furthermore, because the amounts deducted were not considered taxable income, she will have to pay income tax on the money she will receive.

You cannot process the check until after her resignation is effective, so you will mail it to her. You have her home address on file; if she's moving, she needs to let you know where to send the check. Processing the check may take two to three weeks.

Write a memo to Michelle.

Analysis of the Problem

P What are your **purposes** in writing or speaking?

To tell her that she will get only her own contributions, plus 4% interest compounded quarterly; that the check will be mailed to her home address two to three weeks after her last day on the job; and that the money will be taxable as income.

To build goodwill so that she feels she has been treated fairly and consistently. To minimize negative feelings she may have.

To close the door on this subject.

A Who is (are) your **audience(s)?** How do the members of your audience differ from each other? What characteristics are relevant to this particular message?

Michelle Jagtiani. Unless she's a personal friend, I probably wouldn't know why she's leaving and where she's going.

There's a lot I don't know. She may or may not know much about taxes; she may or may not be able to take advantage of tax-reduction strategies. I can't assume the answers because I wouldn't have them in real life.

I What **information** must your message include?

When the check will come. The facts that the check will be based on her contributions, not her employer's, and that the money will be taxable income. How lump-sum retirement benefits are calculated. The fact that we have her current address on file but need a new address if she's moving.

B What reasons or reader **benefits** can you use to support your position?

Giving the amount currently in her account may make her feel she is getting a significant sum of money. Suggesting someone who can give free tax advice (if the company offers this as a fringe benefit) reminds her of the benefits of working with the company. Wishing her luck with her new job is a nice touch.

O What **objections** can you expect your reader(s) to have? What negative elements of your message must you deemphasize or overcome?

She is getting about half the amount she expected, because she gets no matching funds.

She might have been able to earn more than 4% interest if she had invested the money herself. Depending on her personal tax situation, she may pay more tax on the money as a lump sum than would have been due had she paid it each year as she earned the money.

C How will the **context** affect the reader's response? Think about your relationship to the reader, morale in the organization, the economy, the time of year, and any special circumstances.

The stock market has been doing poorly; 4% interest is pretty good.

(continued)

Source: Brad Wieners, "Lego Is for Girls," *Bloomberg Businessweek,* December 14, 2011, http://www.businessweek.com/printer/articles/21120-lego-is-for-girls.

Though more education typically translates into more income and higher job satisfaction, a recent study by GfK Custom Research North America suggests employees with the most education also experience the most workplace stress. Concerns about job security and dwindling workplace resources are affecting Americans with advanced degrees, leading to a rise in voluntary workplace turnover despite tough economic times. What seems like an obvious benefit can sometimes come with hidden detriments.

Source: Chad Brooks, "Best-Educated Americans Experience the Most Stress at Work," *Business News Daily,* June 14, 2011, http://www.businessnewsdaily.com/work-related-stress-1403/.

Figure 11.8 An Unacceptable Solution to the Sample Problem

April 20, 2013

To: Michelle Jagtiani

From   Lisa Niaz *LN*

Subject   Denial of Matching Funds

*Give
reason
before
refusal.*

You cannot receive a check the last day of work and you will get only your own contributions, not a matching sum from the company, because you have not worked for the company for at least five full years.   *Better to be specific*

*This is lifted
straight from
the problem.
The language
in problems
is often
negative and
stuffy; information is
disorganized.*

Your payments and interest come to just over $17,200; the amount could be higher depending on the amount of your last paycheck, which will include compensation for any unused vacation days and sick leave. Furthermore, since the amounts deducted were not considered taxable income, you will have to pay income tax on the money you receive.

The check will be sent to your home address. If the address we have on file is incorrect, please correct it so that your check is not delayed.   *Negative*

*How will reader know what you have on file?
Better to give current address as you have it.*

*Think about the situation, and use your own words to
create a satisfactory message.*

Discussion of the Sample Solutions

The solution in Figure 11.8 is not acceptable. The subject line gives a blunt negative with no reason or alternative. The first sentence has a condescending tone that is particularly offensive in negative messages. The last sentence focuses on what is being taken away rather than what remains. Paragraph 2 lacks you-attitude and is vague. The memo ends with a negative. There is nothing anywhere in the memo to build goodwill.

The solution in Figure 11.9, in contrast, is very good. The policy serves as a buffer and explanation. The negative is stated clearly but is buried in the paragraph to avoid overemphasizing it. The paragraph ends on a positive note by specifying the amount in the account and the fact that the sum might be even higher.

Figure 11.9 A Good Solution to the Sample Problem

April 20, 2013

To: Michelle Jagtiani

From: Lisa Niaz *LN*

Subject: Receiving Employee Contributions from Retirement Accounts

Good to state reason in third-person to deemphasize negative

Employees who leave the company with at least five full years of employment are entitled both to the company contributions and the retirement benefit paycheck deductions contributed to retirement accounts. Those employees who leave the company with less than five years of employment will receive the employee paycheck contributions made to their retirement accounts.

Good to be specific

You now have $17,240.62 in your account, which includes 4% interest compounded quarterly. The amount you receive could be even higher since you will also receive payment for any unused sick leave and vacation days.

Good to show how company can help

Because you now have access to the account, the amount you receive will be considered taxable income. Beth Jordan in Employee Financial Services can give you information about possible tax deductions and financial investments which can reduce your income taxes.

Good to be specific

The check will be sent to your home address on May 16. The address we have on file is 2724 Merriman Road, Akron, Ohio 44313. If your address changes, please let us know so you can receive your check promptly.

Positive

Good luck with your new job!

Forward-looking

Paragraph 3 contains the additional negative information that the amount will be taxable but offers the alternative that it may be possible to reduce taxes. The writer builds goodwill by suggesting a specific person the reader could contact.

Paragraph 4 tells the reader what address is in the company files (Michelle may not know whether the files are up-to-date), asks that she update it if necessary, and ends with the reader's concern: getting her check promptly.

The final paragraph ends on a positive note. This generalized goodwill is appropriate when the writer does not know the reader well.

Figure 11.10

Checklist for Negative Messages

☐ Is the subject line appropriate?

☐ If a buffer is used, does it avoid suggesting either a positive or a negative response?

☐ Is the reason, if it is given, presented before the refusal? Is the reason watertight, with no loopholes?

☐ Is the negative information clear?

☐ Is an alternative given if a good one is available? Does the message provide all the information needed to act on the alternative but leave the choice up to the reader?

☐ Does the last paragraph avoid repeating the negative information?

☐ Is tone acceptable—not defensive, but not cold, preachy, or arrogant either?

And, for all messages, not just negative ones,

☐ Does the message use you-attitude and positive emphasis?

☐ Is the style easy to read and friendly?

☐ Is the visual design of the message inviting?

☐ Is the format correct?

☐ Does the message use standard grammar? Is it free from typos?

Originality in a negative message may come from

☐ An effective buffer, if one is appropriate.

☐ A clear, complete statement of the reason for the refusal.

☐ A good alternative, clearly presented, which shows that you're thinking about what the reader really needs.

☐ Adding details that show you're thinking about a specific organization and the specific people in that organization.

Summary of Learning Objectives

- When you give bad news to superiors, use a subject line that focuses on solving the problem. **(LO 11-1)**
- When you write to peers and subordinates, put the topic (but not your action on it) in the subject line. **(LO 11-1)**
- Organize negative letters in this way: **(LO 11-2)**
  1. Give the reason for the refusal before the refusal itself when you have a reason that readers will understand and accept.
  2. Give the negative just once, clearly.
  3. Present an alternative or compromise, if one is available.
  4. End with a positive, forward-looking statement.
- Organize negative memos to superiors in this way: **(LO 11-2)**
  1. Describe the problem.
  2. Tell how it happened.
  3. Describe the options for fixing it.
  4. Recommend a solution and ask for action.
- When you must pass along serious bad news to peers and subordinates, use a variation of the pattern to superiors: **(LO 11-2)**
  1. Describe the problem.
  2. Present an alternative or compromise, if one is available.
  3. If possible, ask for input or action.

- When the bad news is less serious, use the pattern for negative letters unless your knowledge of the reader(s) suggests that another pattern will be more effective. **(LO 11-2)**
- A good reason must be watertight. Give several reasons only if all are watertight and are of comparable importance. Omit the reason for the refusal if it is weak or if it makes your organization look bad. **(LO 11-2)**
- Giving the reader an alternative or a compromise **(LO 11-2)**
  - Offers the reader another way to get what he or she wants.
  - Suggests that you really care about the reader and about helping to meet his or her needs.
  - Enables the reader to reestablish the psychological freedom you limited when you said *no*.
  - Allows you to end on a positive note and to present yourself and your organization as positive, friendly, and helpful.
- People may respond to limits by striking out in some perhaps unacceptable way. This effort to reestablish freedom is called **psychological reactance. (LO 11-2)**
- When you give an alternative, give the reader all the information he or she needs to act on it, but don't take the necessary

steps for the reader. Letting the reader decide whether to try the alternative allows the reader to reestablish a sense of psychological freedom. **(LO 11-2)**

- Thinking about the legal implications of what you say is particularly important in negative messages. **(LO 11-3)**
  - Think about how a reasonable person might interpret your words.
  - If that interpretation isn't what you mean, revise the passage so that it says what you mean.
- Use a buffer when the reader values harmony or when the buffer serves a purpose in addition to simply delaying the negative. A **buffer** is a neutral or positive statement that allows you to bury the negative message. Buffers must put the reader in a good frame of mind, not give the bad news but not imply a positive answer either, and provide a natural transition to the body of the letter. **(LO 11-4)**

- The kinds of statements most often used as buffers are (1) good news, (2) facts and chronologies of events, (3) references to enclosures, (4) thanks, and (5) statements of principle. **(LO 11-4)**
- Rejections and refusals, disciplinary notices and negative performance appraisals, and layoffs and firings are the most common kinds of negative messages. **(LO 11-5)**
- Use the PAIBOC questions listed in Module 1 to examine the basic points needed for successful informative and positive messages. **(LO 11-6)**

Assignments for Module 11

Questions for Comprehension

11.1 How should a negative letter to customers or clients be organized? **(LO 11-2)**

11.2 Why is giving an alternative or a compromise, if one exists, a good idea? **(LO 11-2)**

11.3 How should a negative memo to a superior be organized? **(LO 11-2)**

11.4 What are the most common types of buffers? **(LO 11-4)**

Questions for Critical Thinking

11.5 How do you use positive emphasis in a negative message? **(LO 11-2, LO 11-3)**

11.6 How do you decide whether to give the negative directly or to buffer it? **(LO 11-4)**

11.7 How do specific varieties of negative messages adapt the basic pattern? **(LO 11-5)**

Exercises and Problems

11.8 Revising a Negative Message (LO 11-1 to LO 11-6)

Rewrite and reorganize the following negative message to make it more positive. Eliminate any sentences that are not needed.

> Dear Renter:
>
> Effective March 1, the rent for your parking space will go up $10 a month. However, our parking lot is still not the most expensive in town.
>
> Many of you have asked us to provide better snow and ice removal and to post signs saying that all spaces are rented so that a car can be towed if it parks in your space. Signs will be posted by March 1, and, if we get any more snow, Acme Company has contracted to have the lot cleared by 7 a.m.
>
> Enclosed is a new parking sticker. Please hang it on your rearview mirror.
>
> Sincerely,
>
> A. E. Jackson

11.9 Rejecting Employees' Suggestions (LO 11-1 to LO 11-6)

For years, businesses have had suggestion programs, rewarding employees for money-saving ideas. Now your city government has adopted such a program. But not all of the suggestions are adopted. Today, you need to send messages to the following people. Because their suggestions are being rejected, they will not get any cash.

1. Diane Hilgers, secretary, mayor's office. Suggestion: Charge for 911 calls. Reason for rejection: "This would be a public relations disaster. We already charge for ambulance or paramedic trips; to charge just for the call will offend people. And it might not save money. It's a lot cheaper to prevent a burglary or murder than to track

down the person afterward—to say nothing of the trauma of the loss or death. Bad idea."

2. Steve Rieneke, building and grounds supervisor. Suggestion: Fire the city's public relations specialists. Reason for rejection: "Positive attitudes toward city workers and policies make the public more willing to support public programs and taxes. We think this is money well spent."

3. Jose Rivera, accountant I. Suggestion: Schedule city council meetings during the day to save on light bills and staff overtime. Reason for rejection: "Having the meetings in the evening enables more citizens to attend.

Open meetings are essential so that citizens don't feel that policies and taxes are being railroaded through."

4. Martin Schultz, data center help desk assistant. Suggestion: Rather than provide free dial-up access, make employees working from home pay for their own Internet connection. Reason for rejection: "The cost of providing access through dial-up is negligible and offset by the increased productivity of employees who voluntarily work from home during times when they would be commuting. Employees also pay their own utility costs and are more likely to work after hours."

Write the messages.

11.10 Telling the Boss about a Problem (LO 11-1 to LO 11-6)

In any organization, things sometimes go wrong. Tell your supervisor about a problem in your unit and recommend what should be done.

As Your Instructor Directs,
a. Prepare notes for a meeting with your supervisor.

b. Write an e-mail message to your supervisor.
c. Write a memo to your supervisor.
d. Give an oral presentation on the problem.
e. Write a memo to your instructor explaining the problem, the corporate culture, and the reasons for your solution.

11.11 Responding to a Demand for a Refund (LO 11-1 to LO 11-6)

You are the regional manager of a movie theater chain. Recently, you received this letter:

I want my money back! I paid $9 to see *The Monster's Bride,* and because the screen was so dark, I could hardly see anything at all. Half the time, the screen was almost pitch black! Besides that, the movie was total garbage and nothing like the advertising suggested. And why did I have to sit through half an hour of trailers before the movie? You should pay me for wasting my time. You guys are a bunch of crooks.

Sincerely,

Glenn McCann

Because individual tastes are varied, your company does not offer refunds when a moviegoer dislikes a film, and trailers before the movie are standard.

However, your theaters recently went to the controversial policy of reducing power on the movie projector bulbs. Doing so cuts electricity costs and may prolong the life of the expensive bulbs. For most films, the difference in screen quality is negligible, but for films with

dark cinematography, like horror movies, some scenes are difficult to see.

Though the tone of Mr. McCann's letter offends you, he might have a valid point about the screen quality. Therefore, you are willing to offer him a 50% discount on his next ticket purchase.

Write a letter to Mr. McCann informing him of your decision.

11.12 A Difficult Negative Message—Taking Away Extra Pay (LO 11-1 to LO 11-6)

Your organization employs far more part-time than full-time workers. Part-timers are paid hourly, up to 15 hours per week, and full-timers are salaried under contract for 40 hours per week.

Both groups share many job responsibilities, though full-timers are also expected to take leadership roles that require their attendance in meetings, on committees, and at community programs. For part-timers, participation is voluntary. To encourage more part-timers to participate, though, one of your managers decided to start paying them extra for their attendance.

Now several full-timers are protesting the move. While they are sympathetic to paying part-timers for additional time, the full-timers note their duties often require them to spend more than 40 hours per week on the job. Because raises and promotions are tied to manager evaluations, they believe they are being pressured to participate without additional compensation. Paying

part-timers but not full-timers for extra time only exacerbates the situation.

The manager believes that part-timers are already underpaid for doing many of the same duties as full-timers, that full-timers should be grateful to have jobs with benefits, and that full-timers should be motivated by more than money to attend. The full-timers should be held to a higher standard as role models for the part-timers.

You checked with your Human Resources Department and found that because attendance by part-timers is voluntary, paying them extra is inappropriate. In addition, recent high-profile lawsuits for overtime pay have resulted in even salaried workers expecting compensation for work beyond 40 hours per week. Therefore, you must end the program started by the manager and find a way to reign in the extra hours full-timers may be working.

Write a memo informing all employees that the extra pay program will end in two weeks.

11.13 Announcing the Elimination of a Position (LO 11-1 to LO 11-6)

Your organization is facing a significant budget shortfall, and in addition to cuts in office supplies and the travel budget, your department must eliminate one position. Though you can make a case for keeping everyone in the department, you have no choice, and the only position that seems possible to cut is Robin's, the department secretary. After much deliberation, you decide to eliminate the position.

Now you must announce this decision to the department. You expect people to be troubled because Robin is a popular and hard worker and has been with the department for three years. There's more, though. Once Robin's position is eliminated, the work must still be done. That means the rest of the staff will have to help cover the phones, make their own copies, process their own paperwork, create files and archive them, and so forth. People are already used to typing their own correspondence, but they will also have to make sure copies are properly filed. People will have to take turns sorting the mail. The list of Robin's duties goes on.

Write an e-mail message to the staff informing them that Robin's last day is in two weeks and that the changes to cover her work will go into effect then.

Hints:

- Think about the emotional impact losing a colleague can have on the department. How can you help soften the blow? What fears might people have about their own job security?
- Care must be taken to avoid the impression that Robin is being let go for any other reason than the budget. Keep in mind, however, that confidentiality issues may affect what you can say and how much.
- You like Robin and regret having to eliminate the position, but is it wise to criticize the company or appear irritated by the decision?

11.14 Telling Retirees They Must Switch to HMOs (LO 11-1 to LO 11-6)

Your company has traditionally provided health insurance not only to employees but also to retirees who have worked for the company for at least 20 years at the time of retirement.

Seven years ago, you cut costs for employee health insurance by switching from open-ended insurance to health maintenance organizations (HMOs). At that time, you kept open-ended insurance for retirees because your employees told you that retirees wanted to keep their current doctors. But the high cost of that program gives you no choice: to continue to insure retirees, you must hold down costs, and HMOs offer the best way of doing that.

Under the current plan, the retiree pays 20% of all costs (up to a yearly ceiling of $10,000 and a lifetime ceiling of $100,000) and you pay 80%. In an HMO, more costs will be covered. Routine doctors' visits, for example, charge only a $10 co-payment. Most tests, such as mammograms, X-rays, and blood work, are covered 100%. Hospitalization is covered completely, and there's much less paperwork. By presenting one's card when one fills a prescription, one pays only the copayment, rather than having to pay the entire amount and then filing for partial reimbursement later.

The bad news for retirees is that they have to go to a physician listed with the HMO. If the current physician is not on the list, the retiree will have to switch doctors to retain benefits. Furthermore, the primary care physician must refer the patient to any other health care providers. That is, someone who wants to see a specialist or go to the emergency room must call the primary care physician first. Primary care physicians always approve such referrals whenever they seem medically advisable, but the requirement does limit the patient's freedom. Further, since HMOs are paid a flat fee and therefore have an incentive to give care that costs less than that fee, some people fear that HMOs will be reluctant to prescribe expensive treatments, even when those treatments are essential.

Your company offers a choice of HMOs. Informational meetings will be held next month for retirees (and anyone else who wishes to attend) to explain the various options. Retirees must return a card within two months, indicating which plan they prefer. The card will be enclosed in the mailing. Anyone who does not return a card will be assigned a plan by the company.

As vice president for human resources, write a form letter to all retirees, explaining the change and telling them how to indicate which HMO they prefer.

Hints:

- Choose a business, government, or nonprofit organization that you know something about.
- About how many retirees do you have? What percentage are "young old" (under 80, in reasonably good health)? What percentage are "old old" (80 and over, sometimes with more serious health problems)?
- How well educated are your retirees? How easy will it be for them to understand the HMO options?
- What times would be convenient for the retirees to come to meetings? Should you have extra times for them, beyond those you've scheduled for employees?

11.15 Telling a Customer an Item Is No Longer Available (LO 11-1 to LO 11-6)

You manage the customer service department for an online company that sells discontinued and out-of-season items from department stores at a discount. Your web page operates 24 hours a day, and you frequently have sales to attract customers to the site. Therefore, the items being offered and their prices can change without warning.

Recently, you received this e-mail message from a customer:

I'm a member of the National Teacher's Federation, which entitles me to a 15% discount on items ordered at your site. Last night, I tried to order a leather chaise lounge. I added the item to my shopping cart, but the discount was not applied. I tried again and got the same result. When I went to the "Online Help" link, an error message said the help function was unavailable. Therefore, I'm contacting you by e-mail.

Would you help me order the chaise with my discount? The item number is 234323ALC2. I'd like it in black, please.

The chaise is a college graduation gift for my daughter, and I've been searching for one like it for months. Right now, you're the only vendor who carries this chaise, so any help you can provide would be much appreciated!

Thank you.

Macy Bergman

You've researched Ms. Bergman's claim and found that she did try to order the chaise the previous evening. While you have no record that the Online Help function was unavailable, it has crashed before.

However, the chaise has already sold out. You can see from the time stamp that two were available when Ms. Bergman e-mailed. The last one sold an hour before you got her message. You've researched the history of the chaise and found that it is part of a discontinued line. You don't expect to get any more.

You can offer her a similar chair in brown leather and give her a coupon worth 5% off (on top of any other discount) on future orders. However, there is nothing you can do about the black leather chaise.

Write a response to Ms. Bergman.

11.16 Rejecting a Suggestion (LO 11-1 to LO 11-6)

Your company has a suggestion system that encourages workers to submit suggestions that will save the organization money or improve safety, customer service, or morale. If a suggestion is accepted that will save the company money, its proposer gets 10% of the estimated first year's savings. If a suggestion is accepted but will not save money, the proposer gets $25. You chair the committee that makes the decisions.

Today, you must tell Wayne Andersen that the committee has rejected his suggestion to buy a second photocopying machine for the sales department. Wayne pointed out that the sales department occupies a whole floor, yet has only one copier. Although the copier is in the center of the room (by the coffee and vending machines), some people have to walk quite a distance to get to it. Of course, they often stop to talk to the people they pass. Wayne calculated how much time people waste walking to the copier and talking to co-workers multiplied by annual salaries compared to the shorter time needed to walk to one of two copiers, each located to serve half the floor. He calculated that the company could save the cost of a $10,000 machine in just six months, with a further $10,000 savings by the end of the first year.

No one on the committee liked Wayne's idea.

"I don't trust his numbers. After all, lots of people combine trips to the copier with a trip to get a cup of coffee or a cola. They'd do even more walking if they had to make two trips."

"He talks about people waiting in line to use the copier, but I'm in sales, and I know the copier really isn't used that much. Sure, there are some bottlenecks—especially when reports are due—but a lot of the time the machine just sits there."

"I'm worried about the economy. I don't think this is the time to spend money we don't have to spend."

"I guess his system would be more efficient. But the real savings comes not from less walking but from less talking. And I think we *want* people to talk to each other. Informal conversations are great for relieving stress, sharing ideas, and strengthening our loyalty to each other and to the company."

"I agree. I think our company is built on informal interchange and a sense that you don't have to account for every single minute. Our people are almost all on salary; they stay overtime without any extra pay. If someone wants to take a break and talk to someone, I think that's OK."

"Well, sometimes we do waste time talking. But his idea isn't really new. Lots of people think we could save money by buying more of every kind of equipment. Even if we get a copier, I don't think he should get any money."

You pointed out that even if a new copier didn't save as much money as Wayne predicted, it would shorten the lines when lots of people have copying to do. You suggested adopting his suggestion but reducing the estimated savings and therefore the award. But the committee rejected your compromise and the suggestion. As chair of the committee, you vote only to break a tie.

Write a message to Wayne, reporting the committee's decision.

Hints:

- What reason(s) should you give for the committee's decision?
- Should you tell Wayne that you disagreed with the majority?
- How can you encourage Wayne to continue to submit suggestions?

11.17 Announcing Cost-Savings Measures (LO 11-1 to LO 11-6)

Your company has to cut costs but would prefer to avoid laying off workers. Therefore, you have adopted the following money-saving ideas. Some can be implemented immediately; some will be implemented at renewal dates. The company will no longer pay for

- Flowers at the receptionist's desk and in executive offices.
- Skyboxes for professional sporting events.
- Employees' dues for professional and trade organizations.
- Liquor at business meals.

Only essential business travel will be approved. The company will pay only for the lowest cost of air travel (coach, reservation 7 to 14 days in advance).

The company will no longer buy tables or blocks of tickets for charitable events and will not make any donations to charity until money is less tight.

11.18 Closing Bill-Payment Offices (LO 11-1 to LO 11-6)

For many years, City Gas & Electric had five suburban offices to which people could take their payments. On the first of the month following next month, you're closing these offices. On that date, 100 local merchants, such as grocers, will begin to accept utility payments. Closing the freestanding

Counters will be put on the photocopiers. People must have access numbers to make photocopies; personal photocopies will cost $ .10 a page.

As the chief financial officer, write a memo to all employees, explaining the changes.

offices will save your company almost $3 million a year. Customers will still be able to mail in payments or have them deducted automatically from their paychecks.

Write a notice that can be inserted in utility bills this month and next month.

11.19 Giving a Customer Less Credit than She Wants (LO 11-1 to LO 11-6)

Yang-Ming Lee applied for your Visa card, asking for a credit limit of $15,000 and a separate card for her husband, Chad Hoang. Her credit references merit granting a credit card. But you generally give new customers only a $7,500 limit, even when the family income is very high, as it is in this case. You might make an exception if your bank had a

previous relationship with the client, but no such relationship exists here. While you have no set policy for reviewing and raising credit limits, normally you would expect at least six months of paying the minimum amount promptly.

Write a letter to Ms. Lee, granting her a credit card with a $7,500 limit.

11.20 Addressing an Allegation about Racism by Employees (LO 11-1 to LO 11-6)

You are the human resources director for Kelly Green's Midwest division. Two of your employees stand accused

of being racist toward a customer. In the customer's letter to you, she states,

---

Today I visited your Kelly Green apparel store in downtown Chicago. In what was probably the most disturbing experience of my life—and I'm a 45-year-old registered nurse—the male clerk decided to verbally attack me, saying, "I really hope you can speak English" and "I don't think someone like you can afford our merchandise." He said this soon after I entered the store.

When I went to try on the silk blouse I'd come to purchase, I heard him outside the dressing room chanting, "Ching chong, ching chong." There was also a female clerk on duty, and I heard them both laughing.

I've been shopping at that Kelly Green store for two years. I've never seen either employee before, and I've certainly never been treated there like this in the past. When my family emigrated to the United States from the Philippines 60 years ago, they met prejudice, but I don't think they could have imagined that in this day and age Americans would still be so pointlessly vicious to other Americans.

I'm not writing to you with the expectation of being compensated nor to threaten a lawsuit. I simply want you to know that you have employees whose idea of civility is deeply flawed. The clerks are young, and I hope you can use this experience to teach them a better understanding of the dignity all people deserve.

Thank you.

Lila Oranto

P.S. I'd still like to shop at Kelly Green, but I'll be driving 30 miles out of my way to avoid returning to that store.

You are understandably shocked by the letter, and your shock grows to dismay when you discover the surveillance video that could provide a visual record of the event has been anonymously erased.

The clerks in question, one a 19-year-old male and the other a 21-year-old female, were both hired at the same time and only a month before. But already the male clerk has been warned about arriving to work late twice, and the female clerk was involved in an argument with a customer over a return.

Kelly Green has a strong policy against discrimination of customers as well as employees, but other than the word of the customer, you have no conclusive proof that the

clerks behaved so inappropriately. They both deny the incident happened. The manager who ordinarily would have been in the store was on her way back from making the afternoon deposit at the bank. At the same time, you see no reason to disbelieve the customer, whose thoughtful tone in particular impresses you.

Your solution, although imperfect, is to document the alleged incident in both clerks' personnel files, along with a reprimand to everyone on duty that day for the surveillance video being erased. In addition to that, you are requiring that all employees in the store attend diversity training.

Write a letter to Ms. Oranto explaining what will be done.

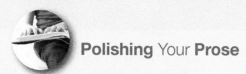

Polishing Your Prose

Parallel Structure

Use parallel structure in lists, headings, and subheadings in documents by using the same grammatical form for ideas that have the same relationship in your sentence. Parallel structure is particularly important in business communication, whose bulleted, vertical lists make parallelism errors obvious.

Not parallel: Good reports are factual, logical, and demonstrate clarity.

It may be easier to see faulty parallelism by listing vertically parts that need to be parallel. Check to make sure each component fits with the words that introduce the list.

Not parallel: Good reports are
Factual
Logical
Demonstrate clarity

Parallel: Good reports are
Factual
Logical
Clear

Make sure all of the list is horizontal or vertical. Don't start a list horizontally and finish it vertically.

Incorrect: As department manager, I supervised eight employees.
• Wrote the department budget.
• Presented our sales strategy to the board of directors.

Correct: As department manager, I supervised eight employees, wrote the department budget, and presented our sales strategy to the board of directors.

Also correct: As department manager, I
• Supervised eight employees.
• Wrote the department budget.
• Presented our sales strategy to the board of directors.

Headings must be parallel throughout the document, but subheads need only be parallel to other subheads in the same section.

Not parallel: Should Ogden Industries Purchase Blue Chip International?
• Short-Term Costs
• What Are Long-Term Gains?

Parallel: Should Ogden Industries Purchase Blue Chip International?
• Short-Term Costs
• Long-Term Gains

In addition to grammatical parallelism, also check your sentences for logical parallelism.

Incorrect: The group ranges from males and females to people in their 20s, 30s, and 40s.
Better: We interviewed men and women ranging in age from 20 to 50.

Gender is one category; age is another.

Exercises

Rewrite the following sentences or headings to make them parallel.

1. Tanika sent copies of the memo to Accounting, the Public Relations Department, the folks in Marketing, and even Purchasing.
2. Some of the undeserved groups in the United States include African Americans, Chinese, Native Americans, and Mexicans.
3. Jayden e-mailed to let us know that customers in our south, north side, and western offices could use more supplies.
4. The awards committee includes Lucas, Mr. Guy Elizondo, Su Yen, Dan "the Man" Jeffries, and Kyle Abrahms.
5. When Esther came to fix the copier, she pointed out that it needed a new toner cartridge, one of those trays for paper, and the replacement of its keypad.
6. We're planning on traveling to Seattle; Columbus, Ohio; the capital of Michigan, and lovely and historic Charleston this year.
7. Make sure you order supplies for the strategic planning retreat: pens, paper, one of those giant notepads, some markers, Post-it Notes, some file folders, and that tape that is sticky on both sides.
8. The best supervisors
   • listen to employees,
   • are really good at valuing diversity in the workplace, and
   • they are moral.
9. Bailey, Valdez, and Shepherd expect to open sales offices in the following countries:
   a. Brazil.
   b. Beautiful Argentina.
   • Our neighbor to the south, Mexico.
   • El Salvador.
10. Issues to consider before making a final commitment:
    a. How does the contract affect the bottom line?
    b. When the contract will take effect.

Check your answers to the odd-numbered exercises at the back of the book.

Persuasive Messages

12

Module 12 shows you how to write successful persuasive messages. After completing the module, you should be able to

LO 12-1	**Compare strategies for persuasive messages.**	**LO 12-5**	**Recognize techniques for more persuasive messages.**
LO 12-2	**Create subject lines for persuasive messages.**	**LO 12-6**	**Apply strategies for common ground solutions.**
LO 12-3	**Apply strategies for persuasive message organization.**	**LO 12-7**	**List common kinds of persuasive messages.**
LO 12-4	**Identify solutions for objections.**	**LO 12-8**	**Apply strategies for persuasive message analysis with PAIBOC.**

In the 21st century, businesses depend more and more on persuasion and "buy-in" to get quality work done. You can command people to make widgets. You can't command people to be creative. And even if you're making widgets, just going through the motions isn't enough. You want people to make high-quality widgets while reducing scrap and other costs. Internal commitment is needed to make that happen.

External motivation doesn't last. Some people will buy a certain brand of pizza if they have a "2 for the price of 1" coupon. But if the coupon expires, or if another company offers the same deal, customers may leave. In contrast, if customers like your pizza better—in other words, if they are motivated internally to choose it—then you may keep your customers even if another company comes in with a lower price.

When a group of students bullied school bus monitor Karen Huff Klein, going so far as to post videos online, they may have thought they were getting the last laugh. Cruel comments like "You're so ugly, your kids should kill themselves" were especially horrific to people who knew that Klein had lost a son to suicide 10 years earlier. After news of the attacks made national headlines, however, outraged and sympathetic donors contributed hundreds of thousands of dollars to a vacation fund set up for Klein. The students were punished. *Cyberbaiting*, a form of bullying where students provoke teachers and other authority figures and then post the results online, is on the rise now that cell phone cameras are so prolific. Bullying generates many results, including ones bullies may not anticipate. Remember, persuasive techniques can be used to any end—think about why you are using them in addition to how.

Sources: Susan Stump, "School Bus Monitor Doesn't Want 'Really Nasty' Kids Charged," *The Today Show,* June 21, 2012, http://today.msnbc.msn.com/id/47896993/ns/today-today_news/t/school-bus-monitor-doesnt-want-really-nasty-kids-charged/; and Susan Donaldson James, "Cyberbaiting on the Rise as Teacher Tantrums Posted to YouTube," *Good Morning America,* January 3, 2012, http://gma.yahoo.com/cyberbaiting-rise-teacher-tantrums-posted-youtube-213036412.html.

Persuasive messages include

- Orders and requests.
- Proposals and recommendations.
- Sales and fund-raising letters.
- Job application letters.
- Reports, if they recommend action.
- Efforts to change people's behavior, such as collection letters, criticisms or performance appraisals where you want the subordinate to improve behavior, and public-service ads designed to reduce drunken driving, drug use, and so on.

All persuasive messages have several purposes:

Primary Purposes:

- To have the reader act.
- To provide enough information so that the reader knows exactly what to do.
- To overcome any objections that might prevent or delay action.

Secondary Purposes:

- To build a good image of the writer.
- To build a good image of the writer's organization.
- To cement a good relationship between the writer and reader.
- To reduce or eliminate future correspondence on the same subject so the message doesn't create more work for the writer.

What is the best persuasive strategy?   LO 12-1

▶ *It depends on how much and what kinds of resistance you expect.*

Four basic short-term strategies exist: direct request, problem-solving persuasion, sales,[1] and reward and punishment. This book will focus on the first two strategies. Rewards and punishment have limited use, in part because they don't produce permanent change and because they produce psychological reactance (◀◀ p. 169). For a major change—such as restoring public confidence in CPA firms and in the stock market—no single message will work. You will need a campaign with a series of messages, preferably from a variety of sources.

Use the **direct request pattern** when

- The audience will do as you ask without any resistance.
- You need a response only from the people who are willing to act.
- The audience is busy and may not read all the messages received.
- Your organization's culture prefers direct requests.

Use the **problem-solving pattern** when

- The audience is likely to object to doing as you ask.
- You need action from everyone.
- You trust the audience to read the entire message.
- You expect logic to be more important than emotion in the decision.

A strategy that works in one organization may not work somewhere else. James Suchan and Ron Dulek point out that Digital Equipment's corporate culture values no-holds-barred aggressiveness: "Even if opposition is expected, a subordinate should write a proposal in a forceful, direct manner."[2] In another organization with different cultural values, an employee who used a hard sell for a request antagonized the boss.[3]

Corporate culture (◀◀ p. 28) isn't written down; it's learned by imitation and observation. What style do high-level people in your organization use? When you show a draft

The Advertising Council creates public service ads. Here, an ad for the Arab American Institute uses emotional appeal to build a common ground and persuade people to reject hate.

Site to See

Go to

http://www. entrepreneur.com/ sales/salestechniques/ article53856.html

for seven tips on writing sales letters.

Site to See

Go to

www.rice.edu/wetlands

Difficult situations arise when multiple stakeholders in an issue have different—perhaps contradictory—points of view. This website, created by faculty and graduate students at Rice University, presents documents, maps, and reports that led to a successful resolution.

to your boss, are you told to tone down your statements or to make them stronger? Role models and advice are two of the ways organizations communicate their cultures to newcomers.

Different ethnic and national cultures also have different preferences for gaining compliance. In one study, students who were native speakers of American English judged direct statements ("Do this"; "I want you to do this") clearer and more effective than questions ("Could you do this?") or hints ("This is needed"). Students who were native speakers of Korean, in contrast, judged direct statements to be *least* effective. In the Korean culture, the study's authors claim, the more direct a request is, the ruder and therefore less effective it is.[4]

What is the best subject line for a persuasive message? LO 12-2

▶ *For direct requests, use the request, the topic, or a question.*
▶ *For problem-solving messages, use a directed subject line or a reader benefit.*

In a direct request, put the request, the topic of the request, or a question in the subject line.

Subject: Request for Updated Software

My copy of HomeNet does not accept the aliases for Magnus accounts.

FYI

"Don't kill the messenger" could certainly apply to Maya society. Before being executed, the scribes of defeated kings often also had their fingers broken, a symbolic muting of their ability to "speak" persuasively on behalf of their leader.

Source: Jeff Grabmeier, "Among the Mayas, Writers for Defeated Kings Met a Cruel Fate," *The Ohio State University Research News,* August 20, 2001, downloaded at http://researchnews.osu.edu/ archive/mayans.htm.

Instant Replay

Use the **direct request** pattern when

- The audience will do as you ask without any resistance.
- You need a response only from the people who are willing to act.
- The audience is busy and may not read all the messages received.
- Your organization's culture prefers direct requests.

Use the **problem-solving pattern** when

- The audience is likely to object to doing as you ask.
- You need action from everyone.
- You trust the audience to read the entire message.
- You expect logic to be more important than emotion in the decision.

Choose the correct persuasive approach for your audience. When Anne Mulcahy, the former chair and CEO of Xerox, decided to purchase a Porsche, she faced two annoyances: the salesperson who assumed she needed to talk to someone, presumably a husband, before making the purchase, and the finance officer, who asked if she needed someone to co-sign her lease. Their attitudes nearly persuaded Mulcahy to drive to another dealership. The situation reminded her of her youth, when, she said, "I was working and was totally financially secure, but I'd have to get co-signatures on my loans because it was the 1970s. Then it was discrimination. Now it's just stupidity."

(continued)

> Subject: Status of Account #3548–003
>
> Please get me the following information about account #3548–003.

> Subject: Do We Need an Additional Training Session in October?
>
> The two training sessions scheduled for October will accommodate 40 people. Last month, you said that 57 new staff accountants had been hired. Should we schedule an additional training session in October? Or can the new hires wait until the next regularly scheduled session in February?

When you have a reluctant reader, putting the request in the subject line just gets a quick *no* before you've had a chance to give all your arguments. One option is to use a **directed subject line** that makes your stance on the issue clear.[5] In the following examples, the first is the most neutral. The remaining two increasingly reveal the writer's preference.

> Subject: A Proposal to Change the Formula for Calculating Retirees' Benefits

> Subject: Arguments for Expanding the Marysville Plant

> Subject: Why Cassano's Should Close Its West Side Store

Another option is to use common ground or a reader benefit—something that shows readers that this message will help them.

> Subject: Reducing Energy Costs in the New Orleans Office

> Energy costs in our New Orleans office have risen 12% in the last three years, even though the cost of gas has fallen and the cost of electricity has risen only 5%.

Although your first paragraph may be negative in a problem-solving message, your subject line should be neutral or positive to show that you are solving a problem, not just reporting one.

Both directed subject lines and benefit subject lines can also be used as report titles.

How should I organize persuasive messages?   LO 12-3

▶ *In direct requests, start with the request.*
▶ *In a problem-solving message, start with the problem you share.*

Start with the request only when you anticipate ready agreement, when you fear that a busy reader may not read a message whose relevance isn't clear, or when your organization's culture prefers direct requests.

Writing Direct Requests

When you expect quick agreement, save the reader's time by presenting the request directly.

1. **Consider asking immediately for the information or service you want.** Delay the request if it seems too abrupt or if you have several purposes in the message.
2. **Give readers all the information and details they will need to act on your request.** Number your questions or set them off with bullets so the reader can check to see that all of them have been answered.

   In a claim (where a product is under warranty or a shipment was defective), explain the circumstances so that the reader knows what happened. Be sure to include all the relevant details: date of purchase, model or invoice number, and so on.

   In more complicated direct requests, anticipate possible responses. Suppose you're asking for information about equipment meeting certain specifications. Explain which criteria are most important so that the reader can recommend an alternative if no single product meets all your needs. You may also want to tell the reader what your price constraints are and ask whether the item is in stock or must be special ordered.
3. **Ask for the action you want.** Do you want a check? A replacement? A catalogue? Answers to your questions? If you need an answer by a certain time, say so. If possible, show the reader why the time limit is necessary.

Figure 12.1 summarizes this pattern. Figure 12.2 illustrates the pattern as did the claim letter in Figure 9.4 (◄◄ p. 131). Note that direct requests do not contain reader benefits and do not need to overcome objections: They simply ask for what is needed.

Direct requests should be direct. Don't make the reader guess what you want.

Indirect request: Is there a newer version of the 2008 *Accounting Reference Manual?*
Direct request: If there is a newer version of the 2008 *Accounting Reference Manual,* please send it to me.

In some direct requests, your combination of purposes may suggest a different organization. For example, in a letter asking an employer to reimburse you for expenses after a job interview, you'd want to thank your hosts for their hospitality and cement the good impression you made at the interview. To do that, you'd spend the first several paragraphs talking about the trip and the interview. Only in the last third of the letter (or even in the postscript) would you put your request for reimbursement.

Similarly, in a letter asking about a graduate program, a major purpose might be to build a good image of yourself so that your application for financial aid would be viewed positively. To achieve that goal, provide information about your qualifications and interest in the field as well as ask questions.

Organizing Problem-Solving Messages

Use an indirect approach and the problem-solving pattern of organization when you expect resistance from your reader but can show that doing what you want will solve

Even reasonable requests from credible sources can meet resistance. Appeals by the captain of a Continental Express jet diverted by weather to Rochester, Minnesota, to let her passengers enter the terminal went unheeded, stranding them for six hours aboard the cramped plane. The Transportation Security Administration (TSA) later blamed Mesaba Airlines, a subsidiary of Delta Air Lines. Its staff, the only ones on duty in the terminal at the time, believed because there were no TSA personnel available, passengers could not deplane. However, regulations allowed for passengers to be taken to a secure area.

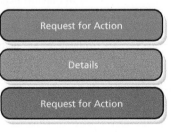

Figure 12.1 How to Organize a Direct Request

Request for Action

Details

Request for Action

Figure 12.2 A Direct Request

BCS Interoffice Memo
Keep each message to one topic.

Date: May 15, 2012

To: Michael Antonucci

From: David Anthony, Chair, BCS Suggestion Committee

Subject: Suggestion #97204 *Topic of request in subject line*

Please evaluate the attached suggestion by May 29. *Put request in ¶ 1.*

Spell out subquestions.
• Should BCS adopt it? Why or why not?
• Will it save the company money? If so, how much a year?
• If the suggestion is adopted, how large an award should be given?

Make action easy. You may put your answers and brief reasons for them at the bottom of this page or send them to me by e-mail (anthony.37@bcs.com). Please get your response in *Ask for the action you want.* by May 29 as the suggestion committee is meeting on May 30.

Thanks! *Reason to act promptly*

a problem you and your reader share. This pattern allows you to disarm opposition by showing all the reasons in favor of your position before you give your readers a chance to say *no*.

1. **Describe the problem you both share (which your request will solve).** Present the problem objectively: Don't assign blame or mention personalities.
2. **Give the details of the problem.** Be specific about the cost in money, time, lost goodwill, and so on. You have to convince readers that *something* has to be done before you can convince them that your solution is the best one.
3. **Explain the solution to the problem.** If you know that the reader will favor another solution, start with that solution and show why it won't work before you present your solution.

   Present your solution without using the words *I* or *my*. Don't let personalities enter the picture; don't let the reader think he or she should say *no* just because you've had other requests accepted recently.
4. **Show that any negative elements (cost, time, etc.) are outweighed by the advantages.**
5. **Summarize any additional benefits of the solution.** The main benefit— solving the problem—can be presented briefly since you described the problem in detail. However, if there are any additional benefits, mention them.
6. **Ask for the action you want.** Often your reader will authorize or approve something; other people will implement the action. Give your reader a reason to act promptly, perhaps offering a new reader benefit. ("By buying now, we can avoid the next quarter's price hikes.")

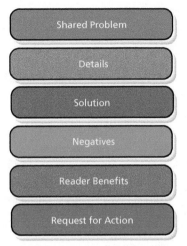

Figure 12.3 How to Organize a Problem-Solving Persuasive Message

Figure 12.3 summarizes the pattern. Figure 12.4 implements the pattern. Reader benefits can be brief in this kind of message because the biggest benefit comes from solving the problem.

How do I identify and overcome objections?   LO 12-4

▶ *Talk to your audience. Then try these strategies.*

The easiest way to learn about objections your audience may have is to ask knowledgeable people in your organization or your town.

- **Phrase your questions nondefensively,** in a way that doesn't lock people into taking a stand on an issue: "What concerns would you have about a proposal to do *x?*" "Who makes a decision about *y?*" "What do you like best about [the supplier or practice you want to change]?"
- **Ask follow-up questions** to be sure you understand: "Would you be likely to stay with your current supplier if you could get a lower price from someone else? Why?"

People are likely to be most aware of and willing to share objective concerns such as time and money. They will be less willing to tell you that their real objection is emotional. Readers have a **vested interest** in something if they benefit directly from keeping things as they are. People who are in power have a vested interest in retaining the system that gives them their power. Someone who designed a system has a vested interest in protecting that system from criticism. To admit that the system has faults is to admit that the designer made mistakes. In such cases, you'll need to probe to find out what the real reasons are.

The best way to deal with an objection is to eliminate it. To sell Jeep Cherokees in Japan, Mitsuru Sato convinced Chrysler to put the driver's seat on the right side, to make an extra preshipment quality check, and to rewrite the instruction booklet in Japanese style, with big diagrams and cartoons.[6]

If an objection is false or based on misinformation, give the response to the objection without naming the objection. In a persuasive brochure, you can present responses with a "question/answer" format. When objections have already been voiced, you may want to name the objection so that your audience realizes that you are responding to that specific

Instant Replay

Organizing a Direct Request

1. Consider asking for the information or service you want.
2. Give readers all the information or details they will need to act on your request.
3. Ask for the action you want.

President Barack Obama, dogged by rumors that he is not a U.S. citizen despite releasing in 2008 a certificate of live birth from Hawaii, did provide a copy of his long form birth certificate a few years later. Nonetheless, detractors continued to cast doubts, with billionaire Donald Trump going so far as to initially comment, "We have to see if it's real, if it's proper." While Trump added that he thought the document likely was real, others with a vested interest in another point of view insist it is a digitally altered fake.

Source: Rachel Rose Hartman, "White House Releases Obama Birth Certificate," April 27, 2011, http://news.yahoo.com/s/yblog_theticket/20110427/ts_yblog_theticket/white-house-releases-obama-birth-certificate.

Figure 12.4 A Problem-Solving Persuasive Message

Memorandum

February 15, 2013

To: All Staff Members

From: Melissa J. Gutridge *MJG*

Subject: Why We Are Implementing a New Sign-Out System

Directed subject line indicates action writer will ask for to solve the problem.

Shared problem

Successfully mainstreaming our clients into the community is very important, and daily interaction with the public is necessary. Our clients enjoy the times they get to go to the mall or out to lunch instead of remaining here all day.   Recently, however, clients have been taken out on activities without a staff member's knowing where the client is and whom the client is with.

Specific example of problem

We need to know where all clients are at all times because social workers, psychologists, and relatives constantly stop by unannounced. Last week, Janet's father stopped by to pick her up for a doctor's appointment, and she was not here. No one knew where she was or whom she was with. Naturally her father was very upset and wanted to know what kind of program we were running. Staff members' not knowing where our clients are and whom they are with is damaging to the good reputation of our staff and program.

Solution presented impersonally

Additional reader benefit

Starting Monday, February 25, a sign-out board will be located by Betty's desk. Please write down where you and the client are going and when you expect to be back. When signing out, help clients sign themselves out. We can turn this into a learning experience for our clients. Then when a social worker stops by to see someone who isn't here, we can simply look at the sign-out board to tell where the client is and when he or she will return.

Ask for action.

Please help keep up the superb reputation you have helped Weststar earn as a quality center for adults with handicaps. Sign out yourself and clients at all times.

objection. However, to avoid solidifying the opposition, don't attribute the objection to your audience. Instead, use a less personal attribution: "Some people wonder . . ."; "Some citizens are afraid that . . ."

If real objections remain, try one or more of the following strategies to counter objections:

1. Specify how much time and/or money is required—it may not be as much as the reader fears.

Distributing flyers to each house or apartment in your neighborhood will probably take two afternoons.

If you can't overcome an objection, admit it. A potential client asked Evonne Weinhaus, "Do you really do anything new in your training?" She looked him in the eye and said, "No, I don't. I just add a twist." After a moment of silence, he said, "That's good. There is nothing new out there, and if you had said 'yes' this lunch would have been over immediately!" They talked about her approach and her "twist" on sales training. The potential client became a real client, signing up for 26 workshops.

2. Put the time and/or money in the context of the benefits they bring.

> The additional $152,500 will (1) allow The Open Shelter to remain open 24 rather than 16 hours a day, (2) pay for three social workers to help men find work and homes, and (3) keep the Neighborhood Bank open, so that men don't have to cash Social Security checks in bars and so that they can save up the $800 they need to have up front to rent an apartment.

3. Show that money spent now will save money in the long run.

> By replacing the boiler now, we'll no longer have to release steam that the overflow tank can't hold. Depending on how severe the winter is, we could save $100 to $750 a year in energy costs. If energy costs rise, we'll save even more.

4. Show that doing as you ask will benefit some cause or group the reader supports, even though the action may not help the reader directly.

> By being a Big Brother or a Big Sister, you'll give a child the adult attention he or she needs to become a well-adjusted, productive adult.

5. Show the reader that the sacrifice is necessary to achieve a larger, more important goal to which he or she is committed.

> These changes will mean more work for all of us. But we've got to cut our costs 25% to keep the plant open and to keep our jobs.

Instant Replay

Organizing a Problem-Solving Message

1. Describe a problem you both share (which your request will solve).
2. Give the details of the problem.
3. Explain the solution to the problem.
4. Show that any negative elements (cost, time, etc.) are outweighed by the advantages.
5. Summarize any additional benefits of the solution.
6. Ask for the action you want.

6. Show that the advantages as a group outnumber or outweigh the disadvantages as a group.

> None of the locations is perfect. But the Backbay location gives us the most advantages and the fewest disadvantages.

7. Turn a disadvantage into an opportunity.

> With the hiring freeze, every department will need more lead time to complete its own work. By hiring another person, the Planning Department could provide that lead time.

What other techniques can make my messages more persuasive? LO 12-5

▶ *Build credibility and emotional appeal. Use the right tone, and offer a reason to act promptly.*

Persuasive messages—whether short-term or long-term—will be more effective if you build credibility and emotional appeal, use the right tone, and offer a reason to act promptly.

Build Credibility

Credibility is the audience's response to you as the source of the message. People are more easily persuaded by someone they see as expert, powerful, attractive, or trustworthy. A sexual abstinence program in Atlanta was effective in large part because the lessons on how to say *no* without hurting the other person's feelings were presented by teenagers slightly older than the students in the program. Adults would have been much less credible.[7]

When you don't yet have the credibility that comes from being an expert or being powerful, build credibility by the language and strategy you use:

- **Be factual.** Don't exaggerate.
- **Be specific.** If you say "X is better," show in detail *how* it is better. Show the reader exactly where the savings or other benefits come from so that it's clear the proposal really is as good as you say it is.
- **Be reliable.** If you suspect that a project will take longer to complete, cost more money, or be less effective than you originally thought, tell your audience *immediately.* Negotiate a new schedule that you can meet.

Build Emotional Appeal

Emotional appeal means making the reader *want* to do what you ask. People don't make decisions—even business decisions—based on logic alone. J. C. Mathes and Dwight W. Stevenson cite the following example. During his summer job, an engineering student who was asked to evaluate his company's waste treatment system saw a way that the system could be redesigned to save the company more than $200,000 a year. He wrote a report recommending the change and gave it to his boss. Nothing

Be sure to analyze all of your audiences carefully for the appropriate persuasive appeal. Tougher audiences require special consideration.

© Mike Baldwin / Cornered

"Excellent proposal. Let's take it upstairs and see if it flies."

Reprinted with permission of CartoonStock.com, www.cartoonstock.com.

happened. Why not? His supervisor wasn't about to send up a report that would require him to explain why *he'd* been wasting more than $200,000 a year of the company's money.[8]

Stories and psychological description (◀◀ p. 116) are effective ways of building emotional appeal. Emotional appeal works best when people want to be persuaded. Even when you need to provide statistics or numbers to convince the careful reader that your anecdote is a representative example, telling a story first makes your message more persuasive. Recent research suggests that stories are more persuasive because people remember them.[9]

Use the Right Tone

When you ask for action from people who report directly to you, you have several choices. Even orders ("Get me the Ervin file") and questions ("Do we have the third quarter numbers yet?") will work. When you need action from co-workers, superiors, or people outside the organization, you need to be more forceful but also more polite.

Avoiding messages that sound parental or preachy is often a matter of tone. Saying "Please" is a nice touch, especially to people on your level or outside the organization. Tone will also be better when you give reasons for your request.

Parental: Everyone is expected to comply with these regulations. I'm sure you can see that they are commonsense rules needed for our business.

Better: Even on casual days, visitors expect us to be professional. So leave the gym clothes at home!

When you write to people you know well, humor can work. Just make sure that the message isn't insulting to anyone who doesn't find the humor funny.

Building Common Ground   LO 12-6

A common ground avoids the me-against-you of some persuasive situations and suggests that both you and your audience have a mutual interest in solving the problems you face. To find a common ground, we analyze the audience; understand their biases, objections, and needs; and identify with them so we can make them identify with us. This analysis can be carried out in a cold, manipulative way. It can also be based on a respect for and sensitivity to the audience's position.

Readers are highly sensitive to manipulation. No matter how much you disagree, respect your audience's intelligence. Try to understand why they believe or do something and why they may object to your position. If you can understand your readers' initial positions, you'll be more effective—and you won't alienate your readers by talking down to them.

The best common grounds are specific. Often a negative—a problem the reader will want to solve—makes a good common ground.

Weak common ground:	This program has had some difficulty finding enough individuals to volunteer their services for the children. As a result, we are sometimes unable to provide the one-on-one mentoring that is our goal.
Improved common ground:	On five Sundays in the last three months, we've had too few volunteers to provide one-on-one mentoring. Last Sunday, we had just two college students to take eight children to the Museum of Science and Industry.

Generalizations are likely to bore the reader. Instead, use the idea behind the generalization to focus on something the reader cares about.

Weak common ground:	We all want this plant to be profitable.
Improved common ground:	We forfeited a possible $186,000 in profits last summer due to a 17% drop in productivity.

In your common ground, emphasize the parts of your proposal that fit with what your audience already does or believes. An employee of 3M wanted to develop laser disks. He realized that 3M's previous products were thin and flat: Scotch tape, Post-it Notes,™ magnetic tape. When he made his presentation to the group that chose new products for development, he held his prototype disk horizontally, so his audience saw a flat, thin object rather than a large, round, recordlike object. Making his project fit with the audience's previous experience was a subtle and effective emotional tool to make it easier for the audience to say *yes*.

Use audience analysis to evaluate possible common grounds. Suppose you want to install a system to play background music in a factory. To persuade management to pay for the system, a possible common ground would be increasing productivity. However, to persuade the union to pay for the system, you'd need a different common ground. Workers would see productivity as a way to get them to do more work for the same pay. A better common ground would be that the music would make the factory environment more pleasant.

When you want people to change their behavior, don't criticize them. Instead, show that you're on their side and that you and they have a mutual interest in solving a problem. Changing attitudes can be extremely difficult, but people can be receptive to changing behavior if they understand why.

Writing to superiors is trickier. You may want to tone down your request by using subjunctive verbs and explicit disclaimers that show you aren't taking a *yes* for granted.

Arrogant:	Based on this evidence, I expect you to give me a new computer.
Better:	If department funds permit, I would like a new computer.

Passive verbs and jargon sound stuffy. Use active imperatives—perhaps with "Please"—to create a friendlier tone.

Stuffy:	It is requested that you approve the above-mentioned action.
Better:	Please authorize us to create a new subscription letter.

Offer a Reason for the Reader to Act Promptly

The longer people delay, the less likely they are to carry through with the action they had decided to take. In addition, you want a fast response so you can go ahead with your own plans.

Request action by a specific date. Always give people at least a week or two: They have other things to do besides respond to your requests. Set deadlines in the middle of the month, if possible. If you say, "Please return this by March 1," people will think, "I don't need to do this till March." Ask for the response by February 28 instead. If you can use a response even after the deadline, say so. Otherwise, people who can't make the deadline may not respond at all.

Show why you need a quick response:

- **Show that the time limit is real.** Perhaps you need information quickly to use it in a report that has a due date. Perhaps a decision must be made by a certain date to catch the start of the school year, the holiday selling season, or an election campaign. Perhaps you need to be ready for a visit from out-of-town or international colleagues.
- **Show that acting now will save time or money.** If business is slow and your industry isn't doing well, then your company needs to act now (to economize, to better serve customers) in order to be competitive. If business is booming and everyone is making a profit, then your company needs to act now to get its fair share of the available profits.
- **Show the cost of delaying action.** Will labor or material costs be higher in the future? Will delay mean more money spent on repairing something that will still need to be replaced?

What are the most common kinds of persuasive messages?   LO 12-7

▶ *Orders, collection letters, performance appraisals, and letters of recommendation.*

Orders, collection letters, performance appraisals, and letters of recommendation are among the most common varieties of persuasive messages.

Orders

Orders may be written on forms, phoned in, or made by clicking boxes on the web. When you write an order,

- Be specific. Give model or page numbers, colors, finishes, and so forth.
- Tell the company what you want if that model number is no longer available.
- Double-check your arithmetic, and add sales tax and shipping charges.

Collection Letters

Most businesses find that phoning rather than writing results in faster payment. But as more and more companies install voice-mail systems, you may sometimes need to write letters when leaving messages doesn't work.

Collection letters ask customers to pay (as they have already agreed to do) for the goods and services they have already received. Good credit departments send a series of letters. Letters in the series should be only a week or two apart. Waiting a month between letters implies you're prepared to wait a long time—and the reader will be happy to oblige you!

Early letters are gentle, assuming that the reader intends to pay but has met with temporary reverses or has forgotten. However, the request should assume that the check has been mailed but did not arrive. A student who had not yet been reimbursed by a company for a visit to the company's office put the second request in the P.S. of a letter refusing a job offer:

> P.S. The check to cover my expenses when I visited your office in March hasn't come yet. Could you check to see whether you can find a record of it? The amount was $490 (airfare $290; hotel room $185; taxi $15).

If one or two early letters don't result in payment, call the customer to ask if your company has created a problem. It's possible you shipped something the customer didn't want or sent the wrong quantity. It's possible that the invoice arrived before the product and was filed and forgotten. It's possible that the invoice document is poorly designed, so customers set it aside until they can figure it out. If any of these situations apply, you'll build goodwill by solving the problem rather than arrogantly asking for payment.[10]

Middle letters are more assertive in asking for payment. Figure 9.2 (◄◄ p. 128) gives an example of a middle letter. Other middle letters offer to negotiate a schedule for repayment if the reader is not able to pay the whole bill immediately, may remind the reader of the importance of a good credit rating (which will be endangered if the bill remains unpaid), educate the reader about credit, and explain why the creditor must have prompt payment.

Unless you have firm evidence to the contrary, assume that readers have some legitimate reason for not yet paying. Even people who are "juggling" payments because they do not have enough money to pay all their bills or people who will put payment off as long as possible will respond more quickly if you do not accuse them. If a reader is offended by your assumption that he or she is dishonest, that anger can become an excuse to continue delaying payment.

Late letters threaten legal action if the bill is not paid. Under federal law, the writer cannot threaten legal action unless he or she actually intends to sue. Other regulations also spell out what a writer may and may not do in a late letter.

Many small businesses find that establishing personal relationships with customers is the best way to speed payment.

Performance Appraisals

At regular intervals, supervisors evaluate, or appraise, the performance of their subordinates. In most organizations, employees have access to their files; sometimes they must sign the appraisal to show they've read it. The superior normally meets with the subordinate to discuss the appraisal.

Figure 12.5 shows a performance appraisal for a member of a student collaborative group.

As a subordinate, you should prepare for the appraisal interview by listing your achievements and goals. Where do you want to be in a year or five years? What training and experience do you need to reach your goals? Also think about any weaknesses. If you need training, advice, or support from the organization to improve, the appraisal interview is a good time to ask for this help.

Appraisals need to both protect the organization and motivate the employee. These two purposes conflict. Most of us will see a candid appraisal as negative; we need praise and reassurance to believe we're valued and can do better. But the praise that motivates someone to improve can come back to haunt the company if the person does not eventually do acceptable work. An organization is in trouble if it tries to fire someone whose evaluations never mention mistakes.

Jonathan A. Segal points out errors managers make when doing performance appraisals. Among them are stereotyping, one-sided dialogue, and using labels rather than behaviors. One, the "like me bias," is so problematic the U.S. Equal Employment Opportunity Commission created a task force to investigate its effect on the workplace. The bias occurs when managers unconsciously hire and then sometimes evaluate employees more favorably simply because they remind the managers of themselves.

Source: Jonathan A. Segal, "The Dirty Dozen Performance Appraisal Errors," *Bloomberg Businessweek,* January 14, 2011, http://www.businessweek.com/managing/content/jan2011/ca20110114_156455.htm.

Figure 12.5 A Performance Appraisal

February 13, 2013

To: Barbara Buchanan

From: Brittany Papper **BAP**

Subject line indicates that memo is a performance appraisal

Subject: Your Performance Thus Far in Our Collaborative Group

Overall evaluation

You have been a big asset to our group. Overall, our business communication group has been one of the best groups I have ever worked with, and I think that only minor improvements are needed to make our group even better.

What You're Doing Well

Specific observations provide dates, details of performance

You demonstrated flexibility and compatibility at our last meeting before we turned in our proposal on February 12 by offering to type the proposal since I had to study for an exam in one of my other classes. I really appreciated this because I really did not have the time to do it. I will definitely remember this if you are ever too busy with your other classes and cannot type the final report.

Another positive critical incident occurred February 5. We had discussed researching the topic of sexual discrimination in hiring and promotion at Midstate Insurance. As we read more about what we had to do, we became uneasy about reporting the information from our source who works at Midstate. I called you later that evening to talk about changing our topic to a less personal one. You were very understanding and said that you agreed that the original topic was a touchy one. You offered suggestions for other topics and had a positive attitude about the adjustment. Your suggestions ended my worries and made me realize that you are a positive and supportive person.

Other strengths

Your ideas are a strength that you definitely contribute to our group. You're good at brainstorming ideas, yet you're willing to go with whatever the group decides. That's a nice combination of creativity and flexibility.

Areas for Improvement

Two minor improvements could make you an even better member.

Specific recommendations for improvement

The first improvement is to be more punctual to meetings. On February 5 and February 8 you were about 10 minutes late. This makes the meetings last longer. Your ideas are valuable to the group, and the sooner you arrive the sooner we can share in your suggestions.

Specific behavior to be changed

The second suggestion is one we all need to work on. We need to keep our meetings positive and productive. I think that our negative attitudes were worst at our first group meeting February 5. We spent about half an hour complaining about all the work we had to do and about our busy schedules in other classes. In the future if this happens, maybe you could offer some positive things about the assignment to get the group motivated again.

Overall Compatibility

Positive, forward-looking ending

I feel that this group has gotten along very well together. You have been very flexible in finding times to meet and have always been willing to do your share of the work. I have never had this kind of luck with a group in the past and you have been a welcome breath of fresh air. I don't hate doing group projects any more!

Arguably, a good sales letter can be a work of art, and there are many approaches to writing one. Microsoft's Joanna L. Krotz offers 11 tips for writing effective sales letters, including building trust in the letter's opening, establishing credibility quickly, adding an incentive, and throwing in a call to action. Colorado State University offers advice at its open-access website, as well as examples of sales letters. Templates for sales letters are included with many word processing programs, but the best letters are created for specific audiences and situations. While there are many approaches to writing a sales letter, there is no single formula, but using the techniques for direct and indirect persuasion described in this module will help you.

Sources: Joanna L. Krotz, "How to Write an Effective Sales Letter: 11 Tips," downloaded on July 14, 2012, at http://www. microsoft.com/business/en-us/ resources/marketing/customer-service-acquisition/how-to-write-an-effective-sales-letter-11-tips. aspx?fbid=GI6G_TpfYbp; and "Writing Guide: Sales Letters," downloaded on May 3, 2012, at http://writing.colostate.edu/guides/ documents/business_writing/ business_letter/Sales_letter/.

Avoid labels, such as *wrong* and *bad,* and inferences. Instead, cite specific observations that describe behavior.

Inference:	Sam is an alcoholic.
Vague observation:	Sam calls in sick a lot. Subordinates complain about his behavior.
Specific observation:	Sam called in sick a total of 12 days in the last two months. After a business lunch with a customer last week, Sam was walking unsteadily. Two of his subordinates have said that they would prefer not to make sales trips with him because they find his behavior embarrassing.

Sam might be an alcoholic. He might also be having a reaction to a physician-prescribed drug; he might have a mental illness; he might be showing symptoms of a physical illness other than alcoholism. A supervisor who jumps to conclusions creates ill will, closes the door to solving the problem, and may provide grounds for legal action against the organization.

Be specific in an appraisal.

Too vague:	Sue does not manage her time as well as she could.
Specific:	Sue's first three weekly sales reports have been three, two, and four days late, respectively; the last weekly sales report for the month is not yet in.

Without specifics, Sue won't know that her boss objects to late reports. She may think she is being criticized for spending too much time on sales calls or for not working 80 hours a week. Without specifics, she might change the wrong things in a futile effort to please her boss.

Good supervisors try not only to identify the specific problems in subordinates' behavior but also in conversation to discover the causes of the problem. Does the employee need more training? Perhaps a training course or a mentor will help. Does he or she need to work harder? Then the supervisor needs to motivate the worker and help him or her manage distractions. Is a difficult situation causing the problem? Perhaps the situation can be changed. If it can't be changed, the supervisor and the company should realize that the worker is not at fault.

Appraisals are more useful to subordinates if they make clear which areas are most important and contain specific recommendations for improvement. No one can improve 17 weaknesses at once. Which two should the employee work on this month? Is getting in reports on time more important than increasing sales? The supervisor should explicitly answer these questions during the appraisal interview.

Phrase goals in specific, concrete terms. The subordinate may think that "considerable progress toward completing" a report may mean that the project should be 15% finished. The boss may think that "considerable progress" means 50% or 85% of the total work.

Letters of Recommendation

In an effort to protect themselves against lawsuits, some companies state only how long they employed someone and the position that person held. Such bare-bones letters have themselves been the target of lawsuits when employers did not reveal relevant negatives. Whatever the legal climate, there may be times when you want to recommend someone for an award or for a job.

Letters of recommendation must be specific. General positives that are not backed up with specific examples and evidence are seen as weak recommendations. Letters of recommendation that focus on minor points also suggest that the person is weak.

Figure 9.3 (◄◄ p. 129) is a letter of recommendation. Either in the first or the last paragraph, summarize your overall evaluation of the person. Early in the letter, perhaps in the first paragraph, show how well and how long you've known the person.

In the middle of the letter, offer specific details about the person's performance. At the end of the letter, indicate whether you would be willing to rehire the person and repeat your overall evaluation.

Experts are divided on whether you should include negatives. Some people feel that any negative weakens the letter. Other people feel that presenting but not emphasizing honest negatives makes the letter more convincing.

In many discourse communities, the words "Call me if you need more information" in a letter of recommendation mean "I have negative information that I am unwilling to put on paper. Call me, and I'll tell you what I really think."

How can I apply what I've learned in this module? LO 12-8

▶ *Plan your activities, and answer the PAIBOC questions.*

Before you tackle the assignments for this module, examine the following problem. Figure 12.6 lists the necessary activities. As in Modules 10 and 11, the PAIBOC questions probe the basic points required for a solution. Study the two sample solutions to see what makes one unacceptable and the other one good.[11] The checklists at the end of the module in Figures 12.9 and 12.10 can help you evaluate a draft.

Problem

In one room in the production department of Golden Electronics Company, employees work on computer monitors in conditions that are scarcely bearable due to the heat. Even when the temperature outside is only 75°, it is over 100° in the monitor room. In June, July, and August, 24 out of 36 workers quit because they couldn't stand the heat. This turnover happens every summer.

Figure 12.6 Allocating Time in Writing a Problem-Solving Persuasive Memo

Memo persuading the boss to approve a major expenditure. Total time: 6 hours

Planning	1½ hours
Figure costs.	
Develop a common ground.	
Answer the PAIBOC questions (◀◀ Module 1).	
Think about document design (◀◀ Module 5).	
Organize the message.	
Writing	1 hour
Draft the memo.	
Revising	3½ hours
Reread draft.	
Measure draft against PAIBOC questions and the checklist for problem-solving persuasive messages (Figure 12.10).	
Revise draft.	
Ask for feedback.	
Revise draft based on feedback.	
Edit to catch grammatical errors.	
Run spell-check.	
Proof by eye.	
Initial memo.	
Give document to boss.	

In a far corner of the room sits a quality control inspector in front of a small fan (the only one in the room). The production workers, in contrast, are carrying 20-pound monitors. As production supervisor, you tried to get air-conditioning two years ago, before Golden acquired the company, but management was horrified at the idea of spending $500,000 to insulate and air-condition the warehouse (it is impractical to air-condition the monitor room alone).

You're losing money every summer. Write a memo to Jennifer M. Kirkland, operations vice president, renewing your request.

Analysis of the Problem

P What are your **purposes** in writing or speaking?

> To persuade Kirkland to authorize insulation and air-conditioning. To build a good image of myself.

A Who is (are) your **audience(s)?** How do the members of your audience differ from each other? What characteristics are relevant to this particular message?

> The operations vice president will be concerned about keeping costs low and keeping production running smoothly. Kirkland may know that the request was denied two years ago, but another person was vice president then; Kirkland wasn't the one who said no.

I What **information** must your message include?

> The cost of the proposal. The effects of the present situation.

B What reasons or reader **benefits** can you use to support your position?

> Cutting turnover may save money and keep the assembly line running smoothly. Experienced employees may produce higher-quality parts. Putting in air-conditioning would relieve one of the workers' main complaints; it might make the union happier.

O What **objections** can you expect your reader(s) to have? What negative elements of your message must you deemphasize or overcome?

> The cost. The time operations will be shut down while installation is taking place.

C How will the **context** affect the reader's response? Think about your relationship to the reader, morale in the organization, the economy, the time of year, and any special circumstances.

> Prices on computer components are falling. The economy is sluggish; the company will be reluctant to make a major expenditure. Filling vacancies in the monitor room is hard—we are getting a reputation as a bad place to work. Summer is over, and the problem is over until next year.

Discussion of the Sample Solutions

Solution 1, shown in Figure 12.7, is unacceptable. By making the request in the subject line and the first paragraph, the writer invites a *no* before giving all the arguments. The writer does nothing to counter the objections that any manager will have to spending a great deal of money. By presenting the issue in terms of fairness, the writer produces defensiveness rather than creating a common ground. The writer doesn't use details or emotional appeal to show that the problem is indeed serious. The writer asks for fast action but doesn't show why the reader should act now to solve a problem that won't occur again for eight months.

Figure 12.7 An Unacceptable Solution to the Sample Problem

Date: October 12, 2013

To: Jennifer M. Kirkland, Operations Vice President

From: Arnold M. Morgan, Production Supervisor *AMM*

Subject: Request for Air-Conditioning the Monitor Room

Request in subject line stiffens resistance when reader is reluctant.

Please put air-conditioning in the monitor room. This past summer, 2/3 of our employees quit because it was so hot. It's (not fair) that they should work in unbearable temperatures when management sits in air-conditioned comfort.

Inappropriate emphasis on writer

(I) propose that we solve this problem by air-conditioning the monitor room to bring down the temperature to 78°.

Attacks reader

Insulating and air-conditioning the monitor room would cost $500,000.

Please approve this request promptly.

Cost sounds enormous without a context.

Memo sounds arrogant.
Logic isn't developed.
This attacks reader instead of enlisting reader's support.

Solution 2, shown in Figure 12.8, is an effective persuasive message. The writer chooses a positive subject line. The opening sentence is negative, catching the reader's attention by focusing on a problem the reader and writer share. However, the paragraph makes it clear that the memo offers a solution to the problem. The problem is spelled out in detail. Emotional impact is created by taking the reader through the day as the temperature rises. The solution is presented impersonally. There are no *I*'s in the memo.

The memo stresses reader benefits: the savings that will result once the investment is recovered. The last paragraph tells the reader exactly what to do and links prompt action to a reader benefit. The memo ends with a positive picture of the problem solved.

Figures 12.9 and 12.10 provide checklists for direct requests and problem-solving persuasive messages.

Figure 12.8 A Good Solution to the Sample Problem

Date: October 12, 2013

To: Jennifer M. Kirkland, Operations Vice President

From: Arnold M. Morgan, Production Supervisor **AMM**

Subject: Improving Summer Productivity

Reader benefit in subject line

Shared problem

Golden forfeited a possible $186,000 in profits last summer due to a 17% drop in productivity. That's not unusual: Golden has a history of low summer productivity. But we can reverse the trend and bring summer productivity in line with the rest of the year's.

Good to show problem can be resolved

Cause of problem

The problem starts in the monitor room. Due to high turnover and reduced efficiency from workers who are on the job, we just don't make as many monitors as we do during the rest of the year.

Additional reason to solve problem

Both the high turnover and reduced efficiency are due to the unbearable heat in the monitor room. Temperatures in the monitor room average 25° over the outside temperature. During the summer, when work starts at 8, it's already 85° in the tube room. By 11:30, it's at least 105°. On six days last summer, it hit 120°. When the temperatures are that high, we may be violating OSHA regulations.

Production workers are always standing, moving, or carrying 20-lb. monitors. When temperatures hit 90°, they slow down. When no relief is in sight, many of them quit.

We replaced 24 of the 36 employees in the monitor room this summer. When someone quits, it takes an average of five days to find and train a replacement; during that time, the trainee produces nothing. For another five days, the new person can work at only half speed. And even "full speed" in the summer is only 90% of what we expect the rest of the year.

More details about problem

Here's where our losses come from:

Normal production = 50 units a person each day (upd)

Loss due to turnover:
loss of 24 workers for 5 days =	6,000 units
24 at $^1/_2$ pace for 5 days =	3,000 units
Total loss due to turnover =	9,000 units

Shows detail— Set up like an arithmetic problem

Loss due to reduced efficiency:
loss of 5 upd × 12 workers × 10 days =	600 units
loss of 5 upd × 36 × 50 days =	9,000 units
Total loss due to reduced efficiency =	9,600 units

Total Loss = 18,600 units

Shows where numbers in paragraph 1 come from

According to the accounting department, Golden makes a net profit of $10 on every monitor we sell. And, as you know, with the boom in computer sales, we sell every monitor we make. Those 18,600 units we don't produce are costing us $186,000 a year.

Figure 12.8 A Good Solution to the Sample Problem

Jennifer M. Kirkland   2   October 12, 2013

Additional benefit

Bringing down the temperature to 78° (the minimum allowed under federal guidelines) from the present summer average of 112° will require an investment of $500,000 to insulate and air-condition the warehouse. Extra energy costs for the air-conditioning will run about $30,000 a year. We'll get our investment back in less than three years. Once the investment is recouped, we'll be making an additional $150,000 a year—all without buying additional equipment or hiring additional workers.

Tells reader what to do

By installing the insulation and air-conditioning this fall, we can take advantage of lower off-season rates. Please authorize the Purchasing Department to request bids for the system. Then, next summer, our productivity can be at an all-time high.

Reason to act promptly

Ends on positive note of problem solved, reader enjoying benefit

Figure 12.9

Checklist for   Direct Requests

☐ If the message is a memo, does the subject line indicate the request? Is the subject line specific enough to differentiate this message from others on the same subject?

☐ Does the first paragraph summarize the request or the specific topic of the message?

☐ Does the message give all of the relevant information? Is there enough detail?

☐ Does the message answer questions or overcome objections that readers may have without introducing unnecessary negatives?

☐ Does the last paragraph ask for action? Does it give a deadline if one exists and a reason for acting promptly?

And, for all messages, not just direct requests,

☐ Does the message use you-attitude and positive emphasis?
☐ Is the style easy to read and friendly?
☐ Is the visual design of the message inviting?
☐ Is the format correct?
☐ Does the message use standard grammar? Is it free from typos?

Originality in a direct request may come from

☐ Good lists and visual impact.

☐ Thinking about readers and giving details that answer their questions, overcome any objections, and make it easier for them to do as you ask.

☐ Adding details that show you're thinking about a specific organization and the specific people in that organization.

Figure 12.10

Checklist for Problem-Solving Persuasive Messages

- [ ] If the message is a memo, does the subject line indicate the writer's purpose or offer a reader benefit? Does the subject line avoid making the request?
- [ ] Is the problem presented as a joint problem that both the writer and reader have an interest in solving, rather than as something the reader is being asked to do for the writer?
- [ ] Does the message give all of the relevant information? Is there enough detail?
- [ ] Does the message overcome objections that readers may have?
- [ ] Does the message avoid phrases that sound dictatorial, condescending, or arrogant?
- [ ] Does the last paragraph ask for action? Does it give a deadline if one exists and a reason for acting promptly?

And, for all messages, not just persuasive ones,

- [ ] Does the message use you-attitude and positive emphasis?
- [ ] Is the style easy to read and friendly?
- [ ] Is the visual design of the message inviting?
- [ ] Is the format correct?
- [ ] Does the message use standard grammar? Is it free from typos?

Originality in a problem-solving persuasive message may come from

- [ ] A good subject line and common ground.
- [ ] A clear and convincing description of the problem.
- [ ] Thinking about readers and giving details that answer their questions, overcome objections, and make it easier for them to do as you ask.
- [ ] Adding details that show you're thinking about a specific organization and the specific people in that organization.

Summary of Learning Objectives

- Use the **direct request pattern** when (LO 12-1)
  - The audience will do as you ask without any resistance.
  - You need a response only from the people who are willing to act.
  - The audience is busy and may not read all the messages received.
  - Your organization's culture prefers direct requests.
- Use the **problem-solving pattern** when (LO 12-1)
  - The audience is likely to object to doing as you ask.
  - You need action from everyone.
  - You trust the audience to read the entire message.
  - You expect logic to be more important than emotion in the decision.
- In a direct request, put the request, the topic of the request, or a question in the subject line. Do not put the request in the subject line of a problem-solving persuasive message. Instead, use a **directed subject line** that reveals your position on the issue or a reader benefit. Use a positive or neutral subject line even when the first paragraph will be negative. (LO 12-2)

- In a direct request, consider asking in the first paragraph for the information or service you want. Give readers all the information or details they will need to act on your request. In the last paragraph, ask for the action you want. (LO 12-3)
- Organize a problem-solving persuasive message in this way: (LO 12-3)

  1. Describe a problem you both share (which your request will solve).
  2. Give the details of the problem.
  3. Explain the solution to the problem.
  4. Show that any negative elements (cost, time, etc.) are outweighed by the advantages.
  5. Summarize any additional benefits of the solution.
  6. Ask for the action you want.

- Readers have a vested interest in something if they benefit directly from keeping things as they are. (LO 12-4)

- Use one or more of the following strategies to counter objections: **(LO 12-4)**
  - Specify how much time and/or money is required.
  - Put the time and/or money in the context of the benefits they bring.
  - Show that money spent now will save money in the long run.
  - Show that doing as you ask will benefit some group the reader identifies with or some cause the reader supports.
  - Show the reader that the sacrifice is necessary to achieve a larger, more important goal to which he or she is committed.
  - Show that the advantages as a group outnumber or outweigh the disadvantages as a group.
  - Turn the disadvantage into an opportunity.
- To make a message more persuasive, build **credibility** and **emotional appeal,** use the right tone and offer the reader a reason to act promptly. **(LO 12-5)**

- To encourage readers to act promptly, set a deadline. Show that the time limit is real, that acting now will save time or money, or that delaying action will cost more. **(LO 12-5)**
- The best common grounds are specific. Often, a negative—a problem the reader will want to solve—makes good common ground. **(LO 12-6)**
- In your common ground, emphasize the parts of your proposal that fit with what your audience already does or believes. **(LO 12-6)**
- Use audience analysis to evaluate possible common grounds. **(LO 12-6)**
- Rejections and refusals, disciplinary notices and negative performance appraisals, and layoffs and firings are the most common kinds of negative messages. **(LO 12-7)**
- Use the PAIBOC questions from Module 1 to analyze persuasive situations. **(LO 12-8)**

Assignments for Module 12

Questions for Comprehension

12.1 How do you decide whether to use a direct request or a problem-solving persuasive message? **(LO 12-1)**

12.2 How do you organize a problem-solving persuasive message? **(LO 12-3)**

12.3 How can you build credibility? **(LO 12-4)**

12.4 How do specific varieties of persuasive messages adapt the basic patterns? **(LO 12-7)**

Questions for Critical Thinking

12.5 What do you see as the advantages of positive and negative appeals? Illustrate your answer with specific messages, advertisements, or posters. **(LO 12-1)**

12.6 Is it dishonest to "sneak up on the reader" by delaying the request in a problem-solving persuasive message? **(LO 12-3)**

12.7 Think of a persuasive message (or a commercial) that did not convince you to act. Could a different message have convinced you? Why or why not? **(LO 12-4, LO 12-5)**

Exercises and Problems

12.8 Asking for Information for an Awards Ceremony (LO 12-1 to LO 12-8)

Your community organization recognizes people who have contributed to the community. Julio Moreno, the chief of police, sent you names and photos of four officers. But you need more information to introduce them and to write the press release you'll send the paper.

In your files, you find this letter used by the previous program chair:

> Thank you for sending me the names of people to recognize. This will be very helpful. However, you did not give me enough information. I need more than just their names. Please give me more information. I want to know how long each person has worked for your organization. Do they have hobbies? (Provide information.) Supply the names of their spouses and children, if any. It would be helpful also to have the children's ages. Additionally, we plan to send special letters to the city council members whose constituents are being recognized. To this end, we need the name or number of the voting ward of each person. It would also be helpful to have the home address of each person because we want to invite both the person to be recognized and his or her spouse or guest to attend the ceremony. What exactly did the person do to deserve recognition? I anxiously await your response at your earliest convenience.

You know this letter is horrible. It's awkward and lacks you-attitude and positive emphasis. The questions aren't arranged or formatted effectively. It doesn't ask for action by a specific date.

As Your Instructor Directs,

a. Identify the problems in this letter.
b. Rewrite the letter, adding information to make it clear and complete.

12.9 Asking for the Right Information (LO 12-1 to LO 12-8)

In today's mail, your insurance agency received the following letter:

> When I called last week to find out about insuring my boat, the clerk told me to include a recent photo. Here it is. Please send me a notice telling me that my boat is now insured—I want to take it out sailing!

The writer, Trevor Bishop, included a photo of himself.

Trevor misunderstood what the clerk said: what you need for insurance purposes is a photo of the boat, not its owner. Write to Mr. Bishop to ask for the photo you need—without making him feel stupid for having misunderstood what your clerk meant.

12.10 Getting a Raise for a Deserving Employee (LO 12-1 to LO 12-8)

A memo from headquarters announces that the maximum merit increase (i.e., a raise when no promotion is involved) is 6%.

You've got a subordinate who, you feel, deserves a bigger raise. A year ago, Sheila Whitfield was promoted into the pre-label division of your packing department. She quickly became proficient in her duties—so much so that now others ask her for advice. You especially like her positive approach to solving problems. She sees obstacles as challenges and more often than not figures out ways to do what needs to be done within the constraints. On her own initiative, she started a program to make others in the company aware of the expense of labels and shipping to better control costs. The program has been very successful, and the company has saved money while still using clear, informative labels with adequate packaging. She has excellent working relationships with label suppliers and her counterparts in other companies.

In her most recent performance appraisal, Sheila had 14 out of 21 boxes checked "Exceptional" (the other 7 were "Commendable," the next highest category). Her overall ranking was "Exceptional." Indeed, the only two suggestions for improvement were minor ones: "(1) Continue to be aggressive, but temper the aggressiveness with diplomacy; (2) continue to expand responsibility in current position."

Write a memo to the Salary Compensation Committee recommending that an exception to the rules be made so that Sheila can be given an 8% raise.

12.11 Asking for a Raise or Reclassification (LO 12-1 to LO 12-8)

Do you deserve a raise? Should your job be reclassified to reflect your increased responsibilities (with more pay, of course)? If so, write a memo to the person with the authority to determine pay and job titles, arguing for what you want.

As Your Instructor Directs,

a. Create a document or presentation to achieve the goal.
b. Write a memo to your instructor describing the situation at your workplace and explaining your rhetorical choices (medium, strategy, tone, wording, graphics or document design, and so forth).

12.12 Writing Collection Letters (LO 12-1 to LO 12-8)

You have a small desktop publishing firm. Unfortunately, not all your clients pay promptly.

As Your Instructor Directs,

Write letters for one or more of the following situations.

a. A $450 bill for designing and printing a brochure for Juggles, Inc., a company that provides clowns and jugglers for parties, is now five weeks overdue. You've phoned twice, and each time the person who answered the phone promised to send you a check, but nothing has happened.
b. A $2,000 bill for creating a series of handouts for a veterinarian to distribute to clients is now 72 days overdue. This one is embarrassing: You lost track of the invoice, so you never followed up on the original (and only) bill.
c. A $3,750 bill for designing and printing a series of 10 brochures for Creative Interiors, a local interior decorating shop, is three weeks past due. When you billed Creative Interiors, you got a note saying that the design was not acceptable and that you would not be paid until you redesigned it (at no extra charge) to the owner's satisfaction. The owner had approved the preliminary design on which the brochures were based; she did not explain in the note what was wrong with the final product. She's never free when you are; indeed, when you call to try to schedule an appointment, you're told the owner will call you back—but she never does. At this point, the delay is not your fault; you want to be paid.

d. A $100 bill for designing (but not actually creating) a brochure for a cleaning company that, according to its owner, planned to expand into your city may be difficult to collect. You got the order and instructions by mail and talked to the person on the phone but never met him.

You tried to call once since then (as much to try to talk him into having the brochures printed as to collect the $100); the number was "no longer in service." You suspect the owner may no longer be in business, but you'd like to get your money if possible.

12.13 Urging Employees to Handle Routine Calls Courteously (LO 12-1 to LO 12-8)

You are manager of the local power company. A recent survey had questions about recipients' attitudes toward the company. On the 7-point "friendly . . . unfriendly" scale, you came out at 2.1—with "1" being the lowest score possible.

The only contact most people have with the power company comes through monthly bills, ads, and phone calls. Many of these calls are about routine matters: whether people can delay payment, how to handle payment when they're away for extended periods of time, how to tell if there's a gas leak, how the budget payment system works. Workers answer these questions over and over and over. But the caller asks because he or she needs to know.

To the worker, the caller is just one more faceless voice; to the caller, the worker is the company.

Write a memo to your staff urging them to be patient and friendly when they answer questions.

Hints:

- In your town, does the power company have a monopoly, or do gas and electricity compete for customers? How might competition affect your message?
- What specifically do you want your staff to do? How could they achieve your general goals?
- How can the job be made more interesting for workers?

12.14 Persuading an Organization to Accept Student Interns (LO 12-1 to LO 12-8)

At City College, you have more would-be interns than internship positions. As Director of the Internship Program, you'd like to line up more companies to accept your students.

If your school already has an internship program, use the facts about it. If it doesn't, assume that internships

- Are open to students who have completed at least two courses in the area of the internship with grades of "B" or better.
- Can be paid or unpaid.
- Must involve substantive work supervised by someone in the organization.

- Must involve at least 100 hours of onsite work experience during the term.

As Your Instructor Directs,

a. Write a form letter that could be mailed to businesses, urging them to set up one or more internships.
b. Pick an organization you know well. Write to a specific person urging him or her to set up internships in that organization.
c. Write a news release about your school's need for more intern positions.

12.15 Helping Students Use Credit Cards Responsibly (LO 12-1 to LO 12-8)

Your college, community college, or university is concerned that some students have high levels of credit card debt and may be using credit cards irresponsibly. Many students—especially those without full-time jobs—pay only part of the bill each month, thus compounding the original amount charged with interest rates that can be 18% annually, or even higher. Nationwide, 20% of students have credit card debt of more than $10,000—and that doesn't count amounts owed for student loans. Excessive credit card debt makes it harder for a student to become financially independent; in extreme cases, students may have to drop out just to pay off the credit card debt.

As Your Instructor Directs,

a. Create a message to urge students on your campus to use credit cards responsibly. Create a document that has the greatest chance of being read and heeded (not just dropped on the ground or in a trash can).
b. Write a memo to your instructor explaining how and when the document would be distributed and why you've chosen the design you have. Show how your decisions fit the students on your campus.

Hints:

- Suggest guidelines for responsible use of credit (limiting the number of credit cards, charging only what one can repay each month except in the case of an emergency, shopping around for a card with the lowest interest rate, and so forth). Suggest a way to test one's own credit savvy.
- Remind students that for continuing expenses, a loan will have a lower interest rate (and may not have to be repaid until after graduation).
- Some students may like the freebies they get with some credit cards (e.g., frequent flyer miles). How can you persuade these students that the freebies aren't worth charging more than they can pay off each month?
- Part of your audience already uses credit responsibly. Be sure the message doesn't offend these people.
- Some students in your audience may already know that they owe too much. What can students do if they already have too much debt?

12.16 Asking to Work at Home (LO 12-1 to LO 12-8)

The Industrial Revolution brought people together to work in factories, and now the Internet Age is making it possible for people to move their work back to their homes. Many kinds of collaboration and communication can take place electronically, so showing up at the office is not essential for getting the job done. Some employees enjoy the social interaction of the workplace. For others, the joy of seeing co-workers just does not make up for the time and discomfort of the daily commute.

Write a memo to your supervisor, requesting that you be allowed a flexible work arrangement in which you do some or all of your work at home. Consider your work requirements, and identify which of them do not require your physical presence. Explain how you will be able to demonstrate that you work at least as effectively at home. Your supervisor will have to be able to justify this arrangement to his or her own boss.

Hints:

- Pick a business, government office, nonprofit agency, or educational institution that you know something about.
- For advice on making the case for working at home, visit www.workoptions.com, www.work-family.com, www.gilgordon.com, www.jala.com, and www.joannepratt.com.
- Will your organization be more persuaded by a dollars-and-cents comparison showing how much this benefit could save the company? Or would stories be more persuasive?

12.17 Persuading Employees to Keep Social Networking Sites Closed (LO 12-1 to LO 12-8)

Your company's regional vice president recently toured your department and was appalled by how many people had Facebook or other social networking sites open on their computers. In most cases, employees had social networking windows open alongside work-related tasks. Your department, which usually gets high marks, received a lower review from the vice president as a result.

While your company's policy is that only work-related sites should be opened on the job, managers and supervisors have been lax in enforcing the rule since work gets done and there have been no complaints. This latest turn of events, however, makes it necessary to remind employees of the policy and penalties, such as written reprimands.

Some employees may be bothered by the reminder. They may feel they are able to effectively multitask and that the policy treats them like children. In addition, some employees are actually responsible for making sure updates about your company are tweeted and posted to the company's Facebook page newsfeed, so they should be allowed to have the sites open at any time.

Write an e-mail message to employees urging them to refrain from opening social networking sites unless doing so is work-related.

12.18 Handling a Sticky Recommendation (LO 12-1 to LO 12-8)

As a supervisor in a state agency, you have a dilemma. You received this e-mail message today:

From: John Inoye, Director of Personnel, Department of Taxation

Subject: Need Recommendation for Peggy Chafez

Peggy Chafez has applied for a position in the Department of Taxation. On the basis of her application and interview, she is the leading candidate. However, before I offer the job to her, I need a letter of recommendation from her current supervisor.

Could you please let me have your evaluation within a week? We want to fill the position as quickly as possible.

Peggy has worked in your office for 10 years. She designed, writes, and edits a monthly statewide newsletter that your office puts out; she designed and maintains the department website. Her designs are creative; she's a hard worker; she knows a lot about computers.

However, Peggy is in many ways an unsatisfactory staff member. Her standards are so high that most people find her intimidating. Some find her abrasive. She's out of the office a lot. Some of that is required by her job (e.g., she takes the newsletters to the post office), but some people don't like the fact that she's out of the office so much. They also complain that she doesn't return voice-mail and e-mail messages.

You think managing your office would be a lot smoother if Peggy weren't there. You can't fire her: State employees' jobs are secure once they get past the initial six-month probationary period. Because of budget constraints, you can hire new employees only if vacancies are created by resignations. You feel that it would be pretty easy to find someone better.

If you recommend that John Inoye hire Peggy, you will be able to hire someone you want. If you recommend that John hire someone else, you may be stuck with Peggy for a long time.

As Your Instructor Directs,

a. Write to John Inoye.
b. Write a memo to your instructor listing the choices you've made and justifying your approach.

Hints:

- What are your options? Consciously look for more than two.
- Is it ethical to select facts or to use connotations so that you are truthful but still encourage John to hire Peggy? Is it certain that John would find Peggy's work as unsatisfactory as you do? If Peggy is hired and doesn't do well, will your credibility suffer? Why is your credibility important?

12.19 Addressing a Passenger Complaint about a Rude Flight Attendant (LO 12-1 to LO 12-8)

As director of customer relations for a major airline, you receive the following letter:

> Recently, I took one of your flights from Portland, Oregon, to St. Louis, Missouri, Flight 2219. Though the flight itself was pleasant (and we even arrived a half hour early!) one of the attendants was rude. He addressed me in a less-than-friendly tone, thrust the cup holding my beverage in my face when serving me, and ran into my shoulder several times while speeding down the aisle for no particular reason. My wife and even the passenger seated next to me were shocked.
>
> I don't know what I did to merit such treatment, but it seems to me that passengers deserve better. I should know. I'm a retired flight attendant from another airline.
>
> Sincerely,
>
> Tim Antilles

You investigate the situation and discover that there was only one male flight attendant on that flight, David. Usually assigned to your airline's regional carrier, which makes short trips on propeller-driven airplanes, he was a last-minute substitution for another attendant who took sick leave.

David has a brief yet spotless record with the airline, but Flight 2219 was on a much larger and more crowded airplane than he usually flies. He may have been overwhelmed by the change. You want to discuss the matter with David before contacting Mr. Antilles, but David is on vacation for nine more days. Rather than leave Mr. Antilles waiting, you decide to contact him to express your concern and to let him know that you will follow up with David.

Write a letter to Mr. Antilles assuring him that the matter will be investigated.

12.20 Persuading Employees that a Security Camera Is Necessary (LO 12-1 to LO 12-8)

To save money, your company orders office supplies in bulk. Each department then gets its allotment of supplies, which are kept in a supply room for employees to access when needed. The room is locked at night, and only you and security guards have the key.

Large amounts of office supplies have been disappearing from your department's supply room for several months. It started with small items, such as pens, tape, and sticky notes. Now, staplers, calculators, and expensive poster and certificate frames are missing. You have no idea who is responsible, but the thefts appear to be happening during regular business hours. The total loss from the thefts is now more than $1,000.

You tried having employees sign materials out on the honor system, but the thefts continued. Security recommends a hidden camera for the room, but the idea of "spying" on employees troubles you. You have agreed to a compromise: a security camera placed in plain view.

You believe the thefts are the work of one person and that the other 90 employees in your department are innocent. Therefore, the camera may offend people and harm employee morale.

Morale already has been down because the company has experienced profit losses the past two quarters due to increased competition. Rumors are spreading that some jobs will be transferred overseas and layoffs are imminent, though you have no solid information on management's plans. Your employees—many of whom have been with the company for more than 10 years—are apprehensive about their future with the company.

But the alternative is to allow the increasingly costly thefts to continue. You also want to avoid having to search employees and their belongings, the next step according to security if the camera fails to discourage the thief.

Write a memo to your employees explaining the need for the camera.

12.21 Asking an Instructor for a Letter of Recommendation (LO 12-1 to LO 12-8)

For a job, for a four-year school, or for graduate school, you need letters of recommendation.

As Your Instructor Directs,

a. Assume that you've orally asked an instructor for a recommendation, and he or she has agreed to write one. "Write up something to remind me of what you've done in the class. Tell me what else you've done, too. And tell me what they're looking for. Be sure to tell me when the letter needs to be in and whom it goes to."

b. Assume that you've been unable to talk with the instructor whose recommendation you want. Write asking for a letter of recommendation.

Hints:

- Be detailed about the points you'd like the instructor to mention.
- How well will this instructor remember you? How much detail about your performance in his or her class do you need to provide?
- Specify the name and address of the person to whom the letter should be written; specify when the letter is due. If there's an intermediate due date (e.g., if you must sign the outside of the envelope to submit the recommendation to law school), say so.

12.22 Recommending Investments* (LO 12-1 to LO 12-8)

Recommend whether your instructor should invest in a specific stock, piece of real estate, or other investment. As your instructor directs, assume your instructor has $1,000, $10,000, or $100,000 to invest.

Hints:

- Pick a stock, property, or other investment you can research easily.

- What are your instructor's goals? Is he or she saving for a house? For retirement? For kids' college expenses? To pay off his or her own student loans?
- How much risk is your instructor comfortable with?
- Is your instructor willing to put time into the investment (as managing a rental house would require)?

*Based on an assignment created by Cathy Ryan, The Ohio State University.

12.23 Retrieving Your Image (LO 12-1 to LO 12-8)

As Director of Business Communication, you get this letter from Sharon Davis, a member of your college advisory board and a major donor:

(The next two inches of the letter are blocked out, and neither the signature nor typed name can be read.)

My bank received this letter from one of your soon-to-be graduates. It seems as though a closer look at writing skills is warranted.

To Whom It May Concern:

This is in reference to the loan soliciation that I received in the mail. This is the second offer that I am now inquiring about. The first offer sent to my previous address I did not respond. But aftersome careful thought and consideration I think it wise to consolidate my bills. Therefore I hope the information provided is sufficient to complete a successful application. I think the main purpose of this loan is to enable me to repair my credit history. I have had problems in the past because of job status as part-time and being a student. I will be graduating in June and now I do have a full-time job. I think I just need a chance to mend the past credit problems that I have had.

As Your Instructor Directs,

Write to

a. The faculty who teach business communication, reminding them that the quality of student writing may affect fund-raising efforts.

b. Ms. Davis, convincing her that indeed your school does make every effort to graduate students who can write.

12.24 Persuading Tenants to Pay the Rent (LO 12-1 to LO 12-8)

As the new manager of an apartment complex, this message is in the files:

ATTENTION!

DERELICTS

If you are a rent derelict (and you know if you are) this communique is directed to you!

RENT IS DUE THE 5TH OF EACH MONTH AT THE LATEST!

LEASE HAS A 5-DAY GRACE PERIOD UNTIL THE 5TH OF THE MONTH NOT THE 15TH.

If rent is not paid in total by the 5th, you will pay the $25.00 late charge. You will pay the $25.00 late charge when you pay your late rent or your rent will not be accepted.

Half of you people don't even know how much you pay a month. Please read your lease instead of calling up to waste our time finding out what you owe per month! Let's get with the program so I can spend my time streamlining and organizing maintenance requests. My job is maintenance only.

RENT PAYMENT IS YOUR JOB!

If you can show up for a test on time, why can't you make it to the rental office on time or just mail it.

P.S. We don't take cash any longer due to a major theft.

This message is terrible. It lacks you-attitude and may even encourage people not to pay until the 5th.

Write to people who have been slow to pay in the past.

12.25 Writing a Performance Appraisal for a Member of a Collaborative Group (LO 12-1 to LO 12-8)

During your collaborative writing group meetings, record specific observations of both effective and ineffective things that group members do. Then evaluate the performance of the other members in your group. (If there are two or more other people, write a separate appraisal for each of them.)

In your first paragraph, summarize your evaluation. Then in the body of your memo, give specific details:

- What specifically did the person do in terms of the task? Brainstorm ideas? Analyze the information? Draft the text? Suggest revisions in parts drafted by others? Format the document or create visuals? Revise? Edit? Proofread? (In most cases, several people will have done each of these activities together. Don't overstate what any one person did.) What was the quality of the person's work?
- What did the person contribute to the group process? Did he or she help schedule the work? Raise or resolve conflicts? Make other group members feel valued and included? Promote group cohesion? What roles did the person play in the group?

Support your generalizations with specific observations. The more observations you have and the more detailed they are, the better your appraisal will be.

As Your Instructor Directs,

a. Write a midterm performance appraisal for one or more members of your collaborative group. In each appraisal, identify the two or three things the person should try to improve during the second half of the term.
b. Write a performance appraisal for one or more members of your collaborative group at the end of the term. Identify and justify the grade you think each person should receive for the portion of the grade based on group process.
c. Give a copy of your appraisal to the person about whom it is written.

12.26 Asking for a Job Description (LO 12-1 to LO 12-8)

Your organization has gone through a lot of changes, and you suspect that the original job descriptions used when people were hired are no longer accurate. So you'd like all employees to list their current job duties. You'd also like them to indicate which parts of their jobs they see as most important and how much time they spend on each part of the job.

Send a message to all employees asking for their job descriptions.

Hints:

- Pick a real business, government, or nonprofit group you know about.
- When is the next cycle of performance appraisals? Will these descriptions be used then?

- People will be reluctant to tell you they're spending lots of time on things that aren't important, and some people may honestly not know how they spend their time. How can you encourage accurate reporting? (If you ask people to keep logs for a week, be sure to also ask them if that week was typical—it may or may not be.)
- Some people will want to change their job descriptions—that is, to change their duties or the proportion of time they spend on each job task. Is that an option in your organization right now? If it isn't (or if it is an option for very few people), how can you make that clear to readers?

Polishing Your **Prose**

Expressing Personality

The words you choose can express personality in speech and writing. What personality do you want in your memos, letters, and reports? Friendly? Assertive? Bureaucratic? Threatening? Confident? These are just a few possibilities.

Consider the personality expressed by billionaire investment guru Warren Buffet in an annual report to the shareholders of Berkshire Hathaway, Inc.:

> Given our gain of 34.1%, it is tempting to declare victory and move on. But last year's performance was no great triumph. Any investor can chalk up large returns when stocks soar, as they did in 1997. In a bull market, one must avoid the error of the preening duck that quacks boastfully after a torrential rainstorm, thinking that its paddling skills have caused it to rise in the world. A right-thinking duck would instead compare its position after the downpour to that of the other ducks in the pond.
>
> So what's our duck rating for 1997? The table on the facing page shows that though we paddled furiously last year, passive ducks that simply invested in the S&P Index rose almost as fast as we did. Our appraisal of 1997's performance then: Quack.

How would you describe the personality of this narrator? Does he sound "folksy"? Fatherly? Grandfatherly? Educated? Confident? How do you know? How does his personality compare to your expectations for someone in the investment field? Someone who is wealthy? Is this someone you would like to know?

Personality is individual. However, we all have control over the words we choose to convey our personalities. To understand your own personality in communication, first see if you can understand the personalities that others convey. Then compare their words and tone to your own.

Exercises

Read the following passages. How would you characterize the narrative voice in each? Which voices seem appropriate for good business communication? Try using your own words to communicate the same basic message.

1. Don't think. Don't talk. Don't even blink. Just do your job!
2. Per the discussion of the 10th and concerning the interested parties, we are establishing the continuance of the aforementioned procedural matters, as referenced by the undersigned in document A, subsection C, paragraphs 1 and 2.
3. What I can't understand—I mean, beyond the fact that some college out there actually granted you a degree—is how that brain of yours actually managed to generate enough power to submit an application to this company in the first place. I mean, you may very well be a modern scientific miracle.
4. Oh, THANK YOU, THANK YOU, THANK YOU, for hiring me!! You WON'T be disappointed!!!!!!!!!!
5. Yeah, thanks for shopping here.
6. BIF AISI BYTM LOL.
7. It's like, you know, the whole thing, okay, and, you know, I'm really glad that we, okay, like, talked about it before we signed any, you know, contract.
8. This is so simple even a man can figure out how to do it.
9. You will no doubt be suitably impressed with the care in which I have completed this report. It is, if I may say so myself, the best work I have ever done.
10. *Yes, sir.* After all, we are after all here to serve customers like you, *sir.* It's our job to make your shopping experience exceptional, *sir.* After all, no matter how outrageous, the customer is always right, *sir.*

Check your answers to the odd-numbered exercises at the back of the book.

E-Mail Messages, Web Writing, and Technology

13

LEARNING OBJECTIVES

Module 13 can help you to write more effectively with e-mail and for the web. After completing the module, you should be able to

LO 13-1 Apply strategies for e-mail message organization.

LO 13-2 Create subject lines for e-mail messages.

LO 13-3 Apply strategies for e-mail message style and content.

LO 13-4 Apply strategies for time management with e-mail and other tasks.

LO 13-5 Identify rules for "netiquette."

LO 13-6 Apply strategies for e-mail attachment use.

LO 13-7 Apply strategies for writing on the web.

LO 13-8 Recognize other technologies for the web.

Technology continues to change the way we work and the way we write. Not too long ago, a pen, typewriter, and telephone were the primary equipment for business communicators; then came word processors, fax machines, and e-mail. Today, we can choose from a host of tools that includes cell phones, web pages, videoconferencing, and instant messaging, each one ever increasing its features and benefits.

Because technology changes so rapidly, so do expectations for how and when to use it. A 21st-century communicator understands that adaptation is the key to staying current, and being open to learning new technologies is a must. Use Module 13 as a starting point, and expect change.

This map represents the path of data sent out to one of 20,000 locations on the internet using a system called Skitter. The lines are color-coded to show the nationality of that part of the internet, for example: USA (pink), UK (dark blue), Italy (light blue), Sweden (light green) and white (unknown).

While texting and using social networking pages are increasingly popular ways to communicate, e-mail remains a common tool in business. Avoid composing e-mails when you are upset. Treat e-mails as professionally as any business message by proofreading and checking for accuracy. Like your authors, Bill Husted recommends giving the reader enough information in any e-mail reply so the reader fully understands your response. If you're not including the original e-mail, at least specify relevant details: "I checked, and I'm free on Wednesday for the short interview" instead of "Wednesday is fine." Andrew Rosen warns against over-relying on e-mail—use a different tool, for instance, if the message is urgent—and failing to use ordinary pleasantries, like a greeting at the beginning and a thank you at the end of the message.

Source: Husted, "Rules to Remember When Sending Your E-Mails," *The Columbus Dispatch*, September 7, 2009, http:// www.dispatch.com/live/content/ business/stories/2009/09/07/ technobuddy_0907.ART_ ART_09-07-09_A7_M7EVEH3. html?sid=101; and Andrew G. Rosen, "18 Common Work E-Mail Mistakes," January 18, 2011, http://finance .yahoo.com/news/18-Common- Work-Email-usnews-1004018741. html?x=0.

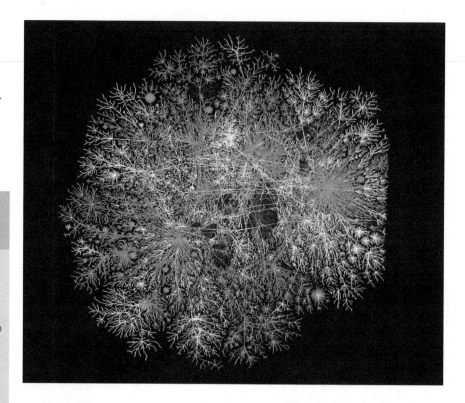

When you start a new job, you may have a short grace period before you have to write paper documents. But most employers will expect you to "hit the ground running" with e-mail. It's likely that you'll respond to—and perhaps initiate—e-mail messages during your very first week at work.

As you write e-mail messages, keep these guidelines in mind:

- Although e-mail feels informal, it is not private, as a conversation might be. Your employer may legally check your messages. And a message sent to one person can be printed out or forwarded to others without your knowledge or consent. Don't be indiscreet in e-mail.
- All the principles of good business writing still apply with e-mail. Remember you-attitude (◄◄ p. 90) and positive emphasis (◄◄ p. 101). Use reader benefits (◄◄ p. 112) when they're appropriate. Use the pattern of organization that fits the purpose of the message.
- Because e-mail feels like talking, some writers give less attention to spelling, grammar, and proofreading. Many e-mail programs have spell-checkers; use them. Check your message for grammatical correctness and to be sure you've included all the necessary information.
- Reread and proofread your message before sending it.
- E-mail messages have to interest the reader in the subject line and first paragraph. If the message is longer than one screen, the first screen must interest the reader enough to make him or her continue. E-mail messages to people who report directly to you are easy because people will read anything from their supervisors. But writing to people who are not in a direct reporting relationship or to people outside your unit or organization takes more care.

How should I set up e-mail messages? LO 13-1

▶ *Formats are still evolving.*

Because there are so many different e-mail programs and formats, for the sake of the discussion here, focus on the general concepts they all share. Then, adapt them to your specific e-mail program.

Most e-mail programs prompt you to supply the various parts of the format. For example, a blank Eudora screen prompts you to supply the name of the person the message goes to and the subject line. *Cc* denotes computer copies; the recipient will see that these people are getting the message. *Bcc* denotes blind computer copies; the recipient does not see the names of these people. Most e-mail programs also allow you to attach documents from other programs. Thus you can send someone a document with formatting, drafts of PowerPoint slides, or the design for a brochure cover. The computer program supplies the date and time automatically. Some programs allow you to write a message now and program the future time at which you want it to be sent.

Some aspects of e-mail format are still evolving. In particular, some writers treat e-mail messages as if they were informal letters; some treat them as memos. Even though the e-mail screen has a "To" line (as do memos), some writers still use an informal salutation, as in Figure 13.1. The writer in Figure 13.1 ends the message with a signature block. You can store a signature block in the e-mail program and set the program to insert the signature block automatically. In contrast, the writer in Figure 13.2 omits both the salutation and his name. When you send a message to an individual or a group you have set up, the "From:" line will have your name and e-mail address. If you post a message to a group someone else has set up, such as a listserv, be sure to give at least your name and e-mail address at the end of your message, as some listservs strip out identifying information when they process messages.

With smartphones now accounting for 54% of the U.S. cell phone market, options to check e-mail and the web continue to evolve and increase. More than half of the smartphones purchased today use the Android operating system.

Source: Nidhi Subbaraman, "Smartphone Sales on the Rise in the U.S., Half of Those Are Androids," *Fast Company*, July 13, 2012, http://www.fastcompany.com/1842795/smartphone-sales-on-the-rise-in-the- us-half-of-those-are-androids.

After one date and then ignored text and voice-mail messages, a rebuffed man tracked down the woman's e-mail address and sent her a 1,600-word screed on the matter. Among his assertions were that she must have found him physically attractive or she would have turned him down in the first place, that she gave all of the classic flirtatious "preening" signs, such as playing with her hair, and that she said, "It was nice to meet you" at the end of the date, an inconclusive statement that contributed to his confusion as to whether they had the potential for a serious relationship. Despite his requests for a second date, the only outcome was the e-mail message went viral on the Internet.

Source: Tara Kelly, "Investment Manager's Embarrassing e-mail Lands on Reddit, Goes Viral," December 9, 2011, http://www.huffingtonpost.com/2011/12/07/investment-manager-embarrassing-email_n_1135279.html.

Figure 13.1 A Basic E-Mail Message in Eudora (direct request)

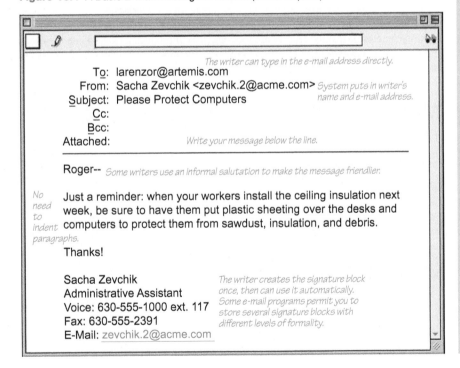

Figure 13.2 An E-Mail Message with an Attachment (direct request)

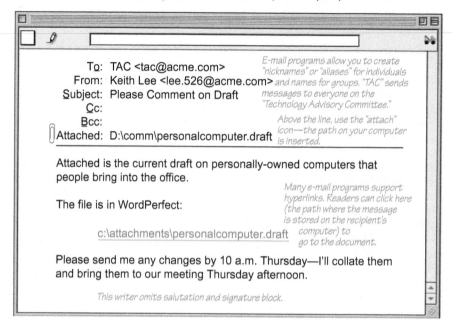

Toː: TAC <tac@acme.com>

From: Keith Lee <lee.526@acme.com>

Subject: Please Comment on Draft

Cc:

Bcc:

Attached: D:\comm\personalcomputer.draft

E-mail programs allow you to create "nicknames" or "aliases" for individuals and names for groups. "TAC" sends messages to everyone on the "Technology Advisory Committee."

Above the line, use the "attach" icon—the path on your computer is inserted.

Attached is the current draft on personally-owned computers that people bring into the office.

The file is in WordPerfect:

c:\attachments\personalcomputer.draft

Many e-mail programs support hyperlinks. Readers can click here (the path where the message is stored on the recipient's computer) to go to the document.

Please send me any changes by 10 a.m. Thursday—I'll collate them and bring them to our meeting Thursday afternoon.

This writer omits salutation and signature block.

When you hit "reply," the e-mail program automatically uses "Re:" (Latin for *about*) and the previous subject. The original message is set off (see Figure 13.3). You may want to change the subject line to make it more appropriate for your message.

If you prepare your document in a word processor, use two-inch side margins to create short line lengths. If the line lengths are too long, they'll produce awkward line breaks as in Figure 13.3. Use two- or three-space tab settings to minimize the wasted space on the screen.

What kinds of subject lines should I use for e-mail messages? LO 13-2

▶ *Be specific, concise, and catchy.*

Subject lines in e-mail are even more important than those in letters and memos because it's so easy for an e-mail user to hit the Delete key. Subject lines must be specific, concise, and catchy. Many e-mail users get so many messages that they don't bother reading messages if they don't recognize the sender or if the subject doesn't catch their interest.

Try to keep the subject line short. If that's difficult, put the most important part into the first few words because some e-mail programs only show the first 28 characters of the subject line.

If your message is very short, you may be able to put it in the subject line. "EOM" (end of message) tells your reader that there is no additional information in the body of the message.

Subject: Will Attend 3 PM Meeting EOM
Subject: Need Password for Survey EOM

Site to See

Go to

www.ftc.gov/bcp/edu/
pubs/consumer/alerts/
alt127.shtm

for tips on avoiding *phishing,* an Internet scam where e-mail or pop-up messages trick people into revealing personal information, such as bank account or Social Security numbers.

Figure 13.3 An E-Mail Reply with Copies (response to a complaint)

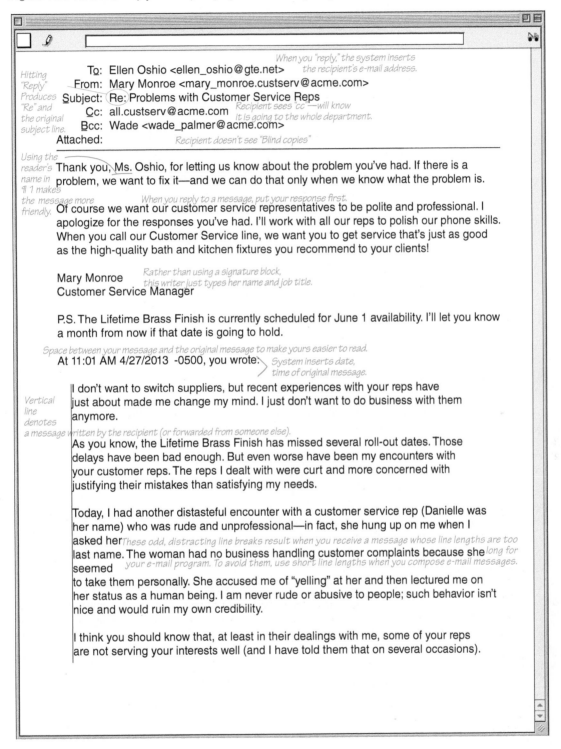

Hitting "Reply" Produces "Re" and the original subject line.

To: Ellen Oshio <ellen_oshio@gte.net> — *When you "reply," the system inserts the recipient's e-mail address.*

From: Mary Monroe <mary_monroe.custserv@acme.com>

Subject: Re: Problems with Customer Service Reps

Cc: all.custserv@acme.com — *Recipient sees "cc"—will know it is going to the whole department.*

Bcc: Wade <wade_palmer@acme.com>

Attached: — *Recipient doesn't see "Blind copies"*

Using the reader's name in ¶ 1 makes the message more friendly. Thank you, Ms. Oshio, for letting us know about the problem you've had. If there is a problem, we want to fix it—and we can do that only when we know what the problem is.

When you reply to a message, put your response first.

Of course we want our customer service representatives to be polite and professional. I apologize for the responses you've had. I'll work with all our reps to polish our phone skills. When you call our Customer Service line, we want you to get service that's just as good as the high-quality bath and kitchen fixtures you recommend to your clients!

Mary Monroe — *Rather than using a signature block,*
Customer Service Manager — *this writer just types her name and job title.*

P.S. The Lifetime Brass Finish is currently scheduled for June 1 availability. I'll let you know a month from now if that date is going to hold.

Space between your message and the original message to make yours easier to read.

At 11:01 AM 4/27/2013 -0500, you wrote: — *System inserts date, time of original message.*

Vertical line denotes a message written by the recipient (or forwarded from someone else).

> I don't want to switch suppliers, but recent experiences with your reps have just about made me change my mind. I just don't want to do business with them anymore.
>
> As you know, the Lifetime Brass Finish has missed several roll-out dates. Those delays have been bad enough. But even worse have been my encounters with your customer reps. The reps I dealt with were curt and more concerned with justifying their mistakes than satisfying my needs.
>
> Today, I had another distasteful encounter with a customer service rep (Danielle was her name) who was rude and unprofessional—in fact, she hung up on me when I asked her last name. The woman had no business handling customer complaints because she seemed to take them personally. She accused me of "yelling" at her and then lectured me on her status as a human being. I am never rude or abusive to people; such behavior isn't nice and would ruin my own credibility.
>
> I think you should know that, at least in their dealings with me, some of your reps are not serving your interests well (and I have told them that on several occasions).

These odd, distracting line breaks result when you receive a message whose line lengths are too long for your e-mail program. To avoid them, use short line lengths when you compose e-mail messages.

Communication technologies are only valuable if they solve problems better than more conventional options.

"Well, I've emailed, faxed, and phoned Dobson.
Maybe I should just walk down the hall
and talk to him..."

Reprinted with permission of CartoonStock.com,
www.cartoonstock.com.

Subject Lines for Informative and Positive E-Mail Messages

If you have good news to convey, be sure it's in the subject line. Be as brief as you can.

The following subject lines would be acceptable for informative and good news e-mail messages:

Subject: Travel Plans for Sales Meeting
Subject: Your Proposal Accepted
Subject: Reduced Prices During February
Subject: Your Funding Request Approved

When you reply to a message, the e-mail system automatically creates a subject line "Re: [subject line of message to which you are responding]." If the subject line is good, that's fine. If it isn't, you may want to create a new subject line. And if a series of messages arises, create a new subject line. "Re: Re: Re: Re: Question" is not an effective subject line.

Subject Lines for Negative E-Mail Messages

When you say "no" to an e-mail request, just hit "reply" and use "Re:" plus whatever the original subject line was for your response. When you write a new message, you will have to decide whether to use the negative in the subject line. The subject line should contain the negative when

- The negative is serious. Many people do not read all their e-mail messages. A neutral subject line may lead the reader to ignore the message.
- The reader needs the information to make a decision or act.
- You report your own errors (as opposed to the reader's).

Thus the following would be acceptable subject lines in e-mail messages:

Subject: We Lost McDonald's Account
Subject: Power to Be Out Sunday, March 12
Subject: Error in Survey Data Summary

E-Mail	Acronyms
ASAP	As soon as possible
BTW	By the way
EOM	End of message
FAQ	Frequently asked questions
FYI	For your information
IMHO	In my humble opinion
TMOT	Trust me on this
LOL	Lots of laughs; Laugh out loud

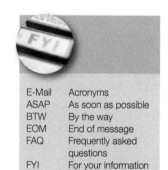
Instant Replay

Keep Subject Lines Short

Try to keep the subject line short. If that's difficult, put the most important part into the first few words because some e-mail programs only show the first 28 characters of the subject line.

In other situations, a neutral subject line is acceptable.

Subject: Results of 360° Performance Appraisals

Subject Lines for Persuasive E-Mail Messages

The subject line of a persuasive e-mail message should make it clear that you're asking for something. If you're sure that the reader will read the message, something as vague as "Request" may work. Most of the time, it's better to be more specific.

Subject: Move Meeting to Tuesday?
Subject: Need Your Advice
Subject: Provide Story for Newsletter?
Subject: Want You for United Way Campaign

A study of more than 977 million e-mail messages by marketer MailerMailer found that shorter subject lines attract more clicks, and any subject line longer than 50 characters is a bad idea.

Source: Julian Sancton, "The Art of the E-Mail Subject Line," *Bloomberg Businessweek,* June 28, 2012, http://www.businessweek.com/articles/2012-06-28/the-art-of-the-e-mail-subject-line/.

Should I write e-mail messages the same way I write paper messages? LO 13-3

▶ *Negative and persuasive messages will be more direct.*

Readers read and reply to e-mail quite rapidly. Dealing with 80 to 100 messages in 20 or 30 minutes is normal. Write e-mail messages so that it's easy for readers to understand and act on them quickly. Writing messages so that the reader can deal with them quickly means taking time to plan, revise, and proofread, just as you do with paper messages. Figure 13.4 shows how a writer might allocate time in responding to a simple e-mail request. Figure 13.5 lists the activities needed for a more complex e-mail message.

Writing Positive and Informative E-Mail Messages

E-mail is especially appropriate for positive and informative messages. Figure 13.3 is an example of a positive response to a customer complaint.

Writing Negative E-Mail Messages

Major negatives, such as firing someone, should be delivered in person, not by e-mail. But e-mail is appropriate for many less serious negatives.

Figure 13.4 Allocating Time in Writing a Simple E-Mail Response (Your time may vary.)

E-mail answering a simple question. Total time: 7 minutes

Planning
    Read the question.
    Gather any information necessary for reply.
    Plan the message.
	2 minutes

Writing Draft the message.	2 minutes

Revising
    Reread draft.
    Make small changes.
    Run spell-check.
    Proof by eye.
    Send the message.
	3 minutes

Figure 13.5 Allocating Time in Writing a Persuasive E-Mail Message (Your time may vary.)

Persuasive request with attachments. Total time: 3 hours	
Planning Understand the situation. Answer the PAIBOC questions (◄◄ Module 1). Think about document design (◄◄ Module 5). Organize the message.	1 hour
Writing Draft the message and attachments.	½ hour
Revising Reread draft. Measure draft against PAIBOC questions and checklist for problem-solving persuasive messages (◄◄ Figure 12.10). Revise draft and attachments. Ask for feedback. Revise draft based on feedback. Edit to catch grammatical errors. Run spell-check. Proof by eye. Send the message.	1½ hours

Never write e-mail messages when you're angry. If a message infuriates you, wait till you're calmer before you reply—and even then, reply only if you must. Writers using e-mail are much less inhibited than they would be on paper or in person, sending insults, swearing, name-calling, and making hostile statements.[1] **Flaming** is the name given to this behavior. Flaming does not make you look like a mature, level-headed candidate for bigger things. And because employers have the right to read all e-mail, flaming—particularly if directed at co-workers, regulators, suppliers, or customers—may cause an employee to be fired.

In the body of the e-mail message, give a reason only if it is watertight and reflects well on the organization. Give an alternative, if one exists.

Edit and proofread your message carefully. An easy way for an angry reader to strike back is to attack typos or other errors.

Remember that e-mail messages, like any documents, can become documents in lawsuits. When an e-mail negative is hard to write, you may want to compose it offline so that you can revise it and even get feedback before you send the message.

Writing Persuasive E-Mail Messages

When you ask for something small or for something that is part of the reader's job duties to provide, your request can be straightforward. (See Figures 13.1 and 13.2.)

- In the body of the message, give people all the information they need to act.
- At the end of the message, ask for the action you want. Make the action as easy as possible, and specify when you need a response. You may want an immediate response now ("Let me know asap whether you can write a story for the newsletter so that I can save the space") and a fuller one later ("we'll need the text by March 4").

When you ask for something big or something that is not a regular part of that person's duties, the first paragraph must not only specify the request but also make the reader view it positively. Use the second paragraph to provide an overview of the evidence that the rest of the message will provide: Use audience analysis (◄◄ p. 19) to find a reason that will convince the reader to do as you ask. Everyone is busy, so you need to make the reader

When Not to Use E-Mail

Managing Your Time LO 13-4

Do you need more time? Welcome to the club! Although researchers claim we have more leisure hours than we did 25 years ago, most of us feel more overworked than ever. And the number of things you'll need to do will only increase as you assume more job responsibilities.

Managing your incoming e-mail is an essential skill for every office worker.

- Create folders, mailboxes, and filters. For example, most e-mail programs allow you to flag messages from your boss in a special color.
- Move items out of your inbox.
- Delete messages after you act on them.
- If you need to save messages, move them to folders on a specific topic or project.
- Create a "delete in 30 days" folder for items you'll need briefly.
- Purge files periodically—at least once a month. (Once a week is better.)

Many workers benefit from managing all their activities (not just their e-mail) more efficiently. To manage your time, divide projects or incoming mail into three piles (real or imaginary). Put urgent items in the *A* pile, important items in the *B* pile, and other items in the *C* pile. Do the *A* items first. Most people find that they never get to their *C* piles.

At the end of the day, make a list of the two most important things you need to do the next day—and leave the paper where you'll see it when you start work the next morning.

If you still don't have enough time to get your *A*s and most of your *B*s done, you're ready for a more systematic approach to time.

1. For at least a week, log how you spend your time. Record what you're doing in 15-minute intervals.

2. Analyze your log to identify patterns, time obligations, time wasters, and frustrations. You may be surprised to find how much time you spend playing computer games. Or you may discover that answering e-mail takes an hour every morning—not the five minutes or so that you'd estimated.

3. Clarify your goals. What do you want to accomplish on the job and in your personal life? What intermediate steps (e.g., taking a course, learning a new skill, or sending out job applications) will you need to do to reach your goals?

4. Set short-term priorities. For the next month, what do you need to accomplish? In addition to goals for school and work, think also about building relationships, meeting personal obligations, and finding time to plan, to relax, and to think.

5. Ask for help or negotiate compromises. Maybe you and another parent can share babysitting so that you each have some time to yourselves. If your responsibilities at work are impossible, talk to your supervisor to see whether some of your duties can be transferred to someone else or whether you should stop trying to be excellent and settle for "good enough." You won't be willing or able to eliminate all your obligations, but sometimes dropping just one or two responsibilities can really help.

6. Schedule your day to reflect your priorities. You don't necessarily have to work on every goal every day, but each goal should appear on your schedule at least three times a week. Schedule some time for yourself, too.

7. Evaluate your new use of time. Are you meeting more of your goals? Are you feeling less stressed? If not, go back to step 1 and analyze more patterns, obligations, time wasters, and frustrations to see how you can make the best use of the time you have.

want to do as you ask. Be sure to provide complete information that the reader will need to act on your request. Ask for the action you want.

Here's why we should do this.

Let me describe the project. Then, if you're willing to be part of it, I'll send you a copy of the proposal.

Major requests that require changes in values, culture, or lifestyles should not be made in e-mail messages.

Site to See

Go to
www.albion.com/
netiquette/netiquiz.html

to test your knowledge of e-mail netiquette.

Like viruses, some spyware programs can infect your computer with malicious code. Your web browser may have security features to block spyware. Popular free spyware detection and clean-up programs include Spybot and Ad Aware, available at www.cnet.com.

Site to See

Go to
www.vmyths.com
to learn whether a rumored virus is real or a hoax.

According to a Pew Research Center study, 51% of Americans preferred vocal communication while only 31% preferred to be contacted via texts. The average adult sends about 10 texts a day but makes 12 phone calls. However, those numbers may differ according to age. An earlier survey by the Nielsen Company found the average 13- to 17-year-old sends and receives 3,339 texts a month, or more than 100 per day. People from ages 45 to 54 sent and received 323 texts a month.

Sources: Erica Ho, "Texting Overtakes Voice Calls for British Mobile Users," *Time,* July 19, 2012, http://newsfeed.time.com/2012/07/19/texting-overtakes-voice-calls-for-british-mobile-users/#ixzz22LxwLhgz; and Katherine Rosman, "Y U Luv Texts, H8 Calls," *The Wall Street Journal,* October 14, 2010, http://online.wsj.com/article/SB10001424052748703673604575550201949192336.html.

What e-mail "netiquette" rules should I follow? LO 13-5

▶ *Lurk before you leap.*

E-mail communities develop their own norms. If possible, lurk a few days—read the messages without writing anything yourself—before you enter the conversation.

Follow these guidelines to be a good "netizen":

- Never send angry messages by e-mail. If you have a conflict with someone, work it out face-to-face, not electronically.
- Use full caps only to emphasize a single word or two. Putting the whole message in caps is considered as rude as shouting.
- Send people only messages they need. Send copies to your boss or CEO only if he or she has asked you to.
- Find out how your recipient's system works and adapt your messages to it. Most people would rather get a separate short message on each of several topics, so that the messages can be stored in different mailboxes. But people who pay a fee to download each message may prefer longer messages that deal with several topics.
- When you respond to a message, include only the part of the original message that is essential so that the reader understands your posting. Delete the rest. If the quoted material is long, put your response first, then the original material.
- When you compose a message in your word processor and call it up in e-mail, use short line lengths (set the right margin at 2.5" or 3"). That's the way to avoid the awkward line breaks of Figure 13.3.

How and when should I use attachments? LO 13-6

▶ *When the reader expects and needs them.*

Any text document can be copied and pasted into the body of your e-mail message. Sending attachments makes the most sense when you send

- A long text document.
- A text document with extensive formatting.
- A nontext file (e.g., PowerPoint slides, html file, spreadsheet).

When you send an attachment, tell the reader what program it's in (see Figure 13.2). Word-processing programs can generally open documents in earlier programs but not later ones.

A computer **virus** is a script that harms your computer or erases your data. You can get a virus through e-mail, and viruses can infect files that are "attached" to e-mail messages or that you download. To stay virus-free,[2]

- Install an antivirus program on your computer, and keep it up-to-date.
- Ask people who send you attachments to include their names in the document titles. Virus titles aren't that specific.
- If you're in doubt about an attachment, don't open it.
- Forward e-mail messages only when you're sure of the source and contents.

What style should I use when writing for the web? LO 13-7

▶ *Use good business writing principles, but consider how people will interact with the text, too.*

Good business writing style basics—being clear, concise, and complete—also work when writing for the web. Unless your page is designed for readers seeking highly technical information, keep your style simple and conversational in tone, and use titles, headings, bulleted lists, and only necessary jargon. Draft your information using a word processor so you can edit and proofread carefully. Module 16 [▶▶ p. 272] provides more information on creating a good business style.

When drafting, think about how readers will use the information. Web surfers generally skim information, at least initially, so lengthy sentences, thick paragraphs, frequent downloads, and too many **hyperlinks,** or jumps to new pages, can discourage surfers from continuing. The same goes for unnecessary graphics or complex introductions that slow loading the page, especially for people using dial-up modems.

Because there is no hard data on how many hyperlinks are too many for readers, use your best judgment when you can't ask your audience directly. One way to check is to highlight hyperlinks in your draft. If they look like too many, they probably are. Consider making some links into buttons, putting links on a separate page, or folding the links' information into the body text. Cut unnecessary links.

Images should support the text. When you write titles and captions, consider telling a story [Module 25 ▶▶ p. 418].

John Morkes and Jakob Nielsen advocate creating "scannable text" to make Web pages accessible:[3]

- Highlight key words.
- Use meaningful, not clever, subheadings.
- Include bulleted lists.
- Use one idea per paragraph.
- Write in the "inverted pyramid" style of organization, with the main idea up front.
- Use half the word count of a printed page.
- Avoid "marketese," or language that is extremely subjective and boastful.

In many organizations, the people who provide written "content" are different than the people who actually design the pages. Where possible, work with designers so that at each stage of the drafting process you can test what you've written for readability against the physical constraints of the layout. For instance, computer screens generally are wider but shallower than a printed page. If you write lengthy paragraphs or long document sections, readers may have to scroll more, which can create eyestrain, especially on monitors whose images seem to flicker due to slower refresh rates. **Frames,** or sections on the page, can organize text and reduce the need to scroll often. Module 5 [◀◀ pp. 78–79] provides information on designing effective screens.

Insist on a clean font, pleasing but contrasting colors, and text-supportive graphics rather than simply decorative ones. Keep in mind, too, that vision-impaired surfers can use the web better if you encourage a layout that accommodates them, such as one using descriptive text links that screen reader software such as Jaws can recognize.

As with any technology, the web is evolving, so expect rules to develop and change. In the meantime, keep a library of web pages you believe work as models, and where possible, test your web pages and content with people who will be using them.

Can I use blogging on the job?   LO 13-7

▶ *Yes, so long as you are professional.*

Creating weblogs, or **blogging,** is an increasingly popular way of communicating on the web. Millions of bloggers post thoughts, images, and links in journal-like entries made available through the Internet and in such languages as Arabic, Chinese, English, French, German, Italian, Japanese, Portuguese, Korean, and Spanish.

Blogging is so popular, some businesses are turning to it to aid in recruiting employees, and CEOs are posting their own blogs in an effort to speak directly to customers and associates. A few people have managed to turn blogging into a career. But blogging

While blogging continues to be popular for many writers, it may be losing its appeal among younger people. According to the Internet and American Life Project at the Pew Research Center, blogging among people ages 12 to 17 fell by half from 2006 to 2009 and by two percentage points in 2010 over two years earlier for people ages 18 to 33. Many younger people prefer instead to use social networking sites like Facebook and Twitter.

Source: Verne G. Kopytoff, "Blogging by Young on Decline," *The Columbus Dispatch,* March 1, 2011, http://www.dispatch.com/live/content/life/stories/2011/03/01/blogging-by-young-on- decline.html?sid=101.

Among the tips offered by Christine Erickson for using social networking tools to market a business are to see if a vanity URL is available, use social plug-ins wherever possible, and provide local content, such as a promotion at a nearby venue or messages customized to languages spoken in an area. A variety of apps exist to help business users, such as Hootsuite, which lets users publish once but distribute messages across multiple tools, such as Facebook, Twitter, LinkedIn, and Google+ .

Source: Christine Erickson, "9 Tips for Small Business Marketing on Facebook," February 20, 2012, http://mashable.com/2012/02/20/facebook-marketing-small-business/.

Derogatory speech is obviously foolish, but posting it in the digital age invites far greater scrutiny than ever before. Recent faux pas include broadcaster Tony Bruno's tweet slamming San Francisco Giants pitcher Ramon Ramirez, originally from the Dominican Republic, as an "illegal alien." The baseless comment was similar to slurs from Mike Bacsik about "Mexicans in San Antonio" that got him fired. University of California at Los Angeles student Alexandra Wallace posted a video titled "Asians at the Library" that, among other things, mocked students calling relatives after the Japan Tsunami. Thousands of Facebook users decried the video, and Wallace later dropped out after reports of death threats. Soon after Amy Winehouse died, Microsoft angered people by tweeting that fans could honor the singer by buying her album from the company's Zune website.

Sources: 'Duk, "Radio Host Tony Bruno Calls Ramirez an 'Illegal Alien' After Plunking," August 6, 2011, http://sports.yahoo.com/mlb/blog/big_league_stew/post/Radio-host-Tony-Bruno-calls-Ramirez-an-8216-il?urn=mlb-wp15190; "Bacsik Fired for Racially Insensitive Tweet," ESPN, April 27, 2010, http://sports.espn.go.com/dallas/mlb/news/story?id=5141002; Simone Wilson, "Alexandra Wallace, UCLA Students, Rants on Asians for Phoning Tsunami victims in the Library," March 14, 2011, http://blogs.laweekly.com/informer/2011/03/alexandra_wallace_ucla_girl_rant_asians_in_the_library.php; and Deborah Netburn, "Microsoft Apologizes for Winehouse Tweet," *The Los Angeles Times,* July 25, 2011, http://latimesblogs.latimes.com/technology/2011/07/microsofts-amy-winehouse-tweet-inspired-disgust-in-twittersphere.html.

in a professional setting is different than blogging in a personal one. For instance, many bloggers feel free to share deeply personal information about themselves or unflattering opinions about people in their lives or the companies they work for. To do so in a business situation might be considered inappropriate. In fact, some employees have been disciplined or fired for doing just that, such as programmer Mark Jen, whose complaints about the health care benefits and free food policy of his employer, Google, got him fired. Retired General Motors (GM) Vice Chairman Bob Lutz joined the growing ranks of top executives who are blogging; his FastLane Blog attracts both supporters and detractors of GM's vehicles, but Lutz's balanced responses have won him praise.[4]

Remember that if companies own or pay for computer resources, they may be entitled to access e-mail and blogs created by employees on their systems. In addition, blogs may be cached just like web pages, meaning that years after the fact someone may be able to access an otherwise nonexistent blog.

Websites such as blogger.com and businessblogconsulting.com provide information on creating blogs and how and where to post them. Search engines for blogs include Google Blog, Technorati, and Blogdigger.

To create a blog for business, Jeff Wuorio suggests these basics:[5]

- Identify your audience.
- Decide where your blog should live.
- Start talking.
- Get into the practice of "blog rolling," or linking to websites and other blogs.
- Emphasize keywords.
- Keep it fresh.
- Watch your traffic closely.

Can I use social networking tools for business situations? LO 13-7

▶ *Yes, as long as you keep things professional.*

Many **social networking tools** are now used by businesses and business professionals to communicate the latest news about themselves, products and services, or even available jobs. While being "plugged in" can provide a greater network of contacts to draw from than in more traditional settings, disclosing information of any kind on the web can expose people to unwanted attention. Choose carefully based on your comfort level.

Be professional when using social networking sites like Facebook or LinkedIn for business. Images, music, and text should be office-appropriate, and avoid criticizing co-workers or past or present employers. You can use social networking to connect with other professionals or even to look for a job.

Many users still blur the line between what is appropriate personally and professionally. A racy photo from a party might be fine with personal friends, but potential or current employers could feel otherwise. Recent awkward situations show the pitfalls of forgetting that the audience for social networking sites, as with blogging, may be larger than users appreciate. For example, after being diagnosed with depression, IBM's Natalie Blanchard began receiving sick leave payments. Months later, they abruptly stopped. She said when she called to find out why, her insurer, Manulife, explained Facebook photos of her having fun at a bar and on the beach showed she was ready to return to work.[6]

Remember, when using a social networking tool in business:

For an organization's social networking pages, also keep in mind:

- Keep things professional. If it's inappropriate at work, it's inappropriate online. That includes comments, images, and music. (◄◄ Module 9 for tips on keeping a professional image.)
- Know who your online friends are, as well as who their friends are. Choose your friends wisely, and set your privacy controls accordingly.
- Know that once information is online, it might be possible to retrieve it again in the future, even after you've deleted items or the page.
- Read user agreements carefully. A site may, for instance, state that in exchange for letting you post, you agree to let it monitor communication or sell personal information to marketers.
- When in doubt, create two pages: one for personal friends and one for business ones.

Sites include tutorials or help functions to get started. Technology evolves quickly, meaning tools and techniques to use them can change at any time. Stay on top of changes by visiting sites often. Upgrade to the latest versions of software when warranted. Understand, too, that just as one tool becomes popular or fades into obscurity, several more are likely on the way.

- Update pages frequently—at least several times a week. Newsfeeds, in particular, must pique the interest of followers with timely information. Post new photos and images. Create events.
- Make one person responsible for updating the company page. Designate someone in a department to be the "point person."
- Consider carefully any decisions to run ads on the company page. Make sure ads and their sponsors match your organization's expectations.
- Understand the value of "word of mouth" advertising. Social networking sites thrive on it.
- Explore the features that social networking sites provide. Facebook, for instance, allows users to locate audiences based on general interests and style. You can also sponsor stories, run your own ads, and even schedule posts ahead of time.

Facebook and MySpace

Though they format information differently, facebook.com and myspace.com both let users create a page with personal information, such as name, photos, and biography. They also have the option to include sound or video, as well as to blog or link to one. Users can make the information public so that all visitors have access, or they can set the page to **private,** meaning only those given permission can view beyond a limited first page. With Facebook and MySpace, users link to **friends,** or specific users within the site's population. When new information is posted, friends can get updates and respond to comments left on their pages. Users can also join groups according to shared interests, such as their hobbies, college, or companies, becoming **fans.**

While basic services are free, there may be paid services available as well. Facebook, for instance, allows users to purchase advertising that targets specific audiences based on interests or affiliation. Users increasingly are turning to Facebook and MySpace to seek out jobs, either through postings or through communicating with their network of friends.

Site to See

Spoke and LinkedIn

Spoke.com and linkedin.com were designed for traditional business networking purposes. As with their more personal counterparts, they let users supply information, such as profession and education; users may also post résumés, look for jobs, list past employers, or in some cases even ask the user community general questions, similar to features found on search engines. The advantage is that users are business professionals, and as this book goes to press, LinkedIn alone reports more than 160 million users, including job recruiters.

Go to
www.fansbuy.org/using-facebook-for-business/
for 20 tips on using Facebook in business. If it doesn't fit, move this Site to See to the column bottom on the next page, please.

Twitter

Twitter integrates computers and cell phones for sharing quick messages, or **tweets.** Snappy blurbs of 140 characters or fewer are the norm, and users can link to friends so that updates are in real time. Like his boss and other high-profile U.S. officials, former White House Press Secretary Robert Gibbs joined the ranks of those tweeting, which also included CEOs like Tony Hsieh and Steve Jobs and celebrities like Jay-Z, Miley Cyrus, and Britney Spears. Users can also find the latest headlines from organizations like CNN and Fox News. DePaul University even offers a class on twittering.[7] The key to effective tweeting is to keep messages brief, timely, and catchy.

YouTube

Youtube.com revolutionized the way people create and access video on the web. Visitors can find everything from amateur skits and home movies to professional training videos, movie trailers, and even some films and television shows. Some professionals upload video résumés [▶▶ Module 28] to the site, which like most sites has a search function.

What other technologies use the Internet?   LO 13-8

▶ *Fax, phone, instant messaging, and videoconferencing services are all available on the web.*

The Internet is making it possible for many services, such as fax and phone, to be handled through the web, sometimes at reduced cost compared to traditional means. Operating systems such as Windows 8 provide rudimentary fax capability.

Keep business tweets simple and professional. Messages must be 140 characters or less. If you have long web addresses to post, free sites like tinyurl.com can shorten them for you. Remember, too, that users are drawn to current information, so frequently tweeting relevant news is a good strategy to keep people following you.

Smartphones continue to evolve quickly in form and function, allowing users to talk, text, e-mail, surf the web, take photos and video, and more. These capabilities will continue to grow in number and sophistication, creating more features but also an ongoing learning curve for users. Many people are concerned about cell phone etiquette, as they are offended by interruptions and loud or inappropriate conversations in such spaces as theaters, classrooms, restaurants, houses of worship, and even restrooms.

Many companies now provide or subscribe to instant messaging services for employees, and companies such as Yahoo! and MSN have instant messaging features for general users. As with a telephone conversation, instant messaging requires people to respond quickly but also to think carefully about what they are going to say. Instant messages can be saved for future reference.

Videoconferencing sites like Skype are making it possible for people in different locations to meet "face-to-face" without ever leaving the office. Rising fuel costs and the drive for greater efficiency are making videoconferencing an attractive alternative to travel, but there are limitations. Cameras still produce two-dimensional images of limited scope, sound may be tinny, and video infrequently captures a person's warmth or physical presence. People speaking into a camera must remember, too, that their movements appear opposite to people watching them—a gesture to the speaker's right, for instance, will appear to the audience's left.

New technologies are often attractive, but choose wisely which is appropriate for you. Remember that technology is only as valuable as it is useful.

(*continued*)

is no expectation of privacy on a business phone, and clarify content and language guidelines for business.

Sources: Joanna Krotz, "Cell Phone Etiquette: 10 Dos and Don'ts," 2011, http://www.microsoft.com/business/en-us/resources/technology/communications/cell-phone-etiquette-10-dos-and-donts.aspx?fbid=GI6G_TpfYbp; Maura Judkis, "N.Y. Philharmonic Phone Disruption: A Cell-Phone Etiquette Reminder," *The Washington Post*, January 13, 2012, http://www.washingtonpost.com/blogs/arts-post/post/ny-philharmonic-phone-disruption-a-cell-phone-etiquette-reminder/2012/01/13/gIQActV9vP_blog.html; and J. J. McCorvey, "How to Create a Cell Phone Policy," *Inc.*, February 10, 2011, http://www.inc.com/guides/how-to-create-a-cell-phone-policy.html.

Summary of Learning Objectives

- Most e-mail programs prompt you to supply the various parts of the format. **(LO 13-1)**
- Some aspects of e-mail format are still evolving. In particular, some writers treat e-mail messages as if they were informal letters; some treat them as memos. **(LO 13-1)**
- If you prepare your document in a word processor, use two-inch side margins to create short line lengths. **(LO 13-1)**
- Subject lines for e-mail messages must be specific, concise, and catchy. **(LO 13-2)**
- If your message is short, you may be able to put it in the subject line. **(LO 13-2)**
- Create e-mail messages that people can read and act on quickly. **(LO 13-3)**
- E-mail is especially appropriate for positive and informative messages. Major negatives, however, should not be delivered by e-mail. **(LO 13-3)**
- Never write e-mail messages when you're angry. **(LO 13-3)**
- **Flaming** is writing insulting or hostile e-mail messages. Avoid this behavior. **(LO 13-3)**
- When you ask in e-mail for something small or part of a reader's job duties, your request can be straightforward. When you ask for something big or outside their normal job duties, let your first paragraph specify the request so the reader views it positively. Let the second paragraph provide an overview of the evidence the rest of the message will provide. **(LO 13-3)**
- Create folders, mailboxes, and filters to keep e-mail messages organized. **(LO 13-4)**
- Use time-saving efforts, such as reviewing time obligations and clarifying your goals, with other activities besides e-mailing. **(LO 13-4)**
- For good "netiquette," in addition to avoiding flaming and writing e-mail messages when angry: **(LO 13-5)**

- Use full caps only to emphasize a single word or two.
- Send people only messages they need.
- Adapt your messages to the recipient's system when possible. Include only the part of your original message needed by the reader when responding to a message.
- Sending attachments makes the most sense when you send **(LO 13-6)**
  - A long text document.
  - A text document with extensive formatting.
  - A nontext file.
- A computer **virus** is a script that harms your computer or erases data. You can get a virus through e-mail and through attachments. Use antivirus software as a defense. **(LO 13-6)**
- Use good business writing principles when writing for the web, but consider how people will interact with the text, too. Where possible, work with web page designers while writing, and test the page and content with people who will be using the page. **(LO 13-7)**
- If you blog on the job, keep it professional. Stay away from sharing deeply personal information about yourself or unflattering opinions about people in your life or the company you work for. **(LO 13-7)**
- You can use social networking sites in business so long as you keep things professional. **(LO 13-7)**
  - If it isn't appropriate for work, it isn't appropriate to post.
- Sites to consider using are MySpace, Facebook, Spoke, LinkedIn, Twitter, and YouTube. **(LO 13-7)**
- Fax, phone, instant messaging, and videoconferencing services are all available on the web. **(LO 13-8)**
- Remember, technology is only as valuable as it is useful. **(LO 13-8)**

Assignments for Module 13

Questions for Comprehension

13.1 How do subject lines for e-mail messages differ from those for paper messages? **(LO 13-2)**

13.2 Should e-mail messages use you-attitude, positive emphasis, and reader benefits? **(LO 13-3)**

13.3 What is flaming? **(LO 13-3, LO 13-5)**

Questions for Critical Thinking

13.4 Why should you be flexible when using different e-mail systems? **(LO 13-1)**

13.5 Why is e-mail better for informative and positive messages than for negative ones? **(LO 13-2)**

13.6 Why is it OK for your boss to send you a message with the subject line "To Do," even though that wouldn't work when you need to ask a colleague to do something? **(LO 13-2)**

13.7 Why should negative and persuasive e-mail messages be more direct than their paper counterparts? **(LO 13-3)**

Exercises and Problems

13.8 Calming an Angry Co-worker (LO 13-1 to LO 13-3)

You're a member of a self-managed team on a factory assembly line. When you check the team's e-mail, you find this message from the factory's Quality Assurance Manager:

Subject: Holes in Your Heads?

Yesterday in the scrap bin I found a casting with three times too many holes in it. How could a machinist make such a mistake? What's going on?

The answer is simple. The extra holes come not from crazy machinists but from crafty ones. Your team uses old machines that aren't computerized. When you make a part on those machines, you have to drill a test piece first to be sure that the alignment and size of the holes are correct. This testing has to be done every time you set up for a new run. Your team has figured out that you can use less material by reusing the test piece until it resembles Swiss cheese, rather than throwing it away after a single testing. Your team is one of the most efficient in the plant, thanks to creative moves like this one. Write an e-mail response.

13.9 Announcing Holiday Diversity (LO 13-1 to LO 13-3)

Your organization has traditionally given employees several holidays off: New Year's; Martin Luther King, Jr., Day; Independence Day; Veterans' Day; Thanksgiving; and Christmas. Employees who celebrate other holidays (e.g., Good Friday, Yom Kippur, Ramadan, Chinese New Year, the Hindu holiday Diwali) have been able to take those days off with the consent of their supervisors. But some employees have complained that it is unfair to depend on the goodwill of supervisors. And now a few other employees have complained that people who honor other holidays are getting "extra" days off since they take those days in addition to the standard holidays.

Therefore, the executive committee of your organization has decided to allow employees any 10 days off for holidays; they will have to tell their supervisors which days they plan to take off. People will be asked in December which holidays they want to take off in the following year. People can change their minds during the year as long as they have not yet taken off the full 10 holidays. Any religious, ethnic, or cultural holiday is acceptable. (Someone who wants to take off *Cinco de Mayo* or Bastille Day can do so.) Vacations, personal days off, and sick days are not affected by this policy.

As vice president for human resources, write an e-mail to all employees, announcing the new policy.

Hints:

• Pick a business, government, or nonprofit organization that you know something about.
• Will the office be "open" every day? If not, do all employees already have keys, or will they need to pick them up so they can get into the office to work days that few other people work?
• See www.holidayfestival.com for a list of holidays in various countries.
• Use your analysis from Problem 2.13.

13.10 Refusing to Pay an Out-of-Network Bill (LO 13-1 to LO 13-3)

Your employees' health insurance allows them to choose from one of three health maintenance organizations (HMOs). Once the employee has selected an HMO, he or she must get all medical care (except for out-of-state emergency care) from the HMO. Employees receive a listing of the doctors and hospitals affiliated with each HMO when they join the company and pick an HMO. They get to choose again each October when they have a one-month "open enrollment period" to change to another of the three HMOs if they choose.

As director of employee benefits, you've received an angry e-mail from Alvin Reineke. Alvin had just received a statement from his HMO stating that it would not pay for the costs of his hernia operation two months ago at St. Catherine's Hospital in your city. Alvin is furious: One of the reasons he accepted a job with your company six months ago was its excellent health care coverage. He feels the company lied to him and should pay for his (rather large) hospital bill because the HMO refuses to do so.

The HMO that Alvin had selected uses two hospitals, but not St. Catherine's. When Alvin joined the company six months ago, he, like all new employees, received a thick booklet explaining the HMO options. Perhaps he did not take the time to read it carefully. But that's not your fault. Alvin can change plans during the next open enrollment, but even if he switched to an HMO that included St. Catherine's, that HMO wouldn't pay for surgery performed before he joined that HMO.

Write an e-mail message to Alvin giving him the bad news.

Hints:

- What tone should you use? Should you be sympathetic? Should you remind him that this is his own fault?
- Is there any help you can give Alvin (e.g., information about credit union short-term loans or even information about negotiating payment terms with the hospital)?
- What can you do to make Alvin feel that the company has not lied to him?

13.11 Saying *No* to the Boss (LO 13-1 to LO 13-3)

Today, you received the following e-mail message from your boss:

> Subject: Oversee United Way
>
> I'm appointing you to be the company representative to oversee United Way. You've done a good job the last three years, so this year should be a piece of cake!

It's true that you know exactly what to do. The job wouldn't be hard for you. But that's just the problem. You wouldn't learn anything, either. You'd rather have an assignment that would stretch you, teach you new skills, or enable you to interact with new people. Continuing to grow is your insurance of continued employability and mobility. Three upcoming projects in your division might offer growth: creating videos for a "town meeting" for all employees to be held at the beginning of next quarter, creating an intranet for the company, or serving on the diversity committee. Any of these would be time-consuming, but no more time-consuming than running the United Way campaign.

Write to your boss, asking for something more challenging to do.

13.12 Sending a Question to a Website (LO 13-1 to LO 13-3)

Send a question or other message that calls for a response to a website. You could

- Ask a question about a product.
- Apply for an internship or a job (assuming you'd really like to work there).
- Ask for information about an internship or a job.
- Ask a question about an organization or a candidate before you donate money or volunteer.
- Offer to volunteer for an organization or a candidate. You can offer to do something small and onetime (e.g., spend an afternoon stuffing envelopes, put up a yard sign), or you can, if you want to, offer to do something more time-consuming or even ongoing.

As Your Instructor Directs,

a. Turn in a copy of your e-mail message and the response you received.
b. Critique messages written by other students in your class. Suggest ways the messages could be clearer and more persuasive.

c. Write a memo evaluating your message and the response, using the checklists for Modules 12 and 10, respectively. If you did not receive a response, did the fault lie with your message?
d. Make an oral presentation to the class, evaluating your message and the response, using the checklists for Modules 12 and 10, respectively. If you did not receive a response, did the fault lie with your message?

Hints:

- Does the organization ask for questions or offers? Or will yours "come out of the blue"?
- How difficult will it be for the organization to supply the information you're asking for or to do what you're asking it to do? If you're applying for an internship or offering to volunteer, what skills can you offer? How much competition do you have?
- What can you do to build your own credibility, so that the organization takes your question or request seriously?

13.13 Suggesting a Change in Your Organization's Communication Materials (LO 13-1 to LO 13-3)

Your organization has a web page, but its address isn't on all your business communication materials (stationery, business cards, invoices, product packaging, brochures, catalogs, voice-mail announcements, e-mail signatures, promotional items such as pens, coffee cups, and mouse pads). Adding the URL would promote the website (and suggest that your organization is up-to-date).

As Your Instructor Directs,

a. Identify the person in your organization with the power to authorize adding the URL to physical materials, and e-mail that person asking him or her to authorize this change.
b. Write an e-mail to all employees, asking them to add the URL and a brief message promoting the organization to their e-mail signature blocks.

Hints:

- Pick a business, nonprofit, or government organization you know something about. What materials does it produce? Which lack the URL?
- Will the reader know you? Has your organization asked for suggestions, or will this come "out of the blue"?

- What should be done with materials already printed or manufactured that lack the web address? Should they be discarded, or used until they run out?
- Who in your organization has the authority to authorize this change?
- What exactly do you want your reader to do? What information does your reader need?

13.14 Asking for More Time and/or Resources (LO 13-1 to LO 13-3)

Today, the following message shows up in your e-mail inbox from your boss:

Subject: Fwd: Want Climate Report

This request has come down from the CEO. I'm delegating it to you. See me a couple of days before the board meeting—the first Monday of next month—so we can go over your presentation.

>I want a report on the climate for underrepresented groups in our organization. A presentation at
>the last board of directors' meeting showed that while we do a good job of hiring women and
>minorities, few of them rise to the top. The directors suspect that our climate may not be
>supportive and want information on it. Please prepare a presentation for the next meeting. You'll
>have 15 minutes.

Making a presentation to the company's board of directors can really help your career. But preparing a good presentation and report will take time. You can look at exit reports filed by human resources when people leave the company, but you'll also need to interview people—lots of people. And you're already working 60 hours a week on three major projects, one of which is behind schedule. Can one of the projects wait? Can someone else take one of the projects? Can you get some help? Should you do just enough to get by? Ask your boss for advice—in a way that makes you look like a committed employee, not a slacker.

13.15 Addressing a Customer Complaint about a Coupon (LO 13-1 to LO 13-3)

As manager of consumer affairs for your company, you received the following e-mail message:

My name is Jan Hofbauer, and I recently visited one of your Kelly Green apparel stores in Denver. While I am a long-time customer who enjoys the many great styles you have to offer, I was dismayed by my experience.

I wanted to use a coupon I received via e-mail for 20% off any single item. But when I tried to use the coupon, I was told there were restrictions, including it only being applicable to regularly priced merchandise.

I explained to the manager that nowhere on the coupon was a statement to that effect. When she said the statement appears on the Kelly Green web page, I pointed out I wasn't on the Internet, I was in the store! She would not honor the coupon, but since I had spent 30 minutes of valuable time picking out the sweater, I purchased it anyway.

It's unfair to wait until after a customer has taken time out of her busy schedule to drive to the store to tell her of restrictions. If anything, this all seems like fraud. She should have honored the coupon.

What I want to know now is what are you going to do to keep me as a customer?

Jan Hofbauer

After further research, you discovered the coupon was sent as a promotion for the Kelly Green web page. In fact, in the e-mail message and on the coupon, a statement prominently indicates it is only good for use at the web page and that some restrictions apply. When customers click on the link to the web page, a statement further explaining restrictions appears, including the coupon being for regularly priced items. Therefore, you don't feel it's appropriate to give Ms. Hofbauer a 20% credit on her Visa card.

However, you are willing to give her a 10% credit for being a loyal customer and for her troubles. Write an e-mail message to Ms. Hofbauer explaining your decision.

13.16 Requesting Your Firm Use Social Networking (LO 13-1 to LO 13-3, LO 13-7)

Your small but prestigious financial services firm has a web page that increasingly gets traffic and now you, the communications director, want to convince upper management to branch out to Facebook and Twitter pages. But several of the senior partners think that social networking sites are too trendy and informal and don't accurately reflect the firm's conservative culture. They would prefer that most communication with clients happens by phone, letter, or face to face, and though they are comfortable with e-mail, feel that it is best left for internal communication. You know that convincing the senior partners to adopt more modern strategies will be tough, but you also know the firm stands to lose its competitive edge in a rapidly changing world if they don't.

As your instructor directs,

a. Identify the person or persons in the firm who might help you establish credibility on technical matters. What additional resources might help you to establish a claim that social networking will help the firm? What information might you collect that can further bolster your claims?

b. Write an e-mail message to the senior partners requesting the firm use social networking. (Alternatively, write a paper message if you believe that e-mail is too informal.)

Hints:

• Consider the potential impacts. Clearly, the move to include social networking in marketing and communication efforts reflects a shift in organizational culture. How might you persuade people firmly invested in the status quo that changes are both necessary and beneficial? What objections might they have?

• Do research. Are there examples or case studies of similar organizations adopting social networking? What can you learn from their experiences that would be helpful in your message?

• Think creatively. Is there a way to test social networking out on a smaller scale with the firm before going "live" to clients?

• Consider company resources. What would be needed in terms of finances, training, equipment, and personnel to use social networking? If the needed resources are minimal, how might that make your appeal more attractive?

Polishing Your **Prose**

Making Nouns and Pronouns Agree

Pronouns must agree with the nouns to which they refer in two ways: (1) person and (2) number—singular or plural.

	Singular	Plural
First-person	I, my, mine, me, myself	we, our, us, ourselves
Second-person	you, your, yourself	you, your, our, ours, yourselves
Third-person	he, she, it, him, her, his, hers	they, their, them, themselves

Incorrect: In my internship, I learned that you have to manage your time wisely.

Correct: In my internship, I learned to manage my time wisely.

Incorrect: The sales team reached their goal.

Correct: The sales team reached its goal.

U.S. usage treats company names and the words *company* and *government* as singular nouns. In Great Britain and those countries using the British System, these nouns are plural and require plural pronouns:

Correct (U.S.): Nationwide Insurance trains its agents well.

Correct (U.K.): Lloyds of London train their agents well.

Exercises

Correct any noun–pronoun agreement errors, following U.S. style. Note that some sentences do not contain errors.

1. My college lowered their parking sticker costs about $10 a year.
2. When Kelea and Shawn arrived together from Portland, she both decided to walk rather than take a shuttle to the airport hotel.
3. You have to mind your Ps and Qs, I discovered, if you're going to get ahead in this world.
4. The Building and Zoning Department got their act together and beat the Marketing Department in the final inning of the company softball game.
5. Victor said her greatest achievement was being selected as "Man of the Year" by the Rotary Club.
6. With few changes to their production model, Jacoby, Inc., expects to start manufacturing in a few weeks.
7. My mother told me that when she was a little girl, she learned you can't always believe what you hear.
8. Madison told me their purse got left in the restaurant—his smartphone was inside of it.
9. At Singh and Associates, I told my parents, I learned you have to do your best to get noticed.
10. The best things about Netflix is the way they make sure their procedures are easy to follow.

Check your answers to the odd-numbered exercises at the back of the book.

Unit 3 Cases for Communicators

The Real Price of a Cheap Flight

In July 2012, United Airlines began offering refunds to passengers who had taken advantage of a computer glitch to book flights to Hong Kong or other destinations in Asia that connected to the city in exchange for four frequent flier miles, plus government taxes. A business class seat on United to Hong Kong typically costs about $8,500, or 120,000 frequent flier miles. First class is about $2,000 more, or 20,000 miles.

Before United officials realized the error, people shared news of it on sites throughout the web, and though United won't confirm the final numbers, hundreds, if not thousands, of people bought tickets. However, United eventually stopped selling tickets and announced it wasn't honoring the tickets already sold. Refunds would instead be offered, though people who had already started their trip would be able to finish it.

Complicating the problem, the U.S. Department of Transportation (DOT) had recently enacted rules that prohibit airlines from increasing prices after consumers make their purchase, so some consumers complained that United was violating that rule. At heart is at what point the glitch appeared. Initially, purchasers were given the correct price. It was only after they actually went to the screen to book the fare that the error appeared.

Individual Activity

As the customer service director at United, you have received hundreds of e-mail messages from angry customers who thought they were booking the cheap flights to Hong Kong. In particular, many of them feel that United is ducking responsibility for the error and breaking the law by ignoring the DOT regulations. Write an e-mail message explaining to them that the initial screen at the point of purchase explained the correct amount customers would be charged and that by pressing "Book Flight Now" there, they were acknowledging the correct price, regardless of what showed up on the following screen. United regrets the error but sees it as an honest technical mistake rather than an attempt to avoid honoring a claim.

As you plan your correspondence, consider the following:

- What should my subject line convey?
- How can I organize the message in a positive, problem-solving way?
- Will I include reader benefits in the message?

As you evaluate your draft, consider these questions:

- Is my subject line specific, concise, and clear?
- Did I organize this message using the following pattern for positive messages?

> Main Point
> Details
> Negatives
> Reader Benefits
> Goodwill Ending

- Did I use PAIBOC (Purpose, Audience, Information, Benefits, Objections, Context) to help me write a positive message?
- Did I successfully create you-attitude in this message?

Be sure to check your grammar and proofread the message by eye as well as by spell-check!

Group Activity

You want the Department of Transportation to understand that United operated in good faith when the computer glitch occurred, and you want to allay any concerns that similar problems will happen in the future. In particular, you want the DOT to know that once the company was aware of the error, the site was shut down and refunds were immediately processed. However, you have heard that some irate customers are lobbying the agency to consider legal action against United.

Your IT Department has provided a report on what went wrong. Maintenance on the web page was actually done by a third party, subcontracted through the department. Responsibility for making sure information on the site was current and correct was that company's, and there is an indemnity clause in the contract stating that United will not be held liable for any mistakes made by the third party. Regardless, however, of who ultimately is held fiducially responsible, the damage to United's reputation from a DOT investigation could be great and affect future sales.

Write a letter to DOT officials explaining the results of United's internal investigation and requesting that no further action be taken regarding whether United violated DOT regulations. Before you write the letter, discuss the following issues with your colleagues:

- What should the subject line convey, if anything?
- Which persuasive strategy—direct request or problem solving—is appropriate in this situation?
- Which of the following patterns is better?

> Shared Problem
> Details
> Solution
> Negatives
> Reader Benefits
> Request for Action
>   Or
> Request of Action
> Details
> Request for Action

- What types of possible objections or responses are expected?
- What benefits, if any, could be highlighted?

Use your answers to these questions to draft the letter. Then work together with your group to craft the final language for this message. As you write, ask these questions:

1. Did we include information to negate possible objections or responses to the message?
2. Did we follow the correct organization for the persuasive strategy we are using?
3. Did we use PAIBOC (Purpose, Audience, Information, Benefits, Objections, Context) to help us write a persuasive message?
4. Did we successfully create you-attitude in this letter?

Watchdog audiences like the DOT are key to the success of United, so be sure to think carefully about the tone of the letter. Remember, these folks have a stake in United's future, too!

Source: Scott Mayerowitz, "The Battle Over $33 Flights to Hong Kong," July 19, 2012, http://news.yahoo.com/battle-over-33-flights-hong-kong-200052930-finance.html.

Polishing Your Writing

Polishing Your Writing 4

Module **14** Editing for Grammar and Punctuation

Module **15** Choosing the Right Word

Module **16** Revising Sentences and Paragraphs

14 | Editing for Grammar and Punctuation

LEARNING OBJECTIVES

Module 14 focuses on solutions to common errors with grammar and punctuation. After completing the module, you should be able to

LO 14-1 **Apply strategies for professional image creation with grammar and mechanics.**

LO 14-2 **Apply principles for common grammatical error correction.**

LO 14-3 **Apply principles for sentence error correction.**

LO 14-4 **Evaluate situations for comma use.**

LO 14-5 **Apply principles for punctuation use inside sentences.**

LO 14-6 **Apply principles for source quotation.**

LO 14-7 **Apply principles for number and date use.**

LO 14-8 **Apply standard proofreading marks throughout the writing process.**

With the possible exception of spelling, grammar is the aspect of writing that writers seem to find most troublesome. Faulty grammar is often what executives are objecting to when they complain that college graduates or MBAs "can't write."

The modules in this unit gather advice about grammar, punctuation, words, and sentence and paragraph revision. Many of these topics are also treated in the Polishing Your Prose sections at the end of each module. For a list, see the inside front cover.

Creating a Professional Image, 2 LO 14-1

Grammar and mechanics present a paradox. On the one hand, grammar and punctuation are the least important part of any message: The ideas and their arrangement matter far more.

On the other hand, many business leaders see good grammar and mechanics as essential to creating effective messages—and to demonstrating quality. The College Board's National Commission on Writing found 95.2% of survey respondents said spelling, punctuation, and grammar were "important" or "extremely important." Companies surveyed included American Express, Boeing, Ford Motor Company, IBM, J. P. Morgan Chase, MetLife, Pfizer, Sears, and Verizon Communications.

"In most cases, writing ability could be your ticket in . . . or it could be a ticket out," noted one participant, while another said of promotion, "You can't move up without writing skills."

Errors also create a negative image of the writer. Professor Larry Beason found that businesspeople judged the authors of errors to be not only poor writers but also poor businesspeople. Negative judgments included the following:

- Careless and hasty
- Uncaring (about reader or message)
- Problems with thinking and logic
- Not a detail person—what will you do with numbers?
- Poor oral communicator
- Uneducated

So grammar and punctuation can be the most important part of your message.

Occasionally, errors in grammar and punctuation hide the writer's meaning. More often, it's possible to figure out what the writer probably meant, but the mistake still sends the wrong message (and can be an excuse for a hostile reader or an opposing attorney).

Don't try to fix errors in your first and second drafts. The brain can't attend both to big ideas and to sentence-level concerns at the same time. But do save time to check your almost-final draft to eliminate any errors in grammar, punctuation, and word choice.

Most writers make a small number of grammatical errors repeatedly. Most readers care deeply about only a few grammatical points. Keep track of the feedback you get (from your instructors now, from your supervisors later) and put your energy into correcting the errors that bother the people who read what you write. A command of standard grammar will help you build the credible, professional image you want to create with everything you write.

Sources: Writing: A Ticket to Work . . . Or a Ticket Out: A Survey of Business Leaders, Report of The National Commission on Writing for America's Families, Schools, and Colleges, College Entrance Examination Board, September 2004; and Larry Beason, "Ethos and Error: How Business People React to Errors," *CCC* 53:1, September 2001.

What grammatical errors do I need to be able to fix? LO 14-2

▶ *Learn how to fix these six errors.*

Good writers can edit to achieve subject–verb and noun–pronoun agreement, to use the right case for pronouns, to avoid dangling and misplaced modifiers, and to correct parallel structure and predication errors.

Agreement

Subjects and verbs agree when they are both singular or both plural.

Incorrect:	The accountants who conducted the audit was recommended highly.
Correct:	The accountants who conducted the audit were recommended highly.

Subject–verb agreement errors often occur when other words come between the subject and the verb. Edit your draft by finding the subject and the verb of each sentence.

U.S. usage treats company names and the words *company* and *government* as singular nouns. British usage treats them as plural:

Correct (U.S.):	State Farm Insurance trains its agents well.
Correct (Great Britain):	Lloyds of London train their agents well.

Rutgers University Professor Jack Lynch sees attention to grammar as at least as much an issue of class warfare as it is of making communication understandable. Correcting a split infinitive—such as *Star Trek's* "to boldly go"—gives people "access to power," not because all grammarians agree that splitting an infinitive in English is wrong but because people in power may think it is.

Source: Laura Miller, "Memo to Grammar Cops: Back Off!" *Salon,* April 18, 2010, http://www.salon.com/books/laura_miller/index.html.

Site to See

Go to

http://grammar.
quickanddirtytips.com/

for Grammar Girl's tutorials on
fixing common errors.

There's only one English today,
right? Not if you ask officials
at the Voice of America, who
have reduced conversational
English to only 1,500 words,
called "specialized English."
Aerospace and Defense Simplified Technical English is used
by the European aerospace
industry to streamline communications, and some Christian
missionaries practice Easy-
English when abroad. These
forms of "simple English" are
designed to reduce problems
with bad grammar and to make
it easier to communicate with
non-native speakers of English.

Source: J. David Goodman, "List of
'Special English' Words Increases,"
The Columbus Dispatch, January
2, 2008, downloaded at www.
dispatch.com/live/content/life/
stories/2008/01/02/1A_SIMPLE_
ENGLISH.ART_ART_01-02-08_D1_
CD8T4TT.html?sid=101.

Site to See

Go to

www.iei.illinois.
edu/grammarsafari/
grammarsafari.html

Especially for ESL students,
Grammar Safari helps you hunt
grammar in real language.

Use a plural verb when two or more singular subjects are joined by *and.*

Correct: Larry McGreevy and I are planning to visit the client.

Use a singular verb when two or more singular subjects are joined by *or, nor,* or *but.*

Correct: Either the shipping clerk or the superintendent has to sign the order.

When the sentence begins with *Here* or *There,* make the verb agree with the subject that follows the verb.

Correct: Here is the booklet you asked for.
Correct: There are the blueprints I wanted.

Note that some words that end in *s* are considered to be singular and require singular verbs.

Correct: A series of meetings is planned.

When a situation doesn't seem to fit the rules, or when following a rule produces an awkward sentence, revise the sentence to avoid the problem.

Problematic: The Plant Manager in addition to the sales representative (was, were?) pleased with the new system.
Better: The Plant Manager and the sales representative were pleased with the new system.
Problematic: None of us (is, are?) perfect.
Better: All of us have faults.

Errors in **noun–pronoun agreement** occur if a pronoun is of a different number or person than the word it refers to.

Incorrect: All drivers of leased automobiles are billed $100 if damages to his automobile are caused by a collision.
Correct: All drivers of leased automobiles are billed $100 if damages to their automobiles are caused by collisions.
Incorrect: A manager has only yourself to blame if things go wrong.
Correct: As a manager, you have only yourself to blame if things go wrong.

The following words require a singular pronoun:

everybody	everyone	nobody
each	neither	a person
either		

Correct: Everyone should bring his or her copy of the manual to the next session on changes in the law.

If the pronoun pairs necessary to avoid sexism seem cumbersome, avoid the terms in this list. Instead, use words that take plural pronouns or use second-person *you.*

Each pronoun must refer to a specific word. If a pronoun does not refer to a specific term, add a word to correct the error.

Incorrect: We will open three new stores in the suburbs. This will bring us closer to our customers.
Correct: We will open three new stores in the suburbs. This strategy will bring us closer to our customers.

Hint: Make sure *this* and *it* refer to a specific noun in the previous sentence. If either refers to an idea, add a noun ("this strategy") to make the sentence grammatically correct.

Use *who* and *whom* to refer to people and *which* to refer to objects. *That* can refer to anything: people, animals, organizations, and objects.

Correct: The new Executive Director, who moved here from Boston, is already making friends.
Correct: The audit, which we completed yesterday, shows that the original numbers are incorrect.
Correct: This confirms the price that I quoted you this morning.

Case

Case refers to the grammatical role a noun or pronoun plays in a sentence. Figure 14.1 identifies the case of each personal pronoun.

Use **nominative** pronouns for the **subject** of a clause.

Correct:	Shannon Weaver and I talked to the customer, who was interested in learning more about integrated software.

Use **possessive** pronouns to show who or what something belongs to.

Correct:	Microsoft Office will exactly meet her needs.

Use **objective** pronouns as **objects** of verbs or prepositions.

Correct:	When you send in the quote, thank her for the courtesy she showed Shannon and me.

Hint: Use *whom* when *him* would fit grammatically in the same place in your sentence.

I am writing this letter to (who/whom?) it may concern.

I am writing this letter to him.

Whom is correct.

Have we decided (who, whom?) will take notes?

Have we decided he will take notes?

Who is correct.

Use **reflexive** and **intensive** pronouns (the form with *self* or *selves*) to refer to or emphasize a noun or pronoun that has already appeared in the sentence.

Correct:	I nominated myself.

Do not use reflexive pronouns as subjects of clauses or as objects of verbs or prepositions.

Incorrect:	Elaine and myself will follow up on this order.
Correct:	Elaine and I will follow up on this order.
Incorrect:	He gave the order to Dan and myself.
Correct:	He gave the order to Dan and me.

Note that the first-person pronoun comes after names or pronouns that refer to other people.

Forty-five percent of employers surveyed recently said they were increasing training to improve grammar and other skills in their employees. Confusion over rules, the informality of social networking, and valuing speed over accuracy may be culprits in why grammar skills suffer in the workplace.

Source: Sue Shellenbarger, "This Embarrasses You and I: Grammar Gaffes Invade the Office in an Age of Informal E-mail, Texting, and Twitter," *The Wall Street Journal*, June 19, 2012, http://online.wsj.com/article/SB100014240527023034104045774666662919275448.html?KEYWORDS=grammar.

Figure 14.1 The Case of the Personal Pronoun

	Nominative (subject of clause)	Possessive	Objective	Reflexive/ Intensive
Singular				
1st person	I	my, mine	me	myself
2nd person	you	your, yours	you	yourself
3rd person	he/she/it	his/her(s)/its	him/her/it	himself/herself/itself
	one/who	one's/whose	one/whom	oneself/(no form)
Plural				
1st person	we	our, ours	us	ourselves
2nd person	you	your, yours	you	yourselves
3rd person	they	their, theirs	them	themselves

Dangling Modifier

Modifiers are words or phrases that give more information about the subject, verb, or object in a clause. A modifier **dangles** when the word it modifies is not actually in the sentence. The solution is to reword the modifier so that it is grammatically correct.

Incorrect:	Confirming our conversation, the truck will leave Monday.
	[The speaker is doing the confirming. But the speaker isn't in the sentence.]
Incorrect:	At the age of eight, I began teaching my children about American business.
	[This sentence says that the author was eight when he or she had children who could understand business.]

Correct a dangling modifier in one of these ways:

- Recast the modifier as a subordinate clause.

Correct:	As I told you, the truck will leave Monday.
Correct:	When they were eight, I began teaching my children about American business.

- Revise the main clause so its subject or object can be modified by the now-dangling phrase.

Correct:	Confirming our conversation, I have scheduled the truck to leave Monday.
Correct:	At the age of eight, my children began learning about American business.

Hint: Whenever you use a verb or adjective that ends in *-ing,* make sure it modifies the grammatical subject of your sentence. If it doesn't, reword the sentence.

Misplaced Modifier

A **misplaced modifier** appears to modify another element of the sentence than the writer intended.

Incorrect:	Customers who complain often alert us to changes we need to make.
	[Does the sentence mean that customers must complain frequently to teach us something? Or is the meaning that frequently we learn from complaints?]

Correct a misplaced modifier by moving it closer to the word it modifies or by adding punctuation to clarify your meaning. If a modifier modifies the whole sentence, use it as an introductory phrase or clause; follow it with a comma.

Correct:	Often, customers who complain alert us to changes we need to make.

Parallel Structure

Items in a series or list must have the same grammatical structure.

Not parallel:	In the second month of your internship, you will
	1. Learn how to resolve customers' complaints.
	2. Supervision of desk staff.
	3. Interns will help plan store displays.
Parallel:	In the second month of your internship, you will
	1. Learn how to resolve customers' complaints.
	2. Supervise desk staff.
	3. Plan store displays.
Also parallel:	Duties in the second month of your internship include resolving customers' complaints, supervising desk staff, and planning store displays.

Hint: When you have two or three items in a list (whether the list is horizontal or vertical), make sure the items are in the same grammatical form. Put lists vertically to make them easier to see.

Predication Errors

The predicate of a sentence must fit grammatically and logically with the subject.

In sentences using *is* and other linking verbs, the complement must be a noun, an adjective, or a noun clause.

Incorrect: The reason for this change is because the SEC now requires fuller disclosure.
Correct: The reason for this change is that the SEC now requires fuller disclosure.

Make sure that the verb describes the action done by or done to the subject.

Incorrect: Our goals should begin immediately.
Correct: Implementing our goals should begin immediately.

How can I fix sentence errors?   LO 14-3

▶ *Learn to recognize main clauses.*

A **sentence** contains at least one main clause. A **main clause** is a complete statement. A **subordinate** or **dependent clause** contains both a subject and verb but is not a complete statement and cannot stand by itself. A phrase is a group of words that does not contain both a subject and a verb.

Main Clauses

Your order will arrive Thursday.

He dreaded talking to his supplier.

I plan to enroll for summer school classes.

Subordinate Clauses

if you place your order by Monday

because he was afraid the product would be out of stock

although I need to have a job

Phrases

With our current schedule

As a result

After talking to my adviser

A clause with one of the following words will be subordinate:

after	if
although, though	when, whenever
because, since	while, as
before, until	

Using the correct punctuation will enable you to avoid four major sentence errors: comma splices, run-on sentences, fused sentences, and sentence fragments.

Instant Replay

Dangling Modifiers

A modifier dangles when the word it modifies is not actually in the sentence.

Comma Splices

A **comma splice** or **comma fault** occurs when two main clauses are joined only by a comma (instead of by a comma and a coordinating conjunction).

Incorrect: The contest will start in June, the date has not been set.

Correct a comma splice in one of the following ways:

• If the ideas are closely related, use a semicolon rather than a comma. If they aren't closely related, start a new sentence.

Kyle Wiens, CEO of iFixIt and founder of Dozuki, requires all job applicants to take a grammar test. With a self-described "zero tolerance" for grammar errors, he notes that in his experience, sloppiness with writing corresponds to sloppiness in other job duties. How strict are his standards? "If you think a semicolon is a regular colon with an identity crisis, I will not hire you. If you scatter commas into a sentence with all the discrimination of a shotgun, you might make it to the foyer before we politely escort you from the building."

Source: Kyle Wiens, "I Won't Hire People Who Use Poor Grammar. Here's Why," *Harvard Business Review,* July 20, 2012, http://blogs. hbr.org/cs/2012/07/i_wont_hire_ people_who_use_poo.html.

Many business professionals bemoan the errors they see as the result of the speed and informality of electronic communication for some people, whether they're typos or grammatical issues like run-on sentences and sentence fragments. Yet, there may be trade-offs. A study of Twitter users showed that while they had 20% more grammatical errors than non-tweeting counterparts, they were only about half as likely to have spelling errors.

Source: Andy Jordan, "RT@gooseGrade: Twitters Good at Spelling, Bad at Grammar. #whatwouldmomsay?" *The Wall Street Journal,* July 6, 2009, http://blogs.wsj .com/digits/2009/07/06/ rtgoosegrade-twitterers-good- at-spelling-bad-at-grammar- whatwouldmomsay/tab/ article/.

Correct: The contest will start in June; the exact date has not been set.

• Add a coordinating conjunction.

Correct: The contest will start in June, but the exact date has not been set.

• Subordinate one of the clauses.

Correct: Although the contest will start in June, the date has not been set.

Remember that you cannot use just a comma with the following transitions.

however   nevertheless

therefore   moreover

Instead, use a semicolon to separate the clauses or start a new sentence.

Incorrect: Computerized grammar checkers do not catch every error, however, they may be useful as a first check before an editor reads the material.

Correct: Computerized grammar checkers do not catch every error; however, they may be useful as a first check before an editor reads the material.

Run-On Sentences

A **run-on sentence** strings together several main clauses using *and, but, or, so,* and *for.* Run-on sentences and comma splices are "mirror faults." A comma splice uses *only* the comma and omits the coordinating conjunction, while a run-on sentence uses *only* the conjunction and omits the comma. Correct a short run-on sentence by adding a comma. Separate a long run-on sentence into two or more sentences. Consider subordinating one or more of the clauses.

Incorrect: We will end up with a much smaller markup but they use a lot of this material so the volume would be high so try to sell them on fast delivery and tell them our quality is very high.

Correct: Although we will end up with a much smaller markup, volume would be high since they use a lot of this material. Try to sell them on fast delivery and high quality.

Fused Sentences

A **fused sentence** results when two or more sentences are *fused* or joined with neither punctuation nor conjunctions. To fix the error, add either punctuation or a conjunction.

Incorrect: The advantages of intranets are clear the challenge is persuading employees to share information.

Correct: The advantages of intranets are clear; the challenge is persuading employees to share information.

Also correct: Although the advantages of intranets are clear, the challenge is persuading employees to share information.

Sentence Fragments

In a **sentence fragment,** a group of words that is not a complete sentence is punctuated as if it were a complete sentence. Sentence fragments often occur when a writer thinks of additional detail that the reader needs. Fragments are acceptable in résumés and sales letters, but they're rarely acceptable in other business documents.

Incorrect: Observing these people, I have learned two things about the program. The time it takes. The rewards it brings.

To fix a sentence fragment, either add whatever parts of the sentence are missing or incorporate the fragment into the sentence before it or after it.

Correct: Observing these people, I have learned that the program is time-consuming but rewarding.

Remember that clauses with the following words are not complete sentences. Join them to a main clause.

after	if
although, though	when, whenever
because, since	while, as
before, until	

Incorrect: We need to buy a new computer system. Because our current system is obsolete.
Correct: We need to buy a new computer system because our current system is obsolete.

Should I put a comma every place I'd take a breath? LO 14-4

▶ *No! Commas are not breaths.*

Some people have been told to put commas where they'd take breaths. That's bad advice. How often you'd take a breath depends on how big your lung capacity is, how fast and how loud you're speaking, and the emphasis you want. Commas aren't breaths. Instead, like other punctuation, they're road signs.

Punctuation marks are road signs to help readers predict what comes next (see Figure 14.2).

When you move from the subject to the verb, you're going in a straight line; no comma is needed. When you end an introductory phrase or clause, the comma tells readers the introduction is over and you're turning to the main clause. When words interrupt the main clause, like this, commas tell the reader when to turn off the main clause for a short side route and when to return.

What punctuation should I use inside sentences? LO 14-5

▶ *Use punctuation to make your meaning clear to your reader.*

The good business and administrative writer knows how to use the following punctuation marks: apostrophes, colons, commas, dashes, hyphens, parentheses, periods, and semicolons.

Apostrophe

1. Use an apostrophe in a contraction to indicate that a letter has been omitted.

> We're trying to renegotiate the contract.

> The 1990s were years of restructuring for our company.

Instant Replay

Comma Splices

A **comma splice** or **comma fault** occurs when two main clauses are joined only by a comma (instead of by a comma and a coordinating conjunction).

The late, great television commentator Andy Rooney stopped using apostrophes, even in his books. According to Bob McTeer, Rooney said that since he wrote things to read on TV, he didn't see the need for most apostrophes.

Source: Bob McTeer, "Have You Ever Wondered?" *Forbes,* November 8, 2011, http://www.forbes.com/sites/bobmcteer/2011/11/08/have-you-ever-wondered/.

Figure 14.2 What Punctuation Tells the Reader

Mark	Tells the Reader
Period	We're stopping.
Semicolon	What comes next is closely related to what I just said.
Colon	What comes next is an example of what I just said.
Dash	What comes next is a dramatic example of or a shift from what I just said.
Comma	What comes next is a slight turn, but we're going in the same basic direction.

Using poor grammar is a crime to many readers.

"Sorry, but I'm going to have to issue you a summons for reckless grammar and driving without an apostrophe."

Copyright © Michael Maslin/The New Yorker Collection, www.cartoonbank.com.

Site to See

Go to
www.illiteratebusinesses.
ca/

for examples of typos in
business messages.

Instant Replay

Sentence Fragments

In a **sentence fragment**, a group of words that is not a complete sentence is punctuated as if it were a complete sentence.

2. To indicate possession, add an apostrophe and an *s* to the word.

> The corporation's home office is in Houston, Texas.

Apostrophes to indicate possession are especially essential when one noun in a comparison is omitted.

> This year's sales will be higher than last year's.

When a word already ends in an *s*, add only an apostrophe to make it possessive.

> The meeting will be held at New Orleans' convention center.

With many terms, the placement of the apostrophe indicates whether the noun is singular or plural.

Incorrect: The program should increase the participant's knowledge.
[Implies that only one participant is in the program.]
Correct: The program should increase the participants' knowledge.
[Many participants are in the program.]
Hint: Use *of* in the sentence to see where the apostrophe goes.

> The figures of last year = last year's figures

> The needs of our customers = our customers' needs

Possessive pronouns (e.g., *his, ours*) usually do not have apostrophes. The only exception is *one's*.

> The company needs the goodwill of its stockholders.

> His promotion was announced yesterday.

> One's greatest asset is the willingness to work hard.

3. Use an apostrophe to make plurals that could be confused for other words.

> I earned A's in all my business courses.

However, other plurals do not use apostrophes.

Colon

1. Use a colon to separate a main clause and a list that explains the last element in the clause. The items in the list are specific examples of the word that appears immediately before the colon.

> Please order the following supplies:
>
> Printer cartridges
>
> Computer paper (20-lb. white bond)
>
> Bond paper (25-lb., white, 25% cotton)
>
> Company letterhead
>
> Company envelopes.

When the list is presented vertically, capitalize the first letter of each item in the list. When the list is run in with the sentence, you don't need to capitalize the first letter after the colon.

> Please order the following supplies: printer cartridges, computer paper (20-lb. white bond), bond paper (25-lb., white, 25% cotton), company letterhead, and company envelopes.

Do not use a colon when the list is grammatically part of the main clause.

Incorrect: The rooms will have coordinated decors in natural colors such as: eggplant, moss, and mushroom.

Correct: The rooms will have coordinated decors in natural colors such as eggplant, moss, and mushroom.

Correct: The rooms will have coordinated decors in a variety of natural colors: eggplant, moss, and mushroom.

If the list is presented vertically, some authorities suggest introducing the list with a colon even though the words preceding the colon are not a complete sentence.

2. Use a colon to join two independent clauses when the second clause explains or restates the first clause.

> Selling is simple: Give people the service they need, and they'll come back with more orders.

Comma

1. Use commas to separate the main clause from an introductory clause, the reader's name, or words that interrupt the main clause. Note that commas both precede and follow the interrupting information.

> R. J. Garcia, the new sales manager, comes to us from the Des Moines office.

While poor spelling and grammar may impede success, even great leaders have been known to exhibit lapses. A handwritten letter by President Abraham Lincoln recently drew scrutiny from modern readers, who noted such errors as an apostrophe inserted into the possessive pronoun "its" and an apostrophe missing in "nations" when meant possessively. Said Harold Holzer, an expert on the 16th U.S. President: "Lincoln was not the best speller in the world."

Source: "Lincoln Letter Shows Grammatical Errors," *The Times of India,* March 19, 2010, http://timesofindia.indiatimes.com/world/us/Lincoln-letter-shows-grammatical-errors/articleshow/5699886.cms.

Eats, Shoots & Leaves: The Zero Tolerance Approach to Punctuation by Lynne Truss explores with humor how improper punctuation mangles sentence meaning. The title came from a description of panda eating habits, but the misplaced comma suggests a more destructive event!

A misplaced comma cost cable television giant Rogers Communications more than $2 million. The company thought it had an ironclad agreement with Aliant Telecom to use telecommunication poles for five years, but Aliant terminated the contract after only one year. A court upheld the move after ruling the errant comma changed the meaning of a contract clause, supporting Aliant's decision.

Source: William Loeffler, "Punctuation Errors Can Cost Jobs, Money, Esteem," *The Pittsburgh Tribune-Review,* September 20, 2009, http://www.pittsburghlive.com/x/pittsburghtrib/ae/more/s_643648.html.

A **nonessential clause** gives extra information that is not needed to identify the noun it modifies. Because nonessential clauses give extra information, they need extra commas.

> Sue Decker, who wants to advance in the organization, has signed up for the company training program in sales techniques.

Do not use commas to set off information that restricts the meaning of a noun or pronoun. **Essential clauses** give essential, not extra, information.

> Anyone ☐ who wants to advance in the organization ☐ should take advantage of on-the-job training.

Do not use commas to separate the subject from the verb, even if you would take a breath after a long subject.

Incorrect: Laws requiring anyone collecting $5,000 or more on behalf of another person to be bonded, apply to schools and private individuals as well to charitable groups and professional fund-raisers.

Correct: Laws requiring anyone collecting $5,000 or more on behalf of another person to be bonded ☐ apply to schools and private individuals as well to charitable groups and professional fund-raisers.

2. Use a comma after the first clause in a compound sentence if the clauses are long or if they have different subjects.

> This policy eliminates all sick leave credit of the employee at the time of retirement, and payment will be made only once to any individual.

Do not use commas to join independent clauses without a conjunction. Doing so produces comma splices.

3. Use commas to separate items in a series. Using a comma before the *and* or *or* is not required by some authorities, but using a comma always adds clarity. The comma is essential if any of the items in the series themselves contain the word *and.*

> The company pays the full cost of hospitalization insurance for eligible employees, spouses, and unmarried dependent children under age 23.

Dash

Use emdashes to emphasize a break in thought.

> Ryertex comes in 30 grades—each with a special use.

To create a dash in Microsoft Word, type in a word, followed immediately by two hyphens and then a second word, with no space between the hyphens and the two words. Add a space after the second word and the hyphens instantly change to a dash.

Hyphen

1. Use a hyphen to indicate that a word has been divided between two lines.

> For reimbursement, attach the original receipts for lodging, transportation, and registration fees.

Divide words at syllable breaks. If you aren't sure where the syllables divide, look up the word in a dictionary. When a word has several syllables, divide it after a vowel or between two consonants. Don't divide words of one syllable (e.g., *used*); don't divide a two-syllable word if one of the syllables is only one letter long (e.g., *acre*).

2. Use hyphens to join two or more words used as a single adjective.

> Order five 10- or 12-foot lengths.

> The computer-prepared Income and Expense statements will be ready next Friday.

The hyphen prevents misreading. In the first example, five lengths are needed, not lengths of 5, 10, or 12 feet. In the second example, without the hyphen, the reader might think that *computer* was the subject and *prepared* was the verb.

Parentheses

1. Use parentheses to set off words, phrases, or sentences used to explain or comment on the main idea.

> For the thinnest Ryertex (.015″) only a single layer of the base material may be used, while the thickest (10″) may contain over 600 greatly compressed layers of fabric or paper. By varying the fabric used (cotton, asbestos, glass, or nylon) or the type of paper, and by changing the kind of resin (phenolic, melamine, silicone, or epoxy), we can produce 30 different grades.

Any additional punctuation goes outside the second parenthesis when the punctuation applies to the whole sentence. It goes inside when it applies only to the words in the parentheses.

> Please check the invoice to see if credit should be issued. (A copy of the invoice is attached.)

2. Use parentheses for the second of two numbers presented both in words and in figures.

> Construction must be completed within two (2) years of the date of the contract.

Period

1. Use a period at the end of a sentence.
2. Use a period after some abbreviations. When a period replaces a person's name, leave one space after the period before the next word. In other abbreviations, no space is necessary.

> R. J. Tebeaux has been named Vice President for Marketing.

> The U.S. division plans to hire 300 new M.B.A.s in the next year.

The tendency is to reduce the use of punctuation. It would also be correct to write

> The US division plans to hire 300 new MBAs in the next year.

Use the pattern your organization prefers.

Site to See

Go to
www.grammarbook.com
The Blue Book of Grammar and Punctuation is online.

Semicolon

1. Use semicolons to join two independent clauses when they are closely related.

> We'll do our best to fill your order promptly; however, we cannot guarantee a delivery date.

Using a semicolon suggests that the two ideas are very closely connected. Using a period and a new sentence is also correct but implies nothing about how closely related the two sentences are.

2. Use semicolons to separate items in a series when the items themselves contain commas.

> The final choices for the new plant are El Paso, Texas; Albuquerque, New Mexico; Salt Lake City, Utah; Eureka, California; and Eugene, Oregon.

> Hospital benefits are also provided for certain services such as diagnostic admissions directed toward a definite disease or injury; normal maternity delivery, Caesarean-section delivery, or complications of pregnancy; and in-patient admissions for dental procedures necessary to safeguard the patient's life or health.

Hint: A semicolon could be replaced by a period and a capital letter. It has a sentence on both sides.

What do I use when I quote sources?   LO 14-6

▶ *Quotation marks, square brackets, ellipses, and underlining or italics.*

Quotation marks, square brackets, ellipses, and either underlining or italics are necessary when you use quoted material.

U.S. writers put periods and commas inside closing quotation marks; English writers put them outside the quotation marks. Spanish writers also put sentence-ending punctuation outside.

Source: Based on Complete Translation Services, "A History of Punctuation," www. completetranslation.com, downloaded July 23, 2005.

Quotation Marks

1. Use quotation marks around the names of brochures, pamphlets, and magazine articles.

> Enclosed are 30 copies of our pamphlet "Saving Energy."

> You'll find articles like "How to Improve Your Golf Game" and "Can You Keep Your Eye on the Ball?" in every issue.

In U.S. punctuation, periods and commas go inside quotation marks. Colons and semicolons go outside. Question marks go inside if they are part of the material being quoted.

2. Use quotation marks around words to indicate that you think the term is misleading.

> These "pro-business" policies actually increase corporate taxes.

3. Use quotation marks around words that you are discussing as words.

> Forty percent of the respondents answered "yes" to the first question.

> Use "Ms." as a courtesy title for a woman unless you know she prefers another title.

It is also acceptable to underline or italicize words instead of using quotation marks. Choose one method and use it consistently.

4. Use quotation marks around words or sentences that you quote from someone else.

> "The Fog Index," says its inventor, Robert Gunning, is "an effective warning system against drifting into needless complexity."

Square Brackets

Use square brackets to add your own additions to or changes in quoted material.

Senator Smith's statement:	"These measures will increase the deficit."
Your use of Smith's statement:	According to Senator Smith, "These measures [in the new tax bill] will increase the deficit."

The square brackets show that Smith did not say these words; you add them to make the quote make sense in your document.

Ellipses

Ellipses are spaced dots. In typing, use three spaced periods for an ellipsis. When an ellipsis comes at the end of a sentence, use a dot immediately after the last letter of the sentence for a period. Then add another three spaced dots.

1. Use ellipses to indicate that one or more words have been omitted in the middle of quoted material. You do not need ellipses at the beginning or end of a quote.

> *The Wall Street Journal* notes that Japanese magazines and newspapers include advertisements for a "$2.1 million home in New York's posh Riverdale section . . . 185 acres of farmland [and] . . . luxury condos on Manhattan's Upper East Side."

2. In advertising and direct mail, use ellipses to imply the pace of spoken comments.

> If you've ever wanted to live on a tropical island . . . cruise to the Bahamas . . . or live in a castle in Spain . . .

> . . . you can make your dreams come true with Vacations Extraordinaire.

Underlining and Italics

1. Underline or italicize the names of newspapers, magazines, and books.

The Wall Street Journal	*The Wall Street Journal*
Fortune	*Fortune*
The Wealth of Nations	*The Wealth of Nations*

Titles of brochures and pamphlets are put in quotation marks.

2. Underline or italicize words to emphasize them.

> Here's a bulletin that gives you, in handy chart form, *workable data* on over 50 different types of tubing and pipe.

You may also use boldface to emphasize words. Bolding is better than either underlining or italics because it is easier to read.

How should I write numbers and dates?   LO 14-7

▶ *Usually, spell out numbers under 10 and at the beginning of sentences.*

Spell out **numbers** from one to nine. Use figures for numbers 10 and over in most cases. Always use figures for amounts of money.

Spell out any number that appears at the beginning of a sentence. If spelling it out is impractical, revise the sentence so it does not begin with a number.

> Fifty students filled out the survey.

> In 2002, euro notes and coins entered circulation.

When two numbers referring to different nouns follow each other, use words for the smaller number and figures for the larger number.

In **dates,** use figures for the day and year. The month is normally spelled out. Be sure to spell out the month in international business communication. U.S. usage puts the month first, so that *1/10/08* means *January 10, 2008.* European usage puts the day first, so that *1/10/08* means *October 1, 2008.* Modern punctuation uses a comma before the year only when you give both the month and the day of the month:

> May 1, 2009

but

> Summers 2004–07

> August 2003

> Fall 2006

No punctuation is needed in military or European usage, which puts the day of the month first: 13 July 2005. Do not add a space before or after the slash used to separate parts of the date: 10/03–5/07.

Use a dash to join inclusive dates.

> March–August 2007 (**or write out:** March to August 2007)

> 05–08

> 1999–2009

Note that you do not need to repeat the century in the date that follows the dash: 2007–09. But do give the century when it changes: 1999–2008.

How do I mark errors I find in proofreading?   LO 8

▶ *Use these standard proofreading symbols.*

Use the proofreading symbols in Figure 14.3 to make corrections when you no longer have access to a computer. Figure 14.4 shows how the symbols can be used to correct a typed text.

Typos can have stunning repercussions. In 2005, a typing error caused Mizuho Securities Co. to lose at least 27 billion yen, or $225 million. The trader had meant to sell 1 share at 610,000 yen, or $5,041, but inputted 610,000 shares at 1 yen, or less than a penny. Even top news outlets can slip. A CNN story on the search for Osama Bin Laden was mistakenly titled "Where's Obama?" resulting in multiple apologies to Senator Barack Obama, who later announced his candidacy for U.S. president.

And while many people complain about the high cost of cable TV, few expect to receive a bill like Daniel DeVirgillo's. "All I want to do is watch March Madness," the Ohioan said. The problem was Time Warner said he owed $16.4 million in late charges.

Sources: "$225 Mil. Typo: Not 610,000 Shares, Just One Please," *Chicago Sun-Times,* December 10, 2005, downloaded at http://findarticles.com/p/articles/mi_qn4155/is_20051210/ai_n15921111; Jennifer Millman, "Barack 'Osama'? CNN Says 'Sorry' for Botched Broadcast," *DiversityInc.,* January 3, 2007, downloaded at www.diversityinc.com/public/1096.cfm?sd=151; and Dave Larsen, "Time Warner Charges Wright-Patt Engineer $16.4 Million for Cable," *Springfield News-Sun,* March 24, 2011, http://www.springfieldnewssun.com/news/business/time-warner-charges-wright-patt-engineer-164-milli/nMqHp/.

Figure 14.3 Proofreading Symbols

⌒	delete	[	move to left
ℛ	insert a letter	]	move to right
¶	start a new paragraph here	⌐	move up
(stet)	stet (leave as it was before the marked change)	⌐	move down
(tr) ⌐	transpose (reverse)	#	leave a space
(lc)	lowercase (don't capitalize)	⌒	close up
≡	capitalize	//	align vertically

Figure 14.4 Marked Text

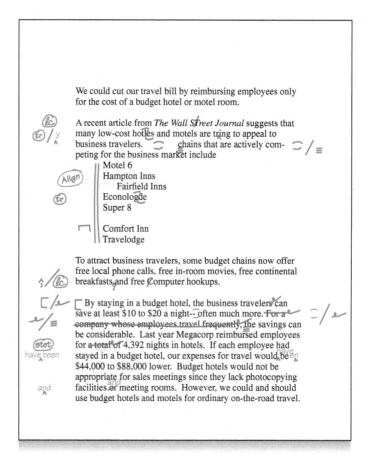

Assignments for Module 14

Questions for Comprehension

14.1 Why is it better to fix errors in grammar and punctuation only after you've revised for content, organization, and style? **(LO 14-1 to LO 14-7)**

14.2 What words make clauses subordinate and thus require more than a comma to join clauses? **(LO 14-2)**

14.3 What is parallel structure? When should you use it? **(LO 14-2)**

14.4 What is a sentence fragment? How do you fix it? **(LO 14-3)**

Questions for Critical Thinking

14.5 Consuela sees a lot of errors in the writing of managers at her workplace. If they don't know or don't care about correctness, why should she? **(LO 14-1)**

14.6 After surveying readers in her workplace (problem 14.15), Camilla finds that most of them are not bothered by errors in grammar and punctuation. Does that mean that she doesn't need to fix surface errors? **(LO 14-1)**

14.7 Joe knows that his variety of English isn't the privileged variety, but he is afraid that using standard edited English will make him seem "uppity" to people in his home community. Should he try to use standard grammar and pronunciation? Why or why not? **(LO 14-1)**

Exercises and Problems

14.8 **Identifying Audience Concerns about Grammar (LO 14-1 to LO 14-7)**

Most readers care passionately about only a few points of grammar. Survey one or more readers (including your boss, if you have a job) to find out which kinds of errors concern them. Use a separate copy of this survey for each reader.

Directions: Each of the following sentences contains some error. Please circle Y if the error bothers you a good bit; S if the error bothers you slightly; and N if you would not be bothered by the error (or perhaps even notice it).

Y S N	1. She brung her secretary with her.
Y S N	2. Him and Richard were the last ones hired.
Y S N	3. Wanted to tell you that the meeting will be November 10.
Y S N	4. Each representative should bring a list of their clients to the meeting.
Y S N	5. A team of people from CSEA, Human Services, and Animal Control are preparing the proposal.
Y S N	6. We cannot predict, how high the number of clients may rise.
Y S N	7. He treats his clients bad.
Y S N	8. She asked Darlene and I to give a presentation.
Y S N	9. Update the directory by reviewing each record in the database and note any discrepancies.
Y S N	10. He has went to a lot of trouble to meet our needs.
Y S N	11. She gave the report to Dan and myself.
Y S N	12. I was unable to complete the report. Because I had a very busy week.
Y S N	13. The benefits of an online directory are a. We will be able to keep records up-to-date;

b. Access to the directory from any terminal with a modem in the county.
c. Cost savings.

Y S N	14. By making an early reservation, it will give us more time to plan the session to meet your needs.
Y S N	15. She don't have no idea how to use the computer.
Y S N	16. The change will not effect our service to customers.
Y S N	17. Confirming our conversation, the truck will leave Monday.
Y S N	18. The sessions will begin January 4 we will pass around a sign-up sheet early in December.
Y S N	19. I will be unable to attend the meeting, however I will send someone else from my office.
Y S N	20. Its too soon to tell how many proposals we will receive.

Compare your responses with those of a small group of students.

- Which errors were most annoying to the largest number of readers?
- How much variation do you find in a single workplace? In a single type of business?

As Your Instructor Directs,

a. Present your findings to the class in a short group report.

b. Present your findings to the class in an oral presentation.

14.9 **Making Subjects and Verbs Agree (LO 14-2)**

Identify and correct the errors in the following sentences.

1. Corinne are going to tour the Hokaido facility in December.
2. We is planning to take the GMAT at the same time to simplify things.
3. While Lani Esposito were our first choice, she declined the job offer.
4. Tyler and Jorge is taking one of the pool cars to the regional meeting.
5. Ephraim reminded us that the first and third Wednesdays of the month are when timecards are due.

14.10 **Using the Right Pronoun (LO 14-2)**

Identify and correct the errors in the following sentences.

1. Bryan e-mailed Todd Winthrop at our Southfield office yesterday, but they didn't receive the message till Thursday.
2. I, Ramon, and Paulette reserved a company car for the three-hour trip to Anaheim this afternoon.
3. We was wondering if anyone contacted the Finance Department to ask them for copies of our annual report.

4. If employees are in uniform, he should understand that he is representing the company, whether on duty or not.

14.11 Fixing Dangling and Misplaced Modifiers (LO 14-2)

Identify and correct the errors in the following sentences.

1. Eleanor reported there were two delayed flights at the staff meeting.
2. At the age of 15, my mom let me drive the car around the block for the first time.
3. Expressing herself with confidence, I was impressed with Lee's answers during the interview.

14.12 Creating Parallel Structure (LO 14-2)

Identify and correct the errors in the following sentences.

1. To narrow a web search,

   - Put quotation marks around a phrase when you want an exact term.
   - Many search engines have wild cards (usually an asterisk) to find plurals and other forms of a word.
   - Reading the instructions on the search engine itself can teach you advanced search techniques.

2. Men drink more alcoholic beverages than women.
3. Each issue of *Hospice Care* has articles from four different perspectives: legislative, health care, hospice administrators, and inspirational authors.
4. The university is one of the largest employers in the community, brings in substantial business, and the cultural impact is also big.

14.13 Correcting Sentence Errors (LO 14-3)

Identify and correct the errors in the following sentences.

1. You can expect our fleet cars to be in pristine working order you can also enjoy such amenities as cruise control, GPS tracking, and satellite radio.
2. Without filling out the appropriate requisition form, the disciplinary action report indicated that Kelly purchased two fax machines for the department.
3. Customers can order through the web page or they can order through our 1-800 number or they can order through traditional mail.

14.14 Providing Punctuation within Sentences (LO 14-5)

Provide the necessary punctuation in the following sentences. Note that not every box requires punctuation.

1. Office work☐☐ especially at your desk☐☐ can create back☐ shoulder ☐neck☐ or wrist strain.
2. I searched for ☐vacation☐ and ☐vacation planning☐ on Google and Alta Vista.
3. I suggest putting a bulletin board in the rear hallway☐ and posting all the interviewer☐s☐ photos on it.
4. Analyzing audiences is the same for marketing and writing☐ you have to identify who the audiences are☐ understand how to motivate them☐ and choose the best channel to reach them.
5. The more you know about your audience ☐who they are☐ what they buy☐where they shop☐☐the more relevant and effective you can make your ad.

5. Jeff Yee and me took a few moments to thank the marketing team for their great work on the December sales promotion.

4. With a broad smile on his face, we watched Alistair accept the Lifetime Achievement Award.
5. Thinking our plane would be delayed due to bad weather, the meeting was rescheduled to 3 p.m.

5. These three tools can help competitive people be better negotiators.

   - Think win–win.
   - It's important to ask enough questions to find out the other person's priorities, rather than jumping on the first advantage you find.
   - Protect the other person's self-esteem.

   These three questions can help cooperative people be better at negotiations.

   - Can you developing a specific alternative to use if negotiation fails?
   - Don't focus on the "bottom line." Spend time thinking about what you want and why you need it.
   - Saying "You'll have to do better than that because . . ." can help you resist the temptation to say "yes" too quickly.

4. They spent the month visiting our satellite offices and meeting their staff. In Fort Wayne. In Lawrence. In Flint. And in Dayton.
5. Zane and me prepared the cover for the annual report and then we gave it to Nardos for review so she will let us know tomorrow if there are any revisions.

6. The city already has five☐ two☐hundred ☐bed hospitals.
7. Students run the whole organization☐ and are advised by a Board of Directors from the community.
8. The company is working on three team☐related issues☐ interaction, leadership, and team size.
9. I would be interested in working on the committee☐ however I have decided to do less community work so that I have more time to spend with my family.
10. ☐You can create your own future☐☐ says Frank Montaño☐ ☐You have to think about it☐ crystallize it in writing☐ and be willing to work at it☐ We teach a lot of goal☐setting and planning in our training sessions☐☐

14.15 Fixing Errors in Grammar and Punctuation (LO 14-5)

Identify and correct the errors in the following passages.

a. Company's are finding it to their advantage to cultivate their suppliers. Partnerships between a company and its suppliers can yield hefty payoffs for both company and supplier. One example is Bailey Controls, an Ohio headquartered company. Bailey make control systems for big factories. They treat suppliers almost like departments of their own company. When a Bailey employee passes a laser scanner over a bins bar code the supplier is instantly alerted to send more parts.

b. Entrepreneur Trip Hawkins appears in Japanese ads for the video game system his company designed. "It plugs into the future! he says in one ad, in a cameo spliced into shots of U.S kids playing the games. Hawkins is one of several US celebrities and business people whom plug products on Japanese TV."

c. Mid size firms employing between 100 and 1,000 people represent only 4% of companies in the U.S.; but create 33% of all new jobs. One observer attributes their success to their being small enough to take advantage of economic opportunity's agilely, but big enough to have access to credit and to operate on a national or even international scale. The biggest hiring area for midsize company's is wholesale and retail sales (38% of jobs), construction (20% of jobs, manufacturing (19% of jobs), and services (18% of jobs).

Polishing Your Prose

Matters on Which Experts Disagree

Any living language changes. New usages appear first in speaking. Here are five issues on which experts currently disagree:

1. Plural pronouns to refer to *everybody, everyone,* and *each.* Standard grammar says these words require singular pronouns: *his or her* rather than *their.*
2. Split infinitives. An infinitive is the form of a verb that contains *to: to understand.* An infinitive is **split** when another word separates the *to* from the rest of an infinitive: *to easily understand, to boldly go.* The most recent edition of the *Oxford English Dictionary* allows split infinitives. Purists disagree.
3. *Hopefully* to mean *I hope that. Hopefully* means "in a hopeful manner." However, a speaker who says "Hopefully, the rain will stop" is talking about the speaker's hope, not the rain's.
4. *Verbal* to mean *oral. Verbal* means "using words." Therefore, both writing and speaking are verbal communication. Nonverbal communication (for example, body language) does not use words.
5. Comma before *and.* In a series of three or more items, some experts require a comma after the next to last item (the item before the *and*); others don't.

Ask your instructor and your boss whether they are willing to accept the less formal usage. When you write to someone you don't know, use standard grammar and usage.

Exercises

Each of the following sentences illustrates informal usage.
(a) Which would your instructor or your boss accept?
(b) Rewrite each of the sentences using standard grammar and usage.

1. Hopefully, we can expand our marketing efforts to Canada in the next few months.
2. Max told us that everybody gets their chance eventually. The trick is to be ready to take it when it happens.
3. Though Gregory said he had a verbal agreement with Parker, Sandy reminded him that it should have been in writing.
4. He said it was more important to successfully serve customers than to simply sell products.
5. Sue Ellen wondered if the plan to quickly go to the supply store before the meeting would instead make them late.
6. The department's best employees are Kai, Paul, Giselle, Timothy, and Elizabeth.
7. While they had a verbal disagreement on the phone yesterday, they stayed professional and patched things up today.
8. Each manager should make sure their department has a box for the Operation Feed campaign.
9. Carolyn said she expects that the Purchasing, Public Relations, and Building Management Departments will each send their representatives to the meeting.
10. The fourth shipment got delayed in transit, but Jenny said hopefully everybody will get their order within 72 hours.

Check your answers to the odd-numbered exercises at the back of the book.

15 | Choosing the Right Word

Module 15 will help you to choose the right words for your business messages. After completing the module, you should be able to

LO 15-1 **Recognize value in using the right words.**

LO 15-2 **Apply strategies for critical thinking in reading, writing, and beyond.**

LO 15-3 **Explain principles for word definition.**

LO 15-4 **Distinguish acceptable jargon from other types.**

LO 15-5 **Define words with similar sounds but different meanings.**

The best word depends on context: the situation, your purposes, your audience, and the words you have already used. As you choose words,

1. Use words that are accurate, appropriate, and familiar.

   Accurate words mean what you want to say.

   Appropriate words convey the attitudes you want and fit well with the other words in your document.

   Familiar words are easy to read and understand.

2. Use technical jargon only when it is essential and known to the reader. Eliminate business jargon.

Does using the right word really matter?   LO 15-1

▶ *The right word helps you look good and get the response you want.*

Using the right word is part of the way you demonstrate that you're part of a discourse community (◀◀ p. 28). Using simple words is part of the way you create a friendly image of yourself and your organization. Using words that are part of standard edited English helps you build credibility and demonstrate your professionalism.

Getting Your Meaning Across

When the words on the page don't say what you mean, the reader has to work harder to figure out your meaning. According to one report, "The western part of Ohio was transferred from Chicago to Cleveland."[1] In fact, Ohio did not move. Instead, a company moved responsibility for sales in western Ohio. Sometimes your audience can figure out what you mean. Sometimes, your meaning will be lost. Sometimes the wrong word can cause you to lose a lawsuit.

Denotation is a word's literal or dictionary meaning. Most common words in English have more than one denotation. The word *pound,* for example, means, or denotes, a unit of weight, a place where stray animals are kept, a unit of money in the British system, and the verb *to hit.* Coca-Cola spends an estimated $20 million a year to protect its brand names so that *Coke* will denote only that brand and not just any cola drink.

When two people use the same word to mean, or denote, different things, **bypassing** occurs. For example, negotiators for Amoco and for the Environmental Protection Agency (EPA) used *risk* differently. At Amoco, *risk* was an economic term dealing with efficiency; for the EPA, the term "was a four-letter word that meant political peril or health risk."[2] Progress was possible only when they agreed on a meaning.

Accurate denotations can make it easier to solve problems. In one production line with a high failure rate, the largest category of defects was *missed operations.* At first, the supervisor wondered if the people on the line were lazy or irresponsible. But some checking showed that several different problems were labeled *missed operations:* parts installed backward, parts that had missing screws or fasteners, parts whose wires weren't connected. Each of these problems had different solutions. Using accurate words redefined the problem and enabled the production line both to improve quality and cut repair costs.[3]

Getting the Response You Want

Using the right word helps you shape the audience's response to what you say. **Connotation** means the emotional colorings or associations that accompany a word. A great many words carry connotations of approval or disapproval, disgust or delight. Words in the first column in the accompanying list suggest criticism; words in the second column suggest approval.

Negative Word	Positive Word
guess	assume
nosy	curious
haggle	negotiate
fearful	cautious
nit-picking	careful
obstinate	firm
wishy-washy	flexible

A supervisor can "tell the truth" about a subordinate's performance and yet write either a positive or a negative performance appraisal, based on the connotations of the words

U.S. presidents, as well as presidential hopefuls, are known for sometimes choosing words poorly. When President George W. Bush declared the war against terrorism a "crusade," the word troubled many observers, who noted its connotation, especially in the Middle East, might be terrifying to more than just the nation's enemies. His successor, President Barack Obama, also got into trouble. "The private sector is doing fine" may have been his biggest gaffe, a statement made during his 2012 reelection campaign against Mitt Romney. Though supporters argued it was interpreted out of context, the comment seemed similar to one by Senator John McCain during the 2008 presidential campaign that drew sharp criticism from the Obama camp. Romney made Obama's phrase the cornerstone of TV commercials. Romney himself got into trouble with remarks to British interviewers that preparations, including security, for the 2012 Summer Olympics in London were "disconcerting." Tabloids had a field day, referring to the former governor and 2002 Winter Olympics chairman as "Mitt, the Twit." Even Prime Minister David Cameron was critical.

Source: Glen Johnson, "President Obama's 'Private Sector' Gaffe a Possible Window to Soul Like Other Recent Gaffes," *The Boston Globe,* June 11, 2012, http://www.boston.com/politicalintelligence/2012/06/11/president-obama-private-sector-gaffe-possible-window-soul-like-other-recent-gaffes/mVfqps0bbcMa5nS20I5fcP/story.html; and Holly Bailey, "British Media Hammer Romney on Olympic Comments," July 26, 2012, http://news.yahoo.com/blogs/ticket/british-media-hammer-romney-olympic-comments-103800909.html.

in the appraisal. Consider an employee who pays close attention to details. A positive appraisal might read, "Terry is a meticulous team member who takes care of details that others sometimes ignore." But the same behavior might be described negatively: "Terry is hung up on trivial details."

Advertisers carefully choose words with positive connotations. Expensive cars are never *used;* instead, they're *preowned, experienced,* or even *preloved.* An executive for Rolls-Royce once said, "A Rolls never, never breaks down. Of course," he added, with a twinkle in his eye, "there have been occasions when a car has failed to proceed."[4]

Words may also connote status. Both *salesperson* and *sales representative* are nonsexist job titles. But the first sounds like a clerk in a store; the second suggests someone selling important items to corporate customers.

Use familiar words that are in almost everyone's vocabulary. Try to use specific, concrete words. They're easier to understand and remember.[5] Short, common words sound friendlier.

Stuffy: Please give immediate attention to ensure that the pages of all reports prepared for distribution are numbered sequentially and in a place of optimum visibility.[6]

Simple: Please put page numbers on all reports in the top outer corner.

The following list gives a few examples of short, simple alternatives.

Formal and Stuffy	Short and Simple
ameliorate	improve
commence	begin
enumerate	list
finalize	finish, complete
prioritize	rank
utilize	use
viable option	choice

There are four exceptions to the general rule that "shorter is better."

1. Use a long word if it is the only word that expresses your meaning exactly.
2. Use a long word or phrase if it is more familiar than a short word. *Send out* is better than *emit* and *a word in another language for a geographic place or area* is better than *exonym* because more people know the first item in each pair.
3. Use a long word if its connotations are more appropriate. *Exfoliate* is better than *scrape off dead skin cells.*
4. Use a long word if the discourse community prefers it.

Connotations may differ among cultures. Even within a culture, connotations may change over time. The word *charity* had acquired such negative connotations by the 19th century that people began to use the term *welfare* instead. Now, *welfare* has acquired negative associations. Most states have *public assistance* programs instead.

How positively can we present something and still be ethical? Referring to a product as *probiotic* is probably better than saying it's infused with bacteria similar to those in your digestive system.[7] *Pressure-treated lumber* sounds acceptable. But naming the product by

Prune

Dried Plum

Sales of prunes fell 14% from 1993 to 1999. To stop the slide, the California Prune Board decided to change the product's name (and its own). To do so required approval from the U.S. Food & Drug Administration, which regulates food labels. Now you can't buy prunes; you buy "dried plums." By July 2001, sales had risen 5.5% over the previous 12-month period.[8]

Thinking Critically   LO 15-2

Like many terms, **critical thinking** has more than one meaning.

In its most basic sense, critical thinking means using precise words and asking questions about what you read and hear.

Vague: This *Wall Street Journal* story discusses international business.

Precise: This *Wall Street Journal* story

    tells how Walmart plans to expand into Europe.

    challenges the claim that a U.S. company needs a native partner to succeed in international business.

    gives examples of translation problems in international business.

    compares and contrasts accounting rules in Europe and in Asia.

    tells how three women have succeeded in international business.

Questions about a *Wall Street Journal* story might include

- What information is the story based on? Did the reporter interview people on both sides of the issue?
- When was the information collected? Is it still valid?
- Does evidence from other newspapers and magazines and from your own experience tend to confirm or contradict this story?
- How important is this story? Does it call for action on your part?

Critical thinking is especially important to business in the 21st century, so much so that the narrow focus on traditional business skills in MBA programs earned criticism from management guru Warren Bennis. He noted, "They are teaching courses to middle managers when they need to prepare leaders." To help students learn to think "out of the box," some MBA programs now include courses in law, poetry, entrepreneurship, and biotechnology.

In a more advanced sense, critical thinking means the ability to identify problems, gather and evaluate evidence, identify and evaluate alternate solutions, and recommend or act on the best choice—while understanding that information is always incomplete and that new information might change one's judgment of the "best" choice.

In its most advanced sense, critical thinking means asking about and challenging fundamental assumptions. For example, as companies shift from a domestic business model to a global

one, they must question whether their values fit into new marketplaces.

That's what U.S. companies wishing to attract China's youth market—whose annual incomes total $40 billion—did, finding that while Chinese youth want to express themselves, images of extreme rebellion were distasteful to them.

"Chinese youth are not becoming Western. You don't scrub away 5,000 years of Confucian values with a couple of ads for McDonald's and Pepsi," said Tom Doctoroff, a marketing expert and CEO in Shanghai.

Even as they dye their hair wild colors or get body piercings, Chinese youth are still concerned with values like good grades and pleasing their parents. So, American companies Coca-Cola, McDonald's, and the National Basketball Association identified four "passion points" that aligned with Chinese value systems: music, fashion, sports, and technology. They created promotions that appealed to these passion points, using popular Chinese celebrities and athletes in socially acceptable presentations.

Coca-Cola alone saw sales increase in cyber cafés by 30%. Such benefits came from questioning the assumption that young people around the world assert their individuality in the same way and for the same reasons.

A study published in the *Journal of Personality and Social Psychology* found that men who rate themselves as disagreeable, stubborn, and difficult make more money than co-workers, an average of 18% more pay. Judged at face value, such a study suggests rewards for being mean in the workplace. But what is the explanation? Is it because the workplace values being mean? Or are mean men more assertive, and thus more likely to compete harder for raises and promotions? And what are the long-term effects? For instance, do mean men make more money in the short run but less over the course of their careers? Thinking critically about questions like these can lead to meaningful conclusions.

Sources: James Flanigan, "Makeover for MBA Programs," www.latimes.com/business/la-fi-flan26june26,1,5147417.column, June 26, 2005; Normandy Madden, "Reaching China's Youth: A Balancing Act," *Advertising Age,* June 6, 2005, 14; and Liz Goodwin, "Mean Guys Finish First, at Least in Their Paychecks," August 15, 2011, http://news.yahoo.com/blogs/lookout/mean-guys-finish-first-least-paychecks-193159172.html.

the material injected under pressure—*arsenic-treated lumber*—may lead the customer to make a different decision. Wood treated in this way even has been banned from most residential uses in the United States. We have the right to package our ideas attractively, but we have the responsibility to give the public or our superiors all the information they need to make decisions.

How do words get their meanings? LO 15-3

▶ *Most meanings depend on usage.*

Some dictionaries are *descriptive,* that is, their definitions describe the way people actually use words. In such a dictionary, the word *verbal* might be defined as *spoken, not written,* because many people use the word that way. In a *prescriptive* dictionary, words are defined as they are supposed to be used, according to a panel of experts. In such a dictionary, *verbal* would be defined as *using words*—which of course includes both writing and speaking. Check the introduction to your dictionary to find out which kind it is.

We learn meanings by context, by being alert and observant. Some terms will have a specialized meaning in a social or work group. We learn some meanings by formal and informal study: "generally accepted accounting principles" or what the trash can on an e-mail screen symbolizes. Some meanings are negotiated as we interact one-on-one with another person, attempting to communicate. Some words persist, even though the reality behind them has changed. In 9 of the 10 largest U.S. cities, so-called "minorities" are already in the majority.[9] Some people are substituting the term *traditionally underrepresented groups* for *minorities,* but the old term is likely to remain in use for some time.

Some meanings are voted upon. Take, for example, the term *minority-owned business.* For years, the National Minority Supplier Development Council (NMSDC) has defined the term as a business at least 51% of whose owners were members of racial or ethnic minorities. But that made it hard for businesses to attract major capital or to go public, since doing so would give more ownership to European-American investors. In 2000, the NMSDC redefined *minority-owned business* as one with minority management and at least 30% minority ownership.[10]

Is it OK to use jargon? LO 15-4

▶ *If it's essential.*

There are two kinds of **jargon**. The first kind of jargon is the specialized terminology of a technical field. *LIFO* and *FIFO* are technical terms in accounting; *byte* and *baud* are computer jargon; *scale-free* and *pickled and oiled* designate specific characteristics of steel. Using technical terms in a job application letter suggests that you're a peer who also is competent in that field. In other messages, use technical jargon only when the term is essential. Define the term when you're not sure whether the reader knows it.

Instant Replay

Denotation, Bypassing, and Connotation

Denotation is a word's literal or dictionary meaning. **Bypassing** occurs when two people use the same word to mean, or denote, different things. **Connotation** means the emotional colorings or associations that accompany a word.

Site to See

Go to
www.sec.gov/pdf/handbook.pdf

for the Security and Exchange Commission's *A Plain English Handbook.*

Many words are easily confused.

By permission of Rick Detorie and Creators Syndicate, Inc.

If a technical term has a "plain English" equivalent, use the simpler term:

Jargon: Foot the average monthly budget column down to Total Variable Cost, Total Management Fixed Cost, Total Sunk Costs, and Grand Total.

Better: Add the figures in the average monthly budget column for each category to determine the Total Variable Costs, the Total Management Fixed Costs, and the Total Sunk Costs. Then add the totals for each category to arrive at the Grand Total.

The revision here is longer but better because it uses simple words. The original will be meaningless to a reader who does not know what *foot* means.

The second kind of jargon is **business jargon,** sometimes called **businessese:** *as per your request, enclosed please find, please do not hesitate.* If any of the terms in the first column of Figure 15.1 show up in your writing, replace them with more modern language.

Use a long word when

1. It is the only word that expresses your meaning exactly.
2. It is more familiar than a short word.
3. Its connotations are more appropriate.
4. The discourse community prefers it.

What words confuse some writers?   LO 15-5

▶ *Words with similar sounds can have very different meanings.*

Here's a list of words that are frequently confused. Master them, and you'll be well on the way to using the right word.

1. accede/exceed
   accede: to yield
   exceed: to go beyond, surpass

   I accede to your demand that we not exceed the budget.

2. accept/except
   accept: to receive
   except: to leave out or exclude; but

   I accept your proposal except for point 3.

Go to
www.yourdictionary.com/ fun.html
for links to word games on the web.

Figure 15.1 Getting Rid of Business Jargon		
Instead of	Use	Because
At your earliest convenience	The date you need a response	If you need it by a deadline, say so. It may never be convenient to respond.
As per your request; 55 miles per hour	As you requested; 55 miles an hour	*Per* is a Latin word for *by* or *for each.* Use *per* only when the meaning is correct; avoid mixing English and Latin.
Enclosed please find	Enclosed is; Here is	An enclosure isn't a treasure hunt. If you put something in the envelope, the reader will find it.
Forward same to this office	Return it to this office	Omit legal jargon.
Hereto, herewith	Omit	Omit legal jargon.
Please be advised; Please be informed	Omit—simply start your response	You don't need a preface. Go ahead and start.
Please do not hesitate	Omit	Omit negative words.
Pursuant to	According to; or omit	*Pursuant* does not mean *after.* Omit legal jargon in any case.
Said order	Your order	Omit legal jargon.
This will acknowledge receipt of your letter.	Omit—start your response	If you answer a letter, the reader knows you got it.
Trusting this is satisfactory, we remain	Omit	Eliminate *-ing* endings. When you are through, stop.

- Octoberfest is held in September.
- The Big 10 has 12 teams.
- The principal ingredient in sweetbread is neither sugar nor bread but the cooked pancreas or thymus of a young animal, usually a calf.

Site to See

Go to

www.wsu.edu/~brians/ errors

for an even longer list of errors (and words that may sound wrong but are really right).

Instant Replay

Two Kinds of Jargon

Technical jargon includes words that have specific technical meanings. Use this kind of jargon in job application letters. Avoid other technical jargon unless it's essential. **Business jargon** or **businessese** are words that do not have specialized meanings. Never use these terms.

3. access/excess
   access: the right to use; admission to
   excess: surplus

   As supply clerk, he had access to any excess materials.

4. adept/adopt
   adept: skilled
   adopt: to take as one's own

   She was adept at getting people to adopt her ideas.

5. advice/advise
   advice: (noun) counsel
   advise: (verb) to give counsel or advice to someone

   I asked him to advise me but I didn't like the advice I got.

6. affect/effect
   affect: (verb) to influence or modify
   effect: (verb) to produce or cause; (noun) result

   He hoped that his argument would affect his boss' decision, but so far as he could see, it had no effect.

   The tax relief effected some improvement for the citizens whose incomes had been affected by inflation.

7. affluent/effluent
   affluent: (adjective) rich, possessing in abundance
   effluent: (noun) something that flows out

   Affluent companies can afford the cost of removing pollutants from the effluents their factories produce.

8. a lot/allot
   a lot: many (informal)
   allot: divide or give to

   A lot of players signed up for this year's draft. We allotted one first-round draft choice to each team.

9. amount/number
   amount: (use with concepts that cannot be counted individually but can only be measured)
   number: (use when items can be counted individually)

   It's a mistake to try to gauge the amount of interest he has by the number of questions he asks.

10. are/our
    are: (plural linking verb)
    our: belonging to us

    Are we ready to go ahead with our proposal?

11. assure/ensure/insure
    assure: to give confidence, to state confidently
    ensure: to make safe (figuratively)
    insure: to make safe, often by paying a fee against possible risk

    I assure you that we ensure employees' safety by hiring bodyguards.

    The pianist insured his fingers against possible damage.

12. attributed/contributed
    attributed: was said to be caused by
    contributed: gave something to

    The rain probably contributed to the accident, but the police officer attributed the accident to driver error.

13. between/among

between: (use with only two choices)
among: (use with more than two choices)

> This year the differences between the two candidates for president are unusually clear.

> I don't see any major differences among the candidates for city council.

14. cite/sight/site

cite: (verb) to quote
sight: (noun) vision, something to be seen
site: (noun) real or virtual location

> She cited the old story of the building inspector who was depressed by the very sight of the site for the new factory.

15. complement/compliment

complement: (verb) to complete, finish; (noun) something that completes
compliment: (verb) to praise; (noun) praise

> The compliment she gave me complemented my happiness.

16. compose/comprise

compose: make up, create
comprise: consist of, be made up of, be composed of

> The city council is composed of 12 members. Each district comprises an area 50 blocks square.

17. confuse/complicate/exacerbate

confuse: to bewilder
complicate: to make more complex or detailed
exacerbate: to make worse

> Because I missed the first 20 minutes of the movie, I didn't understand what was going on. The complicated plot exacerbated my confusion.

18. describe/prescribe

describe: list the features of something, tell what something looks like
prescribe: specify the features something must contain

> The law prescribes the priorities for making repairs. His report describes our plans to comply with the law.

19. discreet/discrete

discreet: tactful, careful not to reveal secrets
discrete: separate, distinct

> I have known him to be discreet on two discrete occasions.

20. do/due

do: (verb) act or make
due: (adjective) scheduled, caused by

> The banker said she would do her best to change the due date.

> Due to the computer system, the payroll can be produced in only two days for all 453 employees.

21. elicit/illicit

elicit: (verb) to draw out
illicit: (adjective) not permitted, unlawful

> The reporter could elicit no information from the Senator about his illicit love affair.

While spell-checkers are getting better at finding mistakes, they still typically get tripped up by homonyms, or words that sound alike, and correctly spelled words that are being used incorrectly. Watch out for "affect" instead of "effect," for instance, or saying "I would of" instead of "I would have." Word processing programs have customizable features to help. Microsoft Word, for instance, can use multiple dictionaries so foreign or technical words can be checked for different kinds of writing projects. One way to check for homonyms is to exclude them from the dictionary so they are flagged every time. Grammar checkers may also catch some of these types of errors, but the best final step is still to know the correct words and phrases and review documents manually for errors.

Source: Kaboodle.com, "11 Common Spelling Errors Spell Check Won't Catch," April 16, 2012, http://shine.yahoo.com/work-money/11-common-spelling-errors-spell-check-won-8217-172300248.html; Helen Bradley, "10 Spelling Checker Secrets for Microsoft Word," *PC World,* March 13, 2012, http://www.pcworld.com/businesscenter/article/251766/10_spelling_checker_secrets_for_microsoft_word.html.

With foreclosure imminent, some homeowners found a three-word phrase to stave off banks and lending companies: *Produce the note.* Many mortgages had been bundled and sold during the real estate boom, sometimes repeatedly, and not every company claiming ownership of a mortgage had the documentation to prove it. As a result, homeowners slowed or stopped foreclosure or even convinced lenders to renegotiate the mortgage.

Source: Mitch Stacy, "Homeowner's Rallying Cry: Produce the Note," *The San Francisco Chronicle,* February 17, 2009, http://www.sfgate.com/cgi-bin/article.cgi?f=/n/a/2009/02/17/national/a120919S63.DTL.

22. eminent/immanent/imminent
    eminent: distinguished
    immanent: dwelling within tangible objects
    imminent: about to happen

> The eminent doctor believed that death was imminent. The eminent minister believed that God was immanent.

23. fewer/less
    fewer: (use for objects that can be counted individually)
    less: (use for objects that can be measured but not counted individually)

> There is less sand in this bucket; there are probably fewer grains of sand, too.

24. forward/foreword
    forward: ahead
    foreword: preface, introduction

> The author looked forward to writing the foreword to the book.

25. good/well
    good: (adjective, used to modify nouns; as a noun, means something that is good)
    well: (adverb, used to modify verbs, adjectives, and other adverbs)

> Her words "Good work!" told him that he was doing well.

> He spent a great deal of time doing volunteer work because he believed that doing good was just as important as doing well.

26. i.e./e.g.
    i.e.:   (*id est*—that is) introduces a restatement or explanation of the preceding word or phrase
    e.g.:   (*exempli gratia*—for the sake of an example; for example) introduces one or more examples

> Although he had never studied Latin, he rarely made a mistake in using Latin abbreviations, e.g., *i.e., etc.,* because he associated each with a mnemonic device (i.e., a word or image used to help one remember something). He remembered *i.e.* as *in effect,* pretended that e.g. meant *example given,* and used *etc.* only when *examples to continue* would fit.

27. imply/infer
    imply: suggest, put an idea into someone's head
    infer: deduce, get an idea out from something

> She implied that an announcement would be made soon. I inferred from her smile that it would be an announcement of her promotion.

While *fast food* may not imply *romance* to many people, it did for customers participating in White Castle's Valentine's Day experience at select locations. To date, nearly 4,000 couples have enjoyed the holiday trimmings at 157 of the chain's 419 locations, and one couple even wed in a Louisville, KY, restaurant. The cake was shaped like a "slider" hamburger.

Source: Emily Bryson York, "White Castle Taking Reservations for Valentine's Day," *Advertising Age,* January 19, 2010, http://adage.com/adages/post?article_id=141584.

28. it's/its
    it's: it is, it has
    its: belonging to it

> It's clear that a company must satisfy its customers to stay in business.

29. lectern/podium
    lectern: raised stand with a slanted top that holds a manuscript for a reader or notes for a speaker
    podium: platform for a speaker or conductor to stand on

> I left my notes on the lectern when I left the podium at the end of my talk.

30. lie/lay
    lie: to recline; to tell a falsehood (never takes an object)
    lay: to put an object on something (always takes an object)

> He was laying the papers on the desk when I came in, but they aren't lying there now.

31. loose/lose
    loose: not tight
    lose: to have something disappear

    > If I lose weight, this suit will be loose.

32. moral/morale
    moral: (adjective) virtuous, good; (noun: morals) ethics, sense of right and wrong
    morale: (noun) spirit, attitude, mental outlook

    > Studies have shown that coed dormitories improve student morale without harming student morals.

33. objective/rationale
    objective: goal
    rationale: reason, justification

    > The objective of the meeting was to explain the rationale behind the decision.

34. personal/personnel
    personal: individual, to be used by one person
    personnel: staff, employees

    > All personnel will get new personal computers by the end of the year.

35. possible/possibly
    possible: (adjective) something that can be done
    possibly: (adverb) perhaps

    > It is possible that we will be able to hire this spring. We can choose from possibly the best graduating class in the past five years.

36. precede/proceed
    precede: (verb) to go before
    proceed: (verb) to continue; (noun: proceeds) money

    > Raising the money must precede spending it. Only after we obtain the funds can we proceed to spend the proceeds.

37. principal/principle
    principal: (adjective) main; (noun) person in charge; money lent out at interest
    principle: (noun) basic truth or rule, code of conduct

    > *The Prince,* Machiavelli's principal work, describes his principles for ruling a state.

38. quiet/quite
    quiet: not noisy
    quite: very

    > It was quite difficult to find a quiet spot anywhere near the floor of the stock exchange.

39. regulate/relegate
    regulate: control
    relegate: put (usually in an inferior position)

    > If the federal government regulates the size of lettering on county road signs, we may as well relegate the current signs to the garbage bin.

40. residence/residents
    residence: home
    residents: people who live in a building

    > The residents had different reactions when they learned that a shopping mall would be built next to their residence.

Consider how words can be presented in headlines, on signage, and anywhere else. Company and domain names may run together, for instance, creating unexpected results. Some rumors about problems are true. Snopes.com, which investigates the authenticity of urban legends, verifies that Italy's Powergen indeed found itself with powergenitalia.com when it created a website, and Experts Exchange, a site for computer programmers, initially could be found at expertsexchange.com.

Source: Downloaded on January 27, 2008, at www.snopes.com/business/names/domains.asp.

41. respectfully/respectively

respectfully: with respect
respectively: to each in the order listed

> When I was introduced to the queen, the prime minister, and the court jester, I bowed respectfully, shook hands politely, and winked, respectively.

42. role/roll

role: part in a play or script, function (in a group)
roll: (noun) list of students, voters, or other members; round piece of bread; (verb) move by turning over and over

> While the teacher called the roll, George—in his role as class clown—threw a roll he had saved from lunch.

43. simple/simplistic

simple: not complicated
simplistic: watered down, oversimplified

> She was able to explain the proposal in simple terms without making the explanation sound simplistic.

44. stationary/stationery

stationary: not moving, fixed
stationery: paper

> During the earthquake, even the stationery was not stationary.

45. their/there/they're

their: belonging to them
there: in that place
they're: they are

> There are plans, designed to their specifications, for the house they're building.

46. to/too/two

to: (preposition) function word indicating proximity, purpose, time, etc.
too: (adverb) also, very, excessively
two: (adjective) the number 2

> The formula is too secret to entrust to two people.

47. unique/unusual

unique: sole, only, alone
unusual: not common

> I believed that I was unique in my ability to memorize long strings of numbers until I consulted *Guinness World Records* and found that I was merely unusual: Someone else had equaled my feat in 1997.

48. verbal/oral

verbal: using words
oral: spoken, not written

> His verbal skills were uneven: His oral communication was excellent, but he didn't write well. His sensitivity to nonverbal cues was acute: He could tell what kind of day I had just by looking at my face.

Hint: Oral comes from the Latin word for mouth, *os.* Think of Oral-B Toothbrushes: For the mouth.
Verbal comes from the Latin word for word, *verba.* Nonverbal language is language that does not use words (e.g., body language).

49. whether/weather

    whether: (conjunction) used to introduce possible alternatives

    weather: (noun) atmosphere: wet or dry, hot or cold, calm or storm

    > We will have to see what the weather is before we decide whether to hold the picnic indoors or out.

50. your/you'rer

    your: belonging to you

    you're: you are

    > You're the top candidate for promotion in your division.

Summary of Learning Objectives

- **Denotation** is a word's literal or dictionary meaning. **(LO 15-1)**
- **Bypassing** occurs when two people use the same word to mean, or denote, different things. **(LO 15-1)**
- **Connotation** means the emotional colorings or associations that accompany a word. **(LO 15-1)**
- Generally, short words are better. But use a long word when **(LO 15-1)**
  1. It is the only word that expresses your meaning exactly.
  2. It is more familiar than a short word.
  3. Its connotations are more appropriate.
  4. The discourse community prefers it.
- In its most basic sense, **critical thinking** means using precise words and asking questions about what you read and hear. **(LO 15-2)**
- In a more advanced sense, critical thinking means the ability to identify problems, gather and evaluate evidence, identify and evaluate alternate solutions, and recommend or act on the best choice. **(LO 15-2)**

- Some dictionaries are *descriptive,* meaning their definitions describe the way people actually use words. *Prescriptive* dictionaries define words the way a panel of experts say they should be used. **(LO 15-3)**
- We also learn meanings through context and formal and informal study. Some meanings are voted upon by groups, such as professional or regulatory organizations. **(LO 15-3)**
- **Jargon** is acceptable if it is essential, such as necessary technical terms. Avoid **business jargon,** or **businessese,** which includes trite phrases like *as per your request* and *please do not hesitate.* **(LO 15-4)**
- Words that sound similar to each other but have different meanings often confuse people. These words include *accept/except, affect/effect, discreet/discrete, forward/foreword, it's/its, loose/lose, personal/personnel, principal/principle, quiet/quite, respectfully/respectively, their/there/they're,* and *to/too/two.* **(LO 15-5)**
- Other words that seem similar and are frequently confused include *between/among, fewer/less, good/well,* and *verbal/oral.* **(LO 15-5)**

Assignments for Module 15

Questions for Comprehension

15.1 What is the difference between *denotation* and *connotation?* **(LO 15-1)**

15.2 What is *bypassing?* **(LO 15-1)**

15.3 Why are short, simple words generally best? **(LO 15-1)**

15.4 What are the two kinds of jargon? Which is OK to use at times? **(LO 15-4)**

Questions for Critical Thinking

15.5 If you were going to buy a new dictionary, would you want a descriptive or a prescriptive one? Why? **(LO 15-3)**

15.6 Why is it desirable to use technical jargon in a job letter and a job interview? **(LO 15-4)**

15.7 How can you avoid confusing words that sound or seem similar? **(LO 15-5)**

Exercises and Problems

15.8 Identifying Words with Multiple Denotations (LO 15-1)

    a. Each of the following words has several denotations. How many do you know? How many does a good dictionary list?

        browser   link   sample

    b. List five words that have multiple denotations.

15.9   Explaining Bypassing (LO 15-1)

Show how bypassing is possible in the following examples.

a. France and Associates: Protection from Professionals

b. We were not able to account for the outstanding amount of plastic waste generated each year.

c. I scanned the résumés when I received them.

15.10   Evaluating Connotations (LO 15-1)

a. Identify the connotations of each of the following metaphors for a multicultural nation.

melting pot

mosaic

tapestry

garden salad

stew

b. Which connotations seem most positive? Why?

15.11   Evaluating the Ethical Implications of Connotations (LO 15-1)

In each of the following pairs, identify the more favorable term. Is its use justified? Why or why not?

1. wastepaper   recovered fiber
2. feedback   criticism
3. scalper   ticket reseller
4. budget   spending plan
5. caviar   fish eggs

15.12   Correcting Errors in Denotation and Connotation (LO 15-1)

Identify and correct the errors in the following sentences.

1. Louie speaks pretty good English for a guy from the south side.
2. I literally exploded with joy when I found out I got the job.
3. Thank goodness Carl, the senior vice president, is older than dirt and has the memory of an elephant.
4. For a woman, JoAnn is remarkably stable—she might just have what it takes for management.
5. Marti estimated the air fare would be $324.34 for a roundtrip flight to Spokane. She said we could rent a car and drive instead for about $231.41.

15.13   Using Connotations to Shape Response (LO 15-1)

Write two sentences to describe each of the following situations, one with positive words, the other with negative words.

1. Lee talks to co-workers about subjects other than work, such as last weekend's ball game.
2. Lee spends a lot of time sending e-mail messages and monitoring e-mail newsgroups.
3. As a supervisor, Lee rarely gives specific instructions to subordinates.

15.14   Choosing Levels of Formality (LO 15-1, LO 15-3)

Identify the more formal word in each pair. Which term is better for most business documents? Why?

1. adapted to   geared to
2. befuddled   confused
3. assistant   helper
4. pilot project   testing the waters
5. cogitate   think

15.15   Identifying Jargon (LO 15-4)

How many of these business jargon terms do you know?

1. Sticky website
2. Alpha geek
3. Road warrior
4. E-tailer
5. Bottom-fish

15.16   Eliminating Jargon and Simplifying Language (LO 15-5)

Revise these sentences to eliminate jargon and to use short, familiar words. You may need to rewrite or add information.

1. With regard to the aforementioned letter of July the 15th, we expect to expedite your order to ship not later than July 21.
2. Jordyn fully appreciates your understanding with regards to the penultimate and ultimate recommendations for your consideration.
3. Your affirmation via signature will conclude all manner of business regarding this transaction.
4. Per your request, please find enclosed the listing of the required nomenclature for the project headings.
5. Proffering the appropriate renumeration for services rendered assists in securing the most adroit and capable person for our employ.

15.17   Choosing the Right Word (LO 15-1 to LO 15-5)

Choose the right word for each sentence.

1. We were waiting for (their/there) fax to come through.
2. A good manager is always aware of the (moral/morale) of his or her employees.
3. (Are/Our) best practices are described on the company web page.
4. Many of the Boca Raton (residence/residents), Lani told us, want to move in by the fifth day of the month their lease begins.
5. It was (quiet/quite) surprising to see Tyree's name missing from the list of Haller-Jacobs Award nominees.

6. We have to be careful not to (loose/lose) the Philmore Company contract because our first-quarter performance will be based on it.
7. When Andre asked me to write the (forward/foreword) to the book, I was honored—he's been my mentor since the day I started working here.

15.18 Choosing the Right Word (LO 15-1 to LO 15-5)

Choose the right word for each sentence.

1. (Their/There/They're) thinking that it's a good idea to hire a consultant to help us plan the festival.
2. While writing his report, Ahmed (implied/inferred) from the data that the next big trend will focus on 3D technology.
3. I asked Jennifer where the slides were, and she said she found them (laying/lying) on the conference table.
4. Tom pointed out we could expect (fewer/less) turbulence in the marketplace this year, as the economy seems to be stabilizing.
5. Though the (amount/number) of typos was small, they were enough to make his résumé seem poor compared to the competition.

15.19 Choosing the Right Word (LO 15-1 to LO 15-4)

Choose the right word for each sentence.

1. The letter said (are/our) books showed we (are/our) in good financial health.
2. Arthur is one of the (principals/principles) at the firm, and as such, he has a duty to oversee operations.
3. (Whether/Weather) we expect to need it or not, it's a good idea to have liability insurance.
4. A (unique/unusual) characteristic of our chroming process is the one-of-a-kind, durable finish.
5. Three attorneys (compose/comprise) the legal team that is reviewing the contracts presented to us by Hynek and Associates.
6. Though it was (implied/inferred) in the proposal that the project could be completed with a minimum of expense,

8. According to Bridget, the decline in sales can be (attributed/contributed) to an overall dip in the economy.
9. Chelsea Lomax stepped right up to the (lectern/podium) and gave the best speech I've ever heard.
10. (Between/Among) you and me, I think the proposal needs a lot more work before we can submit it.

6. When Eliza.beth (accepted/excepted) the position, she said she would be happy to help train her replacement before leaving.
7. Xian submitted a request for additional (personal/personnel) to help with getting our phone system installed by January 10.
8. If managers get questions from staff regarding downsizing—(i.e./e.g.,) which employees will be laid off?—they should direct those employees to the HR Department.
9. The obvious (affects/effects) of having high employee morale are lower turnover, decreased accidents, and better productivity.
10. Make sure that you get the agreement in writing; our legal counsel stresses that a(n) (oral/verbal) agreement is too informal.

Phoebe says we would be wise to budget for several thousand dollars more anyway.
7. Christina pointed out (its/it's) likely that we will see orders pick up the closer we get to the December holidays.
8. Of the many (moral/morale) (principals/principles) that guide our decision making, considering our customers' welfare is the most important.
9. Perhaps (to/too/two) much attention was given to the technical details of the project when more could have been paid to the overall (objective/rationale).
10. Slapping his hand on the (lectern/podium) for emphasis, Brin Maxwell said we could (lose/loose) customers if we (precede/proceed) rashly in our expansion into other markets.

Polishing Your Prose

Run-On Sentences

A sentence with too many ideas, strung together by coordinating conjunctions that lack the required commas, is a *run-on*. (Remember that coordinating conjunctions such as *and, or,* and *but* need a comma to connect independent clauses.)

Run-ons confound readers because there are too many ideas competing for attention and because the missing commas make the ideas harder to follow. The effect is similar to listening to a speaker who does not pause between sentences—where does one point begin and another end?

Test for run-ons by looking for more than two main ideas in a sentence and a lack of commas with coordinating conjunctions:

We installed the new computers this morning and they are running fine but there weren't enough computers for everyone so we are going to purchase more on Wednesday and we will install them and then the department will be fully operational.

Count the number of things going on in this sentence. Where are the commas?

Fix a run-on in one of three ways:

1. For short run-ons, add the missing commas:

Incorrect: The purchasing department sent order forms but we received too few so we are requesting more.

Correct: The purchasing department sent order forms, but we received too few, so we are requesting more.

2. Rewrite the sentence using subordination:

Correct: Because we received too few order forms, we are requesting more from the purchasing department.

3. For longer run-ons, break the run-on into two or more sentences, add missing commas, and subordinate where appropriate.

Correct: We installed the new computers this morning. They are running fine, but because there weren't enough computers for everyone, we are going to purchase more on Wednesday. When we install them, the department will be fully operational.

Exercises

Fix the following run-on errors.

1. Jessica went to college in Texas but her sister stayed in Indiana and attended a local private university.
2. Many of our employees would trade vacation days for shorter work hours in general but we're not sure that the central office would approve of the idea.
3. George said he was going to be late for the meeting but Charlene said she would be there on time so let's plan still getting together at 1 p.m.

4. A few of the employees nearing retirement age want us to hold planning seminars but we don't really have the space for it so please ask someone in HR to locate a room at a conference center.
5. Tucker wants to know if he should stay later tonight but I haven't heard from Andy yet and Paulette told me she would call back in a few minutes.
6. Nabil purchased the stock at the expected price and the order went through but we later got a call from the broker about it.
7. The letter traveled to several offices before it got to me and I only just read it so it may take me a while to consider what it says so you might want to come back in an hour.
8. Joe Dunleavy said he would submit the proposal to the Atlanta office but Karlie DelVechhio thinks it makes more sense to run it past Kevin Green in Legal first and Miranda Kang, who just got her law degree from DePaul, agrees.
9. While St. Augustine was my first choice, I really like Tampa and I found a terrific place to live that is close to the beach but it is very affordable and I think I'm really going to like it here!
10. The Bergerons and the Shimedas said they would be attending the awards dinner but Lou Carlisle said his wife has another commitment so he is attending alone and that means we will need to make sure we have the correct number of seats.

Check your answers to the odd-numbered exercises at the back of the book.

Revising Sentences and Paragraphs

LEARNING OBJECTIVES

Module 16 will help you to make sentences and paragraphs even better. After completing the module, you should be able to

LO 16-1 **Define good style in business messages.**

LO 16-2 **Demonstrate appropriate tone in business messages.**

LO 16-3 **Differentiate rules from writing habits and conventions.**

LO 16-4 **Apply strategies for sentence revision.**

LO 16-5 **Apply strategies for paragraph revision.**

LO 16-6 **Synthesize style with organizational culture.**

Revising sentences and paragraphs can make the difference between a not-so-great document and a really effective paper or e-mail message.

In your first round of revision (◄◄ p. 60), when you focus on content and clarity, you'll add, expand, modify, and perhaps delete sentences and paragraphs. In the second round of revision, as you focus on organization and layout, you change the order of sentences and paragraphs to make them flow better or to put earliest the reader benefit (◄◄ p. 112) that will appeal to most readers. The third round of revision focuses on sentences and paragraphs, as you improve style and tone. In *editing,* you'll again check sentences, this time for grammatical corrections (◄◄ Module 14).

What is "good" style?   LO 16-1

▶ *It's both businesslike and friendly.*

Good business and administrative writing sounds like a person talking to another person. Unfortunately, much of the writing produced in organizations today seems to have been written by faceless bureaucrats rather than by real people.

The style of writing that has traditionally earned high marks in college essays and term papers is arguably more formal than good business and administrative writing. (See Figure 16.1.) However, many professors also like term papers that are easy to read and use good visual impact.

Most people have several styles of talking, which they vary instinctively depending on the audience. Good writers have several styles, too. A memo to your boss complaining about the delays from a supplier will be informal, perhaps even chatty; a letter to the supplier demanding better service will be more formal.

Keep the following points in mind as you choose a level of formality for a specific document:

- Use a friendly, informal style for someone you've talked with.
- Avoid contractions, slang, and even minor grammatical lapses in paper documents to people you don't know. Abbreviations are OK in e-mail messages if they're part of the group's culture.
- Pay particular attention to your style when you have to write uncomfortable messages: when you write to people you fear or when you must give bad news. Reliance on nouns rather than on verbs and a general deadening of style increase when people are under stress or feel insecure.[1] Confident people are more direct. Edit your writing so that you sound confident, whether you feel that way or not.

Good business style allows for individual variation. Depending on the audience and situation, humor may be acceptable.

Figure 16.1 Different Levels of Style

Feature	Conversational Style	Good Business Style	Traditional Term Paper Style
Formality	Highly informal	Conversational; sounds like a real person talking	More formal than conversation would be, but retains a human voice
Use of contractions	Many contractions	OK to use occasional contractions	Few contractions, if any
Pronouns	Uses *I*, first- and second-person pronouns	Uses *I*, first- and second-person pronouns	First- and second-person pronouns kept to a minimum
Level of friendliness	Friendly	Friendly	No effort to make style friendly
How personal	Personal; refers to specific circumstances of conversation	Personal; may refer to reader by name; refers to specific circumstances of readers	Impersonal; may generally refer to readers but does not name them or refer to their circumstances
Word choice	Short, simple words; slang	Short, simple words but avoids slang	Many abstract words; scholarly, technical terms
Sentence and paragraph length	Incomplete sentences; no paragraphs	Short sentences and paragraphs	Sentences and paragraphs usually long
Grammar	Can be ungrammatical	Uses standard edited English	Uses standard edited English
Visual impact	Not applicable	Attention to visual impact of document	No particular attention to visual impact

Using the Right Tone   LO 16-2

Business writing should be businesslike and friendly. But what exactly does it mean to be "friendly"? Well, it depends. It depends on whom you're dealing with, the culture of your workplace, and even the part of the country where you work.

In the past 50 years, social distance in the United States has decreased. In many, perhaps most, workplaces, most people call each other by their first names, whatever their age or rank. But even in cultures that pride themselves on their egalitarianism, differences in status do exist. When you're a newcomer in an organization, when you're a younger person speaking to someone older, or when you're a subordinate speaking to a superior, you're wise to show your awareness of status in the tone you use.

Tone (◀◀ p. 106) is the implied attitude of the speaker or writer toward what the words say. We're usually experts on tone of voice, especially the tones of other people's voices who don't seem to respect us. But sometimes it's harder for us to hear the lack of respect in our own voices as we talk or write to others.

If you're the boss, it's probably OK to e-mail your subordinates, "Let me know when you're free next week for a meeting." But if you're a subordinate trying to line up people on your own level or higher up, politeness pays: "Would you be able to meet next week? Could you let me know what times you have free?"

The difficulty, of course, is that norms for politeness, like those for friendliness, can differ from organization to organization, from group to group, and even in different parts of the country and of the world (◀◀ p. 107). Furthermore, the same words that seem polite and friendly coming from a superior to a subordinate can seem pushy or arrogant coming from a subordinate to a superior. "Keep up the good work!" is fine coming from your boss. It isn't, however, something you would say *to* your boss.

As in other communication situations, you have to analyze the situation rhetorically. Who are your audiences (◀◀ p. 20)? What are your purposes? How do other people in the organization talk and write? What kind of response do you get? If a customer winces when you return her credit card and say, "Have

Dr. Johnnetta B. Cole was president of Bennett College for Women and now chairs the college's Johnnetta B. Cole Global Diversity & Inclusion Institute. Part of her success comes from matching her tone to her audience and the situation. A "force of nature," as peer Antonia Hernandez describes her, Dr. Cole has a demeanor that is "dignified but down to earth." She is pictured here with students Lauren Chanel Thomas, Alissa Johnson, and Ashley Shanelle Cobb.

Sources: "Dr. Johnnetta B. Cole, Keynote Speaker for the 2012 WCTF Conference," downloaded on July 28, 2012, at http://www.cew.umich.edu/dr-johnnetta-b-cole-keynote-speaker-2012-wctf-conference; and C. Stone Brown, "'Sister' Chair of the Board," *Diversity Inc.*, February 2006.

a nice day, Mary," maybe she doesn't appreciate being called by her first name. Talk to your peers in the organization about communication. What seems to work? What doesn't? And talk to a superior you trust. How do you come across? If you're creating the image you want to create, good. But if people think that you're rude, stuck-up, or arrogant, they may be reacting to your tone. A tone that worked for you in some situations in the past may need to be changed if you're to be effective in a new workplace or a new organization.

Are there rules I should follow?   LO 16-3

▶ *Most "rules" are really guidelines.*

Some "rules" are grammatical conventions. For example, standard edited English requires that each sentence has a subject and verb and that they agree. Business writing normally demands standard grammar, but exceptions exist. Promotional materials such as brochures, advertisements, and sales and fund-raising letters may use sentence fragments to gain the effect of speech.

(continued)
Source: Eric Platt, "How a Tenacious Summer Analyst Applicant Got Laughed at by Goldman, Moran, and Everyone Else on Wall Street," February 9, 2012, http://finance.yahoo.com/news/tenacious-summer-analyst-applicant-got-laughed-at-by-everyone-else-on-wall-street.html.

Other "rules" may be conventions adopted by an organization so that its documents will be consistent. For example, a company might decide to capitalize job titles *(Production Manager),* even though grammar doesn't require the capitals, or always to use a comma before *and* in a series, even though a sentence can be grammatical without the comma. A different company might make different choices.

Still other "rules" are attempts to codify "what sounds good." "Never use *I*" and "use big words" are examples of this kind of "rule." These "rules" are half-truths and must be applied selectively, if at all. Think about your audience (◄◄ p. 20), the discourse community (◄◄ p. 28), your purposes, and the situation. If you want the effect produced by an impersonal style and polysyllabic words, use them. But use them only when you want the distancing they produce.

To improve your style,

- Get a clean page or screen, so that you aren't locked into old sentence structures.
- Try WIRMI: *What I Really Mean Is.*[2] Then write the words.
- Try reading your draft out loud to someone sitting at a comfortable personal distance. If the words sound stiff, they'll seem stiff to a reader, too.
- Ask someone else to read your draft out loud. Readers stumble because the words on the page aren't what they expect to see. The places where that person stumbles are places where your writing can be better.
- Read widely and write a *lot.*
- Use the eight techniques in the next two sections.

What should I look for when I revise sentences? LO 16-4

► *Try these six techniques.*

At the sentence level, six kinds of revisions will help make your writing easy to read.

1. Use Active Verbs Most of the Time

"Who does what" sentences with active verbs make your writing more forceful.

A verb is **active** if the grammatical subject of the sentence does the action the verb describes. A verb is **passive** if the subject is acted upon. Passives are usually made up of a form of the verb *to be* plus a past participle. *Passive* has nothing to do with *past.* Passives can be past, present, or future:

were received	(in the past)
is recommended	(in the present)
will be implemented	(in the future)

To spot a passive, find the verb. If the verb describes something that the grammatical subject is doing, the verb is active. If the verb describes something that is being done to the grammatical subject, the verb is passive.

Active	**Passive**
The customer received 500 widgets.	Five hundred widgets were received by the customer.
I recommend this method.	This method is recommended by me.
The state agencies will implement the program.	The program will be implemented by the state agencies.

Verbs can be changed from active to passive by making the direct object (in the oval) the new subject (in the box). To change a passive verb to an active one, you must

make the agent ("by_____" in < >) the new subject. If no agent is specified in the sentence, you must supply one to make the sentence active.

Active	**Passive**
The plant manager approved the request.	The request was approved by the \<plant manager\>.
The committee will decide next month.	A decision will be made next month. No agent in sentence.
[You] send the customer a letter informing her about the change.	A letter will be sent informing the customer of the change. No agent in sentence.

If the sentence does not have a direct object in its active form, no passive equivalent exists.

Active   **No Passive Exists**

I would like to go to the conference.

The freight charge will be about $1,400.

The phone rang.

Passive verbs have at least three disadvantages:

1. If all the information in the original sentence is retained, passive verbs make the sentence longer. Passives take more time to understand.[3]
2. If the agent is omitted, it's not clear who is responsible for doing the action.
3. When many passive verbs are used, or when passives are used in material that has a lot of big words, the writing can be boring and pompous.

Passive verbs are desirable in these situations:

- Use passives to emphasize the object receiving the action, not the agent.

    Your order was shipped November 15.

  The customer's order, not the shipping clerk, is important.

- Use passives to provide coherence within a paragraph. A sentence is easier to read if "old" information comes at the beginning of a sentence. When you have been discussing a topic, use the word again as your subject even if that requires a passive verb.

    The bank made several risky loans in the late 1990s. These loans were written off as "uncollectible" in 2004.

  Using *loans* as the subject of the second sentence provides a link between the two sentences, making the paragraph as a whole easier to read.

- Use passives to avoid assigning blame.

    The order was damaged during shipment.

  An active verb would require the writer to specify *who* damaged the order. The passive here is more tactful.

2. Use Verbs to Carry the Weight of Your Sentence

Put the weight of your sentence in the verb. When the verb is a form of the verb *to be*, revise the sentence to use a more forceful verb.

Weak: The financial advantage of owning this equipment instead of leasing it is 10% after taxes.
Better: Owning this equipment rather than leasing it will save us 10% after taxes.

Better verbs make sentences more forceful and up to 25% easier to read.

Sources: E. B. Coleman, "The Comprehensibility of Several Grammatical Transformations," *Journal of Applied Psychology* 48, no. 3 (1964): 186–90; and Keith Raynor, "Visual Attention in Reading: Eye Movements Reflect Cognitive Processes," *Memory and Cognition* 5 (1977): 443–48.

Nouns ending in *-ment, -ion,* and *-al* often hide verbs.

make an adjustment	adjust
make a payment	pay
make a decision	decide
reach a conclusion	conclude
take into consideration	consider
make a referral	refer
provide assistance	assist

Use verbs to present the information more forcefully.

Weak: We will perform an investigation of the problem.
Better: We will investigate the problem.
Weak: Selection of a program should be based on the client's needs.
Better: Select the program that best fits the client's needs.

3. Tighten Your Writing

Writing is **wordy** if the same idea can be expressed in fewer words. Unnecessary words increase typing time, bore your reader, and make your meaning more difficult to follow, since the reader must hold all the extra words in mind while trying to understand your meaning.

Good writing is tight. Tight writing may be long because it is packed with ideas. In Modules 6–8, we saw that revisions to create you-attitude and positive emphasis and to develop reader benefits were frequently *longer* than the originals because the revision added information not given in the original.

Sometimes you may be able to look at a draft and see immediately how to tighten it. When wordiness isn't obvious, try the following strategies for tightening your writing.

a. Eliminate words that say nothing.
b. Use gerunds (the *-ing* form of verbs) and infinitives (the *to* form of verbs) to make sentences shorter and smoother.
c. Combine sentences to eliminate unnecessary words.
d. Put the meaning of your sentence into the subject and verb to cut the number of words.

The purpose of eliminating unnecessary words is to save the reader's time, not simply to see how few words you can use. You aren't writing a telegram, so keep the little words that make sentences complete. (Incomplete sentences are fine in lists where all the items are incomplete.)

The following examples show how to use these methods.

a. Eliminate Words that Say Nothing

Cut words that are already clear from other words in the sentence. Substitute single words for wordy phrases.

Wordy: Keep this information on file for future reference.
Tighter: Keep this information for reference.
or: File this information.
Wordy: Ideally, it would be best to put the billing ticket just below the screen and above the keyboard.
Tighter: If possible, put the billing ticket between the screen and the keyboard.

Phrases beginning with *of, which,* and *that* can often be shortened.

Wordy: the question of most importance
Tighter: the most important question
Wordy: the estimate which is enclosed
Tighter: the enclosed estimate

Sentences beginning with *There are* or *It is* can often be tighter.

Wordy: There are three reasons for the success of the project.
Tighter: Three reasons explain the project's success.

Ways to Improve Style

- Get a clean page or screen.
- Try WIRMI: *What I Really Mean Is.*
- Read your draft out loud to someone sitting at a comfortable personal distance.
- Ask someone else to read your draft out loud. Revise passages where readers stumble.
- Read widely and write a *lot.*

Active and Passive Verbs

If the verb describes something that the grammatical subject is doing, the verb is active. If the verb describes something that is being done to the grammatical subject, the verb is passive.

Wordy: It is the case that college graduates advance more quickly in the company.
Tighter: College graduates advance more quickly in the company.

Check your draft. If you find unnecessary words, eliminate them.

b. Use Gerunds and Infinitives to Make Sentences Shorter and Smoother

A **gerund** is the *-ing* form of a verb; grammatically, it is a verb used as a noun. In the sentence, "Running is my favorite activity," *running* is the subject of the sentence. An **infinitive** is the form of the verb which is preceded by *to: to run* is the infinitive.

In the revision below, a gerund *(purchasing)* and an infinitive *(to transmit)* tighten the revision.

Wordy: A plant suggestion has been made where they would purchase a fax machine for the purpose of transmitting test reports between plants.
Tighter: The plant suggests purchasing a fax machine to transmit test reports between plants.

Even when gerunds and infinitives do not greatly affect length, they often make sentences smoother and more conversational.

c. Combine Sentences to Eliminate Unnecessary Words

In addition to saving words, combining sentences focuses the reader's attention on key points, makes your writing sound more sophisticated, and sharpens the relationship between ideas, thus making your writing more coherent.

Wordy: I conducted this survey by telephone on Sunday, April 21. I questioned two groups of juniors and seniors—male and female—who, according to the Student Directory, were still living in the dorms. The purpose of this survey was to find out why some juniors and seniors continue to live in the dorms even though they are no longer required by the university to do so. I also wanted to find out if there were any differences between male and female juniors and seniors in their reasons for choosing to remain in the dorms.
Tighter: On Sunday, April 21, I phoned male and female juniors and seniors living in the dorms to find out (1) why they continue to live in the dorms even though they are no longer required to do so, and (2) whether men and women had the same reasons for staying in the dorms.

d. Put the Meaning of Your Sentence into the Subject and Verb to Cut the Number of Words

Put the core of your meaning into the subject and verb of your main clause. Think about what you *mean* and try saying the same thing in several different ways. Some alternatives will be tighter than others. Choose the tightest one.

Wordy: The reason we are recommending the computerization of this process is because it will reduce the time required to obtain data and will give us more accurate data.
Better: We are recommending the computerization of this process because it will save time and give us more accurate data.
Tight: Computerizing the process will give us more accurate data more quickly.
Wordy: The purpose of this letter is to indicate that if we are unable to mutually benefit from our seller/buyer relationship, with satisfactory material and satisfactory payment, then we have no alternative other than to sever the relationship. In other words, unless the account is handled in 45 days, we will have to change our terms to a permanent COD basis.
Better: A good buyer/seller relationship depends upon satisfactory material and satisfactory payment. You can continue to charge your purchases from us only if you clear your present balance in 45 days.

4. Vary Sentence Length and Sentence Structure

Readable prose mixes sentence lengths and varies sentence structure. Most sentences should be 20 words or fewer. A really short sentence (under 10 words) can add punch to your prose. Really long sentences (over 30 or 40 words) are danger signs.

You can vary sentence patterns in several ways. First, you can mix simple, compound, and complex sentences. **Simple sentences** have one main clause:

We will open a new store this month.

LinkedIn's Nicole Williams notes that buzzwords like "creative" and "dynamic" are among the most-used buzzwords on the social networking site, making it harder for potential employers to see what makes a person stand out from the crowd. "It's okay to use some common language," Williams says, "but if everyone is 'creative,' the word becomes null and void." She recommends showing creativity rather than simply using the word. Other common buzzwords on the site include "track record" and "extensive experience."

Source: Diane Stafford, "Buzzwords Won't Motivate Hirers," *The Columbus Dispatch,* December 25, 2011, http://www.dispatch.com/content/stories/business/2011/12/25/buzzwords-wont-motivate-hirers.html.

Instant Replay

Wordiness

Writing is **wordy** if the same idea can be expressed in fewer words.

Site to See

Go to
www.bartleby.com/141/index.html

for the online version of Strunk and White's classic *Elements of Style.*

Compound sentences have two main clauses joined with *and, but, or,* or another conjunction. Compound sentences work best when the ideas in the two clauses are closely related.

We have hired staff, and they will complete their training next week.

We wanted to have a local radio station broadcast from the store during its grand opening, but the DJs were already booked.

Complex sentences have one main and one subordinate clause; they are good for showing logical relationships.

When the stores open, we will have balloons and specials in every department.

Because we already have a strong customer base in the northwest, we expect the new store to be just as successful as the store in the City Center Mall.

You can also vary sentences by changing the order of elements. Normally, the subject comes first.

We will survey customers later in the year to see whether demand warrants a third store on campus.

To create variety, occasionally begin the sentence with some other part of the sentence.

Later in the year, we will survey customers to see whether demand warrants a third store on campus.

To see whether demand warrants a third store on campus, we will survey customers later in the year.

Use these guidelines for sentence length and structure:

- Always edit sentences for tightness. Even a 10-word sentence can be wordy.
- When your subject matter is complicated or full of numbers, make a special effort to keep sentences short.
- Use long sentences

To show how ideas are linked to each other.

To avoid a series of short, choppy sentences.

To reduce repetition.

- Group the words in long and medium-length sentences into chunks that the reader can process quickly.[4]
- When you use a long sentence, keep the subject and verb close together.

Let's see how to apply the last three principles.

Use Long Sentences to Show How Ideas Are Linked to Each Other, to Avoid a Series of Short, Choppy Sentences, and to Reduce Repetition

The following sentence is hard to read not simply because it is long but also because it is shapeless. Just cutting it into a series of short, choppy sentences doesn't help. The best revision uses medium-length sentences to show the relationship between ideas.

Too long: It should also be noted in the historical patterns presented in the summary that though there were delays in January and February which we realized were occurring, we are now back where we were about a year ago, and that we are not off line in our collect receivables as compared to last year at this time, but we do show a considerable over-budget figure because of an ultraconservative goal on the receivable investment.

Choppy: There were delays in January and February. We knew about them at the time. We are now back where we were about a year ago. The summary shows this. Our present collect receivables are in line with last year's. However, they exceed the budget. The reason they exceed the budget is that our goal for receivable investment was very conservative.

Better: As the summary shows, although there were delays in January and February (of which we were aware), we have now regained our position of a year ago. Our present collect receivables are in line with last year's, but they exceed the budget because our goal for receivable investment was very conservative.

Energy and enthusiasm are good. Add standard grammar and accuracy to create good sentences.

By permission of Rick Detorie and Creators Syndicate, Inc.

Group the Words in Long and Medium-Length Sentences into Chunks

The "better" revision above has seven chunks. In the following list, the chunks starting immediately after the numbers are main clauses. The chunks that are indented are subordinate clauses and parenthetical phrases.

1.   As the summary shows,
2.   although there were delays in January and February
3.   (of which we were aware),
4. we have now regained our position of a year ago.
5. Our present collect receivables are in line with last year's,
6. but they exceed the budget
7.   because our goal for receivable investment was very conservative.

The first sentence has four chunks: an introductory phrase (1), a subordinate clause (2) with a parenthetical phrase (3), followed by the main clause of the first sentence (4). The second sentence begins with a main clause (5). The sentence's second main clause (6) is introduced with *but,* showing that it will reverse the first clause. A subordinate clause explaining the reason for the reversal completes the sentence (7). At 27 and 24 words, respectively, these sentences aren't short, but they're readable because no chunk is longer than 10 words.

Any sentence pattern will get boring if it is repeated sentence after sentence. Use different sentence patterns—different kinds and lengths of chunks—to keep your prose interesting.

Keep the Subject and Verb Close Together

Often, you can move the subject and verb closer together if you put the modifying material in a list at the end of the sentence. For maximum readability, present the list vertically.

Hard to read: Movements resulting from termination, layoffs and leaves, recalls and reinstates, transfers in, transfers out, promotions in, promotions out, and promotions within are presently documented through the Payroll Authorization Form.

Smoother: The following movements are documented on the Payroll Authorization Form: termination, layoffs and leaves, recalls and reinstates, transfers in and out, and promotions in, out, and within.

Still better: The following movements are documented on the Payroll Authorization Form:
- Termination.
- Layoffs and leaves.
- Recalls and reinstates.
- Transfers in and out.
- Promotions in, out, and within.

Instant Replay

Sentence Length and Sentence Structure

Readable prose mixes sentence lengths and varies sentence structure. Most sentences should be 20 words or fewer.

Sometimes you will need to change the verb and revise the word order to put the modifying material at the end of the sentence.

Hard to read: The size sequence code that is currently used for sorting the items in the NOSROP lists and the composite stock list is not part of the online file.

Smoother: The online file does not contain the size sequence code that is currently used for sorting the items in the composite stock lists and the NOSROP lists.

5. Use Parallel Structure

Words or ideas that share the same logical role in your sentence must also be in the same grammatical form. Parallelism is also a powerful device for making your writing smoother and more forceful. (See Figure 16.2.) Note the parallel portions in the following examples.

Faulty: I interviewed juniors and seniors and athletes.

Parallel: I interviewed juniors and seniors. In each rank, I interviewed athletes and nonathletes.

Faulty: Errors can be checked by reviewing the daily exception report or note the number of errors you uncover when you match the lading copy with the file copy of the invoice.

Parallel: Errors can be checked by reviewing the daily exception report or by noting the number of errors you uncover when you match the lading copy with the file copy of the invoice.

Also Parallel: To check errors, note

1. The number of items on the daily exception report.
2. The number of errors discovered when the lading copy and the file copy are matched.

Note that a list in parallel structure must fit grammatically into the umbrella sentence that introduces the list.

Eliminate repeated words in parallel lists. (See Figure 16.3.)

Figure 16.2 Use Parallelism to Tighten Your Writing

THESE ARE THE BENEFITS THE CUSTOMER GETS.
- Use tracking information.
- Our products let them scale the software to their needs.
- The customer can always rely on us.

Faulty

CUSTOMER BENEFITS
- Tracking information
- Scalability
- Reliability

Parallel

Figure 16.3 Eliminate Repeated Words in Parallel Lists

POWERPOINT REPORTS
- They work best when the discourse community is well-defined.
- They work best when visuals can carry the message.
- They work best when oral comments can explain and connect ideas.

Wordy

POWERPOINT REPORTS WORK BEST WHEN
- The discourse community is well-defined.
- Visuals can carry the message.
- Oral comments can explain and connect ideas.

Tight

6. Put Your Readers in Your Sentences

Use second-person pronouns *(you)* rather than third-person *(he, she, one)* to give your writing more impact. *You* is both singular and plural; it can refer to a single person or to every member of your organization.

Third-person: Funds in a participating employee's account at the end of each six months will automatically be used to buy more stock unless a "Notice of Election Not to Exercise Purchase Rights" form is received from the employee.

Second-person: Once you begin to participate, funds in your account at the end of each six months will automatically be used to buy more stock unless you turn in a "Notice of Election Not to Exercise Purchase Rights" form.

Be careful to use *you* only when it refers to your reader.

Incorrect: My visit with the outside sales rep showed me that your schedule can change quickly.

Correct: My visit with the outside sales rep showed me that schedules can change quickly.

What should I look for when I revise paragraphs? LO 16-5

▶ *Check for topic sentences and transitions.*

Paragraphs are visual and logical units. Use them to chunk your sentences.

1. Begin Most Paragraphs with Topic Sentences

A good paragraph has **unity;** that is, it discusses only one idea, or topic. The **topic sentence** states the main idea and provides a scaffold to structure your document. Topic sentences are not essential, but your writing will be easier to read if you make the topic sentence explicit and put it at the beginning of the paragraph.[5]

Hard to read (no topic sentence): In fiscal 2003, the company filed claims for a refund of federal income taxes of $3,199,000 and interest of $969,000 paid as a result of an examination of the company's federal income tax returns by the Internal Revenue Service (IRS) for the years 1999 through 2002. It is uncertain what amount, if any, may ultimately be recovered.

Better (paragraph starts with topic sentence): The company and the IRS disagree about whether the company is liable for back taxes. In fiscal 2003, the company filed claims for a refund of federal income taxes of $3,199,000 and interest of $969,000 paid as a result of an examination of the company's federal income tax returns by the Internal Revenue Service (IRS) for the years 1999 through 2002. It is uncertain what amount, if any, may ultimately be recovered.

A good topic sentence forecasts the structure and content of the paragraph.

Plan B also has economic advantages.
(Prepares the reader for a discussion of B's economic advantages.)

We had several personnel changes in June.
(Prepares the reader for a list of the month's terminations and hires.)

Employees have complained about one part of our new policy on parental leaves.
(Prepares the reader for a discussion of the problem.)

When the first sentence of a paragraph is not the topic sentence, readers who skim may miss the main point. Move the topic sentence to the beginning of the paragraph. If the paragraph does not have a topic sentence, you will need to write one. If you can't think of a single sentence that serves as an "umbrella" to cover every sentence, the paragraph lacks unity. To solve the problem, either split the paragraph into two, or eliminate the sentence that digresses from the main point.

Figure 16.4 Transition Words and Phrases

To Show Addition or Continuation of the Same Idea	To Introduce an Example	To Show that the Contrast Is More Important than the Previous Idea	To Show Time
and	e.g.	but	after
also	for example	however	as
first, second, third	for instance	nevertheless	before
in addition	indeed	on the contrary	in the future
likewise	to illustrate		next
similarly	namely		then
	specifically	**To Show Cause and Effect**	until
To Introduce the Last or Most Important Item		as a result	when
	To Contrast	because	while
finally	in contrast	consequently	
furthermore	on the other hand	for this reason	**To Summarize or End**
moreover	or	therefore	in conclusion

(continued)
how celebrity Ryan Dunn had posted a photo of himself drinking with friends an hour before he was killed in a car accident sparked vitriolic debates on Ebert's Facebook page. Though Facebook later apologized and said the page had been removed in error, the company had removed pages before after people flagged content as inappropriate.

Source: John Hudson, "Roger Ebert's the Latest Victim of Facebook's Censorship Problem," *The Atlantic Wire,* June 21, 2011, http://www.theatlanticwire.com/technology/2011/06/roger-ebert-just-latest-victim-facebooks-censorship-problem/39087/.

2. Use Transitions to Link Ideas

Transition words and sentences signal the connections between ideas to the reader. Transitions tell whether the next sentence continues the previous thought or starts a new idea; they can tell whether the idea that comes next is more or less important than the previous thought. Figure 16.4 lists some of the most common transition words and phrases.

How does organizational culture affect style?   LO 16-6

▶ *Different cultures may prefer different styles.*

Different organizations and bosses may legitimately have different ideas about what constitutes good writing. If the style the company prefers seems reasonable, use it. If the style doesn't seem reasonable—if you work for someone who likes flowery language or wordy paragraphs, for example—you have several choices.

- **Use the techniques in this module.** Sometimes seeing good writing changes people's minds about the style they prefer.
- **Help your boss learn about writing.** Show him or her this book or the research cited in the notes to demonstrate how a clear, crisp style makes documents easier to read.
- **Recognize that a style may serve other purposes than communication.** An abstract, hard-to-read style may help a group forge its own identity. James Suchan and Ronald Dulek have shown that Navy officers preferred a passive, impersonal style because they saw themselves as followers. An aircraft company's engineers saw wordiness as the verbal equivalent of backup systems. A backup is redundant but essential to safety, because parts and systems do fail.[6] When big words, jargon, and wordiness are central to a group's self-image, change will be difficult, since changing style will mean changing the corporate culture.
- **Ask.** Often the documents that end up in files aren't especially good. Later, other workers may find these documents and imitate them, thinking they represent a corporate standard. Bosses may in fact prefer better writing.

Building a good style takes energy and effort, but it's well worth the work. Good style can make every document more effective; good style can help make you the good writer so valuable to every organization.

Site to See

Go to
www.gray-area.org/Research/Ambig/

for a collection of ambiguous and often funny sentences from ads, church bulletins, and insurance forms. (Scroll down past the long first page.)

- Good style in business and administrative writing is less formal, more friendly, and more personal than the style usually used for term papers. **(LO 16-1)**
- A good tone is businesslike, friendly, and polite. **(LO 16-2)**
- To create a good tone, analyze communication situations rhetorically: **(LO 16-2)**
  - Who are your audiences?
  - What are your purposes?
  - How do other people in the organization talk and write?
  - What kind of response did you get?
- To improve your style, **(LO 16-3)**
  - Get a clean page or screen, so that you aren't locked into old sentence structures.
  - Try WIRMI: *What I Really Mean Is*. Then write the words.
  - Try reading your draft out loud to someone sitting at a comfortable personal distance. If the words sound stiff, they'll seem stiff to a reader, too.
  - Ask someone else to read your draft out loud. Readers stumble because the words on the page aren't what they expect to see. The places where that person stumbles are places where your writing can be better.
  - Write a lot.

Summary of Learning Objectives

- As you write and revise sentences, **(LO 16-4)**
  1. Use active verbs most of the time. Active verbs are better because they are shorter, clearer, and more interesting.
  2. Use verbs to carry the weight of your sentence.
  3. Tighten your writing. Writing is **wordy** if the same idea can be expressed in fewer words.
     a. Eliminate words that say nothing.
     b. Use gerunds and infinitives to make sentences shorter and smoother.
     c. Combine sentences to eliminate unnecessary words.
     d. Put the meaning of your sentence into the subject and verb to cut the number of words.
  4. Vary sentence length and sentence structure.
  5. Use parallel structure. Use the same grammatical form for ideas that have the same logical function.
  6. Put your readers in your sentences.
- As you write and revise paragraphs, **(LO 16-5)**
  1. Begin most paragraphs with topic sentences so that readers know what to expect in the paragraph.
  2. Use transitions to link ideas.
- Different organizations and bosses may legitimately have different ideas about what constitutes good writing. **(LO 16-6)**

Assignments for Module 16

Questions for Comprehension

16.1 What problems do passive verbs create? When are passive verbs desirable? **(LO 16-4)**

16.2 List two ways to tighten your writing. **(LO 16-4)**

16.3 What is parallel structure? **(LO 16-4)**

16.4 How do topic sentences help readers? **(LO 16-5)**

Questions for Critical Thinking

16.5 Would your other instructors like the style you're learning to use in this class? **(LO 16-1)**

16.6 Can a long document be tight rather than wordy? **(LO 16-1 to LO 16-3)**

16.7 Ask a trusted friend or colleague how your tone comes across in classes and at work. If other people find you shy on the one hand or arrogant on the other, what changes in your tone could you make? **(LO 16-2)**

Exercises and Problems

16.8 Changing Verbs from Passive to Active (LO 16-4)

Identify the passive verbs in the following sentences and convert them to active verbs. In some cases, you may need to add information to do so. You may use different words as long as you retain the basic meaning of the sentence. Remember that imperative verbs are active, too.

1. The car was driven by Lloyd to the airport.
2. A phone call was made by Penelope to the home office.

16.9 Using Better Verbs (LO 16-4)

Revise each of the following sentences to use better verbs.

1. Many of our customers receive the benefits of being a preferred member.
2. Employees who have more than nine months with the company will start to accrue vacation time.

3. Whenever possible, vacations should be taken by employees during summer months.
4. When Deidre calls, she should be told to bring copies of the annual report with her to the meeting.
5. A complete list of all of the attendees was compiled by the Public Relations Office.

3. If Nabil stops by, do be sure to inquire if he plans to participate in the "Race for the Cure" on Saturday.
4. There are a variety of important decisions to be considered carefully before making a purchase.
5. It is extremely doubtful that the sales figures will see an improvement before the end of the quarter.

16.10 Reducing Wordiness (LO 16-4)

1. Eliminate words that say nothing. You may use different words.

   a. Employees who were just hired and are therefore defined as novice employees by the company should take steps to ensure that they attend a mandatory training session that is required of all novice employees.

   b. *Bloomberg Businessweek* magazine printed in its pages a very, very good magazine article on how company executives who work at businesses are currently finding innovative and creative solutions to problems that they encounter with regularity on the job and in the workplace these days.

   c. Employees who come to work on time and ready to work are generally viewed as more professional than employees who don't come to work on time and are not ready to work. Employees who don't come to work on time and are not ready to work are often seen as unprofessional, which means that they are less professional than other employees. Professional employees are more likely to be hired, valued, and promoted than unprofessional employees. Therefore, it's better to be a professional employee rather than an unprofessional employee.

2. Use gerunds and infinitives to make these sentences shorter and smoother.

   a. Customers who want participation in this month's online promotion may find a review of our preregistration process helpful.

16.11 Improving Parallel Structure (LO 16-4)

Revise each of the following sentences to create parallelism.

1. The county will benefit from implementing flextime.
   - Offices will stay open longer for more business.
   - Staff turnover will be lower.
   - Easier business communication with states in other time zones.
   - Increased employee productivity.

2. Newsletters enhance credibility, four times as many people read them as read standard ad formats, and allow soft-sell introduction to prospective customers.

16.12 Putting Readers in Your Sentences (LO 16-4)

Revise each of the following sentences to put readers in them. As you revise, use active verbs and simple words.

1. Proofreading a résumé carefully is vital to ensure that typos are corrected.

2. Working beyond the expected 40 hours per week is allowable, and overtime compensation will be received.

16.13 Editing Sentences to Improve Style (LO 16-4)

Revise these sentences to make them smoother, less wordy, and easier to read. Eliminate jargon and repetition. Keep the information; you may reword or reorganize it. If the original is not clear, you may need to add information to write a clear revision.

b. The production of better but cheaper goods often makes a company more competitive in the sales of merchandise in the marketplace.

c. Whitney said the receipt of company-paid medical insurance is a benefit that many parents today are in consideration of while engaged in the decision process of the acceptance of a job offer.

3. Combine sentences to show how ideas are related and to eliminate unnecessary words.

   a. Michael supervises the archives department. Michael also supervises the data processing department. As supervisor of both departments, Michael has responsibility for the company's archiving and data processing services and oversees 14 employees.

   b. Our employees want our customers to have a positive experience shopping in our store. Our employees are trained to provide good customer service. Our customers expect to have a positive experience shopping in our store. Because both our employees and our customers want the same thing, we have the highest customer satisfaction rating of any store in the company.

   c. The communications department plans to stop printing the company newsletter and instead offer it on the intranet. The format for the newsletter will be the same, but instead of it being printed on paper, it will be available in electronic form. Employees may print a copy of the newsletter or simply read it online. By ceasing to print the newsletter on paper and instead offer it on the intranet, the communications department expects to save several thousand dollars each year.

3. When you leave a voice-mail message,
   - Summarize your main point in a sentence or two.
   - The name and phone number should be given slowly and distinctly.
   - The speaker should give enough information so the recipient can act on the message.
   - Tell when you'll be available to receive the recipient's return call.

3. Annual self-reviews are to be completed by December 12, and meetings with managers are to be scheduled by December 30.

4. Employee friends and family members may use the company gym provided employees preregister them.

5. Staff may attend the training program provided staff obtain permission from a supervisor.

1. The report that was completed by the finance department organizes essential information in a quite unsatisfactory manner.

2. Few of our customers who are most valued seek to obtain goods and services from another vendor, but we must remain ever vigilant in the business environment to better

ensure that these such customers continue in their loyal efforts with our establishment.

3. Per your inquiry, Carla Meier is quite possibly the best and finest member of our staff that we have every had the distinct pleasure to have known and worked with.

4. Following are distinct reasons to retain your current policy with Interstate Insurance:

   - Convenient claims submissions.
   - An agent who is fully prepared to help you to the fullest.
   - web page.

16.14 Using Topic Sentences (LO 16-5)

Make each of the following paragraphs more readable by opening each paragraph with a topic sentence. You may be able to find a topic sentence in the paragraph and move it to the beginning. In other cases, you'll need to write a new sentence.

1. At Disney World, a lunch put on an expense account is "on the mouse." McDonald's employees "have ketchup in their veins." Business slang flourishes at companies with rich corporate cultures. Memos at Procter & Gamble are called "reco's" because the model P&G memo begins with a recommendation.

2. The first item on the agenda is the hiring for the coming year. George has also asked that we review the agency

16.15 Writing Paragraphs (LO 16-5)

Write a paragraph on each of the following topics.

1. Discuss your ideal job.
2. Summarize a recent article from a business magazine or newspaper.
3. Explain how technology is affecting the field you plan to enter.
4. Explain why you have or have not decided to work while you attend college.

5. Planning meetings will be held during next month at different dates and times. These meetings will help us to plan for the upcoming conversion to a revised HR system. Meeting times to devise the plan will be as follows:

   May 3, 2–3 PM

   May 10, 2–3 PM

   May 17, 2–3 PM

goals for the next fiscal year. We should cover this early in the meeting since it may affect our hiring preferences. Finally, we need to announce the deadlines for grant proposals, decide which grants to apply for, and set up a committee to draft each proposal.

3. Separate materials that can be recycled from your regular trash. Pass along old clothing, toys, or appliances to someone else who can use them. When you purchase products, choose those with minimal packaging. If you have a yard, put your yard waste and kitchen scraps (excluding meat and fat) in a compost pile. You can reduce the amount of solid waste your household produces in four ways.

5. Write a profile of someone who is successful in the field you hope to enter.

As Your Instructor Directs,

1. Label topic sentences, active verbs, and parallel structure.
2. Edit a classmate's paragraphs to make the writing even tighter and smoother.

Polishing Your **Prose**

Commas in Lists

Use commas in lists to separate items:

At the office supply store, I bought pens, stationery, and three-ring binders.

Commas show distinctions between items in a list. Technically, the comma before the coordinating conjunction, such as *and* or *or,* is optional, but the additional comma always adds clarity. Use commas consistently throughout your document. Missing or improperly placed commas confuse readers:

We bought the following items for the staff lounge: television cabinet computer desk refrigerator and microwave oven.

Does *television* describe *cabinet* or is it a separate item? Is *computer desk* one item? Or are *computer* and *desk* two separate things? Inserting commas makes the distinction clear:

We bought the following items for the staff lounge: television, cabinet, computer, desk, refrigerator, and microwave oven.

Semicolons replace commas in lists where the items themselves contain commas:

Our company has plants in Blue Ridge, Kentucky; Boise, Idaho; and Saganaw, Michigan.

Exercises

Use commas to make these lists clearer.

1. The best years for our stock were 1995 2004 2010 and 2012.
2. Raises for directors supervisors and managers will be 2.3 2.5 and 2.2 percent, respectively.

3. We've got enough time to tour three of the region's cities, so choose from Nome Alaska Dearborn Michigan Gary Indiana Chicago Illinois or Lexington Kentucky.

4. David said that we need pens pencils erasers notepads folders paperclips note cards and name tags for the strategic planning retreat.

5. I can see that when Juan takes charge in April, we can expect to see profit increases in May June July and August.

6. Sunny forwarded the itinerary for the trip: Xiua will be flying from 9 a.m. till 11:45 a.m. Thursday Alexis will be flying from 10:15 a.m. till 11:25 a.m. on Friday and Jocelyn will be flying from 1 p.m. till 2:35 p.m. on Saturday.

7. Because we only have enough money in the budget for one attendee, we'll have to select Eve Gail Dominic or Lynetta to go.

8. The guest list includes Rick Keri Meyer Tonee Calvin Esteban Christopher Marguerite and Benjamin.

9. Our international division wants the board to tour Kyoto Japan Beijing China Berne Switzerland Mainz Germany and Toronto Canada.

10. So we are prepared for emergencies, the pool cars should have flares gloves blankets warning signs tire pressure gauges portable air compressors and prepaid cell phones.

Check your answers to the odd-numbered exercises at the back of the book.

Unit 4 Cases for Communicators

With the Best of Intentions

The State of Ohio paid a contractor to create and place a road sign above a well-traveled stretch of northern interstate highway. The problem is that the sign misspelled "north" in big white letters as "NORHT."

Though the contractor will replace the sign, the error was reported in one of the region's top newspapers, *The Cleveland Plain Dealer,* and picked up by news outlets around the country. Ohio, a state hit hard by the economic downturn of the past few years, has sought to project a 21st-century image to attract business. The typo doesn't exactly communicate that message.

For now, the contractor has placed an overlay on the typo and corrected the spelling. But the damage to the state's image may be harder to fix. State officials also want to know who approved the sign, which could have proven a distracting safety hazard, before it was placed. They also want to assure taxpayers that the state's beleaguered funds are being spent responsibly.

Individual Activity

Imagine you are the special assistant to the director of the Ohio Department of Transportation (ODOT). Your task is to write a letter to the entire department outlining why errors like these must be prevented in the future.

In your letter, explain the importance of good writing, focusing on editing and proofreading skills. Be sure to include at least three specific points describing how poor writing can affect the perceptions of the writer and the validity of the document and how mistakes can have real consequences for people. Use examples of bad writing for illustration.

As you draft, use WIRMI—What I Really Mean Is—to craft your basic idea. When you're finished, read the draft out loud. Think about these questions as you polish your letter:

- Did I use active verbs most of the time?
- Did I use verbs to carry the weight of my sentences?
- Did I include any words that mean nothing or send the wrong message?
- Can I tighten my writing by combining sentences or using gerunds and infinitives?
- Did I vary sentence length and structure?
- Did I use parallel structure?

- Did I begin most paragraphs with strong topic sentences?
- Did I use transitions to link ideas?

Be sure to carefully edit and proofread your final draft.

Group Activity

Note: To prepare for this group activity, print a new version of your draft, omitting all punctuation and formatting. The end result should be one block of text without any clear sentence or paragraph structure. Then, divide the members of the group into pairs.

The ODOT director has asked to see a copy of the letter you intend to send to the department. Unfortunately, your computer crashes. You recover the document, but it lacks formatting and punctuation. You are pressed for time, but you don't want to give your superior this draft.

Exchange your unformatted draft with you partner. Carefully read through theirs. Using the correct proofreading marks, note where the punctuation and paragraph breaks should go.

Before you return the draft to its author, ask yourself the following questions:

- Did I use the correct proofreading marks?
- Does my edited version of the letter make sense and read smoothly?

Give the edited version of the letter back to your partner. Examine your own draft, now copyedited by your partner, and compare it to your original version. As you do, ask yourself the following questions:

- How does the edited version compare to my draft?
- Are the sentence and paragraph breaks the same?
- Has the meaning or emphasis been changed?
- Did my partner identify any errors (e.g., word usage or punctuation) in my draft?

Note all differences in meaning and structure that you find.

As a group, share your findings. Discuss the ways in which grammar and punctuation affected meaning and structure. What does this experience tell you about the importance of proper grammar and punctuation in business documents?

Source: "Highway Sign for I-71 'Norht' Will Be Replaced," *The Columbus Dispatch,* June 8, 2011, http://www.dispatch.com/live/content/local_news/stories/2011/06/08/ohio-highway-sign-misspelled.html?sid=101.

Research & Reports

21 | Proposals and Progress Reports

Module 21 describes how to write successful proposals and progress reports. After completing the module, you should be able to

LO 21-1   **Define reports in the workplace.**

LO 21-2   **Estimate time for business proposal writing.**

LO 21-3   **Identify sections for business proposal organization.**

LO 21-4   **Identify "hot buttons" for business proposal strategies and beyond.**

LO 21-5   **Identify sections for progress report organization.**

Reports provide the information that people in organizations need to make plans and solve problems.

Writing any report includes five basic steps:

1. Define the problem.
2. Gather the necessary information.
3. Analyze the information.
4. Organize the information.
5. Write the report.

After reviewing the varieties of reports, this module focuses on the first step. Module 22 discusses the second and third steps. Modules 23 and 24 illustrate the fourth and fifth steps.

Other modules that are useful for writing reports are Modules 12, 18, 20, and 25.

What is a "report"? LO 21-1

▶ *Many different kinds of documents are called reports.*

In some organizations, a report is a long document or a document that contains numerical data. In others, one- and two-page memos are called *reports*. In still others, *reports* consist of PowerPoint slides printed out and bound together. A short report to a client may use a letter format. **Formal reports** contain formal elements such as a title page, a transmittal, a table of contents, and a list of illustrations. **Informal reports** may be letters and memos or even computer printouts of production or sales figures.

Reports can just provide information, both provide information and analyze it, or provide information and analysis to support a recommendation (see Figure 21.1). Reports can be called **information reports** if they collect data for the reader, **analytical reports** if they interpret data but do not recommend action, and **recommendation reports** if they recommend action or a solution.

What should I do before I write a proposal? LO 21-2

▶ *Finish at least one-fourth of your research!*

As Figure 21.2 suggests, before you draft a proposal, you not only need to do the analysis that you'd do for any message, but you also need to complete part of your research—usually about one-fourth of the total research you'll need to do for a class project. You'll use this research both to define the problem your report will discuss and to identify the topics you'll investigate. Fortunately, if these parts of the proposal are well written, they can be used with minor changes in the report itself.

Narrow your problem. For example, "improving the college experiences of international students studying in the United States" is far too broad. First, choose one college or university. Second, identify the specific problem. Do you want to increase the social interaction between U.S. and international students? Help international students find housing? Increase the number of ethnic grocery stores and restaurants? Third, identify

---

Figure 21.1 Three Levels of Reports

Reports Can Provide

Information only

- **Sales reports** (sales figures for the week or month).
- **Quarterly reports** (figures showing a plant's productivity and profits for the quarter).

Information plus analysis

- **Annual reports** (financial data and an organization's accomplishments during the past year).
- **Audit reports** (interpretations of the facts revealed during an audit).
- **Make-good** or **pay-back reports** (calculations of the point at which a new capital investment will pay for itself).

Information plus analysis plus a recommendation

- **Feasibility reports** evaluate two or more alternatives and recommend which alternative the organization should choose.
- **Justification reports** justify the need for a purchase, an investment, a new personnel line, or a change in procedure.
- **Problem-solving reports** identify the causes of an organizational problem and recommend a solution.

Feasibility studies often reveal surprising information. A UBS study noted that a plan to fund a $975 million stadium for the Minnesota Vikings mostly with public dollars was a bad idea because "independent academic research studies consistently conclude that new stadiums and arenas have no measurable effect on the level of real income or employment in the metropolitan areas in which they are located." Those words echo findings in Mark Perryman's *Why the Olympics Aren't Good for Us and How They Can Be,* which chronicles bust periods after the Olympics are over, noting in particular how Greece faced a $784 million cost to maintain crumbling facilities after the 2004 games. The price tag of potential accidents from shale gas extraction was calculated by a group of Yale University economics graduates to be $250 million annually—against the estimated $100 billion in yearly economic benefits.

Sources: Mike Ozanian, "Vikings Stadium Not Likely to Help Minnesota's Economy," *Forbes,* May 4, 2012, http://www.forbes.com/sites/mikeozanian/2012/05/04/vikings-stadium-not-likely-to-help-minnesotas-economy/; Mark Perryman, "Do the Olympics Boost the Economy? Studies Show the Impact Is Likely Negative," July 30, 2012, http://www.thedailybeast.com/articles/2012/07/30/do-the-olympics-boost-the-economy-studies-show-the-impact-is-likely-negative.html; and Christopher Helman, "The Arithmetic of Shale Gas," *Forbes,* June 22, 2012, http://www.forbes.com/sites/christopherhelman/2012/06/22/the-arithmetic-of-shale-gas/2/.

Site to See

Go to

www.cdc.gov/mmwr/ mmwr_rr/rr_pvol.html

for sample recommendation reports from the Centers for Disease Control.

The London Business School's John W. Mullins believes that a good business plan starts with a well-defined problem that is supported by convincing evidence gathered from many credible sources. He cites Nike's revolutionary shoe designs as having addressed the real problems of runners: injuries like shin splints and sprained ankles. He also argues for using you attitude: "A Me-First plan sends a clear signal that the writer's priorities are misplaced. What matters more than great technology or a great idea is the problem or pain that the new solution or technology resolves."

Source: John W. Mullins, "Why Business Plans Don't Deliver," *The Wall Street Journal*, June 15, 2012, http://online.wsj.com/article/SB100 01424052970204830304574133501980701202.html.

Site to See

Go to

http://foundationcenter. org/findfunders/

The Foundation Center offers links to grant makers' web pages, information about foundations, and advice about writing proposals.

Figure 21.2 Allocating Time in Writing a Proposal (Your time may vary.)	
Proposal to write a report studying alternative dispute resolution. Total time: 30 hours	
Planning	**15 hours**
Read the Request for Proposal (RFP).	
Gather necessary materials (costs, bios of personnel, etc.).	
Identify and narrow the problem.	
Complete preliminary research.	
Talk to people about the issue.	
Prepare a bibliography and read as many of the sources as possible.	
Construct a questionnaire.	
Identify the topics you'll investigate for the report.	
Answer the PAIBOC questions (◄◄ Module 1).	
Think about document design (◄◄ Module 5).	
Organize the message.	
Writing	**5 hours**
Draft the proposal.	
Revising	**10 hours**
Reread draft.	
Measure draft against PAIBOC questions and RFP.	
Revise draft.	
Ask for feedback.	
Revise draft based on feedback.	
Edit to catch grammatical errors.	
Run spell-check.	
Proof by eye.	
Initial a memo proposal; sign a letter proposal.	
Make the necessary copies and distribute.	

the specific audience that would have the power to implement your recommendations. Depending on the topic, the audience might be the Office of International Studies, the residence hall counselors, a service organization on campus or in town, a store, or a group of investors.

How you define the problem shapes the solutions you find. For example, suppose that a manufacturer of frozen foods isn't making money. If the problem is defined as a marketing problem, the researcher may analyze the product's price, image, advertising, and position in the market. But perhaps the problem is really that overhead costs are too high due to poor inventory management, or that an inadequate distribution system doesn't get the product to its target market. Defining the problem accurately is essential to finding an effective solution.

Once you've defined your problem, you're ready to write a purpose statement. The purpose statement goes both in your proposal and in your final report. A good **purpose statement** makes three things clear:

- The organizational problem or conflict.
- The specific technical questions that must be answered to solve the problem.
- The rhetorical purpose (to explain, to recommend, to request, to propose) the report is designed to achieve.

The following purpose statements have all three elements.

Current management methods keep the elk population within the carrying capacity of the habitat, but require frequent human intervention. Both wildlife conservation specialists and the public would prefer methods that controlled the elk population naturally. This report will compare the current short-term management techniques (hunting, trapping and transporting, and winter feeding) with two long-term management techniques, habitat modification and the reintroduction of predators. The purpose of this report is to recommend which techniques or combination of techniques would best satisfy the needs of conservationists, hunters, and the public.

Report Audience: Superintendent of Yellowstone National Park

When banner ads on web pages first appeared in 1994, the initial response, or "click-through" rate, was about 10%. However, as ads have proliferated on web pages, the click-through rate has dropped sharply. Rather than assuming that any banner ad will be successful, we need to ask, What characteristics do successful banner ads share? Are ads for certain kinds of products and services or for certain kinds of audiences more likely to be successful on the web? The purpose of this report is to summarize the available research and anecdotal evidence and to recommend what Leo Burnett should tell its clients about whether and how to use banner ads.

Report Audience: Leo Burnett Advertising Agency

To write a good purpose statement, you must understand the basic problem and have some idea of the questions that your report will answer. Note, however, that you can (and should) write the purpose statement before researching the specific alternatives the report will discuss.

What should go in a proposal? LO 21-3

▶ *What you're going to do, how and when you'll do it, and evidence that you'll do it well.*

Proposals suggest a method for finding information or solving a problem.[1] (See Figure 21.3.)

Figure 21.3 Relationship among Situation, Proposal, and Final Report		
Company's Current Situation	**The Proposal Offers to**	**The Final Report Will Provide**
We don't know whether we should change.	Assess whether change is a good idea.	Insight, recommending whether change is desirable.
We need to/want to change, but we don't know exactly what we need to do.	Develop a plan to achieve desired goal.	A plan for achieving the desired change.
We need to/want to change, and we know what to do, but we need help doing it.	Implement the plan, increase (or decrease) measurable outcomes.	A record of the implementation and evaluation process.

Source: Adapted from Richard C. Freed, Shervin Freed, and Joseph D. Romano, *Writing Winning Proposals: Your Guide to Landing the Client, Making the Sale, Persuading the Boss* (New York: McGraw-Hill, 1995), 21.

Instant Replay

Purpose Statements

A good **purpose statement** makes three things clear:

- The organizational problem or conflict.
- The specific technical questions that must be answered to solve the problem.
- The rhetorical purpose the report is designed to achieve.

Many business schools hold contests for budding entrepreneurs to pitch their million-dollar ideas as class projects. The contests involve writing business plans and presenting them to judges, with cash prizes of up to $20,000 for winners. However, many ideas never make it to execution. Observes Janet Strimaitis, managing director of Babson College's Arthur M. Blank Center for Entrepreneurship: "You can write a beautiful 50-page business plan without ever talking to a potential customer." And some highly successful businesses failed to earn the top spot in contests. LendingTree, for instance, took second place at the University of Virginia in 1997 and Akamai Technology was only a finalist at the Massachusetts Institute of Technology in 1998. A good business plan, of course, is just a potential foundation for a business. The rest is a combination of talent, tenacity, timing, and luck.

Source: Melissa Korn, "Entrepreneur Contests Take Practical Turn," *The Wall Street Journal,* February 2, 2012, http://online.wsj.com/article/SB10001424052970203920204577196813674180138.html.

As Donna Kienzler points out, proposals have two goals: to get the project accepted and to get you accepted to do the job. Proposals must stress reader benefits and provide specific supporting details.[2] Attention to details—including good visual impact and proofreading—helps establish your professional image and suggests that you'd give the same care to the project if your proposal is accepted.

To write a good proposal, you need to have a clear view of the problem you hope to solve and the kind of research or other action needed to solve it. A proposal must answer the following questions convincingly:

- What problem are you going to solve?
- How are you going to solve it?
- What exactly will you provide for us?
- Can you deliver what you promise?
- What benefits can you offer?
- When will you complete the work?
- How much will you charge?

Government agencies and companies often issue Requests for Proposals, known as **RFPs.** Follow the RFP exactly when you respond to a proposal. Competitive proposals are often scored by giving points in each category. Evaluators look only under the heads specified in the RFP. If information isn't there, the proposal gets no points in that category.

Proposals for Class Research Projects

A proposal for a student report usually has the following sections:

1. In your first paragraph (no heading), summarize in a sentence or two the topic and purposes of your report.
2. **Problem.** What organizational problem exists? What is wrong? Why does it need to be solved? Is there a history or background that is relevant?
3. **Feasibility.** Are you sure that a solution can be found in the time available? How do you know?
4. **Audience.** Who in the organization would have the power to implement your recommendation? What secondary audiences might be asked to evaluate your report? What audiences would be affected by your recommendation? Will anyone serve as a gatekeeper, determining whether your report is sent to decision makers? What watchdog audiences might read the report?

    For each of these audiences and for your initial audience (your instructor), give the person's name, job title, and business address and answer the following questions:
    - What is the audience's major concern or priority?
    - What will the audience see as advantages of your proposal? What objections, if any, is the reader likely to have?
    - How interested is the audience in the topic of your report?
    - How much does the audience know about the topic of your report?

    List any terms, concepts, equations, or assumptions that one or more of your audiences may need to have explained. Briefly identify ways in which your audiences may affect the content, organization, or style of the report.
5. **Topics to Investigate.** List the questions and subquestions you will answer in your report, the topics or concepts you will explain, the aspects of the problem you will discuss. Indicate how deeply you will examine each of the aspects you plan to treat. Explain your rationale for choosing to discuss some aspects of the problem and not others.
6. **Methods/Procedure.** How will you get answers to your questions? Whom will you interview or survey? What published sources will you use? What websites will you consult? Give the full bibliographic references.

Make your proposal persuasive by using benefits that your audience finds important.

"Your Majesty, my voyage will not only forge a new route to the spices of the East but also create over three thousand new jobs."

Copyright © Dana Fradon/The New Yorker Collection, www.cartoonbank.com.

Your Methods section should clearly indicate how you will get the information needed to answer the questions in the Topics to Investigate section.

7. **Qualifications/Facilities/Resources.** Do you have the knowledge and skills needed to conduct this study? Do you have adequate access to the organization? Do you have access to any equipment you will need to conduct your research (computer, books, etc.)? Where will you turn for help if you hit an unexpected snag?

   You'll be more convincing if you have already scheduled an interview, checked out books, or printed out online sources.

8. **Work Schedule.** List both the total time you plan to spend on and the date when you expect to finish each of the following activities:
   - Gathering information
   - Analyzing information
   - Preparing the progress report
   - Organizing information
   - Writing the draft
   - Revising the draft
   - Preparing the visuals
   - Editing the draft
   - Proofreading the report

   Organize your work schedule either in a chart or in a calendar. A good schedule provides realistic estimates for each activity, allows time for unexpected snags, and shows that you can complete the work on time.

9. **Call to Action.** In your final section, indicate that you'd welcome any suggestions your instructor may have for improving the research plan. Ask your instructor to approve your proposal so that you can begin work on your report.

Figure 21.4 shows a student proposal for a long report using online and library research.

Site to See

Go to
http://www.youngmoney
.com/business_planning/
write-a-business-proposal/

A business plan is a special kind of proposal. Young Money offers several articles on creating business plans, as well as other resources.

Figure 21.4 Proposal for a Student Group Report Using Online and Library Research

October 28, 2012

In subject line ① indicate that this is a proposal
② specify the kind of report
③ specify the topic.

To: Steve Kaczmarek

From: Anwar Abbe, Candice Call, Heather Driscoll, Tony Yang

Subject: Proposal to Study the Feasibility of an Alternative Dispute Resolution Program
         for Shepherd Greene Industries

Spell out term the first time you use it, with the abbreviation in parentheses. Then you can use the abbreviation by itself.

Many private companies and government agencies use Alternative Dispute Resolution (ADR) programs to resolve disputes with employees. Adopting an ADR program would save time and money for Shepherd Greene. It would also help reinforce the company's application to manufacture parts for US Air Force combat aircraft.

MLA Style omits the periods in "US."

Summarize topic and purposes of report.

For our report, we plan to research the feasiblility of an ADR program at Shepherd Greene. We hope to recommend a model ADR program for the company based on an existing program with demonstrated success.

↕ *Triple-space (2 empty spaces).*

Background

↕ *Double-space (1 empty space) after heading before first paragraph.*

Founded in 1958, Shepherd Greene Industries is primarily a manufacturer of engine components for civilian aircraft. Since 1997, the company has also produced engine components and wing mount assemblies for military reconnaissance aircraft. The company is privately held.

Bold headings.

Background gives your reader information needed to understand the problem.

Problem

Shepherd Greene wants an alternative to traditional court remedies, which have had mixed results for the company in the recent past. In 1999, an employee fired for poor attendance sued, claiming a manager had illegally altered her time cards. After two years in the courts, Shepherd Greene settled for an undisclosed amount. In 2004, two employees fired for failing on-the-job drug tests unsuccessfully sued the company to get their jobs back, appealing the case all the way to the State of Ohio Supreme Court. In 2009, a coalition of employees sued the company about a management structure that allegedly keeps black employees in low-level jobs. The suit is still pending.

These lawsuits take months or even years to work through the court systems, costing the company thousands of dollars, not including any settlement or judgment cost. Although outside attorneys are also hired, preparing these cases requires hundreds of staff hours and takes the legal staff away from its primary duty of reviewing bids and contracts with Shepherd Greene's customers and suppliers.

Shepherd Greene has another reason to change the way it handles employment disputes. The company has submitted a bid to the US Air Force to manufacture replacement parts for combat aircraft. In addition to adhering to strict manufacturing guidelines and having the highest security clearance, the successful company must demonstrate stability in its labor and management practices. Programs that minimize employee grievances thus would enhance Shepherd Greene's application.

If "Problem" section is detailed and well-written, you may be able to use it unchanged in your report.

Figure 21.4 Proposal for a Student Group Report Using Online and Library Research *(continued)*

Steve Kaczmarek   2   October 28, 2012

Feasibility

Convince your instructor that you have a backup plan if your original proposal proves unworkable.

If our research supports creating an ADR program at Shepherd Greene, we will recommend one based on an existing model. If the research suggests an ADR program is inappropriate for Shepherd Greene, we will recommend the company stay with its current system for handling employee disputes. If our research is inconclusive, we will recommend Shepherd Greene revisit the topic in one year.

Topics to Investigate

Indicate what you'll discuss briefly and what you'll discuss in more detail. This list should match your audience's concerns.

In our report, we will briefly discuss Shepherd Greene's recent litigation history and the general issues in litigating employee grievances. We will focus on the following questions:

All items in list must be grammatically parallel. Here, all are questions.

- What is ADR?
- What organizations use ADR to handle employment disputes?
- How well does ADR work to resolve employment disputes?
- What model ADR programs seem worth imitating?
- What resources are required to create an ADR program?

If it is well-written, the "Topics to Investigate" section will become the "Scope" section of the report—with minor revisions.

Audiences

Identify the kinds of audience and the major concerns or priority of each.

Several audiences have a stake in the findings of our research. Our primary audience is Mr. Richard Yang, Director of Legal Services at Shepherd Greene. He is a 17-year employee with the company and has the authority to submit a plan for ADR to Shepherd Greene's top management for approval. A former trial attorney and member of both the Ohio and New York Bar Associations, Mr. Yang favors reforms to help alleviate the glut of lawsuits in our nation's courts. He is especially interested in our group's ability to apply research to the field of law, as one of the group's members is his son and plans to attend law school.

Vary paragraph lengths to provide good visual impact.

You are our initial audience. Your concern is that we produce a report that is timely, logical, thorough, and well-written. You have told us that you have taken courses in business law and journalism law, so the report topic should interest you.

Secondary audiences for this proposal will include employees in Shepherd Greene's legal and human resources departments, the company's top executives, and union representatives. Each of these audiences must support an ADR program for it to succeed.

Methods

If you're writing a report based on library research, list 10–15 sources that look relevant. Give full bibliographic citations. Here, MLA Style is used.

We will use library research and online research. The following materials on the web or in the Columbus State Community College Educational Resource Center appear to be useful:

Use hanging indents.

Alternative Dispute Resolution: A Resource Guide. US Office of Personnel Management, 2010. Web. 23 Oct. 2012.

Bedikian, Mary A. "Employment ADR: Current Issues and Methods of Implementation." *The Metropolitan Corporate Counsel,* Dec. 2009: 33. Web. 4 Oct. 2012.

Blanchard, Roger, and Joe McDade. Testimony before the US HR Committee on Government Reform Subcommittee on Civil Service, 20 Mar. 2009. Web. 3 Oct. 2012.

MLA no longer requires URLs in citation.

Figure 21.4 Proposal for a Student Group Report Using Online and Library Research *(continued)*

Steve Kaczmarek   3   October 28, 2012

Bresler, Samuel. "ADR: One Company's Answer to Settling Employee Disputes." *HRFocus*, Sept. 2009: 3–5. Print.

Carrell, Michael R., and Christina Heavrin. *Labor Relations and Collective Bargaining: Cases, Practice, and Law.* 9th ed. Upper Saddle River, NJ: Prentice Hall, 2009. Print.

If you'll administer a survey or conduct interviews, tell how many subjects you'll have, how you'll choose them, and what you'll ask them.

Cross, Frank B., and Roger LeRoy Miller. *The Legal Environment of Business: Text, Cases, Ethical, Regulatory, International, and E-Commerce Issues.* 7th ed. Cincinnati, OH: West/South-Western: 2009. Print.

Longstreth, Andrew. "The Softer Side of Sears." *Corporate Counsel Magazine* 9 (2009): 18. *Academic Search Premier Database* Item 6177553. Web. 15 Oct. 2012.

Phillips, F. Peter. "Current Trends in Employment ADR: CPR Institute for Dispute Resolution." *The Metropolitan Corporate Counsel*, Aug. 2008. Web. 8 Oct. 2012.

Senger, Jeffrey M. Testimony before the US HR Committee on the Judiciary, Subcommittee on Commercial and Administrative Law. 29 Feb. 2009, Web. 25 Oct. 2012.

Stone, Katherine V. W. "Employment Arbitration under the Federal Arbitration Act." *Employment Dispute Resolution and Worker Rights in the Changing Workplace.* Ed. Adrienne E. Eaton and Jeffrey H. Keefe. Ithaca: Cornell UP, 2009. 27–66. Print.

If possible, we will also use the library at nearby Ohio State University (OSU). The OSU system is one of the largest in the world and houses significantly more resources than does our own library. As students, we can request materials from the library through OHIOLINK; one of our group members is also a student there.

Qualifications and Resources

Cite knowledge and skills from other classes, jobs, and activities that will enable you to conduct the research and interpret your data.

Here are the strengths we bring to this project:

Bulleted list adds visual variety.

- Anwar Abbe's knowledge of the manufacturing industry will help us better understand labor and management practices in such an environment. He is a second-year student in the Legal Studies Program and already holds a Bachelor's degree in chemistry from The National Somalian University. Anwar also worked for several years for a paint manufacturer in North Carolina.

- With nearly eight years of experience as a personnel clerk for Franklin County, Candice Call's familiarity with legal issues related to human resources will help us understand the workings of current labor law. She is a second-year student in the Human Resources Technology Program, where she had taken a labor relations course whose text talked briefly about ADR.

- Heather Driscoll's expert knowledge of PowerPoint will be invaluable to creating our oral presentation for this project. A second-year student in Multimedia Technology, she is also an expert at research on the web.

- Tony Yang's internship in Shepherd Greene's management program last summer will help our group understand the company's organizational culture. A junior from OSU who is taking business communication here, Tony is majoring in pre-law/English, plans to specialize in labor law, and has already completed a business law course at

Figure 21.4 Proposal for a Student Group Report Using Online and Library Research *(continued)*

Steve Kaczmarek   4   October 28, 2012

OSU. He is also the son of Richard Yang, the director of Shepherd Greene's legal department, and will have access to the company's legal and human resources staff.

Work Schedule

The following schedule will allow us to complete our report by the due date.

Make items in list parallel.

Activity	Responsibility	Total Time	Completion Date
Gathering Information	Anwar, Heather	25 hours	November 15
Preparing the Progress Report	Tony	3 hours	November 19
Analyzing Information	All	10 hours	November 22
Organizing Information	Anwar, Heather	5 hours	November 23
Planning the Draft/Visuals	All	8 hours	November 25
Drafting the Report/Visuals	Tony, Candice	15 hours	November 30
Planning Revisions	All	8 hours	December 2
Revising the Draft/Visuals	Tony, Candice	12 hours	December 7
Editing	Heather	7 hours	December 9
Proofreading	All	3 hours	December 10

Time needed will depend on the length and topic of the report, your knowledge of the topic, and your writing skills.

Allow plenty of time! Good reports need good revision, editing, and proofreading as well as good research.

Call to Action

With Shepherd Greene's legal costs increasing and its bid to the US Air Force under consideration, we urge you to accept this proposal. Let us know if you have suggestions for improving our project. Our team stands ready to begin its research immediately with your approval.

It's tactful to indicate you'll accept suggestions. End on a positive note.

Sales Proposals

To sell expensive goods or services, you may be asked to submit a proposal.

For everything you offer, show the reader benefits (◄◄ Module 8) of each feature, using you-attitude (◄◄ Module 6). Consider using psychological description (◄◄ p. 116) to make the benefits vivid.

Use language appropriate for your audience. Even if the buyers want a state-of-the-art system, they may not want the level of detail that your staff could provide; they may not understand or appreciate technical jargon (◄◄ p. 260).

With long proposals, provide a one-page cover letter. Organize the cover letter in this way:

1. Catch the reader's attention and summarize up to three major benefits you offer.
2. Discuss each of the major benefits in the order in which you mentioned them in the first paragraph.
3. Deal with any objections or concerns the reader may have.

Instant
Replay

Proposal for a Student Report

Include the following sections:

- Problem
- Feasibility
- Audience
- Topics to Investigate
- Methods
- Qualifications
- Work Schedule
- Call to Action

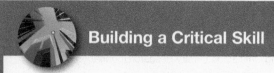

Building a Critical Skill

Identifying "Hot Buttons"   LO 21-4

In a proposal, as in any persuasive document, it's crucial that you deal with the audience's "hot buttons." **Hot buttons** are the issues to which your audience has a strong emotional response.

Study your audience's preferences and motivations. For instance, older, or nontraditional, college students may have different hot buttons than typical 18-to-22-year-old students. Nontraditional students may want remedial skills courses, child or adult day care, 24-hour computer labs, and evening and weekend classes. They may challenge more what they hear in the classroom. Social activities important to traditional students may hold little interest for nontraditional ones. While many traditional students see the workplace as a destination, chances are nontraditional students are already there and have a different work ethic. Nontraditional students also may be more likely to choose a two-year rather than a four-year campus.

Hot buttons sometimes cause people to make what seems like an "illogical" decision—unless you understand the real priorities. A phone company lost a $36 million sale to a university because it assumed that the university's priority would be cost. Instead, the university wanted a state-of-the-art system. The university accepted a higher bid.

When Ernst & Young prepared a proposal to provide professional services to a major automotive company, a team of 15 subject-matter experts spent two intense days working one-on-one with client personnel to learn what issues they cared most about. Reducing work and saving money were concerns, and Ernst & Young proposed redesigning the work to reduce costs and increase return on investment. The focus on value also enabled Ernst & Young to identify an opportunity related to but not part of the original RFP.

But even more important, spending time with the automotive company allowed Ernst & Young to see that a real "hot button" was that the competitor who held the current contract for services seemed to take the automotive company for granted. Ernst & Young exploited this hot button in two ways. First, the proposed work plan included steps to help stakeholders in the company buy into and support the project. Second, the form of the oral presentation of the proposal shouted, "We understand you." Ernst & Young invited the decision makers to come to the Ernst & Young office in Columbus, Ohio, for the presentation. Personnel wore shirts with the company logo, mirroring the uniforms worn at the automotive company. The presentation took place on an office floor that had been designed to mimic the floor plan at the automotive company.

Not only providing logical evidence but also meeting emotional needs won Ernst & Young a seven-figure contract, with the possibility of even more work.

Sources: "Older Students Transforming Some Colleges," July 15, 2005, downloaded at www.cnn.com/2005/EDUCATION/07/15/older.students. ap/; and James Lane to Kitty Locker, March 8, 1999.

Sales proposals must be relevant to discourse communities. Writer Geoffrey James points out engineers and accountants may see the return on investment differently. James maintains "the proposal must state the solution in terms that the customer understands and accepts. In order to provide value, the proposal must address the specific value system and concerns of each set of decision-makers."

Source: Geoffrey James, "How to Write a Killer Sales Proposal," *CBS News*, March 23, 2010, http://www.cbsnews.com/8301-505183_162-28549012-10391735/how-to-write-a-killer-sales-proposal/.

4. Mention other benefits briefly.
5. Ask the reader to approve your proposal and provide a reason for acting promptly.

Proposals for Funding

If you need money for a new or continuing public service project, you may want to submit a proposal for funding to a foundation, a corporation, a government agency, or a religious agency. In a proposal for funding, stress the needs your project will meet and show how your project helps fulfill the goals of the organization you are asking to fund it. Every funding source has certain priorities; most post lists of the projects they have funded in the past.

Figuring the Budget and Costs

A good budget is crucial to making the winning bid. Ask for everything you need to do a quality job. Asking for too little may backfire, leading the funder to think that you don't understand the scope of the project.

Read the RFP to find out what is and isn't fundable. Talk to the program officer and read successful past proposals to find out

- What size projects will the organization fund in theory?
- Does the funder prefer making a few big grants or many smaller grants?
- Does the funder expect you to provide in-kind or matching funds from other sources?

Think about exactly what you'll do and who will do it. What will it cost to get that person? What supplies or materials will he or she need? Also think about indirect costs for using office space, about retirement and health benefits as well as salaries, about office supplies, administration, and infrastructure.

Make the basis of your estimates specific.

Weak: 75 hours of transcribing interviews	$1,500
Better: 25 hours of interviews; a skilled transcriber	
can complete an hour of interviews in 3 hours;	
75 hours @ $20/hour	$1,500

Without inflating your costs, give yourself a cushion. For example, if the going rate for skilled transcribers is $20 an hour, but you think you might be able to train someone and pay only $12 an hour, use the higher figure. Then, even if your grant is cut, you'll still be able to do the project well.

What should go in a progress report?   LO 21-5

▶ *What you've done, why it's important, and what the next steps are.*

When you're assigned to a single project that will take a month or more, you'll probably be asked to file one or more progress reports. A progress report reassures the funding agency or employer that you're making progress and allows you and the agency or employer to resolve problems as they arise. Different readers may have different concerns. An instructor may want to know whether you'll have your report in by the due date. A client may be more interested in what you're learning about the problem. Adapt your progress report to the needs of the audience.

Progress reports can do more than just report progress. You can use progress reports to

- **Enhance your image.** Provide details about the number of documents you've read, people you've surveyed, or experiments you've conducted to create a picture of a hardworking person doing a thorough job.
- **Float trial balloons.** Explain, "I could continue to do X [what you approved]; I could do Y instead [what I'd like to do now]." The detail in the progress report can help back up your claim. Even if the idea is rejected, you don't lose face because you haven't made a separate issue of the alternative.
- **Minimize potential problems.** As you do the work, it may become clear that implementing your recommendations will be difficult. In your regular progress reports, you can alert your boss or the funding agency to the challenges that lie ahead, enabling them to prepare psychologically and physically to act on your recommendations.

Christine Barabas's study of the progress reports in a large research and development organization found that poor writers tended to focus on what they had done and said very little about the value of their work. Good writers, in contrast, spent less space writing about the details of what they'd done but much more space explaining the value of their work for the organization.[3]

Subject lines for progress reports are straightforward. Specify the project on which you are reporting your progress.

> Subject: Progress on Developing a Marketing Plan for TCBY

> Subject: Progress on Group Survey on Campus Parking

Site to See

Go to
http://schools.nyc.gov/Accountability/tools/report/default.htm

to see progress reports on New York City schools.

If you are submitting weekly or monthly progress reports on a long project, number your progress reports or include the time period in your subject line. Include dates for the work completed since the last report and to be completed before the next report.

Make your progress report as positive as you honestly can. You'll build a better image of yourself if you show that you can take minor problems in stride and that you're confident of your own abilities.

Negative: I have not deviated markedly from my schedule, and I feel that I will have very little trouble completing this report by the due date.

Positive: I am back on schedule and expect to complete my report by the due date.

Progress reports can be organized in three ways: to give a chronology, to specify tasks, or to support a recommendation.

Chronological Progress Reports

The following pattern of organization focuses on what you have done and what work remains.

1. **Summarize your progress in terms of your goals and your original schedule.** Use measurable statements.

   Poor: My progress has been slow.
   Better: The research for my report is about one-third complete.

2. **Under the heading Work Completed, describe what you have already done.** Be specific, both to support your claims in the first paragraph and to allow the reader to appreciate your hard work. Acknowledge the people who have helped you. Describe any serious obstacles you've encountered and tell how you've dealt with them.

   Poor: I have found many articles about Procter & Gamble on the web. I have had a few problems finding how the company keeps employees safe from chemical fumes.
   Better: On the web, I found Procter & Gamble's home page, its annual report, and mission statement. No one whom I interviewed could tell me about safety programs specifically at P&G. I have found seven articles about ways to protect workers against pollution in factories, but none mentions P&G.

3. **Under the heading Work to Be Completed, describe the work that remains.** If you're more than three days late (for school projects) or two weeks late (for business projects) submit a new schedule, showing how you will be able to meet the original deadline. You may want to discuss "Observations" or "Preliminary Conclusions" if you want feedback before writing the final report or if your reader has asked for substantive interim reports.

4. **Either express your confidence in having the report ready by the due date or request a conference to discuss extending the due date or limiting the project.** If you are behind your original schedule, show why you think you can still finish the project on time.

The student progress report in Figure 21.5 uses this pattern of organization.

Task Progress Reports

In a task progress report, organize information under the various tasks you have worked on during the period. For example, a task progress report for a group report project might use the following headings:

Finding Background Information on the Web and in Print
Analyzing Our Survey Data
Working on the Introduction of the Report and the Appendices

Under each heading, the group could discuss the tasks it has completed and those that remain.

Apple's annual Supplier Responsibility Report, which chronicles progress in its work with a global network of companies, showed improvements in areas like underage labor violations. At 27 pages, the 2012 report details audits for 97% of its suppliers, finding 6 active and 13 historical instances of underage labor at five facilities, down considerably over previous years. The report also notes two explosions, both in China, which killed 4 people and collectively injured 78. The reports date back to 2007 when, prompted by allegations of worker abuse, Apple began to more closely scrutinize supplier practices.

Source: Phillip Michaels, "Apple Unveils Supplier Names with 2012 Responsibility Report," *Macworld*, January 13, 2012, http://www.macworld.com/article/1164815/apple_unveils_supplier_names_with_2012_responsibility_report.html.

Site to See

Go to

www.who.int/hiv/pub/progress_report2011/en/index.html

for current and past World Health Organization progress reports on the global HIV/AIDS fight.

Figure 21.5 A Student Chronological Progress Report

April 29, 2013

To: Kitty O. Locker

From: David G. Bunnel *DGB*

Subject: Progress on CAD/CAM Software Feasibility Study for the Architecture Firm, Patrick and Associates, Inc.

¶ 1: Summarize results in terms of purpose, schedule. I have obtained most of the information necessary to recommend whether CADAM or CATIA is better for Patrick and Associates, Inc. (P&A). I am currently analyzing and organizing this information and am on schedule.

Work Completed *Underline headings or bold.*

Be very specific about what you've done. To learn how computer literate P&A employees are, I interviewed a judgment sample of five employees. My interview with Bruce Ratekin, the director of P&A's Computer-Aided Design (CAD) Department on April 15 enabled me to determine the architectural drafting needs of the firm. Mr. Ratekin also gave me a basic drawing of a building showing both two- and three-dimensional views so that I could replicate the drawing with both software packages.

Show how you've overcome minor problems. I obtained tutorials for both packages to use as a reference while making the drawings. First, I drew the building using CADAM, the package designed primarily for two-dimensional architectural drawings. I encountered problems with the isometric drawing because there was a mistake in the manual I was using; I fixed the problem by trying alternatives and finally getting help from another CADAM user. Next, I used CATIA, the package whose strength is three-dimensional drawings, to construct the drawing. I am in the process of comparing the two packages based on these criteria: quality of drawing, ease of data entry (lines, points, surfaces, etc.) for computer experts and novices, and ease of making changes in the completed drawings. Based on my experience with the packages, I have analyzed the training people with and without experience in CAD who would need to learn to use each of these packages.

Work to Be Completed

Indicate changes in purpose, scope, or recommendations. Progress report is a low-risk way to bring the readers on board. Making the drawings has shown that neither of the packages can do everything that P&A needs. Therefore, I want to investigate the feasibility of P&A's buying both packages.

Specify the work that remains. As soon as he comes back from an unexpected illness that has kept him out of the office, I will meet with Tom Merrick, the CAD systems programmer for The Ohio State University, to learn about software expansion flexibility for both packages as well as the costs for initial purchase, installation, maintenance, and software updates. After this meeting, I will be ready to begin the first draft of my report.

Whether I am able to meet my deadline will depend on when I am able to meet with Mr. Merrick. Right now, I am on schedule and plan to submit my report by the June 10th deadline.

End on a positive note.

Recommendation Progress Reports

Recommendation progress reports recommend action: increasing the funding for a project, changing its direction, canceling a project that isn't working. When the recommendation will be easy for the reader to accept, use the Direct Request pattern of organization from Module 12 (◄◄ p. 191). If the recommendation is likely to meet strong resistance, the Problem-Solving pattern (◄◄ pp. 191–193) may be more effective.

Summary of Learning Objectives

- **Information reports** collect data for the reader; **analytical reports** present and interpret data; **recommendation reports** recommend action or a solution. **(LO 21-1)**
- A good purpose statement must make three things clear: **(LO 21-2)**
  - The organizational problem or conflict.
  - The specific technical questions that must be answered to solve the problem.
  - The rhetorical purpose (to explain, to recommend, to request, to propose) the report is designed to achieve.
- A proposal must answer the following questions: **(LO 21-3)**
  - What problem are you going to solve?
  - How are you going to solve it?
  - What exactly will you provide for us?
  - Can you deliver what you promise?
  - When will you complete the work?
  - How much will you charge?
- In a proposal for a class research project, use the following headings: **(LO 21-3)**
  - Problem
  - Feasibility
  - Audience
  - Topics to Investigate
  - Methods
  - Qualifications
  - Work Schedule
  - Call to Action
- Use the following pattern of organization for the cover letter for a sales proposal. **(LO 21-3)**

1. Catch the reader's attention and summarize up to three major benefits you offer.
2. Discuss each of the major benefits in the order in which you mentioned them in the first paragraph.
3. Deal with any objections or concerns the reader may have.
4. Mention other benefits briefly.
5. Ask the reader to approve your proposal and provide a reason for acting promptly.

- In a proposal for funding, stress the needs your project will meet. Show how your project helps fulfill the goals of the organization you are asking to fund it. **(LO 21-3)**
- Hot buttons are issues to which your audience has a strong emotional response. Identify hot buttons by studying your audience's preferences and motivations. Then, use the information to help shape your appeals to the audience. What may seem illogical at first may, in fact, reveal what the audience's priorities are. **(LO 21-4)**
- To focus on what you have done and what work remains, organize a progress report in this way: **(LO 21-5)**
  1. Summarize your progress in terms of your goals and your original schedule.
  2. Under the heading "Work Completed," describe what you have already done.
  3. Under the heading "Work to Be Completed," describe the work that remains.
  4. Either express your confidence in having the report ready by the due date or request a conference to discuss extending the due date or limiting the project.
- Use positive emphasis in progress reports to create an image of yourself as a capable, confident worker. **(LO 21-5)**

Assignments for Module 21

Questions for Comprehension

21.1 What three components belong in a purpose statement? **(LO 21-2)**

21.2 What is an RFP? **(LO 21-3)**

21.3 How does the RFP relate to the organization of the proposal? **(LO 21-3)**

Questions for Critical Thinking

21.4 In the budget for a proposal, why isn't it to your advantage to try to ask for the smallest amount of money possible? **(LO 21-3)**

21.5 What should you do if you have information you want to put in a proposal that the RFP doesn't call for? **(LO 21-3)**

21.6 How can you learn your audience's hot buttons? **(LO 21-4)**

21.7 How do you decide whether to write a chronological, task, or recommendation progress report? **(LO 21-5)**

Exercises and Problems

21.8 Writing a Proposal for a Student Report (LO 21-3)

Write a proposal to your instructor to do the research for a formal or informal report. (See Problems 23.9, 23.10, 23.11, 24.8, 24.9, and 24.10.)

The headings and the questions in the section titled "Proposals for Class Research Projects" are your RFP; be sure to answer every question and to use the headings exactly as stated in the RFP. Exception: Where alternate heads are listed, you may choose one, combine the two ("Qualifications and Facilities"), or treat them as separate headings in separate categories.

21.9 Writing a Chronological Progress Report (LO 21-5)

Write a memo summarizing your progress on your report.

In the introductory paragraph, summarize your progress in terms of your schedule and your goals. Under a heading titled "Work Completed," list what you have already done. (This is a chance to toot your own horn: If you have solved problems creatively, say so! You can also describe obstacles you've encountered that you have not yet solved.) Under "Work to Be Completed," list what you still have to do. If you are more than two days behind the schedule you submitted with your proposal, include a revised schedule, listing the completion dates for the activities that remain.

In your last paragraph, either indicate your confidence in completing the report by the due date or ask for a conference to resolve the problems you are encountering.

As Your Instructor Directs,
Send the e-mail or paper progress report to

a. The other members of your group.
b. Your instructor.

21.10 Writing a Task Progress Report (LO 21-5)

Write a memo summarizing your progress on your report in terms of its tasks.

As Your Instructor Directs,

Send the e-mail or paper progress report to

a. The other members of your group.
b. Your instructor.

21.11 Writing a Chronological Progress Report for a Group Report (LO 21-5)

Write a memo to your instructor summarizing your group's progress.

In the introductory paragraph, summarize the group's progress in terms of its goals and its schedule, your own progress on the tasks for which you are responsible, and your feelings about the group's work thus far.

Under a heading titled "Work Completed," list what has already been done. Be most specific about what you yourself have done. Describe briefly the chronology of group activities: number, time, and length of meetings; topics discussed and decisions made at meetings.

If you have solved problems creatively, say so! You can also describe obstacles you've encountered that you have not yet solved. In this section, you can also comment on problems that the group has faced and whether or not they've been solved. You can comment on things that have gone well and have contributed to the smooth functioning of the group.

Under "Work to Be Completed," list what you personally and other group members still have to do. Indicate the schedule for completing the work.

In your last paragraph, either indicate your confidence in completing the report by the due date or ask for a conference to resolve the problems you are encountering.

Polishing Your **Prose**

Mixing Verb Tenses

Normally, verb tenses within a sentence, paragraph, and document should be consistent.

Incorrect: I went to the store yesterday. There, I will buy a new computer, desk, and bookcase. Afterward, I assemble everything and arrange my new home office.

Correct: I went to the store yesterday. There, I bought a new computer, desk, and bookcase. Afterward, I assembled everything and arranged my new home office.

When you have to mix tenses in a document, do so appropriately. The reader must understand the relationship between time and action throughout your document:

Incorrect: By the time you get to the meeting, I drop off the package at FedEx.

Correct: By the time you get to the meeting, I will have dropped off the package at FedEx.

The correct example uses *future perfect tense* to indicate action that has not yet occurred, but will prior to your getting to the meeting (expressed in *simple present tense*).

In general, stick to simple verb tenses in business communication. Standard edited English prefers them. Unless you must indicate specifically when one action takes place with respect to another, the simple tenses work fine.

- Use present tense in résumés and job application letters to describe current job duties; use it in persuasive documents when you want the reader to feel close to the action.
- Use past tense in résumés and job application letters to describe previous job duties; use it in correspondence and reports when action has already occurred.
- Use future tense in messages to describe action that still needs to be completed—in a progress report, any remaining activities; in a résumé or job application letter, when you will graduate from college or complete a job certification program.

Exercises

Fix the verb tense errors in the following sentences.

1. Cason takes the Graduate Record Examination at Sinclair Community College this past Wednesday.

2. Norm gains 38 years of experience working with a diverse range of clients in South and Central America.

3. Prior to working with Locke, Crane, and Bischoff, Natalie will have worked for Microsoft in Redmond, Washington.

4. If we took a plane to Louisville next Friday, we arrived on Saturday afternoon.

5. Doubtless, Jeannie will say at the meeting last week, our customers expect the best in service.

6. After I get home from the sales meeting in Sarasota, I gave you a call.

7. Riana Tilden was vice president of OCSEA in 2015, at which time Denny Chang will become president.

8. George, Deron, and Elissa were planning a surprise party for Alekanekelo on Friday. Let them know if you can attend.

9. Once I pass my last three classes at Michigan State University, I received my Masters in Public Administration.

10. As you saw from my résumé, I will have many experiences from previous jobs that make me an excellent candidate for this position.

Check your answers to the odd-numbered exercises at the back of the book.

Finding, Analyzing, and Documenting Information

Module 22 describes how to collect, analyze, and cite information effectively. After completing the module, you should be able to

LO 22-1   **Apply strategies for print and online information searches.**

LO 22-2   **Apply strategies for web page evaluation.**

LO 22-3   **Apply strategies for survey and interview question use.**

LO 22-4   **Identify respondents for surveys and interviews.**

LO 22-5   **Analyze information from research.**

LO 22-6   **Practice common citation styles for research documentation.**

Research for a report may be as simple as getting a computer printout of sales for the last month; it may involve finding online or published material or surveying or interviewing people. **Secondary research** retrieves information that someone else gathered. Library research and online searches are the best-known kinds of secondary research. **Primary research** gathers new information. Surveys, interviews, and observations are common methods for gathering new information for business reports.

Arguably, research is more important today than ever before. Organizations want reasonable assurances that new ventures will work, governments want to know the best way to use public dollars, and investors want to know that the companies they own are being managed well. Good research helps.

There are many information resources available today—so much so, the amount can be overwhelming. The web has made it possible to find information quickly and efficiently, but the problem is that some of that information is unreliable. It's critical that researchers rely on reputable sources, and that often means looking at who did the research and how, and not just how recent it is or how easy it was to find. The Building a Critical Skill box in this module can help you determine what are good sources.

Splunk is the first "Big Data" company to go public. It specializes in scouring vast amounts of data and mining it for useful information. In particular, fields like health care can benefit from Big Data mining. When Microsoft Research scientist Eric Horvitz and his colleagues analyzed 300,000 emergency room (ER) visits, for instance, they discovered that if a patient stayed in the ER past 14 hours, they were more likely to be readmitted. With 20% of patients released from American hospitals needing to be readmitted within a month, the cost to Medicare alone for inefficiency is $17 billion annually.

Source: Farhad Manjoo, "Big Changes Are Ahead for the Health Care Industry, Courtesy of Big Data," *Fast Company,* June 18, 2012, http://www. fastcompany.com/magazine/167/ big-data-companies-splunk.

How can I find information online and in print? LO 22-1

▶ *Learn how to do keyword searches.*

Keywords are the terms that the computer searches for in a database or on the web. The *ABI/Inform Thesaurus* lists synonyms and the hierarchies in which information is arranged in various databases.

At the beginning of a search, use all the synonyms and keywords you can think of. For example, the report on alternative dispute resolution (▶▶Module 24) used the following search terms:

alternative dispute resolution

ADR

mediation

arbitration

employee grievances

Skim several of the first sources you find; if they use additional or different terms, search for these new terms as well.

Use a Boolean search (Figure 22.1) to get fewer but more useful hits. For example, to study the effect of the minimum wage on employment in the restaurant industry, you might specify

(minimum wage) *and* (restaurant *or* fast food) *and*

(employment rate *or* unemployment)

Without *and,* you'd get articles that discuss the minimum wage in general, articles about every aspect of *restaurants,* and every article that refers to *unemployment,* even though many of these would not be relevant to your topic. The *or* calls up articles that use the term *fast food* but not *restaurant.* An article that used the phrase *food service industry* would be eliminated unless it also used the term *restaurant.*

Use a computer to search for print as well as online sources. Include paper as well as online sources in your research. Information in many periodicals is checked before it goes to print; papers in scholarly journals are reviewed by experts before they are accepted. Thus, print sources are often more credible than web pages, which anyone can post.

Figures 22.2, 22.3, and 22.4 list some of the many resources available.

Figure 22.1 Examples of a Boolean Search

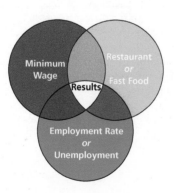

Figure 22.2 Sources for Electronic Research

These databases are available through many university libraries:

Black Studies on Disc

Business Source Premier (full text for more than 2,800 scholarly business journals in management, economics, finance, accounting, international business, and more)

ComIndex (indexes and abstracts of journals in communication)

ERIC (research on education and teaching practices in the United States and other countries)

Foreign Trade and Economic Abstracts

GPO on SilverPlatter (government publications)

Handbook of Latin American Studies

LEXIS/NEXIS Services

Newspaper Abstracts

PAIS International—Public Affairs Information Service

Social Sciences Index

Wilson Business Abstracts

Women's Resources International

Even in the digital age, keeping paper records is important. A Florida man convicted of murder nonetheless was granted a new trial because the court stenographer erased the trial transcript. Though the stenographer backed up files, a virus all but obliterated them, necessitating a new trial.

Source: Katie Kindelan, "Stenographer Error Gives Convicted Florida Murderer New Trial," *Good Morning America,* January 2, 2012, http://gma.yahoo.com/blogs/abc-blogs/stenographer-error-gives-convicted-florida-murderer-trial-192006260.html.

Figure 22.3 Sources for Web Research

Subject Matter Directories

AccountingNet
www.accountingnet.com/

Education index
www.educationindex.com

FINWeb
www.finweb.com/finweb.html

Human resource management resources on the Internet
www.hr-guide.com/

International Business Kiosk
www.calintel.org/kiosk

Management and entrepreneurship
www.lib.lsu.edu/bus/managemt.html

The WWW Virtual Library: Marketing
www.knowthis.com

News Sites

BusinessWeek Online
www.businessweek.com

CNN/CNNFN
www.cnn.com (news)
http://money.cnn.com/ (financial news)

National Public Radio
www.npr.org

NewsLink (links to U.S., Canadian, and international newspapers, magazines, and resources online)
http://newslink.org/

The New York Times
www.nytimes.com

(Continued)

According to a research report by the Joint Center for Political and Economic Studies, college-educated African Americans and Hispanic Americans making more than $50,000 annually are the fastest growing segment of Internet users. When it comes to broadband use, 94 percent of African Americans and 98 percent of Hispanic Americans with college degrees are online.

Source: Lesly Simmons, "Higher Income Minorities Fastest Growing Segment of Web Users," *Black Web 2.0,* March 1, 2010, http://www.blackweb20.com/2010/03/01/higher-income-minorities-fastest-growing-segment-of-web-users/.

Technology is revolutionizing access to data and research. One particular widget—a small computer program that enhances existing web applications—compiled data on the victims of the Haitian earthquake from among many. With thousands of people missing or dead from the quake, Google's Person Finder widget created a portal for users searching for victims.

Source: Andy Carvin, "Using Google's Haiti Missing Persons Widget," *NPR,* January 17, 2010, http://www.npr.org/blogs/inside/2010/01/using_googles_haiti_missing_pe.html.

Figure 22.3 Sources for Web Research *(continued)*

The Wall Street Journal
   http://online.wsj.com/

U.S. Government Information

EDGAR Online (SEC's online database)
   www.edgar-online.com

FEDSTATS (links to 70 U.S. government agencies)
   www.fedstats.gov

STAT-USA (fast-breaking statistics on U.S. trade and economy)
   www.stat-usa.gov

U.S. Census (including Data FERRET)
   www.census.gov

U.S. government publications (search databases online)
   www.gpoaccess.gov/index.html

U.S. Small Business Administration
   www.sbaonline.sba.gov

White House Briefing Room (economic issues)
   www.whitehouse.gov/fsbr/esbr.html

Reference Collections

Hoover's Online (information on more than 13,000 public and private companies worldwide)
   www.hoovers.com

Liszt (mailing lists)
   www.liszt.com

My Virtual Reference Desk
   www.refdesk.com

Web addresses may change. For links to the current URLs, see the BCS website.

Figure 22.4 Print Sources for Research

Indexes:

   Accountants' Index

   Business Periodicals Index

   Canadian Business Index

   Hospital Literature Index

   Personnel Management Abstracts

Facts, figures, and forecasts (also check the web):

   Almanac of Business and Industrial Financial Ratios

   Moody's Manuals

   The Statistical Abstract of the U.S.

U.S. Census reports (also available on the web):

   Census of Manufacturers

   Census of Retail Trade

International business and government:

   Canada Year Book

   Dun and Bradstreet's *Principal International Businesses*

   European Marketing Data and Statistics

   Statistical Yearbook of the United Nations

Using the Internet for Research LO 22-2

Most research projects today include the Internet. However, don't rely solely on the Internet for research. Powerful as it is, the Internet's just one tool. Your public or school library, experts in your company, journals and newspapers, and even information in your files are others.

Finding Web Pages

Use root words to find variations. A root word such as *stock* followed by the plus sign (*stock +*) will yield *stock, stocks, stockmarket,* and so forth.

Use quotation marks for exact terms. If you want only sites that use the term "business communication," put quotes around the term.

Uncapitalize words. Capitalizing words limits your search to sites where the word itself is capitalized; if the word doesn't have to be capitalized, don't.

Some search engines group related sites based on keywords. Look for these links at the top of your search engine.

If you get a broken or dead link, try shortening the URL. For example, if www.mirror.com/newinfo/index.html no longer exists, try www.mirror.com. Then check the site map to see whether it has the page you want.

Evaluating Web Pages

Anyone can post a website, and no one may check the information for accuracy or truthfulness. By contrast, many print sources, especially academic journals, have an editorial board that reviews manuscripts for accuracy and truthfulness. The review process helps ensure that information meets high standards.

For a list of websites about evaluating information, see http://www.vuw.ac.nz/staff/alastair_smith/EVALN/EVALN.HTM

Use reputable sources. Start with sites produced by universities and established companies or organizations. Be aware, however, that such organizations are not going to post information that makes them look bad. To get "the other side of the story," you may need to monitor listservs or access pages critical of the organization. (Search for "consumer opinion" and the name of the organization.)

Look for an author. Do individuals take "ownership" of the information? What are their credentials? How can you contact them with questions? Remember that ".edu" sites could be from students not yet expert on a subject.

Check the date. How recent is the information?

Check the source. Is the information adapted from other sources? If so, try to get the original.

Compare the information with other sources. Internet sources should complement print sources. If facts are correct, you'll likely find them recorded elsewhere.

How do I write questions for surveys and interviews? LO 22-2

▶ *Test your questions to make sure they're neutral and clear.*

A **survey** questions a large group of people, called **respondents** or **subjects.** The easiest way to ask many questions is to create a **questionnaire,** a written list of questions that people fill out. Figure 22.5 shows an example of a questionnaire. An **interview** is a structured conversation with someone who will be able to give you useful information. Surveys and interviews can be useful only if the questions are well designed.

Phrase questions in a way that won't bias the response. Avoid questions that make assumptions about your subjects. The question "Does your spouse have a job outside the home?" assumes that your respondent is married.

Use words that mean the same thing to you and to the respondents. Words like *often* and *important* mean different things to different people. Whenever possible, use more objective measures:

Vague: Do you use the web often?
Better: How many hours a week do you spend on the web?

Site to See

Go to

http://help.surveymonkey.com/app/answers/detail/a_id/101/~/tips-on-creating-and-administering-effective-surveys

for tips on how to do surveys.

Figure 22.5 A Student Questionnaire

In your introductory ¶,
① tell how to return the survey.
② tell how the information will be used.

Survey on Internships

Please answer the following questions and return the completed survey to the person who gave it to you. All information will be confidential and used only for a class project examining the feasibility of establishing an internship program for a particular business.

1. Major _____

2. Rank: First Year _____

   Start with easy-to-answer questions.
   Sophomore _____
   Junior _____
   Senior _____

3. How important it is to you to have one or more internships before you graduate?
   ___ Very important
   ___ Somewhat important
   ___ Not important

   Put directions in parentheses to separate them from the question itself.

   Branch questions allow readers to skip questions.

4. Did you have an internship last summer?
   ___ Yes ___ No (Skip to Question 6.)

5. What were the most beneficial aspects of your internship? (Check all that apply.)
   ___ Work related to my major
   ___ Likely to get a job offer/got a job offer
   ___ Chance to explore my interests
   ___ Made connections
   ___ Worked with clients
   ___ Looks good on my résumé
   ___ Other (Please explain.)

6. How much money did you make last summer? (Approximate hourly rate, before taxes)

   Give readers information they need to understand your question.
   _____
   ❑ Check here if you did not make any money last summer.

7. For next summer, could you afford to take an unpaid internship?
   ___ Yes ___ No

8. For next summer, could you afford to take an internship paying only the minimum wage?
   ___ Yes ___ No

9. How important is each of the following criteria in choosing whether to accept a specific internship?

   These abbreviations are OK when you survey skilled readers.

	Very impt.	Some impt.	Not impt.
a. Money	❑	❑	❑
b. Prestige of company	❑	❑	❑
c. Location near where you live now	❑	❑	❑
d. Quality of mentoring	❑	❑	❑
e. Building connections	❑	❑	❑
f. Chance of getting a job with that company	❑	❑	❑
g. Gaining experience	❑	❑	❑

   Make sure to break up the lines. Leaving an extra space makes it more likely that the respondent will check the right line.

10. How interested are you in a career in managed care?
    ___ Very interested
    ___ Somewhat interested
    ___ Not interested

11. Could you take a job in Cleveland next summer?
    ___ Definitely
    ___ Maybe
    ___ No

12. Have you heard of FFI Rx Managed Care?
    ___ Yes
    ___ No

13. I invite any other comments you would like to make regarding internships.

    Using columns gets the survey on one side, saving money in copying and eliminating the problem of people missing questions on the back. But it leaves almost no room to write in comments.

    Thank you for taking the time to answer this survey. Please return it to the person who gave it to you.

    Repeat where to turn in or mail completed surveys.

Closed questions have a limited number of possible responses. **Open questions** do not lock the subject into any sort of response. Figure 22.6 gives examples of closed and open questions. The second question in Figure 22.6 is an example of a Likert-type scale. Closed questions are faster for subjects to answer and easier for researchers to score. However, since all answers must fit into chosen categories, they cannot probe the complexities of a

Various influences may affect respondents' answers to a question.

subject. You can improve the quality of closed questions by conducting a pretest with open questions to find categories that matter to respondents.

When you use multiple-choice questions, make sure that only one answer fits in any one category. In the following example of overlapping categories, a person who worked for a company with exactly 25 employees could check either *a* or *b*. The resulting data would be unreliable.

Figure 22.6 Closed and Open Questions

Closed Questions

Are you satisfied with the city bus service? (yes/no)

How good is the city bus service?

    Excellent 5 4 3 2 1 Terrible

Indicate whether you agree or disagree with each of the following statements about city bus service:

A D   The schedule is convenient for me.

A D   The routes are convenient for me.

A D   The drivers are courteous.

A D   The buses are clean.

Rate each of the following improvements in the order of their importance to you (1 = most important, 6 = least important)

_____ Buy new buses.

_____ Increase non-rush-hour service on weekdays.

_____ Provide earlier and later service on weekdays.

_____ Increase service on weekends.

_____ Buy more buses with wheelchair access.

_____ Provide unlimited free transfers.

Open Questions

How do you feel about the city bus service?

Tell me about the city bus service.

Why do you ride the bus? (or, Why don't you ride the bus?)

What do you like and dislike about the city bus service?

How could the city bus service be improved?

Tough as it might be to fathom, the U.S. Food and Drug Administration (FDA) is finally requiring tobacco companies to reveal what actually is in cigarettes. Drug companies for years have had to reveal product formulas, but 2010 was the first year the FDA asked tobacco companies to do likewise. Among ingredients in cigarettes are cocoa and menthol for flavor, but up to 4,000 chemicals, including 60 known carcinogens, may be present. The Centers for Disease Control and Prevention estimate 443,000 deaths, or nearly 1 in 5 deaths, are attributable annually to smoking-related diseases.

Source: "What's in a Cigarette? FDA to Study Ingredients," January 18, 2010, http://www.cbsnews.com/stories/2010/01/18/ap/business/main6111057.shtml; and "Smoking and Tobacco Use Factsheet," Centers for Disease Control, downloaded on February 16, 2010, http://www.cdc.gov/tobacco/data_statistics/fact_sheets/health_effects/effects_cig_smoking/.

Research can reveal unusual or counterintuitive findings. Babies born in the fall are more likely to reach age 100 than those born at other times of the year. A study at The Ohio State University found that the more debt college students have, the higher their self-esteem. Asian Americans once led the U.S. in household wealth—with a median of $168,103 in 2005—but dropped behind European Americans a few years later because of the housing market implosion. Whites now top the list, with a median household wealth of $113,149, more than 20 times the median net worth of African Americans and 18 times that of Latino and Hispanic Americans.

Sources: Catherine de Lange, "Autumn Babies More Likely to Hit 100," *NewScientist,* July 12, 2012, http://www.newscientist.com/article/dn22054-autumn-babies-more-likely-to-hit-100.html; Liz Goodwin, "The More Debt College Students Have, the Higher Their Self Esteem," June 16, 2011, http://news.yahoo.com/s/yblog_thelookout/20110616/us_yblog_thelookout/the-more-debt-college-students-have-the-higher-their-self-esteem; and Hope Yen, "Wealth Gap Widens Between Whites, Minorities," July 26, 2011, http://news.yahoo.com/wealth-gap-widens-between-whites-minorities-040224418.html.

Overlapping categories: Indicate the number of full-time employees in your company on May 16:

_____a. 0–25

_____b. 25–100

_____c. 100–500

_____d. over 500

Discrete: categories Indicate the number of full-time employees in your company on May 16:

_____a. 0–25

_____b. 26–100

_____c. 101–500

_____d. over 500

Branching questions direct different respondents to different parts of the questionnaire based on their answers to earlier questions.

10. Have you talked to an academic adviser this year?
yes _____ no _____
(if "no," skip to question 14.)

Use closed multiple-choice questions for potentially embarrassing topics. Seeing their own situation listed as one response can help respondents feel that it is acceptable. However, very sensitive issues are perhaps better asked in an interview, where the interviewer can build trust and reveal information about himself or herself to encourage the interviewee to answer.

Generally, put early in the questionnaire questions that will be easy to answer. Put questions that are harder to answer or that people may be less willing to answer (e.g., age and income) near the end of the questionnaire. Even if people choose not to answer such questions, you'll still have the rest of the survey filled out.

If subjects will fill out the questionnaire themselves, pay careful attention to the physical design of the document. Use indentations and white space effectively; make it easy to mark and score the answers. Include a brief statement of purpose if you (or someone else) will not be available to explain the questionnaire or answer questions. Pretest the questionnaire to make sure the directions are clear. One researcher mailed out a two-page questionnaire without pretesting it. Twenty-five respondents didn't answer the questions on the back of the first page.[1]

How do I decide whom to survey or interview? LO 22-4

▶ *Use a random sample for surveys, if funds permit.*

▶ *Use a judgment sample for interviews.*

The **population** is the group you want to make statements about. Depending on the purpose of your research, your population might be all *Fortune* 1000 companies, all business students at your college, or all consumers.

Defining your population correctly is crucial to getting useful information. For example, Microscan wanted its sales force to interview "customer defectors." At first, salespeople assumed that a "defector" was a former customer who no longer bought anything at all. By that definition, very few defectors existed. But then the term was redefined as customers who had stopped buying *some* products and services. By this definition, quite a few defectors existed. And the fact that each of them had turned to a competitor for some of what they used to buy from Microscan showed that improvements—and improved profits— were possible.[2]

Because it is not feasible to survey everyone, you select a sample. If you take a true random sample, you can generalize your findings to the whole population from which your sample comes. In a **random sample,** each person in the population theoretically has an equal chance of being chosen. When people say they did something *randomly* they often mean *without conscious bias.* However, unconscious bias exists. Someone passing out surveys in front of the library will be more likely to approach people who seem friendly and less likely to ask people who seem intimidating, in a hurry, much older or younger, or of a different race, class, or sex. True random samples rely on random digit tables, generated by computers and published in statistics texts and books such as *A Million Random Digits.*

A **convenience sample** is a group of respondents who are easy to get: students who walk through the student center, people at a shopping mall, workers in your own unit. Convenience samples are useful for a rough pretest of a questionnaire. However, you cannot generalize from a convenience sample to a larger group.

A **judgment sample** is a group of people whose views seem useful. Someone interested in surveying the kinds of writing done on campus might ask each department for the name of a faculty member who cared about writing, and then send surveys to those people. Judgment samples are often good for interviews, where your purpose is to talk to someone whose views are worth hearing.

The response rate—the percentage of people who respond—can differ according to the kind of survey used. According to figures researchers have reported to the Marketing Research Association, telephone surveys averaged 18% (31% when researchers worked from a list), door-to-door surveys averaged 53%, face-to-face surveys in malls and other

Since going public in 2012, Facebook has received greater scrutiny than ever before. One revelation is that as much as 8.7% of the site's billion users may be fakes or duplicates, determined by the company after an internal audit reported to the Security and Exchange Commission. A company called Limited Run stopped advertising on Facebook after it claimed that as many as 80% of the clicks it received on Facebook ads came from bots, or web robots, rather than people.

Source: Tim Sprinkle, "The 7 Ugly Truths About Facebook," August 3, 2012, http://finance.yahoo.com/blogs/the-exchange/7-ugly-truths-facebook-180418410.html.

This shopper works for the marketing firm Team Look-Look, which uses the opinions of in-the-know teens to track trends about what's hot now, or what will be hot in the future.

locations averaged 38%, and web surveys averaged 34%. Good researchers follow up, contacting nonrespondents at least once and preferably twice to try to persuade them to participate in the survey.[3]

Estimates of how much digital data is consumed annually are as high as 9.57 zettabytes, or a stack of books 5.6 billion miles high and stretching from Earth to Neptune more than 20 times. The determination was made by University of California at San Diego scientists, who crunched numbers from the world's 27 million business computer servers. However, since the estimates use 2008 totals, the most recent year they were available, the number could be significantly higher. Such staggering sums may mean little to the average person. When reporter Brian X. Chen asked passersby in Brooklyn to define a megabyte, people spoke in terms of practicality. Said Miranda Popkey, "It's a measure of how much information you store. If there are too many of them, I can't send my e-mail attachment." For the record, a megabyte is 1,000 kilobytes, or about one minute of a downloaded song.

Sources: Catharine Smith, "This Is How Much Information the World Consumes Each Year," April 7, 2011, http://www.huffingtonpost.com/2011/04/06/world-information-consumption_n_845806.html; and Brian X. Chen, "A Ballooning Megabyte Budget," *The New York Times*, April 8, 2012, http://www.nytimes.com/2012/04/09/technology/how-to-budget-megabytes-becomes-more-urgent-for-users.html?pagewanted=all.

How should I analyze the information I've collected? LO 22-5

▶ *Look for answers to your research questions, patterns, and interesting nuggets.*

As you analyze your data, look for answers to your research questions and for interesting nuggets that may not have been part of your original questions but emerge from the data. Such stories can be more convincing in reports and oral presentations than pages of computer printouts.

Understanding the Source of the Data

If your report is based upon secondary data from library and online research, look at the sample, the sample size, and the exact wording of questions to see what the data actually measure. For instance, many polls in the 2004 presidential race showed Americans were closely divided in their choice of a candidate—so close that the difference often was within the margin of error. Thus, pollsters could not confidently say whether President George W. Bush or Senator John Kerry was in the lead. Because the few points of difference between candidates could have been mere chance, pollsters then had to find sample sizes large enough to make poll results meaningful.

Identify the assumptions used in analyzing the data. When Nielsen Media Research estimates the number of people who view television stations, it must make assumptions: how well its People Meter actually tracks whether people are watching and how best to count groups that are hard to measure.

Nielsen recently reported that 18- to 34-year-old males are watching less television, in part because they spend more time with videogames and DVDs. However, television networks complained that the company was underreporting this group's viewing. For example, they said, Nielsen was not counting young people who leave for college, and its sample did not include homes with TiVo or other personal video recorders. Thus, the networks, Nielsen, and advertisers disagree about whether young men are losing interest in television programming.[4]

Evaluating online sources, especially web pages, can be difficult, since anyone can post pages on the web or contribute comments to chat groups. Check the identity of the writer: Is he or she considered an expert? Can you find at least one source printed in a respectable newspaper or journal that agrees with the web page? If a comment appeared in chat groups, did others in the group support the claim? Does the chat group include people who could be expected to be unbiased and knowledgeable? Especially when the issue is controversial, seek out opposing views.

Analyzing Numbers

Many reports analyze numbers—either numbers from databases and sources or numbers from a survey you have conducted.

If you've conducted a survey, your first step is to transfer the responses on the survey form into numbers. For some categories, you'll assign numbers arbitrarily. For example, you might record men as "1" and women as "2"—or vice versa. Such assignments don't matter, as long as you're consistent throughout your project. In these cases, you can report the number and percentage of men and women who responded to your survey, but you can't do anything else with the numbers.

When you have numbers for salaries or other figures, start by figuring the average, or mean, the median, and the range. The **average** or **mean** is calculated by adding up all the figures and dividing by the number of samples. The **median** is the number that is exactly in the middle. When you have an odd number of observations, the median will be the middle number. When you have an even number, the median will be the average of the two numbers in the center. The **range** is the high and low figures for that variable.

Finding the average takes a few more steps when you have different kinds of data. For example, it's common to ask respondents whether they find a feature "very important," "somewhat important," or "not important." You might code "very important" as "3," "somewhat important" as "2," and "not important" as "1." To find the average in this kind of data,

1. For each response, multiply the code by the number of people who gave that response.
2. Add up the figures.
3. Divide by the total number of people responding to the question.

For example, suppose you have surveyed 50 people about the features they want in a proposed apartment complex.

The average gives an easy way to compare various features. If the party house averages 2.3 while extra parking for guests is 2.5, you know that your respondents would find extra parking more important than a party house. You can now arrange the factors in order of importance:

Table 4. "How Important Is Each Factor to You in Choosing an Apartment?"
n = 50; 3 = "Very Important"

Extra parking for guests	2.5
Party house	2.3
Pool	2.2
Convenient to bus line	2.0

Often it's useful to simplify numerical data: round it off and combine similar elements. Then you can see that one number is about 2½ times another. Charting it can also help you see patterns in your data. Look at the raw data as well as at percentages. For example, a 50% increase in shoplifting incidents sounds alarming—but an increase from two to three shoplifting incidents sounds well within normal variation.

Analyzing Words

If your data include words, try to find out what the words mean to the people who said them. Respondents to Whirlpool's survey of 180,000 households said that they wanted "clean refrigerators." After asking more questions, Whirlpool found that what people really wanted were refrigerators that *looked* clean, so the company developed models with textured fronts and sides to hide finger-prints.[5] Also try to measure words against numbers. When he researched possible investments, Peter Lynch found that people in mature industries were pessimistic, seeing clouds. People in immature industries saw pie in the sky, even when the numbers weren't great.[6]

Look for patterns. If you have library sources, on which points do experts agree? Which disagreements can be explained by early theories or numbers that have now changed? By different interpretations of the same data? Having different values and criteria? In your interviews and surveys, what patterns do you see?

- Have things changed over time?
- Does geography account for differences?
- What similarities do you see?

With $1.44 being the average savings per coupon and assuming it takes a minute to clip it, shoppers are saving at the rate of $86.40 per hour, tax-free. Saving $25 a week will net $1,200 a year, or more than $100,000 over a typical lifetime.

Source: Brett Arends, "Doing the Math on Coupons," February 11, 2010, http://customsites.yahoo.com/financiallyfit/finance/article-108816-4123-3-how-to-save-100-in-an-hour?ywaad=ad0035.

Instant Replay

Three Kinds of Samples

In a **random sample,** each person in the population has an equal chance of being chosen. A **convenience sample** is a group of respondents who are easy to get. A **judgment sample** is a group of people whose views seem useful.

With the world watching, Greek triple jumper Paraskevi Papachristou tweeted a racist joke that got her expelled from the 2012 Summer Games. A week later, Swiss soccer player Michel Morganella tweeted racist and threatening messages against South Koreans and was likewise sent packing. Both later apologized, but Papachristou was initially defiant. Measure the impact of words carefully, especially those hurled at other people and at their expense.

(continued)

(continued)
Sources: Alon Harish, "Greek Jumper Expelled from Olympic Team for Racist Tweet," *ABC News,* July 25, 2012, http://abcnews.go.com/International/greek-olympic-jumper-expelled-racist-tweet-defenders-flock/story?id=16856393#.UB_JO01IR55; and "Swiss Olympic Team Expels Player for Racist Tweet," July 31, 2012, http://sports.espn.go.com/espn/wire?section=oly&id=8214115.

American businesses spent $125.9 billion on employee training in 2009 alone, but little research exists on what the return on investment is for much of the training. For "tangible" workshops, where specific skills are taught in areas like sales and product knowledge, measuring results is easier than in "intangible" workshops, where broader skills are taught in areas like leadership and team effectiveness. More than 90% of Fortune 500 CEOs surveyed said they are most interested in learning the business impact of employee training, but less than 10% saw that currently happening in their company.

Source: Gary M. Stern, "Company Training Programs: What Are They Really Worth?" *Fortune,* May 27, 2011, http://management.fortune.cnn.com/2011/05/27/company-training-programs-what-are-they-really-worth/.

Instant Replay

Analyzing Numbers

The **average** or **mean** is calculated by adding up all the figures and dividing by the number of samples. The **median** is the number that is exactly in the middle. The **range** is the high and low figures for that variable.

- What differences do you see?
- What confirms your hunches?
- What surprises you?

Checking Your Logic

Don't confuse causation with correlation. **Causation** means that one thing causes or produces another. **Correlation** means that two things happen at the same time. One might cause the other, but both might be caused by a third.

For example, suppose that you're considering whether to buy cell phones for everyone in your company, and suppose that your surveys show that the people who currently have cell phones are, in general, more productive than people who don't use cell phones. Does having a cell phone lead to higher productivity? Perhaps. But perhaps productive people are more likely to push to get cell phones from company funds, while less productive people are more passive. Perhaps productive people earn more and are more likely to be able to buy their own cell phones if the organization doesn't provide them.

Consciously search for at least three possible causes for each phenomenon you've observed and at least three possible solutions for each problem. The more possibilities you brainstorm, the more likely you are to find good options. In your report, mention all of the possibilities; discuss in detail only those that will occur to readers and that you think are the real reasons and the best solutions.

When you have identified patterns that seem to represent the causes of the problem or the best solutions, check these ideas against reality. Can you find support in the quotes or in the numbers? Can you answer counterclaims? If you can, you will be able to present evidence for your argument in a convincing way.

If you can't prove the claim you originally hoped to make, modify your conclusions to fit your data. Even when your market test is a failure, you can still write a useful report.

- Identify changes that might yield a different result (e.g., selling the product at a lower price might enable the company to sell enough units).
- Discuss circumstances that may have affected the results.
- Summarize your negative findings in progress reports to let readers down gradually and to give them a chance to modify the research design.
- Remember that negative results aren't always disappointing to the audience. For example, the people who commissioned a feasibility report may be relieved to have an impartial outsider confirm their suspicions that a project isn't feasible.[7]

How should I document sources? LO 22-6

▶ *Use MLA or APA format.*

The two most widely used formats for endnotes and bibliographies in reports are those of the Modern Language Association (MLA) and the American Psychological Association (APA). Figure 22.7 shows the MLA and APA formats for books, government documents, journal and newspaper articles, online sources, and interviews. In 2009, MLA Style changed to include such terms as "Print," "Web," or "E-mail" in documentation, and it no longer requires URLs to be included.

In a good report, sources are cited and documented smoothly and unobtrusively. **Citation** means attributing an idea or fact to its source **in the body of the report:** for example, "According to the 2000 Census . . ." or "Jane Bryant Quinn argues that. . . ." Citing sources demonstrates your honesty, enhances your credibility, and protects you from charges of plagiarism. **Documentation** means providing the bibliographic information readers would need to go back to the original source. Note that citation and documentation are used in addition to quotation marks. If you use the source's exact words, you'll use

Figure 22.7 MLA and APA Formats for Documenting Sources

MLA Style

MLA internal citation gives the author's last name and page number in parentheses in the text for facts as well as for quotations (Gilsdorf and Leonard 470). If the author's name is used in the sentence, only the page number is given in parentheses. A list of WORKS CITED gives the full bibliographic documentation, arranging the entries alphabetically by the first author's last name.

Comma — *First name first for second author* — *Put quotation marks around title of article.*

Article in a Periodical

Capitalize all major words in titles of articles, books, journals, magazines, and newspapers.

Gilsdorf, Jeanette, and Don Leonard. "Big Stuff, Little Stuff: A Decennial Measurement of Executives' and Academics' Reactions to Questionable Usage Elements." *The Journal of Business Communication* 38 (2001): 448-75. Print.

Italicize title of journal, magazine, or newspaper. — *Volume number* — *Omit "4" in "475."*

McCartney, Scott. "Why a Baseball Superstar's Megacontract Can Be Less than It Seems." *The Wall Street Journal*, 27 Dec. 2000: B1+. Print.

Use a "plus" when pages are discontinuous.

Article from an Edited Book

Give authors', editors' names as printed in the source.

Killingsworth, M. Jimmie, and Martin Jacobsen. "The Rhetorical Construction of Environmental Risk Narratives in Government and Activist Websites: A Critique." *Narrative and Professional Communication*. Eds. Jane M. Perkins and Nancy Blyler. Stamford, CT: Ablex. 1999. 167-77. Print. *Spell out editors' names. Join with "and."*

Give state when city is not well known.

Article from a Publication on the Web

Greengard, Samuel. "Scoring Web Wins." *Business Finance Magazine*. May 2001. Web. 12 July 2010.

Book

Cross, Geoffrey A. *Forming the Collective Mind: A Contextual Exploration of Large-Scale Collaborative Writing in Industry*. Creskill, NJ: Hampton Press, 2001. Print.

Put in square brackets information known to you but not printed in source.

Book or Pamphlet with a Corporate Author

Citibank. *Indonesia: An Investment Guide*. [Jakarta:] Citibank, 1994. Print.

Date after city and publisher

E-mail message

Kaczmarek, Stephen Kyo. "Planned Revisions for Module 12." Message to Marith Adams. 17 Dec. 2009. E-mail.

day month year — *Abbreviate long months.*

Government Document

United States. Sen. Special Committee on Aging. *Long-Term Care: States Grapple with Increasing Demands and Costs*. 107th Cong., 1st sess. Washington, DC: GPO, 2001. Print.

Omit state when city is well known. — *Abbreviate "Government Printing Office."*

Government Document Available on the Web from the GPO Access Database

United States. General Accounting Office. *Aviation Security: Terrorist Acts Demonstrate Urgent Need to Improve Security at the Nation's Airports*. Testimony before the Committee on Commerce, Science, and Transportation, U.S. Senate (GAO-01-1162T). 20 Sept. 2001. Web. 20 Dec. 2011.

Figure 22.7 MLA and APA Formats for Documenting Sources *(Continued)*

Interview Conducted by the Researcher
> Drysdale, Andrew. Telephone interview. 12 Apr. 2009.

Posting to a Listserv
> Dietrich, Dan. "Re: Course on Report and Proposal Writing." BizCom Discussion Group,
> 31 Aug. 2002. Web. 23. Dec. 2011.

Date of posting   *Date you*
accessed posting

Website
> American Express Company. *Creating an Effective Business Plan*. American Express
> Company, 2001. Web. 20 Dec. 2010.

As of 2009, MLA Style no longer requires URLs in documentation.
However, indicate the basic type of publication.

APA Style

APA internal citation gives the author's last name and the date of the work in parentheses in the text. A comma separates the author's name from the date (Gilsdorf & Leonard, 2001). The page number is given only for direct quotations (Cross, 2001, p. 74). If the author's name is used in the sentence, only the date is given in parentheses. A list of REFERENCES gives the full bibliographic documentation, arranging the entries alphabetically by the first author's last name.

comma   *last name first*   *No quotes around*

Article in a Periodical   *Year (period outside parenthesis).*   *title of article*

In titles of articles and books capitalize only (1) first word, (2) first word of subtitle, (3) proper nouns.

> Gilsdorf, J., & Leonard, D. (2001). Big stuff, little stuff: A decennial measurement of
> executives' and academics' reactions to questionable usage elements. *The Journal of
> Business Communication, 38*, 439-475.

no "pp." when journal   *Capitalize all major words in title of*
Italicize volume.   *has a volume number*   *journal, magazine, or newspaper.*

> McCartney, S. (2000, December 27). Why a baseball superstar's megacontract can be less
> than it seems. *The Wall Street Journal*, p. B1, B3.

Separate discontinuous pages with comma and space.

Article in an Edited Book   *Ampersands join names of co-authors, co-editors.*   *Editors'*
names
have last
names
last.

> Killingsworth, M. J., & Jacobsen, M. (1999). The rhetorical construction of environmental
> risk narratives in government and activist websites: A critique. In J. M. Perkins & N.
> Blyler (Eds.), *Narrative and professional communication* (pp. 167-177). Stamford, CT:

Editors   Ablex.
before book title   *Repeat "1" in 177.*   *Give state when*
city is not well known.

Article from a Publication on the Web
> Greengard, S. (2001, May). Scoring web wins. *Business Finance Magazine*. p. 37.
> Retrieved July 12, 2010, from http://www.businessfinancemag.com/archives/appfiles/
> Article.cfm? IssueID=348&ArticleID=13750   *no punctuation after URL*

Initials only

Book   *Italicize title of book.*

> Cross, G. A. (2001). *Forming the collective mind: A contextual exploration of large-scale
> collaborative writing in industry*. Creskill, NJ: Hampton Press.

Put in square brackets information known to you
but not printed in document.

Book or Pamphlet with a Corporate Author
> Citibank. (1994). *Indonesia: An investment guide*. [Jakarta:] Author.

Indicates that the organization authoring
document also published it

Figure 22.7 MLA and APA Formats for Documenting Sources *(Continued)*

E-Mail Message
[Identify e-mail messages in the text as personal communications. Give name of author and as specific a date as possible. Do not list in References.]

Government Document
Senate Special Committee on Aging. (2001). *Long-term care: States grapple with increasing demands and costs.* Hearing before the Special Committee on Aging, Senate, One Hundred Seventh Congress, first session, hearing held in Washington, DC, July 11, 2001 (Doc ID: 75-038). Washington, DC: U.S. Government Printing Office.

No abbreviations · *Document number* · *APA uses periods for "U.S."*

Government Document Available on the Web from the GPO Access Database
U.S. General Accounting Office. (2001, September 20.) Aviation security: Terrorist acts demonstrate urgent need to improve security at the nation's airports. Testimony before the Committee on Commerce, Science, and Transportation, U.S. Senate (GAO-01-1162T). Retrieved December 20, 2011, from General Accounting Office ReportsOnline via GPO Access: http://www.gao.gov/new.items/d011162t.pdf

Copyright or update date · *Date you visited site* · *Keep "http://"*

Interview Conducted by the Researcher
[Identify interviews in the test as personal communications. Give name of interviewee and as specific a date as possible. Do not list in References.]

Posting to a Listserv
[Identify messages on listservs to which one must subscribe in the text as personal communications. Give name of author and as specific a date as possible. Do not list in References.]

Website
American Express. (2001). Creating an effective business plan. Retrieved August 31, 2010, from the World Wide Web: http://home3.americanexpress.com/smallbusiness/tool/biz_plan/index.asp

Comma · *No punctuation* · *Break long Web address at a slash or other punctuation mark.*

---

the name of the person you're citing and quotation marks in the body of the report; you'll indicate the source in parentheses and a list of References or Works Cited. If you put the source's idea into your own words, or if you condense or synthesize information, you don't need quotation marks, but you still need to tell whose idea it is and where you found it.

Indent long quotations on the left and right to set them off from your text. Indented quotations do not need quotation marks; the indentation shows the reader that the passage is a quote. Because many readers skip quotes, always summarize the main point of the quotation in a single sentence before the quotation. End the sentence with a colon, not a period, because it introduces the quote.

Interrupt a quotation to analyze, clarify, or question it.

Use square brackets around words you add or change to clarify the quote or make it fit the grammar of your sentence. Omit any words in the original source that are not essential for your purposes. Use ellipses (spaced dots) to indicate omissions.

Site to See

Go to
http://owl.english.purdue.edu/owl/

for advice on how to use APA and MLA citation styles.

Summary of Learning Objectives

- **Keywords** are the terms that the computer searches for in a database or on the web. At the beginning of a search, use all of the synonyms and keywords you can think of. Skim several of the first sources you find; if they use additional or different terms, search for these other terms as well. **(LO 22-1)**
- To decide whether to use a website as a source in a research project, evaluate the site's authors, objectivity, information, and revision date. **(LO 22-2)**
- A **survey** questions a large group of people, called **respondents or subjects.** A **questionnaire** is a written list of questions that people fill out. **An interview** is a structured conversation with someone who will be able to give you useful information. **(LO 22-3)**
- **Closed questions** have a limited number of possible responses. **Open questions** do not lock the subject into any sort of response. **Branching questions** direct different respondents to

- different parts of the questionnaire based on their answers to earlier questions. **(LO 22-3)**
- In a **random sample,** each person in the population theoretically has an equal chance of being chosen. Only in a random sample is the researcher justified in inferring that the results from the sample are also true of the population from which the sample comes. A **convenience sample** is a group of subjects who are easy to get. A **judgment sample** is a group of people whose views seem useful. **(LO 22-4)**
- **Causation** means that one thing causes or produces another. **Correlation** means that two things happen at the same time. One might cause the other, but both might be caused by a third. **(LO 22-5)**
- **Citation** means attributing an idea or fact to its source in the body of the report. Documentation means providing the bibliographic information readers would need to go back to the original source. **(LO 22-6)**

Assignments for Module 22

Questions for Comprehension

22.1 What is the difference between open and closed questions? **(LO 22-3)**

22.2 What is the difference between the mean and the median? **(LO 22-5)**

22.3 What is the difference between correlation and causation? **(LO 22-5)**

Questions for Critical Thinking

22.4 How do you decide whether a website is an acceptable source for a report? **(LO 22-2)**

22.5 Why do you need to know the exact way a question was phrased before using results from the study as evidence? **(LO 22-3)**

22.6 Why should you test a questionnaire with a small group of people before you distribute it? **(LO 22-3)**

22.7 Why should you look for alternate explanations for your findings? **(LO 22-5)**

Exercises and Problems

22.8 Evaluating websites (LO 22-2)

Evaluate seven websites related to the topic of your report. For each, consider

- Author(s)
- Objectivity
- Information
- Revision date

22.9 Evaluating Survey Questions (LO 22-3)

Evaluate each of the following questions. Are they acceptable as they stand? If not, how can they be improved?

a. Questionnaire on grocery purchases.
1. Do you *usually* shop at the same grocery store?
   a. Yes
   b. No

Based on these criteria, which sites are best for your report? Which are unacceptable? Why?

As Your Instructor Directs,
a. Share your results with a small group of students.
b. Present your results in a memo to your instructor.
c. Present your results to the class in an oral presentation.

2. How much is your average grocery bill?
   a. Under $25
   b. $25–50
   c. $50–100
   d. $100–150
   e. Over $150

b. Survey on technology
   1. Would you generally welcome any technological advancement that allowed information to be sent and received more quickly and in greater quantities than ever before?
   2. Do you think that all people should have free access to all information, or do you think that information should somehow be regulated and monitored?

c. Survey on job skills

How important are the following skills for getting and keeping a professional-level job in U.S. business and industry today?

	Low				High
Ability to communicate	1	2	3	4	5
Leadership ability	1	2	3	4	5
Public presentation skills	1	2	3	4	5
Selling ability	1	2	3	4	5
Teamwork capability	1	2	3	4	5
Writing ability	1	2	3	4	5

22.10 Designing Questions for an Interview or Survey (LO 22-3)

Submit either a one- to three-page questionnaire or questions for a 20- to 30-minute interview AND the information listed below for the method you choose.

Questionnaire
1. Purpose(s), goal(s)
2. Subjects (who, why, how many)
3. How and where to be distributed
4. Rationale for order of questions, kinds of questions, wording of questions

Interview
1. Purpose(s), goal(s)
2. Subject (who and why)
3. Proposed site, length of interview
4. Rationale for order of questions, kinds of questions, wording of questions, choice of branching or follow-up questions

As Your Instructor Directs,

a. Create questions for a survey on one of the following topics:
   • Survey students on your campus about their knowledge of and interest in the programs and activities sponsored by a student organization.
   • Survey workers at a company about what they like and dislike about their jobs.
   • Survey people in your community about their willingness to pay more to buy products using recycled materials and to buy products that are packaged with a minimum of waste.
   • Survey students and faculty on your campus about whether adequate parking exists.
   • Survey two groups on a topic that interests you.

b. Create questions for an interview on one of the following topics:
   • Interview an international student about the form of greetings and farewells, topics of small talk, forms of politeness, festivals and holidays, meals at home, size of families, and roles of family members in his or her county.
   • Interview the owner of a small business about the problems the business has, what strategies the owner has already used to increase sales and profits and how successful these strategies were, and the owner's attitudes toward possible changes in product line, decor, marketing, hiring, advertising, and money management.
   • Interview someone who has information you need for a report you're writing.

Polishing Your Prose

Using MLA Style

Using MLA requires two steps: gathering all the information you need and then applying it correctly. MLA documentation uses

• The full names of all authors; the full names of editors of an edited book.
• The title and subtitle (if any).
• The title of the edited book or journal, for articles within books and journals.
• For books: city of publication (with state if not well known), publisher, and year of publication.

• For articles in popular periodicals: the date of publication, in as much detail as the periodical gives, and the page on which the article starts.
• For articles in scholarly periodicals: the volume and year and beginning and ending page numbers.
• The specific page(s) on which you find the fact(s) you cite or the sections you quote.

Using MLA Style requires that you look closely at the order of words and at punctuation marks. For example, when you use a short quote (39 words or fewer), the period of your sentence goes outside the parentheses with the page number. In a long indented quote (40 words or more), the parentheses with the page number follows the period at the end of the sentence.

In 2009, MLA Style changed to include such terms as "Print," "Web," or "E-mail" in documentation, and it no longer requires URLs to be included. For more details on how to use MLA Style, see Figure 22.7 or http://owl.english.purdue.edu/owl/.

Exercises

Identify and correct the errors in MLA format in the following Works Cited items.

1. Jonathan B. Wight, interview by Stephen K. Kaczmarek, 04 July 2004.
2. "Report Cards on Governance," by Lauren Young, in BusinessWeek. 6/13/05. Pages 86–87.
3. O'Rourke, P. J. "The CEO of the Sofa." Copyright 2001. Published by Atlantic Monthly Press in New York City, USA.
4. Ameeta Patel and Lamar Reinsch, Companies Can Apologize: Corporate Apologies and Legal Liability, *Business Communication Quarterly*, March 2003, Volume Number 66, Issue Number 1. P. 9–25.
5. EPA. "An Office Building Occupant's Guide to Indoor Air Quality." August 1, 2009. www.epa.gov/iaq/pubs/occupgd.html.
6. July 25, 2012. E-mail message from me.
7. Kaczmarek, Stephen K. and Locker, Kitty O., "Business Communication: Building Critical Skills." 5th Edition. McGraw-Hill/Irwin. Boston. 2011.
8. Thea Singer; Can Business Still Save the World?; "Inc." April 2001. Pp. 58–71.
9. U. of Nebraska. (2004). Husker Fever Card. Retrieved June 20, 2012 from the Internet: http://www.huskerfevercard.com.
10. A Business Call with Adams, Marith, on December 17, 2011.

Check your answers to the odd-numbered exercises at the back of the book.

Short Reports

Module 23 can help you to write the best short reports. After completing the module, you should be able to

LO 23-1 Select patterns for short business report organization.

LO 23-2 Apply strategies for short business report organization.

LO 23-3 Apply principles for good business report style.

LO 23-4 Apply strategies for specific and polite question use.

Whenever you have a choice, write a short report rather than a long one. Never put information in reports just because you have it or just because it took you a long time to find it. Instead, choose the information that your reader needs to make a decision. Should you need to write a longer report, however, the types of reports described here could still be used and expanded. Module 24 provides the key principles for writing a long report.

One report writer was asked to examine a building that had problems with heating, cooling, and air circulation. The client who owned the building wanted quick answers to three questions: What should we do? What will it cost? When will it pay for itself? The client wanted a three-page report with a seven-page appendix showing the payback figures.[1] When Susan Kleimann studied reply forms for a hotel, its managers said they didn't want to read a report. So Kleimann limited the "report" to an executive summary with conclusions and recommendations. Everything else went into appendixes.[2]

Short reports normally use letter or memo format.

Do different kinds of reports use different patterns of organization? LO 23-1

▶ *Yes. Work with the readers' expectations.*

Informative, feasibility, and justification reports will be more successful when you work with the readers' expectations for that kind of report.

Informative and Closure Reports

An **informative** or **closure report** summarizes completed work or research that does not result in action or recommendation.

Informative reports often include the following elements:

- **Introductory paragraph** summarizing the problems or successes of the project.
- **Chronological account** of how the problem was discovered, what was done, and what the results were.
- **Concluding paragraph** with suggestions for later action. In a recommendation report, the recommendations would be based on proof. In contrast, the suggestions in a closure or recommendation report are not proved in detail.

Figure 23.1 presents this kind of informative report.

Feasibility Reports

Feasibility reports evaluate several alternatives and recommend one of them. (Doing nothing or delaying action can be one of the alternatives.)

Feasibility reports normally open by explaining the decision to be made, listing the alternatives, and explaining the criteria. In the body of the report, each alternative will be evaluated according to the criteria. Discussing each alternative separately is better when one alternative is clearly superior, when the criteria interact, and when each alternative is indivisible. If the choice depends on the weight given to each criterion, you may want to discuss each alternative under each criterion.

Whether your recommendation should come at the beginning or the end of the report depends on your reader. Most readers want the "bottom line" up front. However, if the reader will find your recommendation hard to accept, you may want to delay your recommendation till the end of the report when you have given all your evidence.

Justification Reports

Justification reports recommend or justify a purchase, investment, hiring, or change in policy. If your organization has a standard format for justification reports, follow that format. If you can choose your headings and organization, use this pattern when your recommendation will be easy for your reader to accept:

1. **Indicate what you're asking for and why it's needed.** Because the reader has not asked for the report, you must link your request to the organization's goals.
2. **Briefly give the background of the problem or need.**
3. **Explain each of the possible solutions.** For each, give the cost and the advantages and disadvantages.
4. **Summarize the action needed to implement your recommendation.** If several people will be involved, indicate who will do what and how long each step will take.
5. **Ask for the action you want.**

Site to See

Go to

http://www.nwcdc.coop/Resources/OBCFeasibilityReport.pdf

for a copy of the Northwest Co-Operative Development Center's Feasibility Report on biodiesel fuel production and distribution.

General Motors (GM) decided to stop advertising with Facebook after it could no longer justify the cost. According to GM, the third-biggest U.S. advertiser across all media, paid ads on Facebook seemed to have had little impact on car purchases. Kia Motors Corporation also questioned the effectiveness of Facebook ads, but like Subaru, it plans to keep advertising with the company.

Source: Sharon Terlep, Suzanne Vranica, and Shayndi Raice, "GM Says Facebook Ads Don't Pay Off," *The Wall Street Journal*, May 16, 2012, http://online.wsj.com/article/SB10001424052702304192704577406394017764460.html.

Figure 23.1 An Informative Memo Report Describing How Local Government Solved a Problem

 JEFFERSON COUNTY COMMISSIONERS

Use your organization's culture to decide whether to list titles.

April 20, 2013

Informal short reports use letter or memo format.

To: Doug Perrin, Human Resources Director

From: Tamalyn Sykes, Staff Training and Development Manager TS

Subject: Workplace Violence Awareness Training at the Commissioners' Office

First paragraph summarizes main points.

Three months ago, the Commissioners' Office began to offer workplace violence awareness training to all 1,200 Jefferson County employees under its direct authority. The program was held to reduce employee concerns about the possibility of a hostage situation similar to the one in October at the State Workers' Compensation building next to the county courthouse.

Purpose and scope of report.

In this report, I will explain the need for the program, as well as its structure and cost.

Triple-space before heading.   *Capitalize first letter of major words in heading.*

Need for Workplace Violence Awareness Training   *Talking heads tell reader what to expect in each section.*

On October 11, 2010, county employees were shocked to learn of a hostage situation at the State Workers' Compensation building. A 41-year-old man, frustrated that his final benefits appeal had been rejected and facing home foreclosure, walked into a 15th-floor office with a handgun and took five people hostage. He demanded to see the account manager who had denied his original claim.

Double-space between paragraphs within heading.

Reason training is needed.

When the account manager stepped out of her office, she was shot twice by the man, who then turned the gun on himself. Both died. Later, questions abounded: How could the man have entered the building with a handgun? What could have been done to prevent violence? What emergency procedures were in place to protect staff? Why did building security fail to respond soon enough to prevent violence?

Specific impact on organization.

In the weeks that followed, many county employees expressed concern to supervisors that they felt vulnerable—after all, if it happened next door, it could happen here. Calls to the county's Employee Assistance Program for counseling tripled. Supervisors also noted drops in employee attendance; one supervisor reported that half of her staff called off work the week after the shooting.

Figure 23.1 An Informative Memo Report Describing How Local Government Solved a Problem *(continued)*

Short subject (or reader's name)   *Page number*   *Date*

Workplace Violence Awareness Training   2   April 20, 2013

Bold headings.

Structure and Cost of Training

Double-space between paragraphs.

At the November 20 General Session, the Commissioners approved a proposal to initiate workplace violence awareness training to address employee concerns. I then wrote and published the requisite RFP for services, and three training organizations responded with bids. New Horizons Training Services submitted the lowest and best bid.

The Commissioners hired New Horizons to provide 11 training sessions for 100–150 persons each. Sessions were held in the courthouse auditorium twice weekly starting January 7. While managers were allowed to schedule employees for sessions at their discretion, training was mandatory for all 1,200 employees. Employees on vacation or sick leave were required to attend a special "make-up" training session held at New Horizons' headquarters in March.

Indented lists provide visual variety.

The two-and-a-half-hour training sessions consisted of three parts:
- A one-hour video on general issues related to workplace violence.
- A one-hour panel discussion led by New Horizons' staff and featuring members of the county's security department and crisis management team (videotaped for the make-up session.)
- A half-hour question-and-answer session that included a written evaluation of the program.

At the end, the county's "Action Plan" booklet for dealing with workplace violence was distributed. The plan includes emergency telephone numbers, evacuation procedures, an overview of public safety measures at the courthouse, and directions on what to do in a hostage situation.

Be sure to double-check numbers.

The total cost for the sessions was $11,500: $1,000 for each session at the courthouse and $500 for the make-up session held at New Horizons' headquarters.

Employee feedback about the program was overwhelmingly positive.

Alissa Kozuh analyzes the words customers type in on the search feature at www.nordstrom.com. She's found five patterns; customers key in particular items ("shoes"), trends ("leopard prints"), departments from the bricks-and-mortar stores ("Brass Plum," the juniors department), designer names, and special occasions ("prom"). The changes she suggested for the site based on her research increased web sales 32%.

If the reader will be reluctant to grant your request, use this variation of the problem-solving pattern described in Module 12:

1. **Describe the organizational problem (which your request will solve).** Use specific examples to prove the seriousness of the problem.
2. **Show why easier or less expensive solutions will not solve the problem.**
3. **Present your solution impersonally.**
4. **Show that the disadvantages of your solution are outweighed by the advantages.**
5. **Summarize the action needed to implement your recommendation.** If several people will be involved, indicate who will do what and how long each step will take.
6. **Ask for the action you want.**

How much detail you need to give in a justification report depends on your reader's knowledge of and attitude toward your recommendation and on the corporate culture. Many organizations expect justification reports to be short—only one or two pages. Other organizations may expect longer reports with much more detailed budgets and a full discussion of the problem and each possible solution.

Site to See

Go to

www.siemens.com/ sustainability/en/ sustainability/reporting/ current_reporting.htm

for a copy of Siemens' 2011 Sustainability Report.

What are the basic strategies for organizing information? LO 23-2

▶ *Try one of these seven patterns.*

Seven basic patterns for organizing information are useful in reports:

1. Comparison/contrast.
2. Problem-solution.
3. Elimination of alternatives.
4. General to particular or particular to general.

5. Geographic or spatial.
6. Functional.
7. Chronological.

Any of these patterns can be used for a whole report or for only part of it.

1. Comparison/Contrast

Comparison/contrast takes up each alternative in turn, discussing strengths and weaknesses. Feasibility studies usually use this pattern.

A variation of the divided pattern is the **pro and con pattern.** In this pattern, under each specific heading, give the arguments for and against that alternative.

Whatever information comes second will carry more psychological weight. This pattern is least effective when you want to deemphasize the disadvantages of a proposed solution, for it does not permit you to bury the disadvantages between neutral or positive material.

A report recommending new plantings for a university quadrangle uses the pro and con pattern:

> Advantages of Monocropping
>   High Productivity
>   Visual Symmetry
> Disadvantages of Monocropping
>   Danger of Pest Exploitation
>   Visual Monotony

2. Problem-Solution

Identify the problem; explain its background or history; discuss its extent and seriousness; identify its causes. Discuss the factors (criteria) that affect the decision. Analyze the advantages and disadvantages of possible solutions. Conclusions and recommendations can go either first or last, depending on the preferences of your reader. This pattern works well when the reader is neutral.

A report recommending ways to eliminate solidification of a granular bleach during production uses the problem-solution pattern:

> Recommended Reformulation for Vibe Bleach
> Problems in Maintaining Vibe's Granular Structure
>   Solidifying during Storage and Transportation
>   Customer Complaints about "Blocks" of Vibe in Boxes
> Why Vibe Bleach "Cakes"
>   Vibe's Formula
>   The Manufacturing Process
>   The Chemical Process of Solidification
> Modifications Needed to Keep Vibe Flowing Freely

3. Elimination of Alternatives

After discussing the problem and its causes, discuss the *impractical* solutions first, showing why they will not work. End with the most practical solution.

This pattern works well when the solutions the reader is likely to favor will not work, while the solution you recommend is likely to be perceived as expensive, intrusive, or radical.

A report on toy commercials eliminates alternatives:

> The Effect of TV Ads on Children
> Camera Techniques Used in TV Advertisements
> Alternative Solutions to Problems in TV Toy Ads
> > Leave Ads Unchanged
> > Mandate School Units on Advertising
> > Ask the Industry to Regulate Itself
> > Give FCC Authority to Regulate TV Ads Directed at Children

4. General to Particular or Particular to General

General to particular starts with the problem as it affects the organization or as it manifests itself in general and then moves to a discussion of the parts of the problem and solutions to each of these parts. Particular to general starts with the problem as the audience defines it and moves to larger issues of which the problem is a part. Both are good patterns when you need to redefine the reader's perception of the problem in order to solve it effectively.

The directors of a student volunteer organization, VIP, have defined their problem as "not enough volunteers." After studying the subject, the writer is convinced that problems in training, the way work is structured, and campus awareness are responsible both for a high drop-out rate and a low recruitment rate. The general to particular pattern helps the audience see the problem in a new way:

> Why VIP Needs More Volunteers
> Why Some VIP Volunteers Drop Out
> > Inadequate Training
> > Feeling that VIP Requires too Much Time
> > Feeling that the Work Is too Emotionally Demanding
> Why Some Students Do Not Volunteer
> > Feeling that VIP Requires too Much Time
> > Feeling that the Work Is too Emotionally Demanding
> > Preference for Volunteering with Another Organization
> > Lack of Knowledge about VIP Opportunities
> How VIP Volunteers Are Currently Trained
> Time Demands on VIP Volunteers
> Emotional Demands on VIP Volunteers
> Ways to Increase Volunteer Commitment and Motivation
> > Improving Training
> > Improving the Flexibility of Volunteers' Hours
> > Providing Emotional Support to Volunteers
> > Providing More Information about Community Needs and VIP Services

5. Geographic or Spatial

In a geographic or spatial pattern, you discuss problems and solutions by units by their physical arrangement. Move from office to office, building to building, factory to factory, state to state, region to region, and so on.

Is earning a college degree a good alternative to just going straight into the workforce? According to a 2012 Georgetown University report, despite some majors being more employable than others, "extensive research, ours included, finds that a college degree is still worth it." *Hard Times, Not All College Degrees are Created Equal* states the unemployment rate for people without a college degree is more than double that of people with a degree.

Source: Lisa Manterfield, "College Degrees That Hiring Managers Love," downloaded on August 9, 2012, at http://education.yahoo. net/articles/degrees_with_job_ potential.htm?kid=1MNC6.

In any form, good reports always provide enough details for audiences to make sound decisions.

"Sure, we can spend all day nitpicking specifics but aren't
sweeping generalities so much more satisfying?"

Reprinted with permission of CartoonStock.com, www.cartoonstock.com.

With 60% of employers looking
at credit reports for some
or all job candidates, states
are beginning to pass laws
against the practice. California
is among 7 states now
banning companies from
doing credit checks in some
capacity, and 19 other states
have legislation pending. Still,
some research suggests a
correlation between bad credit
and on-the-job problems, with
one study suggesting nearly
a third of employees with
self-reported credit problems
stole, accepted bribes, or did
other "counterproductive work
behavior.

Source: Annamaria Andriotis,
"Hire Hopes for Job Seekers with .
Dodgy Credit," *The Wall Street
Journal: Smart Money,* February
3, 2012, http://www.smartmoney.
com/plan/careers/hire-hopes-
for-job-seekers-with-dodgy-
credit-1328036148030/.

A sales report uses a geographic pattern of organization:

Sales Have Risen in the European Economic Community
Sales Have Fallen Slightly in Asia
Sales Are Steady in North America

6. Functional

In functional patterns, discuss the problems and solutions of each functional unit. For example, a report on a new plant might divide data into sections on the costs of land and building, on the availability of personnel, on the convenience of raw materials, and so forth. A government report might divide data into the different functions an office performed, taking each in turn.

A strategy report for a political party uses a functional pattern of organization:

Current Makeup of the Senate
   Senate Seats Open in 2010
      Seats Held by a Democratic Incumbent
         Races in Which the Incumbent Has a Commanding Lead
         Races in Which the Incumbent Is Vulnerable
      Seats Held by a Republican Incumbent
         Races in Which the Incumbent Has a Commanding Lead
         Races in Which the Incumbent Is Vulnerable
Seats Where No Incumbent Is Running

7. Chronological

A chronological report records events in the order in which they happened or are planned to happen.

Many progress reports are organized chronologically:

Work Completed in October
Work Planned for November

Should I use the same style for reports as for other business documents? LO 23-3

▶ *Yes, with three exceptions*

The advice about style in Modules 15 and 16 also applies to reports, with three exceptions:

1. **Use a fairly formal style, without contractions or slang.**
2. **Avoid the word** *you.* In a document to multiple audiences, it will not be clear who *you* is. Instead, use the company name.
3. **Include in the report all the definitions and documents needed to understand the recommendations.** The multiple audiences for reports include readers who may consult the document months or years from now. Explain acronyms and abbreviations the first time they appear. Explain the history or background of the problem. Add as appendixes previous documents on which you build.

The following points apply to any kind of writing, but they are particularly important in reports.

1. Say what you mean.
2. Tighten your writing.
3. Use blueprints, transitions, topic sentences, and headings to make your organization clear to your reader.

Let's look at each of these principles as they apply to reports.

1. Say What You Mean

Not-quite-right word choices are particularly damaging in reports, which may be skimmed by readers who know very little about the subject. Putting the meaning of your sentence in the verbs will help you say what you mean.

Vague: My report revolves around the checkout lines and the methods used to get price checks when they arise.

Better: My report shows how price checks slow checkout lines and recommends ways to reduce the number of price checks needed.

Sometimes you'll need to completely recast the sentence.

Incorrect: The first problem with the incentive program is that middle managers do not use good interpersonal skills in implementing it. For example, the hotel chef openly ridicules the program. As a result, the kitchen staff fear being mocked if they participate in the program.

Better: The first problem with the incentive program is that some middle managers undercut it. For example, the hotel chef openly ridicules the program. As a result, the kitchen staff fear being mocked if they participate in the program.

Seven Ways to Organize Information

1. Comparison/contrast
2. Problem-solution
3. Elimination of alternatives
4. General to particular or particular to general
5. Geographic or spatial
6. Functional
7. Chronological

"Finely Textured Lean Beef," more commonly known as "pink slime," got the attention of consumers recently when it was revealed that the filler was in 70% of the ground beef sold at supermarkets. Once used only for dog food and cooking oils, pink slime comes from the most contaminated parts of the cow but is simmered and treated with ammonia gas to kill germs. Regardless of which term is more meaningful to people, if they've eaten a hamburger in the past few years, chances are they've sampled the filler.

Source: "Is Pink Slime in the Beef at Your Grocery Store?" *ABC News,* March 8, 2012, http://abcnews.go.com/blogs/headlines/2012/03/is-pink-slime-in-the-beef-at-your-grocery-store/.

Asking Specific and Polite Questions   LO 23-4

Learning to ask the *right* question *the right way* is a critical skill in business. Good business communicators use specificity and politeness.

Specificity

Vague questions often result in vague or rambling answers. Therefore, make sure you ask the right question for the kind of answer you want. To get a short answer,

- Give simple choices:

When you work extra hours, would you prefer overtime pay or comp time (the same number of hours off)?

- Ask the real question.

Not: When do you want to meet?
But: Which day is best for you to meet?

- Ask for a quantifiable or measurable response, such as facts, dates, statistics, and so forth.

What percentage of our customers are repeat business?

When you want longer, more qualitative answers, make your question specific enough for your audience to understand what you're asking:

- Start with one of the five Ws or H: who, what, where, when, why, or how.
- Add concrete language that invites a qualified response:

What reservations do you have about my proposal?

Why do you want to work for this firm?

Politeness

Politeness is a matter of timing, tone, language, and culture (◄◄ Module 3). Remember that when and how you ask the question are almost as important as the question itself. To increase your chances of not offending anyone,

- **Use timing.** Don't assault people with questions the moment they arrive or get up to leave. If someone is upset, give him or her time to calm down. Avoid questions when it's obvious someone doesn't want to answer them.
- **Keep questions to a minimum.** Review all the resources at your disposal first to see if the answers are there.
- **Avoid embarrassing or provocative questions.** Even if *you* are comfortable discussing such issues, don't assume other people are.
- **Avoid language that implies doubt, criticism, or suspicion.**

Rude: You don't really think you can handle this project, do you?
Polite: How do you feel about managing this project?

- **Use you-attitude and empathy.** Try to look at situations from the other person's point of view, particularly if a conflict is involved.

Because culture affects the rules of politeness—and culture changes—keep abreast of what is and isn't acceptable in society. Remember that different cultures have different concepts of politeness.

Instant Replay

2. Tighten Your Writing

Eliminate unnecessary words, use gerunds and infinitives, combine sentences, and reword sentences to cut the number of words.

Wordy: Campus Jewelers' main objective is to increase sales. Specifically, the objective is to double sales in the next five years by becoming a more successful business.
Better: Campus Jewelers' objective is to double sales in the next five years.

3. Use Blueprints, Transitions, Topic Sentences, and Headings

Blueprints are overviews or forecasts that tell the reader what you will discuss in a section or in the entire report. Make your blueprint easy to read by telling the reader how many points there are and numbering them. In the following example, the first sentence in the revised paragraph tells the reader to look for four points; the numbers separate the four points clearly. This overview paragraph also makes a contract with readers, who now expect to read about tax benefits first and employee benefits last.

Paragraph without numbers: Employee Stock Ownership Programs (ESOPs) have several advantages. They provide tax benefits for the company. ESOPs also create tax benefits for employees and for lenders. They provide a defense against takeovers. In some organizations, productivity increases because workers now have a financial stake in the company's profits. ESOPs are an attractive employee benefit and help the company hire and retain good employees.

Revised paragraph with numbers: Employee Stock Ownership Programs (ESOPs) provide four benefits. First, ESOPs provide tax benefits for the company, its employees, and lenders to the plan. Second, ESOPs help create a defense against takeovers. Third, ESOPs may increase productivity by giving workers a financial stake in the company's profits. Fourth, as an attractive employee benefit, ESOPs help the company hire and retain good employees.

Transitions are words, phrases, or sentences that tell the reader whether the discussion is continuing on the same point or shifting points.

There are economic advantages, too.
(Tells the reader that we are still discussing advantages but that we have now moved to economic advantages.)

An alternative to this plan is . . .
(Tells reader that a second option follows.)

These advantages, however, are found only in A, not in B or C.
(Prepares reader for a shift from A to B and C.)

A **topic sentence** introduces or summarizes the main idea of a paragraph. Readers who skim reports can follow your ideas more easily if each paragraph begins with a topic sentence.

Hard to read (no topic sentence): Another main use of ice is to keep the fish fresh. Each of the seven kinds of fish served at the restaurant requires one gallon twice a day, for a total of 14 gallons. An additional 6 gallons a day are required for the salad bar.

Better (begins with topic sentence): Twenty gallons of ice a day are needed to keep food fresh. Of this, the biggest portion (14 gallons) is used to keep the fish fresh. Each of the seven kinds of fish served at the restaurant requires one gallon twice a day ($7 \times 2 = 14$). An additional 6 gallons a day are required for the salad bar.

Headings are single words, short phrases, or complete sentences that indicate the topic in each section. A heading must cover all of the material under it until the next heading. For example, *Cost of Tuition* cannot include the cost of books or of room and board. You can have just one paragraph under a heading or several pages. If you do have several pages between headings, you may want to consider using subheadings. Use subheadings only when you have two or more divisions within a main heading.

Topic headings focus on the structure of the report. As you can see from the following example, topic headings give very little information.

Recommendation
Problem
   Situation 1
   Situation 2
Causes of the Problem
   Background
   Cause 1
   Cause 2
Recommended Solution

Disorganization in writing often causes problems for readers, but disorganization in general can cause problems in business. A survey of 18,000 executives by Express Employment Professionals found that more than half said they lose nine hours a week on the job due to a lack of organization. Disorganized employees who earn $50,000 annually can cost companies $11,000 a year in lost hours.

Source: Janis Petrini, "Business Leaders Lose Hours to Disorganization," July 7, 2012, http://www.corpmagazine.com/management/human-resources/itemid/5887/business-leaders-lose-hours-to-disorganization.

Talking heads, in contrast, tell the reader what to expect. Talking or informative heads, like those in the examples in this chapter, provide an overview of each section and of the entire report:

> Recommended Reformulation for Vibe Bleach
> Problems in Maintaining Vibe's Granular Structure
>   Solidifying during Storage and Transportation
>   Customer Complaints about "Blocks" of Vibe in Boxes
> Why Vibe Bleach "Cakes"
>   Vibe's Formula
>   The Manufacturing Process
>   The Chemical Process of Solidification
> Modifications Needed to Keep Vibe Flowing Freely

Headings must be **parallel** (◄◄ p. 74), that is, they must use the same grammatical structure. Subheads must be parallel to each other but do not necessarily have to be parallel to subheads under other headings.

Summary of Learning Objectives

- For **informative** or **closure reports,** include: **(LO 23-1)**
  - An introductory paragraph summarizing problems or successes.
  - A chronological account of how the problem was discovered, what was done, and what the results were.
  - A concluding paragraph with suggestions for action.
- For **feasibility reports,** include: **(LO 23-1)**
- An opening with explanations of the decision to be made, alternatives, and criteria.
  - A body discussing each alternative.
  - A conclusion with a recommendation. The recommendation could also come at the beginning if that's where the reader wants it.
- For **justification reports,** include: **(LO 23-1)**
  - An indication of what you're asking for and why.
  - A brief discussion on the background of the problem.
  - An explanation for each possible solution.
  - A summary of the action needed to implement your recommendation.
  - A call for action.
- For reluctant readers, use a variation of the problem-solving pattern described in Module 12 for justification reports. **(LO 23-1)**
- **Comparison/contrast** takes up each alternative in turn. The **pro and con pattern** divides the alternatives and discusses the arguments for and against that alternative. A **problem-solving report** identifies the problem, explains its causes, and analyzes the advantages and disadvantages of possible solutions. **Elimination** identifies the problem, explains its causes, and discusses the least practical solutions first, ending with the one the writer favors. **General to particular** begins with the problem as it affects the organization or as it manifests itself in general, then moves to a discussion of the parts of the problem and solutions to each of these parts. **Particular to general** starts with specific aspects of the problem, then moves to a discussion of the larger implications of the problem for the organization. **Geographic or spatial** patterns discuss the problems and solutions by units. **Functional** patterns discuss the problems and solutions of each functional unit. **(LO 23-2)**
- Reports use the same style as other business documents, with three exceptions: **(LO 23-3)**
  1. Reports use a more formal style than do many letters and memos.
  2. Reports rarely use the word *you.*
  3. Reports should be self-explanatory.
- To create good report style, **(LO 23-3)**
  1. Say what you mean.
  2. Tighten your writing.
  3. Use blueprints, transitions, topic sentences, and headings.
- **Headings** are single words, short phrases, or complete sentences that cover all of the material under a heading until the next heading. **Informative** or **talking heads** tell the reader what to expect in each section. **(LO 23-3)**
- Learning to ask the right question the right way is a critical skill in business. Avoid vague questions. Give simple choices if you want a short answer and specific information if you want a longer answer. Be polite. Time your message for the appropriate moment, keep questions to a minimum, avoid embarrassing questions, and avoid language that implies doubt or criticism. Use you-attitude and empathy. **(LO 23-4)**

Questions for Comprehension

23.1 What are the seven basic patterns for organizing information? **(LO 23-1)**

23.2 What is a blueprint? **(LO 23-4)**

23.3 What is a talking head? **(LO 23-4)**

Questions for Critical Thinking

23.4 Why shouldn't you put all the information you have into a report? **(LO 23-1, LO 23-2)**

23.5 Why do reports often use a more formal style than other business documents? **(LO 23-4)**

23.6 Why should you avoid *you* in reports? **(LO 23-4)**

23.7 Why are topic sentences especially useful in reports? **(LO 23-4)**

Exercises and Problems

23.8 Explaining "Best Practices" (LO 23-1 to LO 23-4)

Write a report explaining the "best practices" of the unit where you work that could also be adopted by other units in your organization.

23.9 Recommending Action (LO 23-1 to LO 23-4)

Write a report recommending an action that your unit or organization should take. Address your report to the person who would have the power to approve your recommendation. Possibilities include

• Hiring an additional worker for your department.

• Making your organization more family friendly.
• Making a change that will make the organization more efficient.
• Making changes to improve accessibility for customers or employees with disabilities.

23.10 Writing Up a Survey (LO 23-1 to LO 23-4)

Survey two groups of people on a topic that interests you. Possible groups are men and women, people in business and in English programs, younger and older students, students and townspeople. Nonrandom samples are acceptable.

As Your Instructor Directs,

a. Survey 40 to 50 people.
b. Team up with your classmates. Survey 50 to 80 people if your group has two members, 75 to 120 people if it has three members, 100 to 150 people if it has four members, and 125 to 200 people if it has five members.
c. Keep a journal during your group meetings and submit it to your instructor.
d. Write a memo to your instructor describing and evaluating your group's process for designing, conducting, and writing up the survey. (◄◄ See Module 18 on working and writing in groups.)

As you conduct your survey, make careful notes about what you do so you can use this information when you write up your survey. If you work with a group, record who does what.

Use complete memo format. Your subject line should be clear and reasonably complete. Omit unnecessary words such as "Survey of." Your first paragraph serves as an introduction, but it needs no heading. The rest of the body of your memo will be divided into four sections with the following headings: Purpose, Procedure, Results, and Discussion.

In your first paragraph, briefly summarize (not necessarily in this order) who conducted the experiment or survey, when it was conducted, where it was conducted, who the subjects were, what your purpose was, and what you found out.

In your **Purpose** section, explain why you conducted the survey. What were you trying to learn? Why did this subject seem interesting or important?

In your **Procedure** section, describe in detail *exactly* what you did.

In your **Results** section, first tell whether your results supported your hypothesis. Use both visuals and words to explain what your numbers show. (►► See Module 25 on how to design visuals.) Process your raw data in a way that will be useful to your reader.

In your **Discussion** section, evaluate your survey and discuss the implications of your results. Consider these questions:

1. Do you think a scientifically valid survey would have produced the same results? Why or why not?
2. Were there any sources of bias either in the way the questions were phrased or in the way the subjects were chosen? If you were running the survey again, what changes would you make to eliminate or reduce these sources of bias?
3. Do you think your subjects answered honestly and completely? What factors may have intruded? Is the fact that

you did or didn't know them, were or weren't of the same sex relevant?

4. What causes the phenomenon your results reveal? If several causes together account for the phenomenon, or if it is impossible to be sure of the cause, admit this. Identify possible causes and assess the likelihood of each.

5. What action should be taken?

The discussion section gives you the opportunity to analyze the significance of your survey. Its insight and originality lift the otherwise well-written memo from the ranks of the merely satisfactory to the ranks of the above-average and the excellent.

23.11 Writing a Report Based on Your Knowledge and Experience (LO 23-1 to LO 23-4)

Write a report on one of the following topics.

1. What should a U.S. or Canadian manager know about dealing with workers from _____ [you fill in the country or culture]? What factors do and do not motivate people in this group? How do they show respect and deference? Are they used to a strong hierarchy or to an egalitarian setting? Do they normally do one thing at once or many things? How important is clock time and being on time? What factors lead them to respect someone? Age? Experience? Education? Technical knowledge? Wealth? Or what? What conflicts or miscommunications may arise between workers from this culture and other workers due to cultural differences? Are people from this culture pretty similar in these beliefs and behaviors, or are there lots of variation?

2. Describe an ethical dilemma encountered by workers in a specific organization. What is the background of the situation? What competing loyalties exist? In the past, how have workers responded? How has the organization responded? Have "whistle-blowers" been rewarded or punished? What could the organization do to foster ethical behavior?

3. Describe a problem or challenge encountered by an organization where you've worked. Show why it needed to be solved, tell who did what to try to solve it, and tell how successful the efforts were. Possibilities include

- How the organization is implementing work teams, downsizing, or a change in organizational culture.
- How the organization uses e-mail or voice mail, statistical process control, or telecommuting.
- How managers deal with stress, make ethical choices, or evaluate subordinates.
- How the organization is responding to changing U.S. demographics, the Americans with Disabilities Act, international competition and opportunities, or challenges from dot.com companies.

 Polishing Your **Prose**

Being Concise

Being **concise** in business writing means using only necessary words to make your point, without sacrificing politeness or clarity. Wordy sentences may confuse or slow readers:

Wordy: All of our employees at Haddenfield and Dunne should make themselves available for a seminar meeting on the 5th of August, 2010, at 10 o'clock in the morning. Please make sure you come to the conference room on the 2nd Floor of the Main Complex.

Concise: Please plan to attend a seminar at 10 AM on August 5 in the Main Complex 2nd Floor conference room.

Being concise does not mean eliminating necessary information. Sometimes you'll have to write longer sentences to be clear.

Nor does tightening your writing mean using short, choppy sentences.

Choppy: We have a new copier. It is in the supply room. Use it during regular hours. After 5 PM, it will be shut down.

Concise: A new copier is available in the supply room for use before 5 PM.

Use Concrete Words.

Instead of vague nouns and verbs with strings of modifiers, use specifics.

Vague: The person who drops off packages talked about the subject of how much to charge.

Concrete: The delivery person discussed fees.

Avoid Vague or Empty Modifiers.

Words like *very, some, many, few, much, kind of/sort of,* and *so forth* usually can be cut.

Cut Redundant Words or Phrases.

Don't say the same thing twice. *Cease* and *desist, first* and *foremost,* the *newest* and *latest, official company* policy, 24 *stories tall, said out loud,* and *return* the form *back* to me are all redundant.

Avoid Unnecessarily Complex Constructions.

Instead of *the bid that won the contract,* use *the winning bid.*

Stick to Simple Verb Tenses.

Standard edited English prefers them. Instead of "I *have been attending* the University of Michigan" use "I *attend* the University of Michigan." Instead of "By 2006, I *will have completed* my junior year" use "I *will be* a senior by 2006."

Exercises

Rewrite the following sentences to make them concise.

1. It is very much in the best interest of our business, Sam Chen said out loud, to make our company's buildings at least three stories tall.
2. Please find attached the required and necessary paperwork forms to be completed by yourself at the earliest of your convenience.
3. Take this release to Andrea, please. Ask her to sign it. Bring it back to me. Get it back by 5 p.m.
4. There are a very many people who are kind of aware of the possibility that we may well decide to enter the Asian market.
5. Heather Ansel said out loud that she is planning to come to the event on March the 19th where our celebration for the year will be enjoyed at a formal dinner.
6. First and foremost it is of the utmost importance that we return the proofed copy to the people who are doing the graphic design as quickly as is humanly possible.
7. At about 11:34 a.m., Margaret Kim e-mailed to inform those of us working as a team on the project that we had been awarded a contractual obligation with Tanner, Dempsey, and Mihalek.
8. We should cease and desist at once all official company correspondence with the company that supplies our wholesale goods and services until we determine if it has complied with our official company policies and so forth.
9. I have been attending classes in the field of business at the community college which is local and close to the building at where I am currently employed and my office therein.
10. Derek stopped by at about 1:22 p.m. He wanted to discuss something. He was concerned about our merger with Addison, Plymouth and Partners. He thought we should do the due diligence again. Derek started some of the work. He is a very responsible executive.

Check your answers to the odd-numbered exercises at the back of the book.

Index

A

Abad-Santos, Alexander, 332
Abbreviations
    Latin-based, 264
    Postal Service, 135
ABI/Inform Thesaurus, 360
Abino, I., 529
Abrashoff, D. Michael, 293
Abusive supervisors, 300
accede/exceed, 261
accept/except, 261
access/excess, 262
Accurate words, 256
Active listening, 291, 292. *See also*
    Listening
Active verbs, 274–275
Active voice, 86–87
Addo, Theophilus, 533
Ademola, Esther, 331
adept/adopt, 262
Adjectives, use of, 448
Adjustments, 151–152
Adult literacy, 6
Adverbs, use of, 448
Advertisements, offensive, 52
Advertising Council, 189
advice/advise, 262
affect/effect, 262
Affleck, John, 531
affluent/effluent, 262
Agenda
    elements of, 314–316
    standard, 316–317, 319
Agreement
    noun–pronoun, 235, 240
    subject–verb, 141–142, 239–240
Akil, Bakari, 335
Albers, Susan, 146
Albrecht, Sheri A., 533
Alcorn, Chauncey, 224
Allen, Nancy, 532
Allstate, 313
a lot/allot, 262
Alter, Alexandra, 62
Amabile, Teresa, 105
American Psychological Association
    (APA), 370
America's Job Bank, 440
amount/number, 262
Analytical reports, 343

Andersen, Charlotte, 258
Andersen Consulting, 28
Anderson, Gary, 421
Anderson, Paul V., 532
Anderson, Petra, 165
Anderson, Richard C., 531
Andriotis, Annamaria, 384
Anecdotes, 330–331
Angel, David, 326
Annual reports, 343
Ansberry, Clare, 529
Anxiety, public speaking, 334–335
APA style, 370, 372–373
Apollo 13, 298
Apologies, 107–108
Apostrophes, 100, 111, 122, 245–247
Apple Computer, 11
Appropriate words, 256
Arbeláez, Brenda, 529
Arends, Brett, 369
are/our, 262
Argyle, Michael, 529
Ariely, Dan, 118
Arndt, Michael, 529
Arnold, Carroll C., 532, 533
Arnst, Cathy, 136
Asante, Molefi, 532
Aschauer, Mary Ann, 528
Ashby, Lynn, 531
Asher, J. William, 533
Askling, Lawrence R., 532
Assumptions, 290
assure/ensure/insure, 262
Atkinson, Dianne, 532
Attention, listening and, 289
Attire, job interview, 493
attributed/contributed, 262
Audience. *See also* Reader benefits
    adapting message to, 327–328
    benefits to, 12, 22, 114–115, 119
    communication channels to reach, 31–32
    communication process and, 23–24
    external, 7
    gatekeepers and, 21
    identification of, 20–21
    information needs to analyze, 24–28
    initial, 21
    internal, 7
    needs of, 20, 30
    need to understand, 19

for oral presentations, 326–328
PAIBOC questions and, 22–23
primary, 20
secondary, 20–21
strategies to reach, 29–30
talking to your, 62–63
vested interest of, 193
watchdog, 21
you-attitude and, 91–94
Audit reports, 343
Autocorrect, 80
Average, 369, 370

B

Baby Boomers, 46, 48, 49, 51, 53
Background section, for reports, 411–412
Bacon, Terry, 172
Bacsik, Mike, 228
Badre, Albert N., 79
Bailey, Holly, 257
Bailey, Marissa, 52
Bair, Bettina A., 531
Baker, Stephen, 531
Baldrige National Quality Program, 92
Barabas, Christine Peterson, 533
Bar charts, 418–421
Barna, Laray M., 529
Barrack, Tom, 136
Barron, James, 42
Bassett, Laura, 77
Bayless, Marsha L., 531
Bear, John, 529
Beason, Larry, 239
Bechler, Curt, 532
Beebe, S. A., 533
Begeman, Michael, 319
Behavioral job interviews, 498, 502, 503
Beilock, Sian, 335
Belanger, Kelly, 533
Beliefs, cultural diversity and, 41
Belvedere, 52
Benefits. *See also* Reader benefits
    to audience, 12, 22, 114–115, 119
    details for, 115–117
    extrinsic, 117–119
    intrinsic, 117–119, 150
Besson, Taunee, 534
Best Buy, 315
Beswick, Raymond W., 530
between/among, 263

Bias-free language
  explanation of, 51
  guidelines for, 51–54
Bilingual Canada, 39
Birdwhistell, Ray L., 42, 529
Bischoff, Bill, 534
Bishop, Jerry E., 530
Bissonnette, Zac, 6
Bjerke, Joshua, 495
Blake, Beth, 119
Blanchard, Ken, 27
Blind copies, 132
Block format, for letters, 127, 128, 133
Blocking responses, 292, 300
Blogging, 227–228
Blueprints, 386–387
Blumenstyk, Goldie, 394
Blyler, Nancy Roundy, 532
Body language, 42
Body movements, 42
Boice, Robert, 69, 530
Boilerplate, 67, 69
Bold headings, 80
Bolles, Richard, 441, 533
Booher, Dianna, 66, 528, 530
Boolean search, 360
Borker, Ruth A., 46, 529
Boulton, Clint, 78
Bowers, John Waite, 532, 533
Bowyer, Jerry, 423, 533
Brackets, 250, 373
Bradley, Helen, 263
Brady, Diane, 136
Brainstorming, 62, 113
Branching questions, 366
Breen, Bill, 534
Bregman, Peter, 172
Brehm, Jack W., 169, 531
Briggs, Isabel, 528
British Petroleum (BP), 422
Britt, Robert Roy, 8
Broadhead, Glenn J., 530
Broccoli, Albert R., 353
Brockman, Elizabeth, 533
Brockmann, John, 532
Brooks, Chad, 177, 511
Broome, Benjamin J., 529
Brown, Robert L., Jr., 532
Brown, Vincent J., 528
Bruder, Jessica, 11
Bruno, Tony, 228
Bryner, Jeanna, 102, 116, 300
Budget proposals, 352–353
Buffers, 172–174
Bullets, 80
Bullying, 188
Burck, Charles, 530
Burgarelli, Anthony, 307
Burling, Stacy, 168
Burnett, Rebecca E., 306, 530, 532
Burson-Marsteller, 166
Bush, George W., 257
Business communication. *See also*
    Communication
  audience for, 6, 12

creativity and, 11
culture and, 40–48
nature of, 5–6
purpose of, 6, 12, 22
situations for, 10, 12–13
Businessese, 261, 262
Business jargon, 261, 262
Business plans, 345–347
Buy-in, 30
Buying time, 305
Bypassing, 257, 260

C

Cable, Daniel, 169
Cadrain, Diane, 530
Cage, Sam, 118
Cain, Susan, 302
Cameron, David, 257
Campbell, G. Michael, 533
Campbell, Tom, 29
Canella, Patrick, 336
Capell, Perri, 464
Capelli, Paul, 493
Capitalization, 75, 76
Caprino, Kathy, 326
Careers. *See* Job search
Carell, Steve, 332
Carnegie Speech, 3
Carrasquillo, Adrian, 230
Carvin, Andy, 362
Case, 241
Case, John, 533
Caspers, Carl, 22
Casselman, Cindy, 119
Castillo, Shannon, 106
Castro, Kathy, 530
Causation, 370
Cell phones, 230
Central Connecticut State University, 9
Central Intelligence Agency, 43
Chan, Sewell, 26
Channel overload, 24
Channels, 23. *See also* Communication channels
Chapman, Dan, 44
Charts, 418–421
Chase, Chris, 275
Chatman, Jennifer, 28
Checking account documents, 74
Chen, Brian X., 368
Cheng, Wanla, 50
Chessum, Jake, 20
Chideya, Farai, 529
Choppy writing, 390
Christopher, Robert C., 529
Chronological organization
  explanation of, 333, 385
  in progress reports, 354, 355
  in reports, 378, 385
  in résumés, 452–453, 455, 457
Chronological progress reports, 354, 355
Chronological résumés, 452–453, 455, 457. *See also* Résumés
Citation, 370
cite/sight/site, 263

City Year, 318
Clark, Brian, 203
Clarke, Robyn D., 528
Class research projects, 346–351
Clearview, 77
Clement, Donald R., 533
Cleveland, W. S., 533
Clifford, Mark, 529
Closed body positions, 42
Closed questions, 364–366
Closings
  job interview, 495
  oral presentation, 330–332
Closure reports, 378
Cloud technology, 127
Clustering, 62, 63
Coakely, Caroline Gwynn, 532
Coca-Cola, 259
Cochran, Jeffrey K., 533
Cole, Johnnetta B., 273
Colella, A., 530
Collaborative writing, 306–308
Collection letters, 199–200
College Board's National Commission on
    Writing, 5
College majors, 5–6
Collins, Jim, 299
Collins, Robert, 492
Collins, Scott, 422
Colon, 247
Color
  cultural variations in associations with, 44, 45
  for presentation slides, 79
  in visuals, 421–422
Commas
  in lists, 285–286
  use of, 245, 247–248
Comma splices, 36–37, 243–245
Common ground, 198
Communication. *See also* Business
    communication; Cross-cultural communication
  audience and, 6, 7, 23–24 (*See also* Audience)
  cost of written, 8–9
  effectiveness of, 9
  generational differences in, 49, 51
  importance of, 3–5
  interpersonal, 8, 297
  nonverbal, 4, 41–42
  purpose of, 6–8
  verbal, 4
Communication channels, 31, 32
Comparison/contrast organization, 382
Complaints, responses to, 151–152
complement/compliment, 263
Complete sentence, 278
Complex sentences, 278
Complimentary closes, 127
Compliments, 47
compose/comprise, 263
Conaway, Roger N., 531
Concise writing, 390–391
Concluding paragraphs, in short reports, 378
Condon, John, 529
Confirmations, 151
Conflict, in groups, 302, 303

Conflict resolution
  empathy and, 97
  steps in, 302–304
  you-attitude in, 305
confuse/complicate/exacerbate, 263
Congratulatory notes, 152
Connelly, Phoebe, 145
Connotation, 257–258, 260
Consulting reports, 21
Context, of business communication, 13, 23
Contractions, 100
Convenience sample, 367, 369
Conversational style, 45
Cooper, Charles R., 530
Coordination, 298
Corporate culture. *See* Organizational culture
Correlation, 370
Courtesy titles, 132, 136
Coutu, Diane L., 530
Cowen, Robert, 314
Cox, Taylor H., Jr., 529
Coyle, Jake, 97
Creativity, 11
Credibility, 196
Credit rejection, 64
Critical thinking, 259
Criticism
  delivery of, 312
  responding to, 304–305
Crockett, Roger O., 50
Crosby, Philip B., 531
Cross-cultural communication. *See also*
  Communication; Cultural diversity
  bias-free language and, 51–54
  body language and, 42–43
  nonverbal communication and, 41–42
  oral communication and, 45–48
  personal space and, 43–44
  sensitivity and, 48
  time and, 44–45
Crossen, Cynthia, 532
Crowley, P. J., 28
Cullison, Alan, 307
Cultural diversity. *See also* Cross-cultural
  communication
  bias-free language and, 51–54
  body language and, 42–43
  colors and, 421–422
  conflict and, 302–303
  developing sensitivity to, 48
  Internet use and, 361
  nonverbal communication and, 41–42
  oral communication and, 45–48
  personal space and, 43–44
  persuasion and, 189
  television programming and, 53
  time and, 44–45
  values and beliefs and, 41
  in workplace, 38–39, 49–51
Culture. *See also* Organizational culture
  business communication and, 40–48
  explanation of, 40
  high-context, 40, 41
  low-context, 40, 41
  monochronic, 45, 47
  polychronic, 45, 47

Cuomo, Andrew, 168
Cycle/cycling process, 8
Cycling, 66

D

Dachler, H. Peter, 530
Dahl, Darren, 441
Dahlberg, Nancy, 307
Dana, Rebecca, 266
Dandridge, Thomas C., 531
Dangling modifiers, 163, 242
Darwin, Charles, 266
Dash, 248, 323
Dates, 251, 472
David, Carol, 530
Davis, Alice, 532
Davis, Kenneth C., 60
Davis, Lisa, 529
Davis, Todd, 204
Decision making. *See also* Problem-solving
  messages
  in meetings, 316–318
  styles of, 314
Decode, 23
Defensive body positions, 42
de Lange, Catherine, 366
Dell, Inc., 168
Deloitte Consulting, 49
Delta Air Lines, 44
Demographic data
  explanation of, 25–26
  for U.S and Canadian population, 39
Denham, Thomas J., 317
Denotation, 257, 260
Dependent clauses, 243
describe/prescribe, 263
Design. *See* Document design
Details
  choice of, 30, 448
  in paragraphs, 414
  on résumés, 457
Deutschman, Alan, 11
Deviation bar charts, 421
Dictionary use, 506
Digital Equipment, 188
Dillon, Sam, 5
Dimon, Jamie, 327
Directed subject line, 190
Direct requests
  checklist for, 207
  example of, 192
  explanation of, 189–190
  method to write, 191
Direct response strategy, 188
Disciplinary notices, 175
Discourse community, 28
discreet/discrete, 263
Discrimination, nature of, 50
Diversity. *See* Cultural diversity
Dizik, Alina, 260
Doby, Hersch, 532
Doctoroff, Tom, 259
Documentation, source, 370–373, 375–376
Document design
  of business communication, 6, 30

  capitalization and, 75, 76
  computer use for, 80
  creating professional image with, 130
  effective, 73
  evaluation of, 79–80
  fonts and, 75, 77
  headings and, 74–75
  margins and, 77–78
  planning for, 80–81
  presentation slides and, 78, 79
  revision of, 76
  visuals and, 419–420
  web pages and, 78–79
  white space and, 74
Dod, Glenna, 42
do/due, 263
Dot planning, 317–319
Dotson, Claud, 534
Drafts
  function of, 67, 307
  visuals in, 417
Dress for Success (Molloy), 45
Dreyfuss, Joel, 529
Driskill, Linda, 528, 533
Duckworth, Tammy, 108
Duick, Amber, 224
Duke, Mike, 136
Dulek, Ronald, 188, 531, 532
Dunn, Ryan, 282
Dworkin-McDaniel, Norine, 43
Dykes, Brett Michael, 29, 422
Dyrud, Marilyn A., 54, 530

E

Early letters, 199–200
Easterby, Ronald, 530
Economy, state of U.S., 2–3
Ede, Lisa, 306, 532
Edelman, Benjamin, 266
Editing
  explanation of, 64, 66
  of group documents, 307
Edmondson, Brad, 529
Edmondson, Gail, 529
Eggers, Kelly, 494
Einhorn, Lois J., 497
Eisner, Michael, 5
Ekman, Paul, 529
Elance, 443
Elashmawi, Farid, 41, 46, 48
Elbow, Peter, 530
Elder, Phil, 445, 533
Electronic research, 361. *See also* Research
elicit/illicit, 263
Elimination of alternatives organization,
  382–383
Ellipses, 250
Elsbach, Kimberly, 169
E-mail job application letters, 485–486
E-mail messages
  attachments to, 221, 226
  cautions regarding, 67
  format for, 219–220
  guidelines for, 218
  management of, 225

E-mail messages—*cont.*
  negative, 222–224
  "netiquette" for, 226
  networking through, 317
  persuasive, 224–225
  planning guide for, 64
  positive and informative, 221–223
  résumés in, 468
  subject line for, 220, 222–223
  writing style for, 226–227
eminent/immanent/imminent, 264
Emotional appeal, 196–197
Emotional intelligence (EQ), 97
Empathy, 24, 97
Emphasis. *See* Positive emphasis
Employee termination, 174, 175
Enclosures, 132
Encoding, 23
Eng, Sherri, 534
Engardio, Pete, 529
Engelhart, Katie, 421
Ensign, Rachel Louise, 440
Enthusiasm, 510
Erickson, Christine, 227
Ernst & Young, 352
Essential clauses, 248
Ethical issues
  in use of positive emphasis, 106
  in use of visuals, 422–423
Eure, Jack D., 531
Exaggeration, 46
Excluding alternatives organization, 333
Executive summary, for reports, 410–411
Expectancy theory, 113
External audience, 7
Extrinsic benefits, 117–119
Extroversion–introversion, 26
Eye contact, 42, 335

F

Facebook, 49, 166, 199, 229, 305, 317,
    367, 378
Fadiman, Jeffrey A., 532
Fairchild, Caroline, 382
Familiar words, 256, 258
Fans, 229
Farnham, Alan, 530
Faw, Larissa, 49
Faxes, 230
Fear, of public speaking, 334–335
Feasibility reports, 343, 378
Federal Emergency Management Agency
    (FEMA), 23, 106
Feedback
  checklist for, 67
  function of, 66–67
  revision after, 68
Feller, Ben, 119
Fernandez, Thomas L., 531
Ferrari, Bernie, 292
Ferrazzi, Keith, 317
Ferris, G., 530
fewer/less, 264
Figures, 420
Fiorina, Carly, 29

Firings, 174, 175
Fisher, Anne, 50, 440, 528, 533
Fisher, B. Aubrey, 532
Fishman, Charles, 530
Fitzgerald, Mark, 291
Fixed fonts, 75
Flaming, 224
Flanigan, James, 259
Fleming, John, 25
Florida Atlantic University, 307
Flower, Linda, 530, 532
Flynn, James, 51
Foley, Ryan J., 23
Follow-up letters and calls, 507–509, 511
Fonts, 75, 77
Ford Motor Company, 68
Formality, level of, 30, 339
Formalization, 298
Formal reports, 343
Forman, Janis, 532
Format
  block, 127, 128, 133
  for e-mail messages, 219–220
  explanation of, 126
  for letters, 127–137
  for long reports, 126, 410
  for memos, 137–140
  modified block, 127, 129, 131, 134
  proofreading for, 472
  for short reports, 126
Formation, 298
Form letters, 67, 69
forward/foreword, 264
Foss, Jenny, 508
Frames, 227
Frandsen, Kenneth D., 533
Freed, Richard C., 345, 530, 533
Freed, Shervin, 345
Freeman, Kimberly A., 532
Freewriting, 62
Fried, Jason, 502
Friends, 229
Friesen, Wallace V., 529
Fripp, Patricia, 533
Frost, Peter J., 531
Full justification of margins, 77
Functional organization, 384
Funding proposals, 352
Funk, Jeffrey L., 529
Fused sentences, 244
FYI, 150

G

Gallé, William P., 534
Garlinghouse, Brad, 137
Garrett, Echo Montgomery, 534
Gatekeepers, 21
Gee, Gordon, 327
General Electric Capital, 39
Generalizations, 198
General Motors, 378
General to particular organization, 383
Generation X, 46, 51
Generation y, 49
Geographic organization, 383–384

George, Amiso M., 528
Gerdes, Michelle, 335
Gerunds, 277, 457
Geryk, Bruce, 417
Gestures
  explanation of, 42–43
  for oral presentations, 335
GfK Custom Research, 177
Gies, Florence, 529
Gilbert, Alan, 230
Gillmor, Dan, 532
Glasscock, Gretchen, 531
Glink, Illyce R., 62
Globalization
  communication and, 4
  diversity and, 39, 40
  labor pool and, 438
Gneezy, Avelet, 113
Goldman Sachs, 94
Goldsborough, Reid, 530
Goleman, Daniel, 97
Gongloff, Mark, 533
Gonzalez, Fernando, 291
Gonzalez-Gann, Elizabeth, 291
Goodall, H. Lloyd, Jr., 532
Goodman, Cindy Krischer, 461
Goodman, J. David, 240
good/well, 264
Goodwill, 8, 9
Goodwill endings, 146, 154
Goodwill presentations, 326, 328
Goodwin, Liz, 366
Google, 166, 317
Google Docs, 127
Google Drive, 127
Gordon, Raymond L., 532
Gordon, Thomas, 291, 532
Gouran, Dennis S., 532
Grabmeier, Jeff, 189
Graham, Margaret Baker, 530
Graham, Shawn, 306
Grammar. *See also* Punctuation
  comma splices, 36–37, 243–245
  dangling modifier, 163, 242
  expert disagreement on, 255
  fused sentences, 244
  gerunds, 277
  infinitives, 277
  misplaced modifier, 242
  noun-pronoun agreement, 235, 240
  parallel structure, 186, 242, 280
  professional image and, 239
  run-on sentences, 244, 269–270
  sentence errors, 243–246
  split infinitives, 239
  subject–verb agreement, 141–142
Grammar checkers, 65–66, 72, 263
Granacki, Ann, 534
Grapevine, 8
Graphs. *See* Visuals
Graves, Jada, 439
Greco, Susan, 531
Green, Cheryl, 50
Green, Heather, 531
Green, Whitlowe R., 93

Greene, Robert, 22
Greene, Yvonne A., 533
Greenfield, Jeremy, 528
Gregory, M., 530
Grimm, Matthew, 11
Gross, Samantha, 469
Grouped bar charts, 421
Group presentations, 337
Groups. *See also* Meetings
  analyzing members of, 24–27
  characteristics of successful, 300–301
  collaborative writing in, 306–308
  conflict in, 302–305
  cultural diversity and, 302–303
  developmental stages of, 298
  ground rules for, 298
  groupthink in, 301–302
  leadership in, 300–302
  networking in, 317
  roles in, 298–299, 301
  setting priorities in, 317, 318
Groupthink, 301–302
Gumbinner, Paul S., 152
Gumperz, John J., 529

H

Haas, Christina, 529
Hacker, Carol A., 534
Hagge, John, 108, 530
Hall, Edward T., 45
Hammer, Tove Helland, 530
Happiness, 102, 104
Harish, Alon, 370
Harper, Nance L., 532
Harrington, Frances, 531
Harris, Philip R., 41, 46, 48, 532
Hart, Ariel, 44
Hartigan, John D., 531
Hartman, Rachel Rose, 108, 193
Harty, Martin, 108
Harvard College, 175
Hayes, John R., 530
Hayward, Tony, 108
Headers, 80
Headings
  bold, 80
  explanation of, 74–75, 435
  for letters, 130–131
  parallel, 388
  for reports, 387–388
  talking, 388, 435
  topic, 387
Hearing, 289
Hegarty, Edward J., 533
Helm, Burt, 197
Helman, Christopher, 343
Henley, Nancy M., 529
Herndl, Carl G., 532
Herzberg, Frederick, 117–118
Hess, Pamela, 106
Heussner, Ki Mae, 531
Hidden job market, 443, 445
Hidden negatives, 103
Hierarchy of needs (Maslow), 113–114
High-context cultures, 40, 41

Hill, Kashmir, 175, 463
Hirsch, Penny L., 530
Histograms, 421
History section, for reports, 411–412
Hitzhusen, Fred, 529
Ho, Erica, 226
Hodson, Gordon, 93
Hoger, Beth, 532
Hogg, Sam, 345
Hoholik, Suzanne, 530
Hojda, Vanessa, 450
Holzer, Harold, 247
Horvitz, Eric, 360
Hosking, Robert, 476
Hot button issues, 352
Howe, Neil, 48, 49
Huckin, Thomas N., 532
Hudson, John, 282
Humor, 331, 332, 334
Humphrey, Brad, 5, 528
Hurricane Katrina, 106
Husted, Bill, 218
Hymowitz, Carol, 532
Hyperlinks, 227
Hyphens, 248, 323

I

I, 489–490
IBM, 11
Idioms, 58, 258, 260
i.e./e.g., 264
Illustrations, 54. *See also* Visuals
I/me, 513–514
Imperator, Gina, 532
Impersonal constructions, 93, 94
imply/infer, 264
Indirect requests, 191
Individuals with disabilities, 53–54
Inferences, 305
Infinitives, 277
Informal reports, 343, 378
Information
  analysis of, 394
  business communication as, 6, 12
  role of giving, 8
  strategies to organize, 381–385 (*See also*
    Organizational patterns)
Informational interviews, 441–444
Informational leaders, 300, 302
Informational messages, 298
Information Mapping, 74
Information overload, 24
Informative messages
  checklist for, 156
  e-mail, 221–223
  explanation of, 143
  method to produce, 152–156
  organization of, 145–146
  reader benefits in, 148–150
  subject line for, 144–145
  types of, 144, 150–152
Informative presentations
  examples of slides for, 329
  function of, 326, 328
Informative reports

example of, 379–380
explanation of, 343, 378
-ing, 277
Initial audience, 21
Intel, 314
Internal audience, 7
Internet. *See also* E-mail messages
  blogging and, 227–228
  evaluating information on, 368
  job search and, 440–442
  networking and, 317
  reports on, 409
  social media and, 151, 227–230, 305
  technologies that use, 230–231
  use of, 361
  videoconferencing, 231, 313
  writing strategies for, 226–227
Interpersonal communication, 8, 297
Interpersonal leaders, 300, 302
Interpersonal messages, 298
Interviews
  function of, 363
  informational, 441–444
  job, 491–503 (*See also* Job interviews)
  referral, 443
Intonation, 333
Intrinsic benefits, 117–119, 150
Introductions, for reports, 411
Introductory paragraphs, in short
  reports, 378
Isidore, Chris, 108
Italics, 250–251
Itlaaie, Hillel, 528
it's/its, 100, 264

J

Jablin, Frederick M., 531
James, Geoffrey, 352
James, Susan Donaldson, 188
Jameson, Beverly, 290
Jameson, Daphne A., 7
Jansing, Chris, 25
Jargon, 260–262, 448
Jasper, Jesse, 32
Jayson, Sharon, 529
Jesdanun, Anick, 534
Job application letters. *See also* Résumés
  checklist for, 487
  e-mail, 485–486
  length of, 483
  prospecting, 476, 478–481
  purpose of, 474–475, 481
  solicited, 476–478, 480, 484
  targeting specific company in, 482
  time planning for, 475
  T-letters, 482–484
  tone in, 483, 485
Job benefits, 501
jobhuntersbible.com, 441
Job interviews
  attire for, 493
  behavioral, 498, 502, 503
  body of, 495
  close of, 495
  getting to, 494

Job interviews—*cont.*
 note-taking during, 494
 opening to, 495
 overview of, 491–492
 phone or video, 503
 practice for, 494–496
 responding to questions during,
  496–500, 502
 salary and benefits negotiations
  during, 501
 situational, 502–503
 strategy for, 493
 stress, 495–496
 what to bring to, 494
Job market, 441, 443
Jobs, Steve, 204
Job search. *See also* Job application letters;
  Résumés
 company research and, 439–441
 facing weaknesses and, 444–446
 hidden job market and, 443, 445
 importance factors in, 439–440
 information interviews and, 441–443
 self-knowledge and, 439
 strategies for, 438–439
Job titles, 52
Johnnson, Frank P., 532
Johnson, Angela D., 50
Johnson, David W., 532
Johnson, Glen, 257
Johnson, Scott D., 532
Johnson, W. B., 529
Jones, Carmen, 50
Jones, Del, 44
Jones, Lolo, 275
Jones, T. Boland, 306
Jordan, Andy, 244
Judging–perceiving, 26
Judgment sample, 367, 369
Judkis, Maura, 231
Justification reports
 elements of, 378, 381
 explanation of, 343, 378

K

Kamenetz, Anya, 512
Kaplan, Dan, 266
Karr, Albert R., 534
Katigbak, Everett, 417
Katz, Deanne, 174
Kazoleas, Dean C., 531
Keene, Michael L., 529, 533
Kelleher, Bob, 13
Kelly, Tara, 219
Kershaw, Sarah, 75
Key, Mary Ritchie, 529
Keyes, Jim, 204
Keywords, 360, 462
Kiechel, Walter, III, 533
Kienzler, Donna S., 346, 533, 534
Kiesler, Sara, 531
Kilts, James, 326
Kim, Gina, 118
Kim, Min-Sun, 531
Kindelan, Katie, 361

Kirkland, Jennifer M., 204
Kleimann, Susan, 377, 530, 533
Klein, Karen Huff, 188
Kleinmann, Susan D., 66
Knowledge, 25
Kochman, Thomas, 46, 529
Koen, Deb, 501
Kolodny, Lora, 345
Kopelman, Josh, 144
Kopytoff, Verne G., 227
Korn, Melissa, 346
Kostelnick, Charles, 108, 530
Kotter, John, 30
Koudsi, Suzanne, 501
Kozuh, Alissa, 381
Kramer, Steven, 105
Kratts, Aimee, 321
Kripalani, Manjeet, 529
Krone, Kathleen, 531
Krotz, Joanna, 202, 230, 231
Krumboltz, Mike, 336
Kumayama, Akihisa, 529
Kuneva, Gergana, 42
Kurata, Keisuke, 529
Kurutz, Steven, 531
Kuzak, Derrick, 68
Kwoh, Leslie, 450

L

LaBier, Douglas, 300
Lach, Jennifer, 528
Lahart, Justin, 442
Lamb, Gregory M., 107
Language
 bias-free, 51–54
 boilerplate, 67, 69
 nonracist and nonagist, 53
 nonsexist, 51–53
 to talk about people with disabilities
  and diseases, 53–54
Larson, Christine, 502
Late letters, 200
Lauer, Janice M., 533
LaVallee, Andrew, 39
Lawler, Edward E., III, 530
Lawless, Jill, 424
Layoff messages, 175
Layton, Pamela, 532
Lazarony, Lucy, 53
Leaders
 dictatorial, 301
 informational, 300, 302
 interpersonal, 300, 302
 procedural, 300, 302
Leadership
 in groups, 300–302
 listening skills and, 293
lectern/podium, 264
Lee, Bill, 320
Lee, Matthew, 28
Lee, Sharon, 367
Legal issues, 168
LEGO, 317
Lego Group, 176
Lending Tree, 346

Lenio, Lynze Wardle, 171
Leo, Kevin, 531
Letterhead, 129–130
Letter (memo) of transmittal, 409
Letters
 collection, 199–200
 design of, 80
 explanation of, 126
 following job interviews, 507–509, 511
 form, 67, 69
 format for, 127–137
 improving you-attitude in, 95, 96
 job application, 474–487 (*See also* Job
  application letters)
 organizational patterns for, 63
 prospecting, 476, 478–481
 punctuation in, 127
 of recommendation, 202–203
 solicited, 476–478, 480
lie/lay, 264
Limited agreement, 305
Limited Run, 367
Lin, Jeremy, 275
Lincoln, Abraham, 247
Lindo, Megan, 40
Line graphs, 418, 421
Lingle, Mike, 328
LinkedIn, 229, 317, 499, 508
Listening
 active, 291, 292
 disagreement and, 292–293
 function of, 288–289
 in groups, 300
 importance of, 8
 leading by, 293
 responses to, 292
 strategies for, 289–291
List of illustrations, for reports, 410
Lists, commas in, 285–286
Listservs, 317
Literacy, adult, 6
Lobel, Sharon Alisa, 529
Locke, Gary, 418
Locker, Kitty O., 529, 531–533
Lockhart, Jhaneel, 154
Loeffer, William, 248
Logos, 421, 424
Lohr, Steven, 529
Loneliness, 305
Long reports. *See also* Reports
 background or history for, 411–412
 components of, 394–408
 conclusions and recommendations
  on, 412
 elements of, 382–383
 example of, 395–408
 executive summary for, 410–411
 format for, 126, 410
 introduction for, 411
 letter or memo of transmittal for, 409
 list of illustrations for, 410
 style for, 410
 table of contents for, 409
 time allocation for, 393–394
 title page for, 409
 titles for, 411

Look-Look, 367
loose/lose, 265
Lopez, Julie Amparano, 534
Lorenz, Kate, 493
Louie, David, 9
Low-context cultures, 40–41
Lowry, Tom, 197
Lowy, Joan, 191
Lubell, Jeffrey, 382
Lublin, Joann, 321, 394
Lucas, George, 353
Lundberg, Abbie, 108
Lunsford, Andrea, 306, 532
Luse, Donna W., 534
Lutz, Bob, 228
Lynch, Jack, 239
Lynch, Peter, 533
Lyons, Dan, 166

M

Madden, Normandy, 97, 259
Main clauses, 243
Main points, 333–334
Major, Brenda, 529
Make-good reports, 343
Malik, Tariq, 116
Maltz, Daniel N., 46, 529
Managers, 6–7
Manjoo, Farhad, 360
Mann, Camille, 52
Manterfield, Lisa, 383
Marche, Stephen, 305
Margins, 77–78, 80
Marketing plans, 21
Martin, Joanne, 531
Maslow, Abraham H., 113–114, 530
Masters, Coco, 54
Mathes, J. C., 528, 531
Matson, Eric, 532
Mattioli, Dana, 394, 528
Matuson, Roberta, 304
Mayfield, Jacqueline, 106
Mayfield, Milton, 106
Mayo, Clara, 529
McAdam, Thomas, 274
McCain, John, 257
McCaulley, Mary H., 528
McCord, Elizabeth A., 168
McCorvey, J. J., 230, 231
McDonald's, 39, 54, 97
McFarland, Shannon, 492
McGill, R., 533
McGrane, Victoria, 154
McGuire, Timothy W., 531
McIsaac, Claudia MonPere, 528
McKinsey & Co., 313
McLeod, Poppy Lauretta, 529
McManus, Sean, 530
McQueen, M. P., 51
McTeer, Bob, 245
Mean, 369, 370
Median, 369, 370
Meetings. *See also* Groups
  agenda for, 314–317, 319
  decision-making strategies for, 316–318

effective participation in, 318–319
function of, 312
informal, 319–320
minutes for, 319
planning for, 313–316
types of, 313
virtual, 320–321
Memo of transmittal, 409
Memos
  design of, 80
  example of positive, 149
  explanation of, 126
  format for, 137–140
Menu design, 74
Merchant, Jerrold J., 529
Messages. *See also* E-mail messages;
    Informative messages; Negative messages;
    Persuasive messages; Positive messages
  effectiveness of, 9
  group, 298
  informational, 298
  interpersonal, 298
  procedural, 298
  purposes of, 8
Metcalf, John, 9
Met Life, 101
Meyer, Paul J., 290
Michelin, 39
Microsoft, 78, 168
Microsoft Word, 127
Middle letters, 200
Millennials, 48, 49, 51
Miller, Carolyn R., 532
Miller, Herman, 321
Miller, Jared T., 52
Miller, Karen Lowry, 531
Miller, Laura, 239
Millman, Jennifer, 251
Mills, Robert S., 533
Mintzberg, Henry, 6, 528
Minutes, meeting, 319
Misplaced modifier, 242
Mixed punctuation, 127
Mizuho Securities Co., 251
MLA style, 370–372, 375–376
Mochari, Ilan, 531
Modern Language Association (MLA), 370
Modified block format, for letters, 127, 129,
    131, 134
Modifiers
  avoiding vague or empty, 390
  dangling, 163, 242
  misplaced, 242
Molloy, John T., 45, 106, 493
Monochronic cultures, 45, 47
Monster.com, 440
Moody, Chris, 25
Moore, Teresa, 532
Moore, Tyler, 266
moral/morale, 265
Moran, Robert T., 532
Morgan, Gareth, 531, 532
Morkes, John, 227, 531
Morrison, Denise, 326
Mortgage Resolution Partners, 62
Moss, Frederick K., 528

Mossberg, Walter, 127
Mosvick, Roger K., 532
Motivation, 41
Ms., 136
MSN, 231
MTV, 422
Mueller, Jennifer, 298
Mulally, Alan, 68
Mulcahy, Anne, 190
Mullins, John W., 344
Multiculturalism. *See* Cross-cultural
    communication
Multiple-choice questions, 365, 366
Multi-touch screens, 78
Muoio, Anna, 534
Murray, Sam, 502
Myers-Briggs Type Indicator, 26
MySpace, 199, 229, 317

N

Nadler, Lawrence B., 529
Nadler, Marjorie Keeshan, 529
Narration, 330–331
Nassauer, Sarah, 113
National Assessment of Adult Literacy, 6
National School Boards Association, 300
Nawrocki, Paul, 469
Negative messages
  buffers for, 172–174
  checklist for, 180
  e-mail, 222–224
  explanation of, 164
  legal implications of, 168
  method to produce, 175–179
  misrepresentation in, 150
  organization of, 165–166
  for peers and subordinates, 172
  for people outside your organization,
    166–171
  purposes of, 165
  subject line for, 165
  for superiors, 171, 172
  types of, 174–175
  word use and, 102–104
Negative performance appraisals, 175
Negatives
  deemphasis of, 105–106
  explanation of, 101
  hidden, 103
  justification for, 105
  omission of, 105
Negative words, 102–104, 257
Neilsen, Jakob, 166
Nelson, Beverly H., 534
Nelson, Robert B., 532
Nervousness, 334–335
Netburn, Deborah, 228
Netflix, 13
Netiquette rules, 226
Networking, 317
Newman, Barry, 132
Newton, Isaac, 302
Ni, Preston, 335
Nielsen, Jakob, 78, 227, 530, 531
Nielsen Media Research, 368

Nike, 28, 51
Nine-Curt, Carmen Judith, 529
Nivea, 21
Noise, 23, 24, 320
Nokia, 39
Nolan, Roland, 50
Nonagist language, 53
Nonessential clauses, 248
Nonracist language, 53
Nonsexist language, 51–53
Nonverbal communication, 4, 41–42
Nonverbal symbols, 45
Notes, for oral presentations, 335–336
Note-taking, during job interviews, 494
Noun–pronoun agreement, 235, 240
Nouns
    case of, 241
    concrete, 448
    plural, 122
Nudd, Tim, 393
Numbers, 251, 368–370, 472

O

Obama, Barack, 193, 257
Objections
    of audience, 12, 23
    to persuasive messages, 193–196
Objective pronouns, 241
objective/rationale, 265
O'Connor, Anahad, 104
Odell, Lee, 530
Odum, Charles, 168
O'Keefe, Daniel J., 531
Olofson, Cathy, 532
Ondaatje, Michael, 62
O'Neill, Vincent, 529
One-on-one meetings, 313
1-2-3 organization, 333
Online résumés, 468
Open body positions, 42
Openers
    job interview, 495
    oral presentation, 330–331
Open punctuation, 127
Open questions, 364, 365
Optimism, 103, 104
Oracle Corporation, 31
Oral communication
    complements and, 47
    explanation of, 45–46
    silence in, 47
    understatement and exaggeration in, 46
Oral presentations
    audience for, 326–328
    audience questions following, 336
    delivery of, 334–336
    function of, 325, 326, 328
    group, 337
    openers and closings for, 330–332
    organization of, 332–334
    planning for, 326–327
    types of, 326, 328
    visuals in, 328–330, 335–336, 417, 425
    voice for, 333

Orders, 198
Orenstein, Peggy, 176
Organizational culture. *See also* Cultural
        diversity; Culture
    explanation of, 28, 30
    as learned culture, 188–189
    writing style and, 282
Organizational patterns
    for business communication, 6, 29
    chronological, 385
    comparison/contrast, 382
    elimination of alternatives, 382–383
    functional, 384
    general to particular or particular to general,
        383
    geographic or spatial, 383–384
    for informative and positive messages,
        145–150
    for letters, 63
    for negative messages, 165–166
    for oral presentations, 332–334
    for persuasive messages, 190–193, 195
    problem-solution, 382
    for short reports, 381–385
    types of, 333, 381–382
Organizations
    analyzing people in, 27–28
    cultural diversity in, 38–39
    understanding needs of, 20
Orientation, 298
Orphans, 80
Outzen, Rick, 422
Overview of main points, 333–334
Ozanian, Mike, 343

P

Packer, A. E., 529
Page numbers, 80
Pagonis, William G., 291
PAIBOC questions
    analysis using, 12
    audience and, 22–23
    explanation of, 12
    for informative and positive messages, 152
    for long reports, 410
    for negative messages, 175–176
    for persuasive messages, 203
Paice, Shayndi, 378
Paired bar charts, 421
Palin, Sarah, 335–336
Papachristou, Paraskevi, 369
Pappas, Stephanie, 93
Paradi, Dave, 78
Paragraphs
    concluding, 378
    elements of good, 414
    introductory, 378
    in job application letters, 478, 480–481
    revision of, 281–282
    summary, 476
Parallel headings, 388
Parallel structure, 186, 242, 280
Paraphrasing, 304–305
Parentheses, 249

Parker-Pope, Tara, 130
Parliamentary meetings, 313
Particular to general organization, 383
Partnership for 21st Century Skills, 4
Passive verbs, 93, 94, 274–275
Passive voice, 86–87
Paul, Annie Murphy, 290
Pay-back reports, 343
Peek, Scott, 496
Peer pressure, 301–302
Penkar, Samir, 316
Perchonock, Ellen, 532
Performance appraisals
    example of, 201
    explanation of, 200, 202
    negative, 175
Period, 249
Perryman, Mark, 343
Personal appearance, 130
Personality, 26, 215–216
Personal names, of readers, 136–137
personal/personnel, 265
Personal pronouns, 241
Personal space, 43
Persuasive messages
    checklist for, 208
    e-mail, 224–225
    objections to, 193–196
    organization of, 190–193
    purposes of, 8, 187, 188
    strategies for, 188–189, 203–207
    subject line for, 189–190
    techniques for, 196–199
    tone for, 106–107, 197
    types of, 188, 199–203
Persuasive presentations, 326, 328
Petrini, Janis, 387
Pettit, John D., 531
Petzinger, Thomas, Jr., 534
Pew Charitable Trust, 74
Philbin, John P. "Pat," 106
Phillips, Matthew, 446
Phishing, 220
Phone calls, following job interviews,
        507–509, 511
Phone job interviews, 503
Photographs. *See also* Visuals
    bias-free, 54
    guidelines to use, 30
Phrases
    nonsexist, 51
    in sentences, 243
    transition, 282
Pictograms, 421
Piëch, Anton, 47
Pie charts, 418–420
Pitch, 333
Planning
    for document design, 80–81
    function of, 60
    for meetings, 313–316
    strategies for, 62–64
Planning guides, 63, 64
Plural nouns, 122
Plural possessives, 111, 122

PNC, 119
Podmolik, Mary Ellen, 532
Point of view, 97
Polishing Your Prose
    active and passive voice, 86–87
    answers to, 524–527
    combining sentences, 295–296
    commas in lists, 285–286
    comma splices, 36–37
    concise writing, 390–391
    dangling modifiers, 163
    delivering criticism, 312
    details, 448
    dictionary use, 506
    expert disagreement on grammar and
        punctuation, 255
    expressing personality, 215–216
    formality level, 339
    hyphens and dashes, 323
    idioms, 58
    I/me, 513–514
    it's/its, 100
    MLA style, 375–376
    noun–pronoun agreement, 235
    paragraphs, 414–415
    parallel structure, 186
    plurals and possessives, 122
    proofreading, 472
    run-on sentences, 269–270
    sentence fragments, 18
    singular and plural possessives, 111
    spell/grammar checkers, 72
    subject lines and headings, 435
    subject–verb agreement, 141–142
    verb tenses, 357–358
    who/whom, 513–514
    you/I use, 489–490
Politeness, 107, 386
Polychronic cultures, 45, 47
Pondy. Louis R., 531
Pope, Justin, 528
Population, 366
Porter, Natalie, 529
Positive emphasis
    apologies and, 108
    ethics and, 106
    explanation of, 102
    justifying negative information by
        offering, 105
    methods to create, 102–106
    tone and, 106–108
Positive messages
    checklist for, 156
    e-mail, 221–223
    examples of, 147–149
    explanation of, 143
    method to produce, 152–156
    organization of, 145–146
    reader benefits in, 148–150
    subject line for, 144–145
    types of, 144, 150–152
Positive words, 257–258
Posner, Andrew, 5
Possessive pronouns, 241, 246
Possessives, 111, 122

possible/possibly, 265
Postal Service abbreviations, 135
Posture, 42, 335
Poulton, E. C., 530
PowerPoint slides, 78
Powers, Melanie E., 531
precede/proceed, 265
Predication errors, 243
Prejudice, 93
Presentations. See Oral presentations
Presentation slides
    design of, 78, 79
    guidelines for, 328, 330
    for informative presentations, 329
Presenting problem, 304
Primary audience, 20
Primary research, 359
principal/principle, 265
Print preview, 80
Print research sources, 362
Private, 229
Pro and con pattern, 382
Problem-causes-solution organization, 333
Problem-solution organization, 382
Problem-solving messages. See also Decision
        making
    example of, 194
    organization of, 191–193, 195
    pattern for, 188, 190
    time allocation for, 203
Problem-solving reports, 343
Procedural leaders, 300, 302
Procedural messages, 298
Pro-con organization, 333
Procrastination, 69
Procter & Gamble, 9, 317, 457
Product placements, 197
Professional image, 239
Progress reports
    chronological, 354, 355
    explanation of, 353–354
    recommendation, 355
    task, 354
ProLiteracy, 8
Pronouns
    agreement between nouns and, 235, 240
    case of, 241
    nonsexist, 52–53
    objective, 241
    personal, 241
    possessive, 241, 246
    second-person, 281
    third-person, 281
Proofreading
    of collaborative documents, 307
    explanation of, 64, 66
    guidelines for, 472
    importance of, 69
    marking errors when, 251–252
    of résumés, 451
Proofreading symbols, 252
Proportional fonts, 75
Proposals
    budget and costs, 352–353
    business plans as, 345–347

    for class research projects, 346–351
    elements of, 346
    explanation of, 345
    funding, 352
    planning guide for, 64
    procedure prior to writing, 343–345
    sales, 351–352
Prospecting letters, 476, 478–481
Psychographic characteristics, 26
Psychological description, 116–117
Psychological reactance, 169
Punctuation. See also Grammar
    apostrophe, 100, 111, 122, 245–247
    brackets, 250, 373
    colon, 247
    comma, 245, 247–248
    dash, 248, 323
    ellipses, 240
    expert disagreement on, 255
    hyphen, 248, 323
    in letters, 127
    parentheses, 249
    period, 249
    professional image and, 239
    proofreading for, 472
    quotations, 249–251, 373
    semicolon, 249
    square brackets, 250
Purdy, Kevin, 69
Puri, Manju, 104
Purpose statements, 344–346
Puzzanghera, Jim, 74

Q

Quam, Ross, 440
Quarterly reports, 343
Questionnaires, 363, 364, 366
Questions
    audience, 336
    branching, 366
    closed, 364–366
    job interview, 496–500, 502
    multiple-choice, 365, 366
    open, 364, 365
    for oral presentation opener, 331
    polite, 386
    specific, 386
    survey, 363–366
Quick, Becky, 191
Quickcorrect, 80
quiet/quite, 265
Quintanilla, Carl, 533
Quintura, 418
Quotation marks, 249, 250
Quotations
    for oral presentation opener, 331
    punctuation of, 249–251
    in reports, 373

R

Ragged right margins, 77–78
Ramirez, Ramon, 228
Rampell, Catherine, 103
Random sample, 367, 369

Range, 369, 370
Reader benefits. *See also* Audience
  criteria for use of, 117–118, 120, 151
  detail guidelines for, 115–117
  explanation of, 112–114
  identification of, 113–115
  in informative and positive messages,
    148–150
  for specific audiences, 119
  you-attitude and, 120
Reading skills, in United States, 5
Recommendation letters, 202–203
Recommendation progress reports, 355
Recommendation reports, 343
Reder, Stephen, 5
Redundancy, 390
Reference line, in letters, 127
Referral interviews, 443
Referrals, 443
Refusal messages, 174–175
Regular staff meetings, 313
regulate/relegate, 265
Reichheld, Frederick F., 533
Reinsch, N. Lamar, Jr., 101, 530
Rejection messages, 174–175
Reports
  analytical, 343
  annual, 343
  closure, 378
  examples of, 379–380, 395–408
  explanation of, 343
  feasibility, 343
  formal, 343, 392
  informal, 343, 378
  informative, 343, 378–380
  justification, 343, 378, 381
  levels of, 343
  long, 392–412 (*See also* Long reports)
  make-good, 343
  progress, 353–355
  purpose of, 345
  short, 377–388 (*See also* Short reports)
  steps to write, 342
  types of, 343
Requests
  direct, 189–192
  indirect, 191
  purpose of, 8
Research
  analysis of, 368–370
  on companies, 439–441
  documenting sources of, 370–373, 375–376
  electronic, 361
  Internet use for, 360–363
  primary, 359
  print, 362
  secondary, 359, 368
  surveys and interviews and, 363–368
residence/residents, 265
Resilience, 107
respectfully/respectively, 266
Respondents, 363
Résumés. *See also* Job application letters
  action verbs for, 457, 458
  career objectives on, 463

checklist for, 469
chronological, 452–453, 455, 457
computer use to create, 451
educational background on, 462–463
explanation of, 449
honors and awards on, 463–464
keywords for jobs on, 462
layout and design of, 451
length of, 465
online, 468
proofreading, 451
references on, 464
scannable, 465–468
skills, 452, 454, 456, 458–461
strategies for, 451–452
summary of qualifications on, 461–462
time planning for, 450
video, 468–470
Rettner, Rachel, 93
Reverse chronology, 452
Revision
  after feedback, 68
  checklist for, 65
  of collaborative documents, 307
  explanation of, 64, 66
  function of, 60, 64, 271
  guidelines for, 273–274
  to improve you-attitude, 94–96
  of paragraphs, 281–282
  strategies for, 274–281
Revkin, Andrew C., 168
Reynolds, Fred, 64, 530
Reynolds, Linda, 530
Rice, Anne, 62
Richey, Warren, 336
Rico, Gabriela Lusser, 530
Rigdon, Joan E., 532
Ritchie, Karen, 529
Robbins, Stephen P., 304, 532
Roberts, David D., 533
Robinson, David T., 104
Robinson, Ray, 534
Rogers, Priscilla S., 531
role/roll, 266
Romano, Joseph D., 345
Romney, Mitt, 257
Rondthaler, Ed, 266
Roney, Luke, 476
Rooney, Andy, 245
Roosevelt, Theodore, 266
Rose, Barbara, 529
Rose, Richard C., 534
Rosenbaum, David, 108
Rosman, Katherine, 226
Rothchild, John, 533
Rothenberger, Cecilia, 28, 528
Rowland, Kenneth, 530
Rowley, Laura, 119
Rozhon, Tracie, 533
Rubin, Harriet, 50
Run-on sentences, 244, 269–270
RunPee.com, 97
Rutherford, LeAne, 533
Ryan, Kevin, 27
Rydholm, Erik, 498

S

Saatchi & Saatchi, 224
Safer, Morley, 20
Sahadi, Jeanne, 440
Salary/benefits negotiation, 501
Sales proposals, 351–352
Sales reports, 343
Saliard, Shannon, 10
Salutation, 127
Same-sex couples, touch in, 43
Samples, survey, 366–369
Sancton, Julian, 197
Sands, Judith Gordon, 291, 532
Sans serif fonts, 77
Santos, Fernanda, 331
Saville-Troike, Muriel, 529
Savin, Harris B., 532
Scannable résumés, 465–468
Schawbel, Dan, 27, 443
Schellhardt, Timothy D., 533
Scherer, Michael, 29
Schmandt-Besserat, Denise, 13
Schmid, Randolph E., 118
Schoenberger, Chana R., 169
Schrage, Michael, 151, 532
Schuessler, Jennifer, 153
Schullery, Nancy, 532
Schultz, Beatrice, 532
Schultz, Howard, 327
Search engines, 317, 418. *See also specific
  search engines*
Secondary audience, 20–21
Secondary research, 359, 368
Second-person pronouns, 281
Segal, Jonathan A., 176, 200
Segmented bars, 421
Self-image, 113
Seligman, Martin, 101
Semicolon, 249
Sensing–intuition, 26
Sentence fragments, 18, 244–246
Sentences
  basic pattern for, 414
  comma splices, 36–37, 243–244
  complex, 278
  compound, 278
  explanation of, 243
  fused, 244
  method to combine, 277, 295–296
  punctuation inside, 245–249 (*See also*
    Punctuation)
  run-on, 244, 269–270
  simple, 277
  summary, 476
  topic, 281, 387
  varying length and structure of, 277–280
  you-attitude in, 91–94
Serif fonts, 75, 77
Sexist language, 51–53
Shanahan, Danny, 500
Shapley, Dan, 106
Sharkey, Joe, 3
Shelby, Annette N., 101, 530
Shellenbarger, Sue, 241, 316, 320, 534
Shepardson, David, 135

Sherman, Mark A., 530
Short reports. *See also* Reports
    feasibility, 378
    format for, 126
    function of, 377
    informative or closure, 378–380
    justification, 378, 381
    organizational patterns for, 381–385
    writing style for, 385–388
Shriver, Marcelle, 120
Shwom, Barbara L., 530
Siebel Systems, 31
Siegel, Jane, 531
Siegel, Matt, 528
Signature block, 136
Signposts, 334, 336
Silence, 47
Silverman, Rachel Emma, 314, 417, 501,
    530, 534
Simmons, Lesly, 361
Simmons, Sophie, 119
Simons, Tad, 533
Simple sentences, 277
simple/simplistic, 266
Simpson, Adrian J., 532
Singular possessives, 111
Situational job interviews, 502–503
Skills résumés, 452, 454, 456, 458–461. *See*
    also Résumés
Skyfall, 197
Skype, 231
Slides. *See* Presentation slides
Sloan, Steven, 501
Sloate, Laura, 319
Slocombe, Mike, 530
Smartphones, 231
Smith, Ben, 493
Smith, Catharine, 368
Smith, Greg, 94
Smith, Jacquelyn, 496
Smith, Rebecca, 462, 534
Smith, W. J., 533
Snow, Craig, 532
Social networking
    business applications for, 228–230
    complaints and, 151
    job applicants and, 492
    loneliness and, 305
    strategies for, 227
Solicited letters, 476–478, 480
Solomon, Caleb, 531
Solutions Marketing Group, 50
Southwest Airlines, 510
Space, personal, 43
Spatial arrangements, 43–44
Spatial organization, 383–384
Speaking rate, 289
Spell-checkers, 66, 72, 263, 472
Spielberg, Steven, 353
Spilka, Rachel, 62, 530
Split infinitives, 239
Splunk, 360
Spoke.com, 229
Sprinkle, Tim, 367
Sprung, Shlomo, 499

Spyware programs, 226
Square brackets, 250, 373
Stableford, Dylan, 165
Stacked bars, 421
Stacy, Mitch, 264
Stafford, Diane, 277, 501
Standard agenda, 316–317, 319
stationary/stationery, 266
Steinmail, Joanna Pearl, 120
Stern, Gabriella, 531
Stern, Gary M., 370
Stevenson, Dwight W., 528, 531
Stokes, Jeff, 5, 528
Storyboard, 63
Strauss, Valerie, 24
Strauss, William, 48, 49
Stress Interviews, 495–496
Strickland, Ashley, 60
Strimaitis, Janet, 346
Struzik, Ed, 457
Stump, Susan, 188
Style. *See* Writing style
Subbaraman, Nidhi, 219
Subdivided bars, 421
Subject lines
    directed, 190
    for e-mail messages, 220, 222–223
    explanation of, 144, 435
    for informative or positive messages, 144–145
    in letters, 127
    for negative messages, 165
    for persuasive messages, 189–190
Subject–verb agreement, 141–142, 239–240
Subordinate clauses, 243
Suchan, James, 188, 531, 532
Suddath, Claire, 319
Sullivan, John, 440
Sullivan, Patricia, 533
Summaries, 151
Summary paragraphs, 476
Summary sentences, 476
Sun Microsystems, 31
Supervisors
    abusive, 300
    informal meetings with, 319–320
Surveys
    explanation of, 363
    questions for, 363–366
    sample choices for, 366–369
Symbols, nonverbal, 45

T

Table of contents, for reports, 409–410
Tables, 418–420
Tabs, 80
Tab settings, 80
Talking heads, 388, 435
Tang, ZhaoHui, 418
Tannen, Deborah, 529, 534
Tanner, Lindsay, 531
Task progress reports, 354
Taylor, Lynn, 478
Taylor, Marisa, 26
Team meetings, 313
Teams. *See also* Groups

    collaborative writing in, 306–308
    function of, 297
    virtual, 306
Technology. *See also* E-mail messages; Internet
    cloud, 127
    grammar checkers and, 65–66, 72, 263
    impact of, 217
    job applications and, 474, 492
    research and, 360–363
    social networking and, 227–230
    spell-checkers and, 66, 72
    trends in Internet-based, 230–231
    videoconferencing and, 231, 313
Telecomcareers.net, 440
Telfer, Lauren, 119
Templates, 451
Temple-Raston, Dina, 291
Tempo, 333
Tenses, verb, 357–358, 391
Terberg, Julie, 533
Terlep, Sharon, 378
Tesla Motors, 8
Testa, Garry, 320
Text messages, 218, 231
Thank-you notes, 152
Theibert, Phil, 533
their/there/they're, 266
Thinking–feeling, 26
Third-person pronouns, 281
Thompson, Andrea, 116
Thompson, Carolyn, 32
Thorell, L. G., 533
Thralls, Charlotte, 532
Tibbets, Arn, 532
Tilghman, Kelly, 50
Time, perception of, 44–45
Time planning
    for e-mail messages, 223–225
    for job application letters, 475
    for problem-solving messages, 203
    for proposal writing, 344
    for report writing, 393–394
    for résumés, 450
    strategies for, 61, 62
Title page, for reports, 409
Titles, for reports, 411
to be, 275
Tommasini, Anthony, 60
Tone. *See also* Writing style
    choice of appropriate, 273
    for job application letters, 483, 485
    for persuasive messages, 106–107, 197
Topic headings, 387
Topic sentences, 281, 387
Toppo, Greg, 6
to/too/two, 266
Touch, 43, 116
Townsend, Alan, 168
Townsend, Linda, 168
Toyoda, Akio, 107
Toyota, 107–108, 224
Trade journals, 441, 442
Transitions
    in paragraphs, 414
    words and phrases for, 282, 387, 414

Translations, 47
Transmit, 23
Transmittals, 150–151
Trip reports, 64
Tropman, John E., 302, 532
Trump, Donald, 193
Truncated visuals, 422–424
Truss, Lynne, 248
Tufte, Edward R., 533
Tugend, Alina, 104
Tulgan, Bruce, 49
Tumposky, Ellen, 21
Turner, Ted, 5
Twain, Mark, 266
Twitter, 151, 230
Tyler, Lisa, 530
Typos, 9, 251
Typo-squatters, 266

U

UBS, 493
Ulijin, J. M., 46
Underlining, 250–251
Understatement, 46
Unemployment rate, 3, 445–446
Unified paragraphs, 414
unique/unusual, 266
U.S. Census Bureau, 48, 53
U.S. Postal Service abbreviations, 135
Unity, 281
University of California, Berkeley, 93
University of Wisconsin Writing Center, 66

V

Valdes, Manuel, 492
Values
  cultural diversity and, 41
  explanation of, 26–27
Values and Lifestyles (VALS) profiles, 27
Vample, Ron, 274
Vanac, Mary, 97
Van Allen, Fox, 67
Vance, Ashley, 320
Vargas, Marjorie Fink, 529, 533
Variety, in paragraphs, 414
Venkataraman, Nitya, 11
Venting, 302
Verbal communication, 4
verbal/oral, 266
Verbs
  action, 457, 458
  active, 274–275
  agreement between subject and, 141–142,
    239–240
  concrete, 448
  function of, 274–275
  object of, 241
  passive, 93, 94, 274–275
  in sentences, 279–280
Verb tenses, 357–358, 391
Vergara, Eva, 69
Versis, 113
Vested interest, 193
Vickers, Yvette, 305

Victor, David, 40
Victor, David A., 529
Videoconferencing, 231, 313
Video job interviews, 503
Video résumés, 468–470
Virginia Polytechnic Institute and State
  University, 61
Virtual job interviews, 503
Virtual meetings, 320–321
Virtual teams, 306
Virus, computer, 226
Visuals. *See also* Presentation slides
  bias-free, 54
  color and clip art as, 421–422
  design conventions for, 419–422
  ethical use of, 422–424
  function of, 6, 416–417
  guidelines to use, 30, 418, 422–424
  integration of, 424
  in presentations, 328–330, 335–336,
    417, 425
  types of, 418–419
Voice
  active and passive, 86–87
  for oral presentations, 333
Volume, voice, 333
Vranica, Suzanne, 378

W

Wallace, Alexandria, 228
Walsh, Joe, 108
Wanous, John P., 530
Warshaw, Michael, 119
Watchdog audience, 21
Watson Wyatt Worldwide, 9
Webb, John, 529
Weber, Harry R., 44
Weber, Lauren, 457
Web pages. *See also* Internet
  analysis of, 363
  design of, 78–79
Weeks, Francis W., 531
Weger, John J., 530
Weinhaus, Evonne, 195
Weiss, Piper, 144, 275
Weissman, Jerry, 326
Welsh-Huggins, Andrew, 327
Wendleton, Kate, 534
whether/weather, 267
Whitbourne, Susan Krauss, 289
Whiteman, Doug, 327
White space, 74
who/whom, 513–514
Widows, 80
Wieners, Brad, 177
Wiens, Kyle, 244
Wilder, Claudyne, 330
Williams, Andrea, 532
Williams, Nicole, 277
Williams, Ray B., 528
Wills, J., 533
Wilson, Simone, 228
Windolf, Jim, 353
W.L. Gore & Associates, 11
Wolvin, Andrew D., 532

The Woman's Dress for Success Book
  (Molloy), 45
Wong, Shantel, 97
Woodruff, David, 531
Woods, Tiger, 50
Wooley, Ryan, 51
Word choice
  appropriate, 256
  to express personality, 215–216
  for reports, 385
Wordiness, 276–277, 386
Word (Microsoft), 127
Word-processing programs, 80
Words
  accurate, 256
  analysis of, 369–370
  concise, 390
  confusing, 261–267
  connotation of, 257–258, 260
  denotation of, 257, 260
  familiar, 256, 258
  jargon, 260–261
  meaning of, 260
  negative, 102–104
  nonsexist, 51
  positive, 257–258
  redundant, 390
  transitional, 282, 387
  unnecessary, 276–277
Workplace
  abusive supervisors in, 300
  communication skills for, 3–5
  creating professional image in, 130
  cultural diversity in, 38–39, 49–51
  depressed workers in, 154
The World Factbook, 43
Wozniak, Steve, 302
Writer's block, strategies to overcome, 69
Writing process
  collaborative, 306–308
  design as element of, 80–81
  feedback and, 66–68
  form letters and, 67, 69
  planning and, 60, 61–63
  procrastination and, 69
  revision and, 60, 64–66, 68, 94–96,
    274–281, 307
  strategies for, 60–61
  writer's block and, 69
Writing style. *See also* Tone
  of business communication, 6
  concise, 390–391
  conversational, 45
  to express personality, 215–216
  formality of, 30, 339
  guidelines for, 29, 272, 273–274
  levels of, 272
  organizational culture and, 282
  for reports, 385–388, 410
  revision and, 274–282
  tightening up your, 276–277
Written messages. *See also* Messages
  cost of, 8–9
  cultural contrasts in, 48
  effectiveness of, 9
Wuorio, Jeff, 531

X

Xerox, 119, 507

Y

Yaffa, Joshua, 77
Yahoo!, 231, 317
Yang, Kelly, 503
Yen, Hope, 39, 366, 441, 528
Yochim, Dayana, 150
York, Emily Bryson, 264
you, 385, 489–490

You-attitude
  in conflict resolution, 305
  explanation of, 90, 92, 94
  in job application letters, 483, 485
  methods to create, 91–94
  positive emphasis and, 104–105
  questions and, 386
  reader benefits and, 120
  revision and, 94–96
  you/I use and, 489–490
your/you're, 267
YouTube, 49, 230

Z

Zack, Liz, 11
Zeebie, Bill, 496
Zelazny, Gene, 533
Zhou, Kevin, 11
Ziomek, Erin, 498
Zolli, Andrew, 107
Zuckerberg, Mark, 49
Zwaga, Harm, 530

Credits

New and Improved Coverage in BCS6e!: *Chapter from Business Communication: Building Critical Skills, Sixth Edition by Locker, Kaczmarek, 2014* xi

Support Materials: *Chapter from Business Communication: Building Critical Skills, Sixth Edition by Locker, Kaczmarek, 2014* xxiv

Building Blocks for Effective Messages

Introduction: *Chapter from Business Communication: Building Critical Skills, Sixth Edition by Locker, Kaczmarek, 2014* 1

1. Business Communication, Management, and Success: *Chapter 1 from Business Communication: Building Critical Skills, Sixth Edition by Locker, Kaczmarek, 2014* 2

2. Adapting Your Message to Your Audience: *Chapter 2 from Business Communication: Building Critical Skills, Sixth Edition by Locker, Kaczmarek, 2014* 19

4. Planning, Writing, and Revising: *Chapter 4 from Business Communication: Building Critical Skills, Sixth Edition by Locker, Kaczmarek, 2014* 59

5. Designing Documents, Slides, and Screens: *Chapter 5 from Business Communication: Building Critical Skills, Sixth Edition by Locker, Kaczmarek, 2014* 73

Creating Goodwill

Introduction: *Chapter from Business Communication: Building Critical Skills, Sixth Edition by Locker, Kaczmarek, 2014* 89

6. You-Attitude: *Chapter 6 from Business Communication: Building Critical Skills, Sixth Edition by Locker, Kaczmarek, 2014* 90

7. Positive Emphasis: *Chapter 7 from Business Communication: Building Critical Skills, Sixth Edition by Locker, Kaczmarek, 2014* 101

8. Reader Benefits: *Chapter 8 from Business Communication: Building Critical Skills, Sixth Edition by Locker, Kaczmarek, 2014* 112

Letters, Memos, E-Mail, and Web Writing

Introduction: *Chapter from Business Communication: Building Critical Skills, Sixth Edition by Locker, Kaczmarek, 2014* 113

9. Formats for Letters and Memos: *Chapter 9 from Business Communication: Building Critical Skills, Sixth Edition by Locker, Kaczmarek, 2014* 114

10. Informative and Positive Messages: *Chapter 10 from Business Communication: Building Critical Skills, Sixth Edition by Locker, Kaczmarek, 2014* 143

11. Negative Messages: *Chapter 11 from Business Communication: Building Critical Skills, Sixth Edition by Locker, Kaczmarek, 2014* 164

12. Persuasive Messages: *Chapter 12 from Business Communication: Building Critical Skills, Sixth Edition by Locker, Kaczmarek, 2014* 187

13. E-Mail Messages, Web Writing, and Technology: *Chapter 13 from Business Communication: Building Critical Skills, Sixth Edition by Locker, Kaczmarek, 2014* 217

Polishing Your Writing

Introduction: *Chapter from Business Communication: Building Critical Skills, Sixth Edition by Locker, Kaczmarek, 2014* 237

14. Editing for Grammar and Punctuation: *Chapter 14 from Business Communication: Building Critical Skills, Sixth Edition by Locker, Kaczmarek, 2014* 238

15. Choosing the Right Word: *Chapter 15 from Business Communication: Building Critical Skills, Sixth Edition by Locker, Kaczmarek, 2014* 256

16. Revising Sentences and Paragraphs: *Chapter 16 from Business Communication: Building Critical Skills, Sixth Edition by Locker, Kaczmarek, 2014* 271

Research & Reports

21. Proposals and Progress Reports: *Chapter 21 from Business Communication: Building Critical Skills, Sixth Edition by Locker, Kaczmarek, 2014* 343

22. Finding, Analyzing, and Documenting Information: *Chapter 22 from Business Communication: Building Critical Skills, Sixth Edition by Locker, Kaczmarek, 2014* 359

23. Short Reports: *Chapter 23 from Business Communication: Building Critical Skills, Sixth Edition by Locker, Kaczmarek, 2014* 377

Index: *Chapter from Business Communication: Building Critical Skills, Sixth Edition by Locker, Kaczmarek, 2014* 537